WILLIAM BYRD

Gentleman of the Chapel Royal

Nicola Haym's 'portraits' of Tallis and Byrd, discussed in
Appendix F. (British Museum.)

WILLIAM BYRD
Gentleman of the Chapel Royal

John Harley

SCOLAR PRESS

Published by
SCOLAR PRESS
Gower House
Croft Road
Aldershot
Hants GU11 3HR
England

Ashgate Publishing Company
Old Post Road
Brookfield
Vermont 05036-9704
USA

British Library Cataloguing-in-Publication Data

Harley, John
    William Byrd: gentleman of the Chapel Royal
    1. Byrd, William   2. Composers − England − Biography
    I. Title
    780.9'2

Library of Congress Cataloging-in-Publication Data

Harley, John
    William Byrd: gentleman of the Chapel Royal / John Harley.
    List of composer's works.
    Includes bibliographical references and index.
    ISBN 1-85928-165-6
    1. Byrd, William, 1539 or 40-1623. 2. Composers − England − Biography.
    I. Title.
ML410.B996H37 1997   96-37221
780'.92 − dc21   CIP
[B]   MN

ISBN 1 85928 165 6

Printed and bound in Great Britain by
Biddles Ltd, Guildford and King's Lynn

CONTENTS

ILLUSTRATIONS

Frontispiece

Nicola Haym's 'portraits' of Tallis and Byrd, discussed in Appendix F. (British Museum.)

Plates (between pages 240 and 241)

1   The Byrd genealogy, recorded by Robert Cooke in 1571. (Queen's College, Oxford, MS 72, f. 72ᵛ.)

2   a. The most elaborate of Byrd's signatures in the account books of Lincoln Cathedral. (Lincolnshire Archives, D&C Bi/2/1, 'liveries' section.)

      b. St Margaret's, Lincoln, where Byrd was married and two of his children were baptized. (Lincoln Cathedral Library.)

3   Byrd's letter of 28 June 1573 to Lord Paget. (Keele University Library, Special Collections and Archives, Early Paget Correspondence, 1/7, f. 40.)

4   Part of a document written by Byrd in 1580, during the dispute over Battyshall Manor. (Public Record Office, SP12/157/59-60.)

5   a. The beginning of a document dated 2 October 1598, in which Byrd gave his age as '58. yeares or ther abouts'. (Public Record Office, STAC5/B27/37.)

      b. Byrd's signature at the end of the same document.

6   Byrd's draft, dated 24 January 1603/4, of a letter for King James to send to Mrs Shelley. (Public Record Office, SP15/36.)

7   Part of a map of c.1700 showing Stondon Place. (Essex Record Office, D/DFa P1.)

8   a. Byrd's signature at the end of his will, dated 15 November
       1622. (Public Record Office, Prob. 10, box 404.)

       b. The churchyard at Stondon Massey, where William and Julian
       Byrd were probably buried. (Essex Record Office, Mint Binder,
       Stondon Massey 1/1. From Slocombe's *Companion to the
       Almanacs for 1851.*)

TABLES

PREFACE

This book has two principal purposes: to summarize the currently available biographical information about Byrd, and to provide a brief account of his music with particular emphasis on its chronology. The division of the book into two parts dealing separately with Byrd's life and works is far from ideal, but has the advantage of enabling each topic to be examined in an orderly fashion. To combine them in a strictly chronological account would not only be be confusing, but in the present state of knowledge impossible. I have however provided an introductory table which relates the composition of Byrd's music to the events of his life.

In the course of assembling biographical data I have been able to add to, and in some instances correct, what has already been published. The first part of this book must nevertheless be regarded as an interim report. I am sure that there is much more to be discovered. Printed calendars and indexes do not always mention the appearance of Byrd's name in documents they cover, and there is a vast amount of unindexed and uncalendared material in which he is likely to figure. This is markedly true of Byrd's involvement with the law. The legal documents quoted in the following pages could easily make a whole book,[1] but there are many others which remain to be examined. There are numerous entries in the Public Record Office indexes to Chancery cases concerning persons named William Byrd, either as plaintiff or defendant. Although some of these people are clearly not the composer, the identity of others is sufficiently doubtful to justify further scrutiny. The records of the Court of Common Pleas have so far proved impenetrable. Since Byrd appeared in the other courts it is a reasonable supposition that he is named somewhere in the records of that court too, but the rough-and-ready indexes alone amount to several hundred sizeable rolls. The enormous labour of searching so many large haystacks straw by straw, in the hope that they may contain a needle, will demand great determination on somebody's part. Their removal from Chancery Lane to Kew makes it improbable that I shall be able to tackle even the rolls of Richard Brownlow, the Court's chief prothonotary, of which some sixty cover the period when Byrd is presumed to have written the keyboard galliard named after Brownlow's daughter Mary.

---

1 There is, indeed, some need for a separate study, transcribing the documents, explaining the legal processes, and investigating Byrd's choice of lawyers and how much he paid in fees and fines.

As far as Byrd's music is concerned, no adequate survey could be made in the space available here. There is so much of it, and so much to say about it, that I have found it necessary to be highly selective. I have not said much about the development of English music before and during Byrd's lifetime, in the belief that readers will turn to works such as *The Oxford history of English music* by John Caldwell, or more detailed studies, for the information they need. I am conscious that I have largely avoided discussion of the merits of Byrd's works relative to one another or to those of other composers. To introduce worthwhile value judgements would have meant establishing criteria and examining individual pieces by Byrd and other composers at some length. I hope that I have nevertheless gone some way towards explaining why he was so great a composer, by drawing attention to the skill with which he handled his materials and his frequent successes in realizing his intentions. I have focused upon the chronology of Byrd's compositions, partly because it complements the account of Byrd's life, and partly because it is essential for future Byrd studies to adopt a chronological approach to his music. There are many areas where a closer examination needs to be made of dates of composition, and many problems to be investigated, for example the apparent absence of vocal music between Byrd's two Marian motets and the motets and Anglican music he is likely to have written at Lincoln. I make no claim to have got everything right, and if disagreement with my suggestions stimulates debate, I shall be well pleased.

Acknowledgements

It is inevitable that the book should deal with the same matters as Edmund H. Fellowes' *William Byrd*, first published in 1936, and follow much the same plan. Nevertheless, almost sixty years have passed since Fellowes' book appeared, and it is now possible to take account of a great deal of subsequent work. Fellowes' preface lists some of the scholars to whom he was indebted, but the number of people to whom I am indebted − directly or indirectly − is much greater, and includes most of the authors listed in Richard Turbet's *William Byrd: a guide to research* (1987) and the supplements in his *Tudor Music* (1994), *Brio* and the *Annual Byrd Newsletter*.

I am deeply grateful to Mr Turbet, whose enthusiasm for Byrd's music has been a constant source of encouragement, and whose advice and practical help have been invaluable. I am also grateful for assistance in one form or another to the Marquess of Abergavenny, the Marquess of Anglesey, Dr Andrew Ashbee, Mr David Baldwin, Miss Janet Clayton, Mr Peter Ll. Gwynn-Jones, Dr David Mateer, Mr

O. W. Neighbour and Dr John Purser. Among the librarians and archivists who have helped me are Dr Nicholas Bennett (Lincoln Cathedral), Mrs Caroline Dalton (New College), Mr Robin Harcourt-Williams (Librarian to the Marquess of Salisbury), Mrs F. M. Piddock (Lincoln College), Miss Helen Powell (Queen's College), Mr Jo Wisdom (St Paul's Cathedral) and the staffs of the British Library, the Centre for Kentish Studies, the Essex Record Office, the Greater London Record Office, the Guildhall Library, Keele University Library, the Archives Department of the London Borough of Lambeth, Lincolnshire Archives, the Local History Library of the London Borough of Greenwich, the Mercers' Company, the Public Record Office, Staffordshire Record Office, Westminster Abbey Muniment Room, and the City of Westminster Archives Centre. I am no less grateful to many others who have responded readily to written enquiries.

Illustrations

Permission to reproduce photographs has kindly been granted by the following: the Marquess of Anglesey (plate 3), the Trustees of the British Museum (frontispiece), Essex Record Office (plates 7 and 8b), the Controller of Her Majesty's Stationery Office (plates 4, 5a, 5b, 6, and 8a), the Dean and Chapter of Lincoln (plates 2a and 2b), and the Provost and Scholars of the Queen's College, Oxford (plate 1).

The name 'Byrd'

The frequent coincidence of names, as it touches not only William Byrd and his family but those surrounding them, has struck me many times during the writing of this book. It is easy to see why researchers have occasionally been misled by it. Byrd itself was a very common surname, and was often combined with one of a few favourite Christian names, especially William, John or Thomas.[1] In London alone a large number of people named Byrd bore them during the composer's lifetime, and throughout England there were very many more. The names occur frequently and confusingly in state papers, legal and private documents, subsidy rolls, lists of recusants, membership lists of city companies and other bodies, court records and parish registers.[2] It is not always clear

---

1   Over half the men baptized in the period 1550-99 were given one of these three names. (Withycombe, 1977, p. xxviii.) The most diverting Christian name given to any Byrd was Avis, conferred on the daughter of a John Byrd; she was baptized at St Michael Crooked Lane on 1 May 1541. (GL, MS 11,367.)

2   Among the many people named William Byrd were a Messenger of the Chamber at

whether a name that recurs belongs to one person or two people, or sometimes more, but although a few references to William Byrd the composer are not explicit in the documents assumed below to refer to him, I believe that his identification is secure except where I have noted the fact.

Spellings

Byrd's name appears in different forms in contemporary documents. The attitude to spelling in the sixteenth and early seventeenth centuries is exemplified by Queen Elizabeth's letters patent conferring a printing monopoly on Byrd and Tallis in 1575. There the name appears three times as 'Bird', twice as 'Birde', and twice as 'Byrde'. At Lincoln Byrd signed for his pay as 'Wyllyam byrde' in 1567, but on other occasions wrote 'Willm birde'. He Latinized his name as 'Guil. Birdus' in the dedication of the *Cantiones Sacrae* of 1575. By 1581 he was writing 'Willm Byrde'. In the first and second books of *Cantiones sacrae* published in 1589 and 1591 he appears as 'Guilielmo Byrd'. In two signatures on a document of February 1597/8 he wrote 'Wyllm Byrde'.[3] In January 1608/9 he again signed himself 'Wyllm Byrde',[4] and that was the form he used in his will, though not long before he witnessed his brother's will as 'Willm Byrd'.[5]

For most of the present century the customary spelling of the composer's surname has been 'Byrd', perhaps because it was used on the title-page of *Parthenia*, which became the most familiar source of his music. It is one of the two common modern spellings (the other, as the London telephone directory reveals, is 'Bird', though it also contains 'Byrde'), and there seems little reason to adopt another, except in

court (Ashbee, 1986-96, vi, p. 78), who may have been the man frequently mentioned as a messenger in the Acts of the Privy Council; a Mercer in the City of London (Mercers' Company records; GL, MSS 641 and 642; Chester, 1880, pp. 53, 54, 137); the 'Customer owtward to the Queenes Mat^y for London' (various references in the *Calendars of state papers domestic* and elsewhere); and a Merchant Taylor who made his will in 1566 (PRO, Prob. 11/48). There was a 'Willm Byrde de Ingatestone' on whom the Essex Archdeaconry court imposed a penance (ERO, D/AEA 10, f. 114^v); and there was a William Byrd of Radwinter in Essex, mentioned by William Harrison in *The description of England*, first published in 1577. Fellowes (1948, pp. 33-35) writes at some length about William Byrd alias Borne; his will is printed by Honigmann and Brock, 1993, pp. 131-132. A few of the others are mentioned in the course of this book.

   3   PRO, STAC5/A14/23.
   4   PRO, E126/1, f. 119^v.
   5   PRO, Prob. 10, box 389.

quotations. The spelling is also used for other people called Byrd, though it may not have been the one they habitually employed.

Other names have also been normalized except in quotations, for example 'Catherine' and 'Katharine' as 'Katherine'. The sixteenth-century spelling 'Symond' is adopted for the name of Byrd's elder brother, and the name of Byrd's brother-in-law is spelled 'Philip Smyth', following his signature, though 'Smith' was sometimes used by other people.

I have, with some regret, decided that the titles of Byrd's compositions should be modernized. Even to adopt the spellings of the earliest or most authoritative sources would be impracticable in dealing with his whole output, and might justifiably be regarded as pedantic.

For convenience, references to modern printed editions are often added to those to original documents. Quotations are however taken from the originals, except in a few cases which should be easily identifiable. The spelling of the original sources has been retained (bearing in mind that upper and lower case initial letters are not always clearly distinguished, and that the handwriting may be difficult to read and is sometimes almost illegible), but modern letter forms have been used: 's' has been substituted for ' ∫ ', and where appropriate 'u' and 'v' have been exchanged, as have 'j' and 'i'. Although 'j' has been retained in the Roman numerals 'ij' etc., I could not bring myself to print 'Jrish' and 'Jnstrumens'. The letters 'y' and 'i' have not been exchanged. Terminal and a few medial contractions are expanded in italics, to avoid the need for special characters, but others are represented by near equivalents: thus 'p' is used for the crossed 'p' representing 'par', 'per' or 'pro', a tilde is used for a tittle or any other superior sign indicating the omission of letters, and the ampersand replaces the Tironian mark for 'and',

Numbering of Byrd's compositions

The numerical identification of Byrd's compositions is by the volume and piece number in *The Byrd Edition* (BE) or the *Musica Britannica* edition (MB), e.g. BE 8/1 means the first piece in *The Byrd Edition*, volume 8.

Dates and money

During Byrd's lifetime the year began on 25 March. The date of an event falling in the period 1 January to 24 March is indicated by combining the old and modern styles, e.g. 1593/4.

Before the introduction of decimal currency in 1971, the English pound was made up of twenty shillings (s.) and a shilling consisted of twelve pence (d., Latin *denarius*, *-i*). In Byrd's time the mark, a denomination of weight for gold or silver, was valued at 13s. 4d., i.e. two-thirds of a pound. The sums 6s. 8d. and 13s. 4d., which occur frequently in documents, were therefore equivalent to half a mark or one mark respectively.

Pitch notation

In the few instances where a note needs to be identified by the octave in which it occurs, its pitch is indicated (from the bass) thus: C to B, c to b, c' (middle C) to b', c" to b".

John Harley

WILLIAM BYRD

Gentleman of the Chapel Royal

INTRODUCTION

There could be no more fitting description of William Byrd than that added to his fourth galliard in *My Ladye Nevells Booke*: 'mr: w: birde: homo memorabilis'.

Byrd's surviving compositions number well over five hundred. They range from short, relatively simple pieces to sizeable works of great complexity. Almost every one, whatever its length, reflects his self-critical habits and his invariably careful overall planning and attention to detail. The best of his work reveals a largeness of spirit and a musical vision that are unsurpassed.

It is astonishing that Byrd managed to combine the production of so large a body of work with his activities as a keyboard player and singer, and with the acquisition and management of property, farming, the pursuits necessary to advancing and securing his social position, his frequent appearances in courts of law, and his religious preoccupations. The conclusion must be that he had abilities of the very highest order, and wrote music with the utmost facility. He possessed one of the most distinguished and naturally musical minds of his or any other age. It is revealed not simply in his remarkable technical skill and originality, but in his access to areas of thought and feeling open only to the greatest composers. The word that repeatedly comes to mind in connection with Byrd and his music is 'authority'.

To consider Byrd's music in isolation from his life would of course be artificial. There must be a link between the father who attempted to secure his children's future through the purchase of land, and the composer who sought to preserve his music in organized collections. The resolute Roman Catholic who appeared time and again in the courts on account of his religion is plainly the musician whose faith is expressed in his works. And it is not hard to see a connection between the man who for more than a decade determinedly opposed Mrs Shelley in the Court of Exchequer, and the tenacious personality behind Byrd's carefully wrought musical structures.

It is difficult to determine within anything but the broadest limits when many of Byrd's compositions were written, let alone to suggest how they might relate to specific events. This book is therefore divided into sections dealing separately with his life and his compositions, and the following brief chronology may prove helpful. A more comprehensive musical chronology is contained in tables 7 and 9.

Table 1 · Outline chronology of Byrd's life and music

1540	William Byrd, one of seven children of Thomas and Margery Byrd of London, born between the beginning of October 1539 and the end of September 1540.
c.1550	WB's elder brothers Symond and John are choristers of St Paul's. WB probably enters the Chapel Royal, where he is trained in singing by Richard Bower and in composition and keyboard playing by Thomas Tallis. After his voice breaks he probably stays on as Tallis's assistant. WB may have become acquainted with the Petre family at this time.
1555	WB's sister Barbara marries the musical instrument maker Robert Broughe.
1562/3	WB succeeds Thomas Appleby as organist and Master of the Choristers at Lincoln Cathedral. One of his singers is John Reason.
1568	WB marries Julian Birley at Lincoln.
1569	WB's son Christopher baptized. WB involved in dispute with Cathedral Chapter over the performance of his duties.
1572	WB's daughter Elizabeth baptized at Lincoln. WB sworn in as Gentleman of the Chapel Royal, where he probably shares the organists' duties and sings. Influential friends secure him an annual payment from Lincoln Cathedral.
1573	First evidence of WB's friendship with the Catholic Lord Paget and other noblemen, including Edward Somerset (later Earl of Worcester).
1574	WB's daughter Mary baptized at St Margaret's, Westminster. (No record known of baptism of WB's daughter Rachel.) WB attempts to buy manor of Battyshall in Essex.
1575	WB and Tallis granted patent for printing music.
1576	WB's son(s) Thomas (and Edward?) baptized at St Margaret's, Westminster. Thomas is named after his godfather, Thomas Tallis.
1577	WB and family living at Harlington, Middlesex. John Reason is one of their servants. The Queen grants WB and Tallis several leases.
1579	Beginning of WB's long dispute over manor of Longney.
1580	Evidence of WB's continued friendship with Paget and other Catholics, possibly including Anthony Babington. Death of Symond Byrd. WB engaged in dispute over manor of Battyshall. Peter Philips probably a pupil of WB at this time.

WB's earliest surviving compositions (all based on cantus firmi) date from the late 1550s. They include *Similes illis fiant*, part of a motet written in collaboration with John Sheppard and William Mundy.

The music of WB's years at Lincoln includes Anglican Preces, Services and psalms, his early fantasias, variations and grounds for keyboard and for viols, and a group of Latin motets.

WB at work on motets which he will publish in 1575. Other music composed at this time probably includes works for the Anglican Church and his earliest pavans and galliards for viols and for keyboard.

WB and Tallis publish *Cantiones sacrae*, dedicated to Queen Elizabeth.

WB at work on motets, songs and keyboard pieces, many of which will be included in his collections of 1588-1591, together with pieces for viol consort and music for the Anglican Church.

Table 1 *continued*

1581	WB's house a resort of Catholics. WB seeks help for Mrs Tempest. WB on visiting terms with Petre family. John Byrd imprisoned.
1583	John Reason first imprisoned. Death of Thomas Tallis.
1584	Evidence that WB had an annuity from Paget. First surviving indictment of WB as a recusant.
1585	WB's house searched. Julian Byrd outlawed.
1586	WB known to move in same circles as Jesuit missionaries.
1587	Christopher Byrd in dispute over land at Harlington.
1588	Outlawry of Julian Byrd and her children Rachel and Elizabeth, with their servants Francis and Elizabeth Welshe.
1589	Julian, Rachel and Elizabeth Byrd outlawed again.
1590	WB engaged in dispute over manor of Horsepath. Last record of Julian Byrd as recusant in Middlesex.
1591	Christopher Byrd marries Katherine, a member of the strongly Catholic Moore family. WB retires from full duties at Chapel Royal about this time.
1592	Last record of WB's recusancy in Middlesex.
1593	
1594	WB and family move to Stondon Massey in Essex, where he and Christopher continue intimacy with the Petre family. WB's grandson Thomas born about this time.
1595	First of a long series of records of the recusancy of WB and his family in Essex. WB and John Byrd become involved in a legal dispute resulting from the second marriage of Hester Cole (née Byrd).
1596	WB's son Thomas at English College at Valladolid, having studied law in England. Expelled 1599.
1597	WB gives evidence concerning imprisonment of Philip Smith (husband of WB's sister Martha). Beginning of WB's twelve-year dispute with Mrs Shelley over the lease of Stondon Place. Thomas Morley dedicates *A plaine and easie introduction* to WB, his 'loving Maister'. John Bull refers to himself as WB's 'scolar'.
1598	Rachel Byrd married to John Hooke by this time. Their children are William and Katherine.
1599	WB engaged in dispute over property at St Peter's Ampney.

WB publishes *Psalmes, sonets, & songs*, dedicated to Sir Christopher Hatton. A song by WB published in Yonge's *Musica transalpina*.

WB publishes *Songs of sundrie natures*, dedicated to Sir Henry Carey, and *Liber primus sacrarum cantionum*, dedicated to the Earl of Worcester. More of WB's music published as *A gratification unto Master John Case*.

WB contributes to Watson's *The first sett, of Italian madrigalls Englished*.

WB publishes *Liber secundus sacrarum cantionum*, dedicated to Lord Lumley. He supervises preparation of keyboard manuscript *My Ladye Nevells Booke*.

WB's Mass for four voices published about this time.

WB's Mass for three voices published about this time.

WB's Mass for five voices published about this time. He begins work on the Masses and motets which will be published as *Gradualia*. He continues writing songs and instrumental music.

Table 1 *concluded*

1600	WB accused of blocking the track to Kelvedon Hatch; the case lasts several years. Elizabeth Byrd married to John Jackson by this time; he dies by 1605 and Elizabeth eventually marries a man named Burdett.
1602	Thomas Byrd deputizes for John Bull as Gresham Professor of Music.
1603	Byrd probably at funeral of Queen Elizabeth and coronation of King James. John Reason dies in gaol.
1605	
1606	Dispute over manor of Longney resumed. WB reported (c.1606) to have played the organ at a house frequented by Catholics.
1607	WB sings when King James is entertained at Merchant Taylors' Hall.
1608	Julian Byrd dies about this time, and is buried at Stondon. Reference made to WB's chamber in John Petre's home, Thorndon Hall.
1610	Mrs Shelley dies, Byrd buys Stondon Place.
1611	Mary Byrd marries Henry Hawksworth c.1611-12; their four sons are William, Henry, George and John.
1613	
1614	
1615	Christopher Byrd dies about this time.
1618	Rachel Hooke (née Byrd) widowed and remarried by this time, to Edward Biggs.
1620	WB's will drafted; it refers to his lodgings at the Earl of Worcester's house in the Strand.
1621	Last reference to WB as a recusant.
1622	John Byrd dies. Thomas Tomkins refers to WB as his 'much reverenced master'.
1623	WB dies. His will expresses his wish to be buried beside his wife at Stondon.

WB publishes the first book of *Gradualia*, dedicated to the Earl of Northampton.

WB publishes the second book of *Gradualia*, dedicated to Lord Petre.

WB publishes *Psalmes, songs, and sonnets*, dedicated to the Earl of Cumberland.
Keyboard music by WB published in *Parthenia*.
WB contributes to Sir William Leighton's *The teares or lamentacions of a sorrowfull soule*.

1

LONDON AND WESTMINSTER · 1540-1562

The Byrd family's genealogy was recorded in 1571, in the course of an heraldic visitation of London by Robert Cooke, Clarenceux King of Arms.[1] The family traced its origins to Richard Byrd, who lived at Ingatestone in Essex in the fourteenth century. The village's parish registers show that people named Byrd continued to live there in the sixteenth and seventeenth centuries.[2]

The composer William Byrd was however a Londoner. The first member of the family to settle in the city, in the fifteenth century, was a Thomas Byrd. His grandson, William, was the composer's grandfather. This William evidently retired to Boxley, near Maidstone in Kent, where he was buried in 1540.[3] One of his four half-brothers was John, the penultimate Abbot of Boxley.

The older William had two sons, Thomas and John. The composer was a son of Thomas and his wife Margery.[4] Little information about them has come to light. They may have lived for a time in the parish of All Hallows Bread Street, where one of their daughters was married in 1555, though it is possible that this was the groom's parish. It is more certain that they lived later in the parish of All Hallows Lombard Street, where two of their other children were married in 1567.[5]

All Hallows Bread Street and All Hallows Lombard Street were among the smaller London parishes. The first lay a little to the east of St Paul's and south of Cheapside. The second, called by John Stow 'Alhallowes Grasse church in Lombard streete', lay a few hundred yards directly north of London Bridge.[6] It is probable, therefore, that Byrd's childhood was passed in the heart of London. By the mid-sixteenth century, although the countryside was nowhere far away, the city had spread to the north and west well beyond the line of its ancient walls. Its

---

1 Queen's College, Oxford, MS 72, f. 72ᵛ. See p. 373; pl. 1.

2 Registers in the Essex Record Office.

3 See p. 382 for his will.

4 The composer's father was not, as sometimes supposed, the Gentleman of the Chapel Royal named Thomas Byrd, as the latter's will proves. (See p. 394.) No relationship has been discovered, though it cannot be ruled out.

5 The church of All Hallows Bread Street was destroyed in the Fire of London. All Hallows Lombard Street was demolished in 1938-39.

6 Stow, 1908, i, pp. 346, 202. 'Grasse church' or 'Gracechurch' from the proximity of the former grass market.

population was in the region of seventy thousand — a huge number when there were fewer than three million people in the whole of England — and there were expanding centres of population in nearby Westminster and across the river in Southwark, while new suburbs were growing up to the east. There were at the same time considerable fluctuations in the total due to influenza and the plague. Just how deadly disease was in the sixteenth century is illustrated by the burial at All Hallows Lombard Street, during the space of a few weeks in July and August 1569, of seven members of the Hutton family.[7]

If the composer's father was engaged in business of some kind he probably belonged to a city company. Since, as will appear below, his son-in-law Robert Broughe was a member of the Fletchers' Company, it is conceivable that he was the Thomas Byrd who appears from 1559 to 1573 in the Company's rolls of 'ffreemen of the crafte of ffletchers of the citie of London', though it is hard to explain why his name is absent before 1559.[8] The name William Byrd also occurs in the rolls from 1519 to 1527, and from 1535 to 1545. If it refers to one person, it may be Thomas's father. Another William Byrd and a Symond Byrd who are listed in the rolls could be two of Thomas's sons: that is to say, the composer and the elder of his brothers. This does not necessarily mean that they followed the fletchers' trade. Fletchers originally made or sold arrows, but — particularly as the demand for arrows declined — members of the Company had all manner of occupations.[9] There is nevertheless some reason for speculating whether the family could, like Broughe, have been connected with the woodworking trades, and even perhaps have made musical instruments. This would explain why Thomas's sons all received a musical training. Some notable composers, such as Giles Farnaby and John Jenkins, emerged from just such a background.

7   See Schofield, 1994, on the London known to William Byrd. Before the Black Death the population of England was between 4.5 and 6 million. It had been reduced to about 2 million in the middle of the fifteenth century, but grew to some 4 million by the end of the sixteenth century. (Wrigley and Schofield, 1981.) The population of London reached some 150,000 by about 1600. London's growth is traced by Youings, 1984, pp. 66, 128, 149-150, and Williams, 1995, pp. 162-169. Hutton family: GL, MS 17613.

8   GL, MS 5977/2; description of the company quoted from 1560 roll, but typical of others. The rolls have been indexed by P. E. Jones. (GL, MS 21030.) Some of Thomas Byrd's descendants belonged to the Haberdashers' Company, but he is unlikely to have been the Thomas Byrd who became free of that company as late as 24 September 1563. (GL, MS 15857/1, f. 101^r, compiled 1607-c.1641 from earlier records of the Haberdashers' Company.) Welch (1908) lists apparently unrelated freemen named Byrd.

9   Oxley, 1968.

Table 2 · Historical background 1539-1562

1539   Act of Six Articles. Reaffirmation of clerical celibacy. First commission to sell Crown lands.

1540   Thomas Cromwell's execution marks end of Henrician Reformation.

1542   Witchcraft and other occult arts made felonies. Reminting of silver coinage (with lower content of pure silver) begun.

1543   Henry VIII marries Catherine Parr. War against France (until 1546). English litany separately printed. Reading of Bible restricted to men of yeoman class and above, and noble or gentle women. Hardyng, *Chronicle of England*.

1545   The King's Primer. Taking of interest up to ten per cent permitted (to 1552).

1547   Henry Howard (Earl of Surrey) executed. Death of Henry VIII, succession of Edward VI (aged nine). Somerset appointed Lord Protector. Repeal of treason and heresy laws. Compulsory assessments in London for support of poor. Sternhold and Hopkins, *Psalms* (expanded 1549, 1562). *Book of Homilies* (promoted by Cranmer).

1548   First Enclosure Commission. Subsidy Act (taxes on sheep, wool and exported broadcloth). Latimer resumes preaching. Licences to preach suspended. Communion Service introduced. First volume of Erasmus's paraphrase of the New Testament (trans. Udall; completed anon. 1549).

1549   Subsidy Act repealed. Execution of Thomas Seymour. Knox returns to England. First Act of Uniformity. First Edwardian Prayer Book. Priests allowed to marry. War with France. Kett's rebellion. South-western rebellion. Overthrow of Somerset. Treasons Act. Suspension of all service books but the Prayer Book and Primer.

1550   Warwick (Northumberland) becomes Lord President of the Council. Cecil made Secretary of State (to 1553). The Ordinal (governing structure and functions of church hierarchy). Expulsion of Catholics from the Council. Removal of altars. Statute requiring destruction of religious images and relics. Poor harvest. Halle, *Chronicle*. Langland, *Vision of Pierce the Plowman* (first printing).

1551   Coinage revalued. Severe slump in cloth industry. Sweating sickness. More, *Utopia* in English (trans. Robynson).

1552 Somerset executed. Second Act of Uniformity. Second Prayer Book.

1553 Forty-two Articles (Cranmer). Death of Edward VI. 'Reign' of Lady Jane Grey (6-19 July), succession of Mary. Northumberland executed. *Great Harry* destroyed by fire. Sir Hugh Willoughby sets out to search for north-eastern passage to Cathay and India.

1554 Wyatt's rebellion. Execution of Lady Jane Grey. Queen Mary marries Philip of Spain. Spanish alliance. Arrival of Cardinal Pole in England as papal legate.

1555 Repeal of Henry VIII's antipapal laws. Restoration of papal authority and laws against heresy. Rogers (first Protestant martyr) burned at Smithfield. Ridley and Latimer martyred at Oxford. Cranmer deprived of archbishopric, Pole replaces him. Muscovy Company chartered.

1556 Epidemic of sweating sickness begins (most serious 1557-59). Worst harvest of century. Cranmer burned.

1557 England drawn into war between Spain and France. Surrey, *Virgil's Æneis*. Tottel, *Songs and Sonnets*. Stationers' Company incorporated. Pole deprived of legislative powers.

1558 Loss of Calais. Death of Mary, succession of Elizabeth. Sir William Cecil (later Lord Burghley) reappointed Secretary. Robert Dudley made Master of the Horse (quickly becomes favourite of the Queen). Knox, *First Blast of the Trumpet against the Monstrous Regiment of Women*.

1559 Acts of Supremacy and Uniformity. Elizabethan Prayer Book. Marian bishops deprived. Minor religious orders abolished. Peace with France. Knox arrives in Scotland. English support Scots against the French. Baldwin, *Mirror for Magistrates*.

1560 Treaty of Edinburgh. Merchant Adventurers given monopoly of exporting cloth to Germany and the Netherlands. New currency issued. Death of Dudley's wife (Amy Robsart). Scotland breaks with Rome.

1561 Mary Stuart (Queen of Scots) returns to Scotland. Calvin's *Institution of Christian Religion* (trans. Norton). Chaucer, *Works* printed (ed. Stow). Hoby, *The Courtyer* (from Castiglione). *Gorboduc* acted. St Paul's fired by lightning.

1562 Hawkins takes slaves from West Africa to West Indies. The Queen nearly dies of smallpox. Unsuccessful attempt to support French Huguenots. Sternhold and Hopkins, *Whole Book of Psalms* (complete).

Thomas and Margery had seven children. Their four daughters were Alice, Barbara, Mary and Martha. Their first son was Symond (also spelled Symon), and their second son was named John. William was the youngest son. There was a general requirement for parish priests to keep registers from 1538, but many volumes containing early entries have perished and no record of William's birth or baptism has ever been found.[10] A statement in his will has hitherto been accepted as evidence that he was born in or just before 1543. The will is dated 15 November 1622, and his description of himself as 'nowe in the Eightieth yeare of myne age' has been taken to mean that he was seventy-nine but was not yet eighty. The will seems however to have been drafted a few years before a fair copy was prepared for Byrd's signature. In testimony submitted to the Court of Star Chamber, in his own hand and dated 2 October 1598, he described himself as '58. yeares or ther abouts'.[11] This places his birth towards the end of 1539 or in 1540.

A Thomas Byrd was buried at All Hallows Lombard Street on 12 November 1575, but as with most parish register entries of the time there is no information which allows him to be identified with assurance.[12] The date is concordant with the Fletcher Thomas Byrd's absence from the rolls of the Company after 1573, although the family genealogy can be read as suggesting that Symond Byrd was already head of the family in 1571.[13] It is possible that Thomas moved out of London,

10   For London registers surviving from an early date (and, by implication, those which have not survived) see Guildhall Library, 1990.

11   PRO, STAC5/B27/37. (See pl. 5.) The date was probably added by a clerk, but must have been inserted when Byrd wrote the document or within a few days; it is consistent with dates in associated documents and the progress of the case being heard. (See pp. 118-120.) The day of the month is a little blotted, but is almost certainly 'ij'; the year is given as 40 Elizabeth. The formula 'or thereabouts' was commonly added to ages in legal documents to avoid the necessity of adding months and days to the number of years.

12   GL, MS 17613.

13   The Thomas Byrd buried at St Andrew by the Wardrobe on 15 February 1568/9 was probably related to Joseph Byrd and Isabell Byrd, who were buried there in the same year, and to Elizabeth and William Byrd, buried there in 1569/70 and 1575. (GL, MS 4507/1.) Thomas Byrd who made his will in 1573 lived in the parish of St Botolph Aldersgate, and was the son of John Byrd of the Drapers' Company. (GL, MS 9051/4.) Thomas Byrd, a citizen and Painter, was married to Alice and lived in the parish of St Olave Hart Street. (GL, MS 9171/11, f. 113^r; Fitch, 1974, p. 29.) Thomas Byrd, citizen and Draper of the parish of St Antholin, who made his will in 1602, was a brother of Andrew and Robert Byrd. (Probate copy: PRO, Prob. 11/100, f. 55^v.) A Margery Byrd was buried at St Botolph Bishopsgate on 22 December 1592, but seems not to have

like his father and his son William, and like his son-in-law Philip Smyth who eventually settled at Henley-on-Thames.[14] It may be that his will and the record of his burial should be sought elsewhere.

Symond and John Byrd at St Paul's

On high ground towards London's western gateways rose the gothic bulk of old St Paul's. It was here that William Byrd's elder brothers became choristers.[15] The basis of the cathedral choir was a group of six lay vicars and ten boy choristers or 'queresters'. This fundamental group remained unchanged from the one envisaged in the statutes of the Guild of Jesus in 1507.[16] The boys were supervised by 'oon of the Vicaries, Maister of the seid Queresters for the tyme being', who was responsible for their instruction in singing and reading.[17] A document thought to belong to the early sixteenth century mentions payments 'To the Elemosiner for his Commons, for feeding days of 10 Choristers'.[18]

The singers' names are given in two sets of documents. In 1554 the wardens, petty canons and singers of St Paul's submitted petitions for the payment of annuities lost because of the dissolution of the monasteries and the closure of chapels.[19] Annuities paid to the cathedral's lay vicars and boy choristers from 1555 to 1557 are entered in the books recording payments which would have been made by the Court of Augmentations, had it not been dissolved in 1554.[20]

belonged to the composer's family. (Hallen, 1885-94, i, p. 304.)

14   ERO, D/DM T56, bundle 1.

15   On the training they would have received, see Flynn, 1995.

16   Simpson, 1873, p. 447; Harrison, 1980, pp. 13-14, 183.

17   Simpson, 1873, p. 449.

18   Transcript made in 1785 by the Rev. John Pridden, from 'a M.S.S. in the Possession of Andrew Colter Ducarell', the present whereabouts of which is unknown. (St Paul's Cathedral Library, MS 51.D.6, i; photocopy: GL, MS 5872A/1.) Pridden's transcripts include references to payments to each of the ten choristers of one gastell (loaf of wastel bread) for the Feast of the Conversion of St Paul and on other occasions. There are also references to later matters of musical interest.

19   PRO, E159/334, mm. 232, 238 and 262.

20   PRO, E405/501 (1 & 2 Philip and Mary), E405/561 (Easter, 1 & 2 Ph. and Mary to Michaelmas, 2 & 3 Ph. and Mary), E405/504 (Michaelmas, 2 & 3 Ph. and Mary), E405/506 (Easter, 2 & 3 Ph. and Mary), E405/505 (Easter, 3 & 4 Ph. and Mary). These books are not foliated, but the entries for St Paul's appear in the London sections. E405/509, another volume in the series to which these belong, includes part of the original cover made from a leaf of vellum on which plainsong is written. The Court of Augmentation was founded in 1537 for the control of property taken from monasteries by

The lists of choristers are headed by John Byrd, who is followed by Symond Byrd.[21] While John Byrd was a common name, Symond Byrd was not, which removes all but the slightest doubt as to whether the choristers were the future composer's brothers.[22] If William was born in 1539 or 1540, Symond cannot have been less than fifteen years old in 1554, and John cannot have been less than fourteen. On the other hand, Symond cannot have been much more than fifteen or sixteen, or his voice would have changed, and John cannot have been more than fourteen or fifteen. Although the original list displays every sign of having been copied uncritically from year to year, a new list prepared in 1561 shows that the brothers had left the choir.[23]

At the head of the lists of lay vicars is the name of Sebastian Westcote, who succeeded John Redford as almoner and Master of the Choristers.[24] Symond and John Byrd probably began their musical training under Redford, who did not die until 1547, the year in which religious zealotry led to the great crucifix on the altar of St Paul's being 'cast down by force of instruments, several men being wounded in the process and one killed'.[25] Westcote's patent was not issued until

the Crown.

21   See p. 399. for a full list of names. Payments were also made to the apparently unrelated Henry Byrd of Whittington College, and to a Thomas Byrd, described either as of the church of St Botolph by London Bridge, i.e. in Billingsgate Ward (PRO, E405/561), or of 'St Rother' by Billingsgate (E405/501). There was a Rother Lane in Billingsgate Ward. Another document connected with St Paul's names Edmund Byrd of St Martin Vintry. (GL, MS 9537/2, f. 25ʳ.)

22   There was nevertheless at least one other Symond Byrd of approximately the same age in London, living in the parish of All Hallows Barking by the Tower. His son John was baptized and buried on 7 November 1563, before the composer's brother Symond married. (Blewett, 1984 and 1986.)

23   GL, MS 9537/2, ff. 17ᵛ and 19ᵛ. Payne, 1993, p. 14, draws attention to evidence that boys' voices usually broke between the ages of thirteen-and-a-half and fifteen at the latest. See also Bowers, 1987, p. 48, note 3.

24   Redford's will describes him as 'master of the almonre', and names Westcote as his executor. (Probate copy: PRO, Prob. 11/31, f. 392ʳ⁻ᵛ). Westcote's will (made 3 April 1582, proved 14 April 1582) describes him as 'Almener of the cathedrall churche of Sᵗ. Pawle in London, being greved with syknes'. (PRO, Prob. 10 box 105; probate copy, Prob. 11/64, ff. 99ʳ-100ᵛ, confirmed at ff. 235ᵛ-236ʳ; printed by Honigmann and Brock, 1993, pp. 48-53.) This will is a most interesting document. It names numerous members of Westcote's family and household, gives details of his possessions, and is enlightening about his colleagues and life at St Paul's.

25   Hume and Tyler, 1912, p. 222.

1 February 1553/4,[26] but the choristers were already in his charge when they presented a play before the then Princess Elizabeth at Hatfield House in 1552.[27] Symond and John Byrd may still have been young enough to be among them. They were probably too old to have taken part in recorded dramatic performances at the house of Sir William Petre, the father of William Byrd's future patron John Petre.[28]

The boys of St Paul's played before Queen Elizabeth many times after her accession in 1558.[29] Under Westcote's direction they contributed importantly to the development of Tudor drama, as did the choristers of the Chapel Royal under Richard Bower and those of St George's, Windsor, under Richard Farrant.[30] The success of the St Paul's actors may have contributed to Westcote's ability to escape the more severe penalties of Catholicism. Nicholas Sanders said that Westcote was willing to give up his post in the church, but was allowed to keep it because he was a favourite of Queen Elizabeth and did nothing schismatic.[31] A list of prisoners in the Marshalsea, Southwark, in 1577 includes 'Papistes at libarty', among whom is 'Sebastian Wescot sent in by comaundement from the honarable lords of the conscell for papistry 21 of Desember Aᵒ 1577 and was discharged by my sayd lords of the Counscell the 19 daye of Marche Aᵒ 1577'.[32]

Besides acting, the children of the London choirs played viols. On 30 September 1553, as Queen Mary rode through London towards

26   Westcote's patent confirms him in the post of 'Elemozinarie' (almoner) and refers to 'John Redfurthe' as his predecessor. (GL, MS 25630/1, ff. 276ʳ⁻ᵛ.) Although there seems to have been no specific post of organist at St Paul's at this time, the amount of organ music Redford composed makes it likely that he undertook the duty, in which he was followed by Westcote. Nicholas Sanders called Westcote 'Sebastianus, qui organa pulsabat apud D. Paulum Londini'. (Vatican Archives, Arm. LXIV, xxviii; Catholic Record Society, 1905, p. 21.) The organist's responsibilities were probably shared; the lists of lay vicars include the organist and composer Philip ap Rhys, also named in a keyboard manuscript as 'Off Saynt Poulls in london'. (BL, Additional MS 29996, f. 28ᵛ.)

27   Camden Miscellany, 1853, p. 37 (from f. 10ᵛ of an unidentified document).

28   At the wedding of Sir William Petre's daughter Dorothy to Nicholas Wadham in London in September 1555 (ERO, D/DP A6), at Petre's town house in Aldersgate Street in 1559, and again, for the wedding of his daughter Thomasine, in February 1559/60 (D/DP A8). Mentioned by Emmison, 1961, p. 215. See also note 34 below.

29   Ashbee, 1986-96, vi, as indexed under 'Westcote'.

30   Hillebrand, 1926, particularly pp. 117ff on Westcote; Cunningham, 1842, pp. xxvii-xxix.

31   Catholic Record Society, 1905, p. 21. Westcote is included in a list compiled c.1560 of annuities granted by successive sovereigns. (PRO, E405/487.)

32   PRO, SP12/140/40; Catholic Record Society, 1905, p. 70.

Westminster following her accession, 'Then was there a pageant made against the deane of Paules gate, where the quéeristers of Paules plaied on vials and soong'.[33] Symond and John Byrd may have been among them.[34] There are no references to William as a player, but he too must have gained some knowledge of the viol, even if it was not his chosen instrument.

William Byrd's early training

It has been speculated that, as choristers of the Cathedral, Symond and John Byrd may have attended St Paul's School.[35] It is possible that William too began his education there, but improbable that any evidence remains to show whether he did or not.

Byrd has been regarded as a pupil in music of the composer Thomas Tallis, who was an organist in the Chapel Royal. The evidence lies in a Latin poem prefacing *Cantiones, quae ab argumento sacrae vocantur,* published jointly by Byrd and Tallis in 1575.[36] The author of the poem was the composer and courtier Ferdinand Richardson.[37] He first addressed Tallis as 'venerande senex, mihi magne magister' (revered elder, my great master), and then, addressing Byrd, wrote of their common master. Richardson's intention is not beyond doubt, and 'magister' may mean no more than 'a master of his craft', though Tallis certainly had at least one pupil in the court circles to which Richardson belonged. That was the older John Harington, a son-in-law of Henry VIII, who was 'much skilled in musicke which was pleasing to the King, and which he learnt in the fellowship of good Maister Tallis, when a

33   Holinshed, 1807-8, iv, p. 7. Machyn (1848, p. 282) mentions the children of Westminster performing on an occasion when viols were played (11 May 1562), but does not actually say they were playing them. An earlier entry in his diary (16 June 1561) also mentions viols, but again does not say who played them.

34   The choristers played instruments at Thomasine Petre's wedding: 'To the Children of powles playing on the Mariage Day In reward vj^s viii^d & to ij men that caried the chistes wherin there playinge garmentes were & instrument*es* xij^d'. (ERO, D/DP A8.)

35   McDonnell, 1977, p. 36.

36   This collection and *Liber primus* and *Liber secundus sacrarum cantionum* (1589 and 1591) are generally referred to as *Cantiones sacrae*.

37   Facsimile of the poem in Monson, 1977, p. xx; printed with a translation in Boyd 1962, pp. 288-291. Richardson was the alias of Sir Ferdinando Heyborne. (Marlow, 1974.) Towards the end of the next century Anthony à Wood wrote that Byrd was 'bred up to musick under Tho. Tallis', but his notes on Byrd contain nothing that he could not have gleaned from printed sources. (Bodleian Library, Wood MS D 19 [4] 106; transcribed in Turbet, 1987, pp. 329-333.)

young man'.[38] The assumption that Richardson intended 'magister' to be understood as meaning 'teacher' does not however dispose of the question of how Byrd spent his boyhood.

Byrd was too young to have been the 'Wyllyam Byrd' who was a chorister at Westminster Abbey in 1542-43.[39] It is feasible that he followed his brothers into the choir of St Paul's Cathedral. The relationship between the musicians of St Paul's and the Chapel Royal was a close one, and Westcote may well have recognized in him a talent he could not train adequately and sent him to Tallis for lessons. When Byrd was himself a Gentleman of the Chapel Royal he appears to have given lessons to the young Peter Philips, who not only worked at St Paul's but lodged with Westcote.[40] An association of this kind between Westcote and the young Byrd would go some way to explaining the latter's adherence to Catholicism. There is however no mention of William Byrd in the surviving records of St Paul's. Rimbault's statement that Byrd was the senior chorister of St Paul's was made on the flimsiest of evidence, and is almost certainly inaccurate.[41] It makes better sense to accept an alternative hypothesis that he was a boy chorister in the Chapel Royal, where Tallis was one of the Gentlemen.[42] This might account for his later friendship with the Petre Family. Sir William Petre's interest in the Chapel is shown by a payment of forty shillings recorded in his accounts for 31 January 1554/5: 'To m^r bower m^r of the Children of the Chapell for his paynes taken wth bentley and for his meate and drinke wth hym to this day'.[43] John Bentley was brought up in the Petre household as the personal servant of John Petre. He was one of the family's music copyists, and remained with them until his death in 1597. In his will he left songbooks and music for the virginals.[44]

The Chapel Royal is the group of priests and others serving the religious needs of the monarch and royal household. In the sixteenth century, as now, it was headed by the Dean and Subdean, who were

38   Letter from the younger Sir John Harington to Lord Burghley. (Harington, 1769, pp. 132-133.)

39   Westminster Abbey Muniment Room, MS 37045, f. 3^r.

40   See pp. 62, 364.

41   See p. 397.

42   Tallis's name was included in a lay subsidy roll of 1543/4, when he was probably already a Gentleman of the Chapel. (ERO, E179/69/36; Ashbee, 1986-96, vii, p. 91.) He remained there until his death in 1585. (Rimbault, 1872, p. 4.)

43   ERO, D/DP A6.

44   Edwards, 1975, pp. 31-34; ERO, D/ABW 5/365; and the account of Bentley's life in Dr David Mateer's forthcoming article William Byrd, John Petre and Oxford, Bodleian MS Mus. Sch. E.423.

answerable to the Lord Chamberlain, and who were supported by a number of other priests and officers. Music was provided by the Gentlemen of the Chapel Royal, a group of singing men and organists. Their number hovered around twenty-four throughout the reigns of Queen Elizabeth and King James. There were also twelve boy singers, for whose training and care the Master of the Children was responsible.[45] One of the Gentlemen was chosen to be the Clerk of the Cheque, who had a responsibility for minor disciplinary matters, and kept a record of the Chapel's affairs in the Old Cheque Book, still preserved by the Chapel Royal. This sets out regulations for the ordering of the Chapel and the conduct of its members, and records privileges (such as feasts and the 'Auntient tymes of lyberty and playinge weekes') and financial 'benevolences' traditionally accorded to the Gentlemen.[46]

Unfortunately there is no documentary evidence to confirm Byrd's presence among the Chapel boys, who were not considered worthy of individual mention even when they were cited as a group. The lists of named musicians, priests and others who received mourning liveries for the funeral of Edward VI in 1553 refer simply to '12 Children of the kinges Chappell', or include some similar phrase.[47] Although there were other posts at court which a musical youth might have filled, the occupants are correspondingly anonymous.[48]

A further problem is that Tallis's responsibility for the training of boys is not clear. Their education was formally the duty of the Master of the Children, who was also responsible for boarding them. The Master throughout the period when Byrd could have been a boy singer was Richard Bower.[49] On the other hand Tallis and Bower were the joint recipients of a lease from Queen Mary,[50] which may indicate that each

45   Ashbee, 1986-96, vi, pp. 1-4 et passim; iv, passim.

46   Rimbault, 1872, pp. 62ff. See also Woodfill, 1953, pp. 161-176, and Baldwin, 1990, pp. 272-289.

47   Ashbee, 1986-96, vii, pp. 127ff. A few boys can be identified from miscellaneous references (Smith, 1965, p. 46), and entries in the Old Cheque Book describing newly appointed Gentlemen as having been children of the Chapel, e.g. Tallis's replacement, Henry Eveseed, and William Bodinghurst's replacement, John Bull (Rimbault, 1872, p. 4).

48   At the beginning of Queen Mary's reign the lutenist and viol player Peter van Wilder was paid 'for fyndyng of six singĩge children belongynge to the pʳvye chamber'. (Ashbee, 1986-96, vii, p. 318.)

49   Ibid., vii, p. 96; vi. p. 3. The terms of Bower's appointment in 1545 specify his responsibility for teaching the boys, and for their exhibition, vesture and bedding. He lived until 1561, when the post went to Richard Edwards. (Ibid., vi, pp. 10, 174.)

50   Ibid., vii, p. 143.

held a senior position. Byrd could well have been trained by Bower as a singer, and as a keyboard player and composer by Tallis. The several evidences of a close relationship between Byrd and Tallis, and the former's choice of the latter as the godfather of his son Thomas, argue a bond that might have existed between a pupil and a teacher who had no son of his own.[51] It is difficult to resist the notion that there may have been further unrecorded grounds for their friendship, since before Tallis joined the Chapel Royal he occupied several posts which could have brought him into contact with Byrd's family and patrons.[52]

Byrd's youthful musical skills in any case suggest early recognition and training of the kind he might have received in the Chapel Royal. He would have begun both his musical and his academic education at about the age of seven.[53] There is no doubt of his ability to express himself

51   Tallis's will refers to his godson. (See p. 383.) Although he had no son, a relation of his wife seems to have been brought up as his daughter. Among the names in Tallis's will is that of 'Joane Pearc my wieffs sisters daughter'. Joane Tallis's will mentions 'Joane Paire' as her 'cosen', a term frequently applied to a niece. Kimbell (1816) however prints 'The decree of the Commissioners of Charitable Uses, respecting Stanton, ... Tallis, and Halder's charities', dated 1622. This says (p. 57) that 'John Pare took to wife Joan Tallis, daughter and heir of the aforesaid Joan Tallis [wife of the composer], deceased'. There may be some confusion with the step-daughter of Joane Tallis, the will of whose first husband Thomas Bury refers to his daughter 'Johan bury by my wyfe Jane'. Bury's will, witnessed by Thomas Tallis, has been located by Dr Andrew Ashbee at the Centre for Kentish Studies. (DRb/Pwr 11, f. 254^r.) Drake (1886, p. 89), drawing on extracts made by Thomas Streatfield from the manuscripts of William Lambarde, mentions her first marriage to Bury, and refers to an entry for 8 July 1586 concerning Lambarde's sale of land and buildings to Joane Tallis. (See p. 385, 'Lambert'.)

52   Tallis's name appears in a list of those associated with Waltham Abbey at the time of its dissolution, which was carried through by William Petre. (PRO, E117/11/24; Emmison, 1961, p. 18.) This does not however state Tallis's position at the abbey. Both men served Henry VIII and the three succeeding sovereigns, so they probably had at least a superficial acquaintance. A family friendship with the Byrds could have been formed earlier, while Tallis was a conduct (singing clerk) of St Mary at Hill in the years 1536-1538. (Littlehales, 1905.) Or it could have sprung from the Kentish connections of Byrd and his friends the Roper family, who had lands in Kent and were patrons of Tallis. (Bennet, 1988.) Like Tallis, Ferdinando Heyborne, author of the commendatory poem in *Cantiones sacrae*, had connections with Walthamstow. (Metcalfe, 1878-89, ii, p. 583; Marlow, 1974.)

53   The apprenticeship and training of sixteenth-century musicians has yet to be fully investigated, but see Flynn, 1995, and Woodfill, 1953, p. 122 et passim. It does not appear that formal bonds of apprenticeship (lasting seven years) were usual in the Chapel and cathedrals at this date, as they seem to have been among musicians belonging to

freely in written English, and if he composed his Latin prefaces unaided he benefited from the customary grounding in that language as well. He would have enjoyed the usual privileges accorded to the boys,[54] and taken part in the plays they presented.[55] But above all his life would have centred on the cycle of services and ceremonies in which the choristers participated. He would undoubtedly have sung at the funeral of Edward VI, and experienced the liturgical changes introduced with Queen Mary's accession and the restoration of Roman Catholicism. A major event was the marriage of Queen Mary to Prince Philip of Spain, who brought forty-two musicians to England with him. These included twenty-one singers, a large group of instrumentalists, and two organists.[56] The marriage took place in Winchester Cathedral in 1554, and − in the words of John Elder − 'duryng hie masse tyme the Quenes Chapell matched with the quire, and the organs, used suche swete proporcyon of musicke and harmonye, as the like (I suppose) was never beefore invented or harde'.[57] It is just possible that all three Byrd brothers were still of an age to have taken part when, later in the year, the Spaniards sang with the choirs of the Chapel Royal and St Paul's Cathedral. Machyn entered the following account of the occasion in his diary.

municipal guilds. For the part played by the Master of the Grammar in the education of the boys of the Chapel Royal, see Baldwin, 1990, pp. 319-320.

54   In 1553 Bower received a payment for 'largesse to ye children at high fests'. (Ashbee, 1986-96, vii, p. 123.)

55   If Byrd was in the choir at Christmas 1553-54 he may have taken part in *Respublica*, possibly played at that time. (Hillebrand, 1926, pp. 68-69.) The Gentlemen of the Chapel, who also had a dramatic tradition, put on a play as part of the celebrations for Queen Mary's coronation in 1553. (Ashbee, 1986-96, vii, p. 131.) Performances by the Chapel children seem not to be recorded during much of Byrd's boyhood, but it is unlikely that there was a complete break in the tradition exemplified by performances in 1539, 1559-60 and 1567/8. (Ashbee, vii, p. 79; Feuillerat, 1908, p. 34; Ashbee, vi, p. 96).

56   The musical activities are described more fully in Ward, 1969. See also Anglés, 1944, pp. 124-136.

57   Elder, 1555; Nichols, 1850, p, 142. Another account is given by the Windsor Herald, Charles Wriothesley (1875-77, ii, pp. 118-121). 'The 23 of Julie the Prince of Spayne came to Winchester about vi of the clock at night ... and came to the Cathedrall churche ... and then the Lord Chauncellor began Te Deum, the organs playinge and the quier singinge the rest ...'. On 25 July, 'After the marriage knott thus knitt the King and Queen came hand in hand under a rich canopie ... the trumpetts then blowinge tyll they came into the quier, where all the priestes and singinge men all in riche copes began to sing a psalme used in marriages ...'.

The ij day of desember dyd come to powll*es* all prest*es* & clarkes wth ther copes & c*r*osses & all ye craft*es* in ther leverey & my lord mayre & ye althermе*n* agaynst my lord cardenall*es* comȳg & at ye bysshopes of london plase my lord chãsseler & all ye bysshopes tarehyng for my lord cardenall commyng y^t was at ix of ye cloke for he landyd at beynard castyll & ther my lord mayre reseyvyd hym and browgth im[58] to ye powllse & so my lord chanseler & my lord cardenall & all ye byshopes whent up in to ye quer w^t ther meytry*es* [mitres] & at x of ye cloke ye kyng grace cam to powll*es* to her mase w^t iiij c [hundred] of ye gaard on c englys men on c he almen [High Almains] on c spane*ardes* on c of swechenar*es* [Switzers] & mony lord*es* & knyght*es* & hard masse boyth ye quen chapell & ye kyng*es* and powll*es* quer sang.[59]

It has reasonably been suggested that Tallis's Christmas Mass *Puer natus est nobis* was sung by the combined choirs of the English and Spanish royal chapels a few days later.[60]

Among Prince Philip's musicians were the Spaniard Antonio de Cabezón and the Netherlander Phillipe de Monte. The young Byrd may have been impressed by the organ-playing of the former, but contrary to a view once held there is no evidence that his own keyboard style was influenced by Cabezón's music.[61] It is more credible that Byrd's later exchange of motets with Monte may have originated in an acquaintance formed at this time.[62] Although Monte was a good deal older than Byrd, he was said to have been unhappy as the only non-Spanish member of Prince Philip's musical entourage,[63] and could well have passed some of his time in the company of Tallis and his protégé.

Byrd would have been uncomfortably aware of the arrest in 1555 of William Hunnis, one of the Gentlemen of the Chapel, for complicity in a plot to overthrow the Queen and her Spanish husband.[64] If he retained a

58   'browgth' smudged; 'browgt him' intended?

59   BL, MS Cotton Vitellius F. V; Machyn, 1848, p. 78.

60   The Queen was rumoured to be pregnant. See Doe, 1976, p. 21; Wulstan, 1985, pp. 295-296; Kerman, 1993.

61   Ward (1969) stresses the many unsupported assumptions behind the belief that Cabezón influenced English keyboard music. See also Neighbour, 1978, pp. 145-146.

62   The exchange is not reported earlier than 1763, in John Alcock's annotations. (BL, Additional MS 23624, ff. 101^r and 107^r.)

63   Doorslaer, 1921, p. 217, prints a letter written on 22 September 1555 by Seld, the Viennese Imperial Vice-Chancellor, while on a mission to Paris. It says, in part: 'in des Königs Capell nit wol zu pleiben hat, dieweil die andern singen all Spanier und er allain ain Niderlander'.

64   Ashbee, 1986-96, vii, p. 422. Hunnis survived to succeed Edwards as Master of

place in the Chapel when his voice changed, he probably attended Mary's funeral in 1558 and the coronation of Queen Elizabeth, though he was not among the named members of the Chapel who received liveries for these occasions.[65] He may have been required to take the Oath of Supremacy, and would certainly have felt the effects wrought by the restoration of the English church.

Although this is reasonable conjecture, it is still conjecture. So is what Byrd did immediately before he went to Lincoln in 1563. His fluent literacy and his readiness in later life to write legal documents half inspire the notion that he may have studied the law, as his son Thomas was to do later, but it is hard to see how he could then have gained the musical skills that fitted him in his early twenties for the post of Organist and Master of the Choristers at Lincoln Cathedral. It seems instead almost certain that he acted as assistant organist in the Chapel Royal, and helped to rehearse the singers.[66]

There is little doubt that Byrd underwent an intensive training in composition at this time. His early music contains obvious traces of Tudor methods of teaching, which required the pupil to write counterpoint to a cantus firmus. 'I praie you set me a plaine song, and I will trie how I can sing upon it', says Thomas Morley's scholar Philomathes.[67] Byrd's early canons suggest the instruction he received from Tallis, a notable exponent of the form. Cantus firmi and canon are the foundation of almost everything − and maybe everything − Byrd wrote up to the time of his departure for Lincoln.

In addition to his studies with Tallis, Byrd worked with other seasoned composers, and the association connects him more securely with the Chapel Royal. A setting of the plainsong psalm *Similes illis fiant*, ascribed to 'mr birde',[68] forms the second section of the collaborative composition *In exitu Israel*. It can be dated to Queen Mary's reign because it was designed for the Sarum use, which was discarded on Mary's death, and because the first section is by John

the Children in 1566. (Rimbault, 1872, p. 1.)

65   Two yards of black cloth, to make mourning clothes, was allocated to each of the twelve children of the Chapel for the burial of Queen Mary. The same allowance of red cloth was made for the coronation of Queen Elizabeth. The Gentlemen each got seven yards for the funeral, with a smaller allowance for their servants, and four yards for the coronation. (Ashbee, 1986-96, vi, pp. 1-4.) Could Byrd have been a 'servant'?

66   There is no record of payments to support or invalidate the conjecture. It was not uncommon at a later date for musicians of the royal household to be admitted without fee until a post fell vacant.

67   Morley, 1597, p. 72 (1952 ed., p. 144). See also Flynn, 1995.

68   BL, Additional MSS 17802-5.

Sheppard, a Gentleman of the Chapel Royal who died in 1558.[69] The
third section is by William Mundy, who during Mary's reign was the
parish clerk of St Mary at Hill.[70] St Mary's had a strong musical
tradition, and links with the Chapel Royal; Tallis was a singing clerk
there in 1536-1538, and members of the Chapel sang at the church in
1554.[71] The knowledge that Byrd was born in 1539 or 1540, and not
1543 as thought until now, relieves doubt about whether even a gifted
boy could have worked with these older composers.

Byrd's brothers and sisters

While Byrd was receiving his musical training, his brothers and sisters
were marrying and having children. Symond, the elder of his brothers,
married Anne Bridges at All Hallows Lombard Street on 28 April
1567.[72] Assuming that he was the Symond Byrd whose name appears in
the rolls of the Fletchers' Company from 1566, he became a liveryman
in 1572.[73] Symond's daughter Mary was two years and nine months old
when Cooke recorded the family's genealogy in April 1571. In due
course she married a man named Farrant.[74] It has not been discovered
whether he was a son of the composer and playwright Richard Farrant.[75]
A second daughter, Martha, was born to Symond and Anne in March

69   Sheppard was a member of the Chapel Royal by 1553. (Ashbee, 1986-96, vii,
p. 124.) He was buried at St Margaret's, Westminster, on 21 December 1558. (Burke,
1914, p. 401; Wulstan, 1994.)

70   Baillie, 1962. Mundy had been the head chorister at Westminster Abbey in 1543,
when a 'Wyllyam Byrd' was also a chorister. (Pine, 1953, pp. 48-49). He occupied posts
at St Martin Vintry and St Mary at Hill; and was at St Paul's Cathedral by 1559.
(Lambeth Palace Library, Carte Antique et Miscellanee, XIII.57, f. 1ʳ.) He entered the
Chapel Royal in February 1563/4. (Rimbault, 1872, p. 1.) From 1528 to 1538 a John
Byrd was a warden of St Mary at Hill (Littlehales, 1905), but no connection with the
composer's family is known. Baillie's suggestion of such a connection is unconvincing.

71   Littlehales, 1905.

72   GL, MS 17613. Is it more than coincidence that in 1567 William Byrd's future
patron, John Petre, paid a servant 'for bryngyng Mʳ Brugges lute to my chamber'? (ERO,
D/DP A17, unfoliated.)

73   GL, MSS 5977/2 and 21030.

74   John Byrd's will. See p. 387.

75   Richard Farrant was a Gentleman of the Chapel Royal who married Anne, a
daughter of Richard Bower, Master of the Children of the Chapel. In 1564, despite being
a Roman Catholic, Farrant became Master of the Children at St George's Chapel,
Windsor. He returned to the Chapel Royal as Master of the Children in 1569.

1571. No record of the children's baptisms has yet been found, and these may have taken place outside London.

By October 1577 John Byrd, the second of the brothers, was living in the parish of St John Zachary, where he was assessed for subsidy purposes.[76] This was just to the north of St Paul's. If John went into business he was undoubtedly successful, as his bequests show. It has not been established whether he was a member of a city company; he was generally described as 'John Byrd of London, gentleman' with no other indication of status.[77] His court cases strongly suggest that the lending of money was a principal source of his income, and on more than one occasion he was accused of engaging in usury.[78]

On 11 December 1588 John Byrd was granted administration of the goods of 'Suzanne Burd', a widow who has not so far been identified.[79] His own will, drawn up on 2 January 1621/2, and twice amended, provides information about many members of the family. It however gives no clue as to whether he was married, though the churchwardens' accounts show that a 'Mistris Bird' was buried at St John Zachary shortly before his death at the end of the month.[80]

76   PRO, E179/145/252. An assessment roll of 1582 also names John as living in the parish. (PRO, E179/251/16; Lang, 1993, p. 122.) His will confirms his continued residence there. A different John Byrd was assessed in the nearby parish of St Botolph's without Aldersgate.

77   The name John Byrd was, if anything, more common than William Byrd. Privy Council, 1901, p. 111, refers to a John Byrd who married Hester Godscall (or Godschalke), the sister of a Dutchman named James Godscall. (Marriage recorded in the register of St Nicholas Acons, 26 January 1590/1. See Brigg, 1890, p. 63.) William Byrd's brother however mentioned no one called Godscall in his will. He could not have been the John Byrd whom Court Minute Book P of the Goldsmiths' Company refers to as being in extreme poverty. (Company records at Goldsmiths' Hall.) Nor does he seem to have been a Draper, as suggested in McMurray, 1925, p. 437. The Draper appears in PRO, REQ1/15, ff. 20[v], 22[v], etc, and is perhaps named in the will of 'Rose Trott of London wydowe', since it includes bequests to the Drapers' Company: 'Item to m[r] Burde & his wief to hym a gowne & to her a cassok of pewk'. (ERO, D/DC 27/211, dated 20 January 1573.) John Byrd, a Brewer, is mentioned in REQ1/15, f. 319[r-v].

78   The third verse of psalm 15, twice set by William Byrd, describes the virtuous man who does not put his money out to usury.

79   GL, MS 9050/2, f. 16[r]. The wife of John Byrd of Southwark was named Susan, but he is not known to have been related to the composer's family. (Privy Council, 1903, pp. 215, 256-257.)

80   GL, MS 590/1, f. 99[r].

William Byrd's sisters all married. Alice married William Duffing, but nothing more is at present known of her.[81]

Barbara married Robert Broughe at All Hallows Bread Street on 21 July 1555.[82] Broughe was a maker of virginals and organs, who was born about 1530. He was a vestryman of St Martin's Ludgate from 1586 to 1600, when he lived 'wthout the gate'.[83] He was a liveryman of the Fletchers' Company 1566-73; a warden in 1574, 1582, and 1600-1601; and an assistant 1575-1603.[84]

Mary's first husband was William Ireland; her second husband, whom she married before 1571, was Edward Pryce.[85] The William Ireland who witnessed John Byrd's will must have been Mary's son from her first marriage. There were several people named William Ireland in London, but a chain of associations focuses interest on the one who held several minor offices at Westminster Abbey. He was a 'cousin' (relation) of William Heyther (or Heather), who gave his name to the Oxford chair of music.[86] Heyther was a lay clerk of Westminster Abbey from 1586 until 1615, when he became a Gentleman of the Chapel Royal. William Byrd and Heyther were among those who dined at Magdalen Herbert's house in 1601.[87] Heyther was a close friend of the historian William Camden, who was headmaster of Westminster School from 1593 to 1597. Magdalen Herbert's son George Herbert was a pupil at the school from about 1605, under 'the care of Mr. *Ireland*, who was then chief Master of that School'.[88] The schoolmaster was however Richard

---

81   Queen's College, Oxford, MS 72, f. 72^v.

82   GL, MS 5031; Bannerman, 1913, p. 96. He may have been related to George Broughe, who became free of the Haberdashers' Company in 1587 (GL, MS 15857), and whose children were baptized at All Hallows Bread Street between 1597 and 1604. (Bannerman, pp. 13-15, 168.)

83   Broughe's trade and age: PRO, STAC5/A43/35. Vestryman: GL, MS 1311/1 part 1, ff. 83^r-94^v.

84   GL, MS 5977/2; GL, MS 21030. See also Oxley, 1968, p. 104.

85   Queen's College, Oxford, MS 72, f. 72^v. As no one named Pryce is mentioned in John Byrd's will, it is likely that there was no son of Mary's second marriage.

86   William Heyther, c.1563-1627, was born at Harmondsworth, Middlesex, not far from Harlington, where William Byrd was living by 1577. Neither Ireland's will (1638) nor Heyther's (1627) casts any light on a possible family relationship to William Byrd. (Westminster Archives Centre, Todd 1634-41, ff. 101^v-105^v; Camden 1622-35, ff. 98^v-100^v.)

87   Charles, 1974.

88   Walton, 1675 (1927, p. 262). George Herbert, 1593-1633, cleric, poet, recreated himself with music from an early age: 'the greatest diversion from his Study, was the practice of Musick, in which he became a great Master'. (Walton, 1927, p. 269).

Ireland,[89] who may have had a brother named William, though the relationships within what appears to be one Ireland family in Westminster are not always clear, and need further investigation.[90] Unhappily, the identity of Byrd's nephew and the William Ireland of Westminster Abbey is not confirmed by their signatures.[91]

Martha Byrd married Philip Smyth at All Hallows Lombard Street on 26 January 1567/8. Philip was the second son of Robert Smyth of Corsham in Wiltshire.[92] He was born about 1540.[93] Like John Byrd, Philip was styled 'of London, gentleman', and the brothers-in-law worked together. By 1583 Philip Smyth was sufficiently well off to buy Battyshall manor from John.[94] About 1592 he seems to have lived in the parish of All Hallows Barking by the Tower,[95] but when he sold the manor in 1594 he was described as a 'Citizen and Haberdasher of London' (that is a member of the Haberdashers' Company), who lived at

89   Barker and Stenning, 1928, ii, p. 504. Interestingly, in view of Byrd's Catholicism, Richard Ireland became a Catholic and went to France in 1610; he was back in London as a priest in 1623.

90   It is not certain that they are invariably given correctly in the printed sources mentioned here.

91   The signature of William Ireland of Westminster appears on various documents, e.g. Westminster Abbey, MS 41350 ('The Smiths bill of worke done for the College of Westm^r', 1610), and MS 41547 (1619). The Abbey's Muniment Room has an index of documents concerning people named Ireland. One (MS 53317, reproduced in Musicians' Company, 1909, p. 334) is a note of 1625 to William Ireland from the Abbey's organist, Orlando Gibbons, assuring him that a bill submitted by the organ-maker John Burward is 'very resonable for I have alredy Cut him off ten shillings'. For further information about Ireland see Chester and Armytage, 1886, p. 19, and Burke, 1914, pp. 319 and 80, note 2. It is an open question whether the Abbey's William Ireland could have been the son of Richard 'Yearlande' of Westminster. (Register of St Margaret's, Westminster, 6 June 1579.) A William Ireland is mentioned in a document signed by William Shakespeare, but he has not been identified. The document is dated 10 March 1612/13 and concerns Shakespeare's purchase of a property 'abutting upon a streete leading downe to Pudle wharffe' and 'now or late being in the tenure or occupacōn of one William Ireland or of his assignee or assignes'. (GL, MS 3738.)

92   London and Rawlins, 1963, p. 80.

93   PRO, REQ2/224/42.

94   ERO, D/DM T56, bundle 1.

95   PRO, REQ2/224/42 and REQ2/273/46. A list of citizens made c.1589, and bound into Queen's College, Oxford, MS 72, also mentions a Philip Smyth under the heading of 'All saints Barking S^t donstanes St Claires and Allhallowes pishes'. On the nature of this list, see Lang, 1993, p. xv.

Henley-on-Thames.[96] He had probably become free of the Company in 1566.[97]

The 'Philip Smith' whom John Byrd's will identifies as his nephew was presumably the second son of Philip and Martha.[98] Their first son, Thomas, evidently died young. They also had five daughters: Elizabeth, born in 1568, Mary, Alice, Sara and Judith. By 1622 Mary had a son and daughter of her own.[99]

96   ERO, *D/DM T56*, bundle 1. The sale document is signed 'Philipp Smyth'. A release in the same bundle is signed by John Byrd.

97   GL MS 15857/1, f. 103[v], records the freedom through the Haberdashers' Company of 'Phillip Smith per Thomas Smith', 7 February 1566.

98   A freedom by patrimony was granted through the Haberdashers' Company to Philip Smith on 6 February 1600. (GL, MS 15857/1, f. 146[v].) The freedom granted to 'Symon Bird p Phillip Smith' on 12 May 1598 indicates a connection with William Byrd's family. (See the list of John Byrd's legatees on pp. 389-391.) Other Haberdashers' Company freedoms which may be connected with the Byrd family are 'Thomas Birde p William Grove' (1 August 1589) and 'Symon Smith p Patrimony' (12 October 1604), but no definite association has been established.

99   Queen's College, Oxford, MS 72, f. 72[v]; John Byrd's will.

2

LINCOLN · 1563-1572

In 1562 a replacement was needed for Thomas Appleby, who was to retire from the post of Organist and Master of the Choristers at Lincoln Cathedral, where he had served with only one short break since 1537.[1] William Byrd was a candidate who was little short of ideal: an accomplished organist with experience in training the choir of the Chapel Royal, who had moreover begun to show unusual skill as a composer. Although such a youthful appointment was not wholly exceptional — Robert White, who was probably no more than a couple of years older than Byrd, had shortly before succeeded his father-in-law Christopher Tye as Master of the Choristers at Ely Cathedral — it is hard to see where the Dean and Chapter could have found another young man of anything like equal ability.[2] Appleby was probably in touch with Tallis and others who would have known of Byrd's promise and would gladly have endorsed his candidacy.[3]

Byrd must have travelled to Lincoln to present himself to the Chapter early in 1562/3. The scene that greeted him on his arrival cannot have been greatly different from the one described by the antiquary John Leland, who visited the city in the years before Byrd's birth. He noted particularly the surrounding walls, the outlying suburbs and villages, the two arms of the river and the bridges over them, and the many parish churches. He paid special attention to the great cathedral set on top of a hill overlooking the scene.[4]

Following their meeting with Byrd the Chapter determined on 6 February to grant him and his assigns the nearby rectory of Hainton, and presumably the income which went with it, for forty-one years.[5] On

1   Shaw, 1991, p. 155. Appleby died shortly afterwards. On 1 June 1564 'Mariam Appleby relict' agreed to the reassignment of her late husband's house. (LA, D&C A/3/7, f. 36ʳ, housed in Lincoln Cathedral Library at the time of writing; D&C A/3/8, f. 13ᵛ.)

2   An examination of Shaw, 1991, shows that the field from which the Lincoln Chapter had to choose was very small indeed. White was probably born c.1538. (Grove, 1980, s.v. 'White, Robert', following 'Dotted Crotchet', 1905, and Mateer, 1974.)

3   Suggested by BL Additional MSS 17802-5, which as well as music by Tallis and other Chapel Royal composers contains Byrd's early *Similes illis fiant* and a Mass 'for a Mene' by Appleby.

4   Leland, 1964, i, pp. 29-32; v, pp. 120-123.

5   LA, D&C A/3/7, f. 27ʳ; D&C A/3/8, f. 4ᵛ. Hainton is on the Roman road from Lincoln to Louth.

Table 3 · Historical background 1563-1571

1563   Measures for controlling enclosures, paupers and vagabonds, the importation of clothing, ornaments and weapons, and the licensing of middlemen in food trades. Statute of Artificers (direction of labour, stabilization of employment, and wage-regulation). Thirty-nine Articles drafted. Marriage negotiations between Queen Elizabeth and Archduke Charles. Restoration of currency. Plague kills 20,000 in London (almost one person in four). Foxe, *Book of Martyrs*.

1564   Dudley created Earl of Leicester. Hawkins' second slaving expedition. Peace with France. Merchant Adventurers receive new charter. Queen visits Cambridge. Shakespeare and Marlowe born.

1565   Mary Queen of Scots marries Lord Darnley (her English Catholic cousin).

1566   Queen Elizabeth resists Parliamentary pressure to marry. Queen visits Oxford. Udall, *Ralph Roister Doister*.

1567   Start of Hawkins' disastrous third expedition. Carré starts producing large quantities of cheap window glass. Darnley murdered, Mary marries Bothwell, a Protestant, and is compelled to abdicate.

1568   Mary flees to England. Catholic English College established at Douai.

1569   Suppression of Northern Rebellion (led by Northumberland and Westmorland). Norfolk sent to Tower. *Declaration of the Queen's Proceedings in Church and State*.

1570   Pope excommunicates Elizabeth. Ascham, *The Schoolmaster*.

1571   Opening of London Stock Exchange. Taking of interest up to ten per cent permitted. Re-enactment of treason laws. Ridolfi Plot (involving Norfolk). Puritan *Admonitions to Parliament* (also 1573). English Catholics ordered to return from Continent. Penalties for Catholic activism increased. Universities of Oxford and Cambridge incorporated.

---

17 September 1541 it had been granted to George Heneage, the Dean and Archdeacon of Lincoln, as his canonical farm for a term of forty-one years, but without specific mention of the rectory.[6] As Heneage had died in 1549 the lease was in the hands of his assigns and ran until 1582. An indenture confirming the grant to Byrd was however signed and sealed on 27 February 1562/3.[7] Why the grant was made, and took the form it

6   Cole, 1917, p. 54.
7   LA, D&C A/3/7, f. 27ʳ; D&C A/3/8, f. 4ᵛ. By the seventeenth century land in the

did in the circumstances, are questions yet to be answered, though it is
not difficult to imagine it being offered to Byrd as an inducement to take
the job; nor is it difficult to imagine some connection between Byrd and
the Heneage family. John Heneage's home was at Hainton, and his son
Sir Thomas, George Heneage's eldest brother, was buried there. It was
this Thomas Heneage who, in 1537, contributed to 'the brotherhoods of
Jesus at Powles in London' and sponsored 'a child that Phelips of the
Chapel teacheth'.[8] Sir Thomas's nephew, also Sir Thomas
Heneage, Vice-Chamberlain of Queen Elizabeth's household, had
numerous connections both with Lincolnshire and with Essex, the county
from which Byrd's family originally came.[9]

Byrd's appointment ran from 25 March 1563, and was formalized by
letters patent recorded in a minute of 24 April. The Latin of the copy
entered in the Chapter Acts, and marginally headed 'Littere Pateñ Willmi
bird m[r] choristare', is so full of contractions and abbreviations that a
quotation from part of Shaw's translation makes easier reading than the
original:

> Know ye that we, the aforesaid dean and chapter, have given, granted and by
> this confirmed to our beloved in Christ William Byrde, for the term of his
> life for his good service already rendered and hereafter to be rendered to us
> and the aforesaid church, the post of song master or master of the chorister
> boys of the said church of Lincoln with all singular wages, fees, rights and
> profits whatever pertaining or belonging to the said post, namely six pounds
> thirteen shillings and fourpence of legal English money, to be paid annually
> by the hands of the master or steward for the time being of the house of the
> said choristers by equal portions at the feasts of St Michael the Archangel
> and the Annunciation of the Blessed Virgin Mary.
>
> We have also granted and by these presents have conceded to the same
> William Byrde the post of pulsator or player at the organs of the said church
> of Lincoln with all and singular wages, fees and profits whatever pertaining

countryside owned by the Chapter was usually let for leases of twenty-one or forty years.
These terms rarely ran their full course, the normal period for renewal being every seven
years for a twenty-one year lease and every fourteen years for a forty year lease. (Jones,
1984, p. 5.) A later reference to Byrd's lease may therefore exist in a document that is
still to be found.

8   PRO, SP1/241, f. 262; Letters and papers, 1929, pp. 437-438. Sir Thomas Heneage
also maintained a yeoman named Byrd. 'Phelips' was presumably Robert Philip(s),
Gentleman (formerly a child) of the Chapel Royal. (Ashbee, 1986-96, vii, as indexed.)

9   He was a member of Parliament for Stamford in 1552, for Lincolnshire in 1571 and
1572, and for Essex from 1584. He received many grants of land from the Queen, chiefly
in Essex where he built Copt Hall.

or belonging to which post, namely six pounds thirteen shillings and fourpence of legal English money, of which we wish and assign five marks to be paid to the said William Byrde by the hands of the clerk of the fabric of the said church and the remaining five marks by the hands of the clerk of the common fund of the said church, by equal portions at the abovesaid feasts. The said posts to be had, enjoyed, occupied and exercised by the same William Byrde together with all and singular wages, fees, liberties and profits aforesaid from the feasts of the Annunciation of the Blessed Virgin Mary recently past to the end and for the term of his natural life if the said William Byrde is willing so long to occupy and exercise the said post in his own person.

We allow also that if it should happen that the said William Byrde is hindered by any reasonable cause in the future in discharging the said posts in his own person, for example the following reasons, namely sickness, feebleness of mind or old age, then it shall be permitted to exercise and carry out the said posts by sufficient deputy to be admitted with the consent of the dean and chapter in that regard.

Provided always that he and his deputy shall from time to time well and diligently instruct and teach the choristers for the time being of the said church in knowledge of the art of music and shall also well and diligently exercise and occupy the post of player or pulsator at the organs of the said church.[10]

Byrd was therefore to be paid ten marks as Master of the Choristers and another ten as Organist. This was the salary received by Appleby, and payments from the specified accounts started with the new year on 25 March. Byrd was also given a livery allowance of nine shillings a year.[11]

10   Translation: Shaw, 1967; original: LA, D&C A/3/7, f. 27ᵛ, and D&C A/3/8, f. 4ᵛ. The reference to 'service already rendered' may mean that Byrd had begun work before 25 March, and that this has something to do with the grant of Hainton rectory.

11   Pay: LA, D&C A/3/7, f. 4ᵛ, entry for 23 March 1559/60. Livery: D&C Bi/2/1, section 3, unfoliated; Bi/5/12(20), f. 17r; and elsewhere in the books of payments made by the Clerk of the Common Fund. Shaw (1967, p. 53) says with authority that the total of £13 6s 8d paid to Byrd was above the general level for such posts and quotes examples. It is however hard to compare Byrd's income at Lincoln with payments elsewhere, because of hidden extras. Dr Andrew Ashbee has kindly supplied the information that at Rochester the organist's fee seems to have been £10 a year in 1594, but in 1577 Peter Rowle received a gift of £14 a year for teaching the choristers well. (Centre for Kentish Studies, DRc/Ac1.A; see also Shaw, 1991, p. 233.) Dr Ashbee adds that at Canterbury, on 25 November 1603, George Marson was appointed Organist and Master of the Choristers 'with the usuall fee of £12'. (Chapter Acts.) Comparison with the income of

Organist and Master of the Choristers

Byrd began work at Lincoln at a time when the future of church music was uncertain. The injunctions issued during the course of a royal visitation in 1559 reflected something of the Queen's own taste, and encouraged music provided it was not too elaborate, but at Convocation in 1562 it became clear that many of those present would have been glad to see severe restrictions placed on the use of music in church, including the abolition of organs.[12] The influence of those who harboured such sentiments may have been abated at Lincoln by the presence of the musical Francis Mallett as Dean,[13] but in 1562 the appointment as Archdeacon of John Aylmer can have created nothing but difficulties for Byrd. Strype says 'he first purged the Cathedral Church of *Lincoln*, being at that Time a Nest of unclean Birds; and next in the County, by preaching and executing the Commission, he so prevailed, that not one Recusant was left in the Country, at his coming away'.[14] It may have been more than a dash of personal feeling that led Byrd to set the psalm *Ad Dominum cum tribularer* while he was at Lincoln: 'Heu mihi! quia incolatus meus prolongatus est' (*Woe is me! that my stay is prolonged*).[15]

musicians employed at court is difficult because (1) there were differences in the prestige attaching to their posts, and between the cost of living and other factors in a cathedral city and in London, (2) no record remains of musicians' income from outside sources, such as teaching (Byrd claimed his had been reduced by his leaving Lincoln), and (3) the royal musicians received payments from a variety of sources, and these included gifts and special grants. (See Ashbee, 1986-96, iv and vi.)

12   le Huray, 1978, pp. 32-36. The injunctions of 1559 were issued on the Queen's authority because no bishops had been appointed.

13   '... when he was bot x yere of age he cūth have song discant plaid of thorgans recorderes of lute wᵗ other instruments in so much Lord Latymer had such plesoʳ in hym that he lay wᵗ hym nyghtly'. (John Wilson, Prior of Mountgrace de Ingleby, writing about the young Mallett to Nicholas Metcalfe, Master of St John's College, Cambridge; printed in *The Eagle*, xvii, 1893, pp. 478-479.) Mallett was Dean from 1554 until his death in 1570, when he was succeeded by John Whitgift.

14   Strype, 1701, p. 21. James Bass Mullinger (Dictionary of National Biography) described him as a man of 'arbitrary and unconciliatory disposition'. Aylmer's own spelling of his name, when he signed for his livery at Lincoln, was 'Ælmer' (e.g. LA, D&C Bi/2/1, part 3).

15   Psalm 119 in the Vulgate; the Authorized Version (Psalm 120) is slightly different. A similar construction might be put on the anthem *How long shall mine enemies*; see p. 187.

The organ nevertheless remained in use at Lincoln, despite the dismantling of those in a few other cathedrals. In 1563, soon after Byrd's arrival, £2 13s 6d was spent 'on the emendation and repair' of an instrument which had been built by John Clymowe of London and installed in the 1530s.[16]

The singers Byrd inherited numbered twelve vicars choral and nine boys. There were four senior vicars choral (priests) and eight junior (lay).[17] There had been twelve boy choristers,[18] but on 2 March 1559/60 three were made poor clerks (lay singers below the rank of junior vicar choral), and it was decided not to replace them for the time being.[19] It appears that the number sometimes fell below twelve, and Byrd was reimbursed for journeys to recruit choristers, presumably from other choirs.[20] He visited Louth in 1562-3, and about the same time Henry Horner, one of the vicars choral, was paid for going to Lancashire for a chorister.[21] Byrd went to Louth and Newark in 1564-5, and Newark again in 1565-6.[22] On 20 March 1567/8 his agreement was sought to the admission as a chorister of a Burghersh chanter nominated by the Precentor.[23] There was a difference of opinion about the boys' role in the

16   LA, D&C, Bi/3/6, f. 138ᵛ: 'pro emēdacõe et repacõne organorum'. The repaired instrument was described as being below the choir ('infra chorum'). An engraving made by Wenceslaus Hollar in the seventeenth century however shows a small organ above the stalls on the north side of the choir. (Engraving after Hollar in Dugdale, 1817-30, vi, following p. 1266.)

17   Payne, 1993, pp. 12, 185-186, drawing partly on unpublished notes of Dr Roger Bowers. See also Maddison, 1885.

18   Cole, 1917, p. 176.

19   LA, D&C A/3/7, f. 9ʳ. For the names and ages of Byrd's choristers see Garton, 1983, pp. 721-731. The admission of choristers and vicars choral before Byrd's time can be traced in Cole, 1917 and 1920. For an examination of the sources concerning choral forces at Lincoln over more than a century see Payne, 1993, pp. 12, 185-186.

20   According to the injunctions received by the Cathedral authorities in 1548, 'the Chaunter of the church for the tyme beyng shall have the puttyng in and Admission of the Choristers in the service of the Choristership'. (Bradshaw, 1892-97, ii., p. 595.) Smith (1968, p. 111) presents evidence that in some dioceses a cathedral or other large church may have been empowered to impress choristers from parish churches.

21   LA, D&C Dv/2/2(b), f. 5ᵛ.

22   LA, D&C Bi/3/6, ff. 152ᵛ and 179ᵛ.

23   LA, D&C A/3/7, f. 61ʳ. 'Edward III granted £60 yearly in fee out of the farm of the City to Bartholomew Burgersh (brother of Henry Burghersh, bishop of Lincoln), who granted it to the chapter as part of the endowment of the Burghersh chantry.' (Hill, 1965, p. 243.) When chantries were dissolved, soon after the accession of Edward VI, the funds became available to support a number of boy singers in addition to the choristers proper.

singing of psalms, and on 28 June 1567 Byrd was ordered to ensure that they participated fully.[24]

Byrd's responsibilities may have included the instruction of the boys on keyboard instruments. This duty was at any rate among those of previous incumbents of his posts. In 1535 the cathedral authorities had disallowed a claim for providing the twelve choristers with commons, robes, and instruction in singing, organ-playing and grammar.[25] When James Crawe was appointed as Organist and Master of the Choristers in 1539 it was envisaged that he should duly and diligently instruct and teach the chorister boys, both in 'sciencia cantus viz playn songe, prykyd songe, ffaburdon, discante, et Countor', and in playing the organ ('pulsacione organorum').[26] The organ was to be taught especially to two or three boys whom Crawe or his deputy should find fit, docile, and suitable for instruction on the clavichord ('instrumentes vocates clavicordes'), provided that they should pay for this instrument themselves.[27] When Thomas Appleby was reappointed in 1541 after an absence at Lincoln College, Oxford, it was ruled that his letters patent should have the same form and effect as Crawe's.[28]

How far Byrd was responsible for the general education of the choristers is unclear. His approval was sought before Christopher Wormehall was appointed as a teacher of the choristers on 24 January 1567/8.[29] Payments to provide writing materials for the choristers suggest Byrd's responsibilities, and his successor Thomas Butler received similar payments.[30] But the Masters of the Choristers can have played only a minor part in the boys' formal schooling. During the first five years of Byrd's tenure as Master there were two grammar schools in Lincoln: the Chapter's school in the Close, and the city school supervised jointly by the Dean and Chancellor and the Common

The distinction is still made between two groups of boy choristers at Lincoln, funded from different sources. It is reflected in the fact that 'the four senior boys are choristers, and wear the distinctive black copes, while all the other boys are Burghersh chanters'. (Turbet, 1993(b), p. 7.)

24   LA, D&C A/3/8, f. 36ᵛ.

25   Cole, 1917, p. 176.

26   LA, D&C A/3/5, f. 169ᵛ and 171ᵛ; Cole, 1917, pp. 27, 31-32.

27   'Clavichord' was a general term for stringed keyboard instruments, and the virginals are probably meant. See p. 190, note 10.

28   LA, D&C A/3/5, f. 193ᵛ.

29   LA, D&C A/3/7, f. 61ʳ.

30   Examples in LA, D&C Bi/5/12(34), e.g. f. 5ʳ: 'Pro pergameno papiro et enchausto' (For parchment, paper and ink).

Council.[31] Most of the young singers must have attended the first, and any additional need could surely have been met by the second. The master of the Close school was John Plumtree, who gave up his post in 1565 on account of his Roman Catholicism.[32] He was succeeded by William Sanderson. Then, in 1567, with the provision of a new building for the city school, the Chapter agreed that the two schools should be merged. As this took place on the former Grey Friars site, in the city below the cathedral, the musical training of the choristers must have suffered a considerable disruption.

From the Chapter's point of view the amalgamation proved to be less than satisfactory. John Wintle was appointed as a schoolmaster in 1569, and took charge of the grammar school re-established in the Close in 1573.[33] Wintle was educated at Merton College, Oxford, and one wonders whether he followed the example of another Merton man, Anthony à Wood, by adding 'a' to his name and transforming himself into the John a Wintle who from 1606 to 1610 was involved with Byrd in a dispute over the manor of Longney, near Gloucester.[34]

It was Wintle who revived the presentation of entertainments by the choristers.[35] These had been a feature of celebrations, probably on Twelfth Night, before the schools were merged. They were given before the Archdeacon or the Dean and Chapter, and were associated with

31   Hill, 1956, pp. 102-103.

32   Sanders, 1571, p. 702; LA, D&C Bi/3/6, f. 150^v.

33   LA, D&C Bi/3/6, f. 212^r-213^v; D&C A/3/7, ff. 74^v-75^r. The schools were again united in 1583-4, and remained so. Wintle ('Wintell', 'Winkle', 'Wynkyll') was also, briefly, the seneschal of the choristers' house, with a responsibility for the boys' food and general care. The office was one that had been revived in 1556, when Thomas Paget, a priest, was appointed. Thomas Appleby held the post for a short time in 1559-60. He was followed after some months by Thomas Herbert (or Harbart), a junior vicar, who was appointed in September 1560; there is no information as to how the Dean and Chapter filled the gap between appointments. William Man became seneschal in September 1567. (See Garton, 1983, pp. 718-719.)

34   Wintle was a Fellow of Merton College, 1565; BA, 1565/6; MA, 1570; ordained 1572; rector of Branston, Lincs., 1576. (Foster, 1891-92, p. 1662; Foster, 1911, p. 158.) There were several people named Wintle who came from Gloucester and some were connected with Merton College. (See, for example, PRO, C142/671, m. 154, and Foster, 1891-92, s.v. 'Wintle' and 'Wyntle'.) From 1774 until his death in 1814 Dr Thomas Wintle was the rector of Brightwell, Berkshire, where William Byrd's young relation Thomas was the clerk in 1601. (Foster, 1887-88, iv, p. 1591.)

35   See, for example, LA, Bi/3/6, ff. 125^v and 165^v (payments to John Plumtree, whose pupils played before the Dean and others in 1561, and to William Sanderson, whose boys took part in a festivity in 1565).

feasting and celebration. They may have included plays of the kind acted by boys of the London choirs, but the sketchy entries in the cathedral accounts provide an inadequate basis for assumptions about their nature. The music Byrd wrote for viol consort at Lincoln may mean that viols were − or became − available there,[36] and he may have had a hand in musical aspects of the boys' performances, but there is nothing to connect any of his early consort songs with these occasions.

Marriage and children

The provision of a house free of rent was among the inducements offered to Byrd, and from 1567 he occupied one where where 6 Minster Yard now stands.[37] The previous occupant of Byrd's house was one Thomas Godwin.[38] It was close to the choristers' house, which was on the site of the present 10 Minster Yard.[39]

Under the heading 'Anno Dñi 1568' the register of St Margaret's in the Close records that 'Willm Birde was married the xiiij day of Septembre'.[40] The information that his wife was named Julian, and came from the Lincolnshire family of Birley, is supplied by the heralds' visitations of London (1571) and Essex (1634).[41] Nothing more is at present known of the Birley family.[42] Nor is anything known of whether Julian was a resolute Roman Catholic before her marriage, though there is no doubt that in matters of faith she was to prove extremely strong-minded.

Byrd's first son, Christopher, was baptized at St Margaret's on 18 November 1569. A daughter, Elizabeth, was baptized there on 20 January 1571/2. In neither case is Julian Byrd mentioned in the church register.

Conflict with the Chapter

The day after his son's baptism Byrd appeared before the Chapter to answer for some unspecified action to which they had taken exception

36   See p. 40.

37   Jones, 1984, pp. 39-40. The present house carries a plaque.

38   LA, D&C A/3/7, ff. 36ʳ and 42ʳ, June and November 1564.

39   Jones, 1984, pp. 47-50.

40   Register at LA; Foster, 1915. The church (pl. 2b) was demolished in 1778-81.

41   The Latin form 'Juliana' did not become common in England until the eighteenth century. (Withycombe, 1977, p. 184.)

42   Few surviving Lincolnshire parish registers cover the probable period of Julian's birth. The name given to her first son may have been her father's name.

('ob quasdam causas eidem objectas'), and his salary was suspended. After a few months Byrd sought a further meeting, which took place on 31 July 1570, and the suspension was revoked at his humble request ('ad humilem instantiam dicti Willelmi Byrde').[43] Instructions given on 29 September indicate that Byrd's offence was connected with his duties as an organist, and seem to reflect the strengthening of puritanical attitudes towards music at Lincoln:[44]

> quod exinde organista dicte ecclesiae cathedralis sub forma sequenti tantum modo ad regimen chori in dicta ecclesia organa modulabitur viz ante inchoacionem[45] cantici vocati **Te deum** et cantici vocati **canticum zacharie** ad preces matutinas nec non cantici beate marie virginis vulgariter vocati **magnificat** et cantici Simeonis vulgariter vocati **nunc dimittis** ad preces vespertinas, nec non tempore psallendi le anthem una cum choro psallens idem.

This appears to mean that, whatever Byrd had been doing, he was henceforth to restrict himself to giving the choir their notes before the beginning of the plainsong canticles. When an anthem was performed he was to sing with the choir.[46] While the exact nature of Byrd's transgression remains obscure, there is little doubt that the longest of his keyboard fantasias were written at about this time. If their expansiveness was conveyed into what Byrd had been playing during services, the Dean and Chapter's wish to bring him to heel is entirely understandable.

An apparent increase in the copying of music at Lincoln in 1571 may be a sign that Byrd was angling for a post in the Chapel Royal, and was engaged in collecting his compositions together in an orderly fashion.[47] A

43   LA, D&C A/3/7, f. 66ᵛ; D&C A/3/8, f. 44ʳ.

44   LA, D&C A/3/8, f. 45ᵛ; D&C A/3/7, f. 68ʳ. John Bull was another who had to appear before the Chapter of his cathedral because 'in his capacity as organist he was not following instructions'. (Grove, 1980, iii, p. 438b.)

45   Not 'inchantionem' as read by Shaw, 1967, p. 56.

46   The term 'anthem' seems to have been uncommon and imprecise at this time. Shaw (1967, pp. 56-57) suggests that 'una cum choro' implies that the organ was to double the voices of the choir, but Payne (1993, p. 147) disputes this on the ground that 'play' would be Latinized as 'pulsare' rather than 'psallare'. He also cites the orders given to Thomas Weelkes at Chichester in 1616: 'That the organist remain in the choir until the last psalm be sung, then he go up to the organs, and there having done his duty, to return into the choir again to bear his part all along'. (Quoting Shaw, 1991, p. 75.)

47   Although no connection can be made with the copying of music during Byrd's time at Lincoln, it is of interest that the Cathedral Library possesses fragments of a fifteenth-century Sarum antiphoner that were reused as covers for the tenor and bass part-

hint that Byrd had been paying occasional visits to London is contained in the accounts kept by John Petre when he was a student at the Middle Temple. In January 1567/8 he gave a penny 'To Byrd*es* boye'.[48] The amount of Byrd's music actually sung in the cathedral is a matter of conjecture, but the compilation of music manuscripts and the purchase of printed music had been going on intermittently ever since his arrival. In 1563-64 Thomas Herbert was paid for copying music ('scripturam diversorum librorum Cantacionum'), and he received another payment in 1565-66 for writing and 'prickinge' books for the choir.[49] Books bought for the choir in 1563-64 seem to have been printed volumes; so do the psalters bought in 1566-67.[50] In 1571 a purchase was made of ten large books into which music was copied, perhaps five-part compositions by Byrd.[51] The momentum this appears to have generated continued after Byrd left Lincoln.[52]

It is as certain as it can be that, in his methodical way, Byrd also preserved pieces for the virginals and for viol consort that were written at Lincoln. The identity of friends and local music lovers who heard and played these pieces can only be guessed at. It is conceivable that Byrd was even at this stage in his career an occasional visitor to the Staffordshire homes of the Paget family − though a ride of seventy miles or more across country was not to be accomplished in a day − and that some at least of his music was written for the entertainment of their friends.[53] The first evidence that viols were used at the cathedral is a payment to the 'pedagogo choristar*um*' in January 1594/5 for buying 'chordis & aliis necessariis p̱ violis'.[54] Parts of four pieces of virginal music by Byrd form endpapers to the parish register (1559-1682) of Friskney, about thirty miles from Lincoln, but they cannot be connected with Byrd's period at the cathedral.[55]

books of works by Tallis and Byrd.

48   ERO, D/DP A17.

49   LA, D&C Bi/3/6, ff. 138ᵛ and 166ʳ.

50   Ibid., ff. 138ᵛ and 179ᵛ.

51   Ibid., ff. 224ᵛ and 235ᵛ; Payne, 1993, p. 47.

52   Payne, 1993, p. 48.

53   Byrd's acquaintance with the Pagets is described below (pp. 46-50, 59-63). Their Staffordshire homes were at Burton and Beaudesert.

54   LA, D&C Bi/3/8, f. 321ᵛ.

55   Registers now at LA; see Pacey, 1985. The music is on 6-line staves drawn in red, on large paper cut to fit the narrow pages of the register when it was bound. Only two pieces (MB 27/16a-b) are likely to have been written before 1580. One (MB 27/32a) probably dates from the decade after 1580, and one (MB 28/59b) from after 1591.

3

CLERKENWELL AND WESTMINSTER · 1572-c.1576

In 1572 Byrd left Lincoln to return to London. A vacancy in the Chapel Royal had been created by the drowning of Robert Parsons at Newark upon Trent early in 1571/2.[1] Byrd was chosen to fill the vacancy, and was sworn in as a Gentleman of the Chapel on 22 February.[2] He ceased to sign for money paid to him at Lincoln, and in September his house in the Close was described as his former home.[3]

It is difficult now to imagine the surroundings in which the Queen's musicians worked. Nothing remains of the chapel building at Whitehall Palace, and very little of the surrounding countryside and villages that were already being transformed by the rapid growth of London.[4] Nor is

1   Although Parsons did not join the Chapel Royal until 17 October 1563 (Rimbault, 1872, p. 1), he and Byrd could have known each other. In 1567, on the termination of a lease to John Heneage, Parsons was granted the lease of a rectory at Stainton. (Patent Rolls, 1964, p. 142.) Stainton is near Hainton where Byrd had a lease on a rectory, and Newark too is close to Lincoln. Byrd's acquaintance with Parsons seems to have been assumed by the copyist of the Chirk Castle part-books, who annotated *Deliver me from my enemies* with the words 'some say m^r parsons: m^r Byrde affirmes it to be truth'. (New York Public Library, MS Mus. Res. *MNZ (Chirk), f. 71^v of the medius book.) If, as suggested by le Huray (1982) the manuscript was copied as late as 1620, it would be interesting to know how the note came to be inserted.

2   The Chapel Royal's Old Cheque Book (f. 5^r) says: 'Robt Parsons was drowned at Newark uppon Trent the xxvth of Januarie, And Wm Bird sworne gent. in his place at the first the xxij^{ti} of ffebruarie followinge A^o xiiij^{to}. Lincoln.' (Printed by Rimbault, 1872, p. 2.) A parallel entry is in Bodleian Library MS Rawlinson D318, a composite volume which includes (ff. 24^r-47^v) a smaller cheque book that may have served a less formal purpose than the one preserved by the Chapel Royal. (Printed in Ashbee, 1986-96, viii, pp. 316-333.) This says: 'Robt Parson drowned att Newerk upon trent & Wm Bird sworne Gent in his place the 22th. of ffebruary'. Both cheque books enter Byrd's swearing under 1569, but the regnal year 14 Elizabeth I began on 17 November 1571, a date that accords with the baptism of Byrd's daughter at Lincoln and the appointment of his successor. Parsons was certainly alive at the end of 1571. A certificate of his residence in Greenwich, dated 25 November, describes him as 'Robert psons one of the gentlemen of her ma^{tes} chple'. (PRO, E115/293/10.)

3   LA, D&C Bi/5/12, envelope 23; Bi/3/6, f. 237^r.

4   The chapel at Whitehall Palace is first mentioned in a document of 1541: see London County Council and London Survey Committee, 1930, pp. 53-57, and Colvin, 1963-73, vi, p. 346. The royal palaces where the Chapel Royal attended are described and

Table 4 · Historical background 1572-1576

1572   First of Drake's marauding expeditions. Norfolk executed. St Bartholomew Massacre in France. Society of Antiquarians founded.

1573   Walsingham appointed joint Secretary of State. Walter Devereux (Essex) sets out to colonize part of Ulster. Leicester secretly married.

1574   First Catholic missionaries arrive from Douai. Earl of Leicester's company of actors formed.

1575   *Revenge* launched. Ten-year boom in English trade, industry and agriculture. *Gammer Gurton's Needle*. Festivities at Kenilworth for Queen's visit.

1576   Death of Walter Devereux; his son Robert succeeds to earldom of Essex. Archbishop Grindal suspended. Cathay Company (Frobisher and Lock) seeks North-West Passage (to 1578).

anything left of Henry VIII's chapel at Greenwich, where in 1534, some five years after Wolsey's fall, the Cardinal's arms on 'the grette organes' were painted out and replaced by the arms and badge of Anne Boleyn.[5]

The speed with which Byrd was inducted bears out his claim to have been 'called' to the Queen's service, but there was probably more to his departure from Lincoln than meets the eye. Byrd had formed a close association with a vicar choral named John Reason, who followed him to London and shared his conflicts with the authorities over his Catholic faith. It is a safe guess that they were first drawn together by Catholicism, and that they found life at Lincoln under Aylmer's rule extremely difficult.[6] The opportunity to leave the narrow world of a provinicial cathedral for the service of a queen who often displayed a surprising broad-mindedness in matters of religion was too good for Byrd to miss.

Byrd presumably took the oath of loyalty customarily taken by the Gentlemen, recognizing Queen Elizabeth as the supreme governor of the

depicted in le Huray, 1967, pp. 73-77 and pl. 4, 5, 9, and Baldwin, 1990, pp. 63-111 and illustrations.

5   Colvin, 1963-73, iv, p. 105.

6   Other singers found it hard to give up their beliefs. Henry Horner, who had renounced the bishop of Rome in taking the oath of obedience in 1551, was reminded in 1580 that he should not pray to the Virgin Mary. (Cole, 1920, p. 58; LA, D&C A/3/8, f. 64ᵛ.)

realm in spiritual and ecclesiastical matters as well as temporal.[7] If so, he swore not to 'conceale or keepe secrete any treasons commyted or spoken' against the monarch.[8] There is no evidence that Byrd was ever anything but a loyal subject, but his activities as a Roman Catholic sometimes proved of interest to those with responsibilities for national security.

In March 1571/2 the Archbishop of Canterbury sought the post vacated by Byrd for his own nominee, Henry Lyeth. The Chapter however chose Thomas Butler, one of their own poor clerks whom Byrd recommended.[9] The new appointment was made on 7 December 1572 at a lower salary.[10] Byrd seems to have made an attempt to retain his post as organist at Lincoln while serving in the Chapel Royal, and to have thought of Butler only as a suitable deputy. Thomas Forde's statement that Byrd kept his organist's place 'by Butler his supplitio wh. Org^t of Q^n Eliz chapel', although not made until after 1700, has the ring of truth about it.[11] Ten years after Byrd's appointment as a Gentleman of the Chapel Royal, John Bull was dividing his time in just such a way

7   The oath take by Byrd probably had the same form as the oath of 1558 printed by Rimbault (1872, pp. 107-108) and based on the Act of Supremacy (1 Elizabeth c. 1). The requirement to recognize the Queen as 'supreme governor' in 'spritual and ecclesiastical things' rendered it more acceptable to Catholics than if she had been described as 'supreme head'. (Williams, 1995, p. 455.) Byrd's friend John Case published a picture of the Queen as the primum mobile in *Sphaera civitatis* (Oxford, 1588).

8   Old Cheque Book, f. 16^r; Rimbault, 1872, pp. 107-108.

9   According to O'Dwyer, 1960, p. 136, Butler is to be identifed with Thomas Butler, Doctor of Laws, of New College, Oxford, but this is not borne out by signatures at Oxford (New College archive 7533, for 1559-60) and Lincoln (LA, D&C Bi/5/12 for 1577/8 and 1579/80; and elsewhere in the Cathedral accounts). The Thomas Butler admitted to New College as a probationer on 21 March 1549 came from Radley in Oxfordshire. He became a full fellow two years later, but was removed in 1562 by the Chancellor of the Bishop of Winchester. This must have been a delegated visitation by the Bishop and would almost certainly have been for recusancy. (New College, Registrum Protocollorum, archive 9749, f. 18v and p. 146. Foliation becomes pagination at f./p. 120.)

10   LA, D&C A/3/7, ff. 71^r- 72^v; D&C A/3/8, f. 50^r. The Archbishop was Matthew Parker, who had been Dean of Lincoln from 1552 to 1554.

11   Bodleian Library, MS Mus. e. 17, which bears (f. 1^r) a note that 'This book was wrote and collected by Tho: Forde · Chaplain of Christ Church Oxon'. The inclusion in Forde's notes of the information that Byrd was 'bred up under Tallis & Tutor to Morley' suggests that he knew Anthony à Wood's manuscript.

between the Chapel and Hereford Cathedral, where he was permitted to retain accommodation at the request of the Archbishop of Canterbury.[12]

Like Bull, Byrd was adept at using the Elizabethan system of patronage to forward his career. As a result of certain noblemen and councillors of the Queen writing letters on Byrd's behalf — confirmation that he was already well-connected at this stage in his career[13] — the Lincoln Chapter agreed on 2 November 1573 to grant him an annual payment of £3 6s 8d (the amount by which Butler's pay was reduced) starting on 25 March 1574, and the decision was confirmed on 15 January 1576/7.[14] To ensure that the arrangement was not entirely one-sided, the Chapter required that for the rest of his life Byrd should provide them with 'cantica et Servitia divina bene modulata subministret Ecclesiam predictam scientia et industria suis quam congrue posset decoret' (songs and divine services well set to music, adorning the church aforesaid in appropriate form by his skill and industry). Some of Byrd's Anglican music may have resulted from this bargain, and the compositions he supplied could account for at least some of the subsequent activity in copying music at Lincoln Cathedral. The payments Byrd received from Lincoln came to an end after the financial year 1581-2.[15] There is no explanation for this, but it was in 1582 that Byrd was due to begin enjoying the income from Hainton rectory. In the draft accounts for 1582-3 Byrd's name is crossed out and Butler's substituted.[16] Letters patent formalizing Butler's appointment to the two posts formerly occupied by Byrd were at last issued on 4 February 1582/3, and his salary was increased to the full amount which Byrd had received.[17]

The record of Byrd's work at court lies principally in his compositions; otherwise it is largely undocumented. It is hard to believe that his organ playing during services never attracted attention, or that he never took part as a virginalist in secular entertainments at court, but the records are silent. There are occasional references to him as a singer. He

12   Hereford Cathedral, Acts of the Vicars Choral, 18 January 1590/91. John Hewlett and William Randoll also kept their places at provincial cathedrals for many years after their appointment to the Chapel Royal. (le Huray, 1967, p. 73.)

13   He was friendly with Lord Paget by June 1573.

14   LA, D&C A/3/7, f. 75ʳ; D&C A/3/8, f. 52ᵛ; D&C Bii/2/4, f. 61ᵛ; D&C Bii/3/17, f. 46ᵛ. The payment did not prevent Byrd from complaining that he was the poorer for leaving Lincoln Cathedral to serve the Queen. (See p. 65.)

15   LA, D&C Bi/5/12.

16   Ibid., f. 15ʳ.

17   LA, D&C Bii/3/17, f. 89ᵛ-90ʳ, where no mention is made of Byrd.

was described as a singing-man in 1586,[18] and was said still to have been singing in 1607.[19] His delight in singing is clear from the prefatory matter to his *Psalmes, Sonets, & Songs of Sadness and Pietie* (1589), which includes 'Reasons briefly set downe by th'auctor, to perswade every one to learne to sing'. These end with the couplet: 'Since singing is so good a thing, I wish all men would learne to sing'. It has been suggested that Byrd was a counter-tenor because he was replaced eventually by the counter-tenor John Croker. Some singers were certainly replaced by others with a like voice range,[20] but Byrd probably gave up regular attendance as a Chapel musician thirty-odd years before his place fell vacant.

Some deductions about Byrd's work in the Chapel can nevertheless be made. In the *Cantiones sacrae* of 1575 Tallis and Byrd described themselves as organists as well as Gentlemen of the Chapel Royal ('Serenissimae Regineae Maiestati à privato Sacello generosis, & Organistis'), although at that time no specific reference to a post of organist is to be found in the Chapel's records.[21] Byrd is again described as 'Organista Regio, Anglo' in *Liber Primus* and *Liber Secundus Sacrarum Cantionum* (1589-91), and in *Gradualia* (1605).[22] In *My Ladye Nevells Booke*, a manuscript made by John Baldwin under Byrd's direction in 1591, he is once more referred to as 'organiste of her majesties chappell'.[23]

The two colleagues' use of the title 'organist' may indicate a special role. The work, education and discipline of the boy choristers devolved upon the Master of the Children, and references over many years make apparent that his post was regarded as one of particular importance. But someone had to rehearse the singing men, and quite likely the whole

18   BL, Lansdowne MS 48, f. 180[r]. In the 1580s Robert Dow wrote of Byrd as a singer (Christ Church, Oxford MS Mus. 984), but probably in a poetic sense: 'Cantores inter, quod in aethere sol, bone Birde' (Among singers, you are as the sun in the sky, good Byrd).

19   Nichols, 1828, ii, p. 139.

20   Smith, 1965; Rimbault, 1872, pp. 4, 8-9 (entries for Walter Porter and Roger Nightingale).

21   Tallis was 'joculator organorum' of Dover Priory in 1531-32. (Haines, 1930, p. 448). He probably held a similar post at Waltham Abbey before its dissolution in 1540. (PRO, SP12/99/55.)

22   In *Psalmes, Sonets, & Songs* (1588), *Songs of Sundrie Natures* (1589) and *Psalmes, Songs, and Sonnets* (1611) he is described only as a Gentleman of the Chapel.

23   He is further described as 'gentleman of her majesties chappell', 'gentleman of the queens chappell', and more often simply as 'mr. w. birde'. Other manuscripts written by John Baldwin also refer to Byrd as an organist of the Chapel Royal.

choir. That person must have been the organist. There appear to have been several organists in the Chapel at any one time, which would follow from the use of a duty roster, and it is probable that Thomas Tallis was among those who shared the responsibility for rehearsals.[24] His position was enhanced by his fame and long service. He was about sixty-five years old in 1571, and it would have been natural for him, if he thought of going into semi-retirement, to propose that his brilliant pupil, who had now been in charge of the choir at Lincoln for a decade, should be recalled to take over.

Clerkenwell

It is possible that Byrd had links with Clerkenwell shortly after his return from Lincoln, though there is no reason to suppose that he was related to other people named Byrd who lived there.[25] The evidence is a letter (pl. 3) addressed from 'clarken well' to Thomas, Lord Paget, and signed 'Willm̃ Byrde'.[26] The matter contains nothing that can indisputably be attributed to the composer, but while the writing differs in some respects from his mature hand, it also has a number of similarities to it.[27] The letter seems to represent an intermediate stage in the development of Byrd's writing, between the upright hand of his Lincoln signatures and one more like the hand practised in the circles he now moved in. It

24   Mr David Baldwin, Serjeant of the Vestry, has commented: 'We know what form the Organists' Rota took, and that "the most auncient custom should be observed, which was, and still must be, the most auncient organist shall serve the eeve and daye of evry principall feast ... next Organist in place to serve the second day ... and the third for the third daie if ther be so many Organistes", and that "he that did or shoulde begin the Saturdaie before shall finish up the same weeke, according to the former custom" (Old Cheque Book, 1615). This would seem to point to the opportunity for the Organist in question to have an entire week working on choral pieces with the Gentlemen as necessary'. (Letter to the author.)

25   See the names in Hovenden, 1884-91.

26   Keele University Library, Special Collections and Archives, Early Paget Correspondence, 1/7, f. 40; see also Harrison, 1990-91. A photocopy of the letter is at SRO, numbered D603/K/1/3/27. The D603/K/1 series, to which reference is made below, consists of photocopies of letters among the Anglesey (Paget) papers at Keele University. Thomas Paget, third Baron Paget, was the second son of William, first Baron Paget; matriculated at Cambridge 1559; inherited the title in 1568; imprisoned 1580; released but involved in the Throckmorton plot by his brother Charles, and took flight shortly after Throckmorton's arrest in 1583; died 1590.

27   See Appendix D.

reveals an awareness of his new position in the world, and his adjustment to it.

Receipts that are undoubtedly in Byrd's hand establish that he was acquainted with the Paget family not later than 1576. One reads:

Receyved of Mr Charles Pagett ye xxviijth of marche 1576 the some of vj^{li} xiij^s iiij^d

By me Willm̃ Birde

Another is undated, but has been preserved with papers belonging to the same year. This acknowledges the receipt 'by me Willm̃ Birde' of two shillings for 'three quyres of partician paper' (ruled for writing music) and fifteen pence for 'a payre of showes' (shoes).[28]

Less than a year later, on 28 February 1576/7, Byrd's brother-in-law Robert Broughe signed a receipt to say that he had had 'by the hande of willm̃ warde, for one whole yeares payment for my paynes in tuning his lorships great instrument at Charterhouse the some of twenty sixe shilling*es* and eight pence of lawfull english monye'. On the following 25 January he signed a receipt for £6 6s 8d 'for the alteracõn made by me in his great Instrument at charterhouse'.[29]

The Clerkenwell letter however predates these payments by several years. It runs as follows:

My Good Lord. Althowghe it be needelesse. to suche as be of honor and wysdome. to wryght in short tyme. twyse to one effect./ yet ye importunytye of my powre frend. y^e greate desyre to do hym good. and y^e greate plesure I take in wryghtynge to yor. L. dothe move me at thys present somewhat Inconsyderatelye to do y^t. wch I trust is bothe unneedefull & unnessesarye / What I have spoken & or wryghten In hys comẽndation. I doubt not but his

___

28   SRO, D(W)1734/3/4/98. The D(W) series consists of original documents from the Paget estate housed at the Staffordshire Record Office. 'Partition paper': see Morley, 1597, pp. 34, 103 (1952, pp. 58, 185). Charles Paget was Thomas's younger brother, who matriculated at Cambridge in 1559; he was an untrustworthy double agent, and was involved in the plot that led to the trial of William Shelley and indirectly to Byrd's acquisition of Stondon Place. The documents in BL Egerton MS 2074, in which Byrd's name occurs (see p. 74), include a number concerning the activities of Charles Paget and several dealing with 'The case of Willm̃ shelley how he standeth charged w^t treason'.

29   It seems however to have been from a 'mris Garrard' − the name is all but impossible to read − that Paget bought 'a paire of vyrgynalles for mrs Eli*s*abeth', his step-daughter, on 4 May 1577. At the same time he bought 'a boxe to put thinstrument*es* in'. A payment made on 18 May 1577 was 'To clarck that taught mris Eli*s*abeth the vyrginalles − xiijs iiijd'. (SRO, D(W)1734/3/4/212, nos. 22, 41 and 16.)

desert*es* shall confyrme / yea. yf I had added tryple prayses / The w^ch. / the cawse. / hys deepe povertye. / & great familye consydered. I doubt not but wyll move yor L. to stand hys good Lord. as most hūbly I beseech yor L. to do / In so doinge yor L. shall Justlye procure. hym to be to you. and all yours. a true bedsman. and what heavenlye reward. no yearthlye creature can exprese / and thus w^t my hūble duetye to yor. L. to my good Lady. and to m^r Charles (to whose worke I meane shortlye to addrese me)[30] & w^t my daylye prayer to god for yor increase of vertwe & honor. I hūblye take my leave.

ffrō clarken well w^tin ye close. thys xxviij^th of june 1573

yor lordshypes ever to com̃and

Willm̃ Byrde

The direction on the back says 'To the ryght honorable and hys singuler good Lord. the Lord paget. at burton in staffordshere geve this', and the letter is endorsed '*fr*om mr Birde'.

Clerkenwell Close is to the north of Clerkenwell Green. Although it now seems impossible to discover with whom Byrd was staying, the residents of the Close are known to have included notable families.[31] The district was also a centre of Catholicism to which Byrd might have gravitated; this is clear from the frequency with which it is mentioned in contemporary records of recusancy.[32]

Byrd's friendship with Paget was based on a concurrence of religious views and on music. Sir Francis Walsingham twice wrote to Thomas Paget about his lack of conformity in matters of religion.[33] Paget 'had his

30   Lady Paget was Nazaret, the daughter of Sir John Newton and widow of Sir Thomas Southwell. Charles Paget's 'worke' perhaps concerned the Catholic cause. Even though Charles was evidently knowledgeable enough in music for Lord Herbert to regard him as a competent judge of Thomas's songs (SRO, D603/K/1/5/6), he was probably in his twenties at this time so Byrd is unlikely to have been giving him formal instruction. Moreover, by 1573 Charles may already have left England for Paris, where he made his home.

31   Pinks, 1881, pp. 90-95. Lincoln Cathedral may also have had property in the vicinity, as suggested by several occurrences in the Cathedral accounts (first noticed by Dr Roger Bowers) of the phrase 'ad fontes clericum'. The Cathedral had other property in London, e.g. Barnard's Inn. (Cole, 1917, p. 175).

32   Sir John Arundel and his wife, who often appear with Byrd as recusants in the Middlesex gaol delivery rolls of the 1580s, lived in Clerkenwell. For the discovery of Jesuits in Clerkenwell in the later 1580s see Pinks, 1881, p. 258ff, and State papers, Scotland, 1915, p. 151.

33   SRO, D603/K/1/6/14 (5 September 1580) and D603/K/1/6/24 (24 November

own chaplain who almost certainly continued to say Mass for the household' and 'kept his own choir for liturgical purposes'.[34] It seems to have been about this that Henry Edyall was questioned in September 1586, when he was examined concerning his acquaintance with Paget, Babington and others.[35] He denied being a papist, and claimed to have attended church regularly and received communion. Moreover, he denied expressley 'y^t he ever furnished the sayd L. Padget wth any singing man or p^{r}vided any such for him. or y^t he ever sang any dirige in his howse'; he admitted only that he 'did use himself to singe in his lordships howse songes of m^r byrdes and m^r Tallys. and no other unlawfull songe'.[36]

Paget had inherited his love of music from his father William, Lord Paget, who had employed Thomas Tusser as a musician.[37] Tusser had been a chorister at St Paul's some years earlier than Byrd's brothers, and was trained by John Redford, whom he described in affectionate and admiring terms in *Five hundreth points of good husbandry* (1573). The book was dedicated to Thomas Paget, and to the memory of Paget's late father. The section on 'huswiferie' was dedicated to Lady Paget.

Paget's correspondents not infrequently mentioned his efforts and theirs at composition. In 1570, or possibly earlier, Lord Herbert thanked Paget 'for youer song*es*' and added 'suere ys theye be better then ever'.[38] On 11 October 1581 Francis Talbot wrote in a postscript: 'I have sent yor lo: a songe wch must by yor good helpe be set in part*es* to singe aboute the fier in a wynters night'.[39] Besides providing for the musical education

1580).

34   Harrison, 1990-91, p. 53.

35   Anthony Babington, born 1561. After travelling abroad, including a visit to Rome, he returned in 1585 and became involved with the supporters of Mary Queen of Scots. In April 1586 he took a leading part in a conspiracy to kill Queen Elizabeth and release Mary. He was executed on 20 September 1586.

36   PRO, SP12/193/63, 24 September 1586; State papers, 1865, p. 356. 'Dirige' is the first word of the first psalm antiphon at Vigils of the Dead, and was often applied to the whole Office.

37   Tusser (1524?-1580), was born at Rivenhall, Essex. After St Paul's he went first to Eton and then to Cambridge before entering Paget's service.

38   SRO, D603/K/1/5/6: letter dated 24 June only, and signed E. Herbert. Edward Somerset (c.1550-1627/8) was styled Lord Herbert until February 1588/9, when he became the fourth Earl of Worcester. Byrd's friendship with him is noted on numerous occasions in the following pages.

39   SRO, D603/K/1/7/26. Francis Talbot (c.1550-1582) was the eldest son of the Earl of Shrewsbury; at a very early age (in 1562/3) he was married to Anne, the daughter of William Herbert, first Earl of Pembroke.

of his own children, Paget took an interest in the training given to the children of his friends. On 19 November 1581 Herbert wrote: 'I remayn in musyke still, I have a daughter that will almost serve for a treble at the fyrst sight and my boy cometh well toward*es* the same'.[40] On 7 May 1582 the Earl of Rutland wrote asking 'in the behalf of my daughter that it will please to send her some Italiã & Inglish dittyes to singe'.[41]

A letter from Lord Herbert, probably written in 1573, the year of the Clerkenwell letter, is about a song he had sent to Paget.

My verye good lorde, I have receyved your letters, wherbye I understand that youe thinke there was a berd sange in my ere that made me alter my vayne/ yt is verye true the thing came not to youe w^{th}owt the sight of m^{r} byrde/ saving the last part/ wch he never sawe

He goes on to say that he has had no leisure to talk with Byrd concerning 'the boy', but as soon as he can speak to him he will write to Paget or visit him.[42] The boy is mentioned in two more of Herbert's letters; one of these says, enigmatically, that Byrd has made him believe that some unspecified matter 'wyll prove well'.[43]

The list of Paget's correspondents is a long one, and it is hardly surprising that it includes a number of men who figured in Byrd's life.[44] One was George Heneage. Another was Thomas Heneage, whom Paget addressed as 'cousin', and who wrote on public and private matters. A third, with whom Paget was associated on official business, was William Petre.

Westminster

Whether or not Byrd ever lodged in Clerkenwell, it is likely that he had lodgings close to the Chapel Royal not long after the Clerkenwell letter was written. A William Byrd was the father of children baptized at St Margaret's church, Westminster.[45] His name does not appear in the

---

40   SRO, D603/K/1/7/41.

41   SRO, D603/K/1/8/30. The third Earl of Rutland was Edward Manners (1549-87).

42   SRO, D603/K/1/5/5, dated only 21 May. Quoted in full by Harrison, 1990-91, p. 59. The boy is not Paget's son William.

43   SRO, D603/K/1/5/6, dated 24 June.

44   See the SRO catalogue of documents in the D603/K/1 series.

45   Byrd's servant John Reason lived or lodged in the parish of St Margaret's in 1587 and 1600. (GLRO, MJ/SR 273/63 and MJ/SR 367/23. The latter document apparently belongs to 42 Elizabeth, but is misplaced among documents of 41 Elizabeth. See the note following the calendar entry in Jeaffreson, 1886, pp. 254-255.) Byrd had lodgings in the

overseers' accounts for the parish,[46] so he was probably not a householder, and if he was the musician it is conceivable that he had temporary accommodation within Whitehall Palace or round about.

A degree of faith is involved in accepting that baptismal entries in the register of St Margaret's refer to children of William Byrd the musician, since neither their father's occupation nor their mother's name is mentioned. A Mary Byrd, the daughter of William, was baptized at St Margaret's on 24 January 1573/4.[47] Another Mary, also the daughter of a William Byrd, was baptized in the same church on 13 April 1589. The probability is that, if either Mary was the musician's child, it was the first. The Byrd family was resident at Harlington after 1577, and the composer's daughter Mary was old enough to be listed as a recusant by 1598.[48] On the other hand she was referred to in June 1604 as 'Mariam Byrde puellam'[49] − although that might mean that she was an unmarried woman rather than a child − and she did not marry Henry Hawksworth until 1611 or 1612, after which she had four sons.[50]

No record has been found of the baptism of Byrd's daughter Rachel. It may be that she was born before Mary, so that her baptism coincided with the Byrds' move from Lincoln to London in 1572, and took place elsewhere. This would explain why it was she who was named along with Christopher and Elizabeth in the lease of Stondon Place granted in 1595. They would all have been over twenty-one, while their siblings Mary and Thomas would have been younger.

It is fairly certain that the Thomas Byrd who was baptized at St Margaret's on 30 March 1576 was the composer's second son, since this conforms with other records of his age.[51] His godfather was Thomas Tallis.[52] The thought of the elderly composer, who had served four

Earl of Worcester's house in the Strand in 1622: see Byrd's will, p. 393.

46   Overseers' accounts for 1575-6 at Westminster Archives Centre.

47   Westminster Abbey Muniment Room, register of St Margaret's church; transcribed in Burke, 1914. There are many other entries for people named Byrd in the registers of St Margaret's.

48   ERO, D/AEA 19, f. 48[r], etc.

49   ERO, D/AEA 23, f. 40[v.]

50   It is of course possible that neither Westminster Mary was the musician's daughter.

51   Turbet notes the baptism of a 'Thomas Burde' at St James's, Clerkenwell, on 1 March 1576/7, but the father's Christian name is not given. Florus, the son of 'John Byrde', had been baptized at St James's on 20 January. (Turbet, 1990(a); Hovenden, 1884-91, i, p. 10.)

52   See Tallis's will, p. 383. The fact that Tallis was the godfather strengthens the supposition that Thomas Byrd, the child's grandfather, was dead by then.

sovereigns, holding his small godson is appealing. Thomas seems to have been a twin, for he was baptized at the same time as Edward Byrd.[53] There is no indication of who Edward's godfather was,[54] nor is there any further record of him. He must have died young, but he was not buried at St Margaret's, and he does not appear in the burial registers of Harlington, or in those of nearby parishes.[55] It is possible that he did not die until the family reached Stondon Massey, for which burial registers are not extant, or that the burial of a Catholic child was not recorded.

Besides accommodation at Westminster Byrd must have had need of temporary lodgings elsewhere. The frequency with which the court might move during a royal progress, or when the Queen felt restless, is well illustrated by Sir Francis Walsingham's diary for May 1578. On the seventh 'The Queen's Majestie removed to Theobaldes', and on the tenth 'Her Majestie removed to Mr Bashes house'. On 12 May 'The Queen's Majestie removed to Sir Thomas Henneage his house', and the next day 'Her Majestie removed to my Lord of Leycester's house at Wainsted'. On the sixteenth 'Her Majestie removed from Wainsted to Grenwiche'.[56] The smaller cheque book of the Chapel Royal includes a table of payments for 'Remoovings', with distances between palaces.[57]

Greenwich was one of Queen Elizabeth's preferred residences, and several of her musicians owned houses near the palace. Richard Farrant wrote in his will, made on 30 November 1580, 'I bequeathe to my wieff Anne ffarrante the Lease of my house in the blacke ffriers in London, whiche Lease is in a Cheste at my howse in Grenewiche'.[58] Thomas Tallis's house is traditionally identified as being in Stockwell Street at Greenwich.[59] Whether this is the house mentioned by Joane Tallis in her will, drawn up in 1587, is unclear. There she says her house had been 'lately purchased of Mr Lambert', so perhaps she moved after her

---

53   Westminster Abbey Muniment Room, registers of St Margaret's; Burke, 1914.

54   It is possible that Edward was named after Edward Somerset. See note 38 above.

55   A number of people named Byrd are recorded in the parish registers of Uxbridge, near Harlington, but there is at present no evidence of a family connection.

56   Martin, 1870.

57   Bodleian Library, Rawlinson MS D.318, ff. 45^v-46^v (entered with the book reversed).

58   Proved 1 March 1580/81. (Probate copy: PRO, Prob. 11/63.) The Blackfriars house was probably one leased from Sir William More in December 1576 as a singing school. (Eggar, 1934-35.)

59   Kimbell, 1816, p. 41; Drake, 1886, p. 90; anonymous sketch map of c.1825 in London Borough of Greenwich Local History Library. The house was on the site where Richard Best's house was subsequently built, at the south-east corner of what is now Greenwich market.

husband's death in 1585, or bought one which they had formerly leased.[60]

Byrd's friendship with the Tallises makes it conceivable that he stayed with them from time to time. Joane's will gives a vivid impression of the home he would have been familiar with and how the house of a successful musician was furnished.[61]

Item thre silver spoones Item one Bedsted standinge in the parlour and five curteynes belonginge to the same, one featherbed one bowlster twoe pillowes fower pillowbeers twoe rugges one coverlett of tapisterie of the storye of a shepheard, twoe fustian blankettes thre payer of hollande sheetes and twoe payer of flaxen sheetes of myne owne spyninge Item a wooll mattrice being in the same parlour Item twoe tableclothes of flaxen the one longe and the other shorter a longe flaxen towell and a shorter syx flaxen napkins, the standinge cupborde by the chimnye withe twoe cupbord clothes belonginge to the same the one of Venice and the other of flaxen one bason and ewer of pewter standinge uppon the same cupbord one courte table standinge behinde the parlor dore withe a cupborde cloth therto belonginge Item one chiste of firr standinge in the same parlor by the bedside Item the paynted clothes hanginge and beinge in the parlour Item one longe table withe the frame and twoe venice carpettes belonginge to the same fower joyned stooles six cushions of greene clothe twoe velvett cushion twoe wrought cushions of needle worke one windowe curteyne in the parlour and one scrine Item the settells and waynscott two landirons twoe creepers one payer of tonges one fyre shovell fower flower pottes of pewter Item a barred chest with twoe lockes standinge in the chamber wheare I nowe lye withe a square table withe a cupbord in the same standinge in the same chamber Item a close chayer of joyned worke in the same chamber Item one brasse pott twoe spittes Item the greatest kettell savinge one Item an other kettell somwhat lesser then that Item a cuple of bell candle senkes a cupple of plates a brode plate and a lesser Item a wine quarte and a wine pynte of the new fashion makinge Item one greate charger twoe platters five dishes twoe sowcers and twoe poringers ...

60   Drake, 1886, p. 53, says the house was bequeathed by Joane Tallis to Queen Elizabeth's College (almshouses built in Greenwich in 1575 and entrusted to the Drapers' Company), and escheated to Westcombe Manor.

61   See p. 385, note 8. The Tallises' comparative affluence may have been due in part to the fact that Joane was the widow of Thomas Bury, apparently one of the better off Gentlemen of the Chapel Royal.

The Manor of Battyshall (i)

Byrd came from a middle class which, while often engaged in trade, aspired to the ownership of land. Less than two years after his appointment to the Chapel Royal, Byrd entered into the first of several property transactions. A prominent characteristic of the Elizabethan land market was a growth in the sale of tenancies, usually leases, and he bought the lease of Battyshall manor in Essex, a few miles from Stondon Massey where he was eventually to settle. It is impossible to say whether he still had contacts with his relations at nearby Ingatestone, whether he already knew the Petre family who lived in the vicinity and who were to become close friends, or whether re-establishing a connection with the home of his forbears was simply a romantic idea.

Byrd's account of events was this:

A°. xvi°. of the Q. Thearle of Oxenford made A lease for xxxi[ti] yeares. of the Manor of Battylshall in the Cowntye of Essex. unto. W. Byrde. one of the gent. of her Ma[ties] Chapple. to take place at the deathe of Aubrye veare Esquier. or at the deathe of his Lawfull wyfe[62]

The young seventeenth Earl of Oxford was Edward de Vere, and Aubrey de Vere was his uncle.[63]

Soon after acquiring the lease Byrd was engaged in negotiations for its sale, doubtless with a view to making a profit. The prospective buyer was William Lewen (or Lewyn), who was probably acting for Anthony Luther.[64] Although Byrd agreed orally to sell the lease, he did not regard

---

62   PRO, SP12/157/59-60, formerly m. 26. (See pl. 4.) Comparison with Byrd's signed letters written in support of Dorothy Tempest leaves no doubt that it is in his hand. The regnal year 16 Elizabeth began on 17 November 1573. The manor was variously called 'Battyshall', 'Battelshall' or 'Batayles'. For its history see Powell, 1956, pp. 227-228. ERO has a collection of court rolls and other manorial documents relating to Battyshall, numbered D/DM M172 onwards.

63   Edward de Vere (1550-1604) was born at Castle Hedingham, Essex. As a youth Vere became an inmate of Lord Burghley's house in the Strand. He had a natural taste for music and literature, and was one of the circle of court writers. He married Burghley's daughter Ann (died 1588). See Eggar, 1934-35.

64   Lewen was a Doctor of Civil Law, and Byrd therefore referred to him as 'D. Lewen'. (See Foster, 1891-92, p. 905.) Luther was a member of a prominent Essex family. There is a brass to him and his brother Richard in the church of St Nicholas, Kelvedon Hatch.

the agreement as binding and transferred the lease to his brother John. In 1580 this became the subject of a dispute to be described below.

The monopoly for printing music

On 22 January 1574/5 Tallis and Byrd received from Queen Elizabeth a patent for the printing of music and lined music paper.[65] The preamble claimed that it was granted on account of her affection for 'the science of musick' and to achieve 'the addvauncement thereof'.

The patent ran: 'we gyve and graunt full priviledge and licence unto our welbeloved s^rvant*tes* Thomas Tallys and Willm Byrde two of the gentlemen of our Chappell and to the overlyver [survivor] of them and to the assigne and assignes of them and the overlyver of them'. It permitted them for twenty-one years to 'imprint or cause to be imprinted anye and as many sett songe or songes in partes as to them shall from tyme to tyme seame expedient in the Englishe laten frenche and Italien tonges ... or in any other tong tong*es* or languages that maye serve for the musick either of churche or chamber or otherwise to be songe or playde'. It allowed them to 'rule and cause to be ruled by impression any paper suche as maye serve for the printing or packing[66] of any songe or songes', and to 'sell or utter or cause to be solde or uttered' printed music books and quires of ruled paper. Others were forbidden to import or sell music or ruled paper from abroad, 'uppon payne of our highe induignacon and displeasure'; and those who did so were to forfeit forty shillings to the Crown for each offence, while the offending items were to be confiscated and given to Tallis and Byrd. Stationers and others were enjoined to assist the licensees in the exercise of the privilege, which was apparently not seen as infringing successive patents obtained by John Day, under which he printed many editions of the psalms.[67]

Compared with the Continent, little music had been printed in England, and there is not much doubt that Byrd had a streak of the commercial enterprise evident elsewhere in his family. He and Tallis

---

65   PRO, C66/1129, m. 2; Patent rolls, 1973, p. 471; Turbet, 1987, pp. 325-327. An epitome of the licence was printed at the end of each part-book of the 1575 *Cantiones sacrae*. See the facsimile in Monson, 1977, p. xxiv; see also Steele, 1903, p. 26. Additional references to the printing monopoly appear in Arber, 1875-94, i, pp. 111, 114-116, 144; ii, pp. 10, 15, 775-776. There are numerous other occurrences in the patent rolls of the names William Byrd and John Byrd, but it seems that only the one mentioned here and another concerning the manor of Longney relate to the subject of this book, while it has yet to be determined whether any relates to his brother.

66   *Recte* 'pricking', i.e. writing music by hand.

67   Krummel, 1975, pp. 14-15.

assembled a collection of their own music, which they called *Cantiones quae ab argumeno sacrae vocantur*. They selected as their printer Thomas Vautrollier, 'a Huguenot refugee from Troyes with an incorrigible interest in Protestant propaganda'.[68] They had no choice, since Vautrollier was the only person in England with the music type they needed. He had imported it from France five years earlier for an edition of music by Lassus.[69]

It is uncertain whether Latin motets like those of the *Cantiones* were sung in the Elizabethan Chapel Royal, but the two composers must surely have discussed their projected publication with the Queen's officials, and received no hint that she would find the dedication unacceptable. Latin was a suitably dignified language for both the texts and prefatory matter of the *Cantiones*, and it was one in which the Queen was skilled. It was a language, too, with which many other musical amateurs were acquainted from their schooldays, as the inclusion of a commendatory poem by Richard Mulcaster serves to emphasize.[70] It was consonant with the nobility of the collection's ostensibly patriotic motive of bringing honour to Britain through music.[71] This motive is apparent in the title, which echoes those of Continental publications, for example the several volumes of *Sacrae cantiones* published by Lassus in Nuremberg (1562) and Venice (1566).

The dedication of the book to the Queen was an expression of gratitude for the monopoly under which it was printed, and a declaration of hope that her support would continue. The two musicians needed this sooner they they may have anticipated. In a petition of 1577 they claimed that publication had cost them the tidy sum of two hundred marks. No other book of music was published under their licence during Tallis's lifetime. It looks as if the partners misjudged both the difficulty of

68   Kerman, 1955, p. 73. BL Lansdowne MS 48, f. 180[r], says 'Thomas Vautroller a strang[er] hathe the sole printinge of other latten book*es*', i.e. other than those for grammar schools printed by Thomas Marshe, 'a*nd* the newe Testam[t] & others'.

69   Krummel, 1975, p. 16; Kerman, 1955, p. 71ff.

70   Mulcaster (c.1530-1611) was a schoolmaster in London by 1559; headmaster of the newly-founded school of the Merchant Taylors 1561-1586, where his pupils received daily training in vocal and instrumental music; and High Master of St Paul's School, 1596-1608.

71   Byrd restricted his Latin prefaces to collections of 'sacred songs'. Three of the pieces from the 1575 collection − *Attolite portas*, *Laudate pueri*, and *Memento homo* − had English words fitted to them. (Monson, 1977, pp. vii-viii, and Monson, 1983, pp. xiii-xiv.) The earliest source for any of these adaptations is Bodleian Library, Tenbury College MS 1382, which dates from c.1617, and there is nothing to show whether they were sanctioned by Byrd.

printing music and the demand for copies, while the prohibition on the importation of music printed abroad was unenforceable. Reporting to Burghley in 1582, Christopher Barker, 'her Maties Printer of the English tongue', said: 'The paper is somewhat beneficiall, as for the musick bookes, I would not provide necessarie furniture to have them'.[72]

At the same time, printing monoplies came under attack by London printers. In 1586 they complained that 'The privilidge latelie granted by her Matie under her highness great seale of England to the persons here under written, concerninge the arte of printing of books, hath and will be the overthrowe of the Printers and Stationers w^{th}in this Cittie beinge in number. 175. Beside their wyves children Apprentizes & families'. In listing the various privileges they asserted that 'One Byrde ... hathe a licence for printinge of all musicke books & by that meanes he claimeth the printing of ruled paper'.[73] The petition was supported by a body of named stationers and printers, 'Besides a nomber of Jorneymen & apprentices of Theirs'.[74] This does not mean that others were keen to print music. Another report to Burghley, made by Thomas Norton, one of the Queen's printers, says: 'Bird, and Tallys her ma^{tes} servantes have musike bokes with note, wch. the complainantes confesse they wold not print nor be furnished to print thoughe there were no previlege'.[75]

Tallis died in 1585, leaving his share of the monopoly to Byrd's son Thomas, but there can be no doubt that Byrd remained in control. Vautrollier died in 1587, and his type was acquired by Thomas East. The volumes that East printed for Byrd, including several published after the expiry of Byrd's patent, are indicative of better commercial judgement and an increasing demand.[76]

72   BL, Lansdowne MS 48, ff. 190^r and 192^r; Steele, 1903, pp. 12-15. For examples of the papers sold under the patent see Fenlon and Milsom, 1984.

73   It is curious that the printers did not realize that the patent actually extended to ruled paper.

74   BL, Lansdowne MS 48, f. 180^{r-v}.

75   Ibid., f. 187^v.

76   They include all four editions of *Psalmes, sonets and songs* (first published in 1588), the original edition (1589) and one later edition of *Songs of sundrie natures*, the *Gratification unto Master John Case* (1589), the *Cantiones sacrae* of 1589 and 1591, the three Masses (1592-95) with second editions of those for four and three voices, and the first edition of each volume of *Gradualia* (1605 and 1607). The 'inaccurate and badly printed' third edition (1610) of *Songs of sundrie natures* was the work of East's widow, Lucrezia, and it was his apprentice and son-in-law, Thomas Snodham, who printed *Psalmes, songs and sonnets* (1611). (See Andrews, 1964.) The absence of lute music from this list may betray Byrd's influence. It is notable that as soon as the patent expired in 1596 East began to issue a wider variety of music by other composers.

4

HARLINGTON · 1577-1594

By late 1577 Byrd and his family were installed at Harlington, in Middlesex.[1] Since Harlington was not far from Drayton, where Byrd's patron Lord Paget had an estate, it may not be too much to suppose that they moved there with his encouragement. A few preliminary words must be said about Byrd's continuing association with Paget and his circle.

A list of 'c̃tain parsons who be great frend*es* and ayderes of those [Catholics] beyond the sea*es*', compiled about 1580, refers to 'Mr Byrde at m^r Listers his howse ov^r against S^t dunstons or at the L^d. Padgetts howse in draighton'.[2] Lister was evidently one of Paget's London neighbours.[3] Besides owning property in Stafforshire and at Drayton in Middlesex, Paget had a house in Westminster, just west of Temple Bar in

---

1   For an account of Harlington see Reynolds, 1962, p. 271ff. Concerning the ownership by Gentlemen of the Chapel Royal of houses outside the immediate vicinity of the court, Mr David Baldwin has observed: 'It seems that the transition from residence at Court to private dwelling occurred in 1544, which would leave the way open for Byrd to have lived virtually anywhere that was within practicable reach of his duties as dictated by Rota'.

2   PRO, SP12/146/137, f. 250^r; State papers, 1856, p. 703, where the date 1580 is suggested. The document carries the additional description: 'The names of certain psons who have their sonnes beyond the Seas and the Shires & places of their dwelling'. A different hand has mysteriously added to the entry concerning Byrd: 'The messenger is to tell him things wch he will well lyke'. This document has proved troublesome to Byrd's biographers. It was twice quoted by Rimbault, who gave no reference. (Byrd, 1841; Rimbault, 1872). This caused Squire (1883, p. 299) to remark: 'What this list is, and where Dr. Rimbault obtained a sight of it, we have unfortunately been unable to discover'. It was quoted again by Fellowes (1948, p. 39), whose reference contains a misprint.

3   It is possible that Byrd lodged at Lister's while he was on duty in London, or that the house was a place where Catholics forgathered. Could Lister have been connected with 'John Leycetour', mentioned as living in the parish of St Dunstan in the West in a subsidy roll of 1541? (PRO, E179/144/120; Lang, 1993, p. 76.) St Dunstan in the West is a more likely identification than St Dunstan in the East, although the name 'Leister' appears in the register of the latter for 1575 and 1595. (Clarke, 1939, pp. 143, 29.) This register also lists an Alice Byrd, who married James Fells on 12 June 1581, but she was not the composer's sister Alice, who married William Duffing before 1571.

the parish of St Clement Danes, bordering on the parish of St Dunstan in the West. A subsidy roll of 1575-76 listed Lady Paget as living in the ward of Farringdon Without, which included the parish of St Dunstan in the West, where she was among those paying the clerk's wages.[4]

The accounts of St Dunstan in the West include a great deal of information about the musical resources of the church over a long period. Christmas day and the anniversary of Queen Elizabeth's accession in particular were marked by music; the small group of singing-men received special payments, and sometimes singers came from St Paul's. Expenses during 1574-75 included ten shillings for 'v new bookes for the quier sett out by the Bishopp of Caunterberrye'. The church had at least one organ by 1510, and two organs by 1513. They were maintained by one maker, John Howe, for some thirty years until about 1570, then briefly by William Settle.[5] In 1582/3 they were sold to Robert Broughe for forty shillings.[6] This looks very like a victory for those who opposed the use of organs in churches.[7]

Further evidence of Byrd's association with Paget appears in the account book of the Paget household at Burton, where 'Mr Bird' was a guest from 6 August 1580 at least until 15 August, when the book ends.[8] He arrived as 'Mr Babington' – presumably the future conspirator, whose Catholic stepfather came from Staffordshire – prepared to leave. Anthony Babington had already joined in the formation of a secret society for the protection and maintenance of Jesuit missionaries in England, but among the other guests was a Parson Davys, who is hardly likely to have shared in these objectives.

About 1584 an account was compiled of the possessions of 'Thome Dñi Pagett qui extra hoc regnum fugit sine licencia Regine'.[9] This lists an

4   Lord Paget: PRO, C2/Eliz I C10/46. Lady Paget: PRO, Reading Room typescript from a subsidy roll of 18 Elizabeth; GL, MS 2968/1, f. 311ᵛ, etc. It is not certain whether this was Paget's wife Nazaret or his mother, the dowager Lady Paget.

5   GL, MS 2968/1. The organists and singers are named from time to time. For an account of Howe see Baillie, 1962.

6   GL, MS 2968/1, f. 335ʳ: 'Itm Rec of Mʳ Broughe the xixᵗʰ daye of ffebruarye for the Olde Organs'.

7   See le Huray, 1978, pp. 35-38.

8   SRO, D(W)1734/3/3/280, 'The householde booke declaringe the daylie and weeklie expences from the xvijth day of October 1579'.

9   PRO, SC/6/Elizabeth I 2057, f. 3ᵛ. *An Acte for the Confirmacõn of the Attaynders of Thomas late Lorde Pagett and others* (29 Elizabeth c. 1) was passed on 23 March 1586/7. It names Thomas and Charles Paget, Anthony Babington, and William Shelley, the original owner of Byrd's future house at Stondon Massey.

Table 5 · Historical background 1577-1593

1577 Period in which numerous companies are founded to dominate foreign trade (to 1581). South Seas Project becomes Drake's circumnavigation of the world (until 1580). Archbishop Grindal suspended. Execution of first seminary priest (Mayne). Curtain Theatre opened. Holinshed, *Chronicles*.

1578 Leicester marries Countess of Essex. Hawkins made Treasurer of the Navy. Lyly, *Euphues*.

1579 Catholic English College established in Rome. Lodge, *Plutarch's Lives*. Spenser, *Shepheardes Calendar*. Puritan attacks on stage. First national atlas (Saxton).

1580 Arrival of Jesuit mission led by Campion and Parsons. Stow, *Chronicles of England* (as *Annals*, 1592).

1581 Drake knighted aboard *Golden Hind*. Levant Company established. Treason legislation reinforced. Increased penalties for recusancy. Campion executed.

1582 Jesuits proclaimed traitors. Plague in London (to 1583). Hakluyt, *Diverse Voyages*. Mulcaster, *Elementarie*.

1583 Throckmorton plot. Anti-Puritan Whitgift made Archbishop of Canterbury. Queen's company of actors formed. Smith, *De Republica Anglorum*.

1584 Raleigh despatches expedition (under Grenville and Lane) to Virginia. Commission of enquiry into management of naval funds. Scot, *Discoverie of Witchcraft*.

1585 Raleigh's expedition lands at Roanoke Island. Hawkins given contract for maintenance of navy. Pay of naval ratings increased. Hugh O'Neill made Earl of Tyrone. Drake sacks Vigo and burns São Tiago, then rescues Roanoke Colony. Leicester commands expedition to help United Provinces against Spain. English ships among vessels seized in Spanish Atlantic ports. Central pavilion of Burghley House (Northamptonshire) built. Poor harvest.

annuity of ten pounds paid to William Byrd. The annuity is listed again in a record of the possessions and income of both Thomas and Charles Paget, dated 1585.[10]

10   PRO, E178/3103, f. 25ᵛ. There is no evidence that Byrd purchased the annuity, as he did the one mentioned in his will, and it was possibly a gift from Paget. Although it is

Table 5 *concluded*

1586 Publications lacking ecclesiastical approval banned. Babington executed. Southwell and Garnett in England. Sidney killed at Zutphen. Cavendish circumnavigates the world (to 1588). Camden, *Britannia*. Longleat (Wiltshire) begun.
1587 Execution of Mary Queen of Scots. Leicester recalled. Raleigh made Captain of the Queen's Guard. Second (unsuccessful) attempt to colonize Roanoke Island. Drake attacks Spanish fleet in Cádiz harbour, blockades Lisbon and returns via the Azores. Rose theatre built. First part of Marlowe's *Tamburlaine* performed?
1588 Spanish Armada. Leicester made Captain General of the armies. Expenditure on war and consequent taxation at record levels (to 1603). Martin Marprelate tracts (to 1589). Harriot, *Brief and True Report of the New Found Land of Virginia*. Death of Leicester.
1589 Robert Cecil (later Earl of Salisbury) starts to perform duties of Secretary of State (formal appointment 1596). First of five expeditions sent to northern France. Unsuccessful expedition under Norris and Drake to liberate Portugal. Intermittent English blockade of Spain's Atlantic ports. Hakluyt, *Principall Navigations, Voyages and Discoveries*.
1590 Essex marries Sidney's widow. Death of Walsingham. Sidney, *Arcadia* (posthumous). Spenser, *Faerie Queene*, i-iii.
1591 Essex commands unsuccesful expedition to assist Henry IV. Spaniards attack Howard's squadron off the Azores. Last fight of the *Revenge*. Cavendish's unsuccessful second attempt to circumnavigate the world. Harington, *Orlando Furioso* (trans. from Ariosto). Sidney, *Astrophel and Stella* (posthumous). Earl of Hertford entertains Queen at Elvetham.
1592 Capture of *Madre de Dios*. Shakespeare, *Henry VI, i*. Kyd, *Spanish Tragedy*. Plague in London.
1593 Further legislation enforcing church attendance. Plague closes London theatres. Shakespeare, *Venus and Adonis*. Marlowe killed. Norden, *Speculum Britanniae*, i (part ii published 1598).

difficult to believe that the recipient was not the composer, the inclusion (ff. 18ᵛ-21ʳ) among Paget's tenants of Robert Byrd and Thomas Byrd (and John Bull) is a reminder of the need for caution in assuming that he was. This Thomas Byrd was presumably the one in respect of whom an administration was granted in September 1592. (PRO, Prob. 6/5, f. 29ᵛ.)

It was in 1585, while Paget was abroad, that Byrd's probable pupil Peter Philips entered his service, travelling with him for several years, and visiting Spain, France and the Spanish Netherlands before Paget died in 1590.[11] Philips had grown up as a chorister of St Paul's Cathedral under Sebastian Westcote, who trained William Byrd's brothers Symond and John. He had lodged with Westcote, on whose death in 1582 he received a bequest of £6 13s 4d.[12] He then left England 'po[r] la foy [faith] catholique'.[13] Philips remained in touch with Byrd's Chapel Royal colleague John Bull,[14] who joined him for a time at the Archducal court in Brussels after fleeing from England in 1613.

Paget's correspondent Ralph Sheldon expected that 'Mr Byrde' might be entertained at Drayton in mid-1581, and said he was among Paget's guests at an unspecified location in 1581/2.[15] Another, more curious, letter from Sheldon reads:

> I knoue yor L. wylbe Jelous even whan yow shall understande what pt I have in this berer & houe muche he contentethe him self to bee of o[r] comfort ... Mr Twyneaue. I clayme holy. as he maye do my Self. & all my famylie / of Mr Byrde. yow are not worthie and we take comfort in him as a Leane to. by whom we. are Releved. upon everye casual wreke /.[16]

11   Mary Queen of Scots appointed Paget her special agent in Spain after he offered her his services in February 1584/5.

12   PRO, Prob. 10, box 105; probate copy, Prob. 11/64, ff. 99[r]-100[v], confirmed at ff. 235[v]-236[r]; Honigmann and Brock, 1993, pp. 48-53.

13   Certificate of residence in Brussels, 1597, in Archives du Royaume, Papiers ... de l'Audience, 1398; facsimile in Steele, 1970, p. xxii.

14   Österreichisches Staatsarchiv, Vienna, Belgien PC 46; Grove, 1981, s.v. 'Bull, John'.

15   SRO, D603/K/1/7/5; D603/K/1/6/34. About 1589 a 'Ralf Sheldon', presumably Paget's correspondent, lived in the parish of St Dunstan in the West. (List of residents bound into Queen's College, Oxford, MS 72; London and Rawlins, 1963, p. 159.) Sheldon also had a house at Beoley in Worcestershire, where he was visited by John Petre in 1577. (ERO, D/DP A18; Edwards, 1975, pp. 91-92.) In 1612 the younger Sir William Petre's daughter Elizabeth married William Sheldon of Beoley. (Briggs, 1968, p. 54.) It may have been he who brought a Chancery suit against the contemporary Lord Paget in 1607. (SRO, D603/K/1/11/65.) In 1605 'Raffe Sheldon' of Worcestershire was involved in a dispute with Sir William Roper, arising from the terms of Sheldon's marriage to Jane, the widow of Sir Thomas Tasborowe. (PRO, C3/291/89.)

16   SRO, D603/K/1/7/68. Twyneaue (Twynyho, Twinio) was one of Paget's estate staff.

Whatever lay behind this, it sounds as though Byrd was actively supporting fellow-Catholics. The document linking Byrd, Paget and Lister names 'certen psons havyng their sonnes beyonde the seas brought up w^t papistes', and 'suche as are relivers of papistes and conveyers of money and other thinges unto them beyondes the Seas'. Byrd is unlikely to have had a son beyond the seas at the time the list was compiled; in 1580 his eldest son, Christopher, was only ten. But he might easily have been a 'reliever of papists', both at home and abroad.[17]

Harlington

The first indication of the Byrds' residence in their new home is a certificate of 1577 prepared by the recently consecrated Bishop of London, naming people who refused to attend church within his diocese.[18] The entry for Harlington, which lists 'The wife of William Bird one of the gent of her Maties chappell', also provides the earliest explicit testimony of the Byrd family's adherence to the Roman Catholicism that came to play so important a part in their lives.[19] The Bishop must have smiled, however coldly, for he was John Aylmer, the former Archdeacon of Lincoln, described by his biographer as 'a real Enemy to Popish Errour and Superstition'.[20]

Byrd may at first have rented the property at Harlington, since the manorial courts were held in the name of Anthony Roper until 1583.[21] No help in dating the family's arrival is to be gained from the subsidy rolls. These were compiled by the commissioners responsible for assessing and levying subsidies granted to the Queen by Parliament, and list residents liable for payments in their areas. The extant rolls for the Elthorne hundred of Middlesex, which included Harlington, do not begin

17   PRO, SP12/146/137, f. 250^r; State papers, 1856, p. 703.

18   The certificate was one of those required from bishops throughout England at that time. See State papers, 1856, pp. 559-70. Certificates were also prepared in later years.

19   PRO, SP12/118/73, f. 147^v of a document starting at f. 143^r; Catholic Record Society, 1921, p. 48. On f. 145^r the document also lists 'William Burd a poore man & of no valewe' living in the parish of 'St Botolph next Algate'.

20   Strype, 1701, p. 42. Aylmer was consecrated on 24 March 1576/7. The Dictionary of National Biography says: 'His rule in his diocese was characterized by exceptional severity, fines and sentences of imprisonment being frequently imposed on those who differed from him on doctrinal questions, whether puritans or catholics'.

21   Reynolds, 1962, p. 262. The property was bought by William Roper in 1552. From 1584 the courts were held in Christopher Byrd's name. (GLRO, Acc. 530/11/M10.)

early enough and do not name individuals.[22] Byrd is named in several certificates of residence, but none survives from before 1587, and all describe him as a member of the royal household without giving his home address.[23] Confirmation of the Byrds' residence at Harlington is however given by the parish register, which records the death of Agnes, their maid, who was buried on 8 August 1578.[24]

While Byrd was invariably assessed for subsidies, he was probably excused payment on every occasion. The series of documents prepared in connection with them is now incomplete, but the musicians of the Chapel Royal, like other members of the Queen's household, seem always to have been exempted by letters of privy seal. On 20 December 1593, for example, a direction was given to the Treasury Barons and Chamberlains of the Exchequer, and 'all other our officers'. It said that the chaplains, gentlemen and vestry officers of the Chapel, among whom Byrd was listed, were 'pdoned remytted and released' from payment of the latest subsidy.[25] Surviving certificates issued from the commissioners at court confirm Byrd's residence there, thus precluding any attempt to impose a charge on him in Middlesex. They are typically in the form: 'Willm̃ Byrd gent of the Chappell, being most resyannt and abyding here at the Court in the tyme of taxacon is valued before us after the rate of Eleven pounde in ffee'.[26] A few certificates prepared at court specifically authorize the commissioners of Byrd's home hundred to forbear demanding any payment from him.

The petition of Tallis and Byrd

In 1577, although Byrd was still receiving money from Lincoln, he joined Tallis in petitioning the Queen for the grant of a lease. Queen Elizabeth frequently rewarded service by the gift of leases, usually in

22   PRO, class E179. The class also includes rolls from 1576 to 1609/10 which list Byrd as a member of the royal household; the piece numbers (within E179) are 69/93 (8 July 1576), 266/13 (10 November 1590), 70/107 (22 October 1598), 70/115 (29 April 1602), 70/122 (19 April 1608), 70/121 (1607/8?), and 70/123a (20 March 1609/10).

23   Certificates confirmed the place of residence at the time of taxation and prevented duplicate assessments of people moving from one county to another. The PRO class is E115. The numbers of certificates surviving from Byrd's period of residence at Harlington are 65/117 (30 September 1587), 23/115 (20 December 1589), 34/94 (28 January 1590/1), 59/83 (16 January 1591/2) and 23/59 (31 December 1592).

24   Zouch and Sherwood, 1986, p. 204.

25   PRO, SP46/43, ff. 56-62.

26   PRO, E115/23/59. The sum due to be paid was so much in the pound on the valuation. 'Resiant' means 'resident'.

reversion and without fine, and Byrd may have needed one to help him pay for the manor of Harlington.[27] The petition runs:

The humble suite of Thomas Tallis and William Birde gent of yor Ma^tes chappell: for a lease in rev^rcon w^thoute fyne of the yerely value of xl^li to the ten^antes use in consideracōn of service

To the quenes most excellent Matie

Moste humblie beseache yor Matie. yor poore serv^antes Thomas Tallis and William Birde gent of yor highnes chappell. That whereas the saide Thomas Tallys is now verie aged, and hath served yor Matie. and yor Royall ancesto^res these ffortie yeres, and hadd as yet never anie manner of preferment (Except onely one lease wch yor M^tes. late deare syster quene Marie gave him, which lease beinge now the best pte of his lyvinge, is w^thin one yere of expiracōn, and the rev^rcōn thereof by yor Matie graunted on unto another: And also for that the saide William Birde beinge called to yor highnes se^rvice from the cathedrall churche of Lincolne where he was well setled is now throughe his greate charge of wief and children, fallen into debt & greate necessities, by reason that by his dailie attendaunce in yor Ma^tes saide se^rvice, he is letted from reapinge suche cōmodytie by teachinge, as heretofore he did & still might have done to the greate releyff of him self and his poore famylie: And further where yor Matie of yor princely goodnes, entendinge the benefitt of us your saide poore se^rv^ants did geve unto us about ij° yeres past a lycense for the printinge of musicke. So it is moste gracyous sovereigne that the same hath fallen oute to oure greate losse and hinderaunce to the value of two hundred markes at the least. It might therefore please yor Matie. of yor moste aboundant goodnes, for the bettar releavings of our poore estates To graunte unto us w^thoute ffyne a lease in rev^rcōn for the terme of xxi^ti yeres of the yerely rent of xl^li. to the ten^antes use. So shall we most dutifullie praie unto almightie god for the prosperous preservacōn of you Matie longe to Reigne over us[28]

27   'As most Crown land by this time was under-rented, such leases could be quite profitable acquisitions'. (Youings, 1984, p. 175.)

28   Hatfield House, Cecil papers, clx, ff. 213^r-214^v; Historical Manuscripts Commission, 1888 (Salisbury), p. 155.

The petition is endorsed:

At Grenewiche xxvij^te Junii 1577[29]

It then pleased her Matie to signify her pleas^re that thies peticoners in cõsideracon of their good service don to her highnes shold have (w^thout fine) A lease for xxi^te yeres of lande in possession or Rev^rsion, not exceding the yerely rent of xxx^li. they abyding suche order as shold be taken by the L. Thres. [Lord Treasurer] or Sr Walter Mildmay knight for the behoof of the ten^antes in possession[30]

Thomas Selford

It is a little surprising that Byrd's short service as an adult should justify such a gift, though it was less than the one the petitioners sought. The gift may be a measure of the estimation in which Byrd's talents were held, and by associating himself with Tallis he had reinforced his claim to it.

Five pre-existent leases were sewn together to make one long document, and endorsed at the foot in January 1577/8 to show that they had been made over to Tallis and Byrd for a term of twenty-one years.[31] The leases gave them the income from the tithes of Oversley and Osely in Warwickshire, and of Willersley[32] in Gloucestershire; the manor of Billing Magna in Northamptonshire; the manor of Copford (Copford Hall) in Essex; lands at Drayton and East Camel in Somerset; and the chantry and tithes of Newton Place in Somerset.[33] Some of these

29   Possibly 'xxvj', but read as 'xxvij' by Historical Manuscripts Commission, 1888 (Salisbury), p. 155; Buck, 1928, p. xxiv; and Fellowes, 1948, p. 10 (probably following Buck).

30   The sitting tenants were to be given first refusal if the lease should be re-sold. (Youings, 1984, p. 175.) The Lord Treasurer was Burghley. Sir Walter Mildmay was Chancellor of the Exchequer from 1558/9 until his death in 1589.

31   PRO, E310/40/5, m. 12. The gift was also recorded briefly in February 1577/8: 'A lease in rev^rcõn for xxi yeares, graunted to Thomas Tallys and W^m. Birde two of the gent. of the Chappell and tithes of Oversley and Willersley, and of the mano^r of Billing magna and Copford etc. in the countyes of Warwick, Glouc. Northton & Essex and Som^rset. Rent xxxv^li. v^s. ix^d. And no fyne in consideracõn of service'. (PRO, PSO 5/1, unfoliated.) In E310/41/18, m. 15, letters patent are said to have been issued on 1 March 1577/8.

32   Perhaps to be identified as Willersey.

33   East Camel is more commonly known as Queen Camel; Newton Place is the

properties had come to the Crown with the dissolution of the monasteries. A condition of the Copford lease was that 'Thomas Tallis and William Bird theire Executors & assignes are at theire own cost*es* and expenses, to fynd competent sufficient and convenient drink and lodging for the Queenes ma^*tes* Stuard and Surveyor and their servant*es*, And competent and sufficient hay and provender for their horses at the foresaid manor of Copford, coming thither to keepe cowrt, or to make Survey of the same, from tyme to tyme by the space of one day in every yeere during the said terme'.[34]

Although the lease of Copford Hall, like the other leases, had been for twenty-one years, the Queen made a gift of it again on 6 May 1590.

Hir ma^*ties* pleasure is in consideracon of the service done unto hir by Raphe Battye one of the yeomen of the Pastrye to graunte unto him a lease in Revertion for the terme of one and twenty ycares wth ffyne of the premises ...[35]

No explanation of this is given. It may have been a part of the original gift which fell to Tallis, who died in 1585, or Byrd may have sold it on through the Augmentation Office.

Recusancy

The Roman Catholicism to which William and Julian Byrd and their children adhered offered no easy course. No one else in William's family is known to have been a Catholic. Robert Broughe, Byrd's brother-in-law, was a vestryman of St Martin's Ludgate, and their young relative Thomas Byrd was the parson of Brightwell in Berkshire. The fact that William maintained close ties with his Protestant relations argues that there was tolerance on both sides. As choristers of St Paul's John and Symond Byrd were under the tutelage of Sebastian Westcote, but there is no indication that they absorbed his religious views. A letter of 1594 reveals that 'one Bird Brother to Bird of the Chappel' was acquainted

present parish of North Newton. Court rolls for the manor of Queen Camel, 1577-1638, are held by the Somerset Record Office (DD/MI, box 6), but do not appear to mention either Tallis or Byrd. A note of monies paid into the Exchequer for the tenements of the late William Byrd and of payment by Thomas Strowde for the rectory of Stoke in Somerset, though calendared in the State papers volume covering 1623-25, is dated 1608, and thus concerns another William Byrd. (PRO, SP14/192/9. See also Patent rolls, 1986, p. 162.)

34   PRO, E310/41/18, m. 15.
35   Ibid.

with members of the Catholic Tregian family.[36] This must have been
John Byrd, since Symond was dead, but it says nothing about how well
he knew them.

There is nothing to indicate whether both William and Julian were
Catholics before they married, though their intimate association with the
vicar choral John Reason, whose suffering for his faith is described
below, suggests that, if they were not already Catholics, they were
sympathetic to Catholicism when they lived at Lincoln. It is obvious that
they came to have a strong faith in Catholic doctrines: they could hardly
have survived without it. The personality revealed by Byrd's music
suggests that, given his gift of faith, he might have been drawn to
Catholicism as a comprehensive intellectual system, informed by emotion
and supported by tradition − a framework within which all aspects of
life found a place. And extrapolating from his legal battles, it might be
guessed that he also had a strong dislike of being coerced.

Any explanation of why neither Byrd nor his wife was named as a
recusant before 1577 is bound to involve more speculation. It could be
that their strength of feeling about the Catholic faith grew only
gradually.[37] Probably, too, the level of interest in them was lower before
the Privy Council ordered a census of recusants and the strongly anti-
Catholic Aylmer became Bishop of London.[38] It could be that before the
Byrds moved to Harlington William's attendance at Lincoln Cathedral
and the chapel of the royal household, where Julian perhaps attended
too, was enough to satisfy the authorities. Absence from home on his
Chapel duties may explain why William was not at first indicted along
with Julian as a recusant in Harlington.[39]

36   PRO, SP12/248/118. See p. 362 below.

37   Bossy (1975, p. 121) says that during the first twenty or so years of Elizabeth's
reign almost all Catholics felt Catholic life to be 'compatible with some degree of church
attendance'. Some, like Lord Montague, came to feel that attendance at Anglican services
was a severe lapse. (Manning, 1969, p. 160-161.) Montague was the grandfather of Mary
Browne, whom Byrd honoured with his song *Though I be Brown*.

38   The Privy Council first determined to write to Bishops in November 1575. (Privy
Council, 1894, pp. 40-49.) The year of Aylmer's appointment coincided with another
event of significance for Catholics, the execution of Cuthbert Mayne, 'the first missionary
priest to suffer death ... his host, Sir Francis Tregian, being imprisoned for life'.
(Williams, 1995, p. 468.)

39   Dr David Mateer has very kindly allowed the author to read his article *William
Byrd's Middlesex recusancy* (referred to below as Mateer, 1996) before its publication.
This deals in greater depth with the legal proceedings against Byrd and his family on
account of their recusancy. Where Dr Mateer's researches are the source of information
given here, the fact is acknowledged.

The failure to attend a place of worship had been a statutory offence throughout Elizabeth's reign. *An Acte for the Uniformitie of Common Prayoure and Dyvyne Service in the Churche, and the Administration of the Sacraments*, passed immediately on her accession, required everyone to go to church on pain of 'spiritual censure' and the payment of one shilling to the poor.[40] A statute of 1580, with the same title, imposed new penalties.[41] Breaches were now punished by a fine of twenty pounds a month, instead of one shilling a Sunday, and offenders were to be bound by two securities with a two hundred pound guarantee of future behaviour. Saying or singing Mass was subject to a fine of two hundred marks, and those hearing Mass willingly might be fined one hundred marks; both offences could be punished by a year's imprisonment.

At Harlington, from 1581 to 1592, members of the Byrd family and their household were named repeatedly in the records of the King's Bench,[42] and in General Session of the Peace rolls and gaol delivery rolls.[43] The precise jurisdictional arrangements under which the Byrds

40   1 Elizabeth, c. 2. Justices of Assize might determine offences, and churchwardens were to levy fines.

41   23 Elizabeth, c. 1. This Act was reinforced in 1586 by 28 and 29 Elizabeth c. 6, under which a recusant might lose his goods and chattels to the Crown, along with two-thirds of his lands and tenements, leaving one-third for the maintenance of himself and his family. The 1586 Act explains the powers of Justices of the Peace at Quarter Sessions and Justices of Assize in relation to the prescribed offences. See also Pulman, 1971, p. 128.

42   PRO, King's Bench records, in the following four complementary but incomplete series: KB9 ('ancient' indictments), KB27 (coram rege rolls), KB29 (controlment rolls), and KB37 (brevia regis). Only the documents making up the KB9 rolls (which have been sorted and mounted in books) and the KB29 rolls have been examined comprehensively for the purposes of this chapter. The following Middlesex entries in these have been noted as referring to the recusancy of the Byrds and members of their household:

   KB9: 660/1, m. 42; 663, m. 8; 664, m. 35; 667, m. 54; 670, m. 56; 672, m. 16; 676, m. 106; 679, mm. 17 and 37; 680/1, mm. 43 and 44; 1031, m. 48; 1032, m. 276; 1036, m. 33; 1037 m. 344.

   KB29: 216, m. 12^v; 221, mm. 14^v and 97^v; 222, m. 48^r and 118^r; 223, m. 50^v; 224, mm. 17^r, 43^r, 98^v and 107^v; 225, m. 13^v and 67^r; 226, m. 73^r; 227, m. 17^r and 105^{r-v}; 229, mm. 15^r, 91^v and 94^r. A list of outlawries at the Queen's suit, 2-31 Elizabeth, is contained in KB29/220.

The format of the large and heavy KB27 rolls has been a discouragement to full examination. So has the format of the KB37 rolls; the vellum slips of which they are comprised are still tightly threaded on leather thongs and many are in poor condition. Numbers of rolls in these two series are given when they are quoted below. Additional entries are mentioned by Mateer, 1996.

43   GLRO, MJ/SR series; calendared (with some omissions) and translated from the

came within the purview of the King's Bench at one time and the Sessions at another are unclear, but there appears to have been a large *ad hoc* element in them.[44] The Fire of London is thought to have destroyed any records of appearances the Byrds may have made before the Archdeaconry Court of Middlesex.

The long list of the family's transgressions begins with a gaol delivery and Sessions roll of June 1581, endorsing as a *billa vera*[45] the evidence that 'Juliana Byrde uxor Will*elmi* Byrde de harlington in Com Midd gent & Johes Reason de ead*em* yoman' had failed to attend church from 18 March to 26 June 1581.[46] At about the same time these names were first entered in the rolls of the King's Bench, for 'contemp*tus* contra formam statuti p*ro* uniformitate'.[47] Reason was frequently listed in company with Julian. Although he was said to be a servant,[48] he was no mere domestic. The term 'yeoman' was often used as an indication of seniority among servants, and there is every justification for thinking he was a trusted member of the household, able to look after things when Byrd was away and to carry messages to and from nearby Catholic gentry.

Latin in Jeaffreson, 1886. It is easy to be misled by Jeaffreson's dates (for elucidation see Turbet, 1985; Mateer, 1996) and the order in which he lists the material. The relevant documents are: 230/65, 231/8, 233/1, 234/24, 235/38, 240/25, 241/29, 243/24, 247/59, 248/55, 250/5, 250/7, 253/32, 254/28, 255/27, 257/36, 259/1, 264/18, 265/44, 266/57, 273/63, 291/19, 305/28, 307/11, and 367/23. Besides these documents there are others including the name William Byrd which do not, or may not, refer to the musician. On 28 December 1586, for example, Christopher Jackson gave evidence against a William Byrd at the Sessions of the Peace. (MJ/SR 266/36.) A 'gaol delivery roll' was the list of those to be delivered from gaol (or elsewhere) into court for trial.

44   The presence of the major courts at Westminster Hall influenced the conduct of business in Middlesex, but Byrd may in some instances have obtained a writ of *certiorari*, a direction from a superior court to remove proceedings from an inferior court. He did so in Essex.

45   A 'true bill' was the verdict of a Grand Jury, made up of minor gentlemen and yeomen, that there was enough evidence to go to trial.

46   GLRO, MJ/SR 230/65. The variant spellings of Reason's name (Rayson, Raysonne, Reyson) suggest its pronunciation. A warrant of 5 October 1581 (GLRO, MJ/SR 233/1) ordered the sherrif to apprehend Julian, her servant and others, and procure their appearance before the Justices at the Castle (Sessions House) in St John's Street, Clerkenwell. The writ is endorsed 'non sunt inventi in balliva mea'. (Mateer, 1996.)

47   PRO, KB29/216, m. 12ᵛ.

48   GLRO, MJ/SR 264/18.

Reason was a 'Singingman', originally from Kirton, near Boston.[49] He had been admitted as a chorister at Lincoln Cathedral on 7 May 1547, so he was probably just a little older than Byrd.[50] He was a poor clerk on 10 October 1556, when the Chapter exercised their right to appoint him to the post of Bible clerk at Lincoln College, Oxford.[51] Here he lived in a garret above the library, by the chapel stairs, and 'undertook many tasks of a menial character'.[52] He was the only undergraduate member of the chapel, and was as much a servant as a student. He was responsible for preparing the chapel, ringing the bell for services, and lighting the stairs, and at dinner time he read from the Bible in the College hall. Reason left Oxford without a degree to return to the Cathedral, where he was admitted as a vicar choral 'de secunda forma' in 1561.[53]

Reason had at least two spells in prison. At the Sessions of 18 January 1582/3 he was 'comitted to the Gaiole of newgate from the prison of the Clynk for his disobedience in Religion And the xxiiij[th] of January in the yere Aforesaide the saiede Reason [was] sent Agayne unto the prison of the Clynke ... and is Enclyned to the Romyshe Religion'.[54] He was listed

49   PRO, SP12/159/34; Catholic Record Society, 1906, p. 227. The Kirton parish registers prior to 1559 are not extant. Much of the large parish church known to Reason has been demolished or refashioned.

50   LA, D&C A/3/6, f. 271[v]; Cole, 1917, p. 144. Robert Reson (a younger brother of John?) was admitted as a Burghersh boy at Lincoln Cathedral on 3 December 1558, when he was touching eleven years of age. (A/3/6, f. 437[v]; Cole, 1920, p. 157.) In 1553 a lease was received by Richarde Reyson, a yeoman of the City of Lincoln, whose relationship is unknown. (Cole, 1920, p. 52.)

51   LA, A/3/6, f. 417[r]; Cole, 1920, p. 137; Green, 1977, p. 54. Garton, 1983, pp. 951-953, gives a table of boys nominated to be Bible clerks at Lincoln College.

52   Green, 1977, pp. 24, 27, 53-54. The College's accounts (1530-1580) record various items of expenditure on the chapel, e.g. 'It for ij psalters for y[e] chappell iij[s] iiij[d]'. (Lincoln College library, Computus book 5, f. 13[r].) The College buildings have been much altered since Reason's time.

53   LA, D&C A/3/7, f. 11[v]. (Volume retained in Lincoln Cathedral Library at the time of writing.) Reason's return to Lincoln may have resulted from the dismissal of Catholics from Oxford. Thomas Butler was dismissed from New College soon after. (See p. 43.)

54   PRO, SP12/159/32; Catholic Record Society, 1906, p. 226. Reason was imprisoned on account of his inabilty to pay the £60 fine imposed for three months' recusancy. (GLRO, MJ/SR 240/25; PRO, E372/429 m. 32[v]; Mateer, 1996.) His imprisonment in Newgate and removal is confirmed by SP12/159/36; his continued imprisonment in the Clink on 22 March 1582/3 is confirmed by SP12/159/35-36. Concerning the prisons, see Stow, 1908, i, p. 36 (Newgate, in the northwest corner of the

as one of those committed to the Clink for recusancy since 14 June 1582, and was still there on 22 March 1582/3.[55] He must have been released, since he is included in a list of recusants drawn up in 1584-85, where he is described as resident in Harlington. Reason was indicted as a recusant in Westminster in December 1587,[56] and was again in gaol in 1588, though it was recognized that he was only a recusant, and not like others who were 'by theire owne confessions guyltye of Treason, or ffelonye'.[57] He was freed once more, and in 1592 recognizances in the sum of twenty pounds were taken for his appearance at the next Session of the Peace to be held in Middlesex, where he was 'then & there to aunswere unto suche thing*es* as shalbe objected against hym conceringe his Recusancye in absentinge & absteyninge hym self from devyne servic*e* used in the Churche of England contrarye to her Ma*tes* lawes'. He duly appeared and was released from his bond.[58]

A gaol delivery roll of 1600 records Reason's indictment for not going to any place of Common Prayer for six months.[59] A list of prisoners in the Gatehouse on 6 July 1602 describes him as one of 'two obstinate Recusant*es* that have been there longe'.[60] It is likely that he died in the Gatehouse, since a John Reason was buried at St Margaret's on 2 October 1603, one of the many hundreds killed by the plague between June 1603 and May 1604. An Elizabeth Reason, perhaps his wife, whose entry in the burial register does not indicate that she was a victim of the plague, was buried at St Margaret's on 30 October 1603.[61]

Around 1581 Byrd's house at Harlington was included in a list of 'The places where certaine Recusantes remaine in and about the city of

City); ii, pp. 53-56 (Clink, on Bankside in Southwark); ii, p. 122 (Gatehouse, Westminster).

55　　PRO, SP12/159/34-35.

56　　PRO, E363/9, m. 7; GLRO, MJ/SR 273/63. A note at the foot of the latter document shows that Reason had failed to present himself. (Mateer, 1996.)

57　　BL, MS Lansdowne 58, no. 13 (ff. 26ʳ-28ᵛ), 'Certificat of Seminary Priests and Recusantes in yᵉ Prisons, in, and about London', dated 30 September 1588. (A seminary priest was one ordained abroad, not in England before the accession of Queen Elizabeth.) Another prisoner was William Bray, a Catholic gentleman to whom Byrd's *Pavana Bray* may have been dedicated; he was said to be 'a comon conveyor of prest*es* and recusant*es*, & of naughtye book*es* over the seas, & was taken carryinge the Erle of Arundell over seas'.

58　　GLRO, MJ/SR 305/28.

59　　GLRO, MJ/SR 367/23.

60　　PRO, SP12/284/62i; Catholic Record Society, 1906, p. 288.

61　　Burke, 1914, pp. 480-481.

London: or are to be com by uppon warninge'.[62] His name crops up again in a document dated 26 January 1583/4.[63] This contains a brief narrative that tells how, during Paul Wentworth's search of 'M^ris Hampdens house at Stooke' in Buckinghamshire:

> one whose name ys reason comynge to the gate while the house was in searchinge, he conceavinge sum suspecte of the company wch he sawe, began to ryde backe agayne apace, but he was ov^rtaken and searched, ther was founde abought hym one old prynted songe booke wch was sent unto Carleton as appeard by a letter sent therw^thall, and one other letter, sent unto m^r ffytton from one m^r Byrde of the Quenes Maties Chapple, ther was also founde abought hym the Officin beate marie wch he sayd was hys owne prayer book.[64]

Carleton's chamber and Fytton's chamber, and Mrs Hampden's bedchamber, were among the rooms that were ransacked, no doubt in anticipation of finding objects proscribed by an Act of 1570 that banned the importation of any 'Agnus Dei, or any Crosses Pyctures Beades or such lyke vayne and superstitious Thynges'.[65] The main part of the document is an inventory of the 'Book*es* and other Popishe Reliques' found and carried away.

Fellowes characterized Wentworth's action as 'a mean and wanton act of robbery'.[66] But those in power saw the safety of the state as under threat, and did not always supervise the conduct of their underlings very closely. Official interest in Byrd's activities is signified by a list, covering a period from 1580 to 1587, of people bound by recognizances to appear or answer to charges under various conditions. This contains the entry: '17 ffebruary 1583. Willm̃ Bird gent*leman* bounde in 200^li to be forthcominge at his house at harlington'.[67] There is perhaps a

---

62   PRO, SP12/151/11. 'Wyllm̃ Byrde of the Chappell' appears on f. 46^v.

63   PRO, SP12/167/47; State papers, 1865, p. 155.

64   Several places in Buckinghamshire bear the prefix 'Stoke'; the nearest to Harlington is Stoke Poges. Almost certainly the house was the one near Staines to which Lord Lumley was confined in 1570. (PRO, SP12//18/44; State papers, 1871, p. 284.) Staines and Stoke Poges are in the same general area. Anstruther (1969, p. 407) gives 'Carleton' as the alias of Richard Sherwood, a London Draper committed to the Marshalsea for recusancy in 1582, and ordained in 1588. The *Officium Beatae Mariae* was the Book of Hours, a lay parallel to the Breviary used by those in orders.

65   13 Elizabeth, c. 2. An 'Agnus Dei' was a representation of a lamb bearing a cross or flag.

66   Fellowes, 1948, p. 40.

67   PRO, SP12/200/59. The document is dated 30 April 1587 in the State papers

reference to this in a letter of 22 February 1583/4 written by the Catholic plotter William Parry to Charles Paget, who was then in Paris. This contains the news that 'Mr Byrd is at liberty and hath bene very honorably intreated by my LL. of the Councell'. It may be that the letter was intercepted: at any rate the injunction 'Burne' was not carried out.[68] On 16 May 1585, in the course of a series of examinations that led to Northumberland being sent to the Tower for a second time, Thomas Wylkes, the Clerk of the Privy Council made a note 'Too send for byrd of the chapell and y^t his howse be diligentlye searchyd'.[69] 'Birdes house at Harmonsworth or Craneford' — the geography is vague, but both places are close to Harlington — was included in a list of 21 August 1586 headed 'The houses that are to be searched'.[70] It was then only a week since Anthony Babington and other Catholic conspirators had been arrested near Harrow for their part in a plot to kill Queen Elizabeth and make England into a Catholic realm.

The first surviving indictment to mention William Byrd, in company with Julian, dates from the Michaelmas term of 1584.[71] He was indicted again in 1585.[72] Either Byrd was obedient in surrendering himself, or he was protected by the Privy Council from the results of failing to appear. He certainly had a letter affording him the Council's protection at some stage, but of this most interesting document, and of how Byrd obtained it, there is unfortunately no trace.[73] Julian was less dutiful. She failed to

---

(1865, p. 408), but this is merely the latest date in a record covering the period from 2 March 1580/81. The entry concerning Byrd is for 1583/4.

68   PRO, SP12/168/23.

69   BL, Egerton MS 2074, f. 50^r-51^v (document 33), a 'Memorial for thynges to be presentlie ordered and Don'; Pollen and MacMahon, 1919, p. 123. Henry Percy, Eighth Earl of Northumberland, was born c.1532. In 1571 he offered his service to Mary Queen of Scots. He was sent to the Tower shortly afterwards, but was fined and released. He succeeded to the peerages of Percy and Northumberland in 1572. In 1573 he was permitted to be in London, and took his seat in the House of Lords two years later. After his recommital in 1585 he was found shot dead in his cell.

70   PRO, SP12/192/47-48.

71   PRO, KB9/660/1, m. 42. The terms of the indictment, with a translation, are given by Mateer (1996), who describes subsequent events.

72   PRO, KB9/663, m. 8. See also KB29/221, mm. 14^v and 97^v.

73   Reference to the letter is made in Hatfield House, Cecil papers, Petitions 52; Historical Manuscripts Commission, 1976, p. 219. Mateer (1996) suggests that the grant of the letter may have occurred later than the events described here, and been recorded in the Privy Council registers which are missing for the period 26 August 1593 to 1 October 1595. There is support for this in the fact that an Act of 1592 (35 Elizabeth, c. 2) prohibited Catholic recusants from journeying more than five miles beyond their homes.

appear in court at New Brentford, and a writ of *capias* was issued. She again failed to appear, and was outlawed.[74]

The failure to respond on the part of those 'exacted' by the sheriff grew so serious as to give rise to *An Acte for the more speedie and due execucõn of c'teyne Braunches of the Statute made in the xxiij^{th} yere of the Quenes Majesties Reigne, intytuled An Acte to reteyne the Quenes Majesties Subjectes in their due obeydience.*[75] This provided that 'Upon the Indictment of suche Offender, a *Proc*lamacõn shalbe made, at the same Assises or Gaole Delyverie in whiche thendictment shalbe taken ... by whiche it shalbe cõmaunded that the bodye of such Offender shalbe rendred to the Shirieff of the same Countie, before the saide nexte Assises or Gen^{r}all Gaole Delyverie to be holden in the same Countie; And yf ... the same Offender so *p*claymed shall not make Apparaunce of Recorde, that then upon suche Defaulte recorded, the same shalbe as sufficient a conviccõn in Lawe ... as yf ... a Triall by Verdict thereupon had *p*ceeded and byne recorded'.

Presumably Julian's punishment was compounded by a payment,[76] for

The letter may have contained permission for Byrd to travel to court.

74   Brentford was in the Elthorne hundred, as was Harlington. Outlawry placed a person outside the protection of the law, but was usually little of an inconvenience and could often be reversed or pardoned. Strictly speaking, women were not outlawed (*utlegata*), but 'waived' (*waviata*). The distinction, which is observed in the annotations added to entries concerning the Byrd family, arose in early times because, unlike men, women were not sworn in leets, and were *waiviatae*, i.e. *derelictae*, those left out or not regarded. Julian had probably failed to appear on earlier occasions, since the process of outlawry required the accused to be called to come forth at five county assemblies in succession. The exact timing of events is difficult to determine. PRO, KB29/222, m. 48^{r}, belongs to Hilary term, 28 Elizabeth, i.e. 1585/6; but a note added later suggests that the outlawry was not pronounced until 16 February 29 Elizabeth (i.e. 1586/7). The first of Julian's several outlawries recorded in KB29/220 appears to be the one in the section for Easter 29 Elizabeth.

75   29 Elizabeth c. 6.

76   On 7 November 1581 the Privy Council approved conditions on which recusants might be released on bail. (Privy Council, 1896, p. 41.) Pulman (1971, p. 129) observes that 'the Privy Council registers are full of notations concerning the freeing of recusants, usually in their own recognizances of £100, though the sum exacted depended on the rank of the person involved'. There is no indication that the Byrd family took advantage of the concession, but outlawry could certainly be pardoned for payments in the right quarters. In or about 1590 a proposal was made to increase revenues by granting composition for pardons in matters of outlawry. It was argued that outlawries had come to be held in small regard. At the Parliament of 1589, much to the Queen's displeasure, a quarter of the members of the Lower House were men who had been outlawed.

her indictments continued as usual.[77] The names of Francis and Elizabeth Welshe make their appearance in association with those of the Byrds at this time, as also, fleetingly, does that of Richard Farrington.[78]

The King's Bench records for the Michaelmas term of 1588 show that Julian was again pronounced an outlaw, and so this time were Rachel and Elizabeth Byrd, and both the Welshes.[79] Another entry dated 16 April 1589 tells how Christopher, Elizabeth and Rachel Byrd, with Francis and Elizabeth Welshe, had been summoned to appear at Cranford on 5 June, and failed to do so. They again failed to come forth on 3 July at Stone Cross, on 31 July at Uxbridge, and on 28 August at Cranford.[80] On 25 September Christopher Byrd and Elizabeth Welshe answered the summons; the others did not and were pronounced outlaws.[81] Francis Welshe was dead, however. He was the Frances Wealths 'of Mr Byrds howse' who was buried at the church of St Peter and St Paul in Harlington on 29 December 1588.[82]

A brevia regis roll, which includes several documents relating to the Byrds, suggests the level of fines they must regularly have incurred at this time. Annotations on the backs of four which were dated at Westminster on 30 May 1589, and which relate either to William and Julian Byrd or to William alone, mention payments of five shillings or six shillings and eightpence.[83]

77   PRO, KB9/667, m. 54; KB9/670, m. 56. Also KB29/223, m. 50ᵛ. Julian Byrd and John Reason had appeared steadily in the Middlesex rolls from 1581 to 1585. In 1586-87 they appeared there with William Byrd. (GLRO, MJ/SR 263/18 and 266/57; Jeaffreson, pp. 163, 167.)

78   PRO, KB9/670, m. 56. The Welshes were evidently members of the Byrd household; it is not clear whether Farrington was as well. Francis Welshe and Farrington were both yeoman. Following the defendants' failure to appear, a writ of *capias* was issued (ordering their arrest), and when the sheriff reported that they could not be found an exigent was issued (ordering the sheriff to summon the defendants to appear and deliver themselves up on pain of outlawry). Mateer (1996) suggests the possibility that Byrd and his wife may have been imprisoned as a result of their obduracy, but there is no documentary evidence.

79   PRO, KB29/224, mm. 17ʳ and 17ᵛ (30 Elizabeth).

80   Cranford was in the Elthorne hundred; the stone cross was in the Strand, probably where St Mary's church now is. (Stow, 1908, ii, pp. 91, 93, 96.)

81   PRO, KB37/13/32/1; KB29/225, m. 13ᵛ.

82   Zouch and Sherwood, 1986, p. 206.

83   PRO, KB37/13/32/1; membranes unnumbered. The Byrds' payment of fines needs further examination. Williams (1995, p. 475) says 'recusancy fines were levied with the maximum inefficiency'. See also the conclusions of Mateer (1996) regarding the Byrds' payment of fines. O'Dwyer concluded that 'The Pells Receipt Books and Receipt

The last of the gaol delivery rolls to mention Julian Byrd is dated January 1586/7,[84] but her name occurs in the King's Bench rolls, with her husband's, in several documents of 1590 and 1591.[85] The name of Alice Cole, the wife of Robert Cole, is also introduced. She may have been another of the Byrd's servants. William's name was recorded in a gaol delivery roll of 7 April 1592 and in a King's Bench roll for the Trinity term of that year.[86] A note added to the gaol delivery roll says that Byrd and Elizabeth Willmott were to yield up their bodies before the next general gaol delivery at Newgate. They sued for a writ of *certiorari* and the case was removed to the King's Bench.[87] Eventually the case was halted by order of the Queen.[88]

On the face of things, Byrd's interest was in the promotion of Catholic beliefs and the freedom to practice Catholic rites. At no time was Byrd's loyalty to his Queen and country called into question. It was most likely he who made a setting of the Queen's poem 'Look and bow down Thine ear, O Lord', performed during the victory celebrations at St Paul's on 24 November 1588.[89] No doubt she regarded him in the same light as his friend Edward Somerset, the fourth Earl of Worcester, whom she famously described as having '*reconciled* what she thought *inconsistent, a stiff papist, to a good subject*'.[90] The Queen's gift of the lease of Stondon Place in 1595 implies recognition of Byrd's faithful service.

Rolls show the money that was actually received in the Exchequer, but there were many convicted recusants who did not pay the fines incurred, and against whom no further action seems to have been taken. In ... some years, not every year, there were lists of persons entered in the Recusant Rolls as owing fines, which they never paid'. (O'Dwyer, 1960, p. 199.) O'Dwyer located the name William Byrd in the receipts for 1592-93. He refers on pp. 137-138 to PRO, E401/1328 (a receipt roll) and E401/1849 (a pells book). However, the William Byrd who appears in the former, although indexed as a recusant, possessed lands in Tollesbury, nearly twenty-five miles east of Stondon Massey (to which the composer had not then moved); and the one who appears in a section of the latter following the date 'Termino Pasche ... 1592' was a Suffolk man.

84   GLRO, MJ/SR 266/57.

85   PRO, KB29/226, m. 73ʳ; KB29/227, m. 17ʳ; KB9/676, m. 106; KB9/679, m. 37; KB9/1036, m. 33; KB9/1037, m. 344.

86   GLRO, MJ/SR 307/11; PRO, KB29/229, m. 91ᵛ.

87   PRO, KB 9/680/1, mm. 43-44.

88   PRO, KB 29/229 m. 91ᵛ. Further evidence of intervention on the Byrds' behalf by the Attorney General occurs in KB 29/225, m. 67ʳ (1589) and KB 29/227, m. 17ʳ (1591).

89   Brett, 1976, pp. 197-198. The surviving fragment of the setting is BE 16/41.

90   Lloyd, 1766, i, p. 469.

Yet the feeling lingers that the documents conceal at least as much about Byrd's Catholic connections as they disclose. Delving further into them brings to light hints that, loyal and circumspect as Byrd undoubtedly was, he was more intimately involved in Catholic circles, and probably knew more about Catholic intrigues, than is betrayed by the bare written records. William Vaux's name often occurs at the same time as Julian or William Byrd's in the 1580s.[91] Catholic rites were held in his houses at Hackney and at Harrowden, near Bedford, where he gave shelter to the Jesuit Edmund Campion. In August 1581 the Privy Council committed Vaux to the Fleet for refusing to answer questions. After a trial in the Star Chamber in November he was returned to prison for harbouring Campion, and for contempt of court.[92] Some years later, in 1590, Vaux's son George was wedded to Elizabeth, the daughter of Sir John Roper. The marriage of Byrd's son Christopher to Katherine Moore in the following year created a distant relationship, via the Ropers, between the Byrd and Vaux families.

If an association with Vaux brought Byrd into contact with Campion it may have been the renewal of a boyhood acquaintance, for they were contemporaries and Campion was a pupil at St Paul's School. After being ordained abroad Campion returned to England in 1580 with another Jesuit missionary, Robert Parsons (or Persons). A long pursuit by the government resulted in Campion's capture in July 1581, his torture, and his savage execution with two other priests at Tyburn. The story went about that a spot of his blood fell on the coat of a minor poet, Henry Walpole, who was moved to write the thirty stanzas beginning 'Why do I use my paper, ink, and pen?' Was Byrd at Tyburn too? He set part of the poem, and went so far as to publish his setting in 1588.[93]

91   William Vaux, Lord Vaux of Harrowden. His son Henry Vaux, born c.1558, was arrested in 1586 and committed to the Marshalsea until a few months before his death in 1587. (See State papers, Scotland, 1915, p. 151.) A setting of *The day delayed* by Thomas ('Nicholas') Vaux, Second Baron Vaux of Harrowden (1510-56), the father of William Vaux, appears as BE 15/44 among a group of doubtful and spurious songs which have been attributed to Byrd, notwithstanding the editor's initial inclination to accept it both as Byrd's and as 'exquisite'. (Brett, 1961-62, p. 77.) Vaux's verse might indeed have been set by anyone, since it was well regarded in the sixteenth century. (See Puttenham, 1936, pp. 60, 62, 239-240.)

92   Vaux was probably released at the end of 1588, with other recusants, after the Armada had been defeated; he died in 1595.

93   The setting is no. 33 in *Psalmes, sonets, & songs*. The poem is traditionally ascribed to Henry Walpole, who went abroad, became a Jesuit, returned and was himself executed. According to the memoirs of Father Parsons, more than one author wrote verses on the subject. (Catholic Record Society, 1907, p. 39.) Parsons says Richard

There is no evidence that Byrd supported or even sympathized with the pro-Marian faction among his co-religionists, but he could not have avoided meeting those who wished to place Mary Queen of Scots on the English throne. Did he meet William Kinloch? The Scottish composer was evidently familiar with some of Byrd's music if he did not know the man. Kinloch, who acted on behalf of another musician, James Lauder, as a secret emissary to Mary Queen of Scots while she was in captivity in England, visited London in 1582, and may have done so at other times.[94]

Whatever the extent of his knowledge or involvement, Byrd was keeping dangerous company in the mid-1580s. One of the few glimpses of him is provided by William Weston, a Catholic priest who landed in England in 1584.[95] Weston describes a gathering, which Caraman dates

Vallenger was responsible for one set, for which he was imprisoned and had his ears cut off — a fate that would have befallen Walpole had he been caught. The first stanza of Byrd's text was printed in *A true reporte of the death & martyrdome of M. Campion, Iesuite and priest, & M. Sherwin, & M. Bryan priestes, at Tiborne the first of December 1581*, published without a date in 1583. His second and third stanzas are not among those of the original poem, and were no doubt added to avoid offending too blatantly the authorities who regarded it as recusant propaganda. One of those instrumental in the discovery of Campion had been George Elliot, a former servant of Lady Petre, John Petre's widowed mother. Elliot's testimony, given to the Privy Council in August 1581, seems to have been motivated by his dismissal for embezzlement and attempted rape. (BL, Lansdowne MS 33, ff. 145^r-149^r.)

94   Purser, 1992, pp. 108-112; State papers, Scotland, 1910, p. 185. Dr Purser developed his theme in a stimulating series of broadcasts on BBC Radio Scotland in 1994, under the title 'On the Trail of the Spies'. The evidence of an association between Byrd and Kinloch is entirely circumstantial, but it is not beyond the bounds of possibility that they had common acquaintants. Some of Kinloch's music was known to the copyist of BL Additional MS 30485; he may have been Thomas Weelkes, who may again have been a pupil of Byrd. Brown (1989, pp. xvii-xviii) goes so far as to suggest that Kinloch may have been a fellow pupil, and notes (p. 178) that Kinloch quoted from Byrd's *A voluntary: for my Lady Nevell* (MB 28/46), written about 1591. The conspirator Theophilus Kinloch, perhaps a relation of the musician, was an attorney in London. National Library of Scotland MS 9447, which contains some of Byrd's music as well as a substantial amount of Kinloch's, was once owned by the younger Duncan Burnett. (Purser, 1992, p. 123.) Duncan Burnett the elder was a physician in Norwich, not far from Queen Mary's place of imprisonment; his brother Thomas was a physician in Braintree, Essex, close to Byrd's eventual home.

95   William Weston (1550-1615): Superior of Jesuit mission in England 1584; confined in the Clink prison 1586-88, Wisbeach Castle 1588-98, and the Tower of London 1598-1603; then allowed to withdraw to the Continent, where his autobiography was written.

15-23 July 1586, at the house of Richard Bold, not far from Marlow.[96] The circumstances are of the kind in which Byrd's sacred music may have been performed.

> On reaching this gentleman's house, we were received, as I said before, with every attention that kindness and courtesy could suggest ... [It] possessed a chapel, set aside for the celebration of the Church's offices. The gentleman was also a skilled musician, and had an organ and other musical instruments, and choristers, male and female, members of his household. During those days it was just as if we were celebrating an uninterrupted octave of some great feast. Mr Byrd, the very famous English musician and organist, was among the company.[97]

Weston adds that Byrd 'had been attached to the Queen's chapel, where he had gained a great reputation. But he had sacrificed everything for the faith − his position, the court, and all those aspirations common to men who seek preferment in royal circles as means of improving their fortune'. The second sentence is inaccurate. It may however contain a hint that Byrd had retired from a full role in the work of the Chapel Royal not long before, or it may be that writing some twenty years after the event Weston was confused.

The occasion described by Weston seems to have been the one at which Byrd first met Father Henry Garnett, who was instrumental in sending Byrd's son Thomas to the English College at Valladolid.[98] Father

96   Bold had been Sheriff of Lancashire in 1576, where he had shown an equivocal attitude to Catholicism. He moved to Harlesford, near Marlow and not very far from Harlington, between 1584 and 1586.

97   Weston, 1955, pp. 70-71, 76-77. The original Latin document is at Stonyhurst; translated by Philip Caraman, who worked from a transcript at Rome. The translation given by Morris (1891, p. 145) reads 'singers of both sexes belonging to the family'. Bossy (1975, p. 126) makes the point that a chapel of the sort described was often no more than a room in the house. He says elsewhere: 'In the bigger houses the liturgical cycle merged indistinguishably with the cycle of hospitality. At Easter or Christmas there would be a large company and sung Masses: the musicians who served for the Mass would also serve for the entertainment, and it was presumably on these occasions that Byrd's Masses were first performed'. (Bossy, 1962, p. 40.) Weston's reference to Bold's instruments and singers parallels a description of the musical arrangements at Lady Montague's house at Battle in Sussex: 'she built a choir for singers and set up a pulpit for the priests ... and on solemn feats the sacrifice of the mass was celebrated with singing and musical instruments ...'. (Southern, 1954, p. 43.)

98   See pp. 133-134. Garnett was Superior of the English province from 1587; he was executed in 1606.

Robert Southwell was another who was there.[99]

Byrd's family

Christopher, Elizabeth and Rachel alone among Byrd's children were named as recusants in Middlesex. This can be explained only in part by the terms of the statute of 1580,[100] which did not require regular attendance at church by people under sixteen years of age. Mary, if she was the elder of the children baptized with that name at St Margaret's, Westminster, was sixteen by January 1589/90. The year 1592, in which Thomas probably reached the age of sixteen, saw the passage of a new law, *An Acte to retayne the Quenes subjet[es] in obedyence*.[101] This applied as before to 'any pson or psons above the age of sixtene yeres, wch shall obstynatlye refuse to repaire to some Churche Chappell or usuall place of Cōmon Prayer to heare Devyne Service, established by her Majesties Lawes and Statut*es* in that behalfe made, and shall forbeare to doe the same by the space of a Moneth'.

The later record of Thomas and Mary makes it unlikely that they went to church if they were living at home, and poses the question of whether they might have spent time in London with John Byrd, or with other members of the wider family. It is not impossible that they could have been placed with a noble or wealthy Catholic family to further their education and manners.

The manor of Battyshall (ii)

Byrd's life at Harlington was punctuated by a series of disputes over the ownership of property. One of these concerned the manor of Battyshall, which he had set out to buy in 1573 or 1574.[102]

On the death of Aubrey de Vere in 1580 the manor became available under the agreement made between Byrd and the Earl of Oxford.[103] This opened the question of ownership. The parties were 'Anthonye Luther of the middle temple in London gent Richard Lewther of Greenstead in the

---

99   Southwell arrived in England with Garnett 1586; domestic chaplain to the Countess of Arundel 1589; captured 1592; executed February 1594/5. An Act of 1580 (23 Elizabeth c. 1) imposed severe punishments on proselytizing Catholic priests, and on those they converted. A later Act (27 Elizabeth c. 11) ordered all Jesuits, and seminary and other priests, to leave the country within forty days on pain of death for high treason.

100   23 Elizabeth, c. 1.

101   35 Elizabeth c. 1.

102   See p. 54.

103   Aubrey de Vere made his will on 18 January 1579/80. (Emmison, 1980, p. 18.)

Countie of Essex gent and Willm̄ Lewyn Doctor of the Civil Law on the one pte And Willm̄ Bird of Harlington in the Countye of Middlesex gent John Bird of London gent and Thomas Gibbes of Stapleford Abbott in the foresaid Countie of Essex yoman on the other ptie'.[104] Anthony Luther's claim to the property, which depended on Byrd's oral agreement given in about 1574, was supported by a King's Bench jury. Documents were subsequently produced, on the one hand setting out 'Proofes on the behalfe of Anthony Luther gent. in the cause depending in the King*es* Bench betwene him, and Willm̄ Birde gent', and on the other detailing the practices by which Lewen sought to obtain the lease to Byrd's detriment.[105] There seems to have been no animosity between Byrd and Luther. Byrd's hostility was directed against Lewen, who he alleged had attempted to depreciate the lease.

> Immediatlye uppon the sayde grant. D. lewen. (beinge then in great favor and Creditt about the sayd Earle) gave out speches y^t ther was A former lease for xxi^tie yeares made of the sayde Manor by the sayd Earle. By wch occasion. he procured. y^t none durst deale to bye the Interest from. W. Byrd the thynge beinge verye fytlye for D. lewen and his frends. in the parryshe wher they dwel. uppon wch occassion they greatlye thrysted after yt / And also y^t when. D. lewen saw hys tyme to deale for the sayd lease. he myght by meanes of that speache. obtayne yt for A Tryffell /

> Aboute A°. xvij°. of the Q. D. lewen dealt wth. W. Byrd hym selfe for the byeyng of hys interest./ Affyrmyng styll. y^t ther was A former lease or tow therof. And y^t he Cared not for yt. but for the ten yeares y^t ye lease made to. W. Byrd. had more then the other supposed leases And after manye meetynges about y^t matter. At last uppon A Saturday in the forenoone. D. lewen and. W. Byrd. accorded. what monye should be payde. And what Condicions should passe betwene them. And y^t all shuld be put in wryghtynge agaynst ye afternoone of y^t day. at wch tyme. they bothe appoynted to meete. to make up ther sayd Communicatione of the bargayne / And accordyng to the appoyntment. W. Byrd Came But. D. lewen was Absent. whereuppon ther was nothyng more done /

104   ERO, D/DFa T9.

105   PRO, SP12/157/59-61, formerly mm. 25 and 26. The first bears the pencilled date 1582, probably added in the nineteenth century, but this must be incorrect because of the reference to Aubrey de Vere's death in the 'present year', and since ERO, D/DFa T9 (the arbitration document) is dated 1580. The court was referred to indifferently as the King's Bench or Queen's Bench. Concise information about the courts in which Byrd appeared as plaintiff or defendant can be found in Baker, 1990, and Williams, 1995, pp. 148-152.

This present yeare. Mr Aubrye veare desseassed. and left no wyfe to survyve hym. wherby the sayde lease granted to. W. Byrd is in present possession. being well worth An C. markes A yeare. / Now. D. lewen seinge the benefyt therof. and repentynge. y^t he went not foreward. wth the bargayne when he myght. hathe devysed to get yt by A lease parrall.[106] uppon the private talke y^t was betwene the sayd W. Byrd and hym. vi yeares synce

And because he can not be A wytnes in his owne Casse. he hathe Enfeoffed his brother[107] Anthonye Luther wth the thynge. Affyrmyng. y^t. W. Byrd made hym. An absolute grant parroll therof. for his sayd Brother. / And therfore did Anthonye Luther bryng the sute. by ejectione firma.[108] agaynst the tenant of the Land. and produced his brother Lewen for his wytnes /

D. Lewen depossed flatlye. y^t. W. Byrd made An Assig$n$ment parroll to hym. for his Brother Anthony Luther. And y^t the same was not reffered to wryghtyng / And yet affyrmed he uppon his othe also. y^t he wylled his man to draw the wryghtyngs. and y^t the wryghtyngs weare drawen. / so y^t he must neds make A fal$s$e othe. other in the fyrst parte or in the second /

how unlykelye ys yt. y^t. W. Byrd. shuld make An absolute grant to one whome he never sawe. nor delyvered his lease. nor receyved any monye. / And how unlykelye ys yt. y^t. D. lewen would accept of A grant by speache. wthowt wryghtyngs. of An assyg$n$ment of A lease. y^t was so unsertayne when yt shuld take place / And to what end was ther appoyntment to meete in the after noone. yf the bargayne was fullye dispached in the forenoone how so ever this practyse may be lawfull. it is not expedient for y^t by the lyke devyse. any subjecte of this realme. may be (by the othe of one man). foresworne out of all. that he hathe /

A frendlye Jurye was enpaneled. beinge ye neyghbord. kynffolkes and frends. of Luther and Lewen. and xvi of them appered uppon the fyrst sumuns. and gave ther verdicte agaynst Wm Byrd Whereuppon. he and all his. is lyke to be undone /

The parties eventually agreed to arbitration. The arbitrators were John Talbot of Worcestershire and Sir John Petre.[109] In December 1580,

---

106   'Parol' could include an unsealed writing as well as word of mouth, but the agreement is described below as 'A grant by speache'.

107   Probably brother-in-law.

108   An action *ejectio firmae* could be brought by a tenant who thought he was being ejected before the expiration of his tenancy.

109   Petre was again asked to arbitrate in 1602 (see p. 137), and apparently in 1603.

'havinge at Lengthe heard the allegations', the arbitrators gave their view in a 'Wrytinge of Awarde Indented'. Regarding 'the assignement by worde from the said Willm Bird to the said Anthonye Luther', they found that 'the same was an absolute and Lawfull bargayne'. They nevertheless thought that Luther should surrender his claim on the ground that, since Byrd had guaranteed the lease to his brother John, he would be financially ruined if he could not fulfil his pledge.[110]

The arbitration was however overtaken by events, for in April 1580 the Earl of Oxford had sold the manor to John Byrd for £620. He in turn sold it in 1583 to his brother-in-law Philip Smyth.[111] Smyth held his first court in 1584,[112] and in 1594 sold the manor to Richard Wiseman, a member of the Goldsmith's Company of London.[113]

The manor of Longney (i)

Byrd's ability to pull strings emerges in a letter written in 1579/80 by the Earl of Northumberland.[114] It is addressed 'To the right honnorable my derre good L: and cosen the L: Burghley highe Threr [Treasurer] of England'.

> my dere good lorde I ame ernestly required to be a suiter to your l. for this berer m[r] berde that your lp wyll have hime in remēberance wth your favor towardes hime seinge he cane not injoye that wyche was his ferste sutte and granted unto hime I ame the more importenat to your l. for that he is my frend and cheffly that he is scollemaster to my daughter in his artte the mane is honeste and one whome I knowe your l. may Com̃ande and thus I wyshe to your l. as to my selffe frome my howsse in sancte martenes this laste of februry 1579.

> your l. most affnte
> Cossene
> Northũberlãd

Arbitration was often the preferred method of dealing with disputes.

110   ERO, D/DFa T9.
111   ERO, D/DM T56, bundle 1.
112   ERO, D/DM M175.
113   ERO, D/DM T56; PRO, CP 25(2)/136/1735. The release of 3 July 1594 signed by John Byrd (misdated 1694 on the back) is in ERO, D/DM T56, bundle 1. For the subsequent history of the manor see Powell, 1956, p. 228.
114   BL, Lansdowne MS 29, f. 92[r].

While the context of the letter is not stated, it may have resulted from another of Byrd's property disputes, concerning the manor of Longney, just to the south-west of Gloucester. This began in 1579, although it is not known to have come before the Court of Chancery until many years later.

The 'tenements and Farm' which made up Longney manor were said to have been worth two hundred pounds. The lease had become available to Byrd on the death of the existing tenant, a widow named Elizabeth Spicer. According to his own account he entered into possession on 26 March 1579, and then let the manor to William Mill and Thomas Watkyns. He alleged that on 12 December 1579 Mill and Watkyns were forcibly expelled by Robert Jackson, who attempted to exercise a claim upon the property. Jackson actually obtained a lease, 'by coppy of Court Roll', though Byrd asserted that its preamble 'was untruly sett downe wthout any lawfull warrant' and it was apparently not issued until 1580. He also claimed that the profits from the manor had been taken by the defendants 'ever since the said unlawful entry'. Although it may be unsafe to extrapolate from causes heard in the Star Chamber, this sounds very much as if it could have been one of the fictitious forcible entries created at the time to allow the trial of a title.[115]

The views of the Queen's steward, set out in a letter of 1581 to Sir Thomas Bromley, were quite clear.

m^r chancello^r, where abowt a twelve monethe sence uppon suyte made by me unto my L. Treasurer and yo^w., yo^w revoked a leasse gr^{a}untyd to one Byrde of her ma^{tes}. chappell, of a copyholde lyeng in a manno^r of her ma^{tes}. callyd Longney in the countie of Glouc^r. whereof I am her Highnes Stewarde, and by my deputie gr^{a}untyd then a copie thereof to one Jackson and othe^{rs}./. nowe being enformed by advise of counsell that the graunt by copie cannot be good, sythe the same was before past by Lease, (yor owne opynion as I understand agreyng to the same, willing wthll that the poore man shoulde have it by Lease, so that my consent thereto myghte apeare). These are therefore to signifye yo^w. pytyeng the poore mans case, I do not onlie yelde my consent, but also am hartelie to praye yor furtherance to that ende, and for the same fyne ratyd up̄on his copie, w^{ch}, (as I am adv^{r}tysed) is almost nyne yeres rent. and so wth my verey hartye comendacōns do ende, this iiijth. of maye./ 1581./

yor assured frende
R Lancestar[116]

115   See p. 92 concerning Dawley Downs.
116   PRO, E310/14/53, m. 48.

A lease to Jackson bearing the same date was signed by the Auditor, William Neale, and by Burghley and Sir Walter Mildmay.[117] It carries the following note:

> The p'misses have ben alwaies heretofore letten by copie of courte Rolle, untill of late the same was graunted by lr̃es patent*es* unto Willm̃ Bird one of her ma^ties chappell for the terme of thre lives, which are nowe by composition cancelled, and theruppon the same were gr^aunted againe by copie of courte Rolle for the fyne of xx^li. but noe monye paide, for that the Tenannt doubting of his estate dothe nowe referre him self to yor honors for a lease therof for three lyves, paying the fyne that was assessed by the Stewarde, thone half thereof the teñant*es* of her highnes said Mannor are to be allowed towardes the repc̃ons of the water workes w^thin the same Mannor by vertue of a decree out of the courte of theschequyer.

If Byrd is to be believed, the cancelling of his lease involved some underhand dealings. Part of the story is found in a patent roll of 2 March 1580/81. It begins with the lease to George Clarkson for twenty-one years, from Michaelmas 1580, of the rectory of Walsall in Staffordshire, which had formerly belonged to John, the attainted Duke of Northumberland.[118] Clarkson obtained the lease in return for the surrender of a patent of 1 February 1569/70,[119] and the payment of twenty pounds. Of this sum £1 8s 6d was to be paid at the Exchequer and £18 11s 6d was to go to Byrd in compensation for the similar sum he had paid for the lease of lands in Longney. The patent roll confirms that Byrd's lease was cancelled because the lands were claimed by the tenants of the manor by copy of a court roll.

Byrd alleged in 1608 that Jackson and Neale had fabricated the notion that he wished the fine he had paid for the lease of Longney to be paid instead for the lease of the parsonage of Walsall. He said that George Clarkson, to whom the parsonage had been granted, was someone quite unknown to him.[120] As part of the plot Christopher Smith, the Clerk of the Pipe, had been persuaded to prepare a petition in Byrd's name, but without his knowledge. There was also some juggling with another lease, by means of which the conspirators contrived to pocket an allowance of forty-two pounds (perhaps the 'composition' referred to above) supposedly made to Byrd when his lease was surrendered. Besides this they disposed of a document: 'the Records of the P^lts. lease', Byrd

117 PRO, E310/14/53, m. 49.
118 PRO, C66/1205, mm. 6-7; Patent rolls, 1986, p. 162.
119 See Patent rolls, 1966, p. 2.
120 PRO, C2/James I B16/78.

submitted, 'are imbezeled & not to be found either in the Pipe office wher originally they were nor yet amonge the Records of the Courte of Augmentation'.[121]

An account of what happened when the case eventually came to court, insofar as it can be discovered, is given below.[122] The rights and wrongs of ownership in 1580 may however have been so much water under the bridge. The lease in reversion of the rectory and site of the manor of Longney was obtained by Thomas Blagrave in 1582, and it appears afterwards to have been granted to others.[123]

Symond and John Byrd

The loss of the manor of Longney was not the only blow Byrd suffered at this time. More personal was the death in 1579/80 of his eldest brother Symond.[124] Somewhere there is almost certainly a record of Symond's burial, but it is unlikely that when it is found it will supplement with more than the barest facts the picture of a sad family gathering conjured up by the imagination.

In the summer of 1581 William Byrd's remaining brother, John, was committed to the Fleet prison.[125] The events leading to this did not involve William Byrd directly, but they shed light on his brother's affairs and there was some confusion between the two of them.

The story has to be extracted from the documents spawned by a complaint which John Byrd submitted to the Court of Star Chamber.[126] It

121   Records of various kinds continued to be deposited in the Augmentation Office long after the court was dissolved.

122   See p. 144.

123   PRO, E310/40/10, m. 9. Blagrave may have been the Surveyor of Works in the Tower. (State papers, 1867, p. 553.) In the absence of maps and detailed descriptions it is hard to be sure whether the property leased to Blagrave was precisely the one that had been leased to Byrd, but it seems probable. The manor and rectory of Longney, which had no resident lord of the manor or rector after the twelfth century, passed through many hands, including those of Byrd's friend Lord Lumley. (Elrington and Herbert, 1972, pp. 197, 200.)

124   Assuming him to be the Symond Byrd mentioned in the rolls of the Fletchers' Company. (GL, MSS 5977/2 and 21030.)

125   PRO, KB29/216, m. 100[r]. The Fleet prison was between Fleet Street and Seacoal Lane. (Stow, 1908, ii, 40.) John Byrd may have been there at the same time as William Vaux. (See p. 78.)

126   PRO documents in the STAC5 series are B35/20, B40/26, B49/30, B50/18 and B113/29. The Star Chamber was made up of Privy Councillors sitting as a formal court of law.

emerges that in 1569 he made a loan to Philip Havard, who acknowledged it with a recognizance in statute staple.[127] This conveyed powers similar to those given by a statute merchant, under which the obligee might seize the land of the obligor should the debt not be paid at the appointed time. The property involved was the parsonage of Amberley in Worcestershire. John Byrd made other loans to Havard, who according to the former made excuses for his failure to pay on time but said the sale of lands would enable him to repay a greater sum. The loans were therefore extended for the payment of additional sums.

It was the custom of the time for either party to an action at law to accuse the other of being a scoundrel whose behaviour beggared belief. This makes for entertaining reading, but it is not always easy to unravel the truth. There is no doubt that, in a complex series of manoeuvres, Havard assigned Richard Grene to make part of the repayment. However, behind Havard were Roger Chernock (or Charnocke) of Wellingborough in Northamptonshire, and Robert Mallory. It may have been the passage of the Statute of Usury in 1571 which prompted Chernock and his associates to commence a suit against Byrd in the King's Bench at Westminster.[128] This was to be prosecuted by Jeffery Harris and John Cottrell with the others as witnesses. It proceeded to a trial which went against John Byrd, but there was no judgement because it could not be proved that he had infringed the statute.

In the Easter term of 1574 Chernock and the others procured a new suit in the name of Mallory's nephew, Thomas Davye. They alleged that, for extending the period of loan, John Byrd had received money from Richard Grene on Havard's behalf above the legal rate of interest.[129] The case seems to have come to trial in the King's Bench during Hilary term 1577/8.

Gaps in the story told by the surviving documents make it difficult to be sure of the exact timing of events, but John Byrd entered a complaint to the Court of Star Chamber, asking for his opponents to be punished for practices 'repugnant to yo' ma^ties lawes'.[130] One of the answers to the bill of complaint is dated May 1578, as is Mallory's evidence, so the bill

127 An obligation of record entered into before the mayor of the staple.

128 The statute was 13 Elizabeth c. 8. While embodying the view of Canon law that usury was a sin, it reimposed the ten per cent limit on interest set by 37 Henry VIII c. 9 (1545). 'Mrs Charnock' is mentioned in connection with the Tregian family: see p. 362.

129 The accusation of usury was again strongly made in John Byrd's dispute with Robert Chandler. See p. 119.

130 PRO, STAC5/B40/26. Complaints were addressed to the Queen because the Court of Star Chamber, where it was to be considered, was not originally distinct from her Privy Council.

must have been submitted earlier. The answers confirm Philip Smyth's partnership in John Byrd's dealings, and the defendants' confusion of John Byrd with his brother makes one wonder whether William occasionally had a hand in the business as well. Havard contended that the plaintiff was 'before a Singingeman dealinge therin onely as a Broker and the bargayne maker and yet deliv^{r}inge the monye wth his owne handes', while Chernock, Mallory and Davye said he 'toke upon hym to be a Rymer & Jester and was reported to lende money for one Philip Smythe his brotherinlawe for excessyve usury'. The confusion is more apparent in Chernock's references to 'the skill wch this compl$t$ hathe in the knowledge of musyke' and 'his skill in Tunynge of Vyrgynalls', and in the statement that John Byrd was 'A mynstrell And used to playe in lyncolne'.[131]

The loss of the court's orders and decrees means that details of the dispute cannot be followed further, though John Byrd's commital enables the court's judgement to be guessed. An accommodation was nevertheless reached, with which Davye's attorney and the Attorney General professed themselves satisfied, and John Byrd was released from the custody of the warden of the Fleet.

Whatever the precise nature of John Byrd's activities, he was engaged in dealings involving considerable sums of money. Cases like that just described, or of Symond Wrenche, about whom John Byrd later complained to the Star Chamber,[132] assuredly give no more than a hint of the financial ventures in which he and Philip Smyth were engaged.

These may have begun early. It is impossible to identify with any certainty the subject of Sir William Cecil's response of 26 June 1563 to a memorandum about money paid into the Exchequer, but it reads: 'Make this sum up to 10,000l. with money to be had from Bird'.[133] There is a tantalizing bracketing together of the names 'Burde' and 'Smyth' in a letter sent by Robert Petre to Cecil, now Lord Burghley, on 31 August 1575.[134] This reports that Petre had desired Byrd to make over an additional £1000; and that Byrd had said the Exchange was at present

131 PRO, STAC5/B113/29.

132 PRO, STAC5/B47/4, dated 27 October 43 Elizabeth (1601) on the back, and STAC5/B39/2. Wrenche was a 'Scrivenor & Broker' with a shop in Lothbury. The case involved bonds which were entered into six or seven years earlier. Such arrangements would have been familiar to audiences who saw *The Merchant of Venice*.

133 SP12/11/101; State papers, 1870, p. 539.

134 Robert Petre was Auditor of the Exchequer under Sir Walter Mildmay; he died at Thorndon Hall in 1593 and was buried at Ingatestone.

very dead, but he would do his best, as would Smyth, his principal factor.[135]

An annuity granted by Philip Smyth, from the income of the manor of Faxton in Northamptonshire, was the cause of another complaint by John Byrd in the Court of Star Chamber, when the defendants were Richard Purefey of Faxton and Augustine Nicholas. Although the annuity was for one hundred pounds, very much larger sums were involved in the deal said to have been made, including a recognizance of £3000. On 17 February 1586/7 the Privy Council effectively froze the situation until the court had dealt with it.[136] About the same time the Court of Requests had before it a complaint made by Edmund Huggen (or Hoggin or Hogan), a Mercer, who was one of three people to whom Philip Smyth had lent money under an agreement made at the end of February 1579/80. The principal obligatory was Thomas Dudley; another was Sir Thomas Gresham. The case continued until April 1588.[137]

Dorothy Tempest

Byrd's Catholic connections led him, in 1581, to seek help on behalf of Dorothy Tempest (née Dymoke). She was the wife of Michael Tempest of Holmeside, County Durham, who was attainted as a result of his part in the Northern Rebellion. He escaped to the Continent and entered the service of Philip II.

A letter preserved in the Public Record Office is inscribed on the back 'To ye worshipfull. and my very good frend. m[r] Petre. on of y[e] officers of her Ma[ties] Exchequer at Westminster'. It reads:

---

135 PRO, SP12/105/33, f. 83[r]; State papers, 1856, p. 503. The furnishing of £3000 by Alderman Richard Martin is also mentioned; he became Warden of the Mint in July 1578. The identification of Byrd and Smyth is not entirely secure, since the names occur together in another context: a William Byrd was the Queen's Customer Outward, and Thomas Smith was another customer. (See State papers, Privy Council, etc.)

136 PRO, STAC 5/B5/34, STAC5/B90/6 and PC2/14, p. 273; Privy Council, 1897, pp. 330-331.

137 PRO documents in the REQ2 series are numbered 166/96 (the latest of the documents, referring to the Queen's decree of 26 April 1588 and signed 'Phillipp Smyth'), 219/78 (including papers superscribed with dates in 1586-87), 225/26, 224/42 and 273/46. Some of the court's books of orders and decrees are wanting, including one in which the Queen's decree might be expected to appear. An extant book however contains an injunction, giving a temporary stay of proceedings, issued under the Privy Seal on 8 November 1586. (REQ1/14, f. 210[v].)

Mr Peter. Meetyng you latelye in aldersgat streete at s^r John Petres howse. I Moved you for the payment of the Annuitye dew unto M^{ris} Dorothe Tempest at Michaellmas last past. for ye quarter before passed/. And then you promised me. y^t aboute a fortnight after yf I came unto you. I should receyve yt for her. bringyng a Certificat. y^t she is Alyve / so y^t is .s^r. y^t my attendance heere at the Courte is so Requisite. as I Can not have as yet any spare tyme to Come to London. for the Receipt of the same.[138] But this is most hartelye to desyre you. to accepte of the Certificat under my hand. as you have verye frendlye done heeretofore. / And to deliver unto ye partye y^t shall Bring the same unto you. (wch I thynke wilbe the gentilwoman her selfe.) suche Monye as is now dew. And you shall ever Comande me. in any thing wherin I may plesure you. or any frend of yo^{rs}. while I lyve. / And thus wth my verye hartye Comendations. I Comit you to god. fro the Courte this xvijth of october. 1581.

yor Assured poore frend to Comande
Willm̄ Byrde[139]

Byrd also wrote a certificate that runs:

To all Christian people. to whom this Certificat shall Come or to whom yt may appertayne / Wheras it hathe plessed the. Q. Matie. of her great Clemencye and Goodnes to geve unto Dorothe Tempest. wyfe unto Michaell Tempest Late attaynted. An Annuitye of. xx^{li}. A yeare. for the Releavyng of her. and her fyve Childerne. havyng no other thyng left to Relieve and Mayntayne her and her fyve Childerne wthall But onlye ye sayde anuitye. wch is to be payd quarterlye As by her Maties grant under her privye sceale. More at large dothe and may appeere. Thes are to sertifye you. y^t the sayde Doroth Tempest is Alyve. and in Good healthe. at the Makyng heereof. The xvijth of october. Anno Regni Elizabethae Reginae. xxiij^{mo} / 1581

Willm̄ Byrde[140]

138 Byrd was evidently writing from Greenwich.

139 PRO, document numbered E407/72, but kept separately with Safe Room number SR1/24/2; reproduced in Fellowes, 1948, opposite p. 42. Petre was no doubt Robert Petre. (See note 134 above.)

140 There are two known copies. The above transcription is from BL Egerton MS 3722. (A photograph of this accompanies the letter in PRO; reproduced in Brown, 1976, i, p. xxi, and Grove, 1981, iii, p. 540.) This once belonged to W. Westley Manning, who wrote about it in *The Times*, 12 January 1933. A similar, but not identical, certificate dated 25 June 1581 is owned by Mr O. W. Neighbour, and is reproduced as the frontispiece to Brown and Turbet, 1992.

No further documents have so far come to light to show whether Byrd's appeal was successful, though there may well be some among the Exchequer papers.

Tallis's death

In 1583 Byrd witnessed Thomas Tallis's will, in which he was named as one of the overseers. The other was Richard Granwall, who had entered the Chapel Royal shortly after Byrd.[141] When Tallis died in November 1585 the overseers each received twenty shillings for their pains in carrying out their responsibilities. One of the provisions made by Tallis was for his share of the printing monopoly to pass to his godson Thomas Byrd, and in the event of Thomas's death to William Byrd.

Tallis's widow, Joane, made her will in 1587, naming Byrd as an overseer along with Richard Granwall and Justice Greames. When Joane died in 1589 each of them received forty shillings for his pains. Byrd received 'one greate guilte cuppe withe the cover for the same', and Thomas Byrd received three silver spoons.

Dawley Downs

Byrd's elder son Christopher followed his father in entering disputes over the ownership of property. When he was no more than sixteen he had some arable land in Harlington, called Dawley Downs. It had been part of the manor of Harlington, and adjoined the common land. In an undated bill of complaint he claimed that a riot had occurred on 8 November 1586 because he had made a ditch and quickset hedge on his land to prevent his crops being damaged by stray cattle.[142] The riot was graphically described, though it may never have taken place. The Court of Star Chamber 'was concerned mainly with real property, but petitioners usually complained of riot ... forcible entry, or some other form of oppression, and it was this allegation of misdemeanour which gave the council its theoretical interest in such business. Probably the allegations were often fictitious or exaggerated, and the council was being asked in reality to try title: a task it could not in theory undertake because of the statutes of due process'.[143]

141 The Old Cheque Book misdates Granwall's entry 8 April 1571, but correctly places it in the regnal year 14 Elizabeth, i.e. 1572. For further information about Granwall see pp. 383. 385.

142 PRO, STAC5/B4/35. Interrogatories and answers by the defendants are in STAC5/B23/5 and STAC5/B46/17.

143 Baker, 1990, p. 136. It is not difficult to find probably fictitious allegations

It would be a pity just for that reason to ignore the bill's account of the various husbandmen and labourers of Harlington, 'with many other like evill and lewde disposed persons', and the attack made towards midnight on the ditch and hedge by 'the said ryotuous and disordered persons in Ryotuous and warlike maner beinge also weaponed and well furnished with billes bowes staves, pike staves handgunes crosbowes, dagges, axes, pikeaxes, mattock*es*, pitchfork*es*, swordes, daggers and other weapons'. Another attack was said to have taken place on 22 November.

Since the decrees and orders of the Court of Star Chamber have not survived, it is impossible to say what the outcome was, but the incident reveals that Christopher had a significant stake in the manor of Harlington before the settlement made at the time of his marriage. This is confirmed by the fact that from 1584 to 1593 the manorial courts were held on his behalf.[144]

The Petre family

Sir John Petre (1549-1613) was the son of Sir William Petre (1505?-1572), who for many years served as Secretary of State, an office he shared for a time with Sir William Paget, the father of Byrd's patron Thomas Paget.[145] John was knighted in 1576, sat in Parliament for Essex (1585-86), and was created Baron Petre of Writtle on 21 July 1603. He learned music as a boy,[146] and his accounts for the period from October 1567, when he was a student at the Middle Temple, contain numerous entries connected with his lutes and lute music.[147] His mother and wife were strongly Catholic, and were presented for recusancy, but John Petre's Catholicism seems to have been tempered by an appreciation of the possible results of parading his beliefs too publicly.

---

resembling Christopher Byrd's. In a cause of 1577, in which an unrelated John Byrd was a defendant, a reputed destruction of hedges and mounds at Shobdon in Herefordshire was described in closely similar terms. (PRO, STAC5 series, H74/3 and H28/23.) The list of weapons in the Dawley Downs affair echoes one in a complaint by George Collingwood of Glemsford in Suffolk, when another John Byrd took part with a Thomas Byrd in an attack allegedly carried out in 1593. (STAC5 series, C1/34, C13/40, C46/23, C51/14.)

144   GLRO, Acc. 530/11/M10.

145   See Emmison, 1961, on Sir William Petre.

146   An entry for 19 February 1559/60 in Sir William Petre's London accounts concerns a payment 'for teaching the gentle*men* to play on the virginall*es*'. The gentlemen were 'm^r John Petre and m^r ffarmo^r'. (ERO, D/DP A8.)

147   ERO, D/DP A17.

The Essex homes of John Petre and his son William were Thorndon Hall and Ingatestone Hall.[148] These were at West Horndon and Ingatestone respectively, and the Petre accounts show that Byrd had begun visiting them by 1586.[149] The 'Tempest' letter shows that Byrd visited Sir John Petre's London house in 1581, but they may have known each other well before that time. What is implied by Petre's payment 'To Byrd*es* boye' in January 1567/8 is not clear, since William Byrd was living in Lincoln at the time. It may refer to a different member of the composer's family.[150]

It has been conjectured that Byrd's motet *Petrus beatus* resulted from his friendship with Petre, and belongs to the early 1570s.[151] It is certain that when Byrd later moved to Stondon Massey he was settling not only close to the place from which his ancestors had come, and where he still had distant relations, but to friends of long standing.

An entry in the Petre accounts for October 1586 records a payment 'to John Reynold*es* the lackey fo[r] M[r] Byrd*es* horsemeate & his sonnes at their comyng downe from London'.[152] There is another similar entry for the same month. In January 1586/7 payment was made 'To Thomas Carlton the xvi[th] daye for his dynner & supp at his ryding up to London wth M[r] Byrde'. These visits were all made to Thorndon Hall. Among the other visits made by Byrd was one beginning on 26 December 1589, when Petre sent a servant to London to escort him to Ingatestone Hall, where he remained for the whole Christmas season. The guests included

148 See Briggs, 1968, on the younger William Petre (1575-1637). After the death of the first Sir William his widow continued to live at Ingatestone Hall, and John bought Thorndon Hall. Ingatestone Hall retains much of its Tudor character. The old Thorndon Hall is described and illustrated by Ward and Marshall, 1972. It was demolished in the eighteenth century by Robert, ninth Lord Petre, who replaced it with a Palladian mansion.

149 Entries in ERO, D/DP A20 and A21. There is a four-year gap in the account books prior to 1586. See also Edwards, 1975, p. 73; Price, 1981, pp. 83-91.

150 See p. 40. At least one reference to quite another Byrd appears in the Petre accounts. In April 1594 Isaac Byrde was employed in connection with building work. (ERO, D/DP A22, under 'Buyldinge & Repac̄ons'.)

151 Kerman, 1981, p. 33. *Petrus beatus* is a hymn, like two pieces to which Byrd drew attention in the 1575 *Cantiones*, but no copy is known prior to the one made by John Sadler in 1591. (Bodleian Library, Tenbury MS 1486.) A reason for associating the motet with Petre is the relative obscurity of the text, which occurs in the York and pre-Tridentine Roman rites and might not have sprung to Byrd's mind if his patron had not proposed it as a text. Kerman notes that it is the only hymn to stress the name 'Petrus'.

152 ERO, D/DP A20. Unless 'sonnes' is to be read as a plural it presumably refers to Christopher, who was already farming at Harlington on his own account.

Edward Somerset, the fourth Earl of Worcester, and his wife.[153] At the end of Byrd's stay the steward paid sixty shillings 'To five Musitians of London ye viijth daye for playenge upon the vyolins at Ingatestone by composition [previous agreement] in ye Christmas tyme'.[154] In January 1589/90 reimbursement was made for a sum 'Payd in London by Edward Graye ye viij & ixth dayes of January for iij meales, at his ridynge up wth Mr Byrde'. Entries for June 1590 show that Byrd made another visit to Ingatestone at Whitsun (as always, apparently, without his wife), and there was a further visit in August of that year: 'Paid in London by John Tabo^r fo^r ii gelding*es* one night & half a daye at ye fetchinge downe of m^r Birde'.[155]

The Petre family's accounts reflect the ownership of musical instruments from 1548 onwards. This was not unique in the part of Essex where the Petres lived. In 1583 John Peers of Mountnessing bequeathed to his daughter six viols, a pair of virginals, and his 'great instrument'.[156] Sir William Petre's London account books include several references to William Treasurer, who held the office of tuner of the musical instruments at court from 1551.[157]

153   ERO, D/DP A21.

154   A similar payment was made in January 1593/4: 'To Christopher Anslow musition and ye residue of his companye fo^r playing upon the violins at Ingatstone in the Christmas tyme − lx^s. And geven by the hande of Mr John Petre to John Haydon, one of that companye, who taught hym & Mr Thom*as* to daunce during that tyme − x^s'. (ERO, D/DP A22. John Petre was Sir John Petre's second surviving son; Thomas was his younger brother.) The violins were probably played for dancing. Although terminology was often lax at this time, the same account book makes a clear distinction between the different stringed instruments when it records a payment in September 1594 'To Thom͂s Carleton the xvijth daye fo^r a dosen of string*es* fo^r the vial*les*'. The younger William Petre kept up the practice of having music at Christmas. For example, he gave forty shillings to musicians at Thorndon at Christmas 1602-3. (ERO, ERO, T/A/174.)

155   ERO, D/DP A21.

156   Probate copy PRO, Prob. 11/66, ff. 177^v-178^v (made 19 January 1582/3, proved 24 January 1583/4); Emmison, 1978, p. 235. Six viols made up a 'chest'.

157   ERO, D/DP A6, A7 and A9 (all unfoliated). For Treasurer see also Emmison, 1961, pp. 210-216; Ashbee, 1986-96, vii, pp. 117-118. Treasurer was a German who came to England with Sir John Wallop about 1521. (Kirk and Kirk, 1900-08, i, pp. 359, 413; ii, p. 13.) He often appears in documents simply as 'William', 'Gyllyam', etc. He seems to have lived in Warwick Lane. Littledale (1895, p. 278) mentions the deaths in 1582 (*recte* 1583) of 'Christoner Bell, servant to Mr Gyllame' and 'Agere Holman, servant to Mr Gyllam of Warwick Lane'.

[27 June 1555] In Rewarde to Willm̃ treasurers man for bringing a payer of virginall*es* to my m^r vj^s viij^d and to one that played uppon them iiij^s } x^s viij^d

[14 July 1556] To gylyams man the organmaker for his charge being sent to ingatestone to mend the organs } v^s

[30 November 1561] To gyllm̃ a maker of instrum^{tes} for the making of a Instrum^t for my m^r xl^s and in Rewarde to his man vi^s viij^d besid*es* an other instrum^t wch he had of my m^r and to a carman for b*ringing* home the newe Instrum^t vj^d

The parish books of Christ Church, Newgate Street, a stone's throw from the Petres' London home, record the burial in 1584 of 'Mr Gyllyam, organ maker & servant to the Queene's Majestye'.[158] In October 1586 the Petres began employing a new instrument maker, Byrd's brother-in-law Robert Broughe.

Payed to Mr Brough virginall make^r of London the vijth daye for is half yeares fee to kepe my M^{rs} wynde instrume*n*t at West ho^{r}ndon, this being his firste paym^t, due at ye feast of St Michaell Tharchangell last past − x^s.

The next month another ten shillings was 'Payed to Mr Robt Brough', and in November he supplied 'a payer of small virginalls for Mr John Petre'[159]

1587 saw a series of payments: to Henry Pumfrett 'for his charge & horsemeate ryding up wth Mr Broughe', to William Mekyn 'for his owne horsemeat & Mr Broughes in London', and 'To one y^t brought downe Mr Broughes ho^{r}se'. Another payment was made to William Howell 'fo^r meate fo^r fower horses at ye fetching downe of Mr Byrde & Mr Broughe to Westhorndon'.[160]

Under 'Extraordinary Charges' the accounts for November 1589 include an item for ten pounds, 'Paid to m^{res} Broughe in full payment of fifty pownd*es* for an Instrume*n*t sold by her husband, to my Master'. The instrument which Petre had bought was an organ, for in the following April a payment was made 'To Edward Elmes carman of St Gyles pishe in London ye xxixth daye for bringing downe of ye new Winde Instrume*n*t from London to West Horndon wch was made by m^r Robert Brough'. A supplementary payment was made in May 'for iiij^{or} bedd matt*es* now

---

158 GL, MS 3713/1; Littledale, 1895, pp. 280 ('Gyllyam').

159 ERO, D/DP A20, under 'Charges for children', February 1586/7.

160 ERO, D/DP A20, under 'Ryding Charg*es*' (Pumfrett: January 1586/7; Mekyn and Howell: July 1587).

broughte downe wth his new winde Instrume*n*t to west H. And fo^r a peece of bedd corde wch bow̄d them aboute ye sayd Instrume*n*t in the carte'.[161]

It is not clear whether the new organ replaced the one which Broughe had been engaged to look after in 1586. Nor is it clear whether his contract was continued. There is no information after an entry for May 1590, which reads: 'Payd to Mr Robert Brough Virginall mak^r of London the Third of Maye for one year*es* fee & an halfe ended at o^r Lady daye last for keepinge of ye winde Instrume*n*t at West Horndon after xx^s ye yeare — xxx^s'.[162]

Broughe's instruments must have contained something of Byrd's experience as a performer. Conversely, Byrd's advice that an organ, which John Bull was to have made and sent to the Archduke Albert in Brussels, was not worth a thousand florins, must have been informed by knowledge gained through his association with Broughe.[163]

The Petres' household musician was John Bolt, whose name occurs in a variety of contexts.[164] It first appears in the accounts in 1586/7.[165] In November 1589 Bolt was reimbursed for the expenditure of twelve pence on viol strings.[166] An Ingatestone blacksmith's bill presented in January was for 'a payer of iron Bracket*es* to sett ye dubble virginall*es* upon in the great chamber there', and this was again paid by Bolt.[167] He evidently undertook a range of tasks, and travelled to and from London a number of times.

[November 1589] Payed by Jo: Bolte fo^r my m^{rs} boatehire to Westmester

161   ERO, D/DP A21.

162   Ibid.

163   Letter of 25 February 1610 (new style) from Luis (or Louys) de Groote, writing from Highgate to Monsieur Prats at the Archducal court in Brussels: 'ya he dado qu^a. a V S de como no pude negociar nada con el organista [Bull], que partio para Pleimouth, Despues he sabido de un musico famoso Uamado Burd, m̃o que fue de P^o. flippi, que el organo no Valia mil florines … '. (Österreichisches Staatsarchiv, Vienna, Belgien PC 46.)

164   He is said to have held a place at court. (Morris, 1872, pp. 297-300.) He received a gift under the will of Sebastian Westcote. (PRO, Prob. 10 box 105; probate copy, Prob. 11/64, ff. 99^r-100^v, confirmed at ff. 235^v-236^r; Honigmann and Brock, 1993, pp. 48-53.)

165   ERO, D/DP A20.

166   This was a recurring item of expenditure. In the accounts for 1594 there is an entry for five shillings and sevenpence, 'Paied in London by Thomas Carleton ye last of Aprill fo^r ij dosen & a half of lutestring*es* for my m^{rs} lute, and for a boxe to put them in'. (ERO, D/DP A22.)

167   ERO, D/DP A21; Emmison, 1961, p. 213.

[May 1590] Paid by Edward Graye for his charge*s* in ridinge up to London wth a horse for Jo: Bolte, to come downe upon ye first of Maye, & cõmynge downe ye same daye on foote.

Bolt remained with the Petres until 1593. He then became of interest to the Elizabethan security service and was taken in for questioning. He was interrogated three times, and three statements were drawn up, each of which he signed.[168] The first statement, dated 20 March 1593/4, begins by describing him as 'John Bolt of the cyty of Excester of the age of xxx^te yeares or ther about'. He said that John Petre had discharged him around the previous midsummer, after which he went to Mr Verney's house in Warwickshire to teach Mr Bassett's children to sing and play the virginals. He later stayed with Morgan Robynns, 'a gent that hath a lodging in ffynsbury ffeldes'. The statement concludes with Bolt's explanation of how he came by certain books in his possession.

The next two examinations took place the following day. In the statement drawn up after the first session he is described as 'John Bolt late of Thorndone in the countie of essex, yeoman'. It includes information about people he knew or had known, and contains his confession that five years ago, in London, he copied verses (already set to music by Byrd) beginning 'why do I use my paper penne and Inke &c and endinge thus to Jesus name which such a manne did raise'. During the last examination Bolt admitted that he had not been to church for two years, but refused to say 'who did reconcyle him from the church of England to the Romyshe churche'. Pressed to say what he would do if the Pope or King of Spain invaded England, he gave no answer.[169]

The manor of Horsepath

In 1589 Byrd obtained the deed of a property in Berkshire, about seven miles south-west of Oxford. The manor of Horsepath (or Horspane) had once belonged to Abingdon Abbey.[170] In 1546 William Boxe, a Grocer of

168 PRO, SP12/248/37-39; State papers, 1867, p. 467. The first and last statements were signed also by Edward Vaughan and others as interrogators.

169 O'Dwyer (1960, p. 139), apparently following Morris, says that Bolt owed his life to the intercession of Penelope Riche. He went abroad, was ordained at Douai College, and became a secular priest in the Cambrai diocese. See Morris, 1872, pp. 297-298 (where Bolt is erroneously referred to as 'Best, *alias* Johnson' on p. 297, but correctly as 'Bolt, *alias* Johnson' on p. 298).

170 PRO, C66/580, m. 18 (10); Patent rolls, 1916, pp. 111-112; Page and Ditchfield, 1972, p. 358. The manor should not be confused with the village of Horspath four miles east of Oxford.

London, received from Henry VIII a grant in fee of the lordship and manor of Marcham, the messuage called Horsepath, and a water mill and fishery with other lands in Marcham and nearby, including the possessions of Abingdon Abbey.[171]

Boxe and his son, also William, granted a lease in reversion of the farm called Horsepath to George Garrett and his wife Elizabeth. Before the older William died he entailed all the lands on his son, who had already granted a forty-nine year lease to the Garretts in reversion of someone named Hawkins. He in turn had an estate in being for a term of some dozen years if the Garretts should live that long. To complicate matters further, the younger Boxe sold all his property to Sir Henry Unton, who sold it to Basil Fettiplace (or Pfetiplace) in 1589, the year in which the Garretts executed a deed assigning their remaining term to Byrd.[172] When the Garretts died Byrd sought to claim the property accorded to him by the deed and brought an action against Fettiplace and Boxe in the Court of Requests.

At Greenwich on 20 May 1590 the Queen issued an injuction under the privy seal, requiring 'certen articles and Interrogatories to be mynystred to the witnesses' on Byrd's behalf.[173] A report was to be made to the Court of Requests. The case was before the court on 30 May 1590, when the defendants said they were not ready to examine witnesses.[174] Statements and counterstatements were submitted, and the argument put forward by Fettiplace and Boxe was that the Garretts' interest in the estate had been surrendered to the Boxes while the elder William Boxe was still alive.[175] The defendants' counsel procrastinated successfully, but on 7 July 1590 it was ordered that the matter should be 'published uppon the second day of the nexte Terme Cleard uppon the sixt of the same Terme, w'hout further delay'.[176] A technicality led to the

---

171   PRO, C66/767, m. 10; Letters and papers, 1910, p. 98.

172   There were suggestions that Fettiplace, the Sheriff of Berkshire, and his mother were recusants. (CSDP, 1865, p. 281.)

173   PRO, REQ2/178/48, which includes the interrogatories. Depositions survive in REQ2/164/18, REQ2/178/48 and REQ2/180/14. Fellowes (1948, pp. 12-14) referred to the Queen's injunction issued at Greenwich on 20 May 32 Elizabeth, but dated it 1591 instead of 1590. He believed that Byrd had previously petitioned the Queen seeking her support for his claim and that she had issued an injunction under the privy seal ordering that sworn depositions should be made by witnesses. He dated these events 15 October and 26 October 1590. The source of his information has not been found. The privy seal docquet books for the period are wanting.

174   PRO, REQ1/16, p. 54.

175   PRO, REQ2/178/48.

176   PRO, REQ1/16, pp. 177, 191.

need for a second trial,[177] and on 18 November the case was appointed to be heard 'on Thursday next'.[178] Further orders were given for progressing the case on 5 February 1590/91 and 28 April 1591.[179]

On 10 June 1591 Lord Admiral Howard wrote 'To my very lovinge ffrend*es* Mr D. Aubrey, M^r. Herbert and other the M^rs. of hir Maties Request*es*', reminding them that he had written to them before about the case in which William Byrd was the complainant and Basil Fettiplace the defendant.[180] When it came before them, 'by reason of the wante of some two word*es* that were left forthe', Byrd was driven to commence his suit again, at considerable expense. As the case was at last about to be heard, Howard desired the Masters of Requests to show Byrd 'all lawful favour'.[181]

The court gave its decision two days later on 12 June. It decreed that 'the same cause seemed more aptly to be tryed by the ordinary course of the coṁon lawes then in this said Court', and 'ordered that the same matter be out of this said Court cleerely dismissed by us, & the saide def*endants* licensed at their libertie to depart sine die. And it is further Ordered, that if the said compl^t do hereafter coṁense any acċon at the coṁon lawe for or towching the ṗmisses That then the def^s shall thereunto make answere w^thout delay'.[182] There is no indication that Byrd took any further action, and Robert Hawkins, a yeoman, died seized of the capital messuage called Horsepath farmhouse in 1601.[183]

Christopher Byrd's marriage

In 1591 or 1592 Byrd negotiated the terms of his son Christopher's marriage to Katherine, the daughter of Thomas Moore (or More), who was a grandson of Sir Thomas More, and therefore a cousin of Anthony Roper who had once owned Harlington manor.[184] Moore had been

---

177   See the next paragraph.

178   PRO, REQ1/16, p. 361.

179   PRO, REQ1/16, p. 565 and 706. The second entry appears to duplicate an order in REQ2/180/14, which is dated 18 May 1591 and carries a note dated 21 May 1591.

180   Charles Howard, 1536-1624, Second Baron Howard of Effingham; held the chief command against the Spanish Armada in 1588; created Earl of Nottingham in 1596. The Masters named were Dr William Aubrey and John Herbert. (Foster, 1891-92.)

181   PRO, SP32/17, f. 26^r-v; State papers, 1872, p. 326. 'The preciseness of Latin meant that the omission of a single down-stroke or contraction sign, or an error of Latin accidence, were fatal mistakes in a writ'. (Baker, 1990, p. 103.)

182   PRO, REQ1/16, p. 939.

183   Page and Ditchfield, 1972, p. 358.

184   No record of Christopher's marriage to Katherine has so far been discovered.

committed to the Marshalsea in April 1582 and spent at least six months there from January 1585/6. The greater part of his property, at Barnborough Manor and Moseley Tilte, in the West Riding of Yorkshire, was seized in December 1590 on account of his recusancy, and in 1591 it was let by the Crown to John Southerne.[185] Moore also had an estate at Leyton, in Essex, where he settled in 1582.[186] This estate was free from sequestration, though he frequently suffered penalties for recusancy.

Through his marriage, Christopher became the brother-in-law of a Catholic priest. Thomas Moore, Katherine's brother, was educated abroad and ordained in Rome. From 1594 he was chaplain to Lady Magdalen Montague at Battle Abbey, Sussex.[187]

Patrons

During his later years at Harlington Byrd devoted much time to the collection and publication of his music. All the printed colllections were published by Byrd's sole assignee, Thomas East. The business arrangement between the two men must have covered all the music that East published, not Byrd's alone. How lucrative it was for either is impossible to say, but they obviously found it worth continuing.

Byrd's choice of dedicatees is revealing. His first printed dedication, made jointly with Tallis in their *Cantiones sacrae* of 1575, had wisely been to Queen Elizabeth. They secured a commendatory Latin poem

Thomas Moore (1531-1606) was the son of John Moore, who had married Ann, the wealthy heiress of Edward Cressacre of Barnborough (Barnburgh, Barmborough, Bamborough) in the West Riding of Yorkshire. After her remarriage and the death of her second husband, she conveyed her property to Thomas. In 1553 he married Ann, the daughter of John Scrope of Hambledon, Buckinghamshire. Information about the Moore family is contained in the Dictionary of National Biography, s.v. 'More, Sir Thomas'; McCann, 1986, pp. 122-123; and *The Essex Recusant*, i-vi (genealogical chart in i, pp. 64-65). The last of these shows that Joan Rastall, who was descended from the Moores, married the virginalist and playwright John Heywood (1497-c.1579), a staunch Catholic. Heywood trained Thomas Whythorne and witnessed Thomas Mulliner's ownership of the volume that is now BL Additional MS 30513. Heywood was a favourite of Edward VI and Queen Mary, and Byrd must have known him before he went into exile in 1564.

185   PRO, E372/436, f. 10ᵛ; E372/437 ff. 24ʳ-25ᵛ.

186   ERO, Q/SR 125/32.

187   Southern, 1954, pp. 42-43; Shanahan, 1965; Anstruther, 1969, p. 233. Byrd wrote an elegy, *With lilies white*, on the death of Lady Montague, and the song *Though I be Brown* on the occasion of the marriage of her granddaughter, Mary Browne. (See p. 347.)

from Ferdinand Richardson (the composer Ferdinando Heyborne), a
favourite of the Queen,[188] who claimed in his verses to be a pupil of
Tallis. The eminent schoolmaster Richard Mulcaster was also persuaded
to write a poem.

Byrd made another wise choice in dedicating his first independent
publication, *Psalmes, sonets, & songs* (1588), to Sir Christopher Hatton,
who was prominent in actions against the Catholics.[189] Hatton was on
very intimate terms with the Queen, who visited him daily when he was
ill in 1573, and he prayed in Parliament for her preservation from the
machinations of Jesuits and seminary priests. Hatton became Lord
Chancellor in April 1587.

The choice of Gilbert, Lord Talbot, as dedicatee for *Musica
transalpina* in the same year was most likely made by the publisher,
Nicholas Yonge, although it was 'Imprinted at London by Thomas East,
the assigné of William Byrd'.[190] A more personal note is struck by Byrd's
dedication of *Liber primus sacrarum cantionum* (1589) to his old friend
Edward Somerset, Earl of Worcester. There is no doubt why Byrd
thought it appropriate to dedicate the collection to someone who shared
his religious beliefs, but none of his dedications can be seen as entirely
personal: they were all made to noblemen who regarded patronage of the
arts as a pleasure and a duty, and sometimes as a means of enhancing
their social position. Worcester, like Hatton, was a patron of the firmly
Protestant Edmund Spenser, whose *Prothalamion* of 1596 was written for
the double marriage of 'the two Honorable & vertuous *Ladies the Ladie*
Elizabeth *and the Ladie* Katherine *Somerset*, Daughters to the Right
Honourable the Earle of *Worcester*'. Such connections must have
brought Byrd into contact with a number of the poets of his day, though
only a few have been identified as the authors of verses he set in *Songs
of sundrie natures* (1589). This collection was published with a
dedication to Sir Henry Carey, a first cousin of the Queen through his
mother Mary, the sister of Anne Boleyn. He had become Chamberlain of
the royal household in 1583, and the *Songs* appeared at about the time he
was made Keeper of Tinsdale as a reward for his services in regard to
Scotland.

---

188   Marlow, 1974.

189   Hatton (1540-91) was a patron a Edmund Spenser, Thomas Churchyard, and other
writers. Spenser was a pupil of Richard Mulcaster.

190   Talbot (1553-1616) was the seventh Earl of Shrewsbury. Before his fifteenth
birthday he was married to Mary, the daughter of Sir William Cavendish of Chatsworth.
In 1570-72 he studied in Padua. On Talbot and his connections see Price, 1981, pp. 99-
118.

The compiler of *The first sett, of Italian madrigalls Englished* (1590) was Thomas Watson, who provided translations or alternative lyrics. The collection was dedicated to Robert Devereux, the Earl of Essex, shortly after his recall from an attack on Lisbon, at a time when he was not deeply occupied with home politics and may have felt disposed to indulge his patronage of literature and the drama. Together with the pieces of Italian origin were 'two excellent madrigalls of Master William Byrds, composed after the Italian vaine, at the request of the sayd Thomas Watson', and probably with words by Watson, who may already have supplied some of those for *Psalmes, sonets, & songs*. Watson was born in the parish of St Helen Bishopsgate about 1556, and in 1567 was sent to school at Winchester, where there was a strong Catholic presence and where he met the young Henry Garnett. Watson spent some years abroad, often in Catholic company, but in 1579 he was living in Westminster, where he became friendly with William Camden.[191] By 1581 Watson was probably back in the parish of St Helen's. His days of travel abroad perhaps account for the inclusion of his name in a list of 'strangers that go not to church'.[192] It may have been Watson's sister who married Robert Poley, one of Sir Francis Walsingham's spies and one of those present at the killing of Christopher Marlowe.[193]

The dedication of *Liber secundus sacrarum cantionum* (1591) to Lord Lumley is another to a Catholic nobleman whom Byrd is likely to have known for a long time, and acknowledges his benefactions.[194] Like Byrd's daughter-in-law Katherine, Lumley was descended from the Scrope family. In 1591, despite his Catholicism and terms of imprisonment, Lumley was sufficiently in favour to be able to entertain the Queen at Lewes. Whether there is any significance in this, or in the fact that the dedication was made about the time that Byrd was negotiating his son Christopher's marriage to Katherine, can only be matters for conjecture. So can the questions of whether Byrd knew the

191   See p. 27.

192   BL, Lansdowne MS 33, no. 59, f. 141ʳ.

193   On the connection of Watson and Poley with Marlowe and the spy network, see Nicholl, 1992.

194   John Lumley (c.1534-1609) was the son-in-law of the Earl of Arundel. He was deeply involved in the Ridolfi plot for the re-establishment of Roman Catholicism. He was confined to the Tower in 1569, and in April 1570 he was confined to Mrs Hampden's house near Staines. (See p. 73.) From October 1571 until April 1573 he was held in the Marshalsea prison. Towards the end of 1590 he conveyed the palace and park of Nonesuch to the Queen, but he remained under suspicion. A letter of Benjamin Beard's, addressed to Lord Keeper Puckering on 11 May 1594, refers to Lumley's harbouring of seminary priests. (PRO, SP12/248/102; State papers, 1867, p. 504.)

music books in Lumley's fine library,[195] or played on Lumley's many keyboard instruments at Nonesuch.[196]

A manuscript of keyboard music, copied by John Baldwin, also dates from 1591. The title *My Ladye Nevells Booke* is embossed on the binding, and must have been added soon after Baldwin finished work, but the Lady Nevell for whom the book was compiled has eluded all attempts positively to identify her.[197]

The sale of Harlington manor

Byrd's grandson, Thomas, was probably born within a few years of his parents' marriage.[198] It was he, with his mother Katherine, who in February 1624/5 brought an action in Chancery arising from the marriage.[199] They alleged, in two lengthy documents, that 'By certayne Articles of Agreement or other Writings' between Katherine's father and father-in-law, Moore and Byrd, Harlington had been settled on her at the time of her marriage. Other interesting details of the marriage contract also emerge. Katherine claimed that Byrd had undertaken 'to geve and allow diett and lodging for the said Christopher Bird and yor Oratrix and for such children as they should afterwards have and for one man and one mayde servant*es* and fforty pound*es* ... in money for their maintenance'. Moore was to pay Byrd £250 for a marriage portion, and was also to lend him a great sum of money, which would be repaid in due course.

Katherine went on to say that Byrd had drawn Christopher into 'divers great Engagem^{tes} ... and thereupon afterwards at the earnest request and sollicitačon of the said William Bird to the said Thomas Moore yor said Oratrix ffather' it was agreed 'that the said Manno^r of Harlington might be solde and that yor said Oratrix should Joyne in sale thereof thereby to conclude herself and her children of any Right in and to the same and to wayst moneyes for the paim^t of the detts of the said

195   Milsom, 1993, especially pp. 173-174.

196   Warren, 1968.

197   See Appendix G. It seems likely that any family papers that might have cast light on the matter were destroyed by fire. (Information supplied by Lord Abergavenny in conversation.) A list of 'Catholick*es* banished', dating from 1594 (PRO, SP12/99/55, f. 8^r) includes the names of Sir John Nevell and Christopher Nevell, but this does no more than demonstrate the religious affiliation of some of the Nevells.

198   He was not baptized in the parish church at Harlington. The sixteenth-century parish register of Stondon Massey has perished. Thomas may, of course, have been baptized elsewhere, perhaps by a Catholic priest.

199   PRO, C3/334/3.

William Bird and for the disengagem[t] of the said Christopher'. Byrd promised to double the value of the estate of Christopher and Katherine, and as part of the deal undertook to obtain from Queen Elizabeth the lease of Stondon Place in Essex, 'and of certayne wood*es* there' for the lives of three of his children. 'And the said Willm̃ Bird did confidently affirme that the said Stondon Place was of farre greater value than the said Manno[r] of Harlington w[ch] was by him solde'.[200] Byrd and Thomas Moore 'did mutually agree by other articles in writing under their hand*es* and seales that … one thowsand pound*es* of the money w[ch] should be raysed upon sale thereof should be deposited in a chest, under severall lockes and keyes to be severallie kept by the said Thomas Moore William Bird and Christopher Bird or be putt in some Indifferent land*es* untill the same might be layd out in the p[r]chase of some land*es* of Inheritaunce'. The sale was made to Ambrose Copinger in 1595.[201] The document recording the sale also mentions a Thomas East, probably the music publisher with whom Byrd was closely associated.

The papers relating to the sale of Harlington manor refer to 'William Byrd et Juliana sposem eius'. They do not specifically say she was alive, but they cast doubt on Fellowes' assumption, because he did not find Julian's name in the Middlesex gaol delivery rolls after 1586, that she died shortly afterwards.[202] Her recusancy was in fact recorded in Middlesex in 1591, and if the sale documents mean that she was alive in 1595, it has to be accepted that she moved from Harlington with her family.[203] Evidence that she was still alive in 1608 is presented below.[204]

The Chapel Royal

It appears that Byrd ceased to play a regular part in the affairs of the

---

200 Katherine made no mention of the opportunity for Byrd to settle in the neighbourhood from which his ancestors had come.

201 PRO, C142/286/176. For Ambrose (later Sir Ambrose) Copinger see Reynolds, 1962, p. 262.

202 Fellowes, 1948, p. 249. The present writer was misled into accepting this in Harley, 1992-94, ii, p. 43.

203 A 'Julian Burd' was buried in the London parish of All Hallows the Less on 12 December 1592, but she (if the name was a woman's) was probably related to 'John Byrde' and 'Constance Byrde' who were buried there in 1581 and 1589. (GL, MS 5160/1.) A 'Wyllyam Byrde' married an unnamed widow at the church of St John the Baptist, Hillingdon, on 22 April 1596, but he is likely to have been the son of a Christopher Byrd, who was baptized there on 1 November 1562. (Transcript of register in GLRO; Phillimore, 1910, p. 7.)

204 See p. 145.

Chapel Royal in the early 1590s. In recording his death thirty-odd years later, the Chapel's Old Cheque Book described him as 'a ffather of Musick': that is to say, the longest serving member of the Chapel, who was excused attendance in person or by deputy though still receiving his pay.[205] In a letter written (probably at Greenwich) on 17 October 1581 Byrd complained that because of his attendance at court he had not 'as yet any spare tyme to Come to London', and when his years of service at last earned him freedom from the requirement to be on duty for a month at a time it must have been very welcome.[206]

There is no definite corroboration that Byrd's withdrawal began while he lived at Harlington, but it is a suspicion reinforced by hints. One of these is the appointment of new Chapel Royal organists. In 1592 John Bull was described as 'organiste in her ... Majesties Chappell', the first reference in the Cheque Book to such a post.[207] Bull was present at the organ when Queen Elizabeth received the Sacrament on Easter Day in 1593, an event which the Clerk of the Cheque recounted in detail.[208] He seems to have owed his position to events that took place around the time that John Blitheman died in 1591. Blitheman, who was a noted organist and is reputed to have been Bull's teacher,[209] is likely to have been one of those who shared with Byrd the responsibilities of playing the organ and directing the singers. It appears from the Old Cheque Book that two other organists' posts were filled about the same time. William Randall, who had entered the Chapel in February 1583/4 from Exeter Cathedral, was mentioned as an organist in 1592, and it was in that year that Thomas Morley joined the Chapel, with several years of experience as Master of the Choristers at Norwich.

There are two more pieces of circumstantial evidence that point to Byrd's retirement about 1591 or 1592. First, he was not among the Gentlemen of the Chapel who, from 1592 onwards, added confirmatory signatures to various entries in the Cheque Book. Too much should not

---

205   Mr David Baldwin has drawn attention to this explanation in Serjeant William Lovegrove's memorandum of 1765. (The Chapel Royal's 'Lovegrove' manuscript, f. 173ʳ.) The title 'Brittanicae Musicae Parenti' (Parent of British Music) applied to Byrd in an epigram by 'G Ga.' prefacing the second book of *Gradualia* (1607) means something less specific. Fellowes (1948, p. 240) suggests that 'G Ga.' may have been George Gascoigne.

206   Letter: PRO, E407/72. Duty: Rimbault, 1872, pp. 71-73.

207   Old Cheque Book, f. 17ʳ; Rimbault, 1872, p. 31. The practice of referring to Bull as 'Dr Bull', and his place at the head of a number of subsidy and other lists of the Gentlemen, also suggest that he became the leading figure among the Chapel musicians.

208   Rimbault, 1872, pp. 150-151.

209   BL, Harleian MS 538; Stow, 1908, ii, p. 357.

be made of this, because there are no entries of a prior date with which comparison can be made. Second, the collection of much of Byrd's earlier music was completed in 1591, when *Liber secundus sacrarum cantionum* was published and *My Ladye Nevells Booke* was compiled. A good deal of his time from then on was occupied by the writing of music for private Catholic performance, and he published no more until the first volume of *Gradualia* appeared in 1605.

There is a possibility that Byrd planned his withdrawal even earlier, when he was putting together his initial independent publication, *Psalmes, sonets, & songs of sadnes and pietie*, which appeared in 1588. This was the time when his house was under surveillance and he was first indicted for failing to attend church at Harlington. It may have been with a view to Byrd's eventual replacement that Bull was recruited from his post as Organist and Master of the Choristers at Hereford in January 1585/6. Some support for this view comes from Father Weston's statement that, when he met Byrd in 1586, the composer had given up his post in the Chapel Royal.[210]

Byrd's withdrawal was manifestly not complete, as Weston supposed, and he still described himself in *Gradualia* as 'Organista Regio, Anglo'. He is reported to have performed as a singer as late as 1607.[211] But in all likelihood Queen Elizabeth and King James were content to retain so distinguished a man, at relatively little cost, for occasional services.

---

210   Weston, 1955, pp. 70-71. Another translation is given by Morris, 1875, p. 145.
211   Nichols, 1828, ii, p. 139.

5

STONDON MASSEY · 1594-1623

Stondon Place was in the parish of Stondon Massey.[1] The exact date of Byrd's removal to his new home cannot be discovered, but his family was still living at Harlington in July 1593.[2] In July 1595 it was reported that William and Christopher Byrd and their wives had not been to the parish church of Stondon during the previous six months.[3] This suggests that the move took place in 1594.

No subsidy rolls for the Ongar hundred, which included Stondon Massey, survive from the first few years of Byrd's residence. The earliest is dated 20 October 1598, and includes his name.[4] A series of certificates of residence starts somewhat later.[5] One of the more informative, drawn up by the commissioners who listed members of the royal household, is dated 8 January 1602/3 and addressed 'To the Highe Collecto[rs] and Pettye Collecto[rs] of the Second payement of the Second Subsedye graunted by the Layitie to the Queenes Ma[tie] ... w[th]in the Hundred of Ounger in the Countie of Essex'. It states that 'These be to certifie that Willm̃ Bird ... is discharged of the said second payement ... by vertue of her highnes lẽs of privie seale ... Wherefore you may forbeare to demaund any thinge of him for the said subsedie'.

1   For the history of Stondon Massey see Reeve, 1906; Powell, 1956, pp. 240-249.
2   Records of the manorial court of Harlington. (GLRO, Acc. 530/11/M10.)
3   ERO, Q/SR 130/23.
4   PRO, E179/111/498. The piece numbers of other extant rolls in series E179 which give names for the Ongar hundred, including Byrd's, are: 111/514 (19 October 1599), 111/517 (16 October 1600), 112/578 (19 September 1610). Invariably Byrd was assessed in goods (£8 or £10) at two or three times as much as his neighbours. Subsidy rolls for the royal household for this period (also series E179) are: 70/107 (22 October 1598), 70/115 (29 April 1602), 70/121 (25 April 1607?), 70/122 (19 April 1608), 70/123a (20 March 1609/10).
5   PRO, series E115, pieces numbered 63/190 (1601-1602), 56/11 (8 January 1602), 25/49 (7 June 1602), 56/11 (8 January 1602/3), 57/160 (25 June 1603), 60/54 (25 January 1603/4), 157/42 (10 May 1604), 39/95 (18 July 1606), 58/79 (30 March 1607), 30/54 (17 January 1607/8), 39/45 (19 April 1608), 71/46 (8 March 1608/9), 71/129 (12 April 1611), 45/26 (8 November 1620), and 60/34 (4 October 1621). Inspection of these certificates has inevitably produced more people of the same name, e.g. William Byrd of Edward VI's household (48/28), William Byrd of Hackney (55/24), and Sir William Byrd of Walthamstow (37/41 and 17/44) who is listed in Foster, 1891-92, p. 127.

King James followed precedent in freeing members of his household from the payment of subsidies. A document of 12 October 1610 conveys the King's decree discharging the Chapel Royal from payment 'in consideracon of the true & faithfull service daily done unto us'.[6] The statement in a number of certificates of residence that Byrd was 'abidinge heare at the Court in the tyme of Taxãcon, and for the moste part of the yeare before' is perhaps not to be taken literally, but as a formula excusing him from any contribution. It appears for the last time in a certificate dated 4 October 1621 and countersigned by the musician John Ward, who held an office in the Exchequer.

Welcome as such relief no doubt was, Byrd ought by this time to have been fairly well off. Whether he truly was so is difficult to determine. As a Gentleman of the Chapel Royal his pay amounted to thirty pounds a year, though no record survives of his having signed for it. The sum remained static despite increases in the cost of living, until it was augmented by ten pounds in 1604.[7] He may still have earned something from teaching. There is no evidence that he enjoyed any inherited money or land,[8] though the fact that the men of his family styled themselves 'gentlemen' − an elastic term − hints at the ownership of property. The leases given to him by the Queen in February 1577/8, which had been for twenty-one years, still had a short time to run, though he was unable to enjoy income from Copford Hall.[9] He held other leases which are known because they led to disputes; it is possible that he held some which did not result in legal wrangles, and of which consequently nothing is known.[10] Income from the rectory of Hainton had perhaps become available in 1582.[11]

On the other hand, the circumstances in which he came to take the lease of Stondon Place suggest that he overreached himself, and Katherine Byrd said he had debts at the time of her marriage to Christopher. Although the sale of Harlington manor appears to have raised a sizeable sum, part of this was committed to Christopher and Katherine and there were expenses in connection with the new home.

6   PRO, E179/276/41B.

7   Rimbault, 1872, pp. 60-62; Woodfill, 1953, pp. 167-168.

8   Byrd's pursuit of a musical career may have owed something to his position as a younger son as well as to his immense gifts.

9   See p. 66.

10   The London Borough of Lambeth's archives include four receipts for land in Lambeth naming a William Byrd: II/65 (dated 1576), II/73 and II/75 (1577), and II/84 (1582). They are strips cut from the bottom of larger documents during the nineteenth century, and give no clue to this Byrd's identity.

11   See pp. 30-32.

Table 6 · Historical background 1593-1623

1594   First of four bad harvests. Hooker, *Ecclesiastical Polity*, i-iv. Shakespeare, *Lucrece*.

1595   Raleigh sets out for El Dorado. Spaniards raid Cornish coast. Ulster rebellion. Robert Southwell executed. Expedition to West Indies (deaths of Hawkins, 1595, and Drake, 1596).

1596   Howard, Essex and Raleigh burn Cádiz. Spenser, *Faerie Queene*, iv-vi.

1597   Essex created Earl Marshall and Master of the Ordnance. Unsuccessful Islands Voyage (Essex and Raleigh). Poor Law codifies many existing provisions. Bacon, *Essays* (enlarged 1612, 1625). James VI, *Demonologie*. Shakespeare, *Romeo and Juliet*; *Richard II*.

1598   London offices of Hanseatic League closed. Death of Burghley. Shakespeare, *Henry IV*, i; *Love's Labour's Lost*. Stow, *Survey of London*. Chapman, *Iliad* in translation.

1599   Essex Lord Lieutenant of Ireland. Army sent to Ireland. Globe Theatre opened. Shakespeare, *Julius Caesar* acted?

1600   Essex deprived of offices. East India Company established. Dekker, *Shoemaker's Holiday*. Jonson, *Everyman out of his Humour*. Shakespeare, *Henry V*.

1601   Rebellion and execution of Essex. Spaniards land in south of Ireland to aid Tyrone. Queen Elizabeth's 'Golden' speech. Further Poor Law legislation. Monopolies denounced by Commons; Queen ends all not vindicated in a court of law. Jonson, *Everyman in his Humour*. Shakespeare, *Twelfth Night* acted?

1602   Plague. Bodleian Library opened. Sir John Beaumont, *Metamorphosis of Tobacco*. Surrender of Spanish in Ireland.

1603   Death of Elizabeth I, accession of James I (James VI of Scotland). King grants toleration to Catholics. Jesuits recalled to France. Francis Bacon knighted. Raleigh sent to the Tower. Tyrone makes peace with English. Plague. James I, *True Law of Free Monarchies*. Shakespeare, *Hamlet*. Montaigne's *Essays* (trans. Florio).

1604   Hampton Court Conference. New canons governing church introduced. Peace with Spain. Shakespeare, *Othello* acted.

1605   Gunpowder plot. James I visits Oxford. Jonson and Jones, *Masque of Blackness*. Jonson, Marston and Chapman imprisoned for remarks about the Scots in *Eastward Ho*. Bacon, *Advancement of Learning*.

1606   First Charter of Virginia for London and Plymouth companies. Jonson, *Volpone* acted. Shakespeare, *Macbeth* acted?

Table 6 *concluded*

1607   Commons block union of England with Scotland. Founding of Jamestown, Virginia.

1608   Salisbury Lord Treasurer. Shakespeare, *King Lear*. New Exchange and central tower for old St Paul's (Inigo Jones).

1609   Jonson, *Epicoene* acted. Shakespeare, *Sonnets*.

1610   Commons' Petition on Religion. Jonson, *The Alchemist* acted? Shakespeare, *The Tempest*, *Cymbeline*, *A Winter's Tale* acted 1610-12.

1611   Authorized Version of Bible. Donne, *Anatomy of the World*; *Ignatius his Conclave*.

1612   Deaths of Salisbury and Prince Henry. Webster, *The White Devil*. Cervantes, *Don Quixote*, i (trans. Shelton; ii trans. 1620).

1613   Bacon made Attorney General. Princess Elizabeth marries Frederick V, Elector Palatine. Beaumont and Fletcher, *Knight of the Burning Pestle*. Shakespeare, *Henry VIII* acted.

1614   The Addled Parliament. Proclamation ordering nobility and gentry in London to depart for their homes in the country (repeated 1615 and 1617). Jonson, *Bartholomew Fair* acted. Raleigh, *History of the World*. Napier invents logarithms.

1615   Cockpit Theatre erected. Chapman, trans. *Odyssey*. Overbury scandal begins. Inigo Jones made Surveyor of the King's Works.

1616   Raleigh released for 1617 Orinoco expedition. James I, *Works*. Jonson, *Works*. Queen's House at Greenwich designed.

1617   Bacon made Lord Keeper.

1618   Raleigh executed. Bacon becomes Baron Verulam and Lord Chancellor. Negotiations for marriage of Prince Charles to Spanish Infanta. English West Africa Company founded and occupies Gambia and Gold Coast.

1619   Dulwich College founded (Alleyn). Whitehall Banqueting House begun. Beaumont and Fletcher, *The Maid's Tragedy*.

1620   Pilgrim Fathers sail on *Mayflower*. Inigo Jones investigates Stonehenge. Bacon, *Novum Organum*. Boccaccio, *Decameron* (trans. Jaggard).

1621   Bacon made Viscount St Albans; condemned for accepting bribes. Burton, *Anatomy of Melancholy*. Van Dyck visits England.

1622   Weekly news-pamphlets 'The Corantos' begin. Peacham, *The Compleat Gentleman*.

1623   Prince Charles' trip to Madrid; arrangements for marriage fail. 'First Folio' of Shakespeare. Webster, *Duchess of Malfi*.

The money earned from the sales of Byrd's publications is likely to have been negligible, but their dedication to noble patrons must have had direct as well as indirect value. The annuity Byrd received from Lord Paget presumably ceased when Paget fled overseas, but he is known to have received small gifts from Lord Petre, even if those which are recorded amounted to very little.

Most important, Byrd had a farm which probably enabled his family to be largely self-supporting, and may have made a profit besides. His 'timber trees' at Stondon Massey are mentioned several times, and were a further resource. Living to some extent in retirement he is likely to have spent little on himself, but whatever his needs in that respect he still required a substantial income to meet the mounting cost of his legal expenses.[12] It may be significant that in his will he left little besides the farm and an annuity.

Stondon Place (i)

Stondon Place was a property of some 200 acres, which comprised a house, a farm and other pieces of land. A tiny sketch representing the house is included in a map of about 1700 in the Essex Record Office.[13] This shows a building that may have had an H or Π plan and gabled end sections. It is located just east of the junction of the road leading to Ongar and the road from Kelvedon to Blakemore (modern Kelvedon Hatch and Blackmore).[14]

The history of Stondon Place in the years prior to its acquisition by Byrd is recounted in documents relating to an action he brought against Dyonyce (or Denis) Lolly in 1595.[15] The farm had belonged to William Shelley, in the right of his wife, and in 1582 Shelley let it to the brothers Lawrence and William Hollingworth[16] for twenty-one years. Shelley, an

12   It is uncertain whether the family paid the fines to which they were repeatedly liable for recusancy, and whether these should be added to Byrd's expenses.

13   ERO, D/DFa P1. (See pl. 7.) The house was rebuilt in the eighteenth century, and rebuilt again after a fire in 1877, so that nothing remains of the one occupied by Byrd. The large house which the map shows nearby is Myles's, owned jointly by Richard and Anthony Luther. (Powell, 1956, p. 67.)

14   Kelvedon Hatch is distinct from the Kelvedon lying between Witham and Colchester.

15   PRO, C2/Eliz I B6/56: two statements by Byrd and two by Lolly. When giving evidence in the dispute between Byrd and Mrs Shelley in 1598, Lolly was described as a husbandman of Childerditch, aged about fifty. (PRO, E134/41 & 42 Elizabeth I/Mich 34.) Reeve gathered and indexed information about him in ERO, T/P 188/1.

16   William Hollingworth was reported to the Archdeaconry Court in 1602 for

active Roman Catholic, became involved in a plot to place Mary Queen of Scots on the English throne. Although he avoided execution, to which he was sentenced, his estates were declared forfeit and the Crown became the Hollingworths' landlord.[17]

In March 1589 the brothers divided the property. Lawrence leased most of his moiety to Lolly, reserving for himself only a part known as Malperdus.[18] Lawrence willed his moiety to his nephew John Hollingworth,[19] who sold it back to William. William Hollingworth thus became the sole tenant under the Crown, and mortgaged his lease to William Chambers. In 1593 the two of them assigned their interest to Byrd for three hundred pounds.

Byrd sought to secure the position of his family by obtaining a lease from the Crown for the lives successively of his children Christopher, Elizabeth and Rachel. Burghley signified approval in 1595.[20] It is possible that Thomas and Mary Byrd were not included because, at the time Byrd sought the lease, they had not reached the age of twenty-one.

Lolly still occupied part of the house, but paid rent to Byrd only until Lady Day (25 March) 1595. Byrd then sued him in the Court of Chancery, stating that Lolly was 'divers tymes requested ... in freindly manner to shewe by what title he holdeth the said moyty of the said ffarme', and claiming that he 'hath and doth not onely refuse so to do But also doth still occupy and enjoy the same wthout aunswering the

---

standing excommunicate. (ERO, D/AEA 22, ff. 192^v, 194^v, 206^r, 220^v, 243^r, and D/AEA 23, f. 37^v.)

17   PRO, KB8/47 is the special oyer and terminer roll and file relating to Shelley's trial. He pleaded guilty on 12 February 1585/6, and was sentenced to be executed at Tyburn. See also the *Fourth report of the Deputy Keeper of the Public Records*, 1843, pp. 274-275.

18   'Malperdus' is so written in Byrd's will. There were several versions of the name, including 'Mellow Purgess' and 'Malpergis'. Reaney (1935, p. 81) says it is probably a manorial name from a family called Maupertuis. Malperdus was described in 1604 as 'certayne Closes of pasture and copised wood ground called Malapardus parcell of ye farme of Stondon Place'. (PRO, E134/2 James I/Trinity 5.) Mrs Dawtrey later had some claim upon Malperdus. (Byrd's will; see p. 392.)

19   Curate to the rector of Stondon. (Reeve, 1906, p. 32.)

20   PRO, E310/13/42, m. 5. The lease is also mentioned in C2/Eliz I B6/56. It was enrolled in October 1595. (PRO, E315/228, f. 116^v, and E371/568, rot. 27.) In view of later problems over the ownership of the property, there may be some significance to the words of the scribe who started the document eventually seen by Burghley: 'I cannot certefie the estate of the premisses for want of sight of the lease. More I know not towching dimysing the same in present possession'.

rente'.[21]

Lolly's response was that his agreement with Lawrence Hollingworth gave him the right to Hollingworth's moiety, 'Except one peece of ground called Malapdis conteyninge tenne or twelve Acres more or less'. He was entitled not only to the hall, bedchambers and 'other howses of office', but to 'the whole orchard A larder howse there halfe the gardyn halfe the hopyard his Conyes[22] the Dovehowse and halfe the wood yeard'. He should further have been allowed 'ffree egresse and regresse into the kitchen for bakinge brewinge and Rostinge of meat at his pleasure and the like libertie to goe to the ponde for water as often as need should Require.' Whatever the justice of Lolly's case, the Byrd family could not have found this a happy arrangement.

Lolly's lease was found to be invalid at law, but he received help in the person of Anthony Luther, who had once attempted to buy Battyshall manor. Luther's mediation secured Byrd's agreement to Lolly's continued residence until the supposed lease expired at Michaelmas 1597.[23]

The general disrepair of the premises may have contributed to the Byrds' anxiety to be rid of Lolly. Interrogatories prepared for administration on Byrd's behalf to William Hollingworth during the subsequent quarrel with Jane Shelley include the question: 'whether was not divers parts of the mantion howse, and barnes belonging to the said farme howse in question, so ruynous and decayed when you sould the same to the said p^{lt}, as that there was divers propps of tymber set under the same to hold them up, from falling, yea, or no?'. Hollingworth was asked whether Byrd 'well repaired the most pte of the said howse and Barnes synce his comyng, yea or no? and also brought water to the brewhowse, mylkehowse and Buttery in Pipes of Leade, wch was not there at his comynge, yea, or no?'. Richard Foster, a bricklayer from Ingatestone, and James Glascock, a carpenter from Stondon, were brought in to back up Byrd's implied assertion. From interrogatories to be administered to Mrs Shelley it seems as if Byrd not only set about repairing the buildings, but restoring the farmland and timber plantation as well. Others working for him were the labourers George Pond and

21   After the word 'manner' there is the partly illegible insertion 'both to ... his ... &'.

22   The farm evidently had a rabbit warren.

23   Luther's evidence in Byrd's dispute with Mrs Shelley. (E134/41 & 42 Elizabeth I/ Mich 34.) Lolly was a churchwarden of Stondon, for the second time, in 1596. (Reeve, 1906, p. 33.) This cannot have encouraged a warm relationship with the Byrd family, since he had a duty to report them as recusants.

Thomas Cade of Stondon, both of whom had been set to hedging and ditching.[24]

'Ellen' Byrd

The notion that Julian Byrd died at Harlington was encouraged by references to 'Ellen' or 'Helena' as Byrd's wife in records of their recusancy in Essex.[25] But if the reference to Julian in the document concerning the sale of Harlington genuinely means that she was alive in 1595, and does not refer to her past interest in the property, there is no period in which she might have died and Byrd remarried. 'Willimū Bird et ux eius' are mentioned regularly as recusants from 1595 to 1606. The wish expressed in Byrd's will, 'to be buried neare unto the place where my wife lyest buryed', suggests only one marriage, and a genealogy drawn up in 1634 makes no mention of a second.

The simplest explanation is either that the hard-pressed clerks of the courts were confused, or that John Nobbs, the parson of Stondon, and his churchwardens did not know the name of their difficult parishioner. The occurrence of the error in a certificate produced at greater leisure for the Bishop of London's signature suggests the latter reason.[26] Nobbs must have been familiar with most of the local inhabitants, since before he became rector he had spent a period as curate to William Fering, the former rector.[27] If, however, he was kept at a distance by the newcomers — as his complaints about their utterly refusing 'conference'[28] indicate — he may have known her only as 'Mistress Byrd'.

There is reason to think that Julian was confused with her son's servant Ellen Barcroft. Other confusions exist in the records, such as that made between Christopher and Thomas Byrd in 1597, and between

24   PRO, E134/41 & 42 Elizabeth I/Mich 34.

25   'The common English form of the name has always been *Ellen*, but *Helen* and *Helena* came in at the Renaissance'. (Withycombe, 1977, p. 148.)

26   ERO, Q/SR 171/59-64, f. 59ᵛ.

27   Reeve, 1906, p. 68. It seems that Nobbs was displaced from Stanford Rivers, where Richard Vaughan was the rector for a short time in 1594-95, prior to the appointment of Richard Mulcaster. Two pages in the parish register of Stanford Rivers for 1591-92 are inscribed 'Johannes Nobbs minister'. (ERO, D/P140/1/1, ff. 25ʳ and 86ʳ.) This is not mentioned by Newcourt (1710, pp. 544-555), who does however refer to Nobbs as rector of Stondon Massey. Reeve says that Nobbs became rector in 1596, the year in which his predecessor died, but 1595 is given in the visitations of 1612 and 1615. (GL, MS 9537/11, ff. 8ʳ and 116ᵛ.) The earlier date coincides with the first report of the Byrds' recusancy at Stondon Massey.

28   A discussion of spiritual matters, designed to correct their mistaken beliefs.

Rachel and Katherine Byrd in 1605.[29] The error over Julian seems first to have occurred in March 1599/1600.[30] This was some months after an entry in the Act books of the Archdeaconry Court had identified 'Elena' as Christopher Byrd's servant, who failed to go to church or receive Communion. The entry follows immediately after entries for William and Christopher Byrd and their wives. Later entries refer to a servant of Christopher Byrd named 'Helen' or 'Helena'. Eventually she is named as 'Helena Barcroft' or 'Barcrosse'.[31] The mistake would easily have occurred if Julian had become ill or disabled, or never attended the court for some other reason. The name of Byrd's wife is given correctly as 'Julian' in a document, dated 1608, concerning the manor of Longney in Gloucestershire.[32]

Patrons

Byrd published only three collections of music after he moved to Stondon. Two were printed by Thomas East, but the third was printed, after East's death, by his son-in-law Thomas Snodham, the assignee of W. Barley.

The first volume of *Gradualia* (1605) was dedicated to Henry Howard, Earl of Northampton. Howard was a cousin of Edward de Vere, the Earl of Oxford, whom Byrd had long known. The Queen assumed responsibility for his education, and he became recognized as the most learned nobleman of his time. He was musical, too, and a letter survives in which he sought a teacher, being 'of late very well dysposed to bestowe some ydell tyme upon the lute'.[33] Byrd's dedication says that Howard had often listened to his music with pleasure. Howard was sympathetic to Catholicism when he was young, and in 1582 admitted to having taken part in Catholic worship. His will suggests that he had in fact become a Catholic. He was suspected of conspiracy on behalf of Mary Queen of Scots, and although he cleared himself he was under a cloud. On the rise of Essex he attached himself to the new favourite. He managed to stay on good terms with Cecil, through whose influence he was readmitted to court in 1600, and after the accession of King James his star rose rapidly. He gained a commanding position at court, becoming Earl of Northampton in March 1603/4, a member of the Privy

29   ERO, Q/SR 137/45 and D/AEA 23, f. 137^r.

30   PRO, ASSI 35/42/1, mm. 45 and 60; Cockburn, 1978, p. 495.

31   ERO, D/AEA 19, ff. 221^v, 247^r, 267^v, 287^{r-v}, 312^r, 335^{r-v} and 353^v-154^r. Ellen may have replaced a servant named Martha. (ERO, D/AEA 17, f. 181^r.)

32   See p. 145.

33   BL, Lansdowne MS 109, no. 51., f. 116^r.

Council in May 1603, and a Knight of the Garter in February 1604/5. Byrd could hardly have selected his dedicatee with more care, but he was repaying a debt as well as ensuring the future. He referred to Howard's part in securing pay increases for the royal musicians, and wrote of him as a kind patron in the Byrd family's troubled affairs.[34]

Most of the contents of *Gradualia* must have been written after Byrd left Harlington. In dedicating the second book to Lord Petre in 1607 he said: 'It is from your house (truly most friendly to me and mine) that these musical lucubrations have proceeded, like fruits sprung from a fertile soil'.[35] The dedication to Petre may have been in part an acknowledgement of support given by his son, since it was possibly in connection with the financing of *Gradualia* − hardly likely to have been a sound business proposition − that William Petre lent Byrd a sum of money, perhaps for a term of twelve months. An entry in his accounts for February 1607/8 records that he gave his wife eight pounds 'the xv[th] day w[ch] was parcell of the money I lente M[r] Birde'. The next entry concerns forty shillings 'Given to M[r]. Birde at the same time'.[36]

The Petre family's friendship with Byrd was extended to his eldest son, for a payment of ten shillings was made in August 1599 'to Chrōr Birde in satisfac*tion*'.[37] On 23 December 1609 they dined at Thorndon Hall: 'there came this night to sup m[r] morgin & his ladye m[r] Birde & his sonn. & there were more than ordinary in the hall. xii parsons'.[38] It is easy to believe that it was on some such occasion that Byrd met one of Petre's neighbours to whom he made a gift of the second book of *Gradualia*. The British Library has an incomplete copy with the signature 'Ra: Bosville' on the title-page of the bassus part, and the inscription

34   '... in afflictis familiae meae rebus benignissimum Patronum'.

35   'Preaterea qùod è domo tua (mei meorum*que* meherculè amicissima) hae Musicae Lucubrationes ut ex faecundo solo enatae frùges, ut plurimum prodiêre, fructus*que* ex illa coeli tĕperie, amoeniores et uberiores fecêre'. 'Lucubrationes' could mean that they resulted (actually or figuratively) from labours pursued into the night or from nocturnal meditations, or simply that that they were elaborate works.

36   ERO, T/A/174, a microfilm of a transcript of Folger Library MS 1772.1, the younger William Petre's account book 1597-1610. Unfortunately the transcript was not made directly from the original. For an account of the manuscript see Dawson, 1949-50.

37   ERO, T/A/174, f. 34[v]. Petre's debt to Christopher Byrd may have resulted from a game of some sort. His accounts record frequent losses at cards, at tennis and at bowls. Card-playing seems to have been a popular pastime in the Petre family. The older Sir William had long before met a debt incurred at cards (ERO, D/DP A6, September 1555) and paid 'for mending the playing tables' (ERO, D/DP A8, February 1558/9).

38   ERO, D/DP A26. The 'sonn' is unlikely to have been Thomas, who did not live permanently at Stondon Massey.

'Mr. Wylliam Byrd his last Sett of Songs geven me by him Feb. 1607' on the cover. A Radolphus (Ralph) 'Bossevile' is mentioned in a document of 1573 concerning property at Langford in Essex.[39]

John Byrd and Robert Chantflower

In 1595 Hester Cole had a suit in the Court of Chancery, in which she made a claim against William and Rowland Whittington for six years' income from the parsonage of Notgrove in Gloucestershire.[40] Hester's maiden name had been Byrd. Her parentage is uncertain.[41] She was described as a niece (young kinswoman) of William Byrd's brother John, and her brothers called William and John 'unkle'. Her father must have died and her mother remarried, since her brother Thomas Byrd referred to 'Anne Craddocke mother to the said hester wth zachary her husband'. Thomas Byrd was a clerk of Brightwell in Berkshire, who was twenty-eight years old; Hester's other brothers were Symond Byrd, a Haberdasher of London, who was twenty-four, and John Byrd of Kilburne, gentleman, aged twenty-two.[42] As Hester was a widow, and so unable to pursue the matter in law, the older John Byrd did so for her.[43]

In May 1596 Robert Chantflower (or Chandler), a Salter with a shop in Budge Row in London, became Hester's suitor. He must have been acquainted with the Byrds for some time, because in 1598 Hester's brother Symond said he had known him for six or seven years. It was her brother Thomas who first proposed the match to Chantflower during Easter week 1596, 'beinge at the signe of the Cardinalls hat in

39   ERO, D/DC 23/414.

40   Its progress is recorded in the Chancery books of orders and decrees, PRO series C33, volumes numbered 87 (f. 610[v]), 88 (ff. 186[r], 675[r], 779[v]), 89 (f. 458[v]), 90 (ff. 443[r], 475[v]), 92 (f. 708[v]), 93 (f. 323) and 94 (f. 317[v]). Edward Savaree, a clerk, is sometimes named as one of the defendants.

41   She and her brothers may have been connected with the Byrds of Boxley.

42   'Thomas Birde Clarke parson of the parrishe church of Brightwell' and John Byrd, probably his brother, were the subject of a complaint submitted to the Court of Star Chamber by John Ferne of Brightwell. (PRO, STAC5/F31/24, dated 8 November 1601 on the back; duplicated by STAC5/F27/22.) It was said that Thomas had obtained the parsonage by simony, and let the house and associated property to Ferne. (Simony was prohibited in 1571 by 31 Elizabeth, c. 6.) It was alleged that after Ferne had gathered into the barn the tithes to which he regarded himself as entitled, Thomas with his wife Joan, John Byrd, John Bradford (another clerk) and others had riotously attacked the house and its occupants. See p. 92-93 on similar allegations of attack.

43   'John Byrd made othe for the servinge of a subpoena on the defendant'. (PRO, C33/88, f. 675[r], dated 28 November 1594.)

Readinge', and her brother John supported the idea. It was said that as part of the marriage agreement Chantflower, who appears to have been assisted in the negotiations by Richard Coyse (or Coyshe or Coish),[44] demanded the benefit of the suit against Whittington, and the older John Byrd promised him a hundred pounds regardless of the outcome.[45]

Hester already had a son, William Cole, by her first marriage. She apparently died during 1597, leaving another son, Robert Chantflower. Both children were legatees under John Byrd's will. The court's decree was given on 26 January 1596/7, but on the following 7 November reference was made to 'Hester Cole late pl and Nicholas Cole[46] and Robert Chandflower late husband of the said hester wch nicholas and Robt are Administrators duringe the minority of w^m Cole and Robt Chandflower Infant*es* and Administrators of the said hester pl*aintiff*. It was added that 'Robt Chandflower thelder did this day acknowledge that he hathe Receaved l^li of the said willm̃ whittington to the use of the said Infants wch by a decree of this court was to be pd to the said hester'.[47]

The terms of Hester's marriage to Chantflower led to a writ of *scire facias* being issued on John Byrd's behalf.[48] A hearing took place before the Recorder and a jury in the Lord Mayor's Court at Guildhall on 14 February 1597/8. No documents concerning this survive in the Corporation of London's Record Office. John Byrd then made a complaint against Chantflower in the Court of Star Chamber.[49] One of his concerns was that during the Guildhall hearing Coyse 'most furiouslye in colo^r accused the compl^t of his lendinge money to usury whereof he made no proof'. As with other Star Chamber cases, the

44   It may coincidence that someone named Coyse lived in a house bequeathed to Joane Tallis by her first husband, Thomas Bury. (Bury's will, Centre for Kentish Studies, DRb/Pwr 11 f. 254^r.)

45   All this emerges from the Star Chamber papers listed below.

46   Hester's brother-in-law? There is perhaps a variant of the name 'Cole' in a deposition included in PRO, STAC5/B38/20, where 'Miles Sole of London gent aged 48: yeares' appears to claim a relationship with Hester. The deposition is signed 'My: Sole'. The words 'his kinswoeman' (i.e. John Byrd's) are deleted and 'mye kinswoeman' substituted.

47   The entry of 26 January simply refers to the book's 'fellow'. The entry for 7 November appears twice: in C33/93, f. 323 and C33/94, f. 317^v (quoted). Both entries are signed by Chantflower.

48   A writ requiring matter to be brought to the attention of someone who might then appear to defend his rights.

49   PRO, STAC5/B47/18, dated May 1598 on the back. Other documents in the STAC5 series are B27/37, B38/20 and B71/7. The depositions yield a collection of family signatures.

destruction of the court's books of orders and decrees means that there is no way of discovering its decision.

There are nevertheless several points of interest in the interrogatories and depositions which form part of the documentation. The most important from the point of view of this book is that William Byrd submitted a deposition, which he apparently set down in his own hand on 2 October 1598. It was in this that he gave his age as fifty-eight.[50] It is evident that he knew all about the negotiations for Hester's marriage to Chantflower and subsequent events. Hester's brother Symond said that the matter had been discussed when he and his uncle William 'weare walkinge betwixt Newgate & S^t martyns'.

Of interest too is the variety of people the older John Byrd introduced to give evidence. They included John Kinge, a woollen-draper, and Allen Cotton, a draper, both of Candlewick (now Cannon) Street; Andrew Jones, a goldsmith of Gutter Lane; and Thomas Hussie, a clothworker, and Rowland Hayward, a haberdasher, both of Abchurch Lane.[51]

The Fleet prison

In 1597 Byrd's brother-in-law Philip Smyth was in the Fleet prison.[52] His offence is unknown, but it is conceivable that he was jailed because of his involvement in John Byrd's financial dealings. The prisoners claimed that the warden, George Reynell, was extorting money from them by an improper use of the rules. There was even a suggestion that these had been forged. Smyth and Robert Fisher, a fellow-prisoner, submitted a bill of complaint to the Queen, and Robert Broughe − the brother-in-law of Smyth and Byrd − exhibited an information in the Court of Exchequer.[53]

A large part of Smyth's complaint has been eaten by rats, but what is left affords a fascinating glimpse of the conditions under which the prisoners lived.[54] Orders for the conduct of the Fleet, drawn up by the commissioners, were displayed in the hall of the prison. Smyth alleged that 'in trewthe the orders wrytten in the sayed paper booke and mape or

50   PRO, STAC5/B27/37.

51   The inclusion of a woollen-draper suggests that the trade designations do not necessarily indicate membership of companies.

52   He may have entered the prison some two years previously.

53   'Informations by private persons were encouraged by legislation, from the mid-fifteenth century onwards, as a means of suppressing economic offences, the informer being allowed a share of the penalty'. (Baker, 1990, p. 578.)

54   PRO, STAC5/S21/23.

tabell weare not subscribed by the handes of the sayed commissyoners'. In this he seems to have been wrong, because Lord Burghley gave the opinion, relayed by Anthony Dewe, that the commissioners' signatures were genuine.[55] Smyth went on to say that

George Reynell gent that maryed the sayed Elizabeth the wydoe of the sayed Edward Tyrrell[56] beynge now warden ther in the Righte of his sayed wyffe and desyrous to take the benyfit of the sayed orders and to exacte the ffees and taxes of the prisoners accordinge to the Rate contayned in the sayed booke and tabell, thoughe he did perfectly knowe that the exemplifycation of the sayed orders contayned in the sayed booke & tabell was but a practise to wynne credytt thereunto ... by cowler thereof doe greatly extorte from the prisoners ther to the impovreshinge of the better sorte and to the lamentabell op'ssinge of the poorer sorte ...

Smyth's complaint names individual prisoners and the extortions he believed them to have suffered.

And of your sayed Subject Phillip Smythe the sayed Wardē took vi[s] by the weeke during the space of fower weekes for prisone Roome to set his owne bed in and for that the sayed Smythe Refused to pay xs a weeke for the same prisone Roome the sayed Warden George Reynell Removed him into the comon gayle cawled the Wardes where he hathe lyen ever sythens mydsomer laste and ther he maketh him the sayd Smythe to paye eight pence a nyght for the standinge of his owne bed ...

Smyth, Broughe, William and John Byrd, and their young kinsman William Campe ('of London yeoman aged xx[tie] yeres'), were among those examined on the basis of interrogatories signed by Sir Edward Coke, the Attorney General.[57] Coke's questions were directed to discovering whether witnesses had ever seen a copy of the orders and constitutions for the government of the prison, which had been made under the Great Seal. Had they at any time said that the warden's copy

55   PRO, STAC5/A8/39.

56   A former warden.

57   The documentation is extensive. Items in the PRO's STAC5 series are numbered A8/39, A10/13, A14/22, A14/23, A43/35, and S21/23. There are a number of entries relating to the case in the registers of writs issuing from the Star Chamber, e.g. after Hillary term 41 Elizabeth I and after Michaelmas term 42 Elizabeth I. (PRO, 30/38/9 and 30/38/10.) Only a cursory examination has been made of these books. While they list other disputes involving people named Byrd, such persons cannot be identified unless additional records survive.

had been forged or obtained by indirect or unlawful means?[58] Had they encouraged Broughe 'to exhibit in her ma^*tes* Courte of Exchequer an Information against George Reynell nowe warden of the ffleete[59] for supposed extortion by him comitted in his said office', and had they guided Broughe in drawing up his information, or had they retained an attorney, clerk or counsel for the purpose? Was Broughe promised any money for presenting the information? Did they or anyone else stand to benefit if any money was recovered?

William Byrd was questioned on 21 February 1597/8, John Byrd on 23 February. Much of the evidence, taken down in longhand by a clerk working at speed, approaches illegibilty. Among the others whose evidence was taken were Fisher, the prisoners John Mynors and William Frost, and Reynell and his wife.

In answering most of the questions William Byrd took the line followed by several other witnesses. He said that 'he did never to his Remembrance see the Exemplificacon of the orders & constitutions' which was now shown to him. He did not remember saying that it was forged. He had heard people speak about it, but he could not recall who they were or what they said. He could not remember saying that there was no original copy on record. He did not stand to benefit. When he was asked if he had said anything against the orders, he said he had not; 'but this def*endan*t hath spoken against the disorders & hard dealinge of the now warden of the ffleet against Phillip Smythe this def*tes* brother in law', and 'hath spoken so muche unto the now warden himself before my L. Cheife Baron m^r Baron Ewens & divers others in Serjeant*es* Inne hall in ffleetstreete'.[60] His answer to the question about whether he had encouraged Broughe or employed a lawyer to help him was circumspect: 'concerninge who did it or p̃cured the same to be done this deft under reformacon [subject to correction] taketh it he is not bounde to aunswere for that the Informacõn is ex*hibi*ted into the Excheq^r on her ma^*tes* behalf

---

58   John Mynors had heard that the orders 'were obteyned, & gotten to be exemplified, by sinister & indirecte practices & meanes', and had apparently said as much in a petition to the Lord Treasurer. (PRO, STAC5/A14/23.) This may have been a different petition from Smyth's. Mynors, of Clerkenwell, is named in a gaol delivery roll of 29 Elizabeth with William and Julian Byrd and John Reason. (Jeaffreson, 1886, p. 167, where his name is transcribed as 'Pynors' or 'Rynors'.)

59   Reynell, who came from Ashton in Essex, is described in Broughe's evidence as the 'late warden'. This appears to be an error.

60   PRO, STAC5/A14/23. Matthew Ewens was raised to the bench of Exchequer in 1594; he died in 1598. 'Sargeants Inne, so called, for that divers Judges and Sargeants at the law, keepe a Commons, and are lodged there in Terme time'. (Stow, 1908, ii, p. 47.)

and as this deft beleveth verie orderlye according to the course of her maties Lawes'.

The defendants signed the record of their evidence, William Byrd using his customary formula, 'By me Wyllm̃ Byrde'.[61] On 29 January 1598 he added a paragraph in his own hand, and signed it, affirming that neither he nor any other stood to benefit if Broughe should 'recover' by the information he had submitted.

The record of Robert Broughe's evidence describes him as a Fletcher (member of the Fletcher's Company), aged about sixty-eight, living in the parish of St Martin Ludgate.[62] It was added that he 'saieth that he is a maker of organs, virginalls & other Instrumentes of Musicke & by that meanes doth gett his livinge'. He claimed to have exhibited his information against Reynell in his own name, though Smyth supplied him with notes for it. William Campe said that Broughe had met all the lawyers' fees that had been involved.

Broughe's information was considered by the Privy Council. On 18 April 1598 they ordered him to report to them daily, and on 24 April they referred the matter for investigation to Francis Bacon, the Solicitor-General, and Brian Anesley (or Andslow), a former warden of the Fleet.[63] On the basis of the report submitted by Bacon and Anesley the Privy Council concluded that there was no case against Reynell. They commanded Broughe to appear before them, and ordered him to 'surcease and no further to prosecute the said information, whereunto he yeilded'. On 25 June 1598 he was committed to the Marshalsea prison until he should make a general release to Reynell of all suits and actions, and until he had paid Reynell 'all such charges as he had bin at by the said Brough his wrongful vexation'.

Broughe may have died about 1603,[64] when his name was last recorded in the Fletchers' rolls.

---

61   William Byrd's signature is much the most assured of those in the documents, apart from Coke's. William's brother signed himself 'John byrd', and Smyth signed himself 'Phillipp Smyth'. Broughe signed 'Robert Brough' in a hand that suggests a man getting on in years.

62   PRO, STAC5/A43/35. In the Privy Council records Broughe is described as 'of the Old Bailey'.

63   PRO, PC2/23, pp. 173, 233, 237, 248-9, 304; Privy Council, 1904, pp. 309, 410, 415, 432, 545.

64   June 1603 to May 1604 was a time of severe plague.

St Peter's Ampney

A complaint made by Byrd to the Queen about forcible entry into a house at St Peter's Ampney (also known as Eastington) in Gloucestershire reveals that he had a water mill, houses and grounds there.[65] It appears to be one of the fictitious cases of forcible entry contrived to allow the Court of Star Chamber to try a title. This is borne out by a set of interrogatories that concentrates on the history of the mill's ownership.

According to Byrd he had let the property to John Pitman on 1 September 1598.[66] He alleged that on 2 January 1599, at the instigation of John Partridge, a group of sixteen men entered the house while Pitman was absent, and dragged out his wife, children and servants. They assaulted and beat Thomas Bishop, 'and in very cruell manner pulled hym by the Leggs out of the same house with suche violence as they pulled his knees out of the joynt*es*, and putt hym in great danger of his lief he being a lame man having long sithence lost one of his hands in her Ma*tes* service'.[67] Among the things the invaders took away was the lease.

It was claimed that John Partridge had letters written by his uncle, William Partridge, 'a man learned in the lawes', purporting to show that the latter had bought the title from Robert Cugley, one of the invaders. There was a suggestion that when Cugley broke in he was armed with an order from the Council of the Marches which he pretended gave him authority to take possession of the mill, but in fact the order showed that a lease of the mill made to Cugley by Archad Knight was pawned to Pitman for five pounds.[68] It was further suggested that Byrd had offered Cugley as much for the lease as it had cost him, 'albeit that the same lease was void in lawe'.

65   Eastington is five miles west of Stroud. Byrd addressed the Queen because the Court of Star Chamber derived from the Privy Council.

66   Byrd's complaint is among the documents in PRO, STAC5/B85/14. Other STAC5 documents concerning the case are numbered B37/11, B75/20, B96/3, B97/31, B99/29, B103/22, and B113/19.

67   Bishop, who was about forty, had been pressed into military service, and was wounded in the wars in the Low Countries.

68   The Council of the Principality and Marches of Wales exercised jurisdiction in part of England. In 1604 it was held that Gloucestershire and some other counties were outside its bounds. Byrd's friend the fourth Earl of Worcester was a member of the Council from 1590.

The case continued into the year 1600, but the loss of the orders and decrees of the Star Chamber makes it impossible to know the outcome.

The Chapel Royal

It is hard to say how far Byrd remained involved in the duties of the Chapel Royal in King James's reign. Although he continued to be certified as resident at court for tax purposes, there is no more than a single reference to his participation as a performer. He is said to have been among the men who sang when the King was entertained at Merchant Taylors' Hall on 16 July 1607.[69] John Bull played on 'a very rich pair of organs ... all the dinner-time'. Bull seems to have been the leading figure among the Chapel musicians after Byrd's semi-retirement, and this is borne out by his repeated appearance at the head of subsidy and other lists of the Gentlemen.

Byrd's position as a Gentleman of the Chapel Royal entitled him to mourning livery for the funeral of Queen Elizabeth in 1603.[70] There is nothing to show whether he attended the ceremony, though it would be difficult to imagine him staying away. A tantalizing glimpse of the men and boys of the Chapel is given by a water-colour of them as they appeared in the funeral procession. The men are all bearded in the fashion of the day, and over their cassocks and surplices they are wearing gold embroidered copes of diverse colours. Indeed, they are among the most colourful figures in the procession. But the singers are represented by only four men and four tousled boys carrying music, and it is unlikely that the artist made any attempt to portray individual choristers.[71]

There is no specific mention of Byrd's attendance in the same year at the coronation of King James and Queen Anne in Westminster Abbey, but it is again hard to believe that he was not there. The order of service refers to the singing of hymns, anthems and the offertory, in spite of some curtailment of the service on account of the plague.[72]

69   Nichols, 1828, ii, p. 139.

70   PRO, LC2/4; Ashbee, 1986-96, iv, p. 3.

71   BL, MS Additional 35324, f. 31ᵛ; frequently reproduced, e.g. in Woodfill, 1953, between pp. 48 and 49. Cloth for mourning liveries was allocated to all the musicians taking part, including those of Westminster Abbey. (Ashbee, 1986-96, iv, pp. 1-4.) The boys in the funeral procession are dressed in black, but it is evident from Lavina Teerlinc's miniature of the Royal Maundy service in 1565 that their normal dress was a red cassock and white surplice. (Baldwin, 1990, p. 322.)

72   The order of service is detailed in PRO, SP14/2/77. Although it mentions 'yᵉ: Quere' it does not specify the participation of the Chapel Royal, or say whether the

In addition to their normal duties, the musicians participated in a number of ceremonies described in the Old Cheque Book. One was the marriage in 1604 of Susanna Vere, the Earl of Oxford's daughter, whom Byrd is likely to have known personally.[73]

Byrd received another mourning livery for the funeral of Queen Anne in 1619, though by now his age must have prevented him from taking a very active role in the ceremony.[74]

Recusancy

With the accession of James I Byrd made an attempt to regain a measure of protection from the penalties imposed on Catholic recusants. Among the Cecil papers is a document addressed 'To the moste honorable Lorde, the earle of Salisburie, cheefe secretarie to his Matie.[75] It seems to be a minute from a civil servant covering the submission of a request, possibly in Byrd's hand, which has not survived.

> The humble petition of William Byrd one of the gent: of his Maties: Chapple

> That beinge to crave the Counsailes letter to Mr Atturney Generall to like effect and favor for his recusancye as the late gratious .Q. and her Counsaile gave him, he most humblie beseeches yor Honors good favor therin.

This minute is undated, but the request was obviously made between 4 May 1605, when Robert Cecil became the Earl of Salisbury, and his death in 1612. At a guess Byrd sought help early in this period, when after a brief respite the levying of fines from lay recusants was vigorously resumed. A new code of canon law had been passed by the Convocation of Canterbury on 25 June 1604, and confirmed by Letters Patent on 6 September. Among its many provisions, the code imposed on every parson, vicar or curate the duties of informing himself about, and reporting on, the numbers of popish recusants above the age of thirteen in his parish, and whether they attended church and received communion. The following year saw revised measures against Catholics embodied in *An Acte for the better discovering and repressing of Popish*

Westminster Abbey choristers were present.

73   Rimbault, 1872, p. 160.

74   PRO, LC2/5; Ashbee, 1986-96, iv, p. 50. The organists at this time were Orlando Gibbons and Edmund Hooper.

75   Hatfield House, Cecil papers, Petitions 52; Historical Manuscripts Commission, 1976, p. 219. Robert Cecil was the son of William Cecil (Lord Burghley).

Recusantes.[76] Churchwardens and constables were annually to report to the Sessions the absence of Catholic recusants from church, and the names of their children and servants. Penalties for not receiving the sacrament were set at twenty pounds for the first year, forty pounds for the second year, and sixty pounds for the third. Recusants once convicted were to be fined twenty pounds a month until they conformed; and they might lose two-thirds of their lands. A second Act reimposed restrictions on the places where Catholics might live, and on their freedom to travel more than five miles from home.[77]

Whether Byrd's request to Salisbury was successful is unknown,[78] but he was named repeatedly as a recusant in Essex. He and his family were summoned time and again before justices of the King's Bench at Chelmsford and Brentwood,[79] to the Assizes conducted at Chelmsford or Brentwood by itinerant judges,[80] and to the Quarter Sessions held at Chelmsford, where a mixed tribunal of lawyers and laymen dealt with those serious pleas of the Crown not reserved for Assize judges.[81] The

---

76   3 James I, c. 4.

77   3 James I, c. 5. The restrictions were originally imposed by 35 Elizabeth c. 2.

78   There is evidence of the earlier intervention of the Attorney General on Byrd's behalf in PRO, KB 29/233, m. 92^r (1596) and KB 29/240, m. 97^v (1602).

79   References to the Byrds' recusancy in Essex have been noted as follows in the King's Bench records: KB9 series nos. 691, mm. 62 and 63; 1042, mm. 20 and 21; KB29 series nos. 233, m.92^r; 240, m.97^v; 246, m.52^v; 248, m. 48^r. See p. 69, note 42, concerning the KB27 and KB37 rolls. The interest of the King's Bench in the Byrd family seems to have been limited after they moved to Essex, and to have faded after Christopher Byrd appeared in 1606 (KB29/246) and William Byrd appeared in 1608 (KB29/248).

80   Calendared by Cockburn, 1978.

81   The relevant entries for years up to 1623 in the Sessions rolls (ERO, series Q/SR) are: 130/23 (July 1595), 132/18 (January 1595/6), 133/25 (April 1596), 136/20 (January 1596/7), 137/44 (April 1597), 139/17 (October 1597), 141/21 (April 1598), 147/14 (October 1599), 155/24 (October 1601), 156/20 (January 1601/2), 157/77 (April 1602) 158/27 (July 1602), 159/19 (September 1602), 159/128 (September 1602), 160/32 (January 1602/3), 162/21 (May 1603), 162/24 (May 1603), 165/90 (January 1603/4), 171/59d (April 1605), 172/54 (July 1605), 172/72 (July 1605), 173/76 (October 1605), 174/66 (January 1605/6), 175/53 (May 1606), 177/91 (October 1606), 181/70 (October 1607), 192/131 (October 1610), 193/35 (January 1610/11), 196/118 (October 1611), 199/147 (July 1612), 200/28 (October 1612), 201/35 (January 1612/13), 202/52 (April 1613), 203/53 (July 1613), 208/53 (October 1614), 213/53 (April 1616), 216/73 (January 1616/17), 219/50 (October 1617), 222/25 (October 1618), 224/22 (April 1619), 225/37 (July 1619), 225/56 (July 1619), 227/19 (January 1619/20), 228/17 (April 1620), 229/56 (July 1620: the last entry to mention William Byrd), 230/32 (October 1620), 237/21 (July 1622), 240/29 (April 1623). Apparent gaps suggest that the series is no longer complete.

Byrds' names appear too in the records of the court held at Romford by the Archdeacon of Essex. This was for the correction of moral and disciplinary offences, and its jurisdiction was over all the parishes in the county's deaneries.[82] The records are silent about whether the Byrds were present in person on each occasion, and about what warnings the courts issued when fines were imposed. There is in fact a good deal of difficulty in finding out what took place in the courts. The records were made by men who understood their own procedures, knew what they meant by their abbreviations, and needed only a short reminder of what had occurred. One thing that is sure is that the fines were now stiffer, and that had they been collected − which does not seem always, or even usually, to have been the case − the family would have paid out many hundreds of pounds over the years.[83]

At the sessions held on 3 July 1595 it was asserted that William and Christopher Byrd and their wives had refused to attend the parish church of Stondon for the previous six months.[84] On 26 February 1595/6 it was charged that William, Christopher, Rachel and Elizabeth Byrd, 'dyd not repayre' to any church or chapel, but had 'forborne' to do so since the previous 1 July.[85] An entry in the Acts of the Archdeaconry Court for 11 March 1595/6 says that 'm^r w^m bird & his wife & his son & his wife & his 2 daughters doe not & have not come to o^r churche since they

---

82   The court may have included men who held commissions enabling them to levy fines and imprison offenders as well as imposing the customary penances and excommunications. Anglin, 1965, p. 289, notes that the gentry and upper classes were generally exempt from the archdeacon's jurisdiction; the exception was in cases of recusancy. See also O'Dwyer, 1960. There is a gap in the Act books of the Archdeaconry Court from July 1593 to March 1595. The following entries concerning Byrd's family up to the time of his death have been noted in the surviving books (ERO, series D/AEA): 17 (1595-97), ff. 124^r, 177^v, 181^r, 192^r; 18 (1597-98), ff. 223^{r-v}, 233^r, 259^r; 19 (1598-99), ff. 4^v, 43^r, 48^r, 70^r, 90^{r-v}, 94^r, 99^r, 100^v, 114^{r-v}, 117^r, 133^v, 136^v, 150^v, 153^r, 167^{r-v}, 169^v, 184^v-185^r, 186^v, 221^v, 237^v, 247^r, 267^v, 287^{r-v}, 312^r, 335^{r-v}, 353^v-354^r; 20 (1599-1601), ff. 63^{r-v}, 80^{r-v}, 104^{r-v}, 108^v-109^r; 21 (1601-2) ff. 88^v, 117^r, 121^r, 124^v-125^r, 154^{r-v}, 177^v, 188^r; 22 (1602-4), ff. 7^r, 28^r, 48^r, 192^{r-v}; 23 (1604-6), ff. 37^r, 40^v, 56^v-57^r; 24 (1606-8), f. 126^v; 25 (1608-11), ff. 162^v-163^r; 26 (1611-13), ff. 83^v, 129^{r-v}, 151^r, 189^r, 199^v, 227^r, 245^r, 260^v, 277^v, 288^r; 27 (1613-14), ff. 1^r, 111^v, 300^v; 28 (1614-15), f. 231^v; 29 (1615-17), f. 150^v; 30 (1617-18) appears to contain no Byrd entry; 31 (1618-20), f. 115^r; 32 (1620-22), ff. 24^r, 149^v, 212^r, 283^v; 33 (1622-24) appears to contain no Byrd entry. A few entries may have been overlooked, but those which have been examined are generally very repetitive.

83   O'Dwyer (1960, pp. 204-228) discusses recusant fines in Essex.

84   ERO, Q/SR 130/23.

85   PRO, KB9/691, mm. 62 and 63; KB29/233, m. 92^r.

came to oᵣ pₐrysh to dwell'.[86] So it went on. In April 1597 it was stated that 'we prsent mᵣ burde of Stondon place and his wife and Thomas [*sic*] burde and his wife and old m burdes iij dafters for not comminge to the churche'.[87]

In 1599/1600 events took a slightly different turn. An assize record of 6 March complains that William Byrd, 'Ellen' his wife, and Christopher Byrd, together with Byrd's daughters Elizabeth and Rachel, had not been to church for a month.[88] William traversed his indictment at the winter Assizes of 1601, and in the Trinity term of 1601 it was removed into the King's Bench by writ of *certiorari*. He was presumably trying to have the indictment quashed on procedural grounds.

'A trewe Certificate' of 5 April 1605 signed by Richard Vaughan, the recently preferred Bishop of London, lists the persons reported to him as failing to attend church in Essex.[89] It notes that the parson, churchwardens and sidemen of Stondon Massey 'doe pᵣsente that they have papisticall Recusantₑₛ wᶜʰ utterly refuse to come to the churche', namely William and Christopher Byrd and their wives, and William's daughters Elizabeth and Mary. The Bishop signed a similar certificate on 9 July 1605. This says that the parson and churchwardens of Stondon Massey presented 'William Bird gent and Ellyn his wife, Christopher Bird gent, and Katheryn his wief for absentinge them-selves from their parrishe Churche and from Dyvine servis there read for the space of theis six monethes laste paste'.[90]

Recusancy was not the only offence under the Act of 1592. It was a breach of the law to 'pswade anye other pson whatsoever to forbeare or abstayne' from attending church. A citation of 11 May 1605 accused Byrd of the latter transgression.

Willimu Bird et Ellena eius ux̄   psentat for Popishe Recusantₑₛ he is a gentleman of the kingₑₛ Maᵗⁱᵉˢ Chapell, and as the minister and churchwardens doe heare the said Willā Birde with the asistance of one Gabriel Colford who is nowe at Antwerp hath byn the Chiefe and principall seducer of John Wright sonne and heire of John Wright of Kelvedon in Essex

---

86   ERO, D/AEA 17, f. 124ᵣ.

87   ERO, Q/SR 137/45.

88   PRO, ASSI 35/42/1, mm. 45 and 60; Cockburn, 1978, p. 495. 'Ellen' and Rachel are described as 'spinsters', a designation of occupation rather than married status. Rachel was married by 1598.

89   ERO, Q/SR 171/59-64; the Byrds appear on f. 59ᵛ. A certificate listing the Byrd family and dated 6 April is among the Westmorland papers. (Historical Manuscripts Commission, 1885, p. 486.) Vaughan had once been rector of Stanford Rivers.

90   ERO, Q/SR 172/72, f. 62ᵛ.

gent and of Anne Wright the daughter of the said John Wright thelder[91] And the said Ellen Birde as it is reported and as her servant*es* have confessed have appointed busines on the Saboth daye for her servant*es* of purpose to keepe them from Churche, and hath also done her best indeavour to seduce Thoda Pigbone[92] her nowe mayde servant to drawe her to poperie as the mayd hath confessed And besid*es* hath drawen her mayde servant*es* from tyme to tyme these 7 yeres from comeinge to Churche and the said Ellen refuseth conference and the minister and churchwardens have not as yet spoke with the said Wm Birde because he is from home. − and they have byn exco︆municate these 7 yeares.[93]

The same comprehensive record of the Byrd family's refusal to attend the parish church continues:

χρofer*us* Birde et Catherinā eius uẋ psentat for popishe Recusant*es* they doe utterly refuse conference and they have stood exco︆municate these 7 yeares and they are maynteyned as the minister and churchwardens doe thinke by the said Wm Birde

Thomas Bird psentat for a popishe Recusant, he hath stood exco︆municate these 7 yeares and is manteyned as the minister and churchwardens doe thinke at the charges of the said Wm Birde & he doth resorte often tymes to the howse of the said Will︆m Birde

91   The accusation can hardly have been made by Wright, since like Christopher Byrd's wife he was descended from the More and Scrope families and was himself a Catholic. (*The Essex Recusant*, v, p. 21.) Powell (1956, p. 70) says it is probable that a Catholic priest was maintained from time to time at Kelvedon Hall, but the evidence is from a later date. Colford, whose home was at Navestock, near Stondon Massey, was accused of bringing seditious books into England and imprisoned. (Privy Council, 1901, p. 73, and 1902, p. 10.) He visited the English College in Rome in 1600, the same year in which it was visited by a Thomas Byrd, who may have been the composer's son. (Foley, 1877-84, vi, p. 566 and 571.) Brett (1993(a), pp. xiv-xv) suggests that either of them might have brought William Byrd the Gradual which inspired the plan of his *Gradualia*. (See p. 319.) There were however many foreign books in circulation. John Petre's servant John Bentley left his master a 'new bible in Laten in quarto of venice printe, ymprinted in the yeare of o^r lord god 1587'. (ERO, D/ABW 5/365; Edwards, 1975, pp. 33-34.)

92   Elsewhere called Rhoda Pickbone.

93   ERO, D/AEA 23, f. 136^v-137^r. The Moore family of Leyton, the Byrds' relations by marriage, appear close by (f. 137^v), as they often do in other lists of recusants. (Two leaves have been numbered 137; references are to the first.)

Mariam Birde simile
Elisabetha Jackson viduã simile
ab Stanford Ryvers   Catherinã [*sic*] Hooke ux̃ Johnis Hooke simile[94]

In 1612 it was presented that Byrd 'will not paye to the rate for his land lyinge in the pishe to the repacons of the church and bells wch some is xx^s'. It is ironic that the oldest of the church's bells, probably installed when the belfry was built, was made by a John Byrd early in the fifteenth century.[95]

In June 1615 Byrd 'was sommoned wth his children to appeare to give answer as concerninge theire profession'.[96] The last entry about him in the Act books of the Archdeaconry Court was made in September 1616: 'pntat for a Recusant papist and for absenting him selfe from his pishe church a longe tyme and for standinge excommunicate these seaven yeares'.[97] His recusancy was presented at the Midsummer Sessions in 1620,[98] and was proclaimed according to the statute at the Assizes of 12 March 1620/1.[99] His absence from the records of the courts thereafter may mean that he had become ill, but members of his family continued to be listed.

The occupants of Stondon Place

The Byrd family's recusancy has left a chronicle of the principal

---

94   ERO, D/AEA 23, ff. 136^v-137^r. Stanford Rivers, where Rachel (not Katherine) and John Hooke lived, is a parish close to Stondon Massey. In 1598 Queen Elizabeth presented Byrd's old friend Richard Mulcaster to the rectory there. This is recorded in the parish register. (ERO, D/P140/1/1, f. 145^v.) An entry in the Acts of the Archdeaconry Court for June 1597 seems to refer to 'M^ris ... Mulcaster' of Stanford Rivers, though the title could be construed as 'M^r'. (ERO, D/AEA 18, f. 44^v: dots original.) Mulcaster died and was buried at Stanford Rivers in April 1611.

95   ERO, D/AEA 26, f. 129^v; Powell, 1956, p. 246. In addition to being liable for such payments, the occupant of Stondon Place seems to have had a responsibility for the maintenance of certain parts of the church's property. In July 1602 Byrd was questioned about 'a parte of a pale wch longeth to the fence of the churchyard appointed to stondon place to make it'. (D/AEA 21, f. 177^v.) In 1607 it was presented that Christopher Byrd 'houldeth ground in kelvedon, & was rated to paye certayne monye towards the repayringe of the said churche accordinge to the quantitye of grounde wch he houlds w^thin the said pishe wch he refuse to paie'. (D/AEA 24, f. 126^v.)

96   ERO, D/AEA 28, f. 231^v.

97   ERO, D/AEA 29, f. 150^v.

98   ERO, Q/SR 229/56.

99   PRO, Assizes 35/63/1, m. 6; Cockburn, 1982, pp. 249-250.

occupants of Stondon Place. It is to be supposed that Christopher, the Byrds' older son, increasingly assumed responsibility for the farm, and that his wife Katherine played an important part in running the large household. This included not only William and Julian Byrd and their children, but Thomas, the son of Christopher and Katherine. Two of Katherine's female relations eventually joined her. There was also a number of servants. Julian Byrd had a maidservant named Rhoda Pickbone, who was not a recusant, while Christopher Byrd had the servant named Helena Barcroft, who was a recusant and may have replaced one named Martha. Charles Hill was another recusant servant, who was a member of the household by 1619 and remained until at least 1623.

All Byrd's daughters married, but no marriage agreements are known. Perhaps the modest means of the men they married made it hardly worthwhile. Were the Byrds on friendly terms with the husbands' families? More interestingly, did the Byrds consent to go to church for the weddings? Such information as there is about Byrd's sons-in-law comes from the records of the courts.

It seems that Elizabeth, Rachel and Mary Byrd had husbands who, on the whole, did not share their unbending Catholicism. 'Mr Hoeckes' of Stondon, who was said in 1599 to have been a recusant for three years, may nevertheless have been Rachel's husband.[100] She had wedded John Hooke, a yeoman, by 1598.[101] He was dead in 1612.[102] Their children William and Katherine are named in Byrd's will. Katherine Hooke eventually married Michael Walton.[103] By 1618 Rachel had married again. Her second husband was Edward Biggs, and for a short time they seem to have lived at Warley Magna, a dozen miles south of Stondon Massey.[104] They moved to Doddinghurst, though in October 1621 an entry for Biggs was annotated 'iam habitat in Stondon Massey' and he was thought to be there in June 1622.[105] They lived at Doddinghurst after William Byrd's death.[106] Biggs seems to have been a farmer in a small way, being described variously as a husbandman, a labourer, and at the Midsummer Sessions of 1622 as a farmer bound to keep the peace

100   ERO, Q/SR 147/14.

101   ERO, D/AEA 18, f. 223[r].

102   At the Midsummer and Michaelmas Sessions of 1612 Rachel was referred to as a widow. (Q/SR 199/146-147 and 200/28.)

103   Byrd's will. See p. 393.

104   ERO, D/AEA 31, f. 115[r], July 1619.

105   D/AEA 32, ff. 149[v], 2312[r] and 283[v].

106   ERO, Q/SR 222/24; PRO, E377/57 m. 17[r].

towards Susan Cuper, a spinster.[107] At the Sessions of Michaelmas 1623 he was again bound to keep the peace, this time with Robert Rucke.[108]

Rachel's elder sister Elizabeth was married to John Jackson by 1600, but was widowed by 1605. She was referred to as a widow of Mountnessing in September 1620.[109] She was remarried, to a man named Burdett, when Byrd made his will.

The third daughter, Mary, appears to have spent periods away from home; and although the Act books of the Archdeaconry Court record her as living at Stondon Massey in 1598-99, she is listed separately from the other members of the family on eight occasions, when her name appears between those of John Hayman and John Wibert (or Wybert).[110] Mary married Henry Hawksworth in 1611 or 1612.[111] Their four sons − William, Henry, George and John − are named in William Byrd's will. Hawksworth seems to have died between 1623 and 1634. Mary's second husband was Thomas Falconbridge.

Byrds' son Thomas seems to have lived at Stondon irregularly, although the records do not always distinguish him from his nephew of the same name.[112] As a younger son, who could not expect to inherit the family farm and be a landowner, Thomas had to be educated for a different kind of life. He may be the person who makes a fleeting appearance in the registers of the English College at Valladolid. A Thomas Byrd was admitted to the College on 20 December 1596, with two other young men, John Jones and John Barley. He was then twenty years old, and was said to have been born in London, a description which fits Byrd's son perfectly. In England he had spent a year studying 'humanioribus literis, et legibus municipalibus Angliae', so he is likely to

---

107   PRO, E377/57, m. 17ʳ; ERO, Q/SR 240/28-29 and Q/SR 237/27.

108   ERO, Q/SR 242/79.

109   PRO, ASSI 35/42/1 (6 March 1600); ERO, Q/SR 171/59 and D/AEA 32, f. 24ʳ.

110   ERO, D/AEA 19, ff. 48ʳ-186ᵛ. On f. 242ʳ⁻ᵛ Hayman and Wibert are listed without Mary.

111   The record of the Michaelmas 1611 Sessions (ERO, Q/SR 196/118) refers to 'Mary Byrd'. At the Michaelmas 1612 Sessions (Q/SR 200/28) she was called 'mare hauckes furmerly dafter to willyame burrd'. The partial similarity of her married name to that of her sister Rachel evidently caused confusion, for in the records of the Sessions at Epiphany 1616/17 she was called 'Hoke' (Q/SR 216/72).

112   Problems arise after 1604, when the younger Thomas could have been thirteen and hence old enough to be reported for recusancy. The older Thomas was however identified clearly on occasion, e.g. in the records of the Sessions of 4 October 1605, when he was said to have been absent from church for five years, and at Michaelmas 1612. (ERO, Q/SR 173/76 and Q/SR 200/28.)

have spent some time at one of the Inns of Court.[113] He was born of Catholic parents and had always been an obedient son of the Church, and was recommended by Father Garnett. This Thomas Byrd left the College and returned, but was finally expelled in November 1599.[114] He may have been the 'Thomas Bird of Middlesex' who in April 1600 stayed for eight days at the hospice attached to the English College in Rome.[115]

Thomas was the only one of Byrd's children apparently to become a musician, though the evidence that he did so is indirect, and it is not known whether he was a professional. Writing of John Bull's Gresham professorship, John Ward said:

> In the year 1601 his health was so far impaired, that he was unable to perform the duty of his place; and therefore going to travel was permitted to substitute as his deputy, during his absence, Thomas Birde, master of the same science, and son of William Birde, one of the gentlemen of her majesty's chapel.[116]

This draws directly on the minutes of the comittee of Gresham College.[117] An entry for 5 February 1601/2 reads:

> At the sute and earnest request of doctoᵣ Bull Reader of the Musique Lecture in Gresham howse made unto us the last summer: who thorrowe sicknes hath been inforced to discontynue his exercise there divers termes nowe paste contrarye to the meaninge and intention of the ffowndeᵣ. It is ordered & agreed that Thomas Birde p̲fessoᵣ of the same science of Musique and the sonne of Willm̃ Birde one of the gent of her Matᵉˢ chapple shall hereafter begynne and contynue the readinge of the same publique Lecture in Gresham howse aforesaid as deputie and substitute to doctor Bull duringe his absence.

William Boyce's statement about Thomas Byrd subtly, but probably unintentionally, alters the sense of what Ward wrote. He makes it seem

---

113   On the assumption that 'legibus municipalibus Angliae' means the common law of England. The universities taught Roman, canon and civil law; municipal law did not appear in the academic curriculum until the mid-eighteenth century. (Baker, 1979, p. 194-195.)

114   Henson, 1930, p. 44, where 'Patre Garretio' must be an error for 'Garnetio'. It would not be surprising if Thomas found it difficult to cope with what had been planned for him by an outstandingly able father of powerful personality.

115   Foley, 1877-84, vi, p. 571. Byrd's son Thomas was described many years later as living in Drury Lane, which was then in Middlesex.

116   Ward, 1740, p. 200.

117   Mercers' Hall, Gresham Repertory 1596-1625, pp. 158-159.

as if the substitution applied to Bull's place in the Chapel Royal as well as the professorship.[118]

Bull's admiration for William Byrd is explicit in his 1597 Gresham lecture.[119] Securing the position of deputy for Thomas, who was only twenty-one, could be no more than a reflection of this, or as Bull was still in his mid-thirties it could be that a friendship had grown up between them. Uncertainty about Bull's association with the Catholics, and the motives for his journeys abroad and his activities while he was there, creates a nagging feeling that there may have been more to Bull's illness than is immediately apparent.[120] There is something rather odd in the fact that it required his temporary absence from the Gresham professorship, but that he was fit enough to endure the rigours of Continental travel. When Bull fled abroad in 1613 he claimed to have done so because he was a Catholic, though charges levelled against him in the High Commission Court must have had something to do with it.[121] He was plainly confident of finding a welcome in Brussels at the court of the Archduke, where Peter Philips, who was probably among Byrd's pupils and had himself gone abroad because he was a Catholic, was already well established.[122]

Thomas Byrd's deputyship lasted until 27 June 1603. Two entries for that day read:

This day docter Bull hath given his consent that iiij[li]. x[s]. due unto Jn[o]. Glover shalbe defalked out of his next half yeres allowance.

118   Boyce, 1760-73, iii, p. ix.

119   See p. 365.

120   See Wood, 1813-20, *Fasti* section, cols. 235-236; Boyd, 1962, pp. 318-319. The payment of nine months' salary to Bull on 27 October 1610 evidently followed a journey to Spain, during which he carried letters to Paris. (Ashbee, 1986-96, iv. p. 116 and 87.) But no documentary evidence has ever been put forward in support of statements that Bull was a government spy. (Henry, 1937, pp. 74-77; Dart, 1959(a).) The evidence that Byrd's friend Alfonso Ferrabosco was a spy is set out by Charteris, 1981. Thomas Morley, who may have been a pupil of Byrd, was another involved in the spy network. (Brown, 1959; Dart, 1959(b).)

121   Historical Manuscripts Commission, 1940, pp. 270-271.

122   Letters covering the period March 1609 to September 1610 (Österreichisches Staatsarchiv, Vienna, Belgien PC 45 and 46) make it fairly clear that Philips and Bull were in touch at that time. It is something of a mystery why the Archduke was still willing to receive Bull after his failure to provide an organ for which he had asked an excessive price. (The history of the affair is explicit in Belgien PC 45 and 46, and summarized in Grove, 1981, iii, p. 439, starting halfway down column b.)

This day m^r docter Bull hath here revoked all form^r resignacons of his place made unto m^r Birde or anie others & humbly desireth to be contynued in his place as before.[123]

The track to Kelvedon Hatch

With Stondon Place Byrd gained the associated parcel of land called Malperdus, paying a quit-rent for its freehold to Mrs Dawtrey of Doddinghurst, who with Anthony Luther appears at some stage to have acquired an interest in the property.[124] Across the land of which Byrd was a tenant there had once been a public right of way. This was the subject of dispute between Byrd and Parson Nobbs. There must have been, and may still be, more documents than those which have been discovered, but the outline of the story is clear.

At the Sessions of 7 February 1599/1600 it was claimed that Byrd had enclosed the roads between Stondon and Kelvedon Hatch with a great ditch and hedge, despite their having been from time immemorial common highways for travel by foot, horse and carriage.[125] 'The p^rsentm^t of the greate Inquest' (Grand Jury presentments) at the Brentwood Assizes on 12 March 1601 describe Byrd as having 'stopped upp twoe comon waies leadinge from Styondon aforesaide towardes Kelvedon, to the greate annoyance of her Maie^tes leige people', and it was added that 'he hathe bene heretofore indicted for the same'. A writ was made for his appearance at the next assizes.[126]

123 Mercers' Hall, Gresham Repertory 1596-1625, p. 165. Since the minutes concerning Bull seem never to have been printed before, it is worth adding the first and last (pp. 2, 185). 'Assembly of the comitties at Gresham house the xxxi^th day of March a^o. 1597... It is ordered, and agreed, that the seaven Lecturers shall have and take theire chambers and lodginge, accordinge to th'appoyntm^t here ensuinge. viz [List of lecturers] ... N°. 7: A gallerie and oth^r roomes in m^r Reader handes, are appointed for m^r docter Bull reade^r of the Musick Lecture'. 20 December 1609: 'Upon the resignacon of docto^r Bull late Reader of the Musick Lecture in Gresham howse, Mr Thomas Clayton M^r of arts in the univ^rsity of Oxon was this day ellected to succeed in the same musique Lecture: and to pforme his oration at such convenient tym*es* as s^r Stephen Soam*es* shall appoint'.

124 See Byrd's will, p. 392. The register of St Nicholas, Kelvedon Hatch, includes a note under the year 1627 that Anthony Luther left forty shillings a year to the poor of the parish of Kelvedon to be derived from the sum arising from the lands held by 'Mr Bird de stondon oriente'. (ERO, D/P296/1/1, f. 27^v; Reeve, 1905, p. 36.)

125 ERO, Q/SR 149/51-52. Original in Latin.

126 PRO, ASSI 35/43/1, m. 67; Cockburn, 1978, p. 517. Byrd's case is the third of three to be listed. The first concerns William Neale and John Ashdon, constables of Brentwood, who 'did ᴘmitt & suffer, certeyne minstrelles whose names are unknowne to

Inserted among the Sessions rolls in the Essex Record Office is a letter written in August 1602 by Sir John Petre, from his London house in Aldersgate Street, to Sir Thomas Mildmay.[127] It begins by reminding Mildmay that 'm^r Willm Birde her ma^{tes} servante standeth indited at the Sessyons, & processe from thence awarded agaynst him for stopping up of two supposed highewayes in a farme called Stondon Place'. It goes on to say that Sir John Fortescue[128] had requested Petre and a Mr Weston to see if they could settle the differences between Byrd and the neighbours who opposed him, without prejudice to the Queen's inheritance (that is to say, the property confiscated from Sir William Shelley). Petre was going to be absent from home, and was unable to deal with the matter in time. He therefore asked Mildmay to give an order, when the case came up at the next Sessions, preventing further action until he and Weston had answered Fortescue's request.

On 14 June 1604 depositions were taken at Brentwood concerning the stopping up of the highway, for a case then before the Court of Exchequer.[129] William and Christopher Byrd were now named as plaintiffs and John Nobbs as the defendant. The deponents were John Wright of Kelvedon, whose son and daughter Byrd was accused of seducing to Catholicism, William Hollingworth of Stondon, and other men from round about. Wright acknowledged that 'of late ye said John Nobbs caused ye said Willm Byrd to be endicted for stoppinge upp a comon high way for all ye king^{es} leige people through ye said Malapardus', and that this was 'a common high way, both for horsemen & footemene Cartes and Carriages, leading from Stondon Tye ... towards ... Kelvedon Hatch'. But his evidence was that hedging and ditching had been carried out by Lawrence Hollingworth before the Byrds came to Stondon, and that they were not responsible for 'anie new fence, ditch or hedge to stopp anie passage or comon high waie'. Moreover, he knew that 'William Birde ... hath heretofore stopped a waie leadinge from Stondon Place towardes Kelvedon Churche ... And that he ... hath againe laide open the waie ... by the pswasion of the Lord Petre'. Other witnesses gave a variety of contradictory views, some

wander upp & downe their said Towne'.

127 ERO, Q/SR 155/17. Sir Thomas was a member of the prominent Chelmsford family of that name, and a Sheriff of Essex. The Petre and Mildmay families were neighbours in London as well as Essex, and were often associated in government business over many years.

128 Sir Walter Mildmay's successor as Chancellor of the Exchequer; member of the Privy Council, the Court of Star Chamber, etc.

129 PRO, E134/2 James I/Trinity 5. The documents include interrogatories to be put to the witnesses for both sides.

averring that there had been a common way, and others saying that they knew nothing of it. William Barlie of Norton Mandeville said that the way was 'so fowle, in one place ... that it was not passable'. On 23 June 1604 the court ordered that the depositions should be published, and the causes heard at Serjeants Inn during the third sitting of the next Michaelmas term.[130]

It has not proved possible to substantiate Fellowes' assertion that judgement was given against Nobbs on the grounds that during fifty years or more no one had challenged the position.[131] This looks suspiciously like a misinterpretation of information given in Reeve's history of Stondon Massey. Reeve says 'I have not the judgement before me', but refers to a terrier written by Nobbs in 1618, in which he appears to accept that Lawrence Hollingworth was responsible for blocking the highways. From this Reeve concludes that the findings were in Byrd's favour.[132]

Stondon Place (ii)

William Shelley died in April 1597. His widow Jane was the daughter and sole heiress of John Lyngen (or Lingen) of Sutton Freene in Herefordshire.[133] She suffered a period of imprisonment as a Catholic, and failed in an attempt during Queen Elizabeth's reign to regain the whole of the property she brought to her marriage. According to Mrs Shelley's account it was soon after her husband's death that Byrd began a suit in the Court of Exchequer, in an effort to obtain her ratification of the lease given to him by Queen Elizabeth.[134] The case dragged on until Mrs Shelley's death in 1609/10 and generated much work for the lawyers, not to mention what must have been a substantial amount in fees.[135]

---

130   PRO, E128/17/2, m. 16 (the original order); E123/29, f. 168[r] (copy in the books of orders and decrees).

131   Fellowes, 1948, p. 27.

132   Reeve, 1906, pp. 69, 126. In ERO, T/|P 188/1, pp. 298-304, Reeve states that he transcribed the terrier at the Bishop of London's Registry at St Paul's Cathedral.

133   PRO, Prob. 11/115.

134   PRO, SP14/37/36-36i.

135   The full list of entries in the court's books of orders and decrees is: PRO, E123/24, ff. 254[v], 303[r], 325[v]; E123/26, f. 63[r-v]; E123/27, f. 17[r]; E123/29, f. 133[v]; E124/1, ff. 147[r], 170[v], 172[r], 190[v]; E124/5, ff. 159[v], 162[r], 228[v]; E124/7, ff. 10[r], 68[r], 294[v], 328[r]; E126/1, ff. 113[v] (120[v] in modern numbering), 119[v] (128[v]). Original orders and decrees of the court, now apparently incomplete, are numbered E128. (Many originals, though not those involving the Shelley case, are initialled 'W. B.', presumably

The first entry in the court's books of orders and decrees is dated 19 May 1599. On 3 May in the following year it was decided that 'after longe debatinge of the said cause by the learned Councell on both sides, It is this present daye ordered and decreed for that the matter seemes doubtfull unto the Court, and some question in lawe doth arise thereupon, that a case be drawne and agreed upon betweene the said pties; And that the court will have consideracõn thereof'.[136] Mrs Shelley's motives in withholding the ratification Byrd sought were exposed when, on the same day, the Lord Treasurer[137] told the court that 'he was informed that one Garnett a servant or Solicitor of great trust wth the deft. had reported in the presence of the said deft. and of various witnesses of good credite viz. That it was not meete for the deft. to suffer her Mates: Teñntes to contynewe in possession of her Joyneture for feare they should after her death holde the same possession in the right of her Matie: ... whereby it seemed [to] this court there is a purpose to deseate her Matie: of the inheritance'. The court resolved to look into this; meanwhile Mrs Shelley was to permit the plaintiffs and all other tenants and patentees of the Queen 'to hold and enjoye their severall tearmes interests and possessions therein ... wthout lett or interrupcõn ... untill further order to the contrary'.[138]

Early in the reign of King James, Effingham (William Howard) and others sought to obtain the lands which Shelley had owned. They were however outbidden by Shelley's nephew and heir John Shelley, whose offer to pay £1000 to Effingham and £10,000 into the Exchequer the King found more attractive.[139] Under Letters Patent of 5 September 1603 the lands Mrs Shelley had inherited were restored to her, together with the rents, revenues and profits from them since William Shelley's death.[140] The conflict this created with Queen Elizabeth's grant of a lease to Byrd was bound to cause trouble.

Sir William Byrd: see p. 108, note 5.) In addition to these entries there is a collection of interrogatories and depositions at E134/41 & 42 Elizabeth I/Mich 34.

136   This order is duplicated in a memorandum roll of the Queen's Remembrancer. (PRO, E159/418, m. 169v of the section for the Easter term, 42 Elizabeth). It may also be repeated in the Chancery decree docquets, but PRO class C96 at present has no index to facilitate investigation.

137   Lord Buckhurst, formerly Sir Thomas Sackville, created Earl of Dorset 1603/4.

138   PRO, E123/26, f. 63r-v.

139   PRO, SP14/8/52; State papers, 1857, p. 116. A warrant for the payment to Effingham was issued on 11 July 1604. (PRO, SP38/7, f. 181r; State papers, 1857, p. 131.)

140   PRO, C66/1618/23.

Mrs Shelley now became Byrd's landlord, and tried to evict him. There survives the draft, dated 24 January 1603/4, of a letter designed to express the King's displeasure.[141] It is framed in terms strong enough to suggest Byrd's part in it, were the handwriting not conclusive evidence that he composed the whole thing.

Wher of late. uppon yo[r] hūble sute. we freelye delyvered to you under o[r] great seale. yo[r] joynter land*es*. being o[r] inheritance. w[ch] y[e] late .Q. o[r] deare sister refused to do. and dispenced wth y[e] othe. w[ch] the law in y[t] Case required. being now informed y[t] you wrest o[r] sayd grant contrary to o[r] meanyng. to the undoing of o[r] servant Wyllm̄ Byrd. gent. of o[r] Chapple. who havyng taken leaces of y[e] farme and wood*es* of stondon place in y[e] Cowntye of Essex. (now parcell of yo[r] joynter) from y[e] sayd Late .Q. for three of his Chyldernes lyves. payd fynes and bestowed great Charges of y[e] houses and Barnes ...[142] when he entred. deserved well of you. and you accepted ...[143] his rent. ever synce y[e] death of yo[r] husband. yet notw[th]standyng synce y[e] sayd grant. you go about to thrust hym out of his possession. to his present undoing. (havyng no other house but y[t]) and to y[e] great danger of his Chylderns future estat*es* ...[144] for staying of w[ch] yo[r] hard Course. nether yo[r] owne concience. nor o[r] benignity towards you. nor the Decree of o[r] exchequer Chamber yet in force. nor y[e] letters of y[e] ll[s]. of o[r] pryvye Cownsayle. nor y[e] travayle of y[e] lo: peter. auctorized from them to mediate y[e] sayd cause nor any reasonable composision offered you by o[r] sayd servant. to hold his possession. wth yo[r] good favor. can any whyt move you / being a woman of greate lyvyng. and no Charges. and havyng many better houses then his. to use at yo[r] plesure. growndyng yo[r] Rigor agaynst o[r] sayd servant. uppon y[e] strength of o[r] sayd grant to you wherof we greatlye merveyle. y[t] in thos land*es*. w[ch] so latelye you receyved from us. and w[ch] are o[r] inheritance. you offer so hard mesure to o[r] servant. contrarye to all gratitude & discretion. and Concience / wheruppon (assuryng o[r] selves y[t] y[e] premisses are true.) we do hereby requyre you. to permitt and suffer. o[r] sayd servant and his Chyldern Pattentees of y[e] late .Q. duryng yo[r] tyme quietlye to enjoy ther possession of y[e] sayd farme and wood*es* accordyng to ther sayd grant*es*. paying you ther rent and usyng them selves as good tenant*es* owght to doe

141   PRO, SP15/36/5; State papers, 1872, pp. 438-439. See pl. 6.

142   One or two words are lost through damage at the right hand edge of the paper, followed by an uncertain word at the beginning of the next line.

143   'you accepted' and any following word damaged. Fellowes read 'you accepted of', but this may have been conjecture.

144   The words 'after yo[r] decease' were originally written here. They have been deleted and replaced by 'yf they [rlese?] y[e] present [−?]'.

...[145] also y^t you geve them no just Cause heereafter of any new Complaynt to us. or our Cownsayle toochyng y^t Cause /

Passages have been scored through in the draft, and more concise marginal amendments (now partly obscured by the binding) added in another hand. This argues the intention of an official to submit it to the King, but whether he ever sent a letter is unknown.

By the middle of May 1604 a secondary dispute had arisen because Mrs Shelley and John Prichard, her lawyer, had forbidden the Byrds' workmen to cut wood on the farm. The court put a stay on further cutting, but permitted 'woodes underwoodes and trees allready fallen' to be taken away. Despite this it was alleged in June that the Byrds had continued to cut wood, and an attachment was awarded against them.[146]

The Petre household

After John Bolt left the Petres' service in 1593, no one occupied a similar post until 1608.[147] Byrd may have acted, in effect, as music director at Thorndon Hall in the intervening years. Among the entries in the account books indicating his presence is one for ten shillings given to him in January 1600/1, for a 'calui: curis', and another for twenty shillings given to him in December 1605 'pro xenio'.[148] An inventory of 1608 lists the bedding in 'Mr Bird*es* Chamber' under the headings of 'ffether Bedd*es*', 'Country Coverlett*es*' and 'Blankett*es*'.[149]

145   Obscure word read by Fellowes as 'redely'.

146   PRO, E124/1, f. 147^r and f. 170^v. In 1598 Prichard was described as a gentleman of London, aged about fifty. (PRO, E134/41 & 42 Elizabeth I/Mich 34.)

147   Bennett and Willetts, 1977; Bennett, 1992. The younger Sir William Petre (knighted 1603) seems to have made an unsuccessful attempt to employ a replacement for Bolt. His accounts for June 1605 record a payment 'To Wm Browne y^t shoulde have served mee as a Musitian.' (ERO, T/A/174.) The name William Browne occurs later as that of a servant at Ingatestone, but it is not known whether he was the same man. Petre also employed a musician named Bicley to teach his children, and in January 1606/7 gave him five shillings 'at his goinge away' (marginally headed 'Musitians rewarde').

148   ERO, T/A/174, ff. 34^v and 87^v. The transcript has 'calui: turis', but is amended by Price (1981, p. 89) and Turbet (1987, p. 83), the latter of whom suggests it refers to a lost composition ('I glow with cares'). 'Xenium' means a present.

149   ERO, D/DP F218. One of each item is listed. Against an entry for 'Holmes ffustian & Ticke pillows' the words 'one paire' are scored through. Holmes fustian came from Ulm in Germany. It could be coincidence that Byrd's chamber is mentioned at about the time his wife died, or it could be that providing him with accommodation was a gesture of support following his loss.

John Bolt's replacement, Richard Mico, entered Sir William Petre's service about 1608, and payments to him occur periodically in his master's accounts. Byrd is almost certain to have been consulted about his appointment, as he was about that of 'Andrew fforde that was recom̃ended by M^r. Birde to have waited upon my [Petre's] children'.[150] 'An inventory of the Vial*les*, Lute, & Set*tes* of singing Bookes 1608' drawn up by Mico, shortly after he entered his new post, includes Byrd's *Gradualia* and other books.[151]

A note of Such Singinge bookes, and Instruments wth the keyes belonginge to them as are delivered mee by my Lady to take charge of.

Imprimis the chest of violls wch ar in number 5 viz 2 trebles 2 tenors, and the base, wth bowes to them
Item my Lords Lute wth a case to it
Item 2 Setts of Mr Birds books intituled Gradualia, the first and Second Sett,
Item one other Sett of Mr Birds bookes contayninge Songs of 3. 4. 5. and 6. pts
Item one other Sett of Mr Birds books of 5 pts
Item one other Sett of 3. 4. 5. and 6. pts wch are thick bookes wth end covers not printed but print[152]
Item the key of the wind instrument
Item the key of the greate virginales
Item the key of my Lords Lute
Item the key of the violl chest.

p mr Richard Micoe

The last payment to Byrd in the extant Petre accounts, a sum of ten pounds, was made in June 1608, 'for his riflinge for songe bookes.'[153]

A report of Byrd's performance at a house that could have been one of the Petres' residences was left by a young Frenchman. The four-page letter is annotated 'Charles de Ligny his relation to his Ma^{tes} Embassador in France'.[154] It is undated, but although Ligny describes (in French)

150   ERO, T/A/174, June 1607.
151   ERO, D/DP E2/1; Edwards, 1975, p. 138. Mico was about eighteen years old at the time of his appointment, and remained with the Petre family until 1630, when he became organist to Queen Henrietta Maria. See Briggs (1968, pp. 57-58) for more about the Mico family, and Bennett (1992) for an account of Mico's music.
152   *Recte* 'prict' (manuscript).
153   ERO, T/A/174, f. 107^r.
154   Hatfield House, Cecil papers, cxci, ff. 272^r-273^v; Historical Manuscripts

events that took place before the arrest of Father Henry Garnett in 1605, his account was written after the publication in that year of the first book of Byrd's *Gradualia*.[155]

Ligny says that, as he was on his way from his native Cambrai to England, he fell in with two disguised Jesuits at Gravelines. One was a Dr 'Noiriche',[156] and the other was a servant of Father Garnett named Speelleer. They needed someone who knew Italian, Latin and French, and Ligny agreed to work for them. He became ill, but they carried him to a place of Garnett's five miles from London.[157] When he had recovered he was taken to Speelleer's house between St Paul's and Temple Bar. A thought-provoking sidelight on the religious conflicts of the time is provided by Ligny's reference to Speelleer's brother, an attorney who, though he adhered to the reformed religion, was married to a Catholic.

Eventually Ligny was taken to another house which served as a meeting place for Catholics, at some distance from London. It is possible that this was Thorndon Hall or Ingatestone Hall. There he found Garnett in the company of several Jesuits and gentlemen, who were playing music. They included 'Mre Willaume byrd qui sonnait les organes et plusieurs aultres Instrumens'. This house was visited by many of the nobility and many ladies, chiefly on the solemn days observed by Catholics, though for safety's sake the meeting place was changed from time to time.[158]

Fearing for his safety, Ligny left this company and embarked for Gravelines, carrying letters he had been asked to deliver to the seminary at St Omer and to Jesuits in Brussels. He claimed to have decided to return to London in order to reveal the Jesuits to the authorities. When he was lodging at the Fleur de Lys, near the Tower of London, he was arrested and imprisoned in Newgate on account of 'certains livres

Commission, 1938, pp. 611-612 (where the contents of the document are described at greater length).

155   The resident Ambassador might therefore have been Sir Thomas Parry, or his replacement Sir George Carew.

156   Henry Norwich of Northamptonshire appeared before the Court of Star Chamber in 1578 to accuse his nephews Edward and Symond of papistical activities. (Anstruther, 1953, p. 151.)

157   Almost certainly White Webbs, a large house acquired by Garnett about 1600. It was at Enfield Chase, some twenty miles west of Stondon Massey.

158   Caraman, 1964, p. 317, suggests the house was White Webbs, and is followed by Baker, 1976, p. 249. Although Garnett was musical, there must be doubt about whether his house contained the collection of instruments mentioned by Ligny. 'Priest holes' for the concealment of priests are still exhibited at Ingatestone Hall.

qu'avoit compose Maistre Willaume byrd et Dedie au Seig[re] Henry houardo Du Conseil Privie de sa Maiesté'.[159] The 'livres' must have been the first set of books of *Gradualia*, and as John Reason had discovered earlier, even one printed book of music could be an object of suspicion. Ligny was released because he had a passport from the French Ambassador, and he returned to the Continent.

A letter written by the Jesuit Superior to an English nun at Louvain describes another event that took place not long before Garnett was arrested. Byrd is not mentioned, but even if he was not present he must have attended similar occasions. 'We kept Corpus Christi day with great solemnity and music', the letter reads, 'and the day of the octave made a solemn procession about a great garden, the house being watched, which we knew not till the next day when we departed twenty-five in the sight of all, in several parties, leaving half a dozen servants behind and all is well'. Editors have conjectured that the location was Fremland, not far from Ingatestone.[160]

The manor of Longney (ii)

The ownership of the lease of Longney manor, which Byrd lost about 1581,[161] came before the Court of Chancery nearly thirty years later. What happened in the intervening years has not been discovered.

The first indication in the court's records of Byrd's continued claim to the lease is dated 4 July 1606.[162] Entries refer only to 'the lease in question', but it can be inferred from what took place later that it was the lease of Longney manor. The plaintiffs were 'John Awintle & his wief & W[m] Hayward', and the defendants were 'W[m] Burd & Richard King'. How John a Wintle, Hayward and King came to have an interest is as yet

---

159 Howard became a member of the Privy Council on 4 May 1603. (Privy Council, 1907, p. 496.)

160 Slightly differing versions of the letter are given by Morris (1891, p. 144) and Anstruther (1953, pp. 275-276), the second of whom quotes Foley (1877-84, iv, p. 141). Jackman (1963, p. 36) adds the information that a copy, which takes care not to specify names or places, is in the archives of Stonyhurst College (Coll. MS P, f. 578). Fremland is said by Anstruther (1953, p. 276) to have been the home of Sir Ken Sulyard; but according to Caraman (1964, p. 320) it belonged to Sir John Tyrrel, who married into the Sulyard family.

161 See p. 87.

162 PRO, C33/110, f. 811[v]. Entries do not occur in strict date order, and are split between 'A' and 'B' volumes. Other entries covering the initial stages, all prefixed C33, are 109, f. 876[v]; 110, f. 892[v]; 111, ff. 74[r], 130[r], 140[r], 435[r] and 492[r]; 112, ff. 59[v], 160[v] and 181[r].

unknown, but it is possible that, having acquired a lease, Wintle wanted to be certain that Byrd had no prior claim on the property.[163] The initial entry refers to the plaintiffs and defendants 'clay*m*ing the land*es* in question by severall leases therof'. It bears out what was said in 1581 about Byrd's lease being cancelled by an order of the Exchequer, and adds that 'the possession of the said land*es* contynued wth the Ten*antes* therof according to the lease under wch the *plaintiffs* clayme'. The matter pursued its leisurely way, with witnesses being examined, until at least 28 April 1607. It seems as if the court found in favour of Wintle, but no record has been located.

Another stage in the dispute began in 1608, with 'William Byrd, Julian his wife, and Thomas Byrd ther sonne' as plaintiffs.[164] Their complaint carries the date 13 April and an answer submitted by the defendants, 'Robert Jackson, John a Wintle and Joane his wife', has the date 24 April.[165] An objection to accepting the complaint as evidence that Julian was alive at the time might be made on the grounds that the events described took place so much earlier. It could be argued that the complaint includes Julian's name only because the dispute arose out Byrd's lease of 1579. But it is hard to credit that the complaint would still have carried Julian's name if her death had occurred in the 1590s. There is also the consideration that Thomas would have been only four when Byrd lost the lease of Longney, and a minor until about 1597.[166]

An entry for 1 December 1608 in the court's books of decrees and orders refers to the defendants as 'Robert Jackson et al',[167] but one for 16 April 1610 places Wintle first among them.[168] It also refers to an earlier decree given in favour of Wintle, and says that Byrd's arguments 'for the reverssinge of the said decree shalbe cleerlie and absolutelie dismissed out of the courte'.

163 See p. 37 concerning the possibility that 'Awintle' was John Wintle with whom Byrd was acquainted in Lincoln.

164 The complaint offers the only indication that Byrd's son Thomas may have derived an income from their shared ownership of properties.

165 PRO, C2/James I B16/78. This group of documents includes the initial complaint and replies and counter-replies by each side. On the delays caused by legal processes see Baker, 1990, pp. 77-78.

166 Christopher Byrd may however have entered a complaint in his own name before he was twenty-one. See p. 92.

167 PRO, C33/115, f. 320^r. There is another brief entry on f. 794^r (15 May 1609), which shows how slowly the case progressed. Another is to be found in C33/116, f. 352^r.

168 PRO, C33/118, f. 633^r. The other defendants are given as 'Johan his wief and Robert [*sic*] Birde'. The plaintiffs listed in this entry are again 'William Birde Julian his wief and Thomas Birde theire sonne'.

Stondon Place (iii)

The dispute over the lease of Stondon Place dragged on. Whether or not the King sent Mrs Shelley the letter which Byrd drafted for him in 1603/4, she refused to give up. On 25 January 1607/8 the court warned that if she 'doth trouble the possessyon of the sayde defen*dants* ... or ... doth coṁence suyte or suyt*es* att the coṁon lawe agaynst the sayde Willṁ Byrd ... That then an Injuncõn shalbee awarded agaynst the sayde Jane Shelley'. A few days later the court expressed the need for 'the more speedy expedycõn of the sayde causes'.[169]

Mrs Shelley soon returned to the charge with an obstinacy worthy of Byrd himself, and petitioned Lord Salisbury.

> Your Sup* having in all duetifull respectfulnes receaved your Lo*ps*: pleasure by her Solicito*r* touching Bird*es* contynuaunce in her house at Stondon, (who no doubt by his clamo*r* hath gone about to incense your Lo*p*: against her as he hath done some other great parsonages suggesting unto theire hono*s* that your Sup* intended to take away his living without any just cause or title thereunto).
>
> Nowe, for that it may appeare unto your hono*r* howe injuriouslie the said Bird hathe delt with your Supp* for theis Twelve yeares space, and what smale or no favour he deserveth of your Sup*, she humblie prayeth your Lo*p*: would vouchsafe the reading of the Annexed. And for that your Sup* being aged Threescore and Tenne yeares hath no other house or place of habitation neare the citty of London wherein to rest herselfe in this her period of life, save onely ye said place of Stondon.
>
> Shee most humblie prayeth That with the good likeing of yo*r* hono*r*, shee may quicklie have and enjoye the same, not doubting but that your Lo*p*: in your grave wisdome will putt difference betwene the Landord and Tenaunte, to the end it may Appeare unto your hono*r* with what submissivenes & duetye shee entertayneth you Lo*ps* mocon.[170]

The minute Salisbury added to this on 27 October 1608 was short and to the point:

> This matter hath bene depending in Court and therefore lett her represent unto the Barons [Exchequer judges] that which she hath here delivered unto me, who are better acquainted with the whole procedings than I am and will take some leysure to heare her complaint for I have none

169   PRO, E124/5, ff. 159*v* and 162*r*.
170   PRO, SP14/37/36; State papers, 1857, p. 464..

Salisbury's disinclination to consider the petition cannot have been lessened by the length of the annexe, headed 'M^res Shelleys grievaunces against William Byrde'. This is undoubtedly biased (though no more so than some of Byrd's accusations), but it gives enough of what must be the truth to make it worth printing in its entirety. Mrs Shelley claimed:

1   That Bird being in quiet possession of Stondon place began a suit against your Sup^t in the Excheq^r Chamber Tenne Yeares since, & the same pursued ever sithence in his wiefs & childrens names, praying thereby that the court would order her to ratifie his Lease, which he had from her late Matie for Three Lives.

2   Not prevailing herein, he thereuppon stirred upp all the late Queenes Patentees wth helde any pt of her joyneture land*es*, & did combyme [*sic*] himself with them to mainteyne severall suit*es* against her for the same, wch contynued about eight yeares, & procured her Rent*es* to be sequestered, and hath caused her to expend at least 1000^li in defence of her title.

3   Sr Thomas ffludd Mr Churchyard and the rest of the Queenes Patentees uppon notice of his highnes Lr̄es patent*es* graunted unto your Sup^t for enjoying of her land*es*, did surcease their suits, and all submitted themselves, saving the said Bird and one Petiver, who being encouraged by the said Bird, did along tyme contynue obstinate untill of late he likewise submitted himself. ffor which the said Bird did give him vile and bitter words for doing the same.

4   He hath likewise practized to disgrace her with divers her honorable frends, & others of great quallitie pswading them that she was a woman of no good conscience, and that she went aboute to put him out of his Living without any just cause or title thereunto.

5   And being told by your Sup^tes counsell in her presence, that he had no right to the said Living, hee both then and at other tymes before her said, that yf he could not hould it by right, he would holde it by might, which course he hath pursued ever since.

6   The said Bird hath cutt downe great store of tymber Trees worth one hundreth mark*es* growing in the ground*es* belonging to the said place, hath felled all the underwood*es* worth 100^li & made therein greate spoile, & greater would have made, had not the ho^ble court of Excheq^r taken order to the contrary.

7   The landes in question are yearely worth 100ˡⁱ. for the which he hath onely paid 40 markes p̱ Anñ for syx yeares or thereaboutes. But since the said Lr̄es Patentes, which beare date the ffyft day of September in the ffirst yeare of his highnes Raigne, he hath paid nothing at all; howbeit by the said Lr̄es Patentes she was to receave the meane profyttes thereof ever since the death of her husband, who died about xij yeares since.

8   That for wante of this house, your Supᵗ was inforced in this last plague to remove from Towne to Towne, from whence being driven by Reason of the plague, there, shee was at the last constrayned to lye at a Teññtes house of hers, neare Colchester farre unfitting for her to her great disgrace and to the great hurt of your Supᵗ, being unable in respect of her age to travaile upp and Downe the countrey.

All wᶜʰ notwithstanding in her bounden duety to yoʳ honoʳ, and with a Reverend respect to yoʳ Loᵖˢ: motion; shee wilbe content to Release all her charges & also the moyetie of tharrerages aforesaide, although with exceeding Clamoʳ, he hath justly moved her to Afford him no favour.[171]

Buckhurst, the Lord Treasurer, proposed seeking Mrs Shelley's agreement to arbitration, and the Chancellor of the court, Sir Julius Caesar, attempted to persuade her. She stood firm. It was therefore ordered that Byrd should 'bring all the said rentes behinde and unpayd into this Courte and delyver the same to the handes of his highnes Remembranncer to be left and remayne in deposito' until the court made a further order.[172] A marginal note dated 16 January 1608/9 reads: 'Recyved of mʳ Willm̄ Birde according to this order the suñe of one hundred fiftie eight pounds fower shilinges and fower pence'.

Finally it was Lord Buckhurst who secured Mrs Shelley's agreement to mediation.[173] On 26 January 1608/9,[174] 'Willm̄ Birde one of the saide defendantes being present in courte' it was ordered with the consent of both parties that Byrd and his three children named in the lease should remain in occupation until the Feast of St Michael next (29 September 1609) but no longer. Mrs Shelley agreed to forgo almost half the rent she thought owing to her, and to 'accept of the soñe of fower score poundes

171   PRO, SP14/37/36i.

172   PRO, E126/1, f. 113ᵛ (f. 120ᵛ in modern numbering).

173   PRO, E126/1, f. 113ᵛ (120ᵛ in modern numbering); E124/7, f. 328ʳ and f. 294ᵛ (dated 7 and 13 November 1609, but referring back to earlier events).

174   The date given by Fellowes (1948, p. 25) seems to be a year out. The minute dated 7 November, 7 James I (i.e. in the year beginning 25 March 1609), refers to the decree made on the previous 26 January.

in full satisfacion of and for all the Rents and arrerages due and unpayde and to be due for the premisses (except for the woodes) ... until the said ffeast of S[t] Michaell tharchangell next'. The sum was to be paid 'out of the moneys heretofore left in deposito by the said Willm̄ Birde for the payment whereof this order shalbe unto the said S[r] Henry ffanshawe a sufficient warrant and discharge'. Mrs Shelley's signature, witnessed by John Prichard, shows that she received the agreed eighty pounds on 9 March. Byrd's signature acknowledges repayment of the balance of the money he had left with the court: 'Receyved by mee Willm̄ Byrde of S[r] Henry ffanshawe knight accordinge to this order the som̄e of threescore eighteene pownd*es* fower shilling*es* fower pence'.[175]

When the time came for the Byrds to move they sat tight, and were ostensibly in contempt of court. Their response to John Prichard's complaint was that they had Mrs Shelley's 'lease p*aroll*' (orally agreed lease), which entitled them 'to holde and enjoye the farme' until the next Michaelmas. By this time the court had clearly had enough, and referred the parties to the Common Law, where they might take whatever action counsel advised.[176]

Mrs Shelley was now in her seventies, and at this point in the proceedings she died.[177] Byrd thereupon purchased from her heir John Shelley 'the Redc̃on in ffee of the said Stondon place in the names of John Petre and Thomas Petre Esqrs to the use of him the said Willm̄ Bird and his heires.'[178] But that was far from being the end of dispute over Stondon Place, for shortly after Byrd's death his children embarked on litigation that was to last for many years.[179]

Byrd's later years

Christopher Byrd's father-in-law, Thomas Moore, died at the age of seventy-five. His will was made on 22 July 1606 and proved on

---

175   PRO, E126/1, f. 119[v] (128[v] in modern numbering). Among the names of Byrd's children 'Anne' is mistakenly written instead of Elizabeth. Sir Henry Fanshawe was Remembrancer of the Exchequer.

176   PRO, E124/7, ff. 294[v] and 328[r].

177   Her will was made on 18 February 1609/10 and proved on 30 March 1610. (Probate copy: PRO, Prob. 11/115.)

178   PRO, C3/334/3. The date given for the purchase is 'about the Seaventh yeare of his Ma[tes] Raigne over England'. This was however the year ending 24 March 1610, very soon after Mrs Shelley's death, so unless Byrd worked remarkably quickly the purchase may have been made a little later.

179   See p. 378.

12 September 1606.[180] Among his bequests was one 'To my daughter Katheren the wife of m^r χρofer Bird tenne poundes'.

Byrd's thoughts must have been much preoccupied with human mortality at this time. In the dedication of his second book of *Gradualia* (1607) he wrote: 'I have seen many of my pupils in music, men indeed peculiarly skilful in that art, finish their alloted time while I survived'.[181] He was only in his early sixties, but he was plainly feeling his age.

'Ellen' Byrd was named at the Sessions of 2 October 1606,[182] but starting with the Sessions of 1-2 October 1607, when Christopher and his wife were the only members of the family to be mentioned, William Byrd's wife was no longer listed among the recusants.[183] It is possible that she was alive in April 1608, when 'Julian' was mentioned in connection with the Longney case, but Byrd is listed without his wife in an entry of 13 July 1609 in the Act books of the Archdeaconry Court.[184]

It is to be supposed that she was interred in the churchyard at Stondon Massey, as Byrd's will implies. The burial of Roman Catholics often posed problems for their families and for the church authorities. 'If the dead person had been a recusant, he or she had in principle died excommunicate, and so was not entitled to parish burial; in any event Catholics were not very willing to let the parson read the Anglican burial service over their dead'. This led to the practice, especially common before the Civil War, of burial between dusk and dawn, 'when the most distinctive visual feature of a Catholic funeral, the carrying of candles or tapers, must often have proved both useful and picturesque'.[185] But this was not universally so, and the burials of two of Byrd's staunchly Catholic servants were recorded without comment in the registers of their parish churches.[186]

It may be that immediately upon his wife's death Byrd left Stondon Place in Christopher's hands. He may in fact have done so earlier. This is suggested by the books of orders and decrees of the Court of Exchequer, which reveal that while the dispute with Mrs Shelley was going on Byrd was involved in another. On 9 February 1608/9 the court ordered that he should answer to an action *ejectio firmae* brought against him in the King's Bench by John Penney. The implication is that Penney

180   Probate copy: PRO, Prob. 11/108.
181   Translation from Strunk, 1952, p. 330.
182   Q/SR 177/96.
183   ERO, Q/SR 181/70.
184   ERO, D/AEA 25, f. 162^v.
185   Bossy, 1975, pp. 140-141. Reference kindly supplied by Mr Tony Scull, whose film about Byrd features such a funeral.
186   See pp. 64, 76.

was a tenant whom the Byrds were trying to eject before he considered the term of his tenancy to have expired. On 27 April it was decided that Christopher Byrd should plead to Penney's declaration, both because he was the 'Ejector' and because the court 'was informed this presente day that the sayde Willm̃ Birde dwelleth not upon the premisses'.[187] There is nothing to show where Byrd was. Although it is feasible that he stayed for a short time in the chamber set aside for him at Thorndon Hall, his name does not appear in the Petre accounts after June 1608.

The last of Byrd's individual dedications, attached to *Psalmes, songs, and sonnets* (1611), was to Francis Clifford, Earl of Cumberland. He was born at Skipton Castle in 1559, and held various offices in the north of England. In 1589 he married Grisold, the widow of the older Sir Edward Nevell ('The Deaf'), Lord Bergavenny. Grisold cannot have been the recipient of *My Ladye Nevells Booke*, completed in 1591, since she had married Clifford about 1589, but she links two families whom Byrd counted among his patrons.

The only keyboard music by Byrd to appear in print was given pride of place in *Parthenia*, 'COMPOSED By three famous Masters: William Byrd, Dʳ: John Bull, & Orlando Gibbons, Gentilmen of his Maᵗⁱᵉˢ: most Illustrious Chappell'. The approximate date of publication is established by the engraver's dedication to Princess Elizabeth and Prince Frederick, the Elector Palatine, on the occasion of their betrothal at the end of 1612. The book opens with a revised version, now equipped with a prelude, of Byrd's pavan and galliard bearing the name of Lord Petre's son William, which had been added, apparently as an afterthought, to *My Ladye Nevells Booke*. Among the other pieces by Byrd to be included in *Parthenia* were his last keyboard compositions, the pavan and two galliards marking the recent death of Lord Salisbury.

Lord Petre died at West Horndon on 11 October 1613. Byrd must assuredly have been among the mourners for the burial at Ingatestone, in the church of St Edmund and St Mary. The last that is heard of Byrd's music at Thorndon Hall is an inventory annotated in 1616:

A note of such musique bookes as are left by Rich: Mico in the little cubourd in ye drawing Roome

Imprˢ: 2 setts of mr Birds songes, Intituled Gradualia: on other sett named sacrū cantionū of 5 pts. An other sett of prickt Bookes, of 3, 4. 5 and 6 pts: It His last English sett, : His printed sett of 3 4. 5. and 6 parts;/ An othre

187   PRO, E124/5, f. 228ᵛ. The premises were referred to as 'Stondon ffarme', but this is identical with Stondon Place; E126/1, f. 113ᵛ (or 120ᵛ) refers to 'the ffearme called Stondon Place'. No other documents about this case have yet been found.

sett of bookes of 5 and 6 parts dedicated to my lord Lumley/ watsons sett of 4 5. and 6 parts. It one othre sett of prict bookes wth Black lethre Covres of 5 parts:[188]

No doubt Byrd watched the lives of his children with the alternate joy and sadness experienced by most parents. But he must have suffered a desolating blow with the death of his elder son, Christopher, in whose hands he had evidently hoped to leave Stondon Place. This probably occurred in 1615.[189] It seems likely that Christopher was buried at Stondon, near his mother.

Since a William Byrd received food and alms at the English College's hospice in Rome during November 1616, there is a temptation to think that Byrd's loss caused him to make a pilgrimage to that city.[190] But there is nothing to support the speculation that the traveller was the musician.

Byrd was mentioned in connection with the extraordinary, but extraordinarily modern-sounding, scheme outlined in 1620, for 'The Exercise of many Heroick and Majestick Recreations at his Maties. Amphitheatre'. It was put forward by John Cotton, John Williams and Thomas Dixon, who proposed to build (for about ten or eleven thousand pounds, plus another two thousand for furnishings) a 'house' which was to serve as an arena for sports, contests, military tattoos and pageants, and as a theatre, a concert and masquing hall, a pleasure garden, a bull ring — in short, a home for every imagineable spectacle, display and entertainment. There is no sign that the proposers consulted any of the people they intended to rope in, including 'ffor our severall kindes of Musicke, Mr Alphonso, M^r. Innocent Lanier, Mr Bird, M^r. Johnson, and others great M^rs. in Musick'.[191]

The scheme passed the signet, and a warrant was issued; but it was 'stayed at our Privie Seale'. Clearly the King had second thoughts, and felt the whole thing was getting out of hand. On 29 September he withdrew the warrant and ordered a new one to be prepared for his

---

188   ERO, D/DP E2/8. A note in a later hand has added: 'All wch were delivered into the charge of John Okes the xxviii^th of June 1616./ wth a set of viall*es*'. The reading 'Okes' is partly conjecture. The 'printed sett of 3, 4, 5 and 6 parts' is *Songs of sundrie natures*. The set dedicated to Lumley is *Liber secundus sacrarum cantionum*. Watson's set is *The first sett, of Italian madrigalls Englished*.

189   Christopher is mentioned in the Sessions records of Michaelmas 1614 (ERO, Q/SR 208/52). Those of Easter 1616 (Q/SR 213/52) refer to Katherine Byrd as a widow.

190   Foley, 1877-84, vi, p. 595.

191   Bodleian Library, MS Tanner 89, ff. 50^r-54a^r. 'Mr Alphonso': the son of Byrd's friend, the older Alfonso Ferrabosco. 'M^r. Johnson': the composer and lutenist Robert Johnson.

signature. The Earl of Pembroke, as Chamberlain of the Household, was deputed with others to interview the licensees and explain the King's pleasure.[192] The scheme apparently progressed no further.

Byrd's will shows that, to the end of his life, he had 'lodginge in the Earle of wosters howse in the straund'.[193] The fourth Earl of Worcester was Edward Somerset, whose son Sir Charles left inventories of an extensive collection of music books kept in the family's Strand home.[194] The part Byrd played in building this up can only be guessed at; it includes a wide-ranging selection of English and Italian music, and sacred works perhaps intended for Catholic use in the Earl's private chapel.

No record has yet been found of the deaths of Byrd's sisters, but his brother John died at the end of January 1621/2. The course of John's last illness can be traced all too easily in the progressively weaker signatures he added to his will and its codicils, the last of which is a mark witnessed by William Byrd.[195] The early seventeenth-century burial registers of St John Zachary no longer exist, but the churchwardens' accounts for the period Easter 1621 until Easter 1622 note the receipt of twelve pence, 'the guifte of Mr Burd who died in Mrs Stanninnat*es* house to thuse of the Churche'.[196]

William Byrd's own death is recorded in the Old Cheque Book of the Chapel Royal under the date 1623: 'Willm̃ Bird, a ffather of Musick died

192   Ibid., ff. 55a^{r-v}.

193   In the overseers' accounts for the parish of St Clement Danes, 1610-11, Worcester is listed under 'Noblemen and knightes', At a much later date (1641-42) the churchwardens' and overseers' accounts describe the Worcester home (presumably, at this time, that of Henry Somerset, Lord Herbert of Chepstow, created Marquess of Worcester 2 November 1642) as 'Beyond the Savoy', i.e. towards Whitehall Palace, an area where several noblemen lived. Under the heading 'Midle roe backstrete' the overseers' accounts for 1609-11 list a 'William Burd', but there is no indication that this was the composer; indeed, one might expect to find him among the 'Esquieres and gentlemen' if he was listed at all.

194   Brennan, 1993.

195   See pp. 388-389. The original signed document is stored by the Public Record Office in a box with other wills proved at about the same time. John's will is tied up in a bundle with the will of Walter Burre: a simple statement that he was very sick and left everything to his wife and daughter. On the back of it is the signature 'W: Byrde', which is presumably that of William Byrd (d.1639), the son of Sir William Byrd. He was custos or master of the Prerogative Court of Canterbury. (See Foster, 1891-92, p. 127.)

196   GL, MS 590/1, f. 99^v.

the iiij[th] of July, And John Croker, a conter ten[r] of Westminster was admitted y[e] 24th of December following'.[197]

In his will Byrd expressed a particular wish to be buried at Stondon, near his wife's grave. This was probably outside the church for whose upkeep he had refused to pay.[198] His injunction to his heirs, perhaps to ensure that the Catholic rites were observed, was to see him 'honestly buryed'.

197   Old Cheque Book, f. 7[r]; Rimbault, 1872, p. 10. Also, without the description of Byrd as a Father of Music, Bodleian Library MS Rawlinson D.318, f. 31[v].
198   ERO, D/AEA 26 f. 129[v], dated 1612. See pl. 8b.

6

SOURCES AND CHRONOLOGY OF BYRD'S MUSIC

No music manuscript in Byrd's hand is known to exist, but some two-thirds of his compositions are gathered in collections for which he was responsible. The printed compilations are *Cantiones, quae ab argumento sacrae vocantur* (1575), *Psalmes, sonets, & songs of sadnes and pietie* (1588), *Liber primus sacrarum cantionum* (1589), *Songs of sundrie natures* (1589), *Liber secundus sacrarum cantionum* (1591), *Gradualia: ac cantiones sacrae* (1605), *Gradualia: seu cantionum sacrarum* (1607), and *Psalmes, songs, and sonnets* (1611). A manuscript collection of keyboard music, *My Ladye Nevells Booke* (1591), is assumed to have been prepared under Byrd's supervision and was corrected by him.

There are in addition three printed Masses. These are undated, but Byrd is thought to have published them between 1592 and 1595. *A gratification unto Master John Case* (1589) is a printed madrigal of which only two parts have survived. A few more pieces were printed elsewhere. Nicholas Yonge's *Musica Transalpina* (1588) includes an adaptation of a piece published in *Psalmes, sonets, & songs* during the same year, Thomas Watson's *The first sett, of Italian madrigalls Englished* (1590) contains 'two excellent madrigalls of Master William Byrds', Thomas Morley printed one of Byrd's canons as an example in *A plaine and easie introduction to practicall musicke* (1597), and *Parthenia* (1612-13) contains eight pieces by Byrd, including revised versions of the 'Petre' pavan and galliard from *My Ladye Nevells Booke*.

These sources are of some help in dating the compositions they contain, but of course they provide only *termini ad quem*. All include music composed over extended periods, and some pieces were written as much as twenty years before their collection. The earlier manuscript sources of Byrd's music are similarly helpful as regards dating, but fewer than a dozen can be ascribed to the period before 1590, and no more than half of these were compiled before 1580. While a number of valuable studies have contributed to a better understanding of the chronology of Byrd's music,[1] the attempt to place his pieces in order has frequently to rely on hypotheses about their probable purpose and their connections with dateable events, and on intuitive judgements about style and Byrd's maturity as a composer.

---

1   *The Byrd Edition* and studies by Kerman (1961 and 1981), Neighbour (1978) and Monson (1979 and 1982) are particularly useful.

There is a further matter, bearing on the arrangement of the chapters which follow. It has been said that Byrd customarily undertook a composition with some special technical idea and aesthetic intention in mind, and wrote two closely similar pieces only when his first attempt had not done justice to his conception.[2] Although there are groups of works which display an interest in related problems of composition, or show Byrd's disposition to confer similar characteristics on different pieces, the observation is on the whole true. In consequence, there is not always an easily discernible line of development from one piece to the next. Even if more were known about the dates of Byrd's compositions than is at present the case, this would discourage an attempt to review his progress in all categories simultaneously. It might in addition be a trial for both author and reader to dodge backwards and forwards from one type of piece to another. Yet that is exactly what Byrd did as a composer. Tables 7 and 9 should serve as a corrective to any fragmentary view of Byrd's musical development which may be engendered by the division of the following survey into chapters dealing with one class of composition at a time.

2   Neighbour, 1971, p. 657.

Table 7 · Speculative chronology of Byrd's music to 1571

Not later than 1558 *Motets*: Similes illis fiant BE 8/2 · Alleluia. Confitemini Domino BE 8/1

Before about 1562 *Consort*: Sermone blando BE 17/23 · Christe qui lux es BE17/24-26 · Christe qui lux es BE 8/4 *for viols or voices* · Miserere BE 17/28 · 4-part In Nomines BE 17/16-17 · 5-part In Nomines BE 17/18-19 · Te lucis ante terminem BE 17/32-33 · Salvator mundi BE 17/29 · Sermone blando BE 17/30-31 *Keyboard*: Miserere MB 28/66-67 · Christe qui lux es MB 28/121 · Gloria tibi trinitas MB 28/50 · Salvator mundi MB 28/68-69

About 1562 or 1563 *Keyboard*: Clarifica me MB 28/47-49 · Ut mi re MB 28/65 · Two-part fantasia in C MB 27/28 *Consort*: Sermone blando BE 17/31 · Christe redemptor omnium BE 17/27 · 5-part In Nomines BE 17/20-22

About 1563 to the mid-1560s *Keyboard*: Fantasia in C-A MB 27/27 · Galliard Jig MB 17/18 · Hornpipe MB 27/39 · Wolsey's or Wilson's Wild MB27/37* · Grounds in G MB 27/9, g MB 28/86 and C MB 27/43 · The Gipsies' Round MB 28/80 *Anglican service music and psalms*: Five-part Litany BE 10a/4† · Second Preces† BE 10a/3a and psalms When Israel came out of Egypt, Hear my prayer, and Teach me O Lord‡ BE 10a/3b-d

The mid-1560s to about the end of 1571 *Keyboard*: Fantasia in G MB 28/62 · Prelude and fantasia in A MB 27/12-13 · The Maiden's Song MB 28/82 · Second ground † MB 27/42 *Consort*: Fantasia in F BE 17/11 · Prelude and ground BE 17/9‡ *Motets*: Libera me Domine de morta aeterna BE 1/17 · De Lamentatione Ieremiae prophetae BE 8/5 · O salutaris hostia BE 8/6 · Attollite portas‡ BE 1/5 · Dominum cum tribularer BE 8/7 · Domine quis habitat BE 8/8 · Tribue Domine BE 1/14-16 *Anthems*: How long shall mine enemies BE 11/3‡ · Out of the deep · Save me O God BE 11/9 · O Lord make thy servant Elizabeth BE 11/6‡ *Anglican service music and psalms*: First Preces BE 10a/1a-b and psalms O clap your hands, Save me O God‡ BE 10a/2b-c · Unnumbered Preces and Responses BE 10a/1a-b · Short Service BE 10a/5a-g · Second 'Verse' Service‡ BE 10a/6a-b · Third Service BE 10a/7a-b

*Date very uncertain   †Possibly earlier   ‡Possibly later

7

EARLIEST VOCAL MUSIC

On 17 November 1558 the Catholic Queen Mary died and was succeeded by the Protestant Queen Elizabeth. William Byrd was then eighteen or nineteen years old. Evidence that he was already sufficiently skilled to have collaborated with older and more experienced composers is found in a set of part-books that once belonged to a Dr Gyffard.[1] Since the books' repertoire consists largely of liturgical pieces designed for the Sarum Use, which was discarded on Mary's death, the bulk of their contents can be assigned to her reign (though one of the composers, John Taverner, died before she came to the throne).[2]

The Gyffard part-books are the source of *Similes illis fiant*, which they ascribe to 'mr birde'. This forms the second section of a collaborative four-voice setting of the psalm *In exitu Israel*, in which contrapuntal passages alternate with chant. The first section is by John Sheppard, a Gentleman of the Chapel Royal who died in 1558.[3] The

1   On the Gyffard part-books (BL Additional MSS 17802-5) see Bray, 1969; Mateer, 1993; and Mateer, 1995.

2   The diocesan Use of Salisbury was commonly regarded as the normative English secular use. See Harper, 1991, pp. 202-216.

3   Sheppard was a member of the Chapel Royal by 1553. (Ashbee, 1986-96, vii, p. 124.) He was buried at St Margaret's, Westminster, on 21 December 1558. (Burke, 1914, p. 401; Wulstan, 1994.) Sheppard's influence on Byrd may have been deeper than is sometimes realized. (Turbet, 1993(b), p. 15.) Thomas Whythorne, writing in his personal system of orthography at some time after July 1592, bracketed Sheppard, Tallis and Byrd as 'Ðe most famowz miuzisians in þis tým'. (Whythorne, 1961, p. 302 and plate facing p. 300.) When Whythorne was at Magdalen College, Oxford, in 1542 Sheppard was instructor of the choristers. It was possibly Sheppard's son Nathan who was responsible for educating the younger William Petre. ('Nathan shepard my sonne' is mentioned in Sheppard's will: probate copy in Westminster Archives Centre, Accession 120, 188 Bracy, ff. 146ʳ⁻ᵛ. For his association with Petre during the period December 1580 to September 1581 see the Petre accounts, ERO, D/DP A19, under 'wages & lyvᵗyes'.) The evidence given to the Privy Council by George Elliot in 1581 names Nathan Sheppard as a schoolmaster (and a priest), and this is confirmed by Sessions rolls of 1581-1584 which record his failure to attend church, and gifts made by William Petre to 'Nathan my oulde schoole mastₑr'. (BL, Lansdowne MS 33, ff. 145-9; ERO, Q/SR 78/46, 79/75, 79/100, 80/78, 83/50, 88/48, 90/53, 90/54; ERO, D/DP A33; ERO, T/A/174.) Nathan Sheppard's relationship to Nicholas Sheppard, Sir John Petre's chamberlain, is unknown. For more about his career see Dr David Mateer's forthcoming

third is by William Mundy, who in the reign of Queen Mary was the parish clerk of St Mary at Hill.[4] The knowledge that Byrd was born in 1540, and not 1543 as thought until now, relieves doubt about whether even a gifted boy could have worked with these older composers.[5]

Similes illis fiant (BE 8/2) was intended to be sung during the daily procession of the fonts in Easter week, when it would have been preceded by a setting of the words 'Alleluia. Laudate pueri'. These are combined with words from the Mass on Holy Saturday in the motet *Alleluia. Confitemini Domino* (BE 8/1), which seemingly began life as two separate Alleluia settings for three voices.[6] The liturgical purpose means that this too was written during Queen Mary's reign, and two sources name the composer as William Byrd.[7]

Both *Similes illis fiant* and *Alleluia. Confitemini Domino* proclaim the hand of an apprentice composer. Harmonic organization is rudimentary, though this is partly due to the brevity of the pieces and, in the case of *Similes illis fiant*, to the cantus firmus in the bass.[8] Melodic inspiration is

article *William Byrd, John Petre and Oxford, Bodleian MS Mus. Sch. E.423.*

4   See p. 25.

5   See, for example, the doubts expressed by Harrison, 1980, p. 289. Tests reported by Morehen (1992) cast doubt on the authenticity of *Similes illis fiant*, but it would be no surprise if a student working with two older composers, and perhaps helped by them, produced a piece which failed tests based on his more mature work. Though a misattribution is not impossible, no other musician named Byrd is known as a composer. Morehen (p. 62) acknowledges that the influence of Gregorian chant on the piece could have affected the test results.

6   The term 'motet' was defined by Morley (1597, p. 179; 1952 ed., pp. 292-294) as 'a song made for the church, either upon some hymne or Anthem, or such like ... under which I comprehend all grave and sober musicke'. The broad sense was the one understood by Martin Peerson, who in 1630 published settings of Fulke Greville's poems as *Mottects or Grave Chamber Musique*. The narrower modern use of the word, employed here, means a polyphonic setting of a sacred Latin text, but was 'hardly used by English composers of their Latin works'. (Caldwell, 1991, p. 375.) Byrd published collections of his motets under the title 'sacred songs' (*Cantiones sacrae*).

7   Christ Church, Oxford, Mus. MS 45, dating from the late sixteenth century, and BL MS R.M. 24.d.2, into which John Baldwin apparently copied *Alleluia. Confitemini Domino* before 1591. An early seventeenth-century source, BL Additional MSS 18936-9, simply has 'Mr Byrd'. Morehen supports the authenticity of *Alleluia. Confitemini Domino*.

8   The cantus firmus is a faburden, i.e. an ornamented counterpoint to the chant, deriving from the mediaeval practice of singing an improvised bass below it. *In exitu Israel* contains fourteen statements of the cantus firmus, so that the work is in effect a set of fourteen variations, with Sheppard, the senior partner, supplying seven, and Byrd and

often lacking. Yet, in spite of perceptible shortcomings, contemporaries must have been struck by qualities in these pieces that for us are eclipsed by Byrd's later achievements. The occurrence of *Alleluia. Confitemini Domino* in three comparatively early manuscripts is remarkable, given the few that have survived.

Byrd's ambition at least is manifest. Although in writing *Similes illis fiant* he took suggestions from his collaborators – especially Mundy, whose contribution was plainly finished before Byrd set to work – their sections of *In exitu Israel* offered no model for the younger composer's combination in his middle verse of the cantus firmus with a unison canon and a free canon.[9] (Ex. 1) There are canons too in the first, third and fourth sections of *Alleluia. Confitemini Domino*.

Two further works must be mentioned briefly at this point. One is a five-part setting of the chant *Christe qui lux es* (BE 8/4). As this is closely related to a group of pieces more probably intended for instruments, it is discussed in the the next chapter.[10] The other is the motet *Christus resurgens* (BE 6b/2). Although Byrd published it in his *Gradualia* of 1606, the first part embodies a version of the plainsong which was published in 1558. Kerman suggested that this passage may have been an early composition to which the composer later added a more accomplished second part.[11] His view has held sway until comparatively recently, when an alternative suggestion has been put forward that the whole composition is a late one deliberately written in an archaic style.[12] The issue may never be decided beyond doubt, but it will be convenient to defer discussion for the moment and to consider the piece in the context of the publication in which it appeared.[13]

Mundy three and four respectively.

9   In a strict canon a voice entering after another imitates it exactly, either at the same or a different pitch. The intervals of the second voice may be altered in a free canon, for example to avoid non-key notes.

10   See p. 163.

11   Kerman, 1981, pp. 62-64.

12   le Huray, 1992, p. 23.

13   See p. 330.

Ex. 1

Similes illis fiant (middle section)

8

INSTRUMENTAL WORKS WITH CANTUS FIRMI

Byrd's earliest instrumental compositions are likely to be those which most clearly reflect his tuition in writing counterpoint against a cantus firmus derived from plainchant. This was not so dry an academic exercise as it seems, for in Byrd's boyhood chant was a living thing. He and his brothers must have heard and sung chant melodies every day after they became choristers. Many of his own melodies betray the lasting influence of chant. His earliest lessons at the keyboard are likely to have involved playing plainsong melodies. He would have progressed in time to the improvisation of counter-melodies and to the writing down of contrapuntal pieces of greater complexity, and so to more polished work in the same vein.[1] The survival of several such exercises may be due to Byrd's care, apparent throughout his life, for the preservation of his music. Yet precisely where they lie in relation to *Similes illis fiant* and *Alleluia. Confitemini Domino* − or, for that matter, to each other − is not easy to say.

Two seemingly very early pieces, taking the *Sermone blando* chant as a cantus firmus, were evidently intended for instruments.[2] In the first (BE 17/23) Byrd added two freely imitative voices to the slow notes of the cantus firmus. In the second he added two parts forming a canon at the seventh. These may be a student's tasks, but the new parts are shaped with an eye on repetitions in the chant melody, and achieve a well-regulated intensification of activity within a short span. Even more interesting at this stage of his development, particularly in pieces with a primarily technical purpose, are hints of the dance-like character that so often appears in Byrd's mature music.

Byrd's instrumental pieces are usually assumed to have been written for a viol consort if they were not intended for the keyboard, though the term 'textless' is a more accurate characterization of much that is now

---

1   It is more than likely that Byrd studied some of the theoretical writings of his age as well. He probably knew BL Lansdowne MS 763, a copy of *Musica Guidonis* and other musical treatises, signed by Tallis and taken by him from Waltham Abbey on its dissolution in 1540. He is almost certain to have known some of the authorities listed by Morley at the end of *A plaine and easie introduction to practicall musicke* (1597), and would have had no difficulty with works written in Latin.

2   The ranges of the added parts and the octave leaps they contain are characteristic of instrumental music.

termed 'consort' music.[3] It cannot be certain in every case that Byrd had a specific medium in mind, and it is noticeable that, as a student, he wrote many more 'abstract' pieces than he wrote for voices or keyboard instruments. Most of them are nevertheless suitable for viols. The viol was already well known in England when, in 1540, Henry VIII added to his secular musical establishment a group of foreigners who played bowed instruments, and who continued to serve his successors.[4] By the mid-century an ensemble of viols of different sizes had become a standard musical resource. Since Chapel Royal composers were prominent among those who pioneered new genres with the viol consort in mind, it is to be supposed that the Chapel musicians as well as their secular counterparts were able to play the music they wrote. Indeed, as the secular musicians increasingly resorted to the livelier violin, music for viol consort may have tended to become the preserve of the Chapel Royal.

Among Byrd's early settings are several of the hymn *Christe qui lux es*, which show the influence of five groups written as an exercise by Robert White, his slightly older contemporary.[5] It is quite possible that the two young composers knew each other, since White seems to have grown up in the parish of St Andrew's, Holborn. Byrd in any case knew White's music well, and it is tempting to think that they may have studied together and kept in touch.[6]

Byrd's instrumental settings of *Christe qui lux es* include three printed as BE 17/24, and one printed as BE 17/26. The incipit 'Precamur' in the sources of three more settings (BE 17/25) is from the second stanza of the hymn, and suggests that the pieces of this group were intended to serve as even-numbered stanzas, and to be played between vocal performances of the odd-numbered stanzas. The possibility that Byrd may have had in mind alternative performance by voices, perhaps with odd-numbered stanzas being played on the organ, means that they are printed additionally as BE 8/3.

A *Christe qui lux es* in five parts (BE 8/4) is omitted from the only source to include all Byrd's consort versions, but its connection with White's settings is equally clear.[7] It is written almost entirely in

---

3   Doe, 1979-88, i, p. xviii.

4   Ashbee, 1986-96, vi-vii, passim; Holman, 1993, pp. 78-122, 123-124.

5   Byrd's indebtedness to White is detailed by Neighbour, 1978, pp. 53-56.

6   'Dotted Crotchet' (1905) mentions White's residence in Holborn, but his source may have been destroyed in the Second World War. It is not impossible that White initially sang in one of the London choirs, although he was a chorister at Trinity College, Cambridge, by 1554. (Mateer, 1974.)

7   The collection of consort settings is in Bodleian Library MSS Tenbury 354-358.

unmeasured note against note harmony, and looks even more like a student exercise than the consort settings. The omission of the first and last verses means that the cantus firmus is set five times, once in each voice. Byrd's addition of a short Amen confirms that the piece had no liturgical purpose.[8]

Two *Miserere* settings in four parts (BE 17/28) must also be among the earlier of Byrd's consort pieces, but they already show something of the gravity that complements the popular element in his music. Among the features suggesting an early date, to which Neighbour draws attention, are the unorthodox treatment of dissonances in the first setting and the harmonization of the final as the fifth of the last chord – something that occurs elsewhere among Byrd's instrumental chant settings only in the second verse of *Christe qui lux es*, BE 17/24.[9]

Another pair of *Miserere* settings (MB 28/66-67) survives in the earliest source of keyboard music by Byrd.[10] Like his other keyboard settings of plainsong antiphons and hymns, they were almost certainly intended for the organ. This is borne out by their suitability for the instrument, the sources in which they appear, and similar music written by Byrd's older contemporaries. The plainsong-based organ music that Byrd would have studied and played as a boy is fairly well known, thanks to the survival of a sizeable amount.[11] In the absence of any alternative tradition, organ composers continued to base their music on the Sarum chants which, in pre-Elizabethan times, had served as the foundation of more or less independent pieces within the liturgical scheme.

In the Chapel Royal, besides his master Thomas Tallis, Byrd knew the notable organ composer John Blitheman and must have come into contact with others of an older generation. At St Paul's his brothers had sung with Philip ap Rhys, who doubled as an organist and composer. But it was another musician of St Paul's, the organist, composer and almoner John Redford, whose music made the deepest impression on Byrd.[12] This is evident in the first organ *Miserere*, which embellishes the plainsong and adds a single matching contrapuntal line. Although it finishes awkwardly, 'Byrd shows the same feeling for melodic continuity as

The only source for BE 8/4 is Christ Church, Oxford, Mus. MSS 984-988, which adds a note referring to the setting by White that Byrd imitated.

8   Kerman (1981, p. 33) describes it as 'positively anti-liturgical'.

9   Neighbour, 1978, p. 53.

10   Christ Church, Oxford, MS Mus. 371, probably dating from the 1570s.

11   See Caldwell, 1965(b); Caldwell, 1965(c); Stevens, 1969; Neighbour, 1978, pp. 101-106.

12   Byrd was just old enough to remember Redford, who died in 1547.

Redford, the same understanding of the possibilities of melodic sequence, and the same urge to shape the whole piece entirely by melodic gradation'.[13] The second setting places the chant in long notes in the upper part, while two more parts provide a competent but slightly plodding counterpoint.

An anonymous keyboard *Christe qui lux es* (MB 28/121) appears in close proximity to Byrd's *Miserere* settings, and has a stylistic affinity with the second. It can be attributed to Byrd on the strength of its strong resemblance to the first verse of his second consort setting (BE 17/25). It also reflects a knowledge of Redford's setting of the chant. (Ex. 2, overleaf.)[14]

Growing maturity

A new stage in Byrd's progress may have been reached when he turned to the consort In Nomine, which required the setting of a considerably longer cantus firmus than those used in his other instrumental pieces. The In Nomine was cultivated only in Britain, and was derived from John Taverner's Mass based on the *Gloria tibi trinitas* chant. Taverner's setting of words beginning 'In nomine Domini' in the Benedictus was the only section of his Mass to contain the whole plainsong melody, which was set out in notes of equal length in duple time, with three added parts. It came to be circulated as an independent piece, and served as a model for dozens of compositions on the same cantus firmus for more than a century and a half.[15]

Byrd probably intended his four-part In Nomines (BE 17/16-17) to form a pair, since one begins with a series of descending notes and the other begins with a series of rising notes. Both betray his close study of Taverner's original.[16] He copied Taverner in placing the chant in the part

13   Neighbour, 1978, p. 108.

14   Redford's setting is no. 31 in Thomas Mulliner's collection (BL, Additional MS 30513), which also contains another setting by Redford 'with a meane'. The anonymous keyboard piece is printed in full as no. 34 in Caldwell, 1965(b). The attribution to Byrd is suggested by Brown, 1974 (also Brown, 1976, revised 1985 reprint, p. 211), and Neighbour, 1978, p. 101. Neighbour mentions the possibility of an alternative attribution to White, who is also represented in the manuscript, but plumps for Byrd.

15   See Dart and Donington, 1949; Reese, 1949.

16   Byrd's In Nomines are examined by Neighbour, 1978, pp. 26-50, in the context of contributions to the genre by his predecessors and contemporaries. One of the two sources for BE 17/16 ascribes it to 'Mr Parsons', but Neighbour (p. 85) dismisses doubts about Byrd's authorship.

Ex. 2

a. Redford: beginning of *Christe qui lux es*

b. Byrd(?): beginning of *Christe qui lux es*

second from the top, so allowing himself freedom to shape both the upper and lower outlines. The exact notes of Taverner's opening point occur, with some rhythmic alteration, in the second treble entry of BE 17/16. The belief that it may thus be the first of Byrd's In Nomines is supported by his decision to revise the ending.[17] It is interesting that both the revised and unrevised versions of this youthful piece were in circulation. The revised version shows Byrd once again working on lines similar to those followed by Robert White. Byrd's new ending borrows from a passage in Christopher Tye's In Nomine *Rachel's weeping*, while

17   The weaker, and therefore probably earlier, ending is printed by Elliott, 1971, p. 160.

one of White's In Nomines borrows from the corresponding portion of Tye's In Nomine *Weep no more Rachel.*

The second four-part In Nomine is not so close to Taverner's model as its companion. The opening point and its continuation illustrate two features that were to recur in Byrd's work – his 'propensity, shared by no other composer, to introduce symmetrical periods reminiscent of secular melody into contrapuntal contexts',[18] and his penchant for writing tunes that gently rise and fall, as if under the influence of plainsong but often possessing a slightly greater range than chant melodies. (Ex. 3.)

Ex. 3

In Nomine, BE 17/17

A series of settings of *Te lucis ante terminem* (BE 17/32-33) consists of twelve four-part pieces. Together they make up the number which often formed a single set, although the sources present them as groups of eight and four. Only one is complete, but another can be reconstructed without too much difficulty.[19] As they stand there is little to distinguish their style from the three-part *Sermone blando* settings and the settings of *Christe qui lux es*, but they are clearly later than those very early pieces, even if the diversity of Byrd's more mature variations is missing. The group is uneven in quality, but the one complete setting demonstrates his ability to overcome the limitations of the cantus firmus by writing added parts that are contrapuntally interesting and by his exercise of harmonic

18   Neighbour, 1978, p. 38.
19   BL Additional MS 29246 contains all twelve settings but in a lute intabulation that omits the top parts. The tenth setting survives complete in Bodleian Library MSS Tenbury 354-358. Reconstruction of the fifth is possible because the missing part is the plainsong.

control. The number of settings reflects the fertility of Byrd's invention and his growing confidence.

Two four-part settings of *Salvator mundi* (BE 17/29) and three four-part settings of *Sermone blando* (BE 17/30) are again incomplete,[20] but the missing upper part of the latter group carried the plainsong and can be reconstructed. All the pieces making up the two sets are in a more elaborate melodic style than Byrd's earlier plainsong variations.

Byrd had tackled the composition of a five-part piece in one of his settings of *Christe qui lux es*. Therefore it cannot be assumed that his first five-part instrumental works represent a progression from those in four parts, though it is feasible. One of the five-part In Nomines attributed to Byrd (BE 17/18) is undistinguished, and could well be an early essay. Its authorship is nevertheless a matter of doubt. The piece differs from the five-part In Nomines that are unquestionably by Byrd, in having the cantus firmus in the top part and ending with a *tripla* section.[21] The scribe of the single source at first wrote the composer's name as 'm^r Mundye' before crossing it out and substituting Byrd's name.[22]

The other five-part In Nomines may have been composed in the order in which they appear in the only complete manuscript set.[23] Signs of Byrd's rapid development at least make this a fair supposition. BE 17/19 is Byrd's first response to the intensely imitative style which had developed in the composition of In Nomines, and is a world away from BE 17/18. Its confidence, character and force are immediately audible, and leave little doubt about the reasons for the composer's appointment to a post at Lincoln. But he was still working with other composers' models at his elbow. In this case he drew on Tye's In Nomine *Seldom seen*, from which White too had borrowed.[24] The remaining five-part In Nomines (BE 17/20-22) are dealt with below.

There is no way of deciding with absolute confidence where Byrd's keyboard works of this period fit into the sequence of his consort pieces. The spirit of Redford still hovered close while he was working on his two-part organ setting of *Gloria tibi trinitas* (MB 28/50). The composition has something in common with his two-part *Miserere*, but the ornate upper melodic line and a proportional change place it nearer

---

20   They occur only in BL Additional MS 29246. See the previous note.

21   A *tripla* section is one where a proportional change results in the equivalent of three crotchets being played in the time given to a minim in the preceding section.

22   BL Additional MS 31390, compiled c.1578.

23   The set occurs in Bodleian Library MSS Mus. Sch. d. 212-218, without BE 17/18, but Byrd's pieces are not entered consecutively.

24   Neighbour, 1978, p. 42.

to the first of his settings of *Clarifica me Pater*, which seems likely to have been written shortly before he went to Lincoln.

The last pieces with cantus firmi

Before Byrd embarked on *Clarifica me Pater*, he may have made two keyboard settings of *Salvator mundi* (MB 28/68-69). The first quotes directly from one of Blitheman's six settings of *Gloria tibi trinitas*, suggesting that the pieces were written after 1558, when Blitheman joined the Chapel Royal.[25] But as Blitheman's style is too remote from Byrd's for it to have affected him after he left London, it is fairly certain that Byrd's pieces were written before 1563. Their harmonic language in fact indicates that they were among the latest of Byrd's plainsong settings for the organ.[26]

In setting the *Misere* and *Salvator mundi* chants for organ Byrd chose to write pairs of pieces — at least they were available as pairs to their copyists. In making settings of *Clarifica me* (MB 28/47-49) he extended the number of pieces to three: one with two voices in D, another with three voices and the chant transposed to A, and the last with four voices in D again.[27] Byrd's model may have been Tallis's three *Clarifica me* settings for keyboard, though all are in D, and all are for four voices. Two of Byrd's pieces are however connected with other keyboard works by Tallis. One of these is a *Felix namque* which Tregian dates 1562.[28] It provides both the earliest known example of the proportional time changes adopted by Byrd in his first two settings, and a passage echoed in the second.[29]

The relationship between Byrd's third *Clarifica me* and a piece by Tallis is a different one. Around the chant melody Byrd weaves a

25   Blitheman was among the musicians at Queen Mary's funeral. (Ashbee, 1986-96, vi, p. 2.) The note values of Blitheman's piece are halved by Stevens (1954, no. 92, bars 25-26).

26   Neighbour, 1978, p. 107.

27   The *Clarifica me* settings follow the *Salvator mundi* pair in BL Additional MS 30485. If the copyist was Thomas Weelkes, who may have been a pupil of Byrd, the groupings have a special authority. (See Brown, 1976, ii, p. 198.)

28   *Fitzwilliam Virginal Book*, no [CIX]. It is convenient to refer to Tregian as the copyist of the *Fitzwilliam Virginal Book*, despite questions about his part in its compilation. See p. 362, note 25.

29   Neighbour, 1978, p. 109. It is a pity that the original proportional notation of Byrd's *Clarifica me* settings was not retained in the *Musica Britannica* edition, since it makes it easier to see how the number of 'crotchets' to a semibreve in the added parts increases from four to six and then to nine.

contrapuntal web in three sections, basing each section on its individual point of imitation. In length the sections are roughly in the proportions 1:2:3. Despite the constraints of the chant, Byrd ends each of the outer sections on D, while the central one reaches a cadence a fifth lower on G. A fantasia-like piece by the older composer, based on *Alleluia. Per te*, also consists of three sections with lengths in the proportions 1:2:3, which reach cadences on A, E and A.[30] It would be hard to say which composer copied the other, since they developed the plan in separate ways. Tallis's piece grows entirely out of the opening point; the melody maintains its overall shape and an emphasis on E and A, while expanding in length and range.[31] Byrd would have been familiar with that sort of melodic transformation in the work of other composers, and used it in his slightly later fantasia in G.[32] But his third *Clarifica me* depends instead on a contrast between the sections, combined with a gradual thickening of the texture and an upper melodic outline that rises progressively higher.

The keyboard piece known as *Ut mi re* (MB 28/65) stands somewhere between Byrd's cantus firmus pieces and the keyboard variations to which he was shortly to turn. A case could easily be made for grouping it with the grounds of his Lincoln period.[33] It is however linked to the organ antiphons and hymns by its strong modal characteristics, and conveys the impression that it was written under the influence of both Blitheman and Tallis. The title of the piece comes from the hexachordal names of the three notes with which it begins.[34] Byrd's 'theme' is a curiously mechanical ordering of its notes (Ex. 4), treated simultaneously as a melodic subject and as a ground that is stated fourteen times.

30   The proportions may betray a lingering mediaeval outlook, for they are found as a principle of construction in English music as far back as that of John Dunstable (d. c.1453). Tallis's cantus firmus is explicit in the version of his piece in Christ Church, Oxford, Mus. MS 371, from which Byrd's *Misere* settings come. The version in Christ Church, Oxford, Mus. MS 1034 has lost the cantus firmus at the beginning. The same cantus firmus appears transposed in a piece with the title *Alleluia* attributed to Bull by Messaus. (BL, Additional MS 23623.) Cunningham (1984, pp. 74) identifies the chant.

31   Harley, 1992-94, ii, p. 16.

32   The earliest known secular keyboard piece to depend upon this procedure is a hornpipe by Hugh Aston, which Byrd's own hornpipe resembles.

33   Turbet (1992(b), p. 18) is inclined to do so.

34   A hexachord consisted of six notes with the whole-tone and semitone intervals between them arranged in the order T T S T T. There were several overlapping hexachords, but the notes of each were called by the syllables *ut re mi fa sol la*. The absolute position of any note was defined by its positions in all the hexachords containing it, e.g. middle C was *sol fa ut*. The hexachord was a standard cantus firmus.

Ex. 4

Theme of *Ut mi re*

Since statements of the theme coincide with sections of the piece, the result is in effect a set of variations. It looks very much like an essay in which Byrd presented himself with an interesting compositional problem without solving it wholly satisfactorily, though even comparative failure does not conceal his enquiring mind.[35] He excluded *Ut mi re* from *My Ladye Nevells Booke* in favour of the mature hexachord composition *Ut re mi fa sol la* (MB 28/64). Yet at some stage they were coupled together. The coupling is indicated in the *Fitzwilliam Virginal Book* (the only source for *Ut mi re*), where the later piece is placed first and the word 'Perge' (continue) is written after it.[36]

Byrd returned to the *Sermone blando* chant for two four-part consort settings (BE 17/31) that must have a place among his later pieces for the medium. His skill and the imaginative handling of imitation are more apparent than in his other settings. He delays the entry of the cantus firmus, but since its first few notes are used as the initial point of imitation it is immediately drawn into the melodic scheme. There is more subtlety too in Byrd's approach to harmony, with an increased number of inversions than heretofore, and a greater variety of suspensions over a greater range of bass notes.[37]

Byrd's development as a composer is still more marked in two four-part settings for consort of *Christe redemptor* (BE 17/27), in which the major key of the first is contrasted with the minor key of the second. Here the plainsong melody (the highest part) is elaborated so that it participates in the imitation between the other parts. The decoration of

35   The piece is discussed at length by Neighbour, 1978, pp. 230-232.

36   Another *Ut re mi fa sol la* (MB 28/58) is attributed to Byrd by Tomkins, who describes it as 'a good lesson'. (Bibliothèque Nationale, Paris Conservatoire Réserve 1122.) It was apparently written for a pupil, and must date from later in Byrd's career. The cantus firmus is 'To Be playd By a second person'. The principal keyboard part is interesting for introducing the tunes of two popular songs − 'The Woods so Wild' (bars 25-41) and 'The Shaking of the Sheets' (bars 42 to the end) − but it shows none of Byrd's usual attention to overall structure.

37   Neighbour, 1978, p. 59.

the plainsong and its incorporation into the imitative structure lead the way to the free fantasia. (Ex. 5.)

Ex. 5

Christe redemptor (BE 17/27)

Byrd's latest instrumental compositions based on cantus firmi include the three five-part In Nomines BE 17/20-22. The mood of BE 17/20 is deceptive, for its serenity hides a concentration of imitative activity. Again Byrd demonstrates his alertness to the work of others. The opening point is adapted from one of three five-part In Nomines by the young Italian composer Alfonso Ferrabosco, who was Byrd's junior by three years and had probably arrived in England about the beginning of 1562.[38] Since Byrd was in Lincoln at the beginning of 1562/3, BE 17/20

---

38   Ferrabosco was baptized at Bologna on 18 January 1542/3. A warrant for his payment at the English court is dated 28 March 1562, so he had probably been there for a matter of months. (Charteris, 1981; Ashbee, 1986-96, vi, p. 84.)

may have been written during the previous year. Byrd obviously found things that interested him in Ferrabosco's music, although as a foreigner Ferrabosco was bound to be less familiar than he with the problems of writing In Nomines, which were unknown outside Britain. As it happened, Ferrabosco was also considerably less gifted, despite the fame he was to acquire. Perhaps Byrd was fascinated by a trace of the exotic.[39]

Another of Ferrabosco's In Nomines provided the inspiration for BE 17/21, and Byrd can be seen adapting and improving the Italian's work as he later adapted and improved other composers' keyboard pieces.[40] Byrd's first point is an inversion of Ferrabosco's, and in the later bars he was inspired by Ferrabosco's rapid scalar motives. But Byrd's firmer grasp of structural principles is combined with a greater flexibility apparent in his handling of imitation, and with a wider-ranging expressivity.

The impressive stride forward represented by BE 17/22 argues a period of reflection after the composition of BE 17/21.[41] Its discussion

39   Byrd and Ferrabosco clearly struck up a friendship, but it is difficult to date their competition described by Morley: a 'virtuous contention in love', a contest 'betwixt themselves, made upon the plainsong Miserere'. (Morley, 1597, p. 115; 1952 ed., p. 202.) Ferrabosco left England a number of times for short periods, and left for good about the end of 1577, dying at Bologna in 1588. There is no sign of Byrd's writing plainsong-based pieces after his return from Lincoln in 1572, so the contest may have taken place shortly after he met Ferrabosco, but this cannot be certain. Thomas Robinson's edition of forty canons on *Miserere* by Byrd and Ferrabosco was not licensed for publication until 1603. (See the entry for *Medulla Musicke* in Arber, 1875-94, iii, p. 247.) There are sets of similar pieces. Twenty of Thomas Woodson's 'Forty wayes of 2. pts in one' on the Miserere chant are in BL Additional MS 29996 (with the misleading note 'The rest of these wayes: are prickt In mr: morleys Introduction'). Two sets found their way into print. John Farmer's *Forty several ways of two parts in one made upon a playne song* was published in 1591, and dedicated to Edward de Vere, the Earl of Oxford. William Bathe's *A briefe introduction to the skill of song ... In which work is set downe X. sundry wayes of 2. parts in one upon the plaine songe* is undated but was entered at Stationers' Hall in 1596. No copy is known of Robinson's publication, however, and it may never have appeared. One of Byrd's canons (BE 16/32, probably not from those which Robinson intended to publish) was printed by Morley (1597, p. 103; 1952, pp. 185-186). BE 16/33 is the only one of a number of other canons attributed to Byrd (outside those occurring within larger compositions) which is thought to be genuine.

40   The assumption that Ferrabosco's In Nomine was the earlier depends on Byrd's apparent reaction to features arising from Ferrabosco's Italian training, and Byrd's avoidance of weaknesses in Ferrabosco's piece.

41   Neighbour (1978, p. 62) suggests that BE 17/22 may be later than Byrd's six-part fantasia in F.

here is guided more by literary convenience than certainty that it was composed in London. Wherever the piece was composed, Byrd could have had the Chapel Royal musicians in mind as performers. Doe floats the idea that until about 1575 the In Nomine was less a kind of privately played music than something professionally performed on ceremonial occasions or when a degree of formality was called for.[42] The Chapel musicians would have been well placed to supply such music, both as composers and players. There is no sign that anything of the sort was needed or could have been played at Lincoln.[43]

BE 17/22 was quickly recognized as an exceptional work, and it survives in no fewer than fourteen manuscripts completed by the mid-seventeenth century.[44] In writing it Byrd drew on In Nomines by Robert Parsons and Thomas Tallis.[45] Its construction is extremely skilful, and a brief examination (Table 8) may help to illuminate Byrd's mode of thought, as long as sight is not lost of the expressive intention which guides the development of his ideas. It was surely to this that his contemporaries responded.

Table 8 · Structure of five-part In Nomine (BE 17/22)

BE 17/22 falls into five sections, each of some ten or a dozen bars.

The first section contains the seeds of the whole piece. Above the cantus firmus (second part from the top) Byrd creates an eight-bar melody of singular poise and beauty, to which the lower parts respond. Its rising sixth was probably borrowed from the first point of Parsons' seven-part In Nomine. This interval occurs three times − the second time with an interposed note − in the second bar of each half of the melody and in its four-bar 'coda', and emphasizes the melodic peak f". At the end of the coda the rising sixth is echoed by a rising fifth. In each case the interval leads to a figure composed of a dotted minim and falling notes derived from the beginning of the piece, and forming a principal motive of the imitation. This

---

42   Doe, 1979-88, i, p. xx.

43   There is doubt about the duration of the vogue for textless polyphony which existed in the first ten or fifteen years of Queen Elizabeth's reign. It may have been largely over by the mid-1570s, when some of the principal composers had died (Parsons, and perhaps Tye, in 1572; White in 1574).

44   Two of them, BL Additional MS 31390 and Bodleian Library MS Mus. Sch. e.423, can be dated c.1578 and c.1580 respectively.

45   Detailed by Neighbour, 1978, pp. 46-49, and Turbet, 1988, footnote 1.

Table 8 *concluded*

figure is doubled at the third, tenth or sixth on five of its appearances, and underlines the homophony which becomes an important element of the last section.

Section 2 (from bar 13) employs a point that contrasts with the opening melody in its brevity. It is drawn rhythmically from the motive repeated throughout the first section, but the dotted minim is here followed by a group of rising notes. The melodic peak of the upper part, which is not exceeded until the last section of the piece, is g".

The third section (from bar 24) starts with three emphatic F natural minims doubled at the tenth. They gain particular emotional force from the preceeding F sharp and the leap of a major seventh by which they are reached. The minims are doubled again halfway through the section, and a homophonic tendency appears in the doubling of other figures. Retrospective references appear in dotted notes and rising and falling motives.

The top part of the fourth section (from bar 35) contains a passing reference (bar 37) to material that occurs at the same place in Parsons' popular five-part In Nomine. This section is however concerned largely with motives containing three crotchets that link it to the first and second sections.

In the final section (from bar 45) a figure of three crotchets and a minim in the top part is immediately overlapped below by the same figure in three-part chords, explicitly acknowledging Parsons' five-part In Nomine. A quotation from Tallis also occurs in this section (bars 49-51). Having firmly established B flat as the tonality in which the section begins, Byrd moves rapidly through harmonies that carry him to a long series of alternating chords of G and D, until finally settling on D as the original tonic. Simultaneously, the rapid imitation in the treble and bass of three-crotchet figures derived from Parsons is slowed down as they are lengthened to five crotchets and more, and the upper melodic outline at last rises to a".

Byrd's craftsmanship, even in comparatively early compositions, is often of so high an order that it is almost a hindrance to their full appreciation. So is the apparent absence of any biographical content. It is not that Byrd can have had no emotional life or that it cannot have impinged on his work. The trouble is that we know nothing of it beyond what is discernible in his music. There is a danger of technical skill becoming too much the focus of attention. Yet it is precisely from Byrd's technical skill that the expressivity of his music arises. Feeling is not to be sought as something separate and pre-existent, which the music is written to convey. It is an intimate part of the act of composition, in the course of which it is made manifest. This applies equally to Byrd's instrumental works and his vocal music.[46] The solution of technical problems in writing for the keyboard or viols releases as much emotion as the setting of words. The more complex and more varied the musical structure, the more complex and more varied is the emotional element. Byrd's growing powers in this regard are demonstrated by a series like his In Nomines. The earlier are interesting mainly because Byrd wrote them. The last is interesting by any standard. It was the combined qualities of resourcefulness, musical architecture and emotional insight that, by Byrd's early twenties, marked out his work as exceptional.

46   Kerman (1961, p. 361) observes that 'An instrumental bias is perhaps discernible in all Byrd's vocal music, certainly in the motets published with Tallis in 1575 ...'. This is of course specific in the fashioning of *Laudate pueri* and *In manus tuas Domine* from consort pieces.

9

EARLY MUSIC FOR THE ANGLICAN CHURCH

Byrd was no more than twenty-three when he was appointed Organist and Master of the Choristers at Lincoln Cathedral. It seems probable that someone so alert to musical developments remained as closely in touch with his former colleagues at the Chapel Royal as the Elizabethan mails allowed (how interesting their letters would be had they survived), but he lacked day to day relations with other musicians of standing, and advice of the sort that only an experienced composer like Tallis could give him. He was musically independent and was responsible, under the direction of the cathedral authorities, for his own small musical world. It takes little imagination to see in the pieces he composed at Lincoln a reflection of his personal fortunes and maturation. As a whole they surpass almost everything he had previously written in their vigour, adventurousness, and occasional indisciplines.

A division between chapters at this point nevertheless corresponds only in a very rough way with the break in Byrd's career. One cannot be sure which of the pieces he composed about 1562 and 1563 were written in London and which were written at Lincoln. Nor is it possible to map out an entirely adequate chronology for his Lincoln years. The problem is less one of deciding the order of pieces within a single genre than of being able to identify the relationship between pieces in different genres and of knowing how their composition was spread over the decade.

The problems of dating Byrd's church music with English words are particularly acute. This is due partly to the nature of the sources. Most of them were compiled a long time after the music was written, and almost all were assembled after Byrd's death, sometimes coupling together pieces which were perhaps not originally associated.

It is due too to our ignorance of the circumstances for which the music was composed. Such evidence as there is indicates that in the Elizabethan Chapel Royal musical continuity with Queen Mary's Catholic Chapel was not wholly broken, and that there was room for music of some elaboration. This can hardly have been the case at Lincoln. Although there is next to no information about musical practices at the cathedral, the atmosphere was increasingly severe.[1] The royal injunctions of 1559, which applied everywhere, referred to 'the laudable science of music', and the Queen's intention of avoiding 'the decay of anything that might conveniently tend to the use and continuance of the

---

1 See p. 34.

said science'.[2] But it is unlikely that the cathedral authorities favoured the frequent performance of music that went much beyond the 'modest and distinct' hymn before or after morning and evening prayers for which the injunctions allowed.[3] This is consistent with Byrd's having composed little music for Anglican worship. Nothing he wrote for Lincoln Cathedral can have been been performed there very often, and it is slightly surprising that the Dean and Chapter sought to commit him to provide them with music after his return to the Chapel Royal.[4]

Services

John Barnard's *First Book of Selected Church Musick*, published in 1641, is the earliest source of complete versions of nearly half of the pieces making up Byrd's English services. Barnard's titles, such as 'Second Service', do not indicate the order of composition, and there are questions about whether the customary grouping together of pieces (followed in BE 10a) reflects Byrd's intention, or results instead from their assembly over a period of time to meet practical needs. In a few cases what Byrd wrote may have become obscured. In others the music survives in a fragmentary condition.[5]

The principles underlying music for the Anglican service differed markedly from those which were to inspire Byrd's Latin motets. The object was to present the words in a plain, clear and easily comprehensible manner. Artifice impeding the realization of this intention would be out of place. The resulting note against note chordal writing must have been one of the factors leading to the development of harmonic concepts of composition.

If we date Byrd's earliest Anglican music to his Lincoln years, can we believe that he wrote no vocal works from the end of 1558 to the

2   Frere, 1910, pp. 22-23. The Elizabethan injunctions, administered by Royal Visitors, repeated injunctions issued in 1547 with alterations to suit the new regime and some twenty additions.

3   'Hymn' means an anthem in this context. (Grove, 1980, i, p. 455; Harper, 1991, p. 186.) Monson (1980) suggests that Byrd's earlier Anglican works may have been heard only at major festivals of the church year. Bowers (1994, p. 65) says: 'The early vernacular cathedral service known to Byrd was, like its Catholic predecessor, sung predominantly to plainsong. Perhaps only the anthem concluding Evening Prayer ... was regularly sung in polyphony ... while a small repertory of relatively simple polyphonic settings of the canticles could be deployed to distinguish the greater feast-days'.

4   See p. 44.

5   Editorial problems are detailed in Monson, 1980, and Monson's articles of 1979, 1981 and 1982.

beginning of 1562? There is no satisfactory answer, other than to admit that he may have written some of the pieces dealt with below while he was still in London. Much of Byrd's music complying with the requirements of the Anglican church is nevertheless likely to have been written for Lincoln Cathedral.[6] Byrd was thoroughly professional. He cannot have written his Preces and psalms because the genre excited him, but once faced with the task he brought to it all his energies and produced works which, in their way, are as inventive and carefully crafted as his more spectacular motets.

Presumably he set to work soon after he arrived at Lincoln, in order to present his new employers with samples of his handiwork. A five-part Litany (BE 10a/4) may be the first product of this stimulus, if it was not in his baggage when he arrived.[7] The sole copy, in the Chirk Castle part-books, is poor and probably lacks one voice, but Byrd's reliance on Tallis's Litany is quite clear.[8] He follows Tallis closely in the first two petitions, diverging further — and at times none too expertly — from his model as the piece progresses.

The influence of Tallis is strong in Byrd's Preces and the pieces grouped with them.[9] There are three sets. In apparent order of composition they are the so-called 'Second' Preces, associated with three festal psalms (BE 10a/3a-d); the 'First', associated with two festal psalms (BE 10a/2a-c); and an unnumbered set to which a setting of the Responses is attached (BE 10/1a-b).[10]

The Second Preces are heavily indebted to Tallis's First Preces, the tenor part of which is taken in turn from *The Booke of Common Praier Noted*, published by John Merbecke in 1550.[11] From the phrase 'praise ye the Lord' onward Byrd draws on Tallis's Second Preces as well.[12] It

6   Monson, 1980, p. vii.

7   The Litany is a prayer consisting of a series of supplications, etc., in which the minister leads and the congregation or choir responds. For its early history and exceptional association with music see le Huray, 1978, pp. 4-8, and Harper, 1991 (as indexed under 'Litany, English'). The authorship of a Litany for four voices attributed to Byrd is discussed by Monson, 1979, pp. 265-271.

8   Chirk Castle part-books: New York Public Library MS Mus. Res. *MNZ (Chirk), described by le Huray, 1982(a).

9   'Preces' are the opening versicles and responses in the Anglican offices, i.e. short petitions said (or sung) as verse and response by the minister and congregation (or choir).

10   'Responses' are the versicles and responses sung after the Apostles' Creed.

11   The chants published by Merbecke (or Marbeck) were adapted from plainsong or composed in a similar style, and tend to stress important words.

12   The phrase is where Tallis's reliance on Merbecke ends. Byrd's borrowings are detailed by Monson, 1979.

can be surmised that Byrd copied so extensively from Tallis because he needed something hurriedly on his arrival at Lincoln. The borrowings from others in his early compositions are seldom so prolonged. At the same time the influence of Byrd's always critical ear and his constant urge to improve on his models are distinctly discernible. He expands and enlivens Tallis's harmonies, and his combination of Tallis's two endings produces inner parts that are more interesting than those of either.

Byrd's First Preces (BE 10a/3) seem to result from a more leisurely criticism of his own work, but there is still no place for grand gestures in this music. There is the merest hint of extra decoration, and only an occasional harmony surprises by its boldness. (Ex.6.)

Ex. 6

a. End of the Second Preces

b. End of the First Preces

The unnumbered set of Preces and Responses has a part missing, but its more contrapuntal style is patent. This places it somewhat later in Byrd's output than the other sets, and it is perhaps to be linked with his contrapuntally conceived pieces written further on in the sixties.

The stimulus for the psalms attached to Byrd's First and Second Preces was again provided by Tallis, though only in a general way (unless specific models have disappeared). Indeed Byrd's psalms differ from Tallis's in more or less ignoring the traditional psalm-tones, to which he turns expressly only in *Teach me O Lord*.[13]

The psalms associated with the Second Preces are *When Israel came out of Egypt*, *Hear my prayer*, and *Teach me O Lord*. Those associated with the First Preces are *O clap your hands* and *Save me O God*.[14] They make a more various collection than appears at first sight. *When Israel came out of Egypt* is little more than a short series of harmonies, repeated with small changes half a dozen times alternately by the *cantoris* and *decani* sides of the choir. The word-painting at the first occurrence of 'skipped like rams' is a rare moment of skittishness. Byrd's procedure in *Hear my prayer* and *O clap your hands* is freer. The repetition of the tune in the top part is still emphasized by antiphonal singing, but the homophonic severity is relaxed and the lower parts develop as short variations, so that a structural pattern begins to emerge. *O clap your hands* modestly varies the tune as well, and word-painting is conspicuous at the words 'God is gone up with a merry noise' and 'O sing praises'.[15]

The fundamental framework of *Teach me O Lord* and *Save me O God* is still repetitive, and they retain a great deal of homophonic writing. Novelty resides in their larger scale and their verse and response structure, with passages for a solo singer (in *Teach me O Lord*) or a small group of singers alternating with passages for the full choir (in *Save me O God*). In *Teach me O Lord* the verse and response are in different times, and the solo voice demands an organ accompaniment.[16] Tallis's psalm *O give thanks unto the Lord* may have provided a model for *Save me O God*, but it has survived only as a fragment.[17] As far as can be seen from the evidence that remains, Byrd was exploring largely uncharted territory, and heading in the direction of the verse anthem.

Byrd's Preces and psalms present a chronological puzzle. If a real line of development is to be traced in the psalms, from the simple style of *When Israel came out of Egypt* to the embryonic verse anthem *Teach me O Lord*, it is difficult to see how the First Preces and psalms and the Second Preces and psalms could have been planned originally as two groups. The scoring of the Second Preces and psalms suggests that Byrd

13   A psalm-tone was a melodic formula, in two sections, to which each verse of a psalm was intoned. The *tonus peregrinus* was an addition to the eight principal psalm-tones. In *Teach me O Lord* it occurs in the medius part of the chorus and in the solo line of some verses.

14   The anthem *Save me O God* (BE 11/9) is discussed below (p. 185).

15   In Barnard's version of *O clap your hands* antiphonal singing starts at the phrase 'O sing praises'; until then everything is sung by the full choir.

16   On the problems connected with the extant organ accompaniments to Byrd's service music and anthems, see Monson, 1981.

17   le Huray, 1978, pp. 196-197.

might have planned the pieces as a group, but the First Preces and the related psalms are scored in different ways. In neither the First nor the Second sets is there an obvious liturgical connection between the psalms, and the chronological mixture of styles might mean that the constituent pieces were brought together at some time after they were composed. There must be reservations, too, about whether *Teach me O Lord* and *Save me O God* can have been composed at Lincoln.[18] They are clearly related to Byrd's consort songs with chorus, and there is nothing to show that any of the latter were written before his return to London. On the the other hand, in both sets of Preces and psalms, each piece ends with the chord that begins the next, and similarities can be detected between the constituent pieces.[19] The conclusion must be either that Byrd chose deliberately to write and combine pieces in different styles, or that he (or someone) assembled the two sets of Preces and psalms from pieces written at different times, making such changes as were needed.

The assortment of styles found in Byrd's Preces and psalms is encountered again in his Services. The 'Third' Service (BE 10a/7a-b), apparently the earliest of those written at Lincoln, consists only of the Evensong canticles Magnificat and Nunc Dimittis.[20] The 'Short' Service

18   Wulstan (1992, pp. 69-70) suggests that Byrd's use of two tenors in *Save me O God* and other pieces might indicate that they were written for the Chapel Royal. The likelihood that the Chapel could muster a greater number of tenors than Lincoln Cathedral cannot be overlooked, though not enough is known about the voices available in either place for discussion to proceed beyond speculation. A tabulation of the scoring of all Byrd's sacred vocal music does not seem to yield any pattern that can reliably be used as a basis for dating either his English or Latin pieces, though in some five-voice motets of the 1580s he was drawn to the use of two equal-range upper voices (see Kerman, 1981, p. 155). The possibility suggested by Wulstan is best expressed as 'any piece with two tenors may not belong to Byrd's Lincoln years'; the reverse ('any piece with one tenor is likely to belong to Byrd's time at Lincoln') cannot be true since he did not always use the full resources apparently available to him.

19   For instance, in the First Preces and psalms, the setting of 'and the nations under our feet' in *O clap your hands* is echoed by the setting of 'He shall reward evil unto mine enemies' in *Save me O God*. In the Second Preces and psalms 'The mountains skipped like rams' in *When Israel came out of Egypt* is echoed by 'hide not thyself' in *Hear my prayer O God*. All these examples are rather similar, however. Are the echoes deliberate, or no more than the result of the composer dealing in a similar way with limited material?

20   Monson (1980, p. x) bases his opinion that the 'Third' Service is the earliest on Byrd's 'preoccupation with the working out of details such as quasi-canonic imitation ... and a certain lack of refinement in their treatment ...'. He is supported by Wulstan (1992, p. 70), who refers to the fact that, unlike some probably later works, it uses only one tenor.

(BE 10a/5) sets texts for Matins and Holy Communion as well as Evensong: Venite, Te Deum, Benedictus, Kyrie, Creed, Magnificat and Nunc Dimittis.[21] The number of pre-Restoration sources which include it shows that it became one of the most widely used Services, perhaps second only to Gibbons' Short Service in popularity.[22]

The movements comprising the Services share with Byrd's psalms the practice of repeating melodies and harmonies, but the changes he rings on them, and the fragments of counterpoint that animate the basically 'one note to a syllable' homophony, parallel the style of *Hear my prayer* and *O clap your hands* rather than that of *When Israel came out of Egypt*. Byrd's mastery asserts itself in harmonic subtleties and the freedom he is able to instil into the melodies and variations. Perhaps his most striking achievement is the individual character he manages to confer on each piece.[23] In the Venite the upper voice follows a line that generally undulates over a fairly narrow range. In the Kyrie it twice floats down from g" to a'. The same voice in the Te Deum covers a wider span and embodies conspicuous intervals such as a falling fifth ('aloud', 'therein', 'continually') or easily recognized groups of notes ('the goodly fellowship', 'the noble army'). The Magnificat of the Short Service repeatedly introduces serial false relations, sometimes creating adjacent major and minor chords on the same note.[24]

The 'Second' Service (BE 10a/6a-b) is another early experiment in verse style, with strong passages for the full choir and with the verses sung by one voice or more. Its two movements could be counterparts of the consort songs on which Byrd concentrated after 1574. The chronological link this implies between the Second Service and *Teach me O Lord* is strengthened by the occurrence in both of the *tonus peregrinus*.[25]

---

21   For the order of services see the Book of Common Prayer, 1559, and Harper, 1991, pp. 172-174. 'Canticles' are hymns in the scriptures apart from the psalms; those sung at Morning Prayer are Venite, Te Deum and either Benedictus or Jubilate. The non-existence of the categories 'short' Service and 'great' Service is convincingly propounded by Turbet, 1988, 1990(b), 1992(b) and 1995. Pike (1992) comments on the assertion.

22   le Huray, 1978, p. 234; Monson, 1980, p. ix.

23   There is no single plan, and the musical patterns do not necessarily coincide with those of the words. The plan of the Venite is A, B_1, B_2, C_1, C_2, etc., up to the doxology ('Glory be to the Father …'). The Te Deum takes the form A, B_1, B_2, C_1, C_2, D, E_1, E_2, etc.

24   The juxtaposition of major and minor chords looks very like a device discovered at the keyboard.

25   See note 13 above. The *tonus peregrinus* occurs in the Magnificat of the Second Service, in the treble verse beginning 'As he promised'.

Anthems

The term 'anthem' occurs in instructions given to Byrd by the Dean and Chapter of Lincoln Cathedral in 1570,[26] but it seems not to have been widely used at that time and was certainly not employed with precision.[27] In Morley's mind there was not a great deal of difference between an anthem and a motet.[28] It was perhaps not until the seventeenth century that 'anthem' came generally to mean a composition with English words derived from the Bible or some other religious source. Even then there was scope for the term to be applied to compositions of different kinds. Barnard testifies that Byrd's psalms *Teach me O Lord* and *Save me O God* both came to be sung as anthems.[29] What did 'anthem' mean at Lincoln? The question exposes one of many gaps in our knowledge.

Edwardian anthems were commonly simple, small in scale and for four voices. It appears that in the early years of Elizabeth's reign it was still unusual for anthems to be written on a larger scale. The natural model for anthems according with Byrd's lofty vision was the Latin motet.[30] When he began writing such pieces is unclear. Five of Byrd's anthems occur in manuscripts completed during the 1580s, and seem to be comparatively early works.[31] It would however be difficult to make a case for all of them having been written at Lincoln. Perhaps only *How long shall mine enemies* (BE 11/3), *Out of the deep* (BE 11/7) and *Save me O God* (BE 11/9) can be assigned to that time, with a question mark being placed against *O Lord make thy servant Elizabeth* (BE 11/6).

26   See p. 39.

27   'Anthem' and 'prayer' are synonymous in John Day's *Certaine notes* (1565).

28   See p. 159, note 6. Some of Byrd's anthems occur in secular manuscripts, and may like his motets have been sung as vocal chamber music.

29   Barnard's table of contents lists both with pieces 'many times, Sung instead of Anthems'. Some of Byrd's pieces that have been called anthems in this century are taken from his printed song collections. See Phillips, 1991, pp. 76-78.

30   Monson, 1983, p. v. Some of the English anthems ascribed to Byrd are contrafacta of his Latin motets. (Monson, 1982, pp. 302-304; Monson, 1983, p. xiii.) A contrafactum is a piece in which new words are substituted for the original text. Whether Byrd sanctioned any such pieces is unknown, but at least one was probably used in his lifetime. *Lift up your heads* is based on *Attollite portas*, and follows a four-part version of Byrd's Second Preces in Durham Cathedral Library MSS E4-11 (c.1625) with the note 'Mr Birds preces & Psalmes for Ascension day at evensong'.

31   BL Additional MS 22597 contains BE 11/3; Oxford, Christ Church, MSS Mus. 984-988 contain BE 11/3, 11/6 and 11/8; and BE 11/1 and 11/13 are in Bodleian Library MS Mus. Sch. e. 423.

The authenticity of *Out of the deep* has been questioned, partly because it has been regarded as unrepresentative of Byrd's music, and partly because the contemporary index of a manuscript ascribes it to Gibbons.[32] But Turbet has drawn attention to similar passages in *Out of the deep* and the Venite of Byrd's Short Service.[33] (Ex. 7.) This not only makes it probable that *Out of the deep* is by Byrd, but that it was written at about the same time as the Short Service. The consort fantasia in F (BE 17/11) may also have a chronological connection with *Out of the deep*. Both pieces are in six parts, and in both pieces all the parts sound almost continuously (the passage in Ex. 7 is an exception).

Ex. 7

Venite (bars 38-41) from the Short Service

Out of the deep (bars 46-50)

More serious doubt is justified about the authenticity of *Save me O God*.[34] A manuscript copied in Byrd's lifetime names the obscure Thomas Coste as the composer,[35] an attribution made plausible by the want of Byrd's usual level of competence. No sources attributing the

32   Christ Church, Oxford. Mus. 1001.

33   *Annual Byrd Newsletter*, 1995, p. 4. Turbet makes the point that it would be surprising if Byrd, who seldom repeated himself, had written identical passages.

34   Monson, 1983, p. vi.

35   BL, Additional MSS 29372-7, dated 1616.

anthem to Byrd are earlier than about 1640, and if it is by him it must be a comparatively early work.

How long shall mine enemies (BE 11/3) echoes Tallis's anthem *I call and cry*, the English (and perhaps original) version of his motet *O sacrum convivium*.[36] It may belong to the late 1560s, where the continuous density of its sound would set it alongside *Ad Dominum cum tribularer* and *Domine quis habitat*. In view of Byrd's undoubted practice in the late 1570s and 1580s of setting texts that had a particular meaning for Catholics, the question has to be asked (though it is unanswerable) whether *How long shall mine enemies* carried a personal meaning at this date. Could it have referred to Byrd's difficulties with the authorities of Lincoln Cathedral, or to his feelings as a Catholic working in an atmosphere which he regarded as hostile to his beliefs?[37]

The six-voice anthem *O Lord make thy servant Elizabeth* (BE 11/6) is another of Byrd's densely contrapuntal pieces. The symmetrical construction, readily apparent in the homophony at the beginning and halfway through, seems to link it with the fantasia in F. The possibility that it belongs to the late 1560s is reinforced by the undeveloped nature of the double point introduced where the phrase 'give her her heart's desire' continues with the words 'and deny not the request of her lips'.

The text of *O Lord make thy servant* reworks two verses from Psalm 21. In 1576 the psalm was prescribed for use on the anniversary of the Queen's accession, but the day had been marked at court and in churches for some years. Annual Accession Day tilts at court began about 1570, under the supervision of the Office of Revels, and at St Dunstan in the West payment was made to 'Synginge men that came from powles & other plac*es*' to celebrate the day on 17 November 1571.[38] Byrd's proficiency as an operator in the world of patronage makes it just as credible that he wrote the anthem at that time, when he was perhaps fishing for an appointment to the Chapel Royal, as that he wrote it as a tribute to the Queen once he had landed the post.[39]

---

36   Monson, 1982, pp. 283-286, makes a detailed comparison, and notes that Byrd's anthem is placed near Tallis's in BL Additional MS 22597 and is wrongly ascribed to Tallis in Additional MSS 29247 and 31992.

37   The words are from Psalm 13: 'How long shall mine enemies triumph over me? Consider and hear me O Lord my God. Lighten mine eyes that I sleep not in death, lest mine enemies say, I have prevailed against him...'. See p. 34 for a similar question about *Ad Dominum cum tribularer*.

38   Williams, 1995, p. 405; GL, MS 2968/1, f. 259^v.

39   Wulstan (1992, p. 69) suggests that as *O Lord make thy servant Elizabeth* has two tenor parts it may have been written for the Chapel Royal. On the other hand it seems often to have been sung in five-part versions. (Monson, 1983, p. 210.)

10

EARLY INSTRUMENTAL WORKS
WITHOUT CANTUS FIRMI

The written keyboard repertoire before about 1570 consisted almost entirely of plainsong-based organ works or transcriptions of vocal and instrumental pieces. The handful of surviving keyboard dances, variations and fantasias reflects what must have been a largely improvised art.[1] Byrd's originality and the power of his imagination is nowhere more easily visible than in the edifice he erected on this small foundation.

It is no exaggeration to say that Byrd was the creator of the Elizabethan and Jacobean keyboard school, but the assertion needs qualification. He learned much from the organ composers who preceded him, and he invented no radically new types or forms. The elements of his earliest keyboard music, viewed in isolation, are largely borrowed from the music he grew up with. His achievement was to combine them into something of far greater scope and complexity, charged with a spirit that was at once highly personal and profound. Few English composers have shared Byrd's compulsion to write for the keyboard, or have found in it so direct a means of expression. He evolved a keyboard style that younger composers could adopt and adapt to their own needs. It took about twenty years for a keyboard school to grow out of Byrd's innovative work. In comparison to their predecessors, composers who reached maturity after 1580 committed a considerable body of secular keyboard music to paper.[2]

Keyboard variations

A great deal of improvised keyboard music must have consisted of variations built on the repetition of a tune, or a melodic ground (a predetermined series of notes of given duration, falling short of being a tune, and serving as a kind of cantus firmus), or a harmonic ground (a predetermined series of harmonies of given duration). Since a tune and a melodic ground both imply a more or less fixed set of harmonies, one basis of variation easily merges into another. Some popular tunes such as 'Greensleeves' were constructed on grounds, and some grounds were

---

1   Harley, 1992-94, ii, pp. 3-18.
2   Ibid., pp. 19, 44-46.

associated with particular tunes.[3] This was the compositional basis which Byrd initially substituted for the plainsong cantus firmi that had so far served him in his keyboard music.[4]

Anonymous keyboard variations of a fairly elementary sort, which may have been composed around the middle of the sixteenth century, occur in sources compiled about 1570 or later.[5] Byrd's assimilation of the idiom they represent is clear, but he may have known the one presently surviving English set of keyboard variations which can be assigned with certainty to an earlier date. They are in British Library Royal Appendix 58, a manuscript probably compiled about 1530.[6] A note by the musician and scholar John Stafford Smith indicates that he thought it came from the library of the Earl of Arundel, the father-in-law of Byrd's friend Lord Lumley.[7] A section of the manuscript devoted to music written or adapted for the keyboard starts with a set of variations in the form of a hornpipe by Hugh Aston.[8]

Aston's hornpipe is the single piece of evidence that, by the early sixteenth century, music for the virginals was regarded as a suitable vehicle for a composer's finest skills. Aston's piece is a composition of remarkable energy and technique. If it was seen as exceptional in its day, it would be the natural model for Byrd to follow in writing his own first set of variations for the virginals. But, since nothing similar remains, it is

---

3   The word 'ground' is applied to both the basis of a composition and the composition itself.

4   Byrd never used secular cantus firmi in his sacred vocal music. He left nothing comparable to, say, the *Western wind* Masses of Taverner, Tye and Sheppard.

5   Although Thomas Mulliner's book (BL Additional MS 30513) was begun about 1550, the leaves containing variations seem to have been added as copying neared completion about 1570. The *Dublin Virginal Book* (Trinity College, Dublin, MS D.3.30/i) was probably compiled about the same time.

6   Harley, 1992-94, i, p. 24; ii, pp. 5-8.

7   See Harley, 1992-94, i, pp. 26-27. Smith's note is in Glasgow University Library MS R.d.62, compiled at the end of the eighteenth century. On Lumley's music books, partly inherited from Arundel in 1580, see Milsom (1993), who does not however mention that groups of manuscripts from Lumley's library occur in the Royal Appendix series on either side of MS 58 and the associated MS 56. If MS 58 was indeed the source of Byrd's knowledge of Aston's hornpipe, he was clearly friendly with Lumley or Arundel (whose collection was housed at Nonsuch Palace in Surrey) at an early period in his life.

8   Ibid., ii, pp. 6-7. Aston was Master of the Choristers at St Mary Newarke Hospital and College, Leicester, by 1525; he is thought to have died about 1558.

unclear whether Byrd's early hornpipe takes Aston's as its pattern or mirrors a class of otherwise lost pieces.[9]

The supposition that Aston and Byrd wrote their hornpipes for the virginals depends on a sense of the fitness of these pieces for performance on a plucked keyboard instrument.[10] The variety of the pieces Byrd gathered together in *My Ladye Nevells Booke* is however a strong indication that he saw no hard and fast distinction between those that sound well on one kind of keyboard instrument and those that sound well on another. The probability is that he would have tolerated his secular keyboard music being played on any kind of instrument that was available and was felt by the player to be suitable. More often than not this is likely to have been a pair of virginals, perhaps of a compact design, but chamber organs, claviorgans and regals were also in domestic use.

The differences between Aston's hornpipe and Byrd's (MB 27/39) are more instructive than the similarities. Byrd's piece is considerably longer than Aston's (205 bars against 153). Both pieces are in two large sections, but Aston uses one simple ground throughout, an alternation of G and F. Byrd uses different grounds in his two sections,[11] although the initial two bars of the first ground sometimes carry the same harmonies as the shorter second ground. In (anachronistic but convenient) harmonic terms, Aston alternates two bars of the dominant with two bars of the tonic, though he occasionally treats a note of the ground as belonging to more than one chord. Byrd varies his harmonies in the same way, or substitutes a new chord, but he also breaks frequently into contrapuntal passages where passing notes add to the variety.

Melodically, Aston's piece grows from the first two bars, by a process of continuous melodic and rhythmic transformation. Halfway through the piece the time changes (in modern terms) from 3/2 to 6/4, a dotted minim being played in the time formerly given to an undotted minim. This intensifies the effects of more rapid movement, growing

9   An untitled and unskilled piece which has affinities with Aston's hornpipe was written c.1540 by John Alcestur in the Evesham Abbey Bible, now in the Almonry Museum, Evesham.

10   'Virginals', or 'a pair of virginals', was the usual English term for a plucked keyboard instrument of any design, though it was also called the 'clavicymbals'. 'Clavichords' seems often, if not always, to have been a synonymous term in sixteenth-century England. The keyboard instrument in which the string was struck by a metal tangent instead of being plucked might be distinguished as a 'monochord'. (Harley, 1992-94, ii, pp. 150-155.)

11   C D C C in dotted semibreves occupying four bars, and C C F G in the equivalent of dotted minims occupying two bars.

rhythmic activity, and leaps of increasing size. Byrd's hornpipe is melodically more complex. The first part is filled by simple variations that gradually give way to figures which develop into running semiquavers. The second part is constructed on the same principle. Short snatches of melody or motivic figures are repeated in a varied form until running semiquavers return. The effect is less one of continuous melodic growth and rhythmic thrust than of constantly renewed melodic invention and a forward urge that is no less powerful for being carefully graduated.

The drive Byrd imparts to the hornpipe springs partly from rhythmically insistent root position chords in the left hand. This may be a feature of keyboard style that was once widely used in improvisation.[12] It crops up in two other pieces by Byrd. One is *Wolsey's wild* (MB 27/37), which consists of two repetitions of a set of simple harmonies.[13] Whether the left hand chords mean that it is an early composition, or only that Byrd adopted a simple archaic style in writing something for a pupil, it seems impossible to say.[14] He also made extensive use of chordal accompaniment in a longer piece, curiously named *The galliard jig* (MB 27/18). This is made up of eight sections of eight bars, each of which falls into halves with identical harmonies. The first four sections form an A B C B' pattern, of which the second four are a varied repetition. The piece occurs only in *My Ladye Nevells Booke*, and may be one that Byrd kept by him but which never achieved general circulation.

The unique source for several of Byrd's apparently early compositions is Will Forster's virginal book.[15] This includes two grounds in G (MB 27/9 and 28/86, 'minor' and 'major' respectively) and another

12   Harley, 1992-94, ii, pp. 9, 13, 17.

13   *Wolsey's wild* is Tregian's title. Forster calls it *Wilson's wild*. The tonic, dominant and subdominant harmonies are arranged in blocks of four or two bars, forming the pattern A(4+4) B(2+2) C(4+4).

14   *Malt's come down* (MB 28/107) is still more plainly a teaching piece, with variations of increasing difficulty for each hand separately and the two hands together. Although it is dismissed from the Byrd canon by Neighbour (1978) and Brown (1976), it is not impossible that it is a survival from Byrd's work as a teacher. He must, after all, have provided his pupils with elementary pieces to play. It is conceivable that *A medley* (MB 28/112) is also by Byrd, and was hastily thrown together for a pupil. For an account of this and other medleys attributed to Byrd, see Neighbour, p. 166.

15   British Library, MS R. M. 24.d.3. Nothing is known of Forster, who dated the index of his book 31 January 1624/5, some eighteen months after Byrd's death, and had access to texts of good quality. (A 'Willmus Foster' was baptized at Ingatestone on 30 January 1580, but this may be pure coincidence.) Neighbour, 1978, p. 23, remarks that Forster added Byrd's name to his early pieces, but presented his later compositions anonymously. He also made a number of incorrect attributions to Byrd.

in C (MB 27/43). A date of the middle 1560s cannot be far out for any of them. They are all based on triple-time four-bar sequences of notes that offer few opportunities for straying from the tonic, dominant and subdominant. If they are not drawn from the common stock of the day, they are closely related to it. In each piece Byrd begins by adding dance-like motives to the ground, striving to develop them in ways that are not rigidly dictated by the underlying four-bar pattern, and working towards passages in more or less continuous quavers. In the two grounds in G he introduces a change of time, and starts the process over again. Each piece ends with a broader passage recalling its beginning.

It is plain that all three grounds are the work of someone schooled in the organ music of his time, but there is nothing directly comparable in the surviving keyboard sources. Byrd's compositional skills and the demands made on the performer go well beyond those found in grounds contained in the *Mulliner Book* and the *Dublin Virginal Book*. It is equally obvious that Byrd's grounds are the work of a natural keyboard player. A sense of the composer's fingers on the keys is conveyed by such features as the long series of shakes in the ground in G major, the alternation of major and minor chords at the beginning of the G minor ground, and the flourish that concludes each piece.

Tomkins knew the G major ground, the longest and most enterprising of the group, as Byrd's 'old ground', and listed it with other 'lessons of worthe'.[16] Byrd's own preference was however for his set of variations on a traditional sixteen-bar ground in C (MB 27/40). This was among the compositions which he considered worthy of inclusion in *My Ladye Nevells Booke*, but its place among his early grounds is suggested by the introduction of a tune current in the 1560s,[17] and by flaws which he attempted to correct by omitting one of the original twelve variations and changing the order of others.[18]

The ground formed the bass to a tune known, from words which were sung to it, as 'The hunt's up' or 'Peascod time'.[19] Byrd ignored the tune

16   Bibliothèque Nationale, Paris Conservatoire Réserve 1122, p. 186.

17   Neighbour, 1978, pp. 124-125. The tune occurs in variation 10, using the numbering given in the *Musica Britannica* edition.

18   Both versions appear in the *Fitzwilliam Virginal Book*, where a poor text of the original version appears as no. 59. The revised version, which Byrd presumably prepared for *Nevell*, was copied as no. [276] by Tregian as he neared the end of his collection. The type of writing for the left hand which appears in Byrd's first variation (e.g. bar 4 of variation 4) is found in nos. 1 and 2 of the *Dublin Virginal Book* and elsewhere, and may be indicative of an early date, though Byrd sometimes returned to it in later pieces such as the *Passing measures* pavan.

19   See Chappell, 1893, pp. 86-90. Tregian uses both titles. *My Ladye Nevells Booke*

and used only the sixteen-bar bass. Its length, and the medial cadence on the supertonic, gave him an opportunity not afforded by the short grounds he used initially, of dividing his composition into clearly defined sections. Each is built on a complete statement of the ground. Byrd did not entirely overcome the problems caused by its frequently static nature, but greater difficulties arose in the execution of his overall plan. His intention of ordering the variations by the length of notes and contrasting motives is perceptible as far as variation 6 in the original version. The subsequent variations are muddled, as if Byrd lost control of his plan, though variation 12 was apparently conceived as rounding off the whole set. In revising the piece for *My Ladye Nevells Booke* he tried, with no great success, to remedy matters by leaving out the rather uninteresting sixth variation, and placing later variations in the order 10, 11, 7, 8, 9 and 12.[20]

It is fairly safe to assign the keyboard pieces so far discussed in this chapter to Byrd's years at Lincoln. It is more difficult to be sure about the date of sets of variations which seem to follow them. The best one can do is to note that they may have been composed around the end of Byrd's Lincoln period, and make an arbitrary decision to deal with them here instead of later. One such set is called *The second ground* because it occupies the second position among the grounds in *My Ladye Nevells Booke*. It is closely related to Byrd's consort prelude and ground.[21]

The second ground and the consort ground are based on the popular 'Good night' ground, which Byrd extended from eight bars to twelve by the insertion of two bars in the middle and the addition of two more at the end.[22] (Ex. 8, overleaf.) He may have chosen the ground because it included notes implying chordal inversions, and afforded harmonic variety. In its original form however the ground falls all too easily into two four-bar sections, each of which divides in turn into units of two

---

calls it *The hunt's up*. The title *Corrigiter: or ye old hunts upp* in William Tisdale's manuscript (Cambridge, Fitzwilliam Museum, Mu MS 782) must be the result of a misunderstanding. 'Corrigiter' means that the scribe of a source from which Tisdale's version is derived believed his copy to be correct. Gibbons wrote a set of variations founded partly on the bass and partly on the tune.

20   If variation '5b' is omitted from the *Musica Britannica* edition, the text is that of the second version .

21   See p. 197.

22   Ward (1983, p. 44-45, notes to No. 10) lists eleven other pieces based on the ground, which may have originated as a tune to which the words 'Good night, good rest' were sung. Neighbour (1978, footnote on p. 67) draws attention to echoes of Byrd's version of the ground in other pieces by him, although one of the pieces he mentions is *My little sweet darling*, which Brett (1970) dismisses from the Byrd canon.

bars. Byrd's insertions serve two purposes in addition to lengthening the ground. They emphasize its central division by recapitulating and varying the end of each half, and they render the break between the halves less tiresome by making cadences less regular. In both sets of variations the cadences play an important structural part. This is readily visible in the keyboard set, where Byrd changes the time in variations seven, nine and eleven. It can be seen too in the general layout. *The second ground* develops the kind of pattern which Byrd had sought to create in *The hunt's up*, and does so with notable success. Above repetitions of the ground is erected an ordered series of variations characterized by gradually shorter note values and figures whose evolution and distribution between the hands is linked to the ground's form. Details of outline receive like attention and the harmonies are deftly modified from variation to variation. By placing the ground in the top part from variation twelve onwards Byrd obtains a new set of basic harmonies.

Ex. 8

'Good night' ground, with bars added by Byrd marked +

The structure of the related consort variations is so closely similar that it is hard to say whether they or the keyboard variations were written first, or whether Byrd worked on the two sets simultaneously. It might be supposed that he would initially have explored the possibilities of the ground at the keyboard, but the larger design of the keyboard piece may mean that it was the second to be composed. It is in any case evident that his initial scheme for each piece underwent revision. Byrd's plan for the consort work suggests that he set out to write twelve variations, instead of the present eleven.[23] The plan of the keyboard piece also suggests that Byrd may have set out to compose twelve variations. One explanation of the existing plan may be that at some stage he revised the piece, removing a twelfth variation, and turning the eleventh into a bridge leading to six new variations in which the ground is used as a melody. The number is unusual enough to suggest that the revision may have

23   See pp. 197-198.

taken place in 1575, to honour the seventeenth anniversary of the Queen's succession.[24]

The gipsies' round (MB 28/80) consists of variations on a tune, and is more accomplished than the grounds. The harmonic movement is quicker than in *The hunt's up*, and Byrd has a firmer grasp of his overall plan — unfortunately marred by an error on the part of Tregian (or his source) in copying what is now variation 6, so that it consists of fragments of two contrasting variations.[25] Despite this Byrd's intention remains clear. The harmonic and rhythmic rusticity of the first variation is replaced by imitative quaver figures in the second and third variations, which can be regarded as forming a pair. So can variations 4 and 5, which are linked by running quavers. These, with motives from variations 2 and 3, recur in the defective variation 6. The final variation is almost entirely in crotchets and rounds off the set more soberly. To overcome the repetitiveness inherent in the A A B C C pattern of the tune, Byrd varies corresponding bars within each main variation to produce A A' B C C'.

The gipsies' round, though restricted in vocabulary, contains many of the ideas that inform Byrd's mature variation techniques. It was nevertheless another set of variations on a tune that he selected for inclusion in *My Ladye Nevells Booke*. The melody of *The maiden's song* (MB 28/82) encouraged him to treat it in the tradition of cantus firmus settings. His approach to the melody is very different from the one adopted by the anonymous composer of a setting in the *Mulliner Book*, where it is accompanied almost entirely by chords in root position, as though it were being sung to a lute. As in *The gipsies' round* Byrd worked through imitation towards passages of flowing quavers, but since he now had no need to hammer home the rhythm he was able to maintain a texture that is spare by comparison with that of the earlier piece and is frequently reminiscent of the organ music of his youth. At the same time the almost unbroken polyphony links the piece to his roughly contemporary consort pieces.

Consort works

Byrd had achieved remarkable facility in writing consort music based on plainsong, but freer types of composition introduced new problems. In seeking fresh structural principles he was exploring territory less familiar to English musicians. It may be that he wrote no consort music for two

---

24   See p. 216. on the structure of the 1575 *Cantiones sacrae*. The variations on *Ut re mi fa sol la* (MB 28/64) also have seventeen variations: see p. 254.

25   The first eight bars of the original variation 6, and the last sixteen bars of what should have been variation 7.

or three years after his last In Nomine, preferring to work out new methods in his keyboard music.[26]

Textless compositions from the earlier years of the sixteenth-century are represented by three printed in the collection known as *XX. Songes* (1530). Two of them, in three and four parts, are by William Cornysh, and the other, in four parts, is by Robert Cowper.[27] In the third quarter of the century composers who showed any interest in textless music not based on plainchant worked mostly in five parts and wrote dances, grounds and variations, some ricercare-like compositions, and pieces based on the hexachord and other constructed cantus firmi. Textless music not based on cantus firmi often relied heavily on the power of imitation to bind it together. Byrd rejected this, but his search for a different kind of structure in the six-part fantasia in F (BE 17/11) led to something stiffly and symetrically contrived. In the first section a point is stated by each of the instruments in turn, and then restated six times with minor modifications. Each of the three succeeding sections is repeated without alteration, save for an exchange of parts between instruments of like pitch. The result is a work which lacks the ease characteristic of Byrd's more successful compositions. Regardless of this he thought it worth adapting the fantasia, with minor changes, as the motet *Laudate pueri* (BE 1/7), and including it in the *Cantiones sacrae* of 1575 – even if he did run into difficulties in fitting a continuous text to music that includes repeats.[28]

A view of the fantasia's likely date is influenced by the knowledge that a set of variations on *Browning*, which seems to be Byrd's next-but-one consort composition, was not written until after 1575.[29] There is therefore no need to suppose that the fantasia was written earlier than the mid-1560s, where stylistic considerations appear to place it, though the date poses the unanswerable question of what commission or other cause could have led Byrd to write such a piece at that time.[30]

26   It may of course be that no body of viol players existed at Lincoln.

27   Only the bassus part-book is complete. See Nixon, 1951-52.

28   Some changes could perhaps be more apparent than real. The transformation of an undotted crotchet into a dotted crotchet may be simply a notational difference in rewriting for singers what viol players would instinctively have played as a dotted crotchet. (Compare BE 17/11 and BE 1/7, third note in bar 17, second part from the top, and identical figures elsewhere.) In a letter to the author Dr Richard Rastall has remarked on the potential value of an exploration of Byrd's methods of rewriting pieces for different media, and added that 'a study of this in relation to *Laudate pueri* and *In manus tuas* would be a fascinating start'.

29   See p. 269.

30   To argue that it was not written until Byrd's return to London in 1572 would raise

The consort work which followed the fantasia seems to have been the prelude and ground (BE 17/9) mentioned above in connection with *The second ground*. The belief that the consort ground is later than Byrd's earliest ground-based variations for keyboard is strengthened by this connection, since *The second ground* is plainly more mature than the keyboard grounds in G major and G minor and *The hunt's up*. The case for regarding the consort piece as having been written at Lincoln rests also on Byrd's addition of a prelude to the variations. This suggests contemporaneity with the keyboard fantasia in A minor, and as will be shown in a moment the consort prelude's structure indicates that it may have been written soon after the fantasia for six viols.

The consort prelude and ground is a work carefully planned overall and finely executed in detail, and conveys the impression that Byrd found greater security in its form than he had felt in writing his consort fantasia.[31] It enabled him not only to return to the level of achievement he had reached in his last In Nomine, but to surpass it. The prelude is built from a point and other imitative motives allied to the material of the variations. Despite being in five parts it resembles the consort fantasia in having six entries at distances of one breve, and a highly symmetrical structure. The variations show a comparable concern with design, and are laid out so that several patterns are imposed one upon another.

(1) The notes inserted in the ground by Byrd are given to the bass, which during the first five variations plays nothing else. It continues to have these notes in later variations, though it decorates and varies them and acquires further material. The interjections of the bass accentuate the balanced regularity of the first two variations. In succeeding variations its function is to provide points of reference in a structure that becomes increasingly complex melodically, rhythmically and imitatively. At last, in the ninth variation, the bass is absorbed into a highly elaborate contrapuntal structure.

(2) For the first four variations the ground in its unextended form is given to the tenor, which fills the added bars with free material. The unextended ground is then rotated through the four upper parts, appearing twice in each.

even more difficult questions about its relationship to Byrd's late In Nomines. Neighbour (1978, p. 62) suggests that the fantasia could antedate the last In Nomine. Robert White, who died towards the end of 1574, had written textless pieces not based on cantus firmi, and as on other occasions Byrd may have followed his example. It is as certain as anything can be when there is no documentary evidence that Byrd had given up writing instrumental music based on cantus firmi by about 1562.

31   The quality of the work is somewhat obscured by the sources, both of which are very poor. (BL Additional MSS 17792-6 and Additional MS 32377.)

Since there are only eleven variations, perhaps the result of a decision to conflate the eleventh with a planned twelfth variation, two voices have to share its last appearance.

(3) As in *The second ground*, Byrd allows the extended ground to shape each variation. This can readily be perceived in the first two variations, where the treble is silent while the bass plays the inserted passages. A time change in the ninth variation is also linked to the revised structure of the ground, and occurs at a point where Byrd modified it.[32]

(4) Byrd varies the harmonies throughout, but extends his harmonic resources by transposing the unextended ground when it is in the top and middle parts. The passages inserted by Byrd are never transposed.

(5) The variations are grouped in pairs on the basis of similarities (or a contrast, in the case of the fifth and sixth) between the materials they contain and their layouts.[33] Motives and figuration evolve from the relatively simple to the complex, and their pattern becomes gradually less controlled by the sectionalization of the ground.

Keyboard fantasias

The origin of the free keyboard fantasia, probably at first an improvised genre, lay partly in music based on plainsong melodies. Byrd's little two-voice fantasia (MB 27/28), called 'a verse' by Thomas Tomkins,[34] is unrestricted by a cantus firmus, but it does not differ widely from his two-voice settings of *Clarifica me* and *Gloria tibi trinitas*, and is likely to belong to the same period. There were however various influences at work in shaping pieces of this type. A voluntary by Richard Alwood, who flourished about 1560, betrays in the integrity of its part-writing and its active bass-line a considerable debt to consort music, if it was not a

32   Bar 119 is corrupt in BL Additional MSS 17792-6, and should not require a further time change. See Elliott, 1971, p. 154.

33   Byrd's intention of stating the ground twelve times is borne out by his pairing of related or contrasting variations. It is not clear whether he intended each part to play the ground twice in succession, but this happens only in variations five and six.

34   The two-part fantasia is preserved only in Tomkins' manuscript (Bibliothèque Nationale, Paris Conservatoire Réserve 1122). The term 'verse' seems to imply suitability for performance in church, but terminology was loose, and a piece given that title in one source may be described in another as a 'fantasia', 'fancy' or 'voluntary', synonymous terms carrying overtones of the freedom and spontaneity associated with improvisation.

consort piece originally.[35] The influence of writing for strings is likewise perceptible in an early keyboard fantasia by Byrd (MB 27/27).[36] It is less clearly sectionalized than is usual in Byrd's fantasias (Neighbour calls it 'the most persistently imitative' of Byrd's keyboard works),[37] and there is an awkward join in bar 46, as though two separate compositions have been patched together. The disparity between the two halves is increased by the marked influence of Redford's organ style on the second.

The complete fantasia occurs in only one source.[38] Another manuscript, once owned by Tomkins, ends at bar 46 and calls the truncated piece '3 parts of Mr Birds'.[39] *My Ladye Nevells Booke* contains only the second half, from bar 46 onwards.[40] It may of course be that someone other than Byrd was responsible for joining originally separate fantasias of three parts, but motivic affinities can be detected between them. Although they are in different modes − 'which in fantasie may never be suffered' according to the proscriptive Morley[41] − they make a balanced whole, and a change from the A mode to the C mode (in effect, from the minor to the relative major) makes sense. Perhaps Byrd extended a short composition, but included only the second half in *Nevell* as an example of the 'mean' style, where the middle of three parts moves to and fro between the hands.[42] Whatever the explanation, it is apparent that this piece does not represent Byrd's more seasoned ideas about the fantasia. It is not impossible that the second half of Byrd's fantasia is comparatively early, and the complete work cannot credibly be assigned to a period later than his first months at Lincoln.

Byrd's next fantasia (MB 28/62) is in the 'G major' mode.[43] It is one of his longest, and this is consistent with its having been composed at about the time that he wrote his large-scale psalm-motets. For a young

---

35   No. 17 in the *Mulliner Book* (BL, Additional MS 30513); Stevens, 1954, p. 13 (note-values halved). It begins with a bass initially suggestive of plainsong.

36   The left hand stretch of E-g# in bar 42 could indicate a string origin, but probably means that Byrd had in mind a 'short octave' keyboard, i.e. one without a full set of keys at the bottom end, and on which E is played by the key that usually plays G#.

37   Neighbour, 1978, p. 226.

38   Royal College of Music MS 2093, apparently c.1650 but copied in part from an earlier manuscript.

39   BL, Additional MS 29996. See Caldwell, 1965(a).

40   So does a fourth source of c.1620: Christ Church, Oxford, Mus. MS 1207.

41   Morley, 1597, p. 181 (1952 edition, p. 296).

42   A number of Redford's pieces in the *Mulliner Book* have the mean picked out in black notes.

43   Byrd preferred the G modes for his keyboard music. See Harley, 1992-94, ii, p. 199.

man to write at such length may indicate exuberance, or a desire to show his paces, or that he had not yet learned to express himself concisely; but the effect of working in the vast spaces of Lincoln Cathedral may also have had something to do with it.

The fantasia falls into two contrasted parts of roughly equal length (almost exactly equal if the last twelve bars are regarded as a separate coda). The first half is further divided into two unequal sections.[44] The second half is in four sections. It is evident that a close relationship exists between the points of all the sections, but how far this results from conscious planning is hard to say.[45] (Ex. 9.)

Byrd's methods mirror the techniques of vocal music, where separate points of imitation introduce separate ideas communicated by the words, but he is concerned to characterize each section in purely musical terms. The first two points are treated in an old-fashioned workaday homophonic style. In the second half of the fantasia Byrd shows a growing tendency to use rhythms suggestive of the dance, in contrast to the formal style of the beginning, and the divisions between the sections are often obscured.

Byrd's control of his material throughout his 'old Fancy', as MB 28/62 was known to Tomkins,[46] depends very much on his awareness of harmonic considerations. Although he was working within a system of keyboard modes,[47] there is little doubt that he was already alive to the possibilities of modulation, based on the circle of fifths, long before they were formulated by theoreticians. The first section of the fantasia, ending on the 'tonic', is balanced by the second section, ending on the 'subdominant', rather like the opening of an eighteenth-century

---

44   Neighbour (1978, p. 232) remarks that, 'though unremarkable by continental standards', the treatment of the first point 'is considerably longer than the opening section of any other English piece of the period'. The fantasia was apparently known abroad, for it is in a Continental manuscript of c.1630: Deutsche Staatsbibliothek MS Lynar A2. The other principal sources are BL Additional MS 30485, and the *Fitzwilliam Virginal Book* (which contains a less accurate copy). The point with which Byrd's fantasia begins was borrowed by Peter Philips for a fantasia in the same key (no. 84 in the *Fitzwilliam Virginal Book*). This is in a style that resembles Sweelinck's, and was evidently written after Philips went abroad in 1582.

45   The thematic development is more subtle than that found in Tallis's *Alleluia. Per te*. (See p. 170.) Neighbour (1978, pp. 232-235) examines other characteristics of the points. He notes technical shortcomings in working them out which confirm the piece as one of Byrd's early fantasias.

46   Bibliothèque Nationale, Paris Conservatoire MS 1122, p. 186.

47   On the keyboard modes, see Harley, 1992-94, ii, pp. 196-197.

sonata. Harmonic progress through related keys in the succeeding sections is quicker and more varied.

Ex. 9

Points of the fantasia in G, MB 28/62

A fantasia in A minor (MB 27/13) appears to be coupled with a prelude (MB 27/12). In the *Fitzwilliam Virginal Book*, the only source to contain both pieces, the prelude was entered some time after the fantasia, but Tregian drew attention to what he believed to be their association with the words 'Praeludium to ye Fancie pag. 94'. The prelude's pavan style recurs in the fantasia. In certain passages the latter seems to echo the dotted rhythm in bars 9-10 of the prelude. The prelude's groups of quavers (bars 7-8 and 10), and its descending triadic figure (bar 9), also find their way into the fantasia, which at its end returns to the prelude's style.[48]

If this prelude is a work of Byrd's Lincoln years, as the fantasia seems to be, it is the earliest English keyboard prelude to have survived.[49] The quasi-improvisatory quality shows its descent from a long

48   Neighbour, 1978, pp. 222-223 (and p. 237, concerning a possible association via Tallis's *Felix namque* settings).

49   Improvised introductory passages must long have been played by organists, and

line of unwritten preludes, but the facts that it was written down, and was apparently designed specifically for the fantasia it was to precede, signify the strength of Byrd's urge to create a body of carefully crafted music in a medium where improvisation had previously prevailed.

Even without the prelude the A minor fantasia is as long as Byrd's fantasia in G, but there the similarity ends. It diverges in spirit and construction from its companion, and its greater freedom inspires a belief that it must be the later work. The A minor fantasia begins more clearly than the other in a keyboard idiom, and its harmonic pulse is less leisurely. Although it is again divided into long sections, and these into shorter sections, there is a feeling of altogether greater flexibility in their handling. The first two points have little in common, but the second (bar 17) is the basis of a transition to C, the 'relative major'. It is in this key that the third point appears (bar 41), picking up the four rising quavers of the first point and turning them into semiquavers. The four quavers become six, and then a dozen bars largely in running semiquavers lead back to a cadence on A (bar 77). There the first main section ends. An abrupt transition to F marks the start of the next section.[50] The use of chords a major third apart was never Byrd's most favoured method of linking sections,[51] but the emphasis on F at this spot is absolutely right in a piece which places so much stress on A and C and tonalities related closely to them. As though to compensate for the abruptness of the transition, Byrd binds the new section to the previous one by introducing an inversion of the six-quaver motive already heard. Such brusqueness is found at only one other place in the fantasia (bars 157-158), where a momentary change from a sharp key to a flat key corresponds with a change (shown in proportional notation) equivalent to an increase from six to nine crotchets in the space of a semibreve.

The suggestion of older English organ music is strong throughout the later part of the piece, but the principal influence is that of Tallis's second *Felix namque*, which Tregian dated 1564. This suggests composition in the mid-1560s.[52] Advanced as some of Tallis's ideas

the written-out keyboard prelude had an extensive history in Europe. Preludes from as early as 1448 survive in the tablature of Adam of Ileborgh. (Curtis Institute of Music, Philadelphia.)

50   The transition to F indicates that Byrd was thinking in terms of two major sections. Tregian numbers four sections (his section 2 starts at bar 78, 3 at bar 129, and 4 at bar 166). The numbers do not correspond to the structure of the fantasia, and cannot derive from Byrd.

51   Harley, 1992-94, ii., pp. 201-202.

52   Neighbour, 1978, p. 236-237. The influence is most evident in the proportional changes of time, found in only three other pieces of the sixties: the first of Tallis's *Felix*

undoubtedly were, he was restricted by his cantus firmus. Byrd's freedom from any such constraint in the A minor fantasia enabled him to fashion a structure capable of accommodating a far greater array of ideas and emotions than those encompassed by Tallis's immensely varied but ultimately mechanical figuration. Where Tallis's invention tends to dryness, Byrd's lends expression to a whole range of feelings. With good reason Turbet declares this fantasia to be 'a work of beauty, passion, tenderness, melancholy and high spirits'.[53]

namque settings, and Byrd's settings of *Clarifica me*.
53   Turbet, 1993(b), p. 20.

11

THE FIRST 'SACRED SONGS'

The death of Queen Mary brought about the end of the Sarum rite without bringing about the end of the Latin motet. Nearly half of Tallis's surviving motets are Elizabethan. The freedom from liturgical constraints allowed composers and their patrons to select their own texts. This was to hold great significance for Byrd.

The purposes for which composers set Latin words drawn from religious sources are not absolutely clear, however. Approval given by Queen Elizabeth for the use in the universities and at Eton and Winchester of *Liber precum publicarum*, a Latin version of the *Book of Common Prayer* published by Walter Haddon in 1560, suggests the possibility that spoken Latin as well as the vernacular favoured by reformers may have been used in the Chapel Royal. In the years following the Queen's accession the outward trappings of religion in her Protestant Chapel seemed to some to be uncomfortably close to popery.[1] The tolerance of spoken Latin may on occasion have been extended to sung Latin, and it may be that Tallis's Latin settings of the Magnificat and Nunc Dimittis were written for the Chapel Royal.[2] The possibility cannot be ruled out that Latin motets were also sung extra-liturgically in some churches.[3]

The situation at Lincoln during Byrd's year's as Organist and Master of the Choristers is uncertain, though Aylmer's influence makes it unlikely that any hint of Catholicism was tolerated there. If the injunctions received by the cathedral authorities in 1548 were regarded as still in force, the singing of Latin words by the choir was forbidden. Injunction 25 said:

> they shall fromhensforthe synge or say no Anthemes off our lady or other saynts but onely of our lorde And them not in laten but choseyng owte the best and moste soundyng to cristen religion they shall turne the same into Englishe settyng therunto a playn and distincte note, for every sillable one, they shall singe them and none other.

1 le Huray, 1978, pp. 33-34.

2 A version of the Te Deum from Byrd's Great Service survives with a Latin text in the Peterhouse 'Caroline' MSS at Cambridge.

3 The possibility is suggested by the music preserved in books connected with St Laurence's Church at Ludlow. (Smith, 1968.)

The succeeding injunction required that

> they shall every Sonday Wensday and Fryday and festivall day in this Cathedrall churche afore the high masse in the myddyll of the chore singe thenglishe Letanye and Suffrages the same beyng begunne of hym that excuteth the high masse or by too of the olde vicars, and so done in order as yt is appoynted in the preface before the sayd Englishe letanye.
>   And also they shall have the Epistle and gospell of the high masse redde every day in Englishe and not in laten ...[4]

Any statement that these injunctions continued to be observed seems nevertheless to be lacking, as is any contrary indication that there were exceptional circumstances under which the regime at the cathedral might have been receptive to the singing of music with Latin words.

Some of Byrd's Latin motets of his Lincoln years, if not written for the cathedral, may have been written with an eye on the Chapel Royal. But a further possibility is that he was already receiving commissions from the noblemen who became his patrons, and that the earliest of his Elizabethan motets were intended for performance in their houses. It is apparent from the nature of the extant sources that Latin works were sung privately as 'vocal chamber music'.[5] It is known that, very soon after he left Lincoln, Byrd was friendly with Thomas Paget and others who cultivated the writing and singing of songs – a term which could mean vocal music of any kind. These men were also Catholics, for whom the Latin words would have held a special significance.

On the strength of the evidence to be presented below, Byrd began composing motets around the middle of the 1560s. *De Lamentatione Ieremiae prophetae* and *O salutaris hostia*, each of which in its way tests the boundaries of technique and expression, were probably among the first to be written. *Ad Dominum cum tribularer* and *Domine quis habitabit* are less experimental and appear to have been written a little later. None of these was published, perhaps because they did not fit into the schemes of Byrd's printed collections, or because he thought them either too radical or below standard. Other motets of the same general period appear among the *Cantiones sacrae* printed in 1575. They include *Attollite portas* and *Laudate pueri*, the second of which Byrd adapted from a consort fantasia – though perhaps not until he found himself short of suitable material. They may also include *Libera me Domine de morte aeterna* and *Tribue Domine*.

4   Bradshaw, 1892-97, ii, pp. 592-593.
5   Brown, 1981, p. viii. The point is also made elsewhere, e.g. Bray, 1974, p. 151; Milsom, 1995, p. 163.

The variety of Byrd's early texts is striking. *Ad Dominum cum tribularer* and *Domine quis habitabit* are psalm-motets.[6] The text of the latter is more than a little surprising, considering the financial dealings in which Byrd's brother John was involved. It reads in part:

Pecuniam suam non dedit ad usuram, et munera super innocentem non accepit. (*He has not put his money out to usury, and has not profited at the expense of the innocent.*)[7]

De Lamentatione is a Biblical text used at Matins on Good Friday, *O Salutaris hostia* is a stanza of a hymn, and *Libera me Domine de morte aeterna* takes its words from the Office of the Dead. For *Tribue Domine* Byrd drew upon a variety of sources.[8] The subject matter of these texts is equally diverse: the wrath of God, prayers for strength in the face of oppression and for deliverance on the day of judgement, and adoration of the Trinity combined with a prayer for an increase in faith, hope and charity. Byrd seems to have selected words in which he could see opportunities for musical expression and structure.

Byrd's net was cast just as widely in matters of style. It would be natural to suppose that the five-voice cantus firmus motet *Libera me Domine de morte aeterna* (BE 1/17), an example of a species that was already rather antiquated early in Queen Elizabeth's reign,[9] represents a continuation of his apprentice essays. This is not necessarily so, however, as Byrd went on writing motets with cantus firmi long after he had ceased to use the method in instrumental music. He perhaps saw a traditional technique as specially fitted to the setting of solemn, traditional words, but the need reflected in his instrumental music to explore new methods may explain why *Libera me Domine* is the only cantus firmus motet of his Lincoln years — and, indeed, the only one of Byrd's pieces in the 1575 *Cantiones sacrae* which makes full use of the

6   The term 'psalm-motet' seems to have been coined by Harrison, 1980, p. 345 (originally published in 1958). Kerman (1981, p. 29) recommends that it should be restricted to large-scale settings of complete or nearly complete psalms, or one of the sections of the lengthy Psalm 118, *Beati immaculati*. There is however a danger that the term has led to the perception of a distinction, sharper than any peceived in the sixteenth century, between the motet which takes a psalm as its text and the votive antiphon (another modern term for a genre popular until the eve of the Reformation), and that the notion of one replacing the other is an over-simplification. See Rees, 1992.

7   Psalm 14 (Vulgate numbering). Byrd also set a metrical version of the psalm, *O Lord within thy tabernacle*.

8   Kerman, 1975, pp. 29-30.

9   When Byrd continued to add to it in the 1580s it was unmistakeably so.

cantus firmus technique. It takes suggestions from the responds for the Office of the Dead written by Robert Parsons, who joined the Chapel Royal in October 1563. He in turn seems to have been influenced by Alfonso Ferrabosco, who had perhaps arrived at the English court only a year or so earlier.[10] Byrd's setting is therefore unlikely to have been composed much before 1564, though it may be the first of his Lincoln motets.[11]

Libera me is shaped carefully to the words and the plainsong cantus firmus. Byrd's freedom from a liturgical purpose enables him to delay the first entry of the cantus firmus until the eighth bar, but it is anticipated by the other voices, which all begin with the first few notes of the chant. Thematic unity counterbalances harmonic ambiguity. The first section of the piece never really settles into the tonic key of G,[12] and at the words 'in die illa tremenda' it moves to a firm cadence on A. The passage 'quando caeli movendi sunt et terra' is more securely anchored, and Byrd borrows only two notes of the chant for the other voices. This passage occupies the central bars of the motet, where the soprano cantus firmus describes an arc from its lowest note to a preliminary melodic climax and back again. The true climax, echoing through the other voices, occurs at 'dum veneris iudicare', concurrently with a renewed blurring of the harmony. There is a touch here of the experimentation carried to extremes in Byrd's next two motets.

Byrd's intention in *De Lamentatione Ieremiae prophetae* (BE 8/5) is announced at once by the musical phrase to which the word 'Lamentatione' is sung, a precursor of the fugal opening of Beethoven's late C sharp minor string quartet. Chromatic alterations, contrasts of major and minor, striking modulations, melodic phrases mounting one upon another – all are used to create a work of strong emotional impact. *De Lamentatione* is far from the joyousness and clarity of *Attollite portas*. Whereas that is broken into sections making varied use of different numbers and combinations of voices, the former piece consists of nearly 200 breves of continuous five-voice counterpoint.

The basis of Byrd's design is the text, selected for setting as five sections of roughly equal length, the central three being prefaced by short interludes sung to the Hebrew letters preceding the verses. The tonal plan corresponds to this division of the text, moving by easy steps

10   See Kerman, 1981, pp. 65-66, on these influences.

11   Byrd was evidently in touch with musical life in London. Stylistic considerations which place *Libera me* in the mid-1560s outweigh the possibility that it was written as a memorial tribute to the musician whom Byrd succeeded at the Chapel Royal in 1572. When Kerman (1981, p. 80) suggested this, he thought that Parsons had drowned in 1570.

12   Transposed to A in *The Byrd Edition*.

away from the 'home key' and returning more circuitously. The length of the piece made these procedures a risky business. While Byrd had an advanced harmonic understanding, he was not yet capable of carrying out his plan successfully over so long a stretch.

The Lamentations of Jeremiah provided words for a number of earlier composers, most notably Tallis. *O salutaris hostia* (BE 8/6) tackles another text previously set by Tallis.[13] It is in fact one of Byrd's early attempts to deal with the regular metre of a stanzaic text. It is driven by the same intensity as *De Lamentatione*, but it is a much shorter piece and more firmly controlled. Three parts are in canon, and three are freely imitative. The tight structure can be regarded both as causing the clashes that result from the combination of voices, and as compensating for them. Either way, the impression remains that Byrd was at his most obdurate in trying how far he could push dissonance without the harmonic scheme falling to pieces.

Byrd's recent espousal of composition without cantus firmi may have given rise to the lively, and lightly scored, six-part *Attollite portas* (BE 1/5), although it is extraordinary that he left no similar vocal works leading up to the composition of so accomplished a piece. Nor is there any source earlier than the *Cantiones sacrae* of 1575. It seems to belong with the six-part viol fantasia in F and the Latin motets that are probably to be assigned to Byrd's Lincoln years, but it cannot be dated more accurately.[14]

Attollite portas illustrates admirably the care exercised by Byrd in planning his earlier motets. The four sections of the piece terminate on G, D, D and G, and tonal excursions within each section are defined by the circle of fifths. Virtually the whole tonal scheme of the work is laid out at the beginning, where the six voices enter on D, G, D, G, C and G.[15] The grouping of the voices is organized with equal care. The first

13   It may again be connected with a work by Ferrabosco. See Kerman, 1981, p. 118.

14   Wulstan, 1992, p. 69, points to the 'un-English' angularities of the vocal lines in *Attollite portas*, and suggests that it could date from Byrd's return to the Chapel Royal. Monson, 1975-76, suggests that it followed *Aspice Domine quia facta est* (BE 1/4), which was written in the years 1572-1574, and represents a more successful attempt to deal with similar problems.

15   Transposed up a minor third in BE 1. The question of the transposition of Byrd's vocal works according to a 'clef code' is a vexed one. See Andrews, 1962 (clearly summarized by Turbet, 1987, pp. 207-208); Wulstan, 1985, pp. 203-213; Bowers, 1987 and 1995; and Wulstan, 1992 and 1995. The view expressed by Brett (1989, p. xvi), that 'Absolute pitch ... would not necessarily have been an issue unless the music was accompanied by an organ or other fixed pitch instrument', is more balanced than much that has been written on the topic.

section (bars 1-48) begins with six single imitative entries leading to a long passage of five- or six-part writing. In the second section the voices are grouped mainly in pairs as they ask and answer questions, but they are united to proclaim the Lord of Strength and the King of Glory. For the proclamation of the Trinity in the third section (bars 71-83) they are appropriately grouped in threes, only joining for a short six-voice passage at the end. The voices are again grouped in threes (two in canon, the third free) for a few bars at the beginning of the fourth section, after which the piece concludes with a passage for the full choir. The repetition of the fourth section is a procedure found in Tallis's music and in some of Byrd's consort pieces and songs, but not again in Byrd's motets until *Ave verum corpus*, composed in the late 1590s.

Ad Dominum cum tribularer−*Heu mihi* (BE 8/7)[16] and *Domine quis habitabit* (BE 8/8), for eight voices and nine voices respectively, are in Byrd's most expansive style,[17] and evidently belong to the same period as his two long keyboard fantasias. A new principle of continuous imitation underlies both of them, and may result from the influence of Mundy, whose psalm-motets are based upon it. There is a dark, rather sombre aspect to these pieces. Two basses are included in the scoring of the first and three in that of the second. The number of voices for which they are written may however convey some symbolic meaning. Elders has suggested that the words of *Ad Dominum*, a setting of Psalm 119 (Vulgate numbering), are to be interpreted as referring to the site from which pilgrims travelled to Jerusalem, which is in turn a symbol of eternal salvation. In writing for eight voices, he says, Byrd was appropriately using a numerical symbol of the New Testament and the bliss of eternity.[18] Whether this is true or not, the words of *Ad Dominum* have much in common with Byrd's motets of the 1580s mirroring the unhappy lot of English Catholics.

Domine quis habitabit is said to employ a different symbolism. The words, from the Vulgate text of Psalm 14, refer to human imperfections. Nine, the number of voices for which they are set, was seen as

---

16   Motets in two or more *partes* are indicated where necessary by dashes separating different incipits.

17   The words of both pieces have to be supplied editorially, but a good deal of verbal repetition is necessitated by their length. It is likely that Byrd's text differed in some respects from the Vulgate.

18   Symbolism of this sort is in keeping with the annotations and interpretations included in *The holie Bible faithfully translated into English, out of the authentical Latin*, a version of the Old Testament published at Douai in 1609. The work of translation had been going on for many years, and Byrd would have been familiar with the thinking it embodied. The New Testament in English had been published at Rheims in 1582.

symbolizing imperfection because it was one less than ten.[19] Nine is however three times three, which plays an important part in the scoring of *Tribue Domine*, and perhaps in the layout of *My Ladye Nevells Booke*.[20] There is of course no way of proving or disproving the existence of such symbols in Byrd's works. One may suspect numerical symbolism, and believe that it is not inconsistent with Byrd's mode of thought, without being sure whether or where it is to be found.

There is some possibility that *Ad Dominum* and *Domine quis habitabit* were composed as a pair of related motets, continuing a habit visible in earlier groups of pieces such as the *Miserere* and *Clarifica me* settings for organ.[21] The two motets share a close affinity, both in their density and in the plan that underlies the ending of each. So continuous is the mass of sound that Byrd has to use melodic means to create a climactic conclusion. During the last forty or fifty breves of each piece a lively point of imitation is followed first by a very short phrase, and then by a long final phrase. In both cases the motive of the final phrase contains a seventh that expands to an octave and gives prominence to the melodic peak.

The full choir sings almost throughout *Ad Dominum cum tribularer*, and cadences are disguised by the overlapping of voices. The sense of unity this creates is enhanced by melodic relationships. Each sentence of the psalm is introduced by a new point. It is not apparent that Byrd deliberately strove to derive one point from another by the process of melodic transformation, but certain similarities can be discerned. (Ex. 10.)[22] The point which begins the second part of the motet, *Heu mihi*, starts with four long notes that seem to lie outside these relationships, and act as a kind of interlude.

In turning to the psalm-motet Byrd boldly invited comparison with his predecessors, but his choice of *Domine quis habitabit* as a text was a positive challenge, since it was the psalm most frequently set by English composers.[23] The texture of Byrd's setting is no less dense and unvarying than that of *Ad Dominum cum tribularer*. When the two lowest voices are suspended for twenty breves (bars 60-80), seven voices are still singing.

19   Elders, 1994, pp. 113-117. (See p. 243, note 5.)

20   See pp. 243-244.

21   It was continued in the *Cantiones Sacrae* of 1575, where pieces exploring similar technical problems are paired.

22   All the points appear in a variety of guises. Example 10 presents only one form of each point.

23   Including Tallis, Mundy, White (who made three settings) and Parsons (who made a partial setting).

Ex. 10

Successive points from *Ad Dominum cum tribularer*

In *Tribue Domine—Te deprecor—Gloria Patri* (BE 1/14-16), for six voices, the urge to write on a large scale is expressed in length rather than sustained density. The main components are each as long as many of Byrd's other motets, and in order to fill out Byrd's contribution to the *Cantiones sacrae* of 1575 they were printed as separate pieces.[24] There is however no doubt that they form a single composition, in which two songs of praise (*Tribue Domine* and *Gloria Patri*) frame a prayer (*Te*

24　See Monson, 1975-76. Kerman, 1975, offers evidence that the three pieces make up a single motet, and presents an analysis.

deprecor). A number of factors point to Byrd's having written the piece at Lincoln. The technique is seldom more than elementary, and the cadences and counterpoint are backward-looking. Double imitation and other advanced procedures, found in several of Byrd's other pieces in the printed collection, are absent. The layout of the piece owes much to the early Tudor votive antiphon (here directed to the Trinity rather than the Blessed Virgin), particularly in the juxtaposition of passages for a few voices with others for the full choir. Perhaps Byrd felt the need of a change after the continuous polyphony of *Ad Dominum cum tribularer* and *Domine quis habitabit*. It can hardly be coincidental that his long fantasias contain contrasting passages of horizontal and vertical writing similar to those which perform an important structural function in *Tribue Domine*.

Whereas Byrd's other early motets concentrate mainly on the possibilities inherent in a single idea, *Tribue Domine* assembles an array of musical ingredients. Careful structuring was clearly needed, for so large a design not only provided room for Byrd to survey a range of styles, but scope for things to go badly wrong if control was relaxed. Different vocal groupings and textures, juxtaposed sections of polyphony, homophony, antiphony and melodic climaxes are deployed with what sometimes seems an almost inflexible deliberation. But the musical planning is always responsive to the sense of the words, which acts both as a controlling factor in passages linking the sections together, and as a local determinant of texture and sound.

The linking of the sections is achieved less by musical repetition than by the similar treatment of similar words. The phrases 'sanctam et individuam Trinitatem' (in the *Tribue Domine* section) and 'summae et individuae Trinitati' (*Gloria Patri*) are semi-homophonic, while in 'laudet te lingua mea' (*Tribue Domine*) and 'Te decet laus' (*Gloria Patri*) the voices are paired.

An instance of the way in which the voices are disposed to emphasize the sense of the words is provided by the first main section of the motet. To make this clear it will be helpful to set out the complete text.

Tribue, Domine, ut donec in hoc fragili corpore positus sum laudet te cor meum, laudet te lingua mea, et omnia ossa mea dicant: Domine, quis similis tui? Tu es Deus omnipotens, quem trinum in personis, et unum in substantia deitatis colimus et adoramus: Patrem ingenitum, Filium de Patre unigenitum, Spiritum Sanctum de Utroque procedentem et in Utroque permanentem, sanctam et individuam Trinitatem, unum Deum omnipotentem.

(Grant, O Lord, that so long as I am placed in this fragile body my heart shall praise thee, my tongue shall praise thee, and all my bones shall say: Lord who is like thee?
Thou art God almighty, whom we cherish and adore, three persons and one divine essence:

The Father unbegotten, the only-begotten Son of the Father, the Holy Ghost, proceeding from both and abiding in both, the Holy and undivided Trinity, one omnipotent God.)

The words from 'Tribue Domine' to 'quis similis tui' are set contrapuntally, starting with just three voices that sing of the worshipper's fragile body, but expanding to six for those beginning with 'laudet te cor meum'. The sentence beginning 'Tu es Deus omnipotens' is set in six-voice near-homophony that stresses the idea of three perons united in one divine essence. The three phrases naming the individual members of the Trinity ('Patrem ingenitum', 'Filium de Patre unigenitum' and 'Spiritum Sanctum ... permanentem') are sung antiphonally in three parts (successively by two sopranos and alto, two tenors and bass, and two sopranos and alto), and the full choir sings the phrase describing the undivided Trinity ('sanctam et individuam Trinitatem') – an idea that reappears in the *Gloria Patri* section of the motet.

Table 9 · Speculative chronology of selected works 1572-1591

This table illustrates the scope of Byrd's work at given periods. See the text concerning possible dates of composition, and for other works.

1572-75

Motets: Aspice Domine quia facta est BE 1/4 · Da mihi auxilium BE 1/10 · Diliges Dominum BE 1/12 · Domine secundum actum meum BE 1/11 · Emendemus in melius BE 1/1 · Laudate pueri (*adapted*) BE 1/7 · Libera me Domine e pone me BE 1/2 · Memento homo BE 1/8 · Miserere mihi Domine BE 1/13 · O lux beata Trinitas BE 1/6 · Peccantem me quotidie BE 1/3 · Siderum rector BE 1/9

Anglican music: Arise O Lord BE 11/1 · Prevent us O Lord BE 11/8 (See also pieces marked 'possibly later' in Table 7)

Consort: Pavan BE 17/14

Keyboard: Pavan MB 27/17 · Pavans and galliards MB 27/14, 27/29 · Ut re mi fa sol la MB 26/64 · Hugh Aston's ground MB 27/20 · Fantasia MB 28/63

1575 to about 1581

Motets: Afflicti pro peccatis BE 3/17 · Aspice Domine de sede BE 2/1 · Cunctis diebus BE 3/19 · Descendit de coelis BE 3/14 · Domine exaudi BE 3/6 · Domine praestolamur BE 2/2 · Infelix ego BE 3/16 · Levemus corda BE 3/10 · Memento Domine BE 2/5 · Ne irascaris BE 2/12 · O Domine adiuva me BE 2/3· O quam gloriosum BE 2/13 · Recordare Domine BE 3/11 · Tribulationes civitatum BE 2/14 · Tribulatio proxima est BE 3/5 · Tristitia et anxietas BE 2/4

Anthem: O God whom our offences BE 11/5

Songs: Ah golden hairs BE 15/13 · If in thine heart BE 13 · Lord to thee I make my moan BE 15/5 · The nightingale BE 13 · O God but God BE 15/6 · O Lord how vain BE 15/8 · O that we woeful wretches BE 15/9 · Susanna fair BE 12 · Where fancy fond BE 12

Consort: Browning BE 11/10

Table 9 *concluded*

Keyboard: Variations on All in a garden green MB 28/56, Fortune MB 27/6, Sellinger's round MB 28/84, Walsingham MB 27/8 (Some of these may be a little earlier) · Pavans and galliards MB 27/16, 27/23, 27/30, 27/31, 28/71, 28/72, 28/73, 28/76 (See also Table 16)

About 1582 to 1591

Motets: Apparebit in finem BE 3/7 · Cantate Domino BE 3/18 · Circumdederunt me BE 3/9 · Defecit in dolore BE 2/1 · Deus venerunt gentes BE 2/7 · Domine non sum dignus BE 3/15 · Domine secundum multitudinem BE 2/15 · Domine tu iurasti BE 2/8 · Exsurge Domine BE 3/12 · Fac cum servo tuo BE 3/3 · Haec dicit Dominus BE BE 3/8 · Haec dies BE 3/21 · In ressurectione tua BE 2/10 · Laetentur coeli BE 2/16 · Laudibus in sanctis BE 3/1 · Misere mei Deus BE 3/13 · Quis est homo BE 3/2 · Salve regina BE 3/4 · Vide Domine afflictionem BE 2/6 · Vigilate BE 2/9

Anglican music: Alack when I look back BE 11/11 · Christ rising again BE 11/13 · Exalt thyself O God BE 11/2 · O God the proud are risen BE 11/4 · Great Service BE 10b

Songs: As Caesar wept BE 15/4 · Come to me grief BE 12 · Constant Penelope BE 12 · The greedy hawk BE 13 · I joy not in no earthly bliss BE 12 · Lullaby my sweet little baby BE 12 · My mind to me a kingdom is BE 12 · O dear life BE 13 · O happy thrice BE 16/42 · O that most rare breast BE 12 · O you that hear this voice BE 12 · Penelope that longed BE 13 · Rejoice unto the Lord BE 15/11 · Though Amaryllis BE 12 · Truce for a time BE 15/25· La verginella BE 16/19 · Weeping full sore BE 13 · When first by force BE 13 · Who likes to love BE 12 · Why do I use my paper? BE 12 · Ye sacred muses BE 15/31

Consort: 4-part fantasias BE 17/4, 17/5, 17/34 · 5-part fantasia BE 17/8 · 6-part fantasias BE 17/12, 17/13 · 3-part fantasias BE 17/1, 17/2, 17/3

Keyboard: Variations on The carman's whistle MB 27/36, Lord Willoughby MB 27/7, The woods so wild MB 28/85 · The barley break MB 28/92 · The battle MB 28/94 · Fantasias MB 27/25, 27/26, 28/46, 28/61 · Grounds MB 27/19, 28/57 · Pavans (some with galliards) MB 27/2, 27/3, 27/32, 28/71, 28/74 · Galliard for the victory MB 28/95

12

MOTETS OF THE MIDDLE PERIOD

During the years when Byrd was fully active as a Gentleman of the Chapel Royal, and in the early years of his partial retirement, a stream of music flowed from his pen. He was not nearly as prolific as some Continental composers,[1] but his ability to compose all this music in addition to carrying on his other activities was astonishing. His duties at the Chapel Royal, his farm and his religious, legal and social concerns all made substantial demands on his time. This argues a capacity for formulating and retaining complex musical ideas in his head, leaving the detailed working-out to be done on paper during free moments at home or at his lodgings in London or elsewhere.

Motets composed 1572-1575

The collection of thirty-four motets published by Tallis and Byrd in 1575 under the title *Cantiones, quae ab argumento sacrae vocantur* was dedicated to Queen Elizabeth. She had granted them a monopoly for the printing of music, and in their dedication they praised both the refinement of her voice and the nimbleness of her fingers ('vel vocis elegantia, vel digitorum agilitate').[2] A more subtle tribute to the Queen lay in each composer's inclusion of seventeen compositions in tacit acknowledgement of the seventeen years of her reign, which began on 17 November 1558.[3] The last piece in the book, and the seventeenth of Tallis's contributions, is the seven-part canon *Miserere nostri Domine*, based on a melody of seventeen notes (in the *bassus* part).

The contents of the volume were arranged in groups of three, with the sections of some motets numbered separately to make up the required total.[4] Tallis could draw on a quantity of music composed over many years. His younger colleague Byrd had only a slender portfolio from which to choose, and the almost symmetrical scheme of his contribution suggests that the later pieces were written to fit into it. Kerman

---

1   An idea of the vast output of composers such as Lassus, Monte and Palestrina can be gained from the work lists following articles about them in Grove, 1980.

2   Facsimile in Monson, 1977, p. xvii, translation p. xxv.

3   As an illustration of the regularity with which 17 November was celebrated with music and the ringing of bells, see the churchwarden's accounts of St Dunstan in the West. (GL, MS 2968/1.)

4   Monson, 1975-76.

concluded that the majority of Byrd's contributions to the 1575 *Cantiones* did not circulate for any length of time before publication.[5] They must have been composed following his return from Lincoln, in time for the volume to be assembled in manuscript, set in type, proof-read and printed, before the seventeenth anniversary of the Queen's accession on 17 November 1575. Quite possibly Tallis and Byrd had decided in broad principle what their collection should contain when they sought the printing patent they obtained on 22 January 1574/5. Very little can have been written during the year of publication.

Table 10 · Byrd's contributions to *Cantiones sacrae*, 1575

No.[6]	4 5 6 · 10 11 12 · 17 18 19 · 23 24 25 · 29 30-32 33
Final	g g g G G G F F F A A F G Bb g

g *has one flat, with an informal second flat in some parts where the sixth degree is frequently flattened.* F *has one flat,* Bb *has two flats.*

One determinant in the arrangement of Byrd's pieces is 'key', or − less anachronistically − mode and final. (Table 10.)[7] The organization of collections by mode was known both on the Continent and in Britain, but if the idea was not original the desire to impose order on every aspect of his work still illuminates Byrd's cast of mind.[8] His decision to bring together pieces in the same key reveals something more, namely that despite his forward-looking harmonic sense, he retained an awareness of the characters of the modes. This character is conferred by factors such as the disposition of wholetones and semitones within the modal 'scale',

5   Kerman, 1961, p. 363. This article mentions post-1575 manuscript sources that are unfortunately ignored by BE 1. See also Kerman, 1981, pp. 126-127.

6   See the catalogue of Byrd's music, p. 409.

7   Finals do not necessarily indicate the relative pitches at which pieces were sung. Monson's transcription of the 1575 motets (BE 1) according to the 'clef code' results in most cases in performance a tone or a minor third higher than written pitch. (See p. 208, note 15.)

8   Tallis's contributions were less conformable to arrangement by key, because he was drawing on a stock of pieces written over a long period. A third of them were composed in pre-Elizabethan times. (See the table in Doe, 1976, pp. 66-67.)

whether a given degree supports a major or minor chord, the notes on which cadences typically occur, and the types of cadence which it is possible to form without altering notes.

Byrd was undoubtedly *au fait* with modal classifications and nomenclatures such as those of Glarean and Zarlino, but whether he subscribed to any in particular it is impossible to say.[9] An examination of his keyboard music suggests that it is based on a fairly loose concept of only four modes. These are the 'major' modes of C and G and the 'minor' modes of D and A, with no sharp or flat in the key signature.[10] Additional keys with one flat in their signature (G, D, F) or two flats (C, G, B flat) are formed by transposing the original modes down a fifth (up a fourth) once or twice. Differences between the modes may be obscured by chromatic changes made for a variety of reasons, but it is clear that without such alterations the three G keys (no flat, one flat and two flats) have distinct characters. C (no flat), F (one flat) and B flat (two flats) differ only in terms of absolute pitch and the notes that come readily under the fingers on the keyboard.

It is perhaps more accurate to speak of Byrd's compositions having modal colouration than being in specific modes, but it is to be expected that his feeling for tradition would make him disinclined to disguise their essential modal characteristics. This in fact appears to be the case. In his vocal music Byrd favours the same modes as in his instrumental music. Andrews' opinion was that he also made some use of an E mode and an F mode (no flat).[11] Whether this view is tenable, and indeed in what respects Byrd's compositions are amenable to classification according to the prescriptions of modal theorists, is too large a subject for discussion here. Kerman observes: 'In the Lydian mode the 'informal' flat sometimes added to Dorian compositions is supplied all but invariably, making this mode indistinguishable from Glarean's Ionian'. But he also

9   Byrd must have been acquainted with at least some of the authorities cited by Morley, 1597, last unnumbered page (1952, pp. 319-322).

10   Corresponding, in Glarean's nomenclature, to the Ionian mode (C), Mixolydian (G), Dorian (D) and Aeolian (A). (Heinrich Glarean, Δωδεκαχορδον, Basle, 1547.) For an account of the modal system see Andrews, 1966, pp. 8-38. When British sources refer to the key of a piece they tend to do so by giving the name of the key note in the hexachord system, and whether the key is major or minor, e.g. Gamut flat. For a short summary see Harley, 1992-94, ii, pp. 192ff.

11   Andrews, 1966, pp. 20-21. The E mode is named Phrygian and the F mode Lydian. Kerman, 1981, pp. 68-72, notes that Andrews was in some cases misled by the presence of 'informal' flats in key signatures, i.e. flats not resulting from modal transposition, but inserted in order to save the trouble of writing extra flats if they occur frequently in the course of a piece.

suggests that composers may have regarded the B flat key as 'the Lydian transposed, with a signature consisting of one transposition flat plus one 'informal' one'.[12] This would explain why Byrd took the trouble to write vocal music in B flat rather than C, when he must have expected that it would be performed at whatever pitch the singers found convenient.

Besides grouping his pieces by key, Byrd creates a more intricate pattern by introducing additional factors into the ordering of his pieces. Subject to other considerations he groups together pieces for the same number of voices,[13] and places together those which have features in common. Numbers 17 and 18 (*Laudate pueri* and *Memento homo*), for example, show the same approach to imitation; and though numbers 10 and 11 (*Aspice Domine* and *Attollite portas*) have contrasting texts, their layouts are strikingly similar. Numbers 10, 11 and 12 (*O lux beata Trinitas*) are for two sopranos, two altos, tenor and bass. Numbers 23 and 24 (*Da mihi auxilium* and *Domine secundum actum meum*) are for one soprano, two altos, two tenors and bass, and are grouped with number 25 (*Diliges Dominum*) which adds another tenor and another bass. The remaining groups of three pieces have mixed scorings, but Byrd evidently tried to effect a balance between his first and last groups: number 5 (*Libera me Domine et pone me*), which is sandwiched between two pieces for a different combination of voices, not only begins with the same words as the last piece in the collection (*Libera me Domine de morte aeterna*) but is scored in the same way: soprano, two altos, tenor and bass.

The contributions of each composer to *Cantiones sacrae* sometimes complement those of the other, and reflect the collaborative nature of their venture.[14] *In ieiunio* and *Derelinquat impius* by Tallis, and *Emendemus in melius* by Byrd, are settings of responds from the Roman rite for the First Sunday in Lent, and all are in a style that is modern, free and expressive. Byrd's canon *Miserere mihi Domine* seems to have been written as a smaller counterpart to Tallis's great canon *Miserere nostri Domine*. The largest of Tallis's pieces, the collect *Suscipe quaeso Domine*, is complemented by Byrd's large collect *Tribue Domine*. The latter piece was probably written before Byrd had any thought of publication, but its inclusion gives more than a hint that he was anxious to display the scale of his powers.

Byrd's total contribution to the collection included three previously written motets: *Attollite portas*, *Tribue Domine*, and *Libera me Domine*

12   Kerman, 1981, pp. 69, 71.

13   Most of Tallis's pieces are for five voices; his three pieces for seven voices conclude his contribution (numbers 27, 28 and 34).

14   Kerman, 1981, pp. 34-35.

de morte aeterna. To these he added *Laudate pueri*, an adaptation of an earlier consort fantasia. The remaining pieces, which must have been written in the years 1572-1574, were *Emendemus in melius, Libera me Domine e pone me iuxta te, Peccantem me quotidie, Aspice Domine quia facta est, O lux beata Trinitas, Memento homo, Siderum rector, Da mihi auxilium, Domine secundum actum meum*, and *Diliges Dominum*.[15] Stylistic factors point only uncertainly to a possible order of composition within the later group,[16] and clues to date are disguised by Byrd's arrangement of the pieces. *Memento homo* was probably the first to be written after Byrd's return to London, and *Emendemus in melius* was probably the last to be written before publication.

Motets composed c.1575-1591

Byrd continued steadily to compose 'sacred songs' after the publication of the 1575 collection. *Liber primus* and *Liber secundus sacrarum cantionum* (1589 and 1591) contain between them thirty-seven motets, printed as sixty-one numbers, and more survive only in manuscript.[17] The first book contains songs for five voices. The second contains songs for five and six voices. Each book evidences the same careful arrangement as the *Cantiones sacrae* of 1575. The pieces are ordered by mode and final, in a sequence dictated generally by the circle of fifths but modified by Byrd's wish for the transition from one piece to the next to be as smooth as possible.[18] Byrd's organization spreads across both volumes. The 1589 volume ends with two pieces in C and F respectively (*Domine secundum multitudinem* and *Laetentur coeli*), while the 1591 volume begins and ends with similar pairs (*Laudibus in sanctis* in C and *Quis est homo* in F, and *Domine salva nos* in C and *Haec dies* in F). The pieces in C have somewhat similar thematic material, and so do those in F.[19] (Ex. 11.) Byrd seems to have paid less attention to the order in

15   Respectively numbers 1, 2, 3, 4, 6, 8, 9, 10, 11 and 12 in BE 1. There are no pre-publication manuscripts.

16   See the discussion in Kerman, 1981, ch. 2.

17   Because Byrd used the genitive case the titles of the two books are usually given as *Cantiones sacrae*. For unpublished motets see pp. 224-225 and 424-425.

18   Brown, 1981, p. vi, and 1988, p. vii. *Tribulationes civitatem* in G (two flats) is interposed between pieces in F and C because it begins with a B flat chord. This does not mean that Byrd expected the pieces to be sung one after another, or at the written pitch. Brown suggests that the 'misplacing' of *Domine tu iurasti* may have been dictated by printing needs.

19   Brown, 1981, p. vii.

Ex. 11

Opening points of motets from *Cantiones sacrae* of 1589 and 1591

which his verbal texts appeared, although each volume ends with a song
of rejoicing.

Some of the motets printed in 1589 and 1591 had been circulating for
a considerable time before publication, and the earliest manuscripts
contain a number of readings that differ in various respects from those of
the printed versions. Manuscripts also provide indications of the order of
composition. It cannot be pretended that these are anything but extremely
rough-and-ready, but there is enough agreement to make it worth
tabulating the evidence. Table 11 (overleaf) is based on Bodleian Library
Mus. Sch. e.423, a single partbook compiled for John Petre c.1575-
1589,[20] and Christ Church, Oxford, Mus. 984-988, compiled by Robert
Dow 1581-1588.[21] Studies of these manuscripts have revealed the order

20   Dr Davis Mateer's forthcoming article, 'William Byrd, John Petre and Oxford,
Bodleian MS Mus. Sch. E.423', demonstrates that the manuscript was begun c.1577 and
probably completed by 1589. Periods of copying are marked by the use of different
papers. Byrd's motets appear in the second and third main fascicles.

21   Dow's access to many early versions of Byrd's works points either to a personal
acquaintance with the composer or to friendship with someone close to him, perhaps
Richard Mulcaster or a member of the Catholic community. (Mateer, 1986-87, pp. 6-7.)

Table 11 · Occurrence of motets in selected manuscripts

D = piece number in Dow MSS. (D10-13 copied c.1581, D27-46 c.1581-85, D52 c.1585-88.)
P = page number in Petre MS. (Page numbering interrupted between 140 and 146; pp. 63-140 copied c.1577-c.1582, pp. 146-200 c.1582-1589, pp. 201-233 c.1577-c.1580, pp. 234-294 c.1580-1582, pp. 297-307 c.1582-1589.)

1. Motets from *Cantiones sacrae*, 1589 (BE 2 numbers in parentheses.)

c.1577-82   Aspice Domine de sede (11) *P63*
            Ne irascaris (12) *D9, P65 (dated 1580 by*
               Sadler, 1581 by Add. 47844)[*]
            Memento Domine (5) *P77*
            O Domine adiuva me (3) *D10*
            Tribulationes civitatum (14) *D11, P90*
            Domine praestolamur (2) *D13*
            Trisitia et anxietas (4) *D31, P80*
            O quam gloriosum (13) *D30, P137*

c.1582-89   Domine tu iurasti (8) *D40, P160*
            Laetentur coeli (16) *D46, P164*
            Vide Domine afflictionem (6) *P167*
            In resurrectione tua (10) *D34, P171*
            Domine secundum multitudinem (15) *P176*
            Deus venerunt gentes (7) *D39, P177*
            Vigilate (9) *P189*

No source   Defecit in dolore (1)
before 1589

[*] Perhaps the dates of copying, not of composition. Bodleian Library MSS Mus. e.1-5, copied by John Sadler c.1565-1585 (see Mateer, 1979); British Library Additional MS 47844, a partbook dated 1581.

Table 11 *concluded*

2. Motets from *Cantiones sacrae*, 1591 (BE 3 numbers in parentheses.)

c.1577-80   Infelix ego (16) *P201*
             Cunctis diebus (19) *P206*
             Afflicti pro peccatis (17) *P208*
             Descendit de coelis (14) *P209*

c.1577-82   Levemus corda (10) *P70*
             Domine exaudi (6) *D12, P83*
             Tribulatio proxima est (5) *D27, P132*
             Recordare Domine (11) *P134*

c.1582-89   Apparebit in finem (7) *D32, P155*
             Fac cum servo tuo (3) *D36*
             Haec dicit Dominus (8) *P158*
             Exsurge Domine (12) *D41, P162*
             Circumdederunt me (9) *P166*
             Misere mei Deus (13) *D52, P187*
             Salve regina (4) *P191*
             Quis est homo (2) *P194*

No source   Laudibus in sanctis (1)
before   Domine non sum dignus (15)
1591   Cantate Domino (18)
             Domine salva nos (20)
             Haec dies (21)

in which pieces were entered.[22] Petre has a greater number than Dow of the pieces printed in either book of *Cantiones sacrae*, and has far more of those printed in 1591.[23] Dow gives a more complete version of *Deus venerunt gentes*, which was evidently composed in stages.[24] It is likely that the pieces which begin the printed volumes, and for which there are no early manuscript sources, were written specially for publication, perhaps to offer purchasers something new, and the concluding pieces may also have been recently composed.

It need hardly be stressed that complete reliance cannot be placed on the above indications of date, since they are those of copying, not composition. It is evident, too, that a variety of other considerations needs to be taken into account in determining dates. On stylistic grounds *Laetentur coeli* should perhaps be placed earlier in the sequence, while *Deus venerunt gentes* is likely to have been written in 1582 if the choice of its words reflects, as it seems to do, the execution of Edmund Campion. On the other hand the order of pieces in the manuscripts is sometimes supported by additional evidence. *Infelix ego* and *Cunctis diebus* seem to have been composed as a pair of six-part motets in votive antiphon form, while *Afflicti pro peccatis* and *Descendit de coelis* are both responds for six voices.[25] *Apparebit in finem* and *Domine tu iurasti* both explore modal ambiguity; although published separately they occur at roughly the same point in the manuscripts.

Many of the motets omitted by Byrd from his printed collections occur in sources that point to their composition over the same period as those published in 1589 and 1591.[26] A specific date for the eight-voice

22   Mateer, 1986-87, and Dr Mateer's forthcoming article. The dates and numbering in Table 11 follow these. See also Kerman, 1981, pp. 125-132.

23   In the forthcoming article mentioned above, Dr Mateer writes: 'It is almost as if Bentley [the copyist] had access to the pieces as they were being written, for their succession follows in broad outline the chronology proposed for them by Kerman; while waiting for the next group to become available, the scribe would apparently turn his attention to other genres and/or composers'. Kerman (1981) was, of course, following in part the indications of the Petre manuscript regarding dates.

24   In manuscript sources the third and fourth parts of this motet are generally separated from the first two (which form a tonal unit), as though they were written later. They do not occur at all in the Petre manuscript.

25   Since BE 3/14-21 are for six voices, the implication of the above table is that Byrd abandoned six-voice motets for a decade between about 1580 and 1590.

26   Most of them are for five voices: *Ad punctum in modico* and *Domine Deus omnipotens* (both incomplete), *Ave regina caelorum* and *Petrus beatus* (both of which may have texts drawn from the York rite, and the second of which may be connected with Sir John Petre: see p. 94), *Ne perdas cum impiis* and *Omni tempore benedic Deum* (a pair of

motet *Quomodo cantabimus* comes from the annotation to a copy made
by the organist and composer John Alcock. It says that in 1584 Byrd sent
his motet to Philippe de Monte, whom he may have met thirty years
earlier, and from whom he had received *Super flumina Babylonis* in
1583. The latter date perhaps provides a clue to Monte's reason for
getting in touch with Byrd.[27] It was the year in which Thomas Paget fled
to the Continent, where Peter Philips had gone in 1582. Monte could
have learned, directly or indirectly, from either of them about Byrd's
concern over the treatment of English Catholics. Monte set the first four
verses of Psalm 136 (Vulgate numbering), but rearranged them as though
to refer to the Catholic condition. Byrd's response set verses 4 to 7.[28]

respond settings), *Audivi vocem*, *Benigne fac*, and *Peccavi super numerum*. Those for six
voices are *Circumspice Hierusalem*, *Deus in adiutorium*, and *Domine ante te*. The motets
Ne perdas and *Omni tempore* occur early on in Bodleian Library MS Mus. Sch. e.423,
and must therefore have been composed in the late 1570s. *Ad punctum* appears in the
same source, in a position that suggests composition in the mid-1580s. The sources
containing the foregoing pieces also contain motets of doubtful authenticity: *Decantabat
populus*, *Reges Tharsis*, *Vide Domine quoniam tribulor* and *Sacris solemnis*. The analysis
reported by Morehen (1992, p. 61) indicates a reasonable chance that the first three are
by Byrd; it does not include the last.

27   Monte was presumably at the Habsburg court in either Vienna or Prague. For
Byrd's possible meeting with him in 1554 see p. 23. Against Monte's motet (BL
Additional MS 23624, f. 101[r], modern numbering) Alcock writes: 'This Piece of Musick
was compos'd by Sig[r]: Phillipo de Monte, master of y[e] Children of y[e] Emperor
Maximilian the 2[ds]: Chapel, & sent by him, to M[r]: Bird – 1583'. His note to Byrd's
piece (f. 107[r], modern numbering) is: 'This Piece, was made by M[r]: W[m]: Byrd, to send
unto M[r]: Phillip de Monte, 1584'. Although Alcock's annotations date from c.1763,
Super flumina Babylonis and *Quomodo cantabimus* were circulating together by c.1590.
They occur, separated by two In Nomines, as numbers 19 and 21 in John Baldwin's
commonplace book, BL MS R. M. 24.d.2. (See Bray, 1974.) Another of Alcock's
annotations concerns *Domine tu iurasti* (f. 99[r], modern numbering): 'This Peice in y[e]
Opinion of M[r]: Bird himself, is y[e] best he ever Compos'd'. Alcock appears to have had
access to the now incomplete Bodleian Library MS Tenbury 389 and the privately-owned
'James' part-book.

28   A suggestion that the scoring has a symbolic meaning cannot be proved or
disproved, but it has been said that the eight-part portions of Byrd's motet may symbolize
his longing for eternal salvation, while the three-part canon which it includes may be an
expression of faith that salvation has been ensured by Christ's resurrection. (Elders,
1994, pp. 114-115.)

13

MOTETS: STYLE AND DEVELOPMENT

One of the motets Byrd wrote at Lincoln is for eight voices and one is for nine, but he rarely wrote for more than six voices. Two of his Lincoln motets require five singers, and four need six. The only eight-part motet which he included in the *Cantiones sacrae* of 1575 is the canon *Diliges Dominum*, undoubtedly intended to outdo Tallis's seven-part canon *Miserere nostri Domine*.[1] Eleven of the seventeen pieces he included (counting *Tribue Domine* as three pieces) are for six voices; five are for five voices. The smaller number became his compositional norm for motets. The *Cantiones sacrae* of 1589 are entirely for five voices, while in the 1591 collection there are about twice as many pieces for five voices as for six. Byrd's unpublished motets show the same tendency.[2] He wrote only one more motet for eight voices, when in 1584 he wished to show his paces in *Quomodo cantabimus*, his response to the eight-part motet he had received from Philippe de Monte.[3]

In the *Cantiones sacrae* of 1575 Byrd employed a variety of voice combinations, but seldom used two sopranos in writing for five voices. He used two basses only in the six-part *Laudate pueri*, which began life as a piece for viols, and in the eight-part *Diliges Dominum*. The five-voice scoring he came to use most frequently was for one soprano, two altos, a tenor and a bass. Less often he varied this by the substitution of a soprano or tenor for one of the altos. Both the 1589 and 1591 books of *Cantiones sacrae* contain a number of pieces which do not fit neatly into this pattern, and the need to accommodate an extra voice in the six-part pieces of the second book means that five out of eight require a mezzo-soprano or a baritone voice. As might be expected, Byrd's scoring became more flexible and less regular as he matured.

The 1575 *Cantiones sacrae* were designed to serve a particular set of purposes, not least that of proclaiming Byrd's position as the leading composer of the younger generation. The consistently more modest resources demanded by the later collections may reflect a different intention: to provide a repertoire for recreational singing. An indication that this is so occurs in the dedication of the 1589 collection to the Earl

---

1   Byrd's pupil Peter Philips similarly tried to outdo his teacher. When Philips modelled his *Passamezzo* pavan and galliard on Byrd's he made each dance longer than the original by one statement of the ground.

2   See pp. 224-225.

3   See p. 225.

of Worcester. It was he who, as the young Lord Herbert, wrote that his children were learning to sing and that Byrd had helped him in composing a song.[4]

Byrd's choice of words for his newer motets in the *Cantiones sacrae* of 1575 is as varied as in those he composed at Lincoln.[5] There are five prayers for mercy, three songs of praise, two observations on the human condition, and one rule of conduct. Unlike the texts Byrd was to set after he became more deeply involved in recusant affairs, most carry no secondary political meaning applicable to the lot of English Catholics.[6] Texts such as those of *Emendemus in melius*, *Libera me Domine et pone me iuxta te*, and *Da mihi auxilium* seem to have been chosen because of the scope they allowed for musical expression. Most of the texts which might be put to liturgical use occur in both the Sarum and Roman rites. Only that of *Emendemus in melius*, perhaps the last to be set, occurs solely in the Roman rite and marks a break with pre-Elizabethan custom. Were it not that so much English music from the earlier sixteenth century has been lost, it might almost be suggested that Byrd was trying largely to avoid texts set by his English predecessors.[7] A number of his texts had however been set by Continental composers. This may indicate his knowledge of their music, or it may mean no more than that he settled on the same texts in searching out those with expressive possibilities.[8]

Many of the texts of the *Cantiones sacrae* of 1589 and 1591 express sadness or contrition, and appeal for God's help. More significant is the

4   See p. 50. The dedication may have been inspired partly by Worcester's recent accession to the title (February 1588/89).

5   See p. 206.

6   A possible exception is *Aspice Domine*: 'Behold, O Lord, how the city filled with riches is made desolate. She sits in misery and there is none to comfort her except Thee, our God'.

7   Byrd's 1575 *Cantiones* included the following texts set by English composers or foreigners active in England: *Peccantem me quotidie* (Ferrabosco, Robert Cowper, Parsons), *Aspice Domine quia facta est* (Wilder), *O lux beata Trinitas* (Ferrabosco), *Laudate pueri* (Sheppard), *Libera me Domine de morte aeterna* (Parsons, White). Anonymous settings of *Aspice Domine quia facta est* and *Miserere mihi Domine* occur in English manuscripts. (Hofman and Morehen, 1987.)

8   Clemens's setting of *Peccantem me*, for example, was published in 1547, and settings of *Emendemus in melius*, *Libera me de morte*, *Peccantem me*, *Laudate pueri* and *Domine secundum actum meum* were included in collections of Lassus's music published between 1555 and 1573. English manuscripts contain settings of *Peccantem me* by Orazio Vecchi, and *Aspice Domine quia facta est* by Jacquet. Lumley's library, with which Byrd was almost certainly familiar, contained a number of motet collections published abroad. (See Milsom, 1993.)

number that can be read as references to the plight of Byrd and his fellow Catholics.[9] They were set during the period when Byrd, his family and his servants were repeatedly convicted of recusancy, when his house and the houses of his friends were searched, and when he was associating with Catholic missionaries who risked, and in some cases suffered, death for their beliefs. It takes little effort of imagination either to find half a dozen texts in each volume which speak plainly for a community that felt itself to be beleaguered, or to find others that carry the same import at a deeper level.

> Domine, praestolamur adventum tuum ... dissolvas iugum captivitatis nostrae ... et libera populum tuum. (*Lord, we look for thy coming ... unloose the yoke of our captivity ... and deliver thy people.*)

> Memento, Domine, congregationis tuae ... et mitte eis auxilium. (*Be mindful, O Lord, of thy congregation ... and send them help.*)

> Vide, Domine, afflictionem nostram ... et miserere populi tui gementis et flentis. (*Behold, O Lord, our affliction ... and have mercy upon thy sighing, weeping people.*)

Similar phrases abound: 'Jerusalem is forsaken', 'let us not perish', 'Insults and terrors have I suffered', 'there is hope in thy last days, and thy children shall return to their own borders', 'Unhappy am I, bereft of help on every side', 'Save us, O Lord, for we perish'.

Deus venerunt gentes (BE 2/7), a setting of Psalm 78 (Vulgate numbering), seems to refer specifically to the execution of Thomas Campion and other priests in December 1581, after which their bodies were quartered and nailed to a gate on Tyburn Hill.

> Posuerunt morticina[10] servorum tuorum escas volatilibus coeli, carnes sanctorum bestiis terrae. Effuderunt sanguinem ipsorum tanquam aquam in circuitu Hierusalem, et non erat qui sepeliret. (*They have laid out the dead bodies of thy servants as food for the birds of the air, the flesh of thy saints*

---

9   One of the first to remark on this was Collins (1923, p. 256). For a full discussion see Kerman, 1962(b), and 1981, pp. 39-46. The application of Biblical texts to current circumstances was not unusual. A text of the same type as those set by Byrd appears on the title-page of the tract *A true reporte of the death & martyrdome of M. Campion* (1582): 'These are they that came out of gret tribulation, and have washed their stoles and made them white in the bloud of the Lambe' (Revelation, 7.14).

10   Set by Byrd as 'morticinia'.

for the beasts of the earth. They have poured out their blood like the water round about Jerusalem, and there was no one to bury them.)

Such texts support the belief that the *Cantiones sacrae* were written for domestic performance in the homes of Byrd's Catholic patrons like Paget, Lumley, Petre and Worcester.[11] There seems to be more than a grain of truth in the conventional protestation, in Byrd's dedication of the 1589 volume to Worcester, that he was acceding to the request of friends in publishing accurate versions of his songs. The words may in some cases have been chosen by Byrd's patrons, though as with the *Cantiones* of 1575 a number of the texts had previously been set by Continental composers.[12]

In the 1575 *Cantiones sacrae* Tallis and Byrd pointed out particular types of composition, but probably regarded cantus firmus technique as too well worn to deserve mention. Its presence in *Miserere mihi Domine* and *Libera me Domine de morte aeterna* went unremarked. Byrd's continued use of the technique is however an aspect of the strongly traditional tendency that persisted in his work alongside his exploration of recent innovations. Subsequent cantus firmus motets include *Aspice Domine de sede*, published in 1589, and from the 1591 volume *Descendit de coelis* and, outstandingly, *Afflicti pro peccatis*.[13] Passages written in something like cantus firmus style crop up from time to time in

11   It may therefore be appropriate for the higher parts to be sung by women as well as, or instead of, boys and countertenors. Women took part in the music at Richard Bold's house, when Byrd was present in 1586. (See p. 80.)

12   Among the texts Byrd used for his 1589 collection, only *Laetentur coeli* (set anonymously) is listed by Hofman and Morehen (1987) as occurring in an English manuscript. Four of the texts of the 1591 collection were set by English composers or foreigners active in England: *Quis est homo* (Giles), *Miserere mei Deus* (Gerarde, Mundy, Tye, White), *Cantate Domino* (Nicholson), and *Haec Dies* (Ensdale, Sheppard, and perhaps Tallis). English manuscripts contain anonymous settings of *Domine exaudi*, *Infelix ego* and *Ad te igitur* (the text of the *tertia pars* of Byrd's *Infelix ego*). They also contain settings of *Haec dies* by Palestrina and Pevernage, *Miserere mei Deus* by Formellis, and *Cantate Domino* by Fabritius and Giovanni Gabrielli. Among the texts of Byrd's 1589 collection used in works printed abroad, Lassus's *Laetentur coeli* was published in 1569, and Clemens's *Tristitia et enxietas*, *Vide Domine afflictionem* and *Tribulationes civitatem* in 1547-53. Byrd's 1591 collection included six texts used by Lassus in publications of 1577-1604: *Salve regina mater*, *Domine exaudi*, *Miserere mei Deus*, *Infelix ego*, *Cantate Domino* and *Circumdederunt me*. Clemens's setting of the last was published in 1553. This is by no means a complete list of foreign settings.

13   There are as well three unpublished cantus firmus motets of the same period: *Petrus beatus*, *Ne perdas cum impiis*, and *Omni tempore benedic Deum*.

motets employing an otherwise freely imitative technique. *Aspice Domine de sede* is preceded in the 1589 collection by *In resurrectione tua*, written some years later, where the final 'Alleluia' is underpinned by long notes that resemble a cantus firmus.

Afflicti pro peccatis (BE 3/17) has the cantus firmus in the *sextus* part, the last to enter. Its opening notes are however anticipated by the voices that sing the word 'Afflicti'. Once the cantus firmus has entered 'Afflicti' is sung to a new point. Two other things are worth remarking about the setting of words in the first part of this motet. One is the way in which different groups of words are sung at the same time, as if Byrd has set them only for the benefit of the singers, not for the ready understanding of a congregation. The other, which complements the first, is Byrd's setting of short verbal phrases to overlapping points: 'Afflicti', 'pro peccatis nostris', 'quotidie cum lacrimis', 'expectemus finem nostrum'. It will be necessary to return to this below.[14] The imitative motives of the *secunda pars* largely ignore the cantus firmus, but Byrd once again sets the text phrase by phrase. As interesting as Byrd's setting of the words is his harmonic scheme. The piece as a whole is in G with no flat in the signature, but the note B, which defines the 'major' key, does not occur in the cantus firmus until the forty-seventh semibreve. In the knowledge that the plainsong will lead him to end the first part of the motet with a cadence on F, Byrd flattens B from the outset in other parts, creating minor harmonies appropriate to the sense of the words (sorrow for our sins). The second part − less than half the length of the first − balances harmonies emphasizing F and G, and its tendency to the major parallels the expectation of deliverance from evils described in the text.

The types of composition to which Tallis and Byrd drew attention were hymns and canons. Among the pieces headed 'Hymnus' are Byrd's *Siderum rector* and *O lux beata Trinitas*, both settings of stanzaic metrical texts.[15] As in the case of a number of pieces in the collection, Byrd based his hymns on schemes apparently borrowed from Ferrabosco, who also inspired the light touch that he brings to them.[16] Each of the two verses of the quietly harmonious *Siderum rector* is sung first by a reduced choir and then repeated by the full choir, but as the

---

14   See p. 235.

15   Tallis's hymns are *O nata lux* and *Sermone blando*. The nearest approach to a stanzaic metrical text in Byrd's later books of *Cantiones sacrae* is *Laudibus in sanctis* (1591 collection), paraphrasing Psalm 150 as a sonnet in Latin elegiac verse. Thomas Watson springs to mind as the possible author.

16   Ferrabosco's hymns are *Ecce iam noctis* and *Aurora diem nuntiat*, which occur adjacently in BL Egerton MS 3665.

verses express distinct thoughts they are treated differently. Much of the first verse is set in a syllabic homophonic style; the second verse relies more on counterpoint, but the setting remains largely syllabic. *O lux beata Trinitas* is smoothly written and almost entirely syllabic. Each line of the first two verses is sung twice by antiphonal semichoirs, but − in preparation for the canon in the the the third verse − the second verse is a little more contrapuntal than the first.

Byrd's headings above the music drew special attention to the canon in *O lux beata Trinitas* (BE 1/6), and to those in *Miserere mihi Domine* (BE 1/13) and *Diliges Dominum* (BE 1/12). In *O lux* the canon 'Tres partes in una' appropriately sets words praising the perfect unity of the Father, Son and Holy Ghost. It is formed by the first soprano, the first alto and tenor. *Miserere mihi Domine* is based on two statements of the plainsong cantus firmus, first by the bass and then ornamented by the soprano, so the piece is in effect a pair of variations like some of Byrd's early instrumental works. The canon occurs in the second half of the piece, where the first alto part is a simultaneous inversion of the soprano part, the bass part is a repetition of the second tenor part, and the second alto and first tenor parts are free. *Diliges Dominum* is a canon for eight voices which reverses half-way through. It contains four pairs of melodies. the second half of each melody being the mirror image of the first half of its partner. (Ex. 12, overleaf.)

The use of compositional devices such as canon is a recurring feature of Byrd's work from the very first. Even when the technique is not strictly applied, long stretches of imitative writing like those of *In resurrectione tua* (BE 2/10) may approach canon. Among Byrd's later motets are a number of examples of true canonic writing, most notably in the demonstration piece *Quomodo cantabimus*.[17] His concern was not however with such structures for their own sake, though no doubt he was fascinated by his ability to solve the problems he set himself. It was with the effective presentation of thoughts and feelings that could be embodied in music. A parallel can be drawn with the interest of sixteenth-century English authors in rhetoric and rhetorical techniques, through which they sought the most effective presentation of literary material.[18]

17   Others are *Levemus corda* and *Peccavi super numerum*.

18   The connection between musical and literary rhetoric in England at this period is a subject which has not been much investigated, though as Kerman has noted the English had a 'passion to make music match the quality of the word, phrase, sentence, sonnet, or psalm: to make music rhetoric'. (Kerman, 1966.) See also Butler, 1980. Figuration and ornamentation can be regarded as aspects of rhetoric in music. (Harley, 1992-94, p. 225.)

Ex. 12

Beginning and end of *Diliges Dominum*

Byrd doubtless grew up with an awareness of rhetorical concepts, absorbed in the course of Latin lessons and from contemporary English writers.[19] It is certain that very shortly after his return from Lincoln to London he moved in circles where rhetorical ideas flourished. A series of family connections through marriage meant that the Earl of Oxford, from whom Byrd attempted to buy the manor of Battyshall and whose verses he set, was distantly related to George Puttenham, the probable author of *The arte of English poesie*, a treatise on rhetoric published in 1589 but assembled over a number of years.[20] Puttenham was in turn

19   For example, Thomas Wilson's *The arte of rhetorique* was in print by 1553 (the date of the earliest extant copy) and went through several editions.

20   Puttenham was born about 1529. On his authorship of *The arte of English poesie*, and his family connections, see the introduction to Puttenham, 1936. This deals also with the improbability of *The Arte* having been written by Byrd's friend Lord Lumley, though

related by marriage to Sir Edward Dyer, another of the authors who provided words for Byrd's songs. It is very likely that Byrd came to know Dyer's younger friend Sir Philip Sidney. He too wrote verses set by Byrd, and was the author of the critical essay *The Defence of Poesie* (or *An Apologie for Poetrie*), begun about the end of 1579 though not published until 1595.[21]

Music and words come together in the 'Rules to be observed in dittying' set out by Thomas Morley, who claimed Byrd as his master. Morley insists at some length on the need for the harmonies and melodic and rhythmic movement of the music to be compatible with the words of a vocal composition, and for due attention to be given to other matters connected with 'framing a fit musicke to the nature of a dittie'.[22] Byrd's rhetorical concerns cannot be divorced from his ability to mould the contours of his melodies, to plan long- and short-range harmonic progress, and to feed into his work an inexhaustible supply of fresh, unpredictable, and above all appropriate ideas.[23] He himself recognized the inseparability of music, sentiment and decorum, the last of which was a central theme of writers on rhetoric. In the dedication of *Gradualia* (1605) he was to write:

Quemadmodum enim, in mechanicis; artifici turpe sit, ex preciosissima quapiam materia, impolitum opus effingere: ita profecto, Sacris sententiis, quibus Dei ipsius, caelestiumque Civium, laudes decantantur; nulla nisi caelestis quaedam (quantum eniti possumus) harmonia conveniat. Porro, illis ipsis sententiis (ut experiendo didici) adeo abstrusa atque recondita vis inest; ut divina cogitanti, diligenterque ac serio pervolutanti; nescio quonam modo, aptissimi quique numeri, quasi sponte accurrant sua; animoque minime ignavo, atque inerti, liberaliter ipsi sese offerant.

the hypothesis that it may have been indicates that the study of rhetoric flourished among those with whom Byrd mixed. One of the authors mentioned favourably by Puttenham is Henry Paget, the older brother of Byrd's patron Thomas Paget.

21   Dyer was some eleven years older than Sidney, who lived from 1554 to 1586. The likelihood of Byrd having known Sidney is perhaps greater than allowed by Duncan-Jones, 1990.

22   Morley, 1597, p. 177-178 (1952 ed., p. 290-292).

23   Kerman (1981, pp. 97-98) observes: 'In the music of Byrd's time, a basic tension arose from what may be described as an incipient imbalance between verbal and musical rhetoric ... The pace of Latin prose was not easily accommodated to the pace of sixteenth-century polyphony. As is generally true in such cases, tension within the medium caused composers trouble and also to develop solutions of ingenuity and eloquence. The solutions become, in a sense, an index of the vitality of the style in question.'

(Just as in the craft of construction it would be shameful to make something crude out of the most precious material, so surely nothing but heavenly harmony (insofar as we can achieve it) will do for the sacred sentences in which the praises of God himself and the citizens of heaven are sung. Furthermore (as I have learned from experience) there is such profound and hidden power in the very ideas expressed by the words, that to one reflecting earnestly and attentively on divine things, if his mind is not idle and inactive, the right notes somehow occur spontaneously.)[24]

The last sentence of this passage strongly recalls the spiritual exercises of Saint Ignatius Loyola, and one wonders whether Byrd learned this method of studying texts from his Jesuit friends.[25]

Byrd brought a great variety of patterns and principles of construction to the setting of sacred words. He had at his command all the artifices of vocal and contrapuntal composition. It is noticeable that abstract design and technical devices play a greater part in motets of joy and praise than they do in those with texts expressing contrition and despair, where Byrd's invention is more closely guided by the meaning of the words.[26] This is perhaps the reason why Byrd felt able to fit the words of *Laudate pueri* to existing music.[27]

One of the most significant developments in Byrd's music is his use of rhetorical devices which Morley, who probably learned them from Byrd, wrote of with warm approval:

If you would compose well the best patternes for that effect are[28] the workes of excellent men, wherin you may perceive how points are brought in, the best way of which is when either the song beginneth two severall points in two severall parts at once, or one point foreright and reverted ... this way of

24   Brett (1989, p. xvii) emphasizes the need to consider the complete passage, not just the second sentence which is usually quoted. Irving (1990) seeks to penetrate more deeply into Byrd's meaning.

25   The constitution of the Society of Jesus was approved by Pope Paul III in the year of Byrd's birth. Ignatius of Loyola was made its general in 1541. His exercises, first published in 1548 with the assent of the Pope, initially 'came down in a living tradition through the men who had received them from the lips of St. Ignatius himself'. (Introduction by John Morris to *The text of the spiritual exercises of Saint Ignatius*, fourth edition, London, 1936.)

26   Kerman, 1981, p. 84.

27   Whythorne (1961, pp. 173-174) described himself as writing words to fit music he had already composed, but the fitting of existing Latin words to existing music cannot have been common except in the case of works like the *Western wind* Masses.

28   Morley has 'or'.

two or three several points going together is the most artificiall kinde of composing which hetherto hath beene invented, either for Motets or *Madrigals*, speciallie when it is mingled with revertes, because so it maketh the musick seeme more strange ...[29]

It had long been customary to distinguish different sections of a text by beginning each with a separate point. Morley seems, rather confusedly, to be describing two further procedures. One is the combination of different points, or different versions of one point, in setting one verbal phrase, as though to view it from different angles. The other is the process already noted in *Afflicti pro peccatis*, in which a text is broken into phrases that are set to different overlapping points, with each being treated as a separate unit in the imitative complex.[30] Imitation had progressed from being something applied to music, or to be used schematically, to being a means of examining the innermost meaning of the words.[31] The beginning of *Libera me Domine et pone me iuxta te* (BE 1/2) illustrates the first procedure, with 'one point foreright and reverted'. (Ex. 13a, overleaf.) The second procedure is illustrated by the beginning of *Aspice Domine quia facta est* (BE 1/4), where the words 'Aspice Domine', 'quia facta est' and 'desolata civitas' are set to overlapping fragments of melody treated as independent points (resulting in fact in triple imitation).[32] (Ex. 13b.)

29   Morley, 1597, p. 167 (1952 ed., p. 276). 'Reverted' means inverted in this context.

30   It is the second procedure to which Kerman (1981, p. 98-100) applies the term 'double imitation', which should not be confused with 'double' or 'invertible' counterpoint. (See Morris, 1922, pp. 45-52, and Andrews, 1966, pp. 245-247.) The technique was one particularly used by Byrd (though, as Kerman points out, very little in his instrumental works), but it was not new in English music. It occurs in one of Tallis's contributions to *Cantiones sacrae*, the seven-part motet *Suscipe quaeso Domine*, which may have been written more than twenty years prior to publication. Doe (1976, p. 40), following Noble, connects the motet with the Mass *Puer natus nobis est*. If the association is correct, the three Byrd brothers may have participated in its first performance.

31   In earlier times there seems often to have been a considerable indifference in England to the words of musical settings. Humphreys (1979-80, p. 22) notes that 'almost all known copies of the van Wilder chansons from English scribes are untexted'.

32   Triple imitation appears also in *Libera me Domine et pone me iuxta te*, at the words 'et rursum', 'post tenebras', and 'spero lucem'. Monson (1975-76) draws attention to Byrd's repeated use in *Libera me* of an expressive cadential formula of Continental origin. Kerman (1981, p. 102) suggests a direct debt in Byrd's *Aspice Domine* to Philip van Wilder's setting of the same text, and that it may be a deliberate exercise in the Continental manner. For Wilder's influence on English music, see Humphreys, 1979-80.

Ex. 13

a. *Libera me Domine et pone me iuxta te*

b. *Aspice Domine*

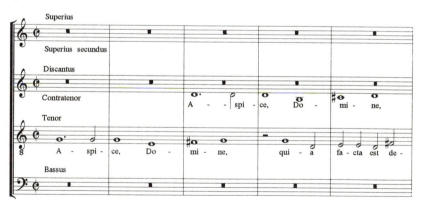

Aspice Domine deals with the desolation of 'the city', that is to say Jerusalem, standing for the English Catholic community. *Libera me Domine et pone me* is an expression of personal torment: 'Dies mei transierunt, cogitationes meae dissipatae sunt, torquentes cor meum' (*My days have passed away, my thoughts are dissipated, wringing my heart*). Byrd's response to the words was dark and passionate. The particular affective quality of his setting is one which surfaces from time to time in subsequent English church music, for example in the work of Orlando Gibbons and Henry Purcell.[33] It parallels an expressionistic trend in the visual arts. On the Continent this led to the anguished expressions and flowing draperies exhibited in baroque paintings and sculptures; but it was not confined to the productions of Continental artists, and appears too in English works such as the *Lamentation over the dead Christ* (1586), one of the few large-scale paintings by the minaturist Isaac Oliver.[34]

In the first part of *Quomodo cantabimus* (BE 9) multiple points become the means of integrating the three-part canon and the free parts. The canon is between the bass voice that enters first and the two altos, the second of which proceeds by inversion. The point with which one of the tenor voices begins the motet, and with which the other four freely imitative voices enter, is based on the first three notes of the canon in its inverted form. This partial relationship between the canon and the free voices is renewed as each phrase of the text becomes the occasion for a fresh point.

It is hardly possible to explore comprehensively within a short space all the technical resources Byrd brought to the composition of motets, and since he did not always proceed in a straight line it is not easy to illustrate his development.[35] Brief examples may nevertheless serve to

---

33   Gibbons' *O Lord in thy wrath* and Purcell's *Lord, how long wilt thou be angry?* are cases in point. For Purcell's interest in Byrd, see Thompson, 1995, pp. 14-15, and Thompson, 1996.

34   Draperies swept by unfelt winds were to appear in the English paintings of Van Dyck, e.g. *Rinaldo and Armida* and the portrait of Mrs Edymion Porter. For an anguished expression and upturned eyes see his *Lamentation*, painted during an absence in Flanders. The uplifted eyes occur in a portrait of Byrd's acquaintance Fr. William Weston, reproduced as a frontispiece to Morris, 1875. Oliver's *Lamentation* (reproduced in Williams, 1995, pl. 13) owes something to Continental influences. So does the spirit that breathes through Byrd's *Libera me Domine et pone me iuxta te*; this is revealed in the opening point and a typical Continental cadence with a suspended seventh, and perhaps transmitted to Byrd by Ferrabosco. (Monson, 1975-76.)

35   Andrews (1966, pp. 2-3) describes Byrd as 'taking the methods of his predecessors, developing and adapting some, transforming others, and rejecting what he

convey something further of his methods. A suitable starting point is provided by two motets that have no cantus firmus, no canon, no multiple points, and little variation in vocal colour: *Memento homo* and *Emendemus in melius*.

It is difficult to be precise about the date of *Memento homo* (BE 1/8), but it must be one of the earlier — perhaps the first — of the motets written in the period 1572 to 1574. It has a short text (only eighteen syllables) conveying the maxim 'thou art dust, and to dust thou shalt return'. Byrd spins it out with much repetition, and treats the words as abstract entities. His setting is so far divorced from the message that the overall effect is of lightness rather than sobriety. The counterpoint is continuous and clear, and while it creates a web of strettos the imitation is seldom more than impressionistic. The principal cadences occur with almost mathematical regularity, and the straightforward harmony, which hardly strays from the guileless Ionian mode, matches the translucency of the texture.

Emendemus in melius (BE 1/1) forms a sharp contrast to *Memento homo*. It was probably the last to be written of Byrd's contributions to the *Cantiones Sacrae* of 1575, and it sums up much that he had learned about rhetorical control. It is reflective, even solemn, and while certainly not overwrought it explores the expressiveness possible in the reticent homophonic style of syllabic declamation, carrying it beyond what he had achieved in *Siderum rector* (BE 1/9) and *O lux beata Trinitas*.[36] Reserve is the overall impression conveyed by the first part of *Emendemus in melius*, and Byrd holds the latent emotion in check and ensures that dissonances are avoided or smoothed away. In the second part that emotion is released. The writing becomes less homophonic and less concise.[37] Cadences are enlivened with dissonance, and the harmonic temperature rises with the introduction of chords foreign to the mode. Tonality is in fact an important constructional element in *Emendemus in melius*. The key is the twice transposed Aeolian (G with two flats), but the opening chords (minor on G, major on E flat and B flat) include two which are to play a role as the motet progresses: a double cadence on B flat emphasizes the words 'die mortis', the *secunda pars* begins with an E flat chord, the word 'Deus' is set by another B flat cadence, and the final

did not find useful'. There was no 'conscious and deliberate break with tradition and the setting up of new styles of composition governed by fashionable trends'.

36   Andrews (1966, pp. 6-7) notes that in *Emendemus in melius* 'technique is no longer a conscious factor standing in the way of free musical expression', as it had been in *Aspice Domine quia facta est*.

37   Although the second part is shorter than the first part, it is not nearly as short as the number of syllables contained in the text would suggest.

'libera nos' again starts with a chord on E flat. Byrd had good reason to place *Emendemus* first among his sequence of motets, where the mastery he could now exercise would be prominently displayed.

Ne irascaris Domine (BE 2/12), perhaps written a couple of years after *Emendemus in melius*, has some of the same reserve, but is differently constructed. It combines homophony, polyphony and antiphony, and its voice combinations change frequently. The two parts of the motet are balanced in method, length, feeling and tonality, and the relationship between them is reinforced by motivic and other links.[38] The emotional depths of the first part remain largely concealed; the composure of the second is pierced by emotion. The first part starts strongly in F, from which it makes a series of short excursions, returning clearly to the home key at the word 'nostrae', and again at the final repetitions of 'respice' and 'omnes nos'. The second part, *Civitas sancti tui*,[39] makes a slightly uncertain journey from F to D, which it reaches with the last repetition of 'facta est deserta' (roughly at the point where the first part reached 'nostrae'). The contrapuntal texture gives way at once to ten homophonic bars proclaiming 'Sion deserta facta est'. They are firmly anchored in F, but embrace acutely affective major chords on E flat.

Homophonic or partly homophonic writing appears too in *Tristitia et anxietas* (BE 2/4), though it can conveniently be bracketed with a small group of other motets of the early 1580s, including *Deus venerunt gentes* (BE 2/7) and *O quam gloriosum* (BE 2/13), in which Byrd appears to have exhausted the possibilities he had found in setting fragments of his texts to separate points. It is a variety of textures that helps to make *Tristia et anxietas* one of Byrd's outstanding imitative motets. The variety is explicit from the beginning, where in singing the phrase 'Tristitia et anxietas' the upper voices work in pairs, and the bass voice pursues an independent course. True imitation occurs only with the phrase 'occupaverunt interiora mea'. The setting of the next sentence, 'Moestum factum est cor meum in dolore, et contenebrati sunt oculi mei', combines homophony and polyphony with sporadic imitation ('in dolore', 'et contenebrati') which becomes more pronounced with the next sentence, 'Vae mihi, quia peccavi'. The imitative nature of the second part of the motet is more marked, and a succession of points culminates in the stretto treatment of 'et miserere mei', with repetitions of the imitative motive closely pursuing one another.

38   Kerman, 1981, pp. 165-166.

39   Modelled to some extent on Wilder's *Aspice Domine*. (Humphreys, 1979-80, p. 30.)

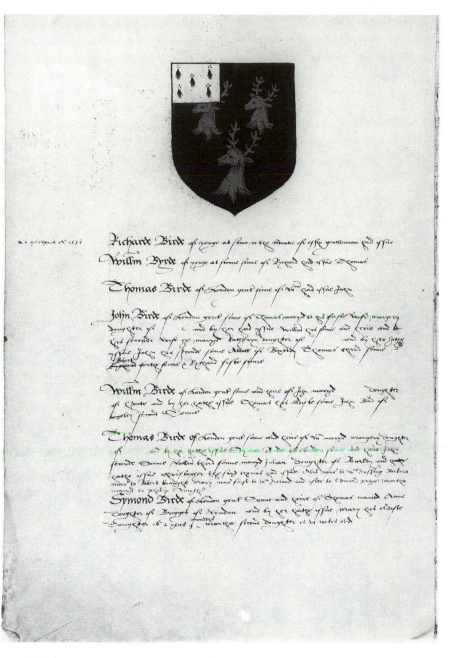

1. The Byrd genealogy, recorded by Robert Cooke in 1571. (Queen's College, Oxford, MS 72, f. 72ᵛ.)

2a. The most elaborate of Byrd's signatures in the account books of Lincoln Cathedral. (Lincolnshire Archives, D&C Bi/2/1, 'liveries' section.)

2b. St Margaret's, Lincoln, where Byrd was married and two of his children were baptized. (Lincoln Cathedral Library.)

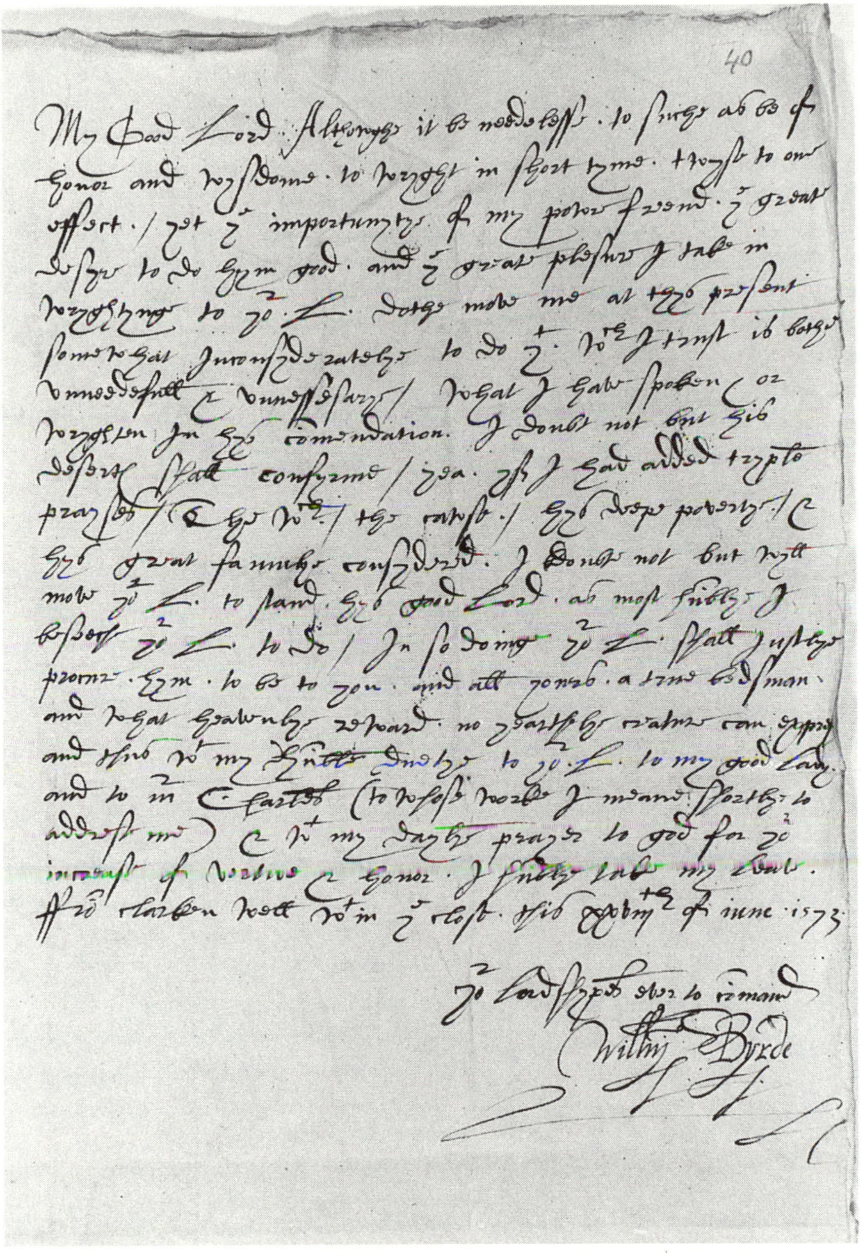
40

My Good Lord . Althoughe it be needeles . to suche as be of
honor and wysdome . to wryght in short tyme . trouble to our
effect . / yet ye importunytye of my poore frend . ye great
desyre to do hym good . and ye great plesure I take in
wrytynge to yor L. doth move me at this present
somewhat inconsyderatelye to do yt . wch I trust is bothe
unneedefull & unnecessarye / what I have spoken or
wrytten in his commendation . I doubt not but his
deserte shall confyrme / yea . yf I had added tryple
prayses / & the wch / the rather . / his deep povertye / &
his great famelye considered . I doubt not but wyll
move yor L. to stand . his good Lord . as most frendly I
beseche yor L. to do / In so doinge yor L. shall justly
procure hym . to be to you . and all yours . a true bedesman .
and what heavenly reward . no yearthly creature can expres
and thus wt my humble dutye to yor L. to my good Lady .
and to mr Charles (to whose worship I meane shortly to
addresse me) & wt my dayly prayer to god for yor
increase of vertue & honor . I humbly take my leave .
ffro Clarken well wt in ye close . this xxviijth of iune 1573

Yor Lordshipps ever to comand
Willm Byrde

3. Byrd's letter of 28 June 1573 to Lord Paget. (Keele University Library, Special Collections and Archives, Early Paget Correspondence, 1/7, f. 40.)

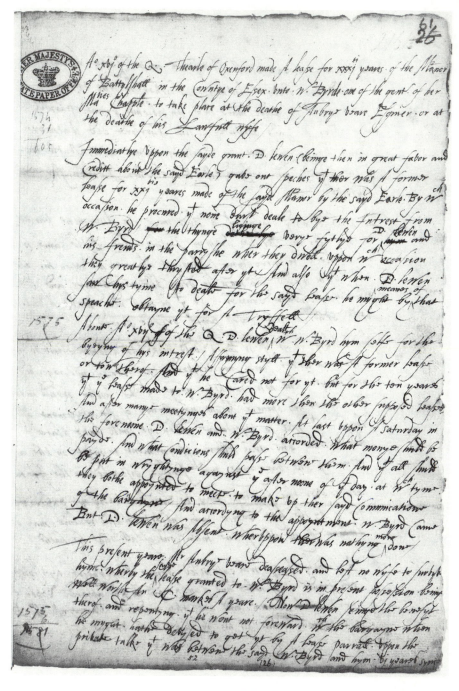

4. Part of a document written by Byrd in 1580, during the dispute over
Battyshall Manor. (Public Record Office, SP12/157/59-60.)

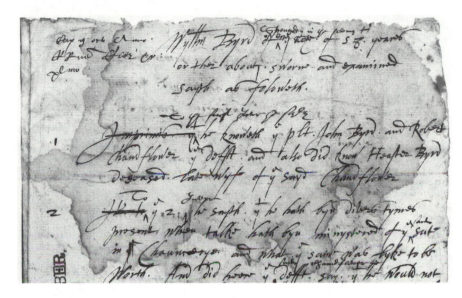

5a. The beginning of a document dated 2 October 1598, in which Byrd gave his age as '58. yeares or ther abouts'. (Public Record Office, STAC5/B27/37.)

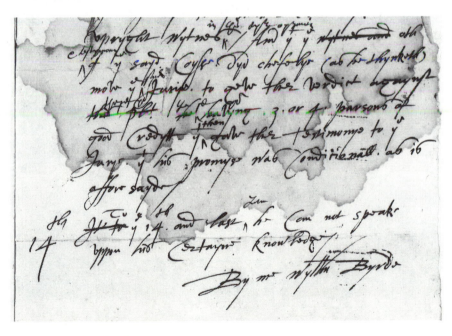

5b. Byrd's signature at the end of the same document.

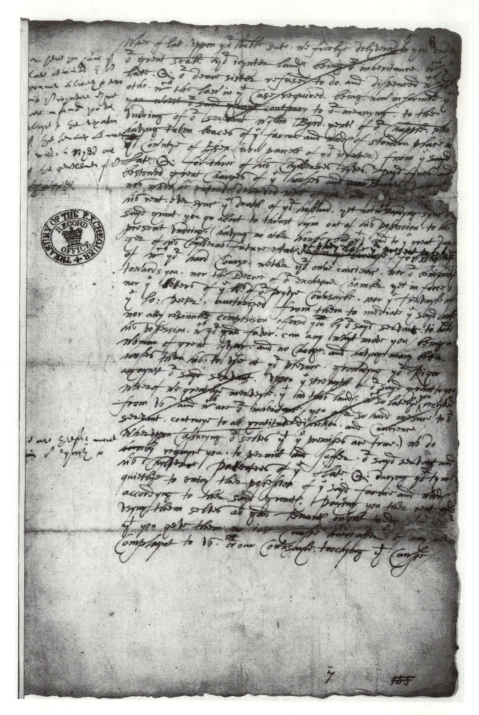

6. Byrd's draft, dated 24 January 1603/4, of a letter for King James to send to Mrs Shelley. (Public Record Office, SP15/36.)

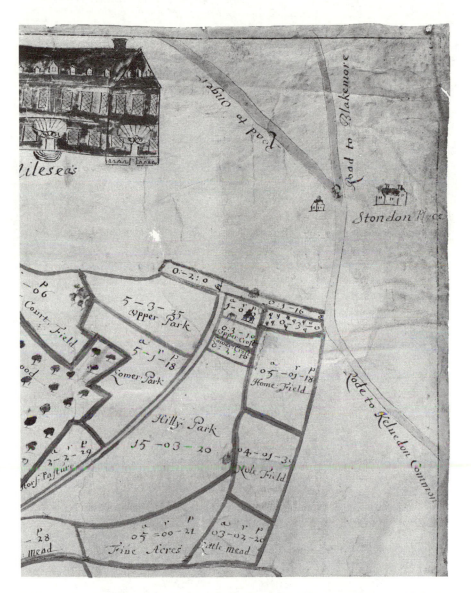

7. Part of a map of c.1700 showing Stondon Place. The large house is Myles's, owned by Richard and Anthony Luther. (Essex Record Office, D/DFa P1.)

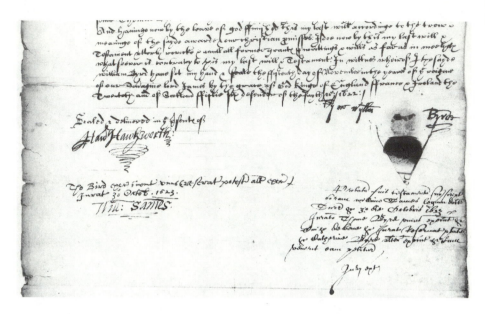

8a. Byrd's signature at the end of his will, dated 15 November 1622. (Public Record Office, Prob. 10, box 404.)

8b. The churchyard at Stondon Massey, where William and Julian Byrd were probably buried. (Essex Record Office, Mint Binder, Stondon Massey 1/1. From Slocombe's *Companion to the Almanacs for 1851*.)

A year or two after he wrote *Tristitia et anxietas* Byrd composed *Haec dicit Dominus* (BE 3/8), a more fully homphonic piece and his most profound and most distinguished in this style. It must have been written during the same period as another homophonic motet, *Vide Domine* (BE 2/6), and one wonders whether they show the effects of Byrd's work on the *Great Service*. For all that, each of the motets is a dark-hued setting of a text which Catholics would have read as a reflection of their tribulations. Dark, certainly − both have a combination of voices used in none of Byrd's other motets: mezzo-soprano, alto, tenor, baritone, bass − but even in Byrd's most sombre pieces there is a humanity, tenderness and an inner radiance. It is as if in his music Byrd had penetrated beyond temporal sorrows to experience the solace for which the text of *Vide Domine* prays, and which that of *Haec dicit Dominus* promises. The full choir sings more or less continuously throughout *Haec dicit Dominus*. Each voice seems at first to seek its own way through a series of predetermined harmonies, for although the voices are not quite free rhythmically the texture is not wholly homophonic. Snatches of imitation between voices are however short-lived. There is no genuine imitative writing until more than half-way through the second part, after the striking setting in breves of 'et es spes' (*and there is hope*). So effectively is the gloom dispelled that at the end Byrd amuses himself with the musical equivalent of word-play in setting 'et revertentur filii ad terminos suos' (*and thy children shall return to their own borders*), where he inverts the point of 'et revertentur' to form the point of 'ad terminos'.

The semi-homophonic style of *Haec dicit Dominus* led Byrd in the direction of the baroque, particularly in the first part. The outer voices play a major role in controlling the shape of the piece. The highest voice (like the inner voices) moves for the most part by small steps, terminating its first phrase on f#', its second on g#', and so rising to a' and b'. The bass line, in true baroque fashion, is often highly active, with leaps of anything up to an octave.

The first two phrases of *Circumdederunt me* closely resemble those of *Haec dicit Dominus*, which it immediately follows in the *Cantiones sacrae* of 1591. *Circumdederunt me* (BE 3/9) is a quiet and reflective motet that seems to belong to the mid-eighties, a prayer for deliverance from sorrow. Frequently, at this stage in his career, Byrd sought to diversify the textures within a single motet. It is often the differences in texture which now distinguish the different phrases of the text. Hints of multiple imitation are only partly developed until the word 'Tribulationem', which begins what is virtually a second part of the motet and triggers off half a dozen pages of alternately homophonic and contrapuntal writing that conclude with a stretto on 'libera animam meam'.

The six-voice motets *Domine non sum dignus* (BE 3/15) and *Domine salva nos* (BE 3/20) are among a number of Byrd's compositions that form pairs of complementary pieces. Another pair is formed by two more motets for six voices composed roughly about the same time, *Cantate Domino* (BE 3/18) and *Haec dies* (BE 3/21). *Domine non sum dignus* and *Domine salva nos* are both prayers, one for a sick son and the other for salvation,[40] and they have similar proportions and the same combination of voices.[41] Kerman calls them 'the most advanced of Byrd's earlier motets', and says they constitute the clearest stylistic link between the *Cantiones sacrae* and the *Gradualia*.[42] Equally marked is their affinity to the two versions of *This sweet and merry month of May*, which Byrd wrote for Thomas Watson's *The first sett, of Italian madrigalls Englished*, published in 1590. Both motets display features of the madrigal style (as indeed do *Cantate Domino* and *Haec dies*), and both have the quality of chamber music – which strengthens the belief that Byrd wrote them for domestic performance. There is no slack in these pieces; the writing is taut and concise. The long vocal lines of earlier motets have given way to short, strikingly moulded motives following one another in a series of strettos that create complex rhythmic patterns, and break up the texts into phrases that would once have provided matter for more leisurely multiple imitation. Implicit tempo changes form an integral part of Byrd's methods of illuminating the texts. In *Domine non sum dignus* the minim pulse changes to a crotchet pulse at 'sed tantum dic verbum'; *Domine salva nos* interrupts the flow with a cry of 'impera' before it settles down again for 'fac Deus tranquilitatem'. In two other motets, *Haec dies* and *Laudibus in sanctis* (BE 3/1), both included in the 1591 book of *Cantiones sacrae*, larger-scale changes between duple and triple time are explicitly indicated. None of these motets has survived in a pre-publication source. It is probable that all were written after Byrd completed work on the 1589 collection of *Cantiones sacrae*, and betray his interest in ideas that were current at the time.

40   Kerman (1981, p. 48) suggests that *Domine non sum dignus* might be connected with the illness of John Petre's youngest child, Robert, who died in infancy on 20 December 1590.

41   Ibid., p. 184.

42   Ibid., p. 187.

14

INSTRUMENTAL WORKS OF THE MIDDLE PERIOD

Keyboard music

It may have been the potential difficulty of setting his keyboard music in type that deterred Byrd from attempting to print it.[1] Instead he collected it in *My Ladye Nevells Booke*, a manuscript copied by John Baldwin, who at the time was a lay clerk of St George's Chapel, Windsor.[2] This is the earliest surviving source to include virginal music by Byrd, as distinct from organ music.[3] Baldwin presumably worked under Byrd's direction, and when he had completed the task he wrote 'finished & ended the leventh of September in the year of our Lord God 1591'. Corrections and alterations seem to have been made by Byrd himself.

My Ladye Nevells Booke consists of thirty-two pieces entered as forty-two numbers.[4] Byrd's intention seems to have been to lay out the contents in three groups: (1) grounds, dances and programmatic pieces, (2) pavans and galliards, and (3) fantasias and variations. Key plays a significant role only in the layout of the central section, where 'major' and 'minor' pieces are carefully disposed. The original plan may have been to include nine pieces in each section, with the first and last sections introduced by extra pieces dedicated to Lady Nevell.[5] (Table 12, overleaf.) If this was indeed Byrd's intention, it was modified by

1 The problem was one of printing simultaneous notes on a single staff. Music was not engraved in England until the publication of *Parthenia* in 1612 or 1613.

2 See Appendix G. Baldwin's three-part song of Coridon and Phyllida was sung before the Queen on 22 September 1591, as part of the Elvetham entertainment. (Brenneke, 1952, p. 36.) He was placed 'next in ordinary' in the Chapel Royal on 3 February 1593/4, was sworn in as a Gentleman without pay on 23 March 1594/5, and appointed to a full place on 20 August 1598. He died on 28 August 1615. (Rimbault, 1872, pp. 35-36, 5, 8.)

3 See p. 190.

4 Thirty-two pieces counting each pavan-galliard pair and the *Battle* sequence as single pieces.

5 The number twenty-seven may have had some meaning for Lady Nevell, or Byrd may have attached some significance to it, say as 3 times 9 or 3 times 3 times 3, though speculation should not be confused with fact. On the subject of numerology in Renaissance music generally see Elders, 1994. Musical symbolism is also explored by Lowinsky, 1946. For an illustrative discussion of similar ideas, see Wells, 1994, pp. 113-142, which deals with symbolic geometry in the Renaissance lute rose.

accidents of copying and a decision to add pieces at the last moment.[6] The resulting collection is listed in the catalogue of Byrd's music and Appendix G.[7] The central group of pavans and galliards nonetheless remains clearly as Byrd planned it, and presents a remarkable conspectus of his development and the variety of his achievement.[8]

Table 12 · Possible original plan of *My Ladye Nevells Booke*

My   Lady   Nevell's   ground
introducing grounds, dances and programmatic pieces

    Qui passe: for my Lady
      Nevell
    The battle sequence
    The barley break
    A galliard jig
    The hunt's up
    Ut re mi fa sol la
    The second ground
    Hugh Aston's ground
    Monsieur's alman

Pavans and galliards

Pavan and galliard in c MB 27/29
Pavan and galliard in G MB 28/71
Pavan and galliard in a MB 27/14
Pavan and galliard in C MB 27/30

Pavan and galliard in c MB 27/31
Pavan and galliard in C MB 27/32
Canonic pavan in G MB 28/74
Pavan in a MB 27/17
Passing measures pavan and
    galliard in g MB 27/2

A voluntary for my Lady Nevell
introducing fantasias and variations

    The woods so wild
    The maiden's song
    Voluntary
    Walsingham
    All in a garden green
    Lord Willoughby's welcome
      home
    The carman's whistle
    Sellinger's round
    A fancy

---

6 *Monsieur's alman*, *Hugh Aston's ground* and *The second ground* slipped out of place. The pavan and galliard dedicated to William Petre were almost certainly new compositions, and the two fantasias which follow them look like afterthoughts. Neighbour (1978, pp. 21-22) makes the alternative suggestion that it is *The hunt's up* and *Ut re mi fa sol la* which are out of place, and that the first section should consist of the two grounds dedicated to Lady Nevell, descriptive music and dances, while the third section should consist of fantasias, grounds and variations.

7 See pp. 406-407 and 414-415.

8 See Neighbour, 1978, p. 179; Harley 1992-94, ii, p. 34-35.

Byrd's plan for *My Ladye Nevells Booke* mixes pieces composed over a span of some twenty years. Five were almost certainly written before 1572 and have been discussed above: *The hunt's up*, *The maiden's song*, *A galliard jig*, *The second ground* and the concluding fantasia (MB 27/27). The dates of a few later pieces in the collection can be deduced as follows:

(a) *Ut re mi fa sol la* (MB 28/64) consists of seventeen variations. The number is so unusual as to suggest that the piece was designed, like the *Cantiones sacrae* of 1575, as a compliment to Queen Elizabeth on the seventeenth anniversary of her succession. Another piece consisting of seventeen variations is *The second ground* (MB 27/42). This may have been revised in the same year from an existing set of twelve variations.[9]

(b) Three pieces were evidently written specially for inclusion in *My Lady Nevells Booke*. They are *My Lady Nevell's ground* (MB 28/57), *Qui passe: for my Lady Nevell* (MB 27/19), and *A voluntary: for my Lady Nevell* (MB 28/61). Number 36 in the collection, *A fancy* (MB 27/25), also has 'for my ladye nevell' written at the end, and may have been a recent composition.

(c) The *Battle* sequence includes an Irish march, which suggests that Byrd had in mind one of the Irish rebellions of the 1570s or early 1580s. The march and the galliard which frame the sequence may have been added to give it the weight needed for its appearance in the collection. The march may have been in existence for some time, but the galliard seems to have been newly composed.[10]

(d) Baldwin added the date 1590 to *The woods so wild*.[11] It cannot be the date of copying, because he is unlikely to have noted this in only one case, or (to judge from his final inscription) to have omitted the day and month. The piece occupies a place in the third section comparable to that of *Qui passe* in the first section, and may have had a special meaning for Lady Nevell.

(e) The pavan dedicated to 'mr. w. peter' and its galliard are separated from the main group of pavans and galliards, and appear to

9   See p. 216 on the structure of the 1575 *Cantiones sacrae*, and pp. 194-195 on *The second ground*. John Bull's chromatic *Ut re mi fa sol la* (MB 14/17) also has seventeen variations. Bull's tonal plan required only thirteen statements of the hexachord to return it to the pitch at which it started. He may have added four more to match Byrd's piece.

10   Neighbour, 1978, pp. 172-174.

11   A revised version with two additional variations appears in *The Fitzwilliam Virginal Book* and Will Forster's manuscript (BL, R. M. 24.d.3).

have been absent from the original plan.[12] Their style suggests recent composition. So does that of *A fancy* (MB 28/46), which has close similarities to the pavan and galliard.[13]

(f) The tune of *Lord Willoughby's welcome home* was also known as 'Rowland'.[14] The title used in *My Lady Nevells Booke* may indicate that Byrd associated it with the words celebrating Willoughby's return from the Low Countries in 1589.

While no definite dates can be assigned to the central group of pavans and galliards in *My Lady Nevells Booke*, stylistic and other evidence points to their composition over the period from 1572 to the late 1580s.[15]

(g) Byrd transcribed the first pavan (MB 27/29) from his consort pavan in C minor (BE 17/14), and Tregian's copy of the keyboard version is annotated 'The first that ever he made'. The consort version must be one of the first pieces Byrd wrote after his return to London, and the keyboard version may have been made soon afterwards.[16]

(h) The eighth pavan (MB 27/17) has a five-part texture which suggests transcription from a lost consort original. Like the first pavan it may be one of Byrd's early essays in the genre.

(i) The fourth pavan (MB 27/30) must be later than the eighth, since it begins by quoting from the eighth's second strain. The quotation cannot be the other way about, since the third strain of the galliard to the fourth pavan continues the quotation. On stylistic grounds the fourth pavan is probably to be placed before the second.

(j) It has been suggested that the inscription 'Fant.', which Tregian attached to the second pavan (MB 28/71), stands for Richard Farrant.[17] Although this explanation is not wholly convincing, the idea that the pavan was a memorial piece for Farrant, who died in November 1580, is not at odds with the stylistic evidence.

(k) An early version of the ninth pavan (*The passing measures pavan*), which is based on the *passamezzo antico* ground, may have

---

12   William Petre was born in 1575. He was knighted in 1603, and in *Parthenia* the pavan is head 'S$^{r.}$ W$^{m.}$ Petre'.

13   *A voluntary* (MB 27/27), an early composition which stands last in the book, may have been added to fill up space.

14   See Brown, 1976, notes to MB 27/7.

15   See Neighbour, 1978.

16   See pp. 261, 269.

17   Brown, 1976, ii, p. 198. The possibility of a family connection between Byrd and Farrant is mentioned above (p. 25).

been known to Peter Philips before he went abroad in 1582, although his own *Passamezzo Pavana* (modelled on Byrd's) could easily have been based on a copy he received later.[18] A date of about 1580 for Byrd's piece however seems consistent with its style.

(l) Dart proposed that, like Byrd's song *Ye sacred muses*, the canonic seventh pavan might be a memorial to Tallis, who grounded Byrd in canon and died in 1585.[19] Dart's hypothesis is not contradicted by the style of the keyboard piece, but it is not supported by documentary evidence. It might equally well apply to the canonic consort fantasia (BE 17/8), which can be dated to the mid-1580s. Byrd may have felt an urge to write canons at that time, without intending to memorialize Tallis.

(m) The sixth pavan is named after Kinborough Good. It was written by 1589, since that is the year in which she changed her name on marriage.[20] It is however possible that it is somewhat earlier.

This leaves the third and fifth and ninth pavans to be fitted into the sequence, on the basis of style. The third seems to be among the earlier *Nevell* pavans, though it is almost certainly later than the eighth. The fifth may come about the middle, and the ninth (the *Passing measures*) at the end.

Keyboard variations

Byrd began working out a virginal style — that is to say, one with sonorities particularly suited to a plucked keyboard instrument — in sets of variations based on harmonic grounds and popular tunes. Most of those discussed in the previous chapter are patently fairly early, though *The second ground* may, in its unrevised form, have been written about the time of Byrd's return to London. *Hugh Aston's ground* and *Ut re mi fa sol la* are apparently later, but not much later. There is of course no means of knowing whether a line between them and those dealt with in chapter 10 is drawn accurately, but there are certain conveniences to dealing with them here. The same can be said of the sets of variations on popular tunes which were apparently written in the seventies or early eighties: *Fortune* (or *Fortune my foe*), *Walsingham*, *All in a garden green* and *Sellinger's round*.

---

18   Byrd's piece also provided inspiration for Morley's *Passamezzo pavan* and *Quadran pavan*. See p. 349, note 34.

19   Brown, 1976, ii, p. 198.

20   See p. 363.

Further sets of variations span a period of approximately a decade from about 1580. This assertion is based partly on their style, but — as indicated above — more precise evidence of date is also available in some cases. The group embraces *My Lady Nevell's ground* and *Qui passe: for my Lady Nevell*, presumably written after Byrd had conceived the idea of a collection dedicated to Lady Nevell, and variations on the tunes *Lord Willoughby's welcome home*, *The carman's whistle* and *Will you walk the woods so wild?*

Table 13 · Tunes used by Byrd as the basis of variations

	Bars	Form	Byrd's key	Chords implied [*]
Maiden's song	16	AABC	G	I II III IV Vma/mi VII
Fortune	12	AABCBC	G(b)	I III IV Vma VII
Garden green	12	ABCDCD	D	Ima/mi IV V VII
Sellinger	20	AABCC	G	I IV Vma/mi
Walsingham	8	ABAC	G(b)	Ima/mi II III Vma/mi VII
Carman's whistle	12	AABB'BB'	C	I IIma/mi IV V
Lord Willoughby	12	AABCBC	G(bb)	I II III Vma/mi VI VII
Woods so wild	8	ABAC	G	Ima/mi II III V VII

[*]*Not in order of occurrence. Other chords may be added by Byrd or result from his counterpoint.*

Byrd's innovations in writing variations were twofold: to bring to what was in essence a popular technique the keyboard skills developed by organists, and to devote to secular music the compositional skills usually reserved for the motet and the Mass. He had vision enough to see the possibility of these things, and the ability as performer and composer to realize his vision.

Just as in his songs Byrd allowed himself to be guided by the structure and sense of the poems he set, so he was guided by the nature of the grounds and tunes on which he composed variations. Each is different from every other, though each is strongly harmonic in its implications. Whereas *The second ground* was based on a series of twenty-eight notes, covering six different degrees of the scale; *Hugh Aston's ground* is thirty-two notes long and is comprised of five different notes. *My Lady Nevell's ground* and the ground of *Qui passe* contain internal repeats, while *Ut re mi fa sol la* is constructed from the ascending and descending notes of the hexachord. The tunes that form the basis of Byrd's variations are as individual as the grounds, and their differences can easily be distinguished in Table 13.[21]

Each repetition of a tune or ground forms the basis of a distinctly characterized section, arranged with other sections into a larger pattern. The fundamentals of the keyboard style Byrd brings to this procedure are most easily discerned in his treatment of popular tunes. He generally preserves the tune, with its implied harmonies, in something recognizably like its original form, and consigns musical development to the added parts. The tune may however appear in the top part or in an inner part. It may be set out plainly in single notes, or decorated (but the freer the decoration the firmer the harmonies). It may be harmonized homophonically or with broken chords, or integrated (perhaps in a fragmented form) into a contrapuntal texture. The counterpoint may involve anything from a single bass line to several imitative parts, or long lines of continuous quavers or semiquavers. Byrd frequently groups his variations according to the procedures they embody, but more than one procedure may occur in a single variation, and the method of one variation may be anticipated or continued in another.

No two sets of variations are laid out in the same way, but the plan of those on *The carman's whistle* will exemplify Byrd's methods.[22] (Table 14, overleaf.) *The carman's whistle* illustrates well the organic growth of Byrd's motives and the part they play in unifying his compositions. Four descending quavers at the end of variation 1 are repeated and preceded by a six-quaver turn-like motive in the middle of variation 2. At the end of variation 2 they are inverted and used in an imitative passage which

21   Grounds and tunes tended to exist in a variety of forms, and Byrd may either have chosen those that best met his needs or adapted them for his purposes. Another possible reason for his choice of tunes may be that some of them were sung with Catholic words. Mr Christopher Hogwood has suggested that such tunes may sometimes be hidden in the inner parts of Byrd's music. The subject has never been explored, however, and there is no readily available collection of Catholic words.

22   The plan of *All in a garden green* is given in Harley, 1992-94, ii, p. 27.

Table 14 · Plan of *The carman's whistle*

Variation	Bars	Main note values	Distribution between hands
1	4	minims/crotchets	both hands
	8	crotchets	
2	3	minims/crotchets	both hands
	3	crotchets	
	6	semiquavers	
3	8	crotchets	both hands
	4	semiquavers	
4	4	crotchets	both hands
	8	semiquavers	
5	6	crotchets/semiquavers	both hands
	6	running semiquavers	alternating
6	12	running semiquavers	alternating
7	8	crotchets	both hands
	4	semiquavers	right then left
8	8	running semiquavers	left hand
	4	running semiquavers	right then both
9	12	mixed	both hands

draws in the second motive. Each of the two motives generates further motives, as well as recurring in its original form. They give rise to the running quavers in variation 5, and the second motive occupies the whole of variation 6, in combination with its inversion. The four descending quavers and their inversion return at the end of the seventh variation to generate another series of running quavers in the eighth, and at the end of variation 9 they conclude the whole piece.

The plan of *Walsingham*, Byrd's largest set of variations (twenty-two in all), though less amenable to tabular simplification than the plan of *The carman's whistle*, is based on the same principles.[23] It demonstrates more clearly than the simpler set Byrd's unflagging attention to detail in shaping a composition over a long span. *Walsingham* requires the full C-a" compass of the instrument for which Byrd wrote in his mature works, but the range of the piece is increased gradually.[24] Until the bass sinks emphatically to D near the end of the fifth variation, it never goes lower than G. It goes down to F three times in variations seven and nine, but does not again descend below G before variations 19 to 21, where it goes down to F, D and F again. It is not until the coda that it twice reaches C at the very bottom of the keyboard. The same process of extension takes place at the top of the keyboard. The highest note played by the right hand is d", until it plays eb" and f" in variation five. It rises to g" in variations eight, ten, thirteen, sixteen and seventeen. The highest note on the keyboard, a", is reached in the nineteenth variation.

Byrd's expansion of the melodic outlines of the *Walsingham* variations is paralleled by an expansion of the harmonic resources he employs. From the outset the harmonies are subtly varied. In the fifth variation, where the upper melodic outline first rises to f", the tune is placed in the bass, altering the harmonies still further. (Ex. 14, overleaf.) In variation nineteen, the extreme melodic peak precedes a change in the final cadence from V-I (present in all the previous variations) to V-IV-I. The IV-I cadence is repeated in the coda.

23 *Walsingham* was a well known tune. (Chappell, 1893, p. 69). It possessed qualities likely to have attracted Byrd, but one cannot help wondering whether he wrote an exceptionally fine and long set of variations on it as a tribute to one of the Walsingham family. While no connection is known, it is not beyond the bounds of possibility. Sir Francis Walsingham (1532?-90), was a zealous Protestant. He was joint Secretary of State from 1573, and controlled an elaborate network of spies. He corresponded with Thomas Paget about the latter's Catholicism (Paget papers at Keele University), and Byrd may have felt it politic to keep on the right side of someone whose agents reported regularly on the activities of Catholics. Sir Francis was, moreover, the father-in-law of Sir Philip Sidney, with whom Byrd may have been on friendly terms. Sir Francis and, more especially, his younger cousin Thomas Walsingham were associated with Byrd's collaborator Thomas Watson. (See Watson's poem *Meliboeus*, 1590.)

24 The contents of *My Ladye Nevells Booke* as a whole require a keyboard with C D E F F# G A Bb B at the lower end, rising chromatically to a" at the top. In other sources Byrd demands G#, showing that he sometimes wrote for an instrument that was chromatic at least from E. Several types of keyboard were however in use, varying in range and chromatic completeness. See Moroney, 1993, and Harley, 1992-94, ii, pp. 160-162.

Ex. 14

Walsingham: beginnings of variations 1, 2, 3 and 5

Byrd's comprehensive designs contrast with many of the poorly planned sets of variations written by his successors. John Bull's set on *Walsingham*, longer and showier than Byrd's but rather ramshackle in its overall construction, bears out Ward's statement that he 'added to it at different times'.[25] The difference of approach between Byrd's set and Bull's is emphasized by the key each composer chose. Byrd placed the tune in G minor, so that the performer feels he is flattening notes altered by an accidental. Bull raised the tune a semitone, so that most of the accidentals are sharps and make the performer feel he is playing a more brilliant piece, in which panache compensates for weaknesses in planning. Bull in fact showed little interest in writing carefully worked out variations on popular tunes. Presumably he could improvise freely

25   Ward, 1740, p. 203.

when called upon, and was satisfied to do so. That was probably the case with Orlando Gibbons too. Gibbons' variations on *The woods so wild* show little recollection of Byrd's, and although brilliant and imaginative have only the loosest overall structure.[26]

Differences in the large-scale planning of Byrd's sets of variations on melodies are mainly those of degree, not principle. His variations on grounds work in much the same way, except that grounds allow Byrd to introduce proportional changes of time. His retention of the old-fashioned *tripla* section, which had been a feature of keyboard music written before he was born, is an aspect of the strongly conservative streak in his make-up.

The organization of *Hugh Aston's ground* is not nearly as unyielding as Table 15 might suggest, but the underlying plan is clear enough.

Table 15 · Plan of *Hugh Aston's ground*

1	⊘/3 (= 3/2 time). Primarily melodic. Minims and crotchets.
2	Mixed minims and crotchets.
3	Mainly crotchets.
4	Mainly crotchets.
5	Crotchets, then quavers.
6	Continuous quavers, first right hand then left.
7	Crotchets. Black notation (= 9/4) from bar 8. Quavers from bar 11.
8	Continuous quavers alternating between the hands.
9	⊘/3. Mixed crotchets and quavers.
10	Quavers, both hands. Black notation from bar 11, crotchets returning to quavers.
11	⊘/3. Quavers.
12	Mixed minims and crotchets.

---

26   The reverse is the case with Gibbons' fantasias.

A break with the conventional ground is marked by *Ut re mi fa sol la* (MB 28/64). Its pairing with the early *Ut mi re* (MB 28/65) has been discussed above.[27] The association is however a little curious, for the earlier piece is not to be compared to the latter in imagination and technique, and is something of an anticlimax if the two are played in the order signified by Tregian. The later work is far less like a set of variations than the earlier, and in some respects resembles Byrd's early keyboard works based on cantus firmi and his keyboard fantasias.[28]

The ground of *Ut re mi fa sol la* consists of an ascending hexachord in semibreves, a semibreve rest, and a descending hexachord in semibreves. Short passages of from one to six semibreves inserted between statements of the ground serve a variety of functions, easing modulations and transitions from one hexachord to another, and preventing the hexachord from imposing too regular and rigid a structure. A lack of rigidity is indeed one of the outstanding qualities of *Ut re mi fa sol la*. While statements of the hexachord provide a framework, they do not inhibit the freedom with which the piece develops. Unlike a cantus firmus the hexachord does not prescribe the harmonic progress of the piece so much as facilitate it, and Byrd greatly extends the range of harmonies available to him. He does so by placing the hexachord in different parts of what is generally a four-part texture, and starting it on different notes (avoiding those which would introduce A flat or G sharp, and cause difficulties of tuning).[29]

Ut re mi fa sol la has an introduction eight breves in length. This is based on the hexachords on G and C, and establishes G as the key. Thereafter the piece falls into four main sections marked by tonic cadences (variations 1-2, 3-6, 7-12, 13-17). The last accommodates the customary *tripla* passage in its first four variations, with hints of the dance — though it is a dance full of complex cross-rhythms. But, as is usual with Byrd's variations, there are several superimposed patterns. A pattern of a sort is formed by the pitch of the hexachords:

G D CCC FGAB♭C GGG D G GG.

There are motivic correspondences between variations, and between the ways in which sections unfold. The highest peaks of the upper outline, on f#", g" and a", are reached consecutively in the three central variations. The different patterns however coincide only approximately

27 See p. 171.

28 Neighbour (1978) in fact discusses Byrd's hexachord pieces with his fantasias.

29 See Harley, 1992-94, pp. 206-210. Byrd was able to use G# during the course of the piece, since in mean-tone tuning it formed an acceptable third with E, but not A♭.

with one another, and with statements of the hexachord and other divisions of the composition. The whole thing is handled with the greatest flexibility, and Byrd achieves an extraordinary equilibrium between rigorous planning and spontaneity.

Byrd never returned to the straightforward keyboard ground, except in pieces where a ground was implied by or coupled with a tune he was setting. *Sellinger's round*, though not actually a ground, incorporates features typical of ground-based popular music. A popular origin is apparent too in *The woods so wild*, where it is only additional harmonies, perhaps introduced by Byrd into bars 6 and 7 of each repetition of the tune, that save the piece from the F−G alternation of Aston's hornpipe.

The preparation of *My Ladye Nevells Booke* called for two pieces with grounds treated in an exceptional manner. *Qui passe* has a bass derived from the tune *Chi passa per questa strada*. This was printed in Filippo Azzaiolo's *Il primo libro de villotte alla padoana*, published in Venice in 1557. The harmonies rather than the tune passed into common currency, and were widely disseminated. Byrd sets out the ground in two repeated sections of eight and twelve bars. The complete ground occurs three times, forming six sections. A similar sort of layout occurs in *My Lady Nevell's ground*, which is composed of three repeated four-bar sections, with the whole stated six times. The relationship between the two works is close, the intervals of the *Qui passe* ground having inspired those of *My Lady Nevell's ground*. In the latter piece, however, Byrd drops the customary *tripla* section, as he did in his fantasias of the time. This seems to confirm that it is the later of the two.

Both *Qui passe* and *My Lady Nevell's ground* exhibit the type of large-scale planning remarked in Byrd's other sets of variations, and motivic growth of the kind described in connection with *The carman's whistle*. In *Qui passe* the last two bars of section 1 extend the figure with which it begins. The varied reprise starts by repeating these bars a fifth higher. Section 1 also generates the repeated chords that begin section 3. These chords appear again in *My Lady Nevell's ground*, at the start of section 6.

Keyboard fantasias

Byrd followed up his long fantasias in G and A (MB 28/62 and 27/13) with a second fantasia in G (MB 28/63). It cannot be dated with certainty, but can plausibly be assigned to the early 1570s. This fantasia is little more than half as long as its predecessor in the same key, and is evidently the product of reflection on the appropriate length for a fantasia. It is closer in duration to the fantasias Byrd composed around 1590.

The second fantasia in G begins, like the fantasia in A, with two brief expositions on the initial point, each ending with a full tonic cadence. The plagal extension of the second cadence has the effect of making what has gone before sound like a short prelude, but it is in fact a succinct substitute for the long, slow opening section of the first fantasia in G. After a brief non-imitative interlude composed of six bars repeated an octave lower, Byrd embarks on two imitative sections (bars 43-79 and 80-85) based on evolving motives. These are followed by a proportional time change and a long final section and coda that sum up much that has gone before.

If the second keyboard fantasia in G truly dates from the early 1570s, Byrd went for a spell of ten years or more before he wrote his next piece in the genre, and that was transcribed from a work for strings. The consort original of the keyboard fantasia in C (MB 27/26) was written by the mid-1580s,[31] and at a guess the keyboard version belongs to the same decade. It is most successful when it fully accepts the new medium.

Byrd's last three keyboard fantasias, in C (MB 27/25), G (MB 28/61) and D (MB 28/46), must all belong to the period when *My Ladye Nevells Booke* was being planned and prepared,[32] but each has a character distinctly its own.

The fantasia in C is a fine work that demonstrates how much Byrd's conception of the keyboard fantasia had matured. Although the sections are no less strongly individualized than those of previous fantasias, the divisions between them are marked less emphatically. Tonality is explored more adventurously, and plays an important part in the structure. Semiquaver passages contribute as much to the characterization of sections as they do to the increasing momentum of the piece, and the usual *tripla* section is replaced, perhaps under the influence of the Italian ricercare, by a varied repetition of the last section (a feature found in the other late keyboard fantasias as well).

The whole piece grows out of the first section of twenty-seven bars, which in *My Ladye Nevells Booke* are marked off by a double bar-line. After six well-spaced entries of the initial point (Ex. 15a), the texture becomes chordal and the first point is inverted (15b). The chordal tendency is stressed at the start of the second section, in bars 28-47 (15c). The rising quavers of the first point reappear in bars 48-67, together with a modified shorter form of the same figure (15d). The

31   See p. 270.

32   Two bear Lady Nevell's name; the third perhaps carries a Catholic message (see p. 259).

descending notes of the first section (15b) are converted into a new motive in bars 68-79 (15e). The opening point recurs in semiquaver form in bars 79-103 (15f), and turns into an undulating passage in semiquavers which is eventually developed in bars 115-135. A new motive at bar 104 (15g) combines features of the second half of the opening point and the semiquaver inversion of the first half. Perhaps because earlier motives are to be recalled in the final section, the motive introduced in bars 135-147 (15h) is not wholly derivative, though it is not wholly new. It bears resemblances to much that has gone before, and like the motive in bars 104-114 it is repeated in a rising sequence. Motives used earlier in the piece are reviewed in bars 147-159, in combination with an ornamented repetition of bars 135-147.

Ex. 15

Fantasia MB 27/25

continued overleaf

Ex. 15 *concluded*

e. Bars 68 - 69

f. Bar 79

g. Bars 104 - 105

h. Bars 134 - 138

Byrd supports the motivic development of the fantasia in C with a strong harmonic framework. The first section (bars 1-27) is strictly Ionian (major), with chord roots on each degree except B. However, the chord of B flat which quickly follows (bar 30) announces Byrd's intention of moving further afield. Several cadences on G (with F sharpened) occur in bars 28-47, before there is a return to a cadence on C. Bars 48-67 introduce C sharp, and modulate to D. In bars 68-79 G sharp is added, and the section reaches a cadence on A. The return journey to C is made in bars 79-103, by way of A minor, D and G. The sections comprised of bars 104-114 and bars 115-135 both end with cadences in A minor, though the second contains an intermediate cadence on G. The final return to C is made in bars 135-147, and the key is reinforced by bars 147-159.

The fantasia in G entitled *Voluntary: for my Lady Nevell* (MB 28/61) is an altogether lighter piece. The opening section is now reduced to a mere eight bars, but it is no less worthy for that. It shows Byrd in a more spring-like mood, and traces of the madrigalesque which appear from time to time in his other keyboard music of the late eighties can be found here too (e.g. bars 41-42).[33]

The fantasia in D (MB 28/46) is weightier, and reflects Byrd's experience in writing for viols.[34] He adopts a pattern established in the four-part consort fantasias in the 'minor' keys of G and A (BE 17/4 and 17/5), where an imitative first section is succeeded by a passage of minim and crotchet syncopations. Neighbour draws attention to material that is shared by the keyboard piece and the consort fantasia in G minor.[35] The beginning of the keyboard work also has a connection with the chant of the antiphon *Salve regina*.[36] This hidden reference to devotion to the Virgin, so peculiarly Catholic and so objectionable to Protestants, would have had a significance for Lady Nevell (once it was pointed out to her) that justified the position which the fantasia may have occupied in Byrd's original plan for the collection. Furthermore, the antiphon, which Byrd twice set for voices, has words that carried a special meaning for members of a Catholic community which felt itself oppressed.

> Salve Regina, Mater misericordiae, vita, dulcedo, et spes nostra: salve. Ad te clamamus exules filii Evae. Ad te suspiramus, gementes et flentes, in hac lachrymarum valle. (*Hail Queen, Mother of mercy, life, sweetness, and our hope: hail. We cry to you, we exiles, we children of Eve. We sigh to you, groaning and weeping, in this vale of tears.*)

Like other mature compositions by Byrd, the fantasia in D (the transposed Aeolian) reveals his keen appreciation of tonality as a means of organization. (Table 16, overleaf.) In this case he indulges in a kind of 'tonal irony'. He never strays far from the tonic minor key, but repeatedly misdirects the listener to the major chord on B flat, the Aeolian sixth. Byrd's perception of the possibility of such an artifice argues his highly developed feeling for key relationships.

33   Bars 54-55 of Byrd's voluntary are quoted in Kinloch's pavan in G (MB 55/11a), bars 49-52.

34   Neighbour (1978, p. 253) suggests that Byrd looked back to his consort In Nomines as well as his consort fantasias.

35   Ibid., p. 249.

36   The extent of the connection is not easy to determine, since the chant appears to be freely paraphrased. The opening of Byrd's fantasia almost certainly lingered in Bull's mind when he made one of his settings of *Salve regina* (MB 14/40) in which a similar technique is adopted. See Apel, 1972, p. 306.

Table 16 · Structure of keyboard fantasia in D (MB 28/46)

I. The section falls into two sub-sections, based on different imitative subjects.

Bars 1-14 are based on the *Salve regina* chant. The contrapuntal texture, drawn from consort models, is generally of four parts. The only major chords are those on D and A, both created by sharpening their thirds to provide leading notes to the tonic and dominant. The section closes with a cadence on D.

Bars 15-29 continue in the manner of the previous sub-section. Interruptions by running semiquavers clearly establish the keyboard idiom. The range of major chords is extended to include F (bar 26) and C (bar 27).

II. Bars 30-44.

The section is marked by a double bar-line. It begins with a series of major chords, including two new ones, Bb and G (with a raised third). There are two repeated passages (bars 30-31 are repeated an octave lower; bars 39-44 are a semi-repetition of bars 34-39, which resume the contrapuntal texture). Bb is emphasized, but overall the tonality is a little ambiguous, and avoids the dominant of Bb. Cadences on D in bars 34 and 44 compensate for the ambiguity.

III. Bars 45-73.

The section is marked by a double bar-line. It again begins with a Bb chord. Major chords on A, Bb, C, D, E, F and G occur in the first six bars. A cadence on the dominant (A) in bar 51 ensures that a sense of the home key is not lost. The dominant serves a different purpose in bars 63-64, where it is treated as the subtonic of Bb, before the music quickly returns to D in bar 66. Bar 67 starts yet again with a Bb chord, and Bb is recalled by the flattened sixth degree in the repeated plagal cadence with which the piece ends.

Two further aspects of the third section should be pointed out. (1) Throughout most of the first ten bars, the bass is formed by a series of semibreves (many of them repeated), which have the appearance of a cantus firmus and may be a reference to another chant. A series of semibreves appears also in the upper parts of alternate bars from 45 to

49, recalling the practice of placing semibreve 'cantus firmi' in the top parts of pavans of the time. (2) In conjunction with the long bass notes Byrd uses the traditional ostinato figure root-octave-fifth-octave.[37] The left hand part of these bars resembles that in the first section of the *Passing measures* pavan. There are other correspondences between these pieces, e.g. bars 64-65 of the fantasia and bars 81-82 of the pavan, but there is a still closer connection between the fantasia at this point and bars 72-75 of the 'Petre' pavan and galliard, which was added to *My Ladye Nevells Booke* after the main body of the collection had been copied.[38]

Such resemblances between passages of Byrd's later works provide a fascinating glimpse into his mind. Although in every piece he set himself the task of creating an individual pattern and of solving a particular set of compositional problems, he drew constantly on the same powerful internal sources of inspiration. His musical personality had become so marked that its occasional manifestation in recognizably similar utterances was unavoidable.

Keyboard pavans and galliards

Several keyboard pavans and galliards in the *Mulliner book* and the *Dublin virginal book* appear either to be transcribed from consort pieces or modelled closely on the consort style. One of the pavans in the latter manuscript in fact exists in consort form.[39] Byrd's point of departure in writing keyboard dances was a similar one. His first keyboard pavan (MB 27/29) is transcribed from a piece for viol consort, and a consort ancestry is evident in a number of other pavans and galliards, including so mature and deeply felt a pair as the one in B flat (MB 27/23).[40]

There is no reason to think that Byrd's first pavan and galliard were composed any earlier than 1572, and it was perhaps his renewed connection with the fashionable world that stimulated him to turn to dance forms. Thanks to Neighbour's careful stylistic analysis, it is possible to suggest approximate periods of composition for Byrd's

37   See Harley, 1992-94, ii, pp. 7-8, 11.

38   Neighbour, 1978, p. 252.

39   No. 21 in the *Dublin virginal book* occurs in the Thomas Wood part-books (altus part in BL Additional MS 33933; tenor and bass in Edinburgh University Library La.III.483; quintus in Trinity College, Dublin, 412, *olim* F.5.13). The earliest English keyboard pavans and galliards, in BL MS Royal Appendix 58, are also derived from pieces for several instruments.

40   MB 27/23 exists in a rather unsatisfactory arrangement for viol and lute in the Weld lute book (Berkshire County Record Office). See North, 1976, no. 3.

Table 17 · Pavans and galliards 1572-1591

The grouping of pieces is a rough guide to the period of composition; the order within groups is not necessarily chronological.

In *Nevell*			Not in *Nevell*		
MB	Key		MB	Key	
27/29	C(bb)	c.1572			
27/17	A	Pavan only	27/4	G(b)	
27/14	A	Later revised	28/75	G	Pavan only
			28/73	G	
			28/72	G	
			28/76	G	Pavan only. Incomplete
			28/77	G	Galliard only. Paired with 28/76?
			27/16	A	
			55/10, 55/15, 55/16, if genuine, belong to this group		
27/31	C(bb)		27/23	Bb	
27/30	C		28/53	D(b)	Galliard only
28/71	G				
27/32	C	Early 1580s			
28/74	G	Pavan only. Canon. 1585?			
27/2	G(b)	Variations on passamezzo antico			
28/95	G	Galliard only. Part of *Battle*			
27/3	G(bb)	1591			

pavans and galliards. (Table 17.) The bulk of them belong to the decade prior to the composition of the pavan in G (MB 28/71), which is inscribed 'Fant.' in the *Fitzwilliam virginal book*. Whether or not that piece is a memorial to Richard Farrant, it is safe to assume that it was composed no later than the early 1580s, and to use it as a benchmark in dating Byrd's other pavans and galliards.

Byrd's pavans usually consist of three sixteen-semibreve strains, though a few have strains of eight semibreves or twelve.[41] Most of his galliards consist of three strains of eight bars (three minims to a bar).[42] Byrd generally extended his pavans and galliards by repeating the strains in a varied form, and linking the two types of dance to form a longer composition. This was a familiar procedure, found in the *Dublin virginal book*. Byrd did not straightforwardly adopt the common practice, also illustrated by that source, of casting the galliard from the same material as the pavan. His methods of coupling the dances were varied and imaginative. A few examples will demonstrate his endless resourcefulness in creating patterns.

Tonality plays a principal part in the structure of the earliest pavan-galliard pair (MB 27/29). The first strain of the pavan is firmly in C minor. The second strain is in the dominant and almost excludes references to the tonic, which is re-established in the third. The galliard pursues its own course, but in a way which establishes links with its partner. Its first strain begins and ends in C, and its second begins and ends in G. The third strain however begins in E flat before making its way back to C minor. E flat is important in relation to the plan of the pavan. This needs a little explanation. The first strain of the pavan ends with a chord on C. Strain 2 begins a tone lower with a chord on B flat and ends with one on G, and strain 3 begins a tone lower on F. There is little doubt that Byrd thought of key relationships as governed by the circle of fifths, but the whole-tone steps by which he moved from one strain of the pavan to the next suggest that, long before key relationships were formulated in the terms of a much later theory, Byrd may have felt B flat as the dominant of C minor's relative major (E flat), and F as the dominant of G minor's relative major (B flat). One would dearly love to know how Byrd described what he was doing.

The consituent dances of a pavan and galliard in A (MB 27/14), perhaps Byrd's first pair conceived at the outset for the keyboard, have a comparable organization. A highly simplified summary like the one in Table 18 (overleaf) ignores the part played in the structure by varied reprises, though these introduce additional patterns. In another early pavan-galliard pair, in G minor (MB 27/4), a pattern is created by differences between the initial statements of strains and their reprises. If, in each dance, the letter A denotes strains in which the initial statement and its reprise have different note-values, and B denotes those in which

---

41   Morley (1597, p. 181; 1952, p. 296) observed that for the benefit of dancers the strain of pavans had to consist of a multiple of four semibreves.

42   The third and fourth strains of MB 27/4 and MB 27/30 consist of four bars.

Table 18 · Structure of pavan and galliard in A (MB 27/14)

The first strain of each dance starts in A, and reaches a central cadence on E;[43] thereafter they part company, the pavan returning to A and the galliard moving on to C. Both first strains contain five chords: on A, C, E and G, plus D in the pavan and F in the galliard. Those on A, D and E may have either a natural or a sharpened third.

Byrd extends his harmonic palette in the second strains, to include chords on A, C, D, E, F and G. The pavan has an additional chord on B. Each second strain begins with an F chord. The pavan reaches a central cadence on A, begins again on F, and moves to E by way of B, the furthest possible distance from F round the circle of fifths. Byrd does not attempt to repeat this bold stroke in the galliard, which moves in the opposite direction, first to E and then to A.

Each last strain begins a fifth below the ending of the previous strain. Each has a central cadence on A. Neither has a chord on B, and an F chord is only a momentary occurrence in each.

they have similar note-values, the pair of dances has the pattern A A B A B A A.[44]

Byrd's pavans and galliards display an increasing subtlety and power in construction and technique. The last pair to be entered in *My Lady Nevells Booke* (BE 27/3), and dedicated to the young William Petre, are united as much by a pervasive intensity of feeling as by their design. The twice-transposed Aeolian mode (G with two flats) is so modified by accidentals that some degrees carry both major and minor chords, but the harmonies of the pavan are progressively restricted. Chords lasting for a semibreve or longer occur on each degree during the first strain, and four take both the major and minor forms. In the second strain the number of degrees bearing chords is reduced to six. Only three chords appear in two forms, and one lasts for no more than a minim. Although

43   The final cadences of Byrd's pavan strains are usually reached in the penultimate bar. The central cadence in a sixteen-semibreve strain is reached where the final cadence would be in an eight-semibreve strain. See Neighbour, 1978, p. 182.

44   The galliard has four strains, the last two of four bars each. The rigidity of the pattern is twice relaxed, where shorter note-values begin before a strain has ended.

the last strain again has chords on each degree, the duration of three is short and only two degrees carry both major and minor chords.

The restriction of harmonic variety contrasts with an increasing melodic complexity, starting from a simple rising and falling melody in the first strain and leading to to a three-part canon in the third. The canon starts (bar 72) on a B flat chord, linking it with earlier excursions into the 'relative major' of the prevailing G minor tonality. When Byrd moves into G major for the original ending of the pavan, he does so with figuration resembling the B flat figuration of the second strain.[45]

The galliard again emphasises the relative major. The first strain begins and ends in G minor; the second (which has less harmonic variety than than the other two) starts in B flat and ends in F. The third strain alternates chords on F and B flat before returning to G.

Byrd's confidence in handling dance-based compositions is exemplified by two which preceded the 'Petre' pieces, the seventh and ninth in the series which stands at the centre of *My Ladye Nevells Booke*. The pavan in G (MB 28/74) contains a canon between the two upper parts, the second following the first at a distance of two semibreves and a fifth below.[46] Byrd contrives to continue the canon through the varied reprises, sometimes allowing the free parts to echo the decorated phrases of one canonic part.

The *Passing measures* pavan and galliard (MB 27/2) in G minor (one flat) are variations on the *passamezzo antico* ground. To produce a pavan of the sixteen-semibreve type, each of the ground's first seven notes is stretched to two semibreves and the remaining two to one semibreve. The same means are used to produce galliard strains of sixteen bars. The first strain of the pavan is restricted harmonically by the ground; thereafter repetitions of the the harmonic pattern are handled with a good deal of freedom, and chords are often modified by the contrapuntal flow. The galliard is harmonically less venturesome.

The *Passing measures* pavan is made up of six variations. The first group of three progresses from a moderate contrapuntal movement that acknowledges the pavan style, to florid writing in semiquavers. The

---

45   When Byrd published the pavan and galliard in *Parthenia* he replaced the pavan's original ending with one that did not weaken the emphasis on B flat in the second strain of the galliard. The G minor prelude (BE 27/1) which Byrd published at the same time, apparently as an adjunct to the pavan and galliard, avoids any anticipation of B flat, but has a strategically placed F chord. The prelude has only one flat in the signature, which would suggest the transposed Dorian mode. But E is flattened on half the occasions on which it occurs, and if mode had any meaning at all in keyboard music the choice of signature was a notational simplification.

46   The start of the canon is preceded by four chords.

second group starts with a single strand of melody, becomes contrapuntal, and ends with a florid passage corresponding with the one that ends the first group. The galliard is divided into three groups of three variations: (1) a contrapuntal group, (2) a group in which continuous quavers are contrasted with chords (though the sixth variation breaks the flow to anticipate what follows), and (3) a group made from a mixture of components, including (in the eighth variation) a quotation from the tune *The lusty gallant*.[47]

Besides exhibiting the features of Byrd's later keyboard manner, the pavan draws initially on the melodic organ style of his predecessors. *Tripla* passages in both pavan and galliard link them with Byrd's other grounds and early fantasias. The dances' function as an historical survey is underscored by occurrences of the old-fashioned root-octave-fifth-octave figure for the left hand. Between them the *Passing Measures* pavan and galliard review the whole of Byrd's development as a keyboard composer, and are a fitting conclusion to *Nevell's* main sequence of pavans and galliards.

Miscellaneous keyboard works

Byrd wrote a number of keyboard pieces that do not require extended consideration here.[48] They include arrangements of popular dance tunes, some of which may stem from his teaching activities or have been written for his friends to play. It is not really possible to date these pieces, though a guess might be hazarded that more of them belong to the 1580s (or perhaps before) than to the 1590s. Three miscellaneous works included in *My Ladye Nevells Booke* deserve closer attention. They are *Monsieur's almain*, *The barley break*, and *The battle*.

Byrd wrote three versions of *Monsieur's almain*.[49] Two are in G (MB 28/87 and 28/88); a third version in C (MB 27/44) is in Byrd's later style and presumably dates from after 1591. The setting in G included in *Nevell* (MB 28/88) is longer and more brilliant than the other in that key (MB 28/87). The original dance consisted of two strains, each of which Byrd elaborated before repeating it in a varied form. He then repeated and varied the whole two times, rather as Philips and Morley repeated

---

47   Illustrated by Neighbour, 1978, p. 136.

48   Three almans, MB 27/10 (*The Queen's alman*), 27/11 and 28/89; MB 28/78 (*The ghost*), which has the characteristics of an alman; a jig, MB 27/22; four corantos, MB 27/21a-c and 28/45, the last of which is also called a jig; and two voltas, MB 28/90 ('L. Morley') and 28/91. For a fuller discussion see Neighbour, 1978.

49   This was 'a dance found mainly in English sources, though apparently named after François Duke of Alençon, who died in 1584'. (Neighbour, 1978, p. 167.)

and varied complete pieces.[50] Perhaps Byrd found the scheme unsatisfactory, and for once he failed to assimilate the units convincingly into a progressively developing pattern.

The barley break is descriptive of a country game. Could the game have been popular among Sidney's friends when he wrote of it about 1581-83, and could this be the date of Byrd's piece?[51] There is little thematic linkage in the work, but Byrd's sense of design asserts itself. The piece is in thirteen sections, largely in dance rhythms. In the first half the sections are paired. Most are eight bars long, and most are repeated and varied. The middle section is however fourteen bars long, and − probably to compensate for the non-repetition of sections 9 to 11 − section 13 is expanded to twenty-four bars.

Byrd's *Battle* sequence (MB 28/94) is the first English example of a whole genre of pieces descriptive of battles.[52] It can claim additional distinction as the first English keyboard suite. The main sequence consists of nine short pieces in the key of C. The materials are simple, and though they are restricted Byrd manages to extract a good deal of variety from very unpromising stuff. *The retreat* shows Byrd in an atypically humorous mood, and the whole suite must have seemed highly entertaining in its day.[53] *The Battle* is framed in *Nevell* by a march and a galliard, both in G and both numbered separately. *The march before the battle* (MB 28/93) has the title *The Earl of Oxford's march* in Tregian's manuscript, and its insistence on the tonic and dominant suggests that it may be a setting of a march originally conceived for trumpets and drums. It was presumably associated with Edward de Vere, the Earl of Oxford.[54] Within the limiting confines of the harmonic scheme Byrd

50   Philips' almain (Christ Church, Oxford, Mus. MS 1113), and Morley's galliard in C (BL, R. M. 23.d.3). Sweelick's variations on a pavan by Philips (Deutsche Staatsbibliothek, MS Lynar A1) follow the same practice. See below concerning the march preceding Byrd's *Battle* sequence.

51   Chappell, 1893, p. 271; Sidney, 1962, pp. 247, 495.

52   Neighbour, 1978, pp. 173-174.

53   It appears in four late sources, with some spurious additions.

54   The tune occurs as an independent piece in later sources, e.g. Thomas Morley, *First book of consort lessons* (1599), and the mid-seventeenth-century lute book of Johannes Thysius of Leiden (in the Bibliotheca Thysiana, which forms part of the Bibliotheek der Rijksuniversiteit, Leiden; see Land, 1882-91). Dr John Purser, in his broadcast series 'On the Trail of the Spies', suggested that the addition of the march to the *Battle* sequence might be a pun on 'Battles Hall'. This was a variation of 'Battyshall', the name of the manor which Byrd attempted to buy from Oxford in 1573 or 1574, and which Oxford sold to Byrd's brother John in 1580. The idea is ingenious, but there is nothing to indicate when the march was written or whether it was linked with the *Battle*

turns it into a genuine keyboard piece, and adds a varied repetition of the whole. The *Galliard for the victory* (MB 28/95) is in a different class. Its overall organization and practised handling of details leave little doubt that it was written only a short time before the 'Petre' galliard.

A note should be added here about the performance of Byrd's songs and consort music at the keyboard. Before a group of Byrd's songs in British Library Additional manuscript 29996, Thomas Tomkins wrote: 'These Following are all w^th^in the Compass of the Hand & so mo*st* Fitt to Be played wth ease'. The songs, all from *Songs of sundrie natures* (1589), are copied on to four staves, without their words.[55] He also played consort music at the keyboard. 'The leaves Bee greene: grownd of Mr Will: Byrd' is one of the pieces copied out on two staves.[56] Tomkins was not the only musician to do this, and several of Byrd's songs and motets exist in anonymous versions which in some cases have undergone no more than a minimum of adaptation for the keyboard.[57]

Consort music

The view was expressed above that Byrd began writing consort pieces without cantus firmi while he was at Lincoln. Behind this lie the assumptions that he had reason to do so, and that he expected his pieces to be played, though too little is known of Byrd's musical and social connections during his Lincoln years to justify speculation about the circumstances of their composition. It might, alternatively, be argued that Byrd delayed writing such pieces until he was settled in London. This would mean that the fantasia in F was not composed until a short time before its adaptation as *Laudate pueri* and that the prelude and ground was composed shortly before *Browning*, with which it has features in common. The pattern of Byrd's development makes this unlikely, however. A tolerable guess is that these pieces were indeed

---

before Byrd began assembling material for *My Ladye Nevells Booke*. By that time Battyshall was in the hands of Byrd's brother-in-law Philip Smyth. Dr Purser additionally pointed out that the battle pieces composed by Byrd and Kinloch may contain a tune celebrating the crushing defeat of the French by Catholics at the battle of Pavia. (Also mentioned in Purser, 1992, pp. 109-110.)

55   The songs, which occur on ff. 110^v^-120^v^, are *Is Love a boy? — Boy pity me*, *Wounded I am — Yet of us twain, From Cytheron — There careless thoughts — If Love be just*, and two choruses, *Rejoice, rejoice* (part of *From virgin's womb*) and *Cast off all doubtful care* (from *An earthly tree*).

56   The same tune as *Browning*. Tomkins' copy of Byrd's consort fantasia BE 17/4, published in *Psalmes, songs and sonnets* (1611), is no. 55 in Brown, 1989 (MB 55).

57   For examples, see Brown, 1989, nos. 48-54.

written at Lincoln, and that Byrd's first consort work after his return to London was inspired by a milieu which encouraged the composition of dances.[58] The five-part consort pavan in C minor (BE 17/14) is without much doubt the original of the first keyboard pavan in *My Ladye Nevells Booke* (MB 27/29a).[59]

The earliest source of what may have been Byrd's next consort work, the variations (BE 17/10) on *Browning* (a tune also known as *The leaves be green*), is British Library Additional manuscript 31390. The date 1578 appears on f. 3[r] (modern numbering), but a different hand entered *Browning* on ff. 124[v]-125[r] after the bulk of the manuscript had been completed. Since by the early or mid-1580s the piece was available to other copyists, it can be dated c.1580.[60]

Ex. 16

The tune of *Browning* as it occurs in Byrd's variations

The tune of *Browning* looks almost like an abridged version of the ground Byrd used in his consort prelude and ground and *The second ground* for keyboard.[61] (Ex. 16.) The similarity underscores the popular nature of the materials on which Byrd consistently based his variations after he gave up using cantus firmi in instrumental music. It may also help to explain why in his variations on *Browning* the tune appears first in the lowest part, as though it is to function as a ground. Henry Stonings and Clement Woodcock both wrote sets of consort variations on the tune, but each of these begins with the bass silent. The tune is placed in the

---

58   Several pavans known or likely to have originated as consort pieces appear in keyboard anthologies of about 1570. For instance, Newman's pavan which occurs towards the end of the *Mulliner Book* looks like a transcription from a piece for viols, and an anonymous keyboard pavan (no. 21 in the *Dublin Virginal Book*) exists as a consort piece in the Wode part-books (no. 78 in Elliott, 1964).

59   BE 17 presents a version reconstructed from BL Additional MSS 37402-6 (an incomplete set of part-books) and the keyboard version. An edition of the complete set of parts in the Murhardsche Bibliotheek der Stadt Kassel und Landsbibliothek (4° Ms. mus. 125) is published as Hunter, 1994.

60   See Neighbour, 1978, pp. 20, 70. *Browning* appears also in BL Additional MS 32377, and in a section of Bodleian Library MS Mus. Sch. e.423 copied c.1582.

61   See p. 194. Both the tune of *Browning* and the ground have a supertonic cadence halfway through.

tenor and given to the bass in the second variation.[62] In Byrd's set, the initial occurrence of the tune in the bass is clearly due to a modification of his preliminary plan. His first intention was to write four groups of variations in each of which the tune would be rotated through the five parts in turn, a procedure he had used long before in variations on *Christe qui lux es* (BE 8/4).[63] What is now the first of Byrd's *Browning* variations was transferred from his third group.

It is possible that the five-part canonic fantasia in C for consort (BE 17/8) was in existence by the mid-1580s, since there is a near quotation from it in one of Byrd's G minor consort fantasias of about that time (BE 17/13). This occurs at the point where the fantasia modulates into a major key.[64] The absence of the fantasia in C from early sources of consort music also points to a date no earlier than the mid-eighties, and the inclusion of a keyboard version (MB 27/26) in *My Ladye Nevells Booke* means that it cannot have been written much after.[65]

A canon at the fourth occurs between the two upper parts. Each strand of the canon consists of phrases that are repeated in a varied or transposed form. In bars 82-89 the canon incorporates the tune to which words beginning 'Sick, Sick' were sung.[66] Byrd's melodic style was such that, even in his most artificial compositions, he could accommodate popular elements without jarring. Although the two canonic parts sometimes overlap, they are antiphonal for much of the time. The other three parts are in imitative counterpoint that frequently borrows motives from the canon. Not only is an exceptionally unified work created by this means, but as Neighbour has observed, almost everything in the fantasia

62   Neighbour (1978, p. 69) demonstrates that Byrd knew the pieces by Stonings and Woodcock, and characteristically borrowed from them, while just as characteristically expanding and improving upon their work.

63   The procedure, also with the tune in the lowest part initially, occurs in keyboard variations under the title *The leaves be green* by William Inglott (or Englitt) in the *Fitzwilliam virginal book* (no. 251). These show the influence of consort music, and may have been adapted from a consort work. Byrd's original plan for *Browning* typically has other plans superimposed upon it. His twenty variations fall into two groups of ten, which are subdivided into smaller groups (and often into pairs) that do not always coincide with the groups defined by the rotation of the tune. Imitative motives are rotated through the parts not containing the tune, but their occurrence may not observe the boundaries marked by repetitions of the tune.

64   Noted by Neighbour, 1978, p. 85; the resemblance is between BE 17/8, bar 111ff, and BE 17/13, bar 49ff. See below for the date of BE 17/13.

65   The keyboard transcription seems to have been made from an earlier version of the consort piece than the one which survives in seventeenth-century copies.

66   Chappell, 1893, pp. 73-75; Neighbour, 1978, p. 78.

can be traced directly or indirectly to the opening melody.[67] It is thus linked to the keyboard fantasia in the same key (MB 27/25), which grows organically from its opening section. However, Byrd's attempt to refashion the consort piece as a keyboard fantasia met with a comparative lack of success, and it may have been this that led him to attempt another keyboard canon in the pavan in G (MB 28/74), which again seems to belong to the mid-1580s.

The chronological relationship between Byrd's six-part fantasias in G minor is far from certain. BE 17/13 was published with small changes in *Psalmes, songs, and sonnets* (1611),[68] but it occurs with BE 17/12 in Bodleian Library manuscript Mus. Sch. e.423. The positions of the fantasias in this manuscript mean that the compiler acquired them for copying in the mid-1580s.[69] The fact that the copyist entered BE 17/12 before BE 17/13 does not necessarily reflect the order of composition, and Byrd's decision to publish one and not the other may have been made on grounds of length or some other consideration rather than on any advance in execution he believed himself to have made.[70] Indeed, BE 17/12 has claims to be the more interesting composition. It shares with the keyboard fantasias the exploration, section by section, of a range of feeling from the formal to the dance-like; but it differs from them in allowing one voice to echo another in a way that would make less sense in keyboard writing.[71] The contrast between sections, and contrasting material within them, provide Byrd with his means of control; harmonic means are of less importance than is often the case in his works. The most striking contrast occurs at bar 92 with the introduction of a galliard, consisting of the customary three strains with varied repeats.[72] A noticeably popular feature of the piece is the emergence of *Greensleeves*, and a variation on it, at bar 84.[73] What is its

67   Neighbour, 1978, p. 75.

68   BE 17/13 is therefore printed also as BE 14/26.

69   They are separated only by a piece by Ferrabosco. See Dr David Mateer's forthcoming article 'William Byrd, John Petre and Oxford, Bodleian MS Mus. Sch. E.423'.

70   BE 17/13 is the shorter by twenty bars.

71   Neighbour (1978, pp. 79-80) suggests that Byrd may have got the idea of 'antiphonal' effects from Parsons.

72   It is possible that this was not part of Byrd's initial plan. See the discussions by Neighbour (1978, pp. 81-83) and Rastall (1996).

73   Fellowes (1948, p. 190) claimed to find *Walsingham* in the fantasia as well. Rastall (1996) says: 'Neighbour assumed that he had recognized *Walsingham* in the third strain of the galliard, but it is more likely that Fellowes heard the tune in the preparation for *Greensleeves*'. The former would imply a reference in the minor to a tune usually in

function? What connotations had it for Byrd? Would his listeners have associated it with some significant verses? The notion that Byrd may have had Catholic words in mind is not hard to entertain, but until they can be discovered it must remain a conjecture of dubious value. The easiest explanation may be that the inclusion of the tune was no more than a *jeu d'esprit*, fostered by Byrd's realization that it fitted neatly into his melodic and harmonic scheme.

The companion six-part fantasia (BE 17/13) is laid out on a comparable plan, and embraces many of the same elements, including similar figuration and a section (starting at bar 80) in the galliard style. It relies on contrasts between sections rather than within them, and largely due to its relative compactness it has been regarded as Byrd's second attempt at working out the details of his general design. If this is so, a certain amount of spontaneity and rude vigour was lost in refining the initial inspiration.[74]

Besides BE 17/13, *Psalmes, songs, and sonnets* contains Byrd's four-part G minor fantasia (BE 17/4, also edited as BE 14/15). This shares material with *A fancy* (MB 28/46), one of the last pieces to be entered in *My Ladye Nevells Booke*.[75] It cannot therefore be later than about 1590, and it does not contain the rapid motivic changes that began to enter Byrd's writing after that date. It plainly inhabits the same world as two keyboard fantasias dedicated to Lady Nevell, MB 27/25 and MB 28/61, both evidently composed for inclusion in the volume presented to her in 1591.[76] BE 17/4 has something of the character of Byrd's motets of the mid-eighties. While there is no precise resemblance, passages of the fantasia could without incongruity be put alongside others from, say, *Haec dicit Dominus*. The motet was one of those in which Byrd sought a diversification of texture. Employed to different ends, the same principle

---

the major. Rastall remarks: 'This is not impossible, and further work is needed to determine Byrd's use (if any) of popular tunes in the wrong mode'. If *Walsingham* is present in the fantasia, there is a question of whether it implies composition about the time that Byrd's keyboard variations on the tune were written, and whether there is a connection with the Walsingham family.

74   Rastall (1996) questions the conclusion of Neighbour (1978, p. 84) that BE 17/13 was written a little time after BE 17/12. He also questions Neighbour's opinion, shared with Fellowes (1948, pp. 188-190), that BE 17/13 is the superior work. See Rastall (1996) for a careful analysis of BE 17/12. See also the forthcoming book on Byrd's G minor fantasias by Dr Richard Rastall and Miss Julie Rayner (entered in the bibliography under Rastall).

75   Neighbour, 1978, p. 249.

76   Neighbour (p. 93) draws attention to correspondences between BE 17/4 and these works.

governs the layout of the fantasia. It can be divided into five sections;[77] the three which are imitative are separated by shorter non-imitative interludes.

Two more four-part fantasias survive incompletely. BE 17/5 in A minor lacks most of the top part, and only one part remains of BE 17/34 in G,[78] which Byrd transcribed for the 1605 book of *Gradualia* as *In manus tuas*. A probable date for the A minor fantasia is c.1590, since it shares with the four-part consort fantasia in G minor (BE 17/4) and the keyboard fantasia in D minor (MB 28/46) a plan in which an imitative first section is succeeded by a passage of minim and crotchet syncopations. The transcription of the fantasia in G suggests that it must have been a little earlier. Neighbour notes that the exchange of parts in double counterpoint which occurs in the consort piece seems to have been conveyed into the keyboard fantasia in C (MB 27/25), and observes that 'Byrd was in the habit of transferring technical features from his consort to his keyboard music, rather than in the reverse direction'.[79] This would place the consort fantasia in the late 1580s.

A group of short three-part fantasias for viols (BE 17/1-3) can conveniently be dealt with here, though they cannot be dated with the same assurance as the consort pieces discussed above. Neighbour is surely right to suggest the influence of Willaert, or that of his followers, on Byrd's three-part fantasias.[80] This connects them with the three-part songs Byrd wrote in the eighties. But other connections can be found, for example between BE 17/1, rhythmically the smoothest of the three-part fantasias, and the Gloria from Byrd's Mass for three voices. (Ex. 17, overleaf.)

A very close connection exists too between Byrd's three-part consort fantasias and the three-part pieces in his *Gradualia*.[81] Is it possible that Byrd remembered the training received from Tallis in his youth, and wrote a few pieces in an untexted medium to prepare himself for his vocal works?

77   Bars 1-28, 28-34, 34-46, 46-50 and 50-61.

78   Reconstruction by Dr Warwick Edwards first published in *Early Music Review*, no. 11, 1995.

79   Neighbour, 1978, p. 92.

80   Neighbour (1978, p. 96), who notes that ricercares by Willaert were to be found in Lord Lumley's copy of *Motetta trium vocum* (1543). (See Milsom, 1993, pp. 161-162.)

81   Mr M. J. Fleming drew attention to this in the *Viola da Gamba Society of Great Britain newsletter*, 92 (January 1996), p. 19. In conversation he has pointed out some general correspondences in Byrd's viol and vocal music: for instance, the opening of *Ave maris stella* (BE 6b/16) almost inverts the beginning of the canonic fantasia (BE 17/8).

Ex. 17

End of Fantasia BE 17/1

End of Gloria from the Mass for three voices

15

SECULAR SONGS OF THE MIDDLE PERIOD

The year 1588 saw the beginning of a great burst of activity in the printing of songs in London. Byrd led the way with two major collections. Thirty-five of his songs were printed as *Psalmes, sonets & songs* in 1588. *Songs of sundrie natures*, published in the following year, contained thirty-four songs printed as forty-seven numbers. Both collections show Byrd's perpetual concern for order in everything he did. In the 1588 collection the songs are divided into 'psalms', 'sonnets and pastorals', and 'songs of sadness and piety'. In the 1589 collection settings of the seven penitential psalms are placed first, but the main consideration is the number of voices for which the pieces are written.[1] This leads to the choruses of some songs being separated from the verses. Within the groups Byrd arranged the songs very loosely by key (final and mode). His need to forgo this arrangement in places may have been dictated by the demands of printing.

Several other songs by Byrd were printed at this time. He adapted *La virginella* from *Psalmes, sonets & songs* as *The fair young virgin,* for inclusion in Nicholas Yonge's compilation *Musica transalpina* (1588). His setting of verses by Thomas Watson, beginning 'Let others praise what seems them best', was printed in 1589 as *A gratification unto Master John Case, for his learned booke, lately made in the praise of musicke.*[2] Watson's publication of 1590, *The first sett, of Italian madrigalls Englished*, included two settings by Byrd of *This sweet and merry month of May*, one for four voices and the other for six.

Byrd included the four-part version of *This sweet and merry month of May* in *Psalmes, songs, and sonnets* (1611), which contained two consort fantasias that had also been written many years earlier. It is uncertain how far this collection drew on other pieces which Byrd had written before 1589 and left unpublished, but he certainly had a stock of songs in hand. A substantial number surviving only in manuscript appear to have

---

1   Thomas Whythorne's *Songes, for three, fower, and five voyces*, published in 1571, was the first collection printed in England to be arranged according to the number of voices. The scheme was passed on by Byrd to subsequent English composers.

2   Case's book was *The praise of musicke* (1586). *A gratification* survives only incompletely; Brett (1976, pp. 16-32) supplies the missing parts. See also Boyd, 1962, pp. 28-33, 292-300; Barnett, 1969; Knight, 1980. On Watson's Catholic associations, which may have brought him into contact with Byrd, see p. 103.

been written during the same period as the songs published in 1588 and 1589.[3]

Before going any further it will be as well to ask what 'song' means in this context. The word embraces two different categories, the solo song accompanied by viols,[4] and the contrapuntal song for several voices. Byrd's 'Epistle to the Reader' in *Psalmes, sonets & songs* states:

> If thou delight in Musicke of great compasse,[5] heere are divers songs, which being originally made for Instruments to expresse the harmonie, and one voyce to pronounce the dittie, are now framed in all parts for voyces to sing the same. If thou desire songs of smal compasse & fit for the reach of most voyces heere are most in number of that sort.

The implication that only some of the five-part songs published in 1588 were at first composed for a solo voice and four viols is disproved by an examination of the songs themselves. It is clear that all were of this type. The original form of many as songs for voice and consort is confirmed by their existence in manuscript copies of early versions, covering all the categories distinguished in the title of the collection. Attention was long ago focused on this, chiefly by Dent,[6] and it is true too of some of the songs in Byrd's collections of 1589 and 1611. These however contain a large number of pieces conceived from the start as unaccompanied polyphonic songs.

Byrd's ability to publish collections of two different kinds of songs within a year of each other means that he had been writing both types over a considerable period, though he apparently turned to writing songs for several voices in response to the growing demand for such pieces in the eighties. His original intention was probably to devote a volume to

---

3   See the catalogue of Byrd's works, p. 423, which however includes later songs discussed on pp. 346-347.

4   The term 'consort song' has come to denote 'the use of a consort of viols together with a solo voice or voices, and it covers the addition of a chorus of voices in a later development which turns the consort song into the secular counterpart of a verse anthem'. (Brett, 1961-62, where the history of the genre in England is outlined.) There is no evidence for the term being so used in Byrd's day. The earliest occurrence noted, in Sir William Leighton's *The teares or lamentacions of a sorrowful soule* (1614), refers to part-songs for four voices accompanied by a 'broken' consort of different sorts of instruments.

5   Byrd apparently means the distance from the lowest bass note to the highest soprano note. He seems to mean the same thing when he presents a table of 'those songs which are of the highest compasse'. See Kerman, 1962(a), p. 103.

6   Dent, 1929. Arkwright and others had previously noted the fact. See also Brown, 1957.

each sort of song. His decision to add words to the viol parts of the consort songs was presumably taken late in the day, when he concluded that he would otherwise be unable to sell enough copies to make publication worthwhile. This suggests either that viol consorts were not widely available to accompany solo singers, or that the vogue for the consort song had waned in the face of competition from the increasingly popular multi-voice song. Possibly both assumptions are true, though Byrd never gave up writing consort songs.

Some at least of Byrd's consort songs must have been composed for the court, where a viol consort and solo singers were available.[7] It may have been this that brought Byrd most intimately into contact with the Queen and her courtiers, and helped to reinforce his position as a favoured servant. Other consort songs may have been written for a few connoisseurs who played the viol or could employ viol players. The songs for several singers were perhaps composed principally for 'Gentlemen and Merchants' like those described by Nicholas Yonge, who − so he said − met daily in his house to make music,[8] or those patrons who encouraged Byrd to write his motets.[9]

7   Brett (1964, p. 63-64) points out that the 1588 collection is the musical equivalent of manuscript anthologies of courtly verse; and that a handful of the verses are known to have been written by courtiers, and may have been set to music for special occasions, such as court entertainments, and ceremonies such as weddings and funerals. Byrd's solo songs require a voice in the soprano range. The National Portrait Gallery's frequently reproduced painting of scenes from Sir Henry Unton's life, probably made soon after his death in 1596, shows four viol players seated round a table with a boy singer. (Reproduced in Woodfill, 1953, following p. 48; Brett, 1974, p. xx; and elsewhere.) There is no direct evidence that a group of singing boys was employed in the privy chamber after Queen Mary's death, but boys could easily have been brought in from the Chapel Royal or one of the other London choirs. Women were not employed as professional singers, but certainly took part in domestic performances: see Herbert's letter about his daughter, quoted on p. 50.

8   Described in the preliminaries of *Musica Transalpina* (1588). Yonge was a singing-man at St Paul's Cathedral.

9   It is possible that Catholic meanings are to be discovered in some of the songs. Dr John Purser has pointed out, in a letter to the author, that in a painting after Nicholas Hilliard in the National Portrait Gallery, Mary Queen of Scots wears a rosary hanging from a cross with an enamel of Susanna and the Elders in the centre. The enamel, symbolizing the triumph of right through divine aid − figuratively, perhaps, true faith withstanding the corruption of Protestantism − is surrounded by a Latin motto signifying 'Trouble on all sides'. A meaning of this sort might well have been understood by a Catholic singing Byrd's settings of *Susanna fair*. Will Forster's manuscript (BL, R. M. 24.d.3) contains a keyboard version of the song (MB 55/50).

It is occasionally said that some of Byrd's songs may have been written for theatres, partly because songs by older composers such as Richard Farrant and Robert Parsons were or seem to have been intended for plays.[10] The only strong evidence of Byrd having composed music for plays concerns the fragmentary *Preces Deo fundamus*, sung during the first act of Thomas Legge's *Ricardus Tertius* at St John's College, Cambridge, and *Quis me statim* (BE 15/37), probably sung during a performance of *Hippolytus* at Christ Church, Oxford.[11] But there may be some significance in the fact that the start of Byrd's song-writing career coincides approximately with the opening of the Paul's theatre in 1575 and the first Blackfriars theatre in 1576.[12]

Early versions of two-thirds of the pieces printed in 1588 were circulating in manuscript copies both before and after Byrd went to press, but only three of those printed in 1589 survive in early versions.[13] He may not have been making a wholly conventional protestation when he declared, in dedicating his 1588 collection to Sir Christopher Hatton, that

> The often desires of many my good friends, Right honorable, and the consideration of many untrue incorrected coppies of divers my songes spread abroad, have beene the two causes, chiefly moving my consent at length to put in Print the fruits of my small skill and labors in Musicke.

Chronology

Dow did not begin collecting Byrd's songs until his anthology had reached an advanced stage, and he was interested in the consort songs, not those for several voices.[14] However, Bodleian Library manuscript

10   Writing of the consort song, Brett (1967, p. xiv) observes: 'Two basic types, each with distinguishing characteristics, can be discerned in the earliest repertory: the strophic song and the dramatic lament. The one comprises settings of metrical psalms ... the other consists of through-composed settings of elegiac verses which appear to derive from tragedies acted by the companies of choirboy players at the Elizabethan court'.

11   The ascription of *Preces deo fundamus* to Byrd is in BL Harleian MS 2412, f. 75ᵛ. Fellowes (1948, pp. 167-169) discusses the piece at some length, but mentions only the 1579 production of the play, not those of 1573 and 1582. (See Ward and Waller, 1910, p. 81.) For *Quis me statim*, which dates from 1592, see p. 346.

12   The boys of St Paul's used a small theatre adjacent to the Chapter House from 1575 to 1590 and again from 1600 to 1606. The new Blackfriars theatre was used by the children of the Chapel Royal from 1576 to 1583/4. (Gurr, 1987, p. 22.)

13   See Brett, 1976.

14   Christ Church, Oxford, Mus. MSS 984-988, compiled by Dow 1581-88, contain

Mus. Sch. e.423, compiled for Lord Petre c.1577-89, is of considerable help in dividing songs into broadly dateable groups.[15]

(a) A part of the manuscript compiled c.1577-c.1582[16] contains *Susanna fair*, *O you that hear this voice*, and *Where fancy fond* (all consort versions of songs published in 1588); *If in thine heart* (published 1589); and *Ah golden hairs*, *Lord to thee I make my moan*, *O God but God*, *O Lord how vain*, and *O that we woeful wretches* (all unpublished).[17]

(b) The following songs are in a part of the manuscript compiled in 1582 or later: *I joy not in no earthly bliss*, *La verginella*, *Lullaby my sweet little baby*,[18] *My mind to me a kingdom is*, *Though Amaryllis*, and *Who likes to love* (all consort versions of songs published in 1588); *Christ rising*, *I thought that love*, and *When first by force* (consort versions of songs published in 1589); and the unpublished songs *As Caesar wept* and *O happy thrice* (a fragment).

(c) *Truce for a time* (unpublished) and *In fields abroad* (published 1588) are in a section of the manuscript copied after 1586.[19] The latter song however shows that even a privileged copyist might occasionally be behind the times, for a keyboard intabulation occurs in a manuscript that may be no later than c.1580.[20]

only *When I was otherwise* from the 1589 collection.

15   See Dr David Mateer's forthcoming article 'William Byrd, John Petre and Oxford, Bodleian MS Mus. Sch. E.423'.

16   This is based on the assumption that *Why do I use my paper?* − the song that ends this group − was composed soon after Campion's execution. See the next page.

17   Since the Byrd Edition volumes containing the collections of 1588 and 1589 are so far unpublished, BE numbers are not given in this chapter for the songs they contain. Reference is made instead to the year in which any song was published. The unpublished songs are printed in BE 15.

18   *Lullaby my sweet little baby* is one of two songs by Byrd that are lullabies; the other is *Come pretty babe* (not published by Byrd). It is an attractive thought that they might have been inspired by the birth of his son Thomas, who was baptized on 30 March 1576, or a younger daughter, but (with the remotely possible exception of *Wedded to will is witless*: see p. 344) there is no indication of Byrd's family life being reflected in his songs. The words of the first song in any case refer to the Christ child, and those of the second are sung by a deserted mother.

19   It includes the funeral songs for Sir Philip Sidney, and *Constant Penelope* (which seems to have been written earlier in the 1580s but has words by Sidney): see below.

20   York Minster Library MS M 91.(S). Printed by Caldwell, 1995 (no. 82).

Dates can be confirmed or determined by other means for a small number of Byrd's published songs, though their reliability varies.

(d) According to Peacham, Byrd and Ferrabosco 'in a friendly aemulation, exercised their invention' in setting *The nightingale*. If this is so, it must have been before Ferrabosco finally left England at the end of 1578. But what was the source of Peacham's information? He was writing more than forty years after the event he describes, and it would be understandable if, inspired by Morley's account of the amiable competition between Byrd and Ferrabosco, he assumed a connection between their songs. Since both are for five voices and they set the same words, the story can perhaps be accepted with reservations. Peacham's words can be read as implying that *Susanna fair* was the subject of a similar 'aemulation', but he does not actually say so and it seems improbable. Neither of Byrd's settings (*a* 3 and *a* 5) uses the words of Ferrabosco's setting (*a* 5).[21]

(e) The first stanza of *Why do I use my paper, ink, and pen?* (printed in 1588) is from *A true reporte of the death & martyrdome of M. Campion ... at Tiborne the first of December 1581*, published not long after the event. It is not too much to assume that the song was written soon afterwards, probably at about the same time as the motet *Deus venerunt gentes*, which also appears to allude to Campion's death.[22]

(f) The last two songs of the 1588 volume, *Come to me, grief* and *O that most rare breast*, are 'funerall songs' for Sir Philip Sidney, who died on 17 October 1586 after being wounded at Zutphen in the Netherlands.[23] After Sidney's body was returned to England it remained unburied until 16 February 1586/7. Perhaps the songs were sung in connection with the funeral eventually held at St Paul's Cathedral.[24]

---

21   Peacham, 1622, pp. 101-102. Ferrabosco and Byrd probably had in mind Lassus's famous songs, *Le rossignol* and *Susanne un jour*. These were published in London by Vautrollier, in *Receuil du mellange d'Orlande de Lassus* (1570), and afterwards with Ferrabosco's settings in Yonge's *Musica transalpina* (1588). Both the translations fitted to Lassus's music were used by Ferrabosco.

22   See p. 228.

23   According to Fellowes (1967, p. 684), the poems may be by Watson. An alternative attribution to Dyer is supported by the version of *O that most rare breast* printed as BE 16/28, which contains the words 'thou dead dost live, thy dier living dieth'.

24   The engravings of the funeral procession published by Thomas Lant in 1587 include a portrayal of Robert Cooke, who drew up the Byrd genealogy in 1571.

(g) It is a reasonable assumption that the settings Byrd provided for Watson's publications of 1589 and 1590 were made not long before they were printed. They are *Let others praise* and two settings of *This sweet and merry month of May*.

To try to determine the dates of Byrd's songs from the time when their words were written is a riskier business, since he drew on a number of older printed sources and had access to verses that circulated in manuscript before publication, but in a few cases the attempt is profitable.

(h) Byrd seems to have written few songs before the mid-1570s, so it is likely that *From Virgin's womb* (published 1589) was composed after 1578, when Francis Kindlemarsh's words appeared in Edwards's *The paradyse of daynty devises*.

(i) *O you that hear this voice* (published 1588) and *O dear life* (1589) are from Sidney's *Astrophil and Stella*. As the poems were probably written about 1582, Byrd's settings cannot be earlier.[25] This is concordant with the position of the first in Bodleian Library manuscript Mus. Sch. e.423, and means that Byrd had access to Sidney's poem as soon as it was written.[26]

(j) It is possible that *Constant Penelope* and *Penelope that longed for the sight of her Ulysses* (published in 1588 and 1589 respectively) are connected with Penelope Rich, the Stella of Sidney's sonnets, and belong to the early 1580's. This is consistent with the conjecture that the author of the first was Thomas Watson.[27] The song *Weeping full*

25   Sidney, 1962, p. 439. On Sidney's authorship of the words of Byrd's uncollected song *O Lord how vain*, dismissed by Ringler (the editor of Sidney, 1962), see Mateer, 1986-87, p. 6.

26   The likelihood that Byrd was acquainted with Sidney is supported by his setting of poems by Sidney and his close friend Dyer, and by the possible acquaintance with Sidney and his circle of Edward Paston, who collected a great deal of Byrd's music and apparently gave some to Petre. (Brett, 1964(a), pp. 54-55.) Brown (1976, ii, p. 201) suggests that Byrd's *Battle* suite may have been based on John Derricke's *The image of Ireland* (1581), dedicated to Sidney and praising his father. Byrd's settings of verses translated or imitated from Jorge de Montemayor's *Diana* may have been encouraged by the interest taken in *Diana* by Sidney's circle. (Byrd wrote unpublished settings of *Ah golden hairs*, a translation, and *As Caesar wept* and *Truce for a time*, both evidently intended as imitations of Montemayor.) Watson may also have been acquainted with this group of writers. (Nicholl, 1992, p. 180.) See, however, Duncan-Jones, 1990.

27   Fellowes, 1967, p. 683. Watson was in London by 1579, and in 1581 dedicated his first book, *Antigone*, to Philip Howard, head of the leading Catholic family in

sore, which in the 1589 collection immediately precedes *Penelope that longed*, contains the line 'This lady rich is of the gifts of beauty'.

(k) The words of *My mind to me a kingdom is* are by Edward Dyer, who may also have been the author of *I joy not in no earthly bliss*.[28] Both songs were published in 1588. If Dyer's poems stem from his friendship with Sidney and Spenser, with whom he joined in a literary group known as the Areopagus, they cannot be earlier than about 1580.[29]

(l) Byrd took the verse for his setting of *The greedy hawk* (1589 collection) from Geoffrey Whitney's *A choice of emblemes*, published at Leiden in 1586. None of the songs in Byrd's 1588 collection draws on this book, although he turned to it twice for songs in his 1611 collection, so it is possible that he did not know Whitney's poems prior to their publication.[30]

There is reason to suppose that thirteen songs in the 1588 collection which do not survive in early versions were the last to be composed before publication, and that Byrd held them back as his plans for the volume matured.[31] A slight doubt is cast on this theory by his release of the two elegies for Sidney, but their special nature may have caused him to make an exception. The songs in question are: *All as a sea, Although the heathen poets, Ambitious love, As I beheld I saw a herdsman, E'en from the depth, Help Lord for wasted are those men, If women could be fair, Mine eyes with fervency, My soul oppressed with care, O God give ear, O Lord how long wilt thou forget, The match that's made,* and *What pleasure have great princes.*

Brett regards as authentic nearly thirty songs which never got into print, but are apparently from the same period as the songs published in 1588 and 1589.[32] Among them:

(m) *Ye sacred muses* (BE 15/32) is an elegy for Thomas Tallis, who died on 23 November 1585.

England. Howard, like Byrd's patron Lord Lumley, was a son-in-law of Henry Fitzalan, the Earl of Arundel.

28   Fellowes, 1967, p. 682.

29   See p. 279 concerning their position in Bodleian Library MS Mus. Sch. e.423.

30   On the other hand, Whitney was a friend of Sidney, Dyer, and Edward Paston. (Brett, 1964(a), p. 55.)

31   Brett, 1964, p. 65.

32   Brett, 1970. Ten of the songs come from one or both of two manuscripts: Bodleian Library, Mus. Sch. e.423, completed in 1586, and Christ Church, Oxford, Mus. MSS 984-988, completed in 1588.

(n) *Rejoice unto the Lord* (BE 15/11) refers to Queen Elizabeth having preserved England in a quiet state 'These eight & twentye yeares'. It could therefore have been sung in 1586 on the anniversary of her accession.

(o) The words of *In angel's weed* (BE 15/31) were perhaps written by Edward Paston as an elegy for Mary Queen of Scots, who was executed in 1587, but they seem to have been fitted to the music of an existing song by Byrd. A fragment of the same music occurs in the incomplete British Library Additional manuscript 31992, and appears from the index to have belonged to a song beginning 'Is Sidney dead?', which must have been written in 1586 or 1587.[33]

None of the above indications of date, with the exception of those for *The nightingale* and perhaps *From virgin's womb*, places the song it refers to earlier than the 1580s. It could well be that the bulk of Byrd's songs was composed after he had finished work on the *Cantiones sacrae* published in 1575, and that most of them belong to the same period as the *Cantiones sacrae* published in 1589 and 1591.

It is a little surprising to find that none of Byrd's songs can safely be identified as the product of his student years or his time at Lincoln. Songs must have been performed in the course of entertainments put on by the boy choristers of Lincoln, and very soon after Byrd's return to London, if not before, he was intimate with a group of noblemen who by their own account not only sang songs at home but wrote songs with his help — though as the word 'song' might be applied to anything from a motet, anthem or part-song to a piece for a solo voice accompanied by a lute it is not easy to be sure what they meant.[34]

Style

In the case of the songs published in 1588 it is obvious from early versions, and from the range, shape and greater activity of the lower parts, and the sometimes awkward or repetitive word underlay, that they were conceived for a solo voice and four viols. Although Byrd sanctioned their performance as part-songs, and although his consort writing is particularly vocal in nature, it cannot be said that they are improved by their metamorphosis. Byrd may have agreed, for in many songs of the 1588 collection the original solo voice is labelled 'The first singing part', with the clear implication that the other parts are really for

33   See Brett, 1970, p. 175.

34   Whythorne (1961, p. 174) and Baldwin (*My Ladye Nevells Booke*, ff. 145ᵛ and 148ᵛ) used 'song' of instrumental pieces.

viols. The first singing part may be recognizable even when it is not so described. Such is not the case with all the songs of 1589, but three are extant in consort form: *When first by force, I thought that Love had been a boy*, and *See those sweet eyes*. Other songs of 1589 have similar features. The late entry of the soprano parts, the silence of these parts while the other parts are sounding, and their general configuration may identify *O Lord my God* and *Wounded I am* as songs for a solo voice and, exceptionally, three viols. If they did not start out as solo songs they retain many of the solo song's characteristics.[35] *When I was otherwise* and *O dear life* seem for the same reasons to have been songs for a solo voice and four viols. The second part of *And think ye nymphs — Love is a fit of pleasure* fairly clearly originated as a song for two voices and four viols.

The voice in Byrd's consort songs is usually, but not always, in the soprano range, and may be either above or below the uppermost viol part. Sometimes it may go below the level of the next highest viol. In *O Lord how long* (1588) it is assigned to the middle of the five parts. There is some indication that the placing of the voice in the second highest part was a common practice in writing for a voice and four viols before the mid-1570s.[36] Unfortunately there is not enough evidence to suggest conclusively that this was a slightly archaic feature when Byrd adopted it in his earlier songs, and in any case he placed the voice below the highest viol part in some of his latest pieces.

It has been argued above that Byrd began writing polyphonic songs for several voices as a result of the demand for such pieces in the 1580s.[37] The popularity of songs for four and six singers is attested by Yonge's *Musica transalpina* (1588) and Watson's *The first sett, of Italian madrigalls Englished* (1590). It was for the latter collection that Byrd wrote four- and six-voice versions of *This sweet and merry month of May*. They followed his six-voice song *Let others praise* (1589). Three-part songs were evidently less in demand, and after the group published by Byrd in 1589 no more were printed until — in a different vein — Morley's *Canzonets* appeared in 1593.

Byrd's songs for three and four voices have a special place in his work. For twenty years or more he had written only incidentally for three voices, and infrequently for four voices. His customary practice in

35   Phillips (1991, p. 93) argues that *O Lord my God* cannot have been composed as a solo song with viol accompaniment, because the words are too closely associated with its structure. 'O lord my God' and 'let flesh and blood thy servant not subdue' are sung to double points which, sung sequentially, form one melodic phrase.

36   See the songs printed in Brett, 1974.

37   See p. 276.

songs, as in motets, was to write in five parts. This is true of his songs for a solo voice and four viols,[38] and of the general run of his a cappella songs. The songs for six voices which Byrd published in 1589 may have been written specially for publication (they do not survive in earlier versions), and perhaps belong to the same spell of six-part writing that produced the later six-part motets in the *Cantiones sacrae* of 1591. Yet, even among these five songs, the first section of *And think ye nymphs—Love is a fit of pleasure* is for five voices, while *Who made thee Hob?* is for two voices and four viols. There are indications that in writing other six-part songs Byrd took vocal duets with viol accompaniment as his pattern. *Behold how good a thing*, *Love is a fit of pleasure* and *Christ rising again* all have two soprano parts.[39]

Byrd's response to the taste of his audience is partly borne out by the words he chose, in spite of his obvious personal liking for older poetry with a moral tone. His 1588 collection contains only three fourteen-line sonnets, and one of these (an elegy for Sidney) was written at the end of 1586. It may have been the growing vogue for the form, which Sidney did much to encourage,[40] that led Byrd to include settings of six poems of this kind in 1589. There are other signs too of his response to changing tastes. Most of the poems grouped as 'sonnets and pastorals'[41] and 'songs of piety and sadness' consist of six-line stanzas, but there are only half as many in the 1589 collection as in the 1588 collection. The number of songs dealing conventionally with love is three times as great in the second publication as in the first.

The poems chosen by Byrd show considerable diversity in their schemes of metre and rhyme. He generally respects these, repeating words chiefly at the very beginning, or for emphasis, or in response to some overriding musical need.[42] Among the assorted verse forms the metrical psalms stand out as almost unswervingly uniform, consisting of four-line stanzas with lines alternately of four and three iambics.[43] This

38   In *Delight is dead* (BE 15/30), for two voices, Byrd dropped one of the viols.

39   The antiphonal three-part passages in *Unto the hills mine eyes I lift* look as if they were intended for voices from the outset.

40   Sidney, 1962, p. lviii.

41   Byrd here used 'sonnet' to mean any short poem of a lyrical or amatory nature, not in the specialized sense of a poem of fourteen decasyllabic lines.

42   On Byrd's word-setting see Brett, 1971-72. He notes (pp. 52-53) that verbal rhymes are often matched by musical rhymes in Byrd's settings.

43   Whether stanzas are printed as lines of four and three feet, or as lines of seven feet (as in BE 15) depends on the rhyme scheme. *Lord to thee I make my moan* (BE 15/5) presents a subtle variation of the customary metrical psalm form, with numerous incomplete feet. Each line of the psalm *The man is blest* (BE 15/4) consists of four feet.

creates a pause equivalent to one silent foot after every two lines, occasioning a rest in Byrd's melody. Among the metrically more unusual poems set by Byrd are *Constant Penelope* and *Come to me grief for ever*. The first was translated (perhaps by Thomas Watson) from Ovid's *Heroides*, and is an experiment in measured verse. In setting the solo voice part so that the long syllables are rendered as minims and the short syllables as crotchets, Byrd reflected the ideas of Baïf and Courville which were transmitted to England by Sidney.[44] He dealt with the metre of the second by applying the same pattern of note values to each of the first three lines of the stanza.[45]

Usually, though not invariably, Byrd set at least two stanzas of a poem as a continuous whole.[46] All four stanzas of *O God give ear* and *Unto the hills* are set in this way. The through-composed four-stanza settings seem to be among Byrd's later metrical psalms, and are given special prominence. The former occupies the first place in the 1588 collection, and the latter the penultimate place in the 1589 collection. (It is followed by a prose text culled from *Romans* and *Corinthians*, to which Byrd must have attached particular importance.) In 1588 Byrd printed the words of additional stanzas (as many as seven or eight) for the majority of songs – something he did rarely in 1589 – but there is often an odd number which does not fit a two-stanza setting, and Byrd may not have expected them to be sung. Moreover, some stanzas do not make sense if they do not follow without a pause from what has gone before.[47]

Frequently Byrd emphasizes the significant conclusion of a verse by repeating it. This was a traditional device in English song. In the case of *Although the heathen poets* (1588), the song is so short that he repeats the whole. *Behold how good a thing it is* (1589) sets three stanzas, but the last is set and printed as a separate section of the song. Byrd divides several other songs into two sections. In the case of the carols of 1589, *From Virgin's womb* and *An earthly tree*, he sets the first sections for

---

When Byrd turned from the all but unrelieved gloom of the psalms he published in 1588 and 1589 (illumined only in 1589 by *Behold how good a thing it is* and *Unto the hills I lift mine eyes*), and set joyful texts for his 1611 collection, he used prose versions.

44   Stevens, 1990. See also Brett, 1976, pp. 192-193.

45   The pattern of minim/two crotchets/four minims is disguised by the breaking of some minims into two notes of different pitch. The word underlay in BE 16/27 is questionable.

46   In *Mine eyes with fervency of sprite* (1588) he sets only one of the stanzas. E'n from the depth (1588) is unusual in possessing just one stanza.

47   For example, stanza three of *Mine eyes with fervency of sprite*, and stanzas three to five of *O Lord who in thy sacred tent*.

one or two voices with a viol consort, and the repeated choruses for four unaccompanied voices. The setting for different combinations of voices of the two stanzas which form a *proposta* and *risposta* of *And think ye nymphs – Love is a fit of pleasure* (1589) points up their different metrical patterns.[48]

Byrd occasionally treated poems with some freedom. The words of *Although the heathen poets* (1588) and *I thought that Love had been a boy* (1589) are obviously incomplete. In the unpublished *Triumph with pleasant melody* (BE 15/12) Byrd interpolated a few words of his own as a brief interlude.[49] The form of the dialogue, mirrored in the setting, is: Christ (4 lines), sinner (2), Christ (4), interpolated interlude, alternate lines allocated to the sinner and Christ (8). It would have been particularly suitable for an entertainment mounted by boy choristers, but it cannot be connected with any and there is a question about the time when such dialogues were popular. William Hunnis's *Seven sobs of a sorrowfull soule for sinne* (1583) contains two similar dialogues, *Arise from sin thou wicked man* (for which Hunnis provided a tune) and *Awake from sleepe and watch awhile*, but it is uncertain when Hunnis wrote them. They were not included with other poems by Hunnis in Richard Edwards's *The paradyse of daynty devises* of 1578, and may be later.

Triumph with pleasant melody (BE 15/12) has characteristics similar to those of Byrd's psalms, though it differs in changing (in modern terms) from 4/2 to 6/2 – a purely musical requirement, not demanded by the sense of the words. It is probably one of Byrd's earlier works in the idiom. By comparison with his mature songs it is unpolished, and the voice part lacks the careful shaping typical of his later work,[50] but it forms a bridge between the psalms and the songs of sadness and piety.

Broad stylistic differences are recognized in the division of Byrd's 1588 book of songs into 'psalms', 'sonnets and pastorals', and 'songs of sadness and piety'. (The funeral songs for Sir Philip Sidney, though

---

48   See Kerman, 1962, pp. 85, 106. Many poems set by composers of the period are irregular in form, so it seems unlikely that Byrd first set, and then brought together, two separate poems.

49   The ascription of the song to 'Thomas Bird' in BL Additional MS 30484 was added in the eighteenth century by John Stafford Smith, and stems from confusion caused by the name of a previous owner, Thomas Hamond. *Triumph with pleasant melody* is one of only three of Byrd's forty-odd unpublished songs to escape the collector Edward Paston. The others are the psalm *O Lord within thy tabernacle* (BE 15/1) and *Thou poets' friend* (BE 15/24.)

50   Brett (1970, p. 171) nevertheless goes too far in his opinion that it is 'crude and unlovely'.

given a separate heading, are a subclass of the songs of sadness.) In some ways these categories match distinctions of style that are present in the work of older composers. Byrd had absorbed a tradition that was well established, however much he surpassed and developed what his predecessors had done.[51] Five unpublished consort psalms (BE 15/1-5)[52] may be earlier than at least the majority of those he published,[53] but in spite of the variety with which he managed to invest his psalms the essentials of his style in such pieces changed little. Perhaps most of them were composed within a short span of time. The vocal parts somewhat resemble the tunes published with the metrical psalms of Thomas Sternhold and others, though as far as is known they are wholly original.[54] They are written mostly in equal note values, and all are in duple or quadruple time. The firm cadences are reminiscent of congregational singing, but pairs of lines containing different numbers of feet help Byrd in placing them irregularly, and gaps may be prolonged and filled by the frequently imitative viol parts. The placing of the voice below the top viol part means that it does not have to share in the imitation in order to be fully integrated into the polyphonic structure.[55] The result is a rather abstract response to the meaning of the words. Occasional word-painting is confined to phrases like 'in Thy most holy hill', where the viols rise and fall and the voice climbs to its highest note.[56]

51   See Brett, 1961-62; Brett, 1971-72, p. 50; Brett, 1974. The viol writing of earlier composers is usually less contrapuntal than Byrd's (Kerman, 1962, p. 105, calls it 'animated homophony'), and more rhythmically straightforward.

52   *O Lord within thy tabernacle*, *The Lord is only my support*, *Have mercy on us Lord*, *The man is blest*, and *Lord to thee I make my moan*. The words of the first are an adaptation of Psalm 15 (Authorized Version), which supplied the text for the motet *Domine quis habitat*. They deal with the evil of usury, of which John Byrd was accused. (See pp. 88, 119.)

53   The psalms of the 1588 collection are: *O God give ear*, *Mine eyes with fervency*, *My soul oppressed with care*, *How shall a young man*, *O Lord how long*, *O Lord who in thy sacred tent*, *Help Lord for wasted are those men*, *Blessed is he that fears the Lord*, and *Lord in thy wrath*.

54   Compare the tunes assembled by Frost, 1953.

55   Brett (notes to BE 15) advances the theory that four settings may have ended in a short chorus, with additional voices singing the parts assigned to the viols. BE 15/3 has a repeat instead of a chorus. *O Lord who in thy sacred tent* (BE 16/8, published in 1588) is another psalm that has every appearance of ending with a chorus.

56   Kerman (1981, p. 149) says that word-painting entered the main stream of English music through Byrd. 'It is used only sporadically and self-consciously, though sometimes very impressively, in the work of older composers.'

Most of the songs of sadness and piety published in 1588 are in the same vein as the psalms.[57] Differences of length and structure are primarily those imposed or suggested by different verse forms or the nature of a particular poem. The repeated refrain of *Lullaby my sweet little baby*, for instance, stimulates Byrd to introduce short passages of vocalise, and to distinguish the main body of the verse by writing it in a different time. *O that most rare breast*, the second of the funeral songs for Sir Philip Sidney, is a through-composed setting of a fourteen-line sonnet, and consequently much longer than the single stanza-setting supplied for its strophic companion, *Come to me grief*. The first four lines of *O that most rare breast* nevertheless have almost the same music as the second four lines. The corresponding lines of two other sonnet settings of 1588, *Ambitious Love hath forced me to aspire* and *As I beheld a herdsman wild*, are given exactly the same music.

In the funeral pieces, as in a number of other songs, Byrd strikes a balance between homophony and imitative polyphony. This characteristic appears in *Rejoice unto the Lord* (BE 15/11), and in the through-composed psalm *O God give ear*, published in 1588 but presumably dating also from the later 1580s.[58] It can be found too in the motets which Byrd wrote at about the same time.

The distinction between homophony and counterpoint running through Byrd's consort songs is clear in three printed in 1588. *I joy not in no earthly bliss* is almost entirely homophonic, but *My mind to me a kingdom is* employs a kind of semi-homophony, reminiscent of Byrd's later Anglican music. *La verginella* alternates short homophonic passages with counterpoint that creates complex cross-rhythms of a sort which occurs frequently in Byrd's songs.[59] (Ex. 18, overleaf.)

57   As are Byrd's unpublished songs of the same type (BE 15/6-12).

58   No 'first singing part' is identified in these two pieces, but in *O God give ear* the soprano clearly fulfils the role. Early versions prove the existence of a first singing part in the funeral songs.

59   This led Fellowes unsuccessfully to try to bar his edition by dividing the song into passages with different time-signatures. He does the same thing elsewhere. Compare, for example, his edition of *O you that hear this voice* (*The English Madrigal School*, volume XIV, pp. 78-83) with Brett's edition of the same piece (BE 16, pp. 102-105).

Ex. 18

La verginella, bars 20-27

The match that's made for just and true respects (1588) takes the process still further. It would be difficult to distinguish the 'Pari jugo dulcis tractus' section of this song, with its change of time, and imitation carried through into the vocal part, from purely instrumental five-part writing.[60]

Insofar as a clear distinction can be made between the lighter 'pastorals' and the pensive 'sonnets', it can be said that rhythmic variety is found more often in the former. Sonnets are invariably in duple or quadruple time (strongly marked, for instance, in *I joy not in no earthly bliss*); pastorals may be in triple time, and have underlying dance rhythms. Both tend to have shorter note-values than the psalms.[61] *Though Amaryllis dance in green* is essentially a galliard, with the galliard's characteristic alternation of 6/4 and 3/2;[62] and the dance informs not only the playful *Who likes to love* and *If women could be fair*, but the serious

60   The Latin refrain of this song is paralleled in a number of early Tudor poems. Byrd may have chosen some old verses to set.

61   For example, the combined parts of *In fields abroad* move almost entirely in crotchets and quavers.

62   Dent, 1929,

My mind to me a kingdom is and *The match that's made.*[63]

Compared with those of earlier consort songs, Byrd's solo vocal parts have a striking tunefulness: 'melodious birde', Baldwin called him.[64] His melodies often have much in common with popular song, particularly in his pastorals, and their contribution to the style of John Dowland and other lutenist song-writers is manifest.[65] The careful attention Byrd devoted to the shaping of his melodies, the placing of melodic peaks, and accentuation is exemplified by his setting of Sidney's *O Lord how vain* (BE 15/8).[66] The peaks, from which the melody gently descends, rise gradually higher, and the word 'Lord' occurs on the highest of all. (Ex. 19.)

Ex. 19

Vocal part of *O Lord how vain*

The progress of Byrd's vocal lines often reflects changes in the thoughts expressed. In *Why do I use my paper, ink and pen?* (1588)

---

63 All these songs are from Byrd's 1588 collection.

64 See p. 367.

65 Spink, 1974, p. 16.

66 Byrd did not publish the song. See p. 281 concerning Sidney's authorship of the poem.

there is a clear alteration in the voice's melody and the harmonies it implies at the words 'I speak of saints'. There is more room for word-painting in the melodies of through-composed songs than in those of strophic songs like the psalms, where different sets of words may be sung to one tune. The vocal part of *Out of the orient crystal skies* (BE 15/10) portrays the skies in a highly active line with many wide leaps. This is not of course a 'natural' manner of singing. Byrd's melodies are not based closely on the inflections of speech, though they are never at odds with speech rhythms. The slightly abstract style this engenders does not mean that the consort songs are without feeling, but the emotion they convey is that of a calm, confident mind, not the anguished emotion of the more baroque motets. While it is true that some songs are less personal than others, there is nothing unfeeling about the joyful chorus of *Christ rising again* or the sorrow of *Ye sacred muses*, Byrd's elegy on the death of Tallis.[67] Turbet has aptly written of Byrd's solo songs as 'music of restraint and subtlety yet also of richness and deep feeling', and of their 'implicit emotion but absence of drama'.[68] In every song the viols help to create the atmosphere as surely as the piano does in a song by Schubert, often setting the mood before the voice enters.[69]

Some of the six-part songs of Byrd's *Songs of sundrie natures* (1589) have been discussed in connection with his consort songs.[70] It is now time to turn to the songs of three, four and five parts from that book.

The musical style of the penitential psalms for three a cappella voices with which Byrd began the collection is as austere as the message of the words. It owes little to the English tradition of three-part songs, and much to the contrapuntal style developed by composers of the Low Countries. The remarkable extent to which Byrd reshaped the song for several singers is revealed by a glance at Thomas Whythorne's *Songes, for three, fower, and five voyces*, published in 1571, shortly before Byrd took up song writing. Whythorne's songs are largely homophonic, and counterpoint results merely from the decoration of music conceived in vertical terms, not from the progress of independent lines.

---

67   Brett (1971-72, p. 54) observes that 'Byrd intended to honour Tallis's memory by a triumph of skill within the conventions of the elegy, not by a mere display of personal grief, which he would have considered imappropriate and unworthy'.

68   Turbet, 1992(c).

69   Brett (1971-72, p. 56) says: 'While his writing for the solo voice barely altered in style, Byrd increasingly found in the instrumental accompaniment another, and more subtle, means of making his song "framed to the life of the words"'.

70   See p. 285. For *If in thine heart* see p. 295.

Byrd's songs for three voices clearly had a role in preparing him for the three-part Mass and the three-part pieces of the *Gradualia*, and there is no doubt that they are connected in some way with his late three-part consort fantasias. It is unknown what inspired him to return to three-part composition after having avoided it since his student days, or what access he had to music on which he might have modelled these pieces. Continental music was probably more widely available in manuscript and in print than surviving copies disclose. One possible source of such music, to which Byrd is more than likely to have been admitted, is the library of Lord Lumley. Neighbour points to the influence of Adrian Willaert, directly or indirectly, upon Byrd's three-part fantasias, and the Lumley library included at least one Flemish-bound book of Willaert's music.[71]

The usual note-length in the three-part psalms[72] is the minim; crotchets are rare and quavers rarer still. The contrapuntal writing necessitates greater repetition of the words than in the consort songs. The verses provide little opportunity for word-painting, and Byrd does not go out of his way to seek it. He illustrates his texts only in the more obvious places ('in thy fury', 'From depth of sin').

Some of the secular three-part songs are a little closer to the spirit of the madrigal and related genres, though this depends on how the madrigal is defined.[73] It cannot be said that they have a great deal in

71   Neighbour, 1978, p. 56; Milsom, 1993, p. 152. Although Willaert spent most of his life in Italy, he was of Flemish origin and seems to have maintained his Flemish contacts. While Willaert's music may contain no exact models for Byrd's songs of three and four parts, it is impossible to read his *Musica Nova* of 1559 (the book owned by Lumley), or his madrigals, without feeling that Byrd must have studied music in the same style.

72   *Lord in thy rage*, *Right blest are they*, *Lord in thy wrath*, *O God which art most merciful*, *Lord hear my prayer*, *From depth of sin*, and *Attend mine humble prayer*.

73   The madrigal, like Byrd's songs, brought together elements that had been around for a very long time. The important thing was the choice of elements and the prominence accorded them. Caldwell (1991, p. 397) defines the madrigal in very broad terms as 'a monostrophic poem, set to music in a way that underlines the verbal and semantic content of the text', and adds (p. 398) that the question of whether he was writing a 'madrigal' probably never entered Byrd's head. Nonetheless, while Byrd never used the term in his printed books of songs, he must have had a clear enough idea of the style in providing samples for Watson in 1590. Kerman (1962), writing specifically about the madrigal, and nearer in time to Fellowes' endeavours to include Byrd among the members of the 'English madrigal school', felt it necessary to distinguish the bulk of Byrd's songs from those of the madrigalists.

common with Morley's Italian-influenced three-part canzonets.[74] Indeed, if Peacham is to be trusted, *The nightingale* and perhaps the three-part setting of *Susanna fair* were composed before the Italian style gained a real hold on English music.[75]

In spite of the lighter mood and shorter note-values of Byrd's three-voice settings of secular lyrics, his polyphony often remains exacting. The fourteen-line sonnet *When younglings first on Cupid fix their sight* makes extensive use of canon throughout its two sections (corresponding to the octet and sestet). At the other extreme the voices in *The greedy hawk* are often individualized and contrasted.

The singing of four-part songs is described in Claude Hollybande's dialogue *The French Schoolemaster* (1573). After Katherin has opened the chest containing music books, Roland − a counter-tenor who advocates the merits of white wine over green as a vocal lubricant − asks, 'Who shall singe with me?' The master, who does not propose to sing himself, replies, 'You shall have cōpanie enough: David shall make the base, Jhon the tenor; and James the treble'.[76] James must have been a boy. The songs he and his fellows sang were probably comparable to the songs for four voices transcribed without words in the *Mulliner book*, which are more homophonic than contrapuntal, and contain few rhythmic complexities.[77] Passages in Byrd's four-voice songs reflect this idiom, but as a whole they spring from different roots.

O Lord my God and *Wounded I am* have been identified above as originating in consort versions. Ignoring the four-part choruses to consort songs, the other songs for four voices in Byrd's 1589 collection are *While that the sun, From Cytheron the warlike boy is fled*, and *Is Love a boy?* They illustrate well the variety of Byrd's methods and how they are influenced by his texts. The poem of *While that the sun* consists of four stanzas with a repeated refrain. Byrd was content to set only the first stanza, leaving the performers to adjust the music if they want to sing the additional stanzas. *From Cytheron* has three stanzas, each of which is given its own music. The reason is clear: any music that fitted the words of all the stanzas would be very dull, and Byrd was interested in the whole poem. The line 'Thereby to train poor misers to the trap' is superficially identical metrically with 'O god, O good, O just, reserve

---

74   Byrd 'avoids all the familiar canzonet clichés with almost ingenious consistency'. (Kerman, 1962, p. 108.)

75   See p. 280.

76   Hollybande, 1573, pp. 126-128.

77   See Stevens, 1954. Examples are *O ye tender babes* and *When shall my sorrowful sighing* by Tallis, the anonymous *I smile to see how you devise*, and similar pieces with English titles.

thy rod', but it needs quite a different musical treatment. *Is Love a boy?* is a fourteen-line sonnet, and the structure of the music follows the structure of the poem. The series of questions in the first four lines is set to a series of different but related points, the longest of which is reserved for the last question at the end of line four. The assertions of the next four lines are set to the same music, a procedure made possible because the text falls into phrases matching those of the first four lines in rhythm and length. Fresh music is provided for the sestet, which is divided into short, distinctly characterized sections of two lines.

It has already been pointed out that most of the songs for five and six voices which Byrd published in 1589 either started life as consort songs or exhibit features of the genre. The one which most clearly has five singing parts is *Of gold all burnished*, and it needs to be singled out because it is a special case in several other ways. The poem, a sonnet that smacks of playhouse declamation, is metrically unusual. What the author intended is not altogether clear, but his poem has six stresses to a line, and each line contains a caesura.[78] Byrd's setting observes the caesura throughout. More importantly, his phrasing follows the sense of the poem.[79] The words govern much else as well. Metrical imitation plays as large a part in the structure of Byrd's setting as melodic imitation.

More typically representative of Byrd's attitude to composition for *a cappella* performance are the five-voice song *Compel the hawk* and the six-voice songs *If in thine heart* and *Unto the hills*. The ambivalence of manner they betray may explain why he chose a severely contrapuntal style for his *a cappella* songs for three and four voices, and shows in any case how firmly he remained wedded to the idea of the consort song.[80]

---

78 Kerman (1962, p. 114) suggests that the poem might be syllabic or be written in an experimental metre, or both.

79 Kerman describes the piece as 'Italianate' in its brief phrases, and its sharp, simple and frequent cadences. In this connection he draws attention to *La verginella*, Byrd's setting of an Italian poem in his 1588 collection (originally a consort song, but newly equipped with words for all the parts). Brett however observes that Byrd treated the Italian words of the single stanza he set as though they were Latin. When *The fair young virgin*, an English version of Byrd's song, was prepared for publication in Yonge's *Musica Transalpina* (1588) the translator fitted his words for the first stanza as best he could to Byrd's existing music; Byrd provided Yonge with a fresh setting of a second stanza, working from the English words. (Brett, 1976, pp. 187-188, 193.)

80 This led Kerman (1962, p. 115) to include them in a group that he termed 'transitional' songs. This should not be allowed to suggest that there were two legitimate methods of song composition, and that some of Byrd's songs fell inconveniently between them. It is more accurate to say that Byrd had a variety of methods at his command, and

In Byrd's consort songs, the first entry of the solo vocal part is often delayed. Something similar happens in *Compel the hawk*, which has two closely imitative soprano parts. The first soprano does not enter until the eighth bar, and the second soprano enters two bars after that. But it is as though the composer thought of the song as a vocal duet while he was setting the first four lines of the poem, and then changed his mind. The fifth line, which forms a couplet with the fourth, is twice set for different combinations of three voices, before all five voices sing the remainder of the first part of the poem. The concluding lines also are set for five voices, and repeated. *If in thine heart* raises fewer questions about Byrd's intentions, and his use of different voice combinations is linked to the form and sense of the poem. The long silences of the upper voice during the first half of the song nevertheless lead to the suspicion that he was not completely happy about adding to the number of parts in which he was accustomed to working.

It was evidently the inclusion of passages for three voices that caused Kerman to group *Unto the hills* with *Compel the hawk* and *If in thine heart*.[81] But while the first entry of the bass is delayed for the space of twelve semibreves, *Unto the hills* is much more credible as a piece intended from the outset for six voices. Byrd must have been working at about the same time on the six-part song *Let others praise what seems them best*, presumably at the request of Watson, who wrote the words. This song was published separately in 1589. Only three parts are known to have survived,[82] but they indicate that the song may have been in a style similar to that of *Unto the hills*.

At the age of fifty Byrd adopted a markedly new approach in making two settings of Watson's poem *This sweet and merry month of May*. There is not much question that the occasion for one or both of the settings was an entertainment designed for the diversion of the Queen; that is confirmed by the emphasis Byrd placed on the words 'Eliza' and 'O beauteous Queen'. It may explain why he embraced so comprehensively a manner that he had previously been cautious about adopting. However little he felt inclined to compete with younger composers in adding to their outpourings in the latest fashion, he did so and became the first English composer whose madrigals appeared in print.[83]

used them at need.

81   Ibid.

82   See pp. 412-413.

83   Leaving aside Byrd's own *The fair young virgin*, which is not strictly in the madrigal style, the madrigals published hitherto in England had been adaptations of Italian compositions. The composer most heavily represented in Yonge's *Musica transalpina*

Ex. 20

Selected motives from the four-voice setting of *This sweet and merry month of May*

In Byrd's four-voice version of *This sweet and merry month of May* the fully developed madrigal style shows itself in the succession of brief motives, strongly characterized melodically and rhythmically, which illustrate short phrases of the text and imply tempo changes as the sense of the poem changes.[84] (Ex. 20.) There are eight such motives in the space of the first twenty-six semibreves, and at least four in the space of the next nineteen semibreves. This necessitates two things if the piece is not going to fall apart: firm harmonic control and an underlying

(1588) was Alfonso Ferrabosco (by then decidedly old-fashioned), followed by Marenzio and Palestrina; almost all the pieces in Watson's *Italian madrigalls Englished* (1590) were by Marenzio. Watson's inclusion in his collection of two settings of one poem by the same composer was original; it did not happen in Italian collections.

84   Each motive occurs in a variety of forms, but retains its essential characteristics.

relationship between the motives. During the first section of the madrigal Byrd achieves harmonic control by the simplest means. He stays close to the home key of A, with emphatic cadences on G (in modern terms the dominant of the relative major), E, A and C. He begins the second section with a bold step to F, but he quickly returns by way of D and G to A and its dominant, and then remains close to them.

The relationship between the motives springs from features such as the alternation of notes a tone or semitone apart, groups of rising notes, broken chords, groups of two or more notes moving downwards in steps. A detailed study of the madrigal would reveal many more common factors.

The six voices of Byrd's other setting of *This sweet and merry month of May* make for greater musical complexity, and commentators have generally felt that his inspiration was more intense,[85] but the piece is informed by the same principles and contains many of the same ideas: 'merry' is repeated and sung to quavers, 'wantons' calls for a dotted figure, 'pleasure' demands triple time, and 'take well in worth a simple toy' is sung (perhaps to make it clearly audible to the Queen) in 'contrapuntal homophony'.

---

85   It was nevertheless the four-voice version that Byrd reprinted in *Psalmes, songs, and sonnets* (1611).

16

ANGLICAN MUSIC OF THE MIDDLE PERIOD

The discussion of Byrd's Anglican music in chapter nine left several problems of dating unresolved. The full and verse anthems dealt with here pose further questions, but they all belong fairly certainly to the years after Byrd left Lincoln.[1] It is not possible to decide whether any of Byrd's Anglican music resulted from his commitment to supply Lincoln Cathedral with 'cantica et Servitia divina' for the rest of his life. Payment of the money which was part of the arrangement began on 25 March 1574, and ended after the financial year 1581-1582.[2] Unless he sent the Dean and Chapter copies of music written for the Chapel Royal, the chances are that most of Byrd's energy was channelled in other directions and the undertaking was soon forgotten,

Full anthems

Arise O Lord—Help us O God (BE 11/1) looks like two unusually concise anthems linked together.[3] The two sections are in different modes and are scored for different forces, and exceptionally among Byrd's anthems the words are taken from two psalms. The stylistic indications are that they were written after Byrd's return from Lincoln. Bold harmonic movement supported by an active bass, and the mixed homophonic and contrapuntal writing, relate both sections to the later of Byrd's motets in the *Cantiones sacrae* of 1575. Although they are separated in some sources, they had become joined by the early 1580s, and perhaps before. *Help us O God* occurs in a section of Bodleian Library manuscript Mus. Sch. e.423 copied between c.1577 and 1582, where it is described as 'Arise O Lord Secunda Pars'. Since the manuscript was copied by John Petre's scribe John Bentley,[4] who

1   A 'full' anthem is sung throughout by several voices. A 'verse' anthem includes sections for soloist(s) and instrumental accompaniment as well as chorus. The term 'verse anthem' appears to be a coinage of the seventeenth or the eighteenth century; the earliest example given by the *Oxford English Dictionary* is from Thomas Busby's *A complete dictionary of music* (London, 1801). John Barnard's *First Book of Selected Church Musick* (1641) distinguishes 'full anthems' and 'anthems with verses'.

2   See p. 44.

3   Compare the keyboard fantasia MB 27/27. (See p. 199.)

4   See Dr David Mateer's forthcoming article 'William Byrd, John Petre and Oxford, Bodleian MS Mus. Sch. E.423'.

apparently received many of Byrd's pieces soon after they were composed, the parts may have been joined by Byrd himself.

The second fascicule of Robert Dow's anthology is opened by a group of three anthems.[5] Although it may be that none of them was entered before 1587, because they are followed by Byrd's elegies for Sidney, two of the anthems, *O Lord make thy servant Elizabeth* and *How long shall mine enemies*, have already been assigned tentatively, though not indisputably, to Byrd's later years at Lincoln. If the third, *Prevent us O Lord* (BE 11/8), was transmitted to Dow with the others, it may belong to much the same period. Since it reflects Byrd's experience in writing the Latin works that led to *Emendemus in melius*, it was probably written not very long after his return to London.[6]

None of Byrd's remaining full anthems appears in a sixteenth-century source. Perhaps the first to be written was *O God whom our offences* (BE 11/5), which bears comparison with such motets of the early 1580s as *Deus venerunt gentes* (BE 2/7) and *O quam gloriosum* (BE 2/13).

O God the proud are risen (BE 11/4), the incomplete but largely reconstructable *Exalt thyself O God* (BE 11/2), and *Sing joyfully* (BE 11/10) form a group related by key and scoring. More than any other pieces among Byrd's English church compositions they have an affinity with the Great Service − for example, in their deployment of two sopranos − and could well be among the last pieces he provided for the Chapel Royal. But when did Byrd write them? *Sing joyfully*, if not the other two anthems, may be out of place in the present chapter. Its insistence on the name 'Jacob' could mean that it was conceived as a tribute to King James, and was not composed before 1603.[7]

A Jacobean date for *Sing joyfully* is not out of the question, given the influences revealed in *O God the proud are risen* and *Exalt thyself O God*. The rapid changes of vocal colour and texture that occur in the first are not found in Byrd's earlier anthems, and the juxtaposition of long and short notes in setting 'slow to anger' is madrigalian enough to suggest the possibility of composition in the 1590s. The short phrases, sharply drawn motives and word repetition of *Exalt thyself* bespeak an equally late date. The same treatment, carried to greater lengths, is invited and received by the text of *Sing joyfully*. Its phrases are distinguished by motives which are imitative without relying on exact repetition. The four entries of the

5   Christ Church, Oxford, MSS Mus. 984-988. The second fascicule is chronologically the last. See Mateer, 1986-87, p. 6.

6   Monson (1983, p. vii) associates both *Arise O Lord – Help us O God* and *Prevent us O Lord* with 'the more expressive and flexible motets of 1575'.

7   Suggested by Mr Richard Turbet. The words are from Psalm 81, which Byrd set in a different translation as *Sing we merrily* and published in 1611.

opening point have different first intervals, prefiguring the freedom that is to follow. Far from fragmenting into short semi-imitative passages, the work is held together by Byrd's harmonic skill, which enables him to work phrase by phrase through a range of more or less closely related keys. In crude terms, the opening section of Byrd's plan takes in the first two cadences on C ('Sing joyfully') and G ('strength'). He then creates one side of a tonal arch: C ('strength'), G ('Jacob'), D ('timbrel'). A modulatory passage ('and the viol') teasingly points in the opposite direction round the circle of fifths, and is followed by a series of chords on F, the relative major of D minor (for the phrase 'Blow the trumpet in the new moon').[8] Byrd however avoids the B flat which would define the key as F, and returns via the other side of the arch through D ('appointed') and G ('feast day') to C ('Israel'). The opening section of the scheme is balanced by the last (repeating the phrase 'and a law of the God of Jacob'), which Byrd treats as a separate and tonally more fluid unit. It quickly reaches a cadence on A − not previously heard, but closely related to the D which stands at the centre of the work's main arch − before returning in a more leisurely fashion to C.[9]

Verse anthems

The roots of the verse style can be traced to the mid-sixteenth century.[10] Solo songs with sacred words seem sometimes to have had choral refrains.[11] By a process of cross-fertilization, initially rather stilted church anthems came to be written with verses sung to the organ. Composers with whom Byrd was closely associated played a part in this development, though the chronology is unclear. It is not possible to establish with certainty the dates of pieces such as Richard Farrant's

8   Byrd characteristically subjected this part of the anthem to revision, among other things giving greater prominence to 'in the new moon', which in the second version is repeated more often. (See Monson, 1983, pp. viii, 216.) Could the anthem have been composed for the coronation of King James, and revised at greater leisure?

9   Another anthem, *O praise our Lord* (BE 11/21), has a text and madrigalian touches that are reminiscent of *Sing joyfully*, though it is less typical of Byrd in style and accomplishment. The question of its authenticity is discussed by Monson, 1983, pp. xi-xii. The ascription to 'Alphonso' (presumably the older Ferrabosco), which occurs in a set of Paston books (BL Additional MSS 18936-9), is unconvincing despite the opinion of Fellowes (1948, p. 138). In other sources (BL Additional MS 31992, another Paston manuscript, and BL Additional MS 17797) the anthem is ascribed to Byrd.

10   le Huray, 1978, pp. 217-225.

11   The modern term 'consort anthem' is sometimes applied to songs designed for domestic devotions.

When as we sat in Babylon and William Mundy's *Ah helpless wretch.*[12] It is nevertheless evident that Byrd's verse anthems run in parallel with his consort songs.

It is difficult to be sure about the original form of a few of Byrd's pieces that occur as verse anthems in comparatively early sources.[13] *Christ rising again* was published by Byrd in 1589 as a song for two sopranos and chorus with viols. The earliest source includes it among a group of secular songs,[14] but a pre-publication version is found in several ecclesiastical sources and it may well have begun life as an anthem. *Alack when I look back* (BE 11/11) survives in two versions. One is a transcription for voice and lute of what was almost certainly a consort song; the other is a verse anthem with choruses and organ accompaniment. The consort song probably came first, and had its origin in words and a tune by William Hunnis, the Master of the Children. He published the words alone in Richard Edwards's *The paradyse of daynty devises* (1578), and with the tune in his own *Seven sobs of a sorrowfull soule for sin*ne (1583).[15] Hunnis himself appears to have made a verse setting which Byrd reworked for his second version, as he reworked material by other composers. He adopted Hunnis's general design but modified the tune and expanded and reharmonized the choruses.[16] Hunnis's piece could have been in existence for some time before the words and tune were printed, but there is nothing to show that Byrd's adaptation was made any earlier than the 1580s.[17]

---

12   Mundy's piece has words by Hunnis, but it is not known when he wrote them. The part of Farrant and Mundy in developing the verse anthem is discussed by le Huray, 1978, pp. 220-222.

13   For songs by Byrd that have been sung as anthems in church see Phillips, 1991, pp. 76-77.

14   Bodleian Library MS Mus. Sch. e.423, where it is in a section copied in 1582 or after.

15   The first line echoes, or is echoed by, Lord Vaux's poem beginning 'When I look back', which also appears in Edwards's collection.

16   Hunnis's setting is incomplete in two Bodleian Library manuscripts: Mus. d. 162 and Tenbury 1382. Byrd's anthem occurs only in seventeenth-century sources.

17   Hunnis was the author of two further poems set by Byrd as verse anthems. The words of *Let us be glad and clap our hands* (BE 11/23) and *Thou God that guid'st* (BE 11/16) succeed *Alack when I look back* in *Seven sobs of a sorrowfull soule*. Byrd's setting of *Let us be glad* has been lost, while his setting of *Thou God that guid'st* has been transmitted in copies which make it difficult to determine what he originally wrote, though it may have been a consort song. See Monson (1983, pp. ix-x and 190-191) on the sources and authorship of the consort setting, and for anthems by Byrd of which only the words have survived.

Behold O God the sad and heavy case (BE 11/12), with its prayer for the preservation of the Queen's health and the thought that 'ev'ry limb will tremble, shake and quake, Till health possess her wonted course again', must refer to one of the many epidemics experienced by Elizabethan England. The piece was not published, and its obviously late position among Byrd's anthems accords with Monson's suggestion that it was occasioned by the serious outbreak of plague in 1592-93.[18] It occurs only in part-books and an organ book from Durham Cathedral, yet it is not radically different from Byrd's settings of other rhymed strophic poems that appear in secular sources, and the organ accompaniment contains passages that could well stem from a consort original.

The Great Service

The 'Great' Service contains the musical material for the morning and evening services and holy communion.[19] It presumably acquired its name because it is longer than Byrd's other Services, not because there was any recognized musical category of 'great services'.[20] The first source to contain any of its movements is John Baldwin's commonplace book, where the Te Deum is described as part of Byrd's 'Long Service'.[21] Incomplete versions of the Te Deum and Benedictus occur on pages which Baldwin copied between about 1600 and 1606, but what is known of Byrd's activities points to the Great Service having been written some years earlier. Monson refers, without being specific, to disparities within the work which encourage the supposition that the movements were composed piecemeal and brought together subsequently,[22] and the description 'sute [suite] of service' in one source seems to indicate that it was regarded as a collection of pieces that could be used separately at need.[23] Fellowes rightly remarks that 'no occasion can be imagined which would have called for the performance of all the seven numbers included in it'.[24] Perhaps the soundest conclusion that can be reached

18   Monson. 1983, p. x.

19   Venite, Te Deum, Benedictus, Kyrie, Creed, Magnificat and Nunc Dimittis.

20   See p. 184, note 21.

21   BL, MS R. M. 24.d.2, f. 82^v.

22   Monson, 1982, p. vi.

23   York Minster Library MS 13, compiled c.1618. Monson, 1982, pp. v-vi, dismisses the suggestion that the word 'new' applied to the Great Service in this source might indicate recent composition. 'Suite' was used in the seventeenth century to mean a group of pieces that were not necessarily connected but which were in the same key or by the same composer. The terminology was very loose.

24   Fellowes, 1948, p. 128. Performance of all the numbers would not have accorded

about its date is that it was composed over the same broad period as Byrd's motets of the later 1580s and perhaps beyond. The repetition of words, the multiplicity of motives, and the word-painting in the Magnificat are so pronounced as to suggest that it could belong to the 1590s.

It is difficult to know whether to interpret certain inconsistencies in the Great Service as betraying spasmodic composition. The Benedictus, Creed, Magnificat and Nunc Dimittis all begin with verses sung by a soprano and alto on the cantoris side, and a soprano and tenor on the decani side, as though Byrd were trying to establish a measure of unity. Three movements do not fit this scheme. The Te Deum begins with two sopranos and two tenors, and the short Kyrie is sung throughout by a full five-voice choir. The Venite is incomplete, but should almost certainly begin with two sopranos and two altos. Andrews focuses attention on Byrd's use of the 'head-motive' technique in a group of movements, though these do not coincide with those connected by the scoring.[25] The movements are the Venite, Benedictus, Magnificat and Nunc Dimittis, each of which begins with a series of notes repeated with more or less consistency. The same series of notes crops up in the course of several of the movements. On some occasions, at least, these resemblances seem to be the result of deliberate planning on Byrd's part, but on others they appear to originate below the level of consciousness.

The Great Service represents the culmination of a process begun in earlier services and paralleled in a number of motets, namely the relaxation of the homophonic writing of earlier Anglican music to a point

with the form of any service specified by the Prayer Book of 1559, and although the Great Service makes superb use of the forces which, probably, were normally on duty in the Chapel Royal, it does not require their augmentation as might be the case if the work had been intended for a special occasion, say at St Paul's. The Armada celebrations of 1588, which seem at first sight to be an event demanding special music, can be ruled out. There was hardly time for Byrd to write the Great Service between the Privy Council's decision on 3 November that thanksgiving services should be held, and Queen Elizabeth's attendance at St Paul's on 24 November. Stow (1605, f. [Nnnn 6]ᵛ) in any case mentions only 'the cleargie singing the Letanie' during the Armada thanksgiving at St Paul's. The 1631 edition of Stow, expanded by Edmund Howes, gives the same information, but Brett (1976, p. 197), writing of the song *Look and bow down*, which was probably performed after the thanksgiving, apparently quotes a different source in saying it followed a Te Deum.

25   Andrews, 1966, pp. 269-270. A head-motive is one which appears at the beginning of several movements and establishes a relationship between them. In the work of English composers the technique can be traced to the fifteenth century, and occurs in the *Sine nomine* Mass of Taverner and the four-part Mass of Tallis.

where Byrd could move with ease between homophony and complex polyphony. This is exemplified on a large scale by the Nunc Dimittis, and on a smaller scale by the last fourteen bars of the Creed. (Ex. 21.) Few syllables are spread over more than one note, but long passages of genuine homophony are rare. Much of the time Byrd employs nothing more rigid than the semi-homophony found in a motet like *Haec dicit Dominus*.

Ex. 21

Creed from the Great Service, final bars

Contrast between the homophonic and contrapuntal is an aspect of the variety with which all movements of the Great Service are invested. Certain passages of the texts are sung rapidly, one note to a syllable, without repetition. Others are dwelt upon, reiterated, or elaborately set. There is an antithesis between melodies with a small vertical range and those which are highly animated. Both types may occur together, but even when the top voice is static the bass is active. (Ex. 22.)

Ex. 22

Te Deum from the Great Service, bars 15-20

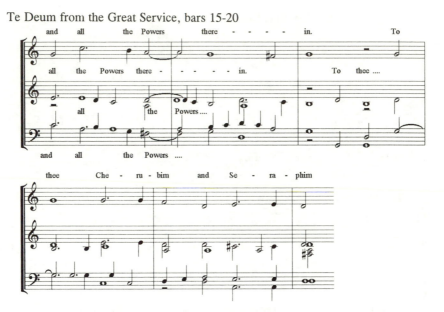

There are contrasts between the cantoris and decani sides, the full choir and small groups of voices, and different voice combinations (Byrd shows a partiality for groups that include two trebles). Vocal colourings and antiphonal effects in the Te Deum are particularly notable. Such devices invariably serve a purpose. Frequent changes of scoring in the Creed counterbalance the predominant homophony.

All Byrd's musical imagination is brought to bear on the task of illuminating the words prescribed for Anglican worship, and presenting them with liturgical propriety. He approaches the English words with no less conviction than he does the Latin words of his motets and Masses.[26]

26   As this book was going to press, Mr Richard Turbet pointed out that a comparison of Byrd's Great Service with Sheppard's Second Service demonstrates Byrd's study of the work of his former mentor. Mr Turbet proposes to publish details of this.

17

MASSES

Byrd made settings of the Ordinary of the Mass for three, four and five voices. The Ordinary consists of texts used throughout the year, and Byrd followed precedent in setting the Kyrie, Gloria, Credo, Sanctus (including Benedictus) and Agnus Dei. He presumably expected the Proper, that is the texts specified for particular feasts or times of year, to be rendered in plainsong settings.[1]

The part-books for each of Byrd's three settings of the Ordinary were published without title-pages or colophons. This suggests the printing of a small number of sets for circulation among Catholics, and in the circumstances it is surprising that as many as half a dozen copies of each Mass have survived.[2] Clulow's careful detective work established that they were printed by Byrd's usual printer, Thomas East, and that the

---

1   The movements of the Ordinary were not meant to be sung straight through, as they are often sung in concert performances and recorded today, nor do they make liturgical sense if sung without Proper texts. For an outline of the mediaeval and post-Tridentine Masses, showing how the various musical units fitted into the whole, see Harper, 1991, pp. 114-125, 161-164.

2   The three Masses were nevertheless known to John Playford, though the source of his information about their existence may have been Thomas East's list of *Musick bookes printed in England*. (See Rimbault, 1847, p. 14.) They appear as 'Kirries' in Playford's *A catalogue of all the musick-bookes that have been printed in England, either for voyce or instruments*, which he published in 1653. This includes:

Birds Kirries 3 parts.
Birds Kirries 4 parts.
Birds Kirries 5 parts.
Birds 5. parts wherein is Lullaby.
Birds 3, 4, 5, 6 parts, English.
Birds 5 parts Latine, *Ne Irascarie*, 1. set.
Birds 5, 6 parts Latine, *Infaelix ego*, 2. set.
Birds 1. set of Gradualia, 5, 4, 3 parts.
Birds 2. set of Gradualia, 4, 5, 6 parts.
Birds 2. set English.

Facsimile in Humphries and Smith, 1954; the original is Harley 5936, part of the Bagford Collection in the British Library's Department of Printed Books. The term 'kyries' is used also in the catalogue of the Lumley library: see Milsom, 1993, p. 166.

Mass for four voices was first published in 1592-93, the Mass for three voices in 1593-94, and the Mass for five voices in 1594-95.[3]

There were good reasons, in the climate of the times, for the publisher's name and the date of publication to be omitted. The Catholic missionary Father Robert Southwell was captured in 1592 and executed in 1594. Byrd and his household were themselves subject to penalties as recusants, and the family of fellow-Catholics into which his eldest son married in 1591 or 1592 had endured the seizure of the greater part of their property. The mere possession of an openly Catholic book could lead to suspicion and interrogation; its printing and publication might incur serious penalties. To write even one Mass was a bold and unusual decision, which could only have been prompted by the strongest personal motivation. The identification of Byrd as the composer at the top right-hand corner of each page was a calculated risk, and must mean that he felt secure in the protection afforded him by the friendship and patronage of some of the most influential men in the realm.

There is little doubt that the Masses were intended for the clandestine services maintained by men like the Petres and the Pastons, and for performance by small groups of singers, probably with one voice to a part.[4] The dates of their publication do not necessarily show when they were written, but there is every reason to think that they were among the first fruits of Byrd's semi-retirement, when he began to concentrate his energies on the composition of music for the Catholic rite. It can be guessed that he started them when collections of his earlier music were completed in 1591, and that he published them as soon as he could after they were finished. This does not inevitably mean that he started with the Kyrie of the four-part Mass and worked steadily through to the Agnus Dei of the five-part Mass. If he occasionally worked on more than one at a time it would help to explain the occurrence of similar material in different Masses.

---

3   Clulow, 1966. Undated second editions of the Masses for four and three voices were published in 1598-1600. Brett (1981(b), p. ix) suggests that John Baldwin's copy of the Mass for three voices, in BL MS R. M. 24.d.2, was made from Byrd's manuscript before it went to the printer. This is doubtful because Baldwin's note of 'proporcions to the minum', which immediately precedes the Mass (no. 123, f. 128^v), is dated 1603. It may of course be that Baldwin worked from a pre-publication copy.

4   Although the Masses are not in Byrd's most elaborate manner, they are not so simple that a group of (perhaps largely) amateur singers could have performed them without skilled direction. Musicians who might have supplied this were employed in some large houses, but not in all. It is entirely possible that Byrd helped to train singers at Ingatestone and Thorndon Hall (the Petres lost John Bolt in 1593/4), and at other houses (such as that of Richard Bold, near Marlow) where he was welcome.

Byrd's Masses were the first to be written in England for over thirty years. Not many English musicians now shared his memory of singing Masses in their boyhood. And while he grew up with composers who had written Masses, there was no active tradition such as gave rise to the vast output of Continental composers like Lassus and Palestrina. Byrd's experience was of writing multi-movement works for the reformed English church. Setting the texts central to Catholic worship required him to tackle a wholly new set of problems. As on other occasions when he tackled a genre for the first time, Byrd began by studying an existing work by an older composer; he had, for example, modelled his keyboard hornpipe on one by Aston, and his Litany on one by Tallis. We are never likely to know what works Byrd had in his personal library — though he must have copied and collected a good deal of music in the course of some forty years — or what he sought out in the libraries of friends,[5] but one work to which he now turned has been firmly identified. It is the 'Meane' (or 'Sine nomine') Mass of John Taverner.[6]

The choice of Taverner's Mass cannot have been casual. It was not only a direct link with pre-Reformation tradition,[7] it had long ago served as a model for Masses by Tye, Sheppard and Tallis,[8] all of which Byrd is likely to have known and perhaps sung in his youth. And it had the virtue, for Byrd's purpose, of brevity. But while he took over a number of Taverner's ideas, the differences in the first of his own Masses are — as always — highly instructive. Taverner divided his work into a large number of short sections, usually containing one imitative point or more; they are often separated by a cadence and a pause, and sometimes by a new time signature. Unity is assisted by head-motives and other thematic relationships; variety is provided by metre, vocal scoring and sometimes texture. Taverner's imaginative structural use of harmony must have appealed particularly to Byrd. He broadly adopted Taverner's overall plan, but generally gave less prominence to divisions between sections. And when he broke up the long texts of the Gloria and Credo, he made divisions that differ from those of his immediate model and almost any other he could have chosen.[9] Thematic links, too, played a less important

5   A source of Masses known to Byrd may have been the Forrest-Heyther part-books. After Forrest's death about 1581 the books passed into the hands of John Baldwin, who for some reason had to recopy or complete one part of the last four Masses. (Bergsagel, 1963.)

6   What follows on this topic is indebted to Brett, 1981(a).

7   Taverner died in 1545.

8   Davison, 1973.

9   See Kerman, 1981, p. 195-197. Kerman's 1981 volume incorporates his article of 1979 on Byrd's Masses.

part in Byrd's thinking. His debt to Taverner is nonetheless explicit in the Sanctus of the Mass for four voices.[10] Taverner's Sanctus begins with two sets of paired entries, employing a point that expands in melodic range. Byrd reworks and enhances the idea, and even incorporates a transcription of a bar from Taverner.[11]

It is more than probable, as Brett conjectures, that Taverner's Mass was open on Byrd's writing table as he worked, but everything in his approach to Mass writing points to his having thought carefully and independently about what he was doing. At one level Byrd's settings are illustrative commentaries upon the words. At another level, they are prayers of petition and thanksgiving, and they are musical records of thoughts and feelings springing from the contemplation of a text which he must have pondered long and often. His words in the first book of *Gradualia* are inevitably recalled: 'to one reflecting earnestly and attentively on divine things, if his mind is not idle and inactive, the right notes somehow occur spontaneously'. Byrd's reading of the text determines the plan of each Mass, and there is a consistency between the settings that suggests he set out with some clear ideas that remained unaltered. But − apart from the fact that Byrd was not a composer to repeat himself − their composition was spread over three or four years in which he must have meditated many times and ever more deeply on the meaning of the words he was setting.

Byrd's first concern was the practical one of how to break the text of the Mass into sections. This was not hard in the case of the shorter movements, but the Credo and Gloria posed a problem. In most respects established practice and his own reading of the text were a satisfactory guide to the task of making broad divisions, and in the Masses for three and five voices he generally stuck to the plan he first laid down in the Mass for four voices.[12] In a few instances this was unconventional. Instead of dividing the Gloria at 'Qui tollis' he chose to do so a phrase earlier, so that he could dwell on the words 'Jesu Christe' at the end of the previous section and place 'Domine Deus, agnus Dei, filius patris' at

10   David Josephson (letter in *Musical Times*, cxvii, 1976, p. 739) gives voice to the 'suspicion' that the 'In nomine' section of the Benedictus of Byrd's five-part Mass owes something to the corresponding part of Taverner's Mass based on the *Gloria tibi trinitas* chant. This would not be surprising, since Byrd's first consort In nomine draws directly on that Mass.

11   Other connections are detailed by Brett, 1981(a). For instance, the final cadence of Byrd's Benedictus is a rearrangement of the one from the same movement of Taverner's Mass. A theme derived from Taverner, and employed in Byrd's four-part Mass, occurs in varied form at the beginning of the Sanctus of Byrd's three-part Mass.

12   See Kerman, 1981, p. 195.

the head of a new one. It was customary to divide the Credo before 'Et incarnatus est', with the obvious intention of highlighting a tenet of faith; Byrd again made his division earlier, at 'Qui propter nos homines'. He held to these divisions in his next two Masses,[13] but in one case he recognized that he had made a mistake. While the division of the Credo immediately before the words 'et unam sanctam' gave prominence to the notion of one holy catholic and apostolic church, he subsequently adopted the traditional division before 'et in spiritum sanctum'. This resulted in better proportions and did not place in a subordinate position a part of the text relating to the Father, Son and Holy Ghost. The initial misjudgement helps to confirm that the four-part Mass was the first to be written.

The larger sections of the text are marked by full cadences and double bar-lines. Within them Byrd picks out phrases and words which he wishes to illuminate or upon which he wishes the listener to reflect. Sometimes he focuses attention by reducing the number of voices,[14] sometimes by setting a few words homophonically or antiphonally, or by introducing a fresh point. In each Mass his pictorial imagination is stirred by phrases such as 'et resurrexit', 'descendit de caelis' and 'ascendit in caelum'. Concepts like 'sepultus est', 'vivificantem' and 'et exspecto resurrectionem' are illustrated more subtly but no less effectively. The procedure is related to the procedures of the madrigal without being in any way madrigalian. The writing has affinities with that of *Domine non sum dignus* and *Domine salva nos* − both prayers, and both published in 1591.

All Byrd's Masses have a certain austerity, attributable in part to their function as spiritual exercises and in part to his concise expression. Without compromising the attention given to every word, Byrd's parsimony with notes is conveyed into the Masses from some of his most recent motets (the two just mentioned are instances). He repeats few words and sets few syllables to more than one note. He resists any temptation to spin out the shorter movements as surely as he rejects any urge to superficiality in the longer ones.[15] The shortest of the Masses, for three voices, is atypical as an example of Byrd's brevity, since his resources limit the opportunities for pursuing imitative motives through voice after voice. His striving for concision is clearer in the five-part Mass, which is slightly shorter overall than the Mass for four voices, and has a Kyrie and a Gloria which are considerably more compressed than their four-voice counterparts. It is sometimes said that the Mass for five

13   There are changes in the proportions of comparable passages.
14   Kerman, 1981, p. 195.
15   Seductions to which his English predecessors and Continental peers often yielded.

voices, Byrd's standard resource in the composition of motets, is more reserved than those for fewer voices.[16] It is true that, because of its comparative brevity, there is less room for emotional indulgence in the five-part Mass than in its four-part companion; but an equally valid opinion is that the richer sonority of the five-part Mass adds to its character as the formal public statement which fittingly concludes the series.

The sections into which Byrd divided the text of the Mass are held together by musical means. The Gloria of the Mass for four voices is as good an example as any of his harmonic methods. (Table 19.)

Table 19 · Mass for four voices: plan of the Gloria

The movement is divided into two principal sections, each of which can be divided for convenience into two subsections. The two main sections explore slightly opposed tonalities. Each has cadences on G, F and D, but the first makes an excursion into C while the second makes a longer excursion into B flat.

I. The first subsection extends to and includes 'glorificamus te'. It begins in G* with a short stretch of two-part counterpoint. Phrases are then singled out by pairs of voices working homophonically, until the subsection is closed in C by a partly imitative passage for four voices.

The second subsection begins in C with 'Gratias agimus tibi' sung in four-part homophony. This gives way to a passage sung by three or four voices, in which separate ideas in the text are characterized by separate imitative motives. It passes through G ('gloriam tuam') and F ('pater omnipotens'), and ends on D ('Jesu Christe').

II. The section starts in G. Up to and including 'suscipe depricationem nostram' the words are sung by different groups of three voices, each group with its own point: (i) ending on F with 'patris', (ii) ending on B flat 'nobis', and (iii) ending on B flat with 'nostram'.

---

16   On occasion by writers who have noted the conviction of Kerman (1981, p. 211), and his complementary view (p. 198) that the four-voice Mass is 'the most intense, personal, and highly coloured'.

Table 19 *concluded*

A passage mainly for four voices, beginning 'qui sedes dexteram patris', starts at the midpoint of the second main section. As before, different textual phrases are distinguished by different imitative points (not always imitated exactly or by all voices). Special emphasis is laid on the first 'Jesu Christe' by a cadence on D, and on then on 'Dei patris', initially by a cadence on B flat and then by a repetition of the phrase as the music makes its way back to G. The home key is re-emphasized by the closing 'Amen'.

* The movement is generally minor. The two flats in the signature suggest the twice-transposed Aeolian mode, but the frequent cancelling of E flat by a natural throughout the Mass may mean either that Byrd thought of it as the once-transposed Dorian, or that he was not overly concerned with the niceties of modal theory.

Each of Byrd's settings of the Mass makes use of head-motives. In the Mass for four voices the Kyrie, Gloria, Credo and Agnus Dei start with material that is closely similar without being identical.[17] The Sanctus (which, as in the other Masses, is combined with the Benedictus) is derived from Taverner and begins differently, but its opening seems to be the source of secondary phrases in the Kyrie and Credo. In the three-part Mass, part of the motive that begins the Kyrie is closely connected with the motive which begins the Benedictus and Agnus Dei. (Ex. 23.)

Ex. 23

Mass for three voices

17   Illustrations are given by Andrews, 1966, p. 267.

The Sanctus is again the odd movement out, but a connection can be
discerned with the Sanctus of the four-part Mass (Ex. 24), and hence
with Taverner's Mass.

Ex. 24

a. Beginning of Sanctus, Mass for three voices

b. Beginning of Sanctus, Mass for four voices

All the movements of the five-part Mass are linked by recurring themes. (Ex. 25.) These are not repeated exactly, even in one movement, but their relationship is clear enough. The themes are of three kinds: (1) the figure which begins the Kyrie , Gloria, Credo and Agnus Dei, (2) the figure which begins the Benedictus, and (3) the figure which winds upwards and follows (1) and (2) in the four movements just mentioned. Versions of figures (2) and (3) occur simultaneously in the Sanctus.

Ex. 25

Mass for five voices

What of other melodic correspondences which occur in the three Masses? Andrews sets out a host of figures among which family likenesses can be distinguished. Kerman, on the other hand, says flatly that Byrd's Masses 'display only a few internal thematic relationships', while acknowledging that Andrews takes a somewhat different view.[18] Probably both opinions have some merit. It would be incautious to maintain that Byrd intentionally introduced all the thematic connections that a dedicated analyst might perceive, but just as imprudent to deny their existence. Like Beethoven's late piano sonatas and string quartets, Byrd's Masses embody many melodic fragments that seem to have risen involuntarily from a common source in the composer's unconscious mind and insinuated themselves into his work in ways of which he may have been unaware. This gives the Masses individually and as a group an extraordinary feeling of unity.[19]

The chief source of the sense of unity however springs from Byrd's perceptions as a composer. He is illustrating and expounding the text for the benefit of the listener, and he is addressing himself to God on his own behalf. Prayers for peace can seldom have been more profoundly expressed than those which close the Masses. But his main preoccupation is the writing of music. In the act of setting words ideas arise which are separated from the meaning of the words, because they are purely musical. It is unnecessary to share Byrd's system of beliefs to wonder at the depth of his penetration into generally inaccessible realms of the mind. His exploration of non-verbal states is universally valuable. His religious notions serve as his starting point, and insofar as the music can give expression to them, it is consonant with them without being 'about' them. Byrd passes beyond concepts which are capable of verbalisation, to areas where questions of truth and falsehood are relevant only in relation to the accuracy with which he communicates his discoveries in musical terms. His Masses are among the great documents of human experience.

18   Kerman, 1981, p. 193; Andrews, 1966, pp. 268-269.
19   Reinforced, in the case of each Mass, by the contrast between the fully choral Ordinary and the chanted Proper.

GRADUALIA

By the time Byrd's last Mass was in print he had moved to Stondon Massey. It was there, and in the houses of his patrons, that the last phase of his work as a composer was completed. This began with two books of *Gradualia, ac cantiones sacrae*, a collection of music for Catholic worship, and the dedication of the second book acknowledges Lord Petre's hospitality as an important factor in its composition.[1]

Byrd's market was ostensibly the same as that for his previous publications: 'Honourable gentlemen who occasionally enjoy singing hymns and spiritual songs to God'.[2] But he clearly had in mind the special requirements of Catholics, and *Gradualia* is a testimony to the dedication of wealthier members of the Catholic community in providing opportunities for music to be sung in a liturgical context. There was no attempt to hide the collection's purpose. In the first book Byrd said:

> the Offices for the whole year which are appropriate to the principal feasts of the Blessed Virgin Mary and of All Saints are set out for your use, together with some other songs for five voices with their words drawn from the fount of sacred writings. Here too is the Office for the feast day of Corpus Christi, together with the more solemn antiphons of the same Blessed Virgin and other similar songs for four voices, and also all the hymns composed in praise of the Virgin. Finally, here are settings for three voices of various songs sung at the feast of Easter. Moreover, so that they may be placed in the correct position in the various parts of the Office, I have added a special index at the end of the book in which all the songs appropriate to the same feasts will easily be found listed together, even though they may differ in the number of voices.[3]

Publication was carried on more openly than had been the case with Byrd's three settings of the Ordinary. Through his printer, Thomas East, Byrd took the precaution of registering both books of *Gradualia* with the Stationers' Company, and of obtaining the approval of Richard Bancroft, first when he was the Bishop of London and then after he had become

---

1   See p. 117.
2   'Quibus volupe sit aliquando (*Generosi Candidissimi*) in hymnis & canticis spiritualibus deo psallere'. (Byrd's note to the reader in the first book.)
3   Original in Latin.

the Archbishop of Canterbury.[4] To do so was prudent, for fierce restrictions had recently been reimposed on Catholics. It turned out to be more foresighted than Byrd could have known. In November 1605, a few months after the first book had appeared, the Gunpowder Plot was discovered. If this put a brake on sales it would help to account for the survival of only one set of part-books of the first issue.[5]

Circumstances perhaps counselled a delay in further publication. The Masses and antiphons for the Feasts of SS Peter and Paul and St Peter's Chains had particularly strong political overtones. The Introit *Nunc scio vere* says 'Now I know truly that the Lord has sent his angel, and has delivered me from the hand of Herod'; but the text was Biblical and its publication could be justified on those grounds. *Tu es pastor ovium*, *Hodie Simon Petrus* and *Solve iubente Deo* have non-Biblical texts affirming the Pope's role as keeper of the keys of heaven, and Byrd printed only the opening words of each. The second book may have been in the hands of the printer, if it was not actually printed, for some time before it was issued. Byrd's dedicatory epistle to Lord Petre, dated 3 April 1607 and presumably added last, refers to the contents as having been 'long since completed by me and committed to the press'.[6]

The first book of *Gradualia* contains sixty-three numbered items, and the second book forty-six, though some items consist of several sections which can be used separately. The components can be combined in a variety of ways to meet different needs, and constitute the most remarkable example of the care Byrd expended on organizing the music of his collections.

A large part of *Gradualia* is devoted to settings of Propers and other texts for a variety of feasts and observances. Byrd gave no indication that he expected the Propers to be sung with his settings of the Ordinary, and indeed there are no Propers corresponding to the Mass for three voices, and no Ordinary to match the *Gradualia* numbers for six voices. Moreover, there is no consistency between the voice ranges of the four- and five-voice Masses and the Propers for the same numbers of voices.

4   Book I was registered on 10 January 1604/5: 'Master Easte. Entred for his Copie under the handes of the late Lord Bishop of LONDON and the wardens ...'. (Arber, 1875-94, iii, p. 279.) Book II was registered on 19 February 1606/7, 'under the handes of my lordes grace of CANTERBURY and the Wardens'. (Ibid., p. 340.) See Nasu, 1995.

5   Andrews, 1964, p. 9. There is also 'a questionable single Bassus book without title-page'. The complete set, at York Minster Library, lacks the introductory matter, which may have been removed by a cautious owner, and the indexes are displaced in most of the part-books.

6   Delay may also have been caused by a lack of money for printing. See p. 117 concerning William Petre's loan to Byrd.

There had been other settings of Proper cycles, for example by the Flemish composer Heinrich Isaac (d. 1517), whose ninety-nine cycles were written in 1507-9 and eventually published as *Choralis constantinus* (Nuremberg, 1550-55). It is impossible to say whether Byrd knew of these, though at least one music book published in Nuremberg was in the library of his friend Lord Lumley.[7] Among other cycles were those by Lassus and Palestrina for the offertory.[8] Nearer home, Byrd would have known the numerous pieces that Sheppard and Tallis wrote for the principal feasts of the Church year.[9] But none of the existing cycles, complete or incomplete, resembles Byrd's singular collection.

It is uncertain what gave Byrd the idea of providing modules that can be variously combined, but it is likely to have been suggested by the layout of the Gradual.[10] The printed *Graduale Romanum* of the late sixteenth century generally provided each chant only once. If it was needed a second time it was referred to in a rubric. When did Byrd conceive his grand scheme? Possibly it grew in his mind as he went along. The first book of *Gradualia* contains many miscellaneous items, and originally gave no hint that a second book was planned.[11] The second book has a greater formal clarity than the first, and includes only three miscellaneous pieces.

Byrd's scheme is not quite complete, and not without its problems.[12] His guidance to users is frequently inadequate, and what contemporaries made of it can only be guessed. Fifty years of the reformed church must have meant that for many people it was no more than a book of vocal music with Latin words, on the lines of Byrd's other collections. The words 'cantiones sacrae' are indeed part of the title. The scheme resulted in an assemblage of motets with words that, as they stand, are unsuited to

7   *Thesaurus musicus* (1564). See Milsom, 1993, p. 152.

8   In a review of Kerman, 1981 (*MLA Notes*, June 1982, p. 827), Richard Taruskin champions the influence on the style and idea of *Gradualia* of Palestrina's *Offertoria totius anni* (1593).

9   Doe (1976, p. 34) says: 'their joint output of both hymns and responds suggests that they had in mind some sort of annual cycle of office polyphony, which surely must have been for Mary Tudor's chapel'.

10   The Gradual contains chants for the Proper of the Mass. The edition examined for the present purpose is *Graduale Romanum de tempore, & sanctis, ad ritum missalis, ex decreto sacrosancti Concilii Tridentini restituti* (Venice,1611; date altered to 1561 in the British Library copy). Byrd may have had a similar edition: see Brett, 1989, p. viii.

11   New title-pages that identified the books as 'Liber primus' and 'Liber secundus' were provided for a second issue in 1610. They are incorrect in stating that this was a second edition.

12   See Brett, 1989, p. xii.

any liturgical need. To take one example, *Diffusa est gratia* (BE 5/22) must be dismembered, and where necessary combined with other units to provide the Gradual and Tract for Mass on the Feast of the Annunciation prior to Easter, the Gradual for Mass on the Feast of the Assumption, and the Offertory for Mass on the Feast of the Purification of the Blessed Virgin Mary. The omission of the words 'et in saeculum saeculi' required for the last purpose is one of Byrd's oversights.

In this century the plan of *Gradualia* remained obscure until it was elucidated progressively by Jackman (1963), Kerman (1981) and Brett (in the relevant volumes of The Byrd Edition).[13]

Book I: Layout

The contents of the first book of *Gradualia* are grouped according to the number of voices required. The items in each group are numbered separately from those in other groups.[14] The five-voice section begins with twenty-five pieces designed for Marian feasts and Votive Masses. To announce at the outset the devotion to the Virgin which is so apparent in many of the pieces amounts almost to a deliberate affront to Protestant reformers.[15]

The operation of Byrd's system can be illustrated by the music for the Feast of the Purification of the Blessed Virgin Mary, observed on 2 February. Byrd's numbering is shown in bold type.

Introit **1** (bars 1-46 repeated at end)
Gradual **1** (bars 1-37), and Verse and Alleluia **2** (bars 24-34 omitted after
    Septuagesima)
Verse and Alleluia **3** (before Septuagesima), or Tract **4** (after Septuagesima)
Offertory **22** (bars 1-27)
Communion **5**

Other feasts for which Propers can be put together from the first twenty-five numbers are:

13   Their explanations are more detailed than the one for which there is room here. One of the few people who recognized the liturgical functions of the various pieces was the musician Samuel Wesley (1766-1837), a Roman Catholic who anthologized *Gradualia* into BL Additional MS 35001.

14   See the catalogue of Byrd's works, pp. 416-418.

15   Henry Horner of Lincoln Cathedral was reminded in 1580 that he should not pray to the Virgin Mary. See p. 42.

Nativity of the Blessed Virgin Mary (8 September) **6-11**
Annunciation (25 March) **16**, **6**, **22** (before Easter) or **20** (after Easter),
    14-15
Assumption of the Virgin (15 August) **23**, **6**, **22-25**

Votive Masses of the Blessed Virgin Mary, suited to the time of year,
can be assembled as follows:

Advent **12-15**
Christmas to the Purification **16**, **6**, **17-18**, **21**, **19**, **11**
Purification to Easter **6-8**, **20-21**, **19**, **11**
Easter to Pentecost **6**, **20**, **10-11**
Pentecost to Advent **6-8**, **18**, **14**, **11**

The same material also provides music for other Marian feasts: the
Visitation (2 July), Presentation (21 November) and Conception
(8 December). All the above pieces are in D with one flat in the
signature. To ease the transition from one module to the next, Byrd
ensures that when a section ends with a cadence on a note other than the
key note it is always one that is closely related.

The pattern of the five-voice section of the first book is interrupted by
three non-liturgical motets in different keys (**26-28**). These are followed
by four pieces (**29-31**) which conclude the five-voice section and provide
music for Mass on the Feast of All Saints (1 November); all are in F,
and the group is complete in itself.

The section for four voices begins with the Propers for Corpus Christi
(**1-4**), celebrated on the second Thursday after Pentecost.[16] The four
pieces are again in one key (G, with no flats in the signature), and
provide all the necessary music except the sequence *Laude Sion*, which
is presumably to be sung to a version of the plainchant melody. Together
with numbers 13, 14 and 16 from *Gradualia* II, they also provide the
music for a Votive Mass of the Blessed Sacrament.[17] The Corpus Christi

16   For a description of a Corpus Christi celebration that took place shortly after the
publication of *Gradualia* I, see p. 144.

17   The conversion of the Corpus Christi Mass into a Votive Mass of the Blessed
Sacrament illustrates the intricacies and ambiguities of Byrd's system of transferable
modules. The Votive Mass has three liturgical forms for use at different times of the
year. Problems arise because certain Alleluias which must be discarded outside Paschal
time are musically integrated into the sections where they occur. For practical purposes,
therefore, small modifications have sometimes to be made to Byrd's music. The presence
in *Gradualia* of the Votive Mass of the Blessed Sacrament hints at Jesuit influence, and
perhaps that of Henry Garnett in particular. Brett suggests the possibility that, together

group continues with a prayer to the Blessed Sacrament (5) in the key of G with two flats, but Byrd returns to the first key for a hymn to the Blessed Sacrament (6) and a Corpus Christi antiphon (7). The move to A for a Corpus Christi processional hymn (8) is dictated by the plainchant which must precede it.[18]

The remainder of the four-voice section of *Gradualia* I consists of antiphons and other settings of sacred texts in a variety of keys (numbers **9-20**). The section for three voices (**1-11**) consists almost entirely of Marian hymns and antiphons, and music for Holy Week and the Easter season. Byrd's intention had been to conclude it with the dramatic *Turbarum voces in passione Domini secundum Joannem*, settings of choruses for the recitation of the Passion at the Mass of the Presanctified on Good Friday. A free space on a sheet of paper added to take part of the index led him to insert *Adorna thalamum tuum*, a Purification antiphon for the procession at the Blessing of Candles.

Book I: Masses

The structure and texts of the Proper of the Mass vary with the feast or time of year. The principal units are the Introit plus psalm verse and doxology (after which the Introit is repeated), the Gradual and verse, the Alleluia (sometimes replaced by the Tract) and verse, the Offertory and the Communion. The Gradual is sometimes omitted and infrequently (at Easter and Whitsun) a Sequence is added.

The texts vary in length. The longer units, with repetitions and verses, occur in the earlier parts of the Mass. Whether Byrd is writing for a choir of six, five or four voices, he always breaks up the long Introit by setting the verse for three voices.[19] A variety of patterns is created by the texts which follow the reading of the Epistle, that is to say the Gradual, Alleluia and their verses. In almost all instances Byrd

with the Corpus Christi antiphons and the Litany of Saints in the first book, it may have been composed for some enactment of the Forty Hours Devotion, which was encouraged by the Jesuit pope Clement VIII, who reigned 1592-1605. (Brett, 1991, p. viii-ix.) He also cites the choruses for the St John Passion as evidence of Byrd's commitment to 'a religion centred firmly on Rome, revitalized by Jesuit fervour'. (Brett, 1993(a), p. xv.) The Passion was of special importance to those who were close to the Jesuit mission.

18   Further Corpus Christi pieces appear as numbers 17 and 18 in *Gradualia* II.

19   He nevertheless includes the verses in the sections of *Gradualia* devoted to the larger numbers of voices. The rubric 'Chorus sequitur' which follows the three-voice Gradual verse *Notum fecit. Alleluia* in the Christmas Mass (Book II) intimates that the section for reduced voices is to be sung by solo singers. This accords with the virtuosic tendency of the writing, and probably applies to all such sections in both books.

reduces the voices for one section or more, though generally he avoids ending any number with reduced voices.[20] It is evident that he regarded the post-Epistle units as a single entity, and sometimes composed them as one number (e.g. in the Masses for the Feasts of All Saints and Corpus Christi). The Offertory and Communion are short, though they may on some occasions be lengthened by an 'Alleluia'. The word 'Alleluia' occurs repeatedly in the Mass and invites special musical treatment; it served for Byrd as a means of intermediate or terminal punctuation.

The first twenty-five numbers of *Gradualia* I furnish the music for four Masses on feasts of the Blessed Virgin Mary and a cycle of five Marian Votive Masses. The first fifteen numbers supply the Propers for three Masses which contain no common units, save that the Mass for the Feast of the Purification shares its Offertory with two Masses partly made up of transferable units. The Purification Mass stands first in the collection, and Kerman was led by some unsureness on Byrd's part to believe that it may have been the first to be written.[21] Since Byrd provided a Tract for this Mass, he may have composed it in a year when a Tract was needed because the Feast of the Purification (2 February) fell after Septuagesima. This happened in 1593/4, 1596/7, 1599/1600 and 1601/2,[22] but one would guess that by the later of these dates Byrd's work on the first book of *Gradualia* was well advanced and the Mass had been in existence for some time.

There is support for the notion that all the sections of the Purification Mass were composed at one time. There are similarities, for example, between the beginning of the Introit *Suscepimus Deus* (BE 5/1), which also serves as the Gradual, and the verse 'Quia viderunt oculi' of the Tract *Nunc dimittis* (BE 5/4). And there are rising and falling lines of crotchets in both *Suscepimus Deus* and the Offertory *Diffusa est gratia* (BE 5/22). Kerman has indeed suggested that although the Offertory is part of one of Byrd's transferrable units, it may have been composed for the Purification Mass and subsequently expanded for other purposes. Its spacious opening point is comparable to that of the Communion, *Responsum accepit Simeon* (BE 5/5). There is a further internal link

---

20   The separate numbering of *Dies sanctificatus* in the Christmas Mass seems to result from an accident of printing, and not from any intention that the preceding number should end with a section for three voices.

21   Kerman (1981, p. 251) points out that part of the doxology seems to be an early model for other doxologies, the Communion is unusually long, the Gradual verse is uncertain in texture, the words of the Offertory are incomplete, and Byrd's indication of the end of the Gradual with a minim rest is unique in *Gradualia* I.

22   R. C. Cheney, *Handbook of dates*, 1945. Kerman (1981, p. 253) seems to be partly mistaken in saying that the years were 1598, 1600 and 1603.

between the opening of the Communion, where one voice sings a cantus firmus-like melody, and the opening of the Tract.

It is difficult to judge the extent to which such parallels result from a deliberate effort to unify the first few Marian Masses. There is a natural tendency to think that a work which is not composed of transferable modules must be more unified than one which is, but the Nativity Mass and the Votive Mass for Advent do not provide much justification for this. It is possible to find similar melodic and rhythmic material in the different sections of each, but it seems to spring from a general 'early Gradualia' style that occurs in more than one Gradualia Mass, and is not dissimilar to the style of the five-part setting of the Ordinary.

The Nativity and Advent Masses come second and third in Gradualia I, and each seems to have generated modules rather than to have taken any from other Masses. If Byrd began Gradualia by writing complete five-part Propers, then the Mass for the Feast of the Assumption may have been written next. Although most of its units occur further on in the five-voice section, the only passage which it indisputably shares with other Masses is the Introit verse and doxology (part of number 6, originally composed for the Nativity Mass). There is nevertheless doubt about whether its Gradual (part of 22) was written separately and then combined with the Offertory of the Purification Mass to form the Gradual and Tract for the Mass of the Annunciation, or whether 22 in its longer form was in existence before Byrd embarked on the Assumption Mass.[23] All one can say for sure is that by the time Byrd composed the Assumption Mass his mood had changed, and is reflected in its livelier vein.

Only after he had completed three or four sets of Propers does Byrd appear to have started composing the units which, together with what he had already written, provide material for four Votive Masses for seasons other than Advent. He probably did so before completing two further Masses which require no transfers, the five-part Mass for the Feast of All Saints and the four-part Mass for the Feast of Corpus Christi.

There are numerous unifying factors in the Mass for the Feast of All Saints. The Introit, its verse, and the verse of the Gradual all start with three rising notes. The rhythmically intricate writing of the second half of the Introit is paralleled in the verse of the Gradual (the 'Inquirentes autem' section of Timete Dominum), and clearly does not result from Byrd's need to set similar words. On a rhythmic level, the All Saints Mass is matched by many of the pieces in Gradualia II, and one might

---

23   Kerman (1981, p. 267) expresses disquiet about the idea that Byrd could have composed the Gradual specially for the Assumption Mass, but observes that he echoed the effect of its transfer (if it was transferred) in the Alleluia verse, Assumpta est Maria.

suppose it to be among the later portions of the first book. Byrd may have been inspired by jubilant sections of the text to write passages paralleling the anthem *Sing joyfully*, which would suggest that the Mass was composed round about 1603. There are parallels too with some of the cheerful songs of *Psalmes, songs, and sonnets*, such as *Sing we merrily* and *Make ye joy to God*, the first of which is almost certainly Jacobean. Yet not all is unalloyed joy. In the Alleleuia verse the words 'omnes qui laboratis et onerati estis' (you who labour and are burdened) cause the superius and tenor to sing b' and bb' simultaneously (BE 6a/5, bar 69). In the Communion (BE 6a/7) Byrd produces a host of C-C# false relations to illustrate a notion very close to the hearts of English Catholics: 'Beati qui persecutionem patiuntur propter justitiam' (Blessed are they who suffer persecution for the sake of justice). For the Offertory *Iustorum animae* (BE 6a/6), with its thoughts of death, Byrd turns to a profoundly expressive semi-homophony in place of the livelier rhythms of the Introit and Gradual.

The Corpus Christi Mass must have been composed as a whole, since it is the only four-part Mass in *Gradualia* I. It provides modules for the Votive Mass of the Blessed Sacrament, but the additional modules needed for that Mass appear in *Gradualia* II, and were presumably written later. An elevated passion glows more evenly in the Corpus Christi Mass than in the All Saints Mass. The music is informed by a smooth melodiousness that finds particular expression in the brief but beautiful Offertory, *Sacerdotes Domini* (BE 6a/10), after which the more vigorous Communion, *Quotiescunque manducabitis* (BE 6a/11), comes as a satisfying contrast. The style of its components gives no reason to doubt that the Corpus Christi Mass post-dates Byrd's decision to write Propers for a variety of Masses, or that it may be one of the later works gathered into *Gradualia* I, but there is no obvious clue that enables it to be dated more narrowly.

Book I: Miscellanea

The first book of *Gradualia* contains a number of pieces that do not form part of a Mass. They are exemplified by the group appropriate to Corpus Christi.[24] This includes two hymns to the Blessed Sacrament, *Ave verum corpus* and *O salutaris hostia* (BE 6a/12-13), the processional hymn *Pange lingua − Nobis datus nobis natus* (BE 6a/15), and the Magnificat

---

24   Byrd's provision of more settings for the Feast of Corpus Christi than any other feast is explained by its elaboration. In the Roman rite it consists of First Vespers, Compline, Matins (First, Second and Third Nocturns), Lauds, Prime, Terce, Mass, Procession, Sext, None and Second Vespers.

antiphon for second Vespers, *O sacrum convivium* (BE 6a/14), which also serves as an antiphon at the procession. Although they appear in the four-voice section of the first book, where they follow the Corpus Christi Mass, there is no reason to believe that they were written at the same time as the Mass or that their performance was reserved for the feast. *Ave verum corpus* appears to be earlier than most of the collection. *Pange lingua — Nobis datus* is a multi-purpose hymn which can be used at the Forty Hours' Prayer or other exposition of the Blessed Sacrament, and if *O sacrum convivium* is deprived of its 'Alleluia' it can function unspecifically as a motet honouring the Blessed Sacrament.

The four- and three-voice sections of *Gradualia* I, then, contain settings of liturgical texts which serve various purposes, including those of general devotion or recreation. They also contain motets that have no place in the liturgy. Although Byrd himself grouped the three-voice Marian hymns and antiphons with the three-voice pieces for Holy Week and the Easter season, it will be convenient to lump together as 'miscellaneous' all the pieces which do not find a place in the Propers.

The All Saints Mass is preceded by three non-liturgical motets, but a change in the nature of the collection is really signalled by *Ave verum corpus*, which follows the Corpus Christi Mass. Its text, like those of many of the 'sacred songs' mentioned in the full title of *Gradualia*, is included in the Primer,[25] and it marks a transition from public ritual to private devotion, from music requiring the presence of a priest for its liturgical performance to music which could appropriately find a place in observances maintained by the laity. A number of pieces in this category relate to the Virgin, a devotion to whom is apparent in much of *Gradualia*.

Indications of date can be found for a good many of the miscellaneous pieces. Apparently early versions of *Ave verum corpus* (BE 6a/12) and *Ecce quam bonum* (BE 6b/1) occur in manuscript sources and suggest the possibility of composition in the late 1590s.[26] *Ave verum corpus* is a prayer to the Blessed Sacrament, and the false relation contained in the second and third chords makes quite clear Byrd's position on the topical issue of transubstantiation.[27] It lays stress on the word 'verum' and the

---

25   'Primer' is the English name for the Book of Hours. Its significance for Elizabethan Catholics is outlined by Brett, 1993(a), pp. vii-ix. Some of Byrd's texts occurring in the Missal and Breviary as well as the Primer have pecularities which identify the last as his source, and it was probably the source of other texts also.

26   Both are in Bodleian Library MSS Mus.f.16-19; the second is also in BL Additional MSS 18936-9.

27   The idea of the false relation may have been suggested by Lassus's setting of the same words, and provides a possible clue to Byrd's familiarity with Lassus's music.

notion that bread and wine are *truly* the body and blood of Christ. Byrd's convictions are translated into music of great fervour, possessing a highly personal quality accentuated by his addition to the text of the repeated words 'miserere mei'. *Ecce quam bonum* is a less intense piece, whose multiplicity of motives also suggests composition in the nineties. Its quietly undulating lines convey the sense in a strikingly different way from Byrd's setting of the same psalm, in a verse translation, as the six-part song *Behold how good a thing it is*.[28]

Adoramus te Christe (BE 6a/1) is another piece that exists in a manuscript copy suggesting derivation from a pre-publication version.[29] Unexpectedly, in the context of *Gradualia*, it is for solo voice and four viols. This exquisite work is unusual among Byrd's consort songs in possessing Latin words. The text had long held a special place in the affections of English Catholics,[30] and as if to give prominence to its traditional aspect Byrd twice set the final words, 'redemisti mundum', to the motive Tallis had used in setting them at the end of his pre-Elizabethan antiphon *Sancte Deus*. To drive the point home the viols play the motive six times in the first six bars[31] and six more times before the piece ends.

Among the *Gradualia* items known to have circulated prior to publication are the Passion choruses, *Turbarum voces in passione Domine secundum Ioannem* (BE 6b/22). Byrd's three-voice setting of the words of the crowd was designed for insertion in the plainchant recitation on Good Friday of the Passion according to St John.[32] English polyphonic settings of scenes for the crowd and minor characters had been made for Passions according to St Matthew and St Luke in the fifteenth century.[33] Byrd may well have known of the tradition from

28   *Songs of sundrie natures* (1589). The words are from psalm 132/133 (Vulgate/Authorized Version).

29   BL, Additional MSS 18936-9.

30   The versicle and response for the Office of the Holy Cross, from the Primer, one of the texts recited by Henry Garnett before his execution in 1606. (See Brett, 1991, p. viii.)

31   Beginning alternately on G and D, thus anticipating the motive's occurrences in the voice part, where it also begins on G and D.

32   The manner of insertion is shown by Brett, 1993(a), pp. xxvii-xxxii. In the Roman liturgy the gospel lessons for specified days were drawn from the Evangelists' accounts of the Passion, and recited to 'lesson tones' with three voice ranges: the lowest for Christ, the middle range for the Evangelist, and the highest for the crowd and other characters. See *Die Musik in Geschichte und Gegenwart*, x, cols. 891-894; Grove, 1980, s.v. 'Passion'; Brett, 1993(a), pp. xiii-xiv.

33   Harrison, 1980, pp. 402-403; Caldwell, 1991, pp. 167, 199.

which these settings came, and something of the many Continental Passions,[34] but Brett discovered that his setting alludes 'constantly and pointedly' to a Roman version of the chant codified by Giovanni Giudetti and published in *Cantus ecclesiasticus passionis Domini nostri* (Rome, 1586).[35] This enables the choruses to be placed precisely in context. It also defines the beginning of the period during which the choruses were written. The end of the period is defined by the entry of the choruses in a manuscript completed before 1600.[36]

A series of interconnections between several of the pieces in *Gradualia* I makes it likely that the choruses belong to the earlier part of this period. The setting of 'Ave Rex Judaeorum' in chorus 6 seems derisively to parody the beginning of *Ave maris stella* (BE 6b/16), a long Marian hymn. *Ave maris stella* occurs in the same sources as three much more concise Marian hymns, *Quem terra pontus aethera*, *O gloriosa Domina* and *Memento salutis auctor* (BE 6b/13-15), which always appear as a group (though in different orders), and in copies that seem to reflect the existence of pre-publication versions.[37] *Quem terra pontus aethera* is connected with Byrd's song *Of gold all burnished*, which begins with an identical tenor solo and a similar choral response. Among the songs Byrd published in 1589, *Of gold all burnished* is the one most clearly composed originally for five singers and not for a solo voice and viols. It may therefore have been one of the later songs of the collection, and *Quem terra pontus* and its companions may belong to the same period in the late eighties.

The four Marian hymns and the Passion choruses are all for three voices. Another three-voice piece can be connected with them, since the second 'crucifige' in chorus 10 of the Passion has the same music as the words 'et laetemur' in *Haec dies* (BE 6b/19, bars 13-14).[38]

A further piece culled from Byrd's stock of existing compositions is *In manus tuas Domine* (BE 6b/7), adapted from a consort fantasia of the late 1580s (BE 17/34) of which only a single part survives.[39] If the fantasia was as little altered in the process of transcription as the existing

---

34   One setting occurs in the Gyffard part-books, which preserve Byrd's earliest vocal works. (See p. 158.) The best known Continental settings were those of Victoria, published in *Officium hebdomadae sanctae* (Rome, 1585).

35   Brett, 1993(a), pp. xiv, 143-168.

36   BL, Additional MSS 30480-4, compiled c.1565-1600.

37   BL Additional MSS 29246 and 34800; Royal College of Music MS 2036.

38   Kerman, 1981, p. 334. Like the Passion, *Haec dies* is for the Easter season, but contemporary service books do not contain the words exactly as Byrd set them. (Brett, 1993, p. xi.)

39   See p. 273.

part suggests, it was because it already owed much to Byrd's vocal style. The debt is particularly marked in the opening bars, where − quite in the manner of a motet − the second half of the initial point is a barely changed inversion of the first half, and assumes a simultaneous independent life.

The inclusion of the above pieces in the first book of *Gradualia* confirms the impression that Byrd's comprehensive plan was formed only slowly. All the same, much of the book must have been written in the years after 1595. The text of *Ave Regina caelorum* (BE 6b/6) comes from a revised Breviary issued in 1602.[40] The work is another through-composed setting of Marian verses − in this case an antiphon, not a hymn, and neither as prolix as *Ave maris stella*, nor as economical as *Quem terra pontus aethera*, *O gloriosa Domina* and *Memento salutis auctor*. Length is nevertheless a controlling factor in its structure. Within each of the two stanzas the lines are set at increasing length, those of the second stanza being slightly longer than comparable lines of the first, until an extra long line rounds the piece off. Byrd could hardly write a piece of music without giving it a pattern of its own.

Ave Regina caelorum must be close in date to *Plorans plorabit* (BE 6a/3). This deeply felt setting of words from *Jeremiah* is an expression of quiet but intense grief over the lot of English Catholics. Its measured counterpoint evokes the style of earlier motets leading to *Defecit in dolore*, the latest in the *Cantiones sacrae* of 1589,[41] but since it refers to a king as well as a queen it must have been written after the accession of James in 1603 − perhaps shortly before publication, when the reimposition of repressive measures against Catholics was in prospect. Nothing could be more pointed than the words of its second section:

Tell the King and Queen, 'Be humbled, sit down, for the crown of your glory has fallen from your head'.

Since *Adorna thalmum tuum* (BE 6b/23) was tacked on to the first book of *Gradualia* at the last moment, there is a possibility that that too had been written shortly before publication. It is among the longest of Byrd's pieces for three voices, but its length depends not on a protracted stanzaic text like that of *Ave maris stella*, nor on repetitions of 'Alleluia' like *Regina caeli*. In setting prose Byrd had the freedom to create an

40   See Brett, 1993(a), pp. ix-x.

41   Byrd must have had in mind the setting of the words 'plorans ploravit' in Tallis's first *Lamentations*, the probable inspiration for his own setting of passages from Jeremiah (BE 8/5).

extended three-part composition in which musical form was independent of poetic form, and he produced a work at once restrained and well-proportioned.

Christus resurgens (BE 6b/2) needs to be discussed with the dateable miscellaneous pieces from *Gradualia*, though its date is open to question. The text is that of an Easter processional antiphon in both the Sarum and Roman uses, and acts for Byrd as a dual reference to the English past and the post-Tridentine present, but the setting includes material that possesses some appearance of having been written much earlier than anything else in the collection. Not only is the presence of a cantus firmus in the first section an archaic feature, but the version of the chant on which Byrd based it was published in 1558.[42] The question this poses is whether *Christus resurgens* is, at least in part, one of Byrd's earliest works. Whatever the answer, its inclusion was a gesture towards the Catholicism of his youth. Settings by John Redford and Thomas Knyght of the customary version of the chant occur with Byrd's *Similes illis fiant* in the Gyffard part-books.[43]

Kerman identifies a number of possibly early features in the first part of *Christus resurgens*: the 'crude' dissonance treatment in the cantus firmus sections, generally colourless motives, and the wide spacing of the upper voices.[44] Brett expresses amazement that Byrd did not sweeten the 'Alleluia' refrain for publication.[45] Both writers believe the second part of the work to be a later addition. Yet in performance the crudities and the sourness do not seem so pronounced, and Kerman quotes the view of H. B. Collins (on whose opinions he elsewhere remarks with favour) that *Christus resurgens* is 'a wonderful meditation on the plainchant'.[46] Its shortcomings might have remained less conspicuous had they not been noticed by scholars of such authority. The possibility that it is a deliberately old-fashioned piece, 'Byrd's last great tribute, perhaps, to the ancient English disciplines of descanting and cantus firmus composition', was first proposed by le Huray.[47] There are a number of reasons for accepting le Huray's conjecture. There is no early source to suggest that *Christus resurgens* was begun before Queen Mary's death in November 1558, that is to say very soon after the chant was published in Antwerp. During the early part of Queen Elizabeth's reign, before Byrd acquired his Catholic patrons, it could only have been composed as an

---

42   Brett, 1993(a), pp. xiii, 142, 175, amending Kerman, 1981, pp. 62-63.
43   See p. 158. For other settings see Hofman and Morehen, 1987.
44   Kerman, 1981, pp. 62-64.
45   Brett, 1993, p. xiii.
46   Collins, 1923. p. 257; Kerman, 1981, p. 62.
47   le Huray, 1992(b), p. 23.

exercise. There is no other example of Byrd writing vocal music for such a purpose,[48] and no manuscript copy of the work to suggest such an origin. What is more, it is hard to see Byrd, at that stage in his career, employing two concurrent imitative motives in each of the three sections into which the piece falls (bars 1-17/18, 18-29/30, 30-43). (Ex. 26.)

Ex. 26

Christus resurgens, bars 19-23

The remaining miscellaneous pieces in the first book of *Gradualia* present an extraordinarily wide array of forms and styles. *O salutaris hostia* (BE 6a/13), *Pange lingua–Nobis datus* (BE 6a/15) and *O sacrum convivium* (BE 6a/14) are all Corpus Christi motets, but there are no early versions or early manuscript sources, and they are unlikely to have been composed at the same time as *Ave verum corpus*, after which they are printed. *O salutaris hostia* is a highly schematic (but not symmetrical) piece of limited harmonic scope, in which each line of text is the

---

48   With the exception of the five-part *Christe qui lux es* (BE 8/4).

occasion for two full expositions of a musical subject. *Pange lingua* has a different schematic design. The text consists of six stanzas, of which Byrd sets the second (starting 'Nobis datus nobis natus'), the fourth, and the fifth (during which the Sacrament is displayed and the celebrants kneel). The other stanzas are sung to the chant, the beginning of which is quoted in long notes by one of the voices at the start of each stanza, but in successively shorter snatches of five, four and two notes. *O sacrum convivium* begins with a series of very calculated imitations, but unfolds as a less formalistic work than *O salutaris hostia* and *Pange lingua*, written in an idiom suggestive of the second book of *Gradualia*. It is probably among the later pieces of *Gradualia* I.

The *Laetania* (BE 6b/8) incorporates the chant of the Litany of Saints as a cantus firmus into a syllabic chordal four-part setting, superficially little different from that of Byrd's Anglican Litany.[49]

Visita quaesumus Domine (BE 6b/3) and *Salve sola Dei genitrix* (BE 6b/9) are both set succinctly for four high voices. The first, for two sopranos, alto and tenor, is a sunny prayer alternating madrigalesque polyphony with homophony. The second is an appeal to the Virgin which at the words 'Miserere tuorum nunc et in extrema' (Have mercy on your people now and at the end) makes a masterly transition of mood in mid-phrase, marking the intrusion of thoughts of death with a striking false relation.

In *Salve Regina* (BE 6b/4) Byrd returned to a text he had set for five voices in the 1580s (BE 3/4), now setting it more flowingly and (except for the first four words addressing the Queen of Heaven) much more concisely for four voices. *Alma redemptoris mater* (BE 6b/5) has a not dissimilar text (both pieces are Marian antiphons), and is set in rather the same way, the sounds of groaning and weeping in the first being matched by the portrayal in the second of people falling and striving to rise.

Senex puerum portabat (BE 6b/10) and *Hodie beata Virgo* (BE 6b/11) are also comparable, as Magnificat antiphons (respectively for the first and second Vespers of the Purification) which indulge in a good deal of semi-homophony until they burst into a final page of polyphony.

The last of the four-voice pieces in the first book of *Gradualia* is an eleven-breve setting of *Deo gratias* (BE 6b/12), with twin points. To find a companion piece it is necessary to turn to the first 'Alleluia' of the first three-part motet provided by Byrd for Holy Week, *Alleluia. Vespere autem Sabbathi* (BE 6b/18).[50]

---

49 The cantus firmus occurs in the tenor except in sections 2, 16 and 18, where it passes to the top voice. The source from which Byrd took the chant has not been discovered.

50 The comparison is tabulated by Kerman, 1981, p. 333.

Among the works for three voices, *Angelus Domini* (BE6b/20) is remarkable for the arpeggio shapes and octave leaps that occur in all the voices. Like *Post dies octo* (BE 6b/21) it is one of Byrd's shorter three-part pieces, rather slight but neatly contrived. *Regina caeli* (BE 6b/17) by contrast shows Byrd at his most eloquent, with each expressive setting of a textual phrase melting expansively into a luxuriant 'Alleluia'. If it is not the last of Byrd's works for three voices it is the peak of his achievement in the three-voice section of *Gradualia*.

Book II: Layout

The plan of the second book of *Gradualia* can be dealt with fairly briskly. Almost all the duplicate texts (e.g. numbers 26 and 28) are now set separately, and the pieces are numbered straight through. The headings from Byrd's index (originally in Latin) are shown below in italics, but it is obvious that a few anomalies result from the grouping of pieces by the number of voices they require.

a 4

Christmas

    Mass of the Nativity (25 December) **1-5**
    Antiphons and responds for the Christmastide **6-9**

Epiphany

    Mass of the Epiphany (6 January) **10-12, 15**
    Motets for the Votive Mass of the Blessed sacrament **13-14**

After Easter

    Music for Corpus Christi and the Votive Mass of the Blessed Sacrament
      16-18
    Hymn for the Ascension **19**

a 5

Easter

    Mass on Easter Day **20-24**

Ascension

> Mass of the Ascension **25-29**
> Magnificat antiphon, second Vespers **30**

Whitsun

> Mass of Pentecost **31-36**
> Magnificat antiphon, first Vespers **37**

a 6

Feast of SS Peter and Paul

> Mass of SS Peter and Paul (29 June) **38-39, 41**
> Magnificat antiphons, first and second Vespers, and Benedictus antiphon,
>   Lauds **42-44**

> Mass of St Peter's Chains **38-40**
> Magnificat antiphon, second vespers **40**

> Miscellaneous motets **45-46**

Book II: Music for feasts, and miscellanea

Byrd's claim that *Gradualia* II had 'long since' been with the printer seems to mean that work on it advanced swiftly after the completion of the first book. Progress was assisted by the clear plan he had now formed, and most of its contents were newly written to suit it. The music for the Feasts of SS Peter and Paul and of St Peter's Chains may be the exception in this last respect. It comprises all the six-part compositions of *Gradualia*, and serves as the culmination of the collection. There can be little question that it was placed last also in honour of the dedicatee of the second book, Lord Petre. The play on the name 'Peter' is wholly in keeping with the puns Byrd and other people made on his own name. The possibility that all the pieces venerating St Peter were composed for one special occasion is reinforced by the fact that Byrd appears to have written only two other six-part motets quite so late in his career; both follow the Petrine group in *Gradualia* and both are in praise of God. Kerman is probably right in proposing 1603 as the year when much, if not all, of the music for the two feasts was composed.[51] It was, as he observes, the year in which John Petre was created Baron Petre of Writtle (21 July); but it was also the year in which his son William was knighted (3 May) after riding north to greet the new king at York. The dual honour done to the family could well have been the cause of a tribute or commission. The conjecture is supported by the modular construction of the Masses, which is consistent with their composition while Byrd was at work on *Gradualia* I. The style of numerous passages recalls the Mass for the Feast of All Saints. A delay in publication is easily explained by Byrd's wish to include them in the second book of the collection, where six-part motets would not be out of place, and to crown his project.

The celebratory nature of the Masses is marked both by the number of voices and by their dense texture. Apart from the Introit verse, which is for three low voices and is matched by the Gradual verse for three high voices, the full choir sings virtually throughout. This is true too of the associated antiphons *Tu es pastor ovium*, *Hodie Simon Petrus*, *Quodcunque ligaveris* and *Solve iubente Deo* (which with an added 'Alleluia' serves as the Alleluia of the Mass for St Peter's Chains). All may belong to much the same period, even if it is not easy to imagine Byrd composing every one in response to the same stimulus.[52]

The likeness of texture extends to the splendid separate six-part motets of *Gradualia* II, *Laudate Dominum omnes gentes* and *Venite exultemus Domino*. These call to mind other six-part motets of different periods, *Laudate pueri* and *Cantate Domino*. All are set for voices which include two basses, and have similar texts. The *Gradualia* motets are of course a great deal later than *Laudate pueri*, published in 1575, but *Laudate Dominum* bears stylistic comparison with *Cantate Domino*, one of the latest motets to be published in 1591, and even begins in somewhat the same way. It is therefore tempting to think that it preceded the Petrine group and may have been written in the 1590s. The date of the more madrigalian *Venite exultemus Domino* is just as hard to determine, but there is no disputing that Byrd's addition of a long 'Alleluia' with no liturgical function enhances its role as a superb conclusion to *Gradualia*.

The considerations that suggest the possibility of Byrd holding back the six-part motets do not apply to another miscellaneous piece, *Iesu nostra redemptio*, a stanzaic hymn for the Ascension which appears alone at the end of the four-part section of *Gradualia* II. Although it has much

---

51   Kerman, 1981, pp. 317-318.

52   The text of *Quodcunque ligaveris* (Matthew 16, xix) is paraphrased in the unpublished motet *Petrus beatus* (BE 8/9), also likely to have been written for Petre.

in common with Byrd's simpler Marian hymns for three voices, the likelihood is that if it had been composed before 1605 it would have found a place in the four-voice section of the first book.

Apart from units of the Petrine Masses and numbers 13, 14 and 16, which enable the Mass for Corpus Christi to be turned into a Votive Mass of the Blessed Sacrament, Byrd's system of transfers does not extend to *Gradualia* II. The Christmas, Epiphany, Easter, Ascension and Whitsun (Pentecost) Masses are complete in themselves, and the units of some show unmistakeable signs of having been composed together. This and other slender pieces of evidence[53] encourage the belief that Byrd laid out the plan of *Gradualia* II and then worked through it, making adjustments where they were required. The method corresponds to the one he apparently adopted in his individual compositions. Finally he added the six-part pieces he had in hand.

The largest group of pieces in *Gradualia* II consists of those which open both the book and the four-voice section, and provide the Proper of the Mass for Christmas Day and Office motets for Christmastide. The group includes two Matins responds, *O magnum misterium* and *Beata Virgo*, examples of a liturgical type that does not otherwise occur in *Gradualia*. The group does not form a fully coherent whole, since *O admirabile commercium* is for the Feast of the Circumcision, which falls a week after Christmas. There are other anomalies too. The usual scoring of the Christmas music, and indeed most of *Gradualia* II, is for two sopranos, tenor and bass. *Puer natus est nobis* (the Introit) and *O magnum misterium* (the Matins respond for Christmas Day) however employ an alto in place of the second soprano, like the Corpus Christi motets in the same book. Nevertheless, although one can imagine Byrd incorporating into his Christmas music a respond that had been written earlier, the idea that he fitted an existing setting of *Puer natus est nobis* into a Mass for different voices is less easy to entertain and weakens any reason for thinking *O magnum misterium* may have been recycled. *Puer natus est nobis* is in fact among the finest motets in Byrd's most advanced manner − though significantly it starts by referring to the chant on which Tallis based his Mass of 1554, and recalling the performance in which Byrd may have participated during Queen Mary's reign.[54] The echoes which its rhythmic complexities find elsewhere in the Christmas pieces, and the impossibility of identifying certainly early features in any member of the group, suggest that none was incorporated from Byrd's available stock of compositions.

53   See p. 339 concerning *O Rex gloriae* and *Spiritus Domini*.
54   See p. 22. The chant and Byrd's piece both begin with a rising fifth.

It is not known why Byrd published the Mass of the Epiphany without the Gradual (which should be a setting of *Omnes de Saba venient*) or the Alleluia verse (*Vidimus stellam*),[55] nor is it known why he set no antiphon for the feast. His replacement of the Gradual verse (*Surge et illuminare Ierusalem, quia gloria Domini super te orta est*) with the words of the Lesson that follows the Collect (*Surge illuminare Ierusalem, quia venit lumen tuum, et gloria Domini super te orta est*) looks like the result of confusion.[56] More interesting than the relatively few errors and omissions in Byrd's unprecedented enterprise is the practised facility that enabled him to marshal and combine an array of technical skills in setting texts which, at first glance, seem less open to expressive interpretation than many others he had tackled. The Introit, *Ecce advenit dominator Dominus*, sets off with a snatch of double canon before easing into free counterpoint, and longer stretches of canon occur in the verse. The hallmark of the Gradual verse, *Surge illuminare Ierusalem*, is its great rhythmic ingenuity. At the start of the Offertory, *Reges Tharsis*, the higher voices sing a canon at the fifth, which the lower voices repeat as a canon at the fourth. The pattern is maintained at different pitches and with greater liberty in the phrase 'et insulae munera offerunt', creating a sparkling rhythmic ostinato in which the motive of 'insulae munera' is continually contrasted with the motive of 'offerunt'. Whatever obstacles other parts of the text may have presented, the words 'et adorabunt omnes reges terrae' moved Byrd to write the finest canonic passage of the piece.

The five-voice section of *Gradualia* II opens with the Easter Mass. Before embarking on *Gradualia* Byrd had set few texts belonging to a majority of the feasts for which the collection provided. The reverse was the case with Easter, and some of the texts he had already set now needed to be set again. He had set the words of the Gradual verse, 'Confitemini Domino', while he was still a pupil of Tallis. Those of the Gradual itself, 'Haec dies quam fecit Dominus: exultemus et laetemur in ea', had occasioned two previous settings; the first, for six voices, was published in the *Cantiones sacrae* of 1591, and the second, for three voices, appeared in the first book of *Gradualia*. Byrd was on familiar ground and responded with one of the best integrated of the *Gradualia* Masses.

It is almost inevitable that 'Resurrexi' (I am risen), the first word of the Introit, should give rise to tone-painting. The figure devised by Byrd

55   He could have supplied the Alleluia verse by adding an 'Alleluia' to his setting of the Communion, which uses the same words.

56   There was a muddle of some kind, for two motets for the Votive Mass of the Blessed Sacrament are inserted among the pieces that form the Epiphany Mass.

occurs in several forms, but it usually begins with an upward step of a fifth (a minor third followed by a major third). In its principal form the figure makes its way to the octave above the first note. (Ex. 27.)

Ex. 27

A closely similar figure, involving a fourth instead of a fifth, begins the Gradual, *Haec dies*, and is echoed at the start of the Communion, *Pascha nostrum*. (Ex. 28.)

Ex. 28

Repeatedly throughout the Mass Byrd either returns to elements of these figures or creates an impression of their recurrence, or introduces new figures with a strong family likeness. The Introit verse starts with a leap of a fifth; another fifth, composed of a major and a minor third, is defined by the first 'exultemus' of *Haec dies*; rows of notes rise or fall an octave (sometimes over- or under-shooting); and figures wind up and down in emulation of the first 'Resurrexi'.

The proportions of the Mass of the Ascension differ from those of the Easter Mass. This is partly because comparable units of the Masses are of different lengths (the Introit and Communion of the Ascension Mass are each shorter than their counterparts by ten breves, while the Offertory is longer by eight breves), and partly because the Ascension Mass has no Gradual (its Alleluia is less than half the length of the long Sequence which forms part of the Easter Mass). The two Masses nevertheless have much in common, notably in the rising figures called for by their texts. Those of the Ascension Mass expand through the sections. The 'Viri Galilaei' and 'ascendentem in coelum' figures of the Introit rise a fifth. The first Alleluia and its first verse 'Ascendit Deus' start with phrases that rise a seventh, while 'ascendens in altum' in the second verse rises a seventh, an octave or a ninth. 'Ascendit Deus' in the

Offertory generally extends over an octave. The Communion's final
Alleluia is preceded by a setting of 'qui ascendit super coelos coelorum'
in which, on the first occurrence of the words, the bass voice climbs a
twelfth. Similar rising figures occur in the Ascension Magnificat
antiphon, *O Rex gloriae*. In its several guises 'qui triumphator hodie'
rises an octave, a ninth and (beginning with an octave leap) a twelfth.

The rising figures of the Ascension Mass penetrate the Whitsun Mass.
They appear in the Introit verse (*Exsurgat Deus*), and at the beginning of
the second Alleluia verse (*Veni Sancte Spiritus reple tuorum corda
fidelium*). But there is an even more striking similarity between the
opening bars of the Introit, *Spiritus Domini*, and the preceding number in
Gradualia II, *O Rex gloriae*. (Ex. 29.) Byrd must have set to work on the
Whitsun Mass almost as soon as he had finished the Ascension antiphon.

Ex. 29

(a)

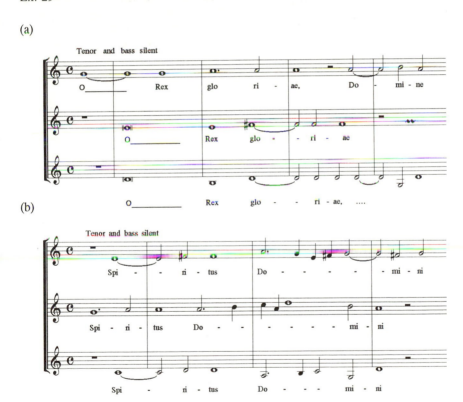

(b)

The Sequence *Veni Sancte Spiritus et emitte coelitus lucis tuae radium*
presented Byrd with one of the longest texts of the *Gradualia* Masses.
His response was to set it in a semi-homophonic style, with one note to a

syllable and barely any repetitions. He introduced textural variety by means of passages for reduced voices in the second and third parts of the Sequence. The Offertory, *Confirma hoc Deus*, on the other hand sets the briefest of texts, starting like a continuation of the Sequence but giving way to counterpoint that leads seamlessly into the Alleluia. (The alto voice in fact gives vent to an 'Alleluia' in mid-text.) The progress of the Communion, *Factus es repente*, is similar, beginning with semi-homophony and progressing to contrapuntal complexities representing the Apostles speaking of the wonders of God.

'Alleluia' is a key word in *Non vos relinquam orphanos*, the Magnificat antiphon for Whitsun, where it occurs twice in the middle and again at the end. Byrd now develops the notion of assimilating the Alleluia, which he had tried out in the Offertory, by introducing the word early and setting it in parallel with the first phrase of the text. The result is an extraordinarily effective verbal, melodic and rhythmic counterpoint.

19

LATER VOCAL AND INSTRUMENTAL MUSIC

Byrd expected *Psalmes, songs, and sonnets* (1611) to be his final publication. In his dedication to the Earl of Cumberland, he said: 'These are like to be my last Travailes in this kind, and your Lordship my last Patron'. His address to 'all true lovers of *Musicke*' echoed the thought: '*Being exited by your kinde acceptance of my former travailes in Musicke, I am thereby much incouraged to commend to you these my last labours, for myne* ultimum vale'. He was however represented in two subsequent publications. His keyboard music was given pride of place in *Parthenia* (1612 or 1613), and he contributed to Sir William Leighton's *The teares or lamentacions of a sorrowfull soule* (1614).

Songs of 1611

'The Naturall inclination and love to the Art of *Musicke*, wherein I have spent the better part of mine age', Byrd wrote in *Psalmes, songs, and sonnets*, 'have become so powrefull in me, that even in my old yeares which are desirous of rest, I cannot containe my selfe from taking some paines therein'. This may be a rhetorical flourish, but there is no reason to doubt its essential truth.[1] Byrd's address to the users of his book speaks again of the trouble he has taken.[2]

Psalmes, songs, and sonnets contains thirty works printed as thirty-two numbers. Their order is governed first by the number of parts and then by key.[3] Byrd's choice of pieces resulted in a very mixed collection, giving the impression that, although he had a number of solo consort songs in hand, he was pushed to find enough material to make a coherent compilation for his 'ultimum vale'.

This conviction is supported by differences of genre. *Ah silly soul* and *How vain the toils* are consort songs. So are *O God that guides* and *Have mercy upon me O God*, but they include choral passages. Byrd must have felt that his decision on this occasion not to add words to parts written for viols justified the inclusion of two old consort fantasias.[4]

---

1   Byrd had, however, been harping on about his old age since the preface to the first book of *Gradualia* (1605).

2   See p. 370.

3   Byrd was more concerned about bringing together pieces in the same key than about the transition from one key to another.

4   The fantasias have already been discussed. See pp. 271-272.

Stylistic indications that the songs were composed over a long period are backed up by the dates that can be attached to a handful of them. Byrd included one song, the four-voice setting of *This sweet and merry month of May*, which had been published in 1590. Three of the songs survive in manuscript sources that are known to pre-date publication by anything up to ten or fifteen years. They are *Crowned with flowers I saw sweet Amaryllis*, *Wedded to will is witless*, and *How vain the toils*.[5]

The poems Byrd set are very like those of his earlier song-books. He began with *The eagle's force*, a verse by Churchyard that had been published in *The mirror for magistrates* in 1563, and he included poems Whitney had published in 1586.[6] Byrd's taste for older moralistic poetry appears in *Let not the sluggish sleep*, the words of which occur in a manuscript of c.1540.[7] There are no more than three strophic poems, and of these only *A feigned friend* is not through-composed.[8] It is notable that Byrd no longer included any metrical psalms. The nine psalm passages he set are all in prose translations,[9] and instead of being gathered together like most of those in Byrd's earlier books of songs they are scattered throughout the collection.

There is no such thing as a typical Byrd three-part song, but generally those of 1611 resemble the secular three-part songs of 1589 or certain three-part pieces in *Gradualia*. They bear less resemblance to the sacred three-part songs of the earlier collection or to the Mass for three voices. This is true not only of those which set poems, but also of those which set prose. They differ from the songs of 1589 in always having two

5   All the sources are from the Paston group of manuscripts described briefly in Brett, 1964(a). *Crowned with flowers* and *Wedded to will is witless* occur in Harvard College Library MS Mus. 30 (*olim* 634.I.703), c.1605; BL, Egerton MSS 2009-12, after 1597; Royal College of Music MS 2041 (c.1610). *How vain the toils* occurs in BL Additional MS 31992 (c.1600). See Morehen, 1987, pp. 178-179, for a comprehensive list of sources.

6   The words of numbers 2-5 and 8 are from Whitney's *A choice of emblemes*. Fellowes (1967) fails to record this as the source of 3 and 4, but pages of the original book are reproduced in Morehen, 1987, pp. xxii-xxv.

7   BL, Additional MS 15233, containing John Redford's play *Wit and science*.

8   Morehen (1987, p. vi) observes that Byrd included a number of verses that seem to reflect his awareness of growing old. This theme runs through his dedication and preface. Morehen notes that the quotation from Seneca used by Byrd to point up his remarks about his age, 'ut esse Phoebi dulcius lumen solet iam iam cadentis' (since the sweeter light of the sun generally occurs at the very moment of his setting), was used for the same purpose by Lassus in his six-part *Cantiones sacrae*, published in the year he died (1594).

9   The beginning of 'I have been young but now am old, yet never did I see' nevertheless shows how naturally English falls into the metre of the metrical psalms.

voices with approximately the same soprano range. This suggests that many, if not all, of the three-part songs published in 1611 were written as a later group.[10] Some of them have madrigal-like features that indicate composition after Byrd's two settings of *This sweet and merry month of May*.

The four-part *Come jolly swains* is in Byrd's madrigalesque manner, and contrasts with the largely homophonic *What is life?* and the distinctly old-fashioned *Let not the sluggish sleep* and *A feigned friend*. The song *Awake mine eyes* falls somewhere between the extremities of style in these pieces. The variety of styles creates a difficulty in dating Byrd's songs. It is reasonable to attach a date after 1590 to those influenced by the madrigal, but there is nothing to show whether he continued to write pieces with an admixture of older traits alongside his more fashionable compositions.

The five-part songs in *Psalmes, songs, and sonnets* are if anything more varied than the four-part songs. Several are psalms which can conveniently be considered below. The most serious of the other five-part pieces is *Retire my soul*, as subtle in its avoidance of the obvious as it is skilful in its balance between the shaping influence of the text and purely musical considerations, and between imitation and continuously variable but unostentatious counterpoint.[11]

Retire my soul is little affected by the madrigal. *Come woeful Orpheus* and *Crowned with flowers* absorb some of the madrigal's attributes into a style that is essentially unmadrigalian. It was inevitable that in *Come woeful Orpheus* the poem's 'strange chromatic notes', 'mournful accents' and 'sourest sharps and uncouth flats' should stimulate Byrd to replicate them in his music, but the piece is semi-homophonic, its rhythm and tempo are steady, and its motives are not strongly defined.[12] The motives of *Crowned with flowers* are more clearly differentiated, and they are organized in contrasting groups, but

10   It is hard to be confident of this in every instance. The publication together of *The eagle's force* and the four-part consort fantasia of the 1580s draws attention to the presence of similar motives in each. Whatever this says about their chronology, it brings home the point that Byrd's consort writing is often very like his writing for voices. This no doubt stems from his early exercises in writing untexted pieces that could be played or sung.

11   Studied in detail by Kerman, 1992.

12   *Come woeful Orpheus* is not one of Byrd's most powerfully felt songs, but the type to which it belongs is indicated by Wells, 1994, p. 202. He observes that 'the most intense emotions were valued as an end in themselves', and refers to Dowland's dedication to Queen Anne of *Lachrimae* (1604): 'pleasant are the teares which Musicke weepes, neither are teares shed alwas in sorrowe, but sometime in joy and gladnesse'.

apart from the illustration of 'a storm of wind and weather' the development of the song is determined by musical rather than literary considerations.[13] The same is true of *Wedded to will is witless*.[14] It begins in exactly the manner applauded by Morley, with 'two severall points in two severall parts at once' combined with 'one point foreright and reverted'.[15] The whole piece is highly inventive in its motivic combination and variation, but only in its repeated setting of the final couplet does it closely approach the madrigal style.

Ah silly soul and *How vain the toils* contain nothing of the madrigal's influence. Both are for a solo voice and five viols, with the voice below the highest part. There is little evidence for the precise date of either beyond the appearance of the second in a manuscript source of c.1600.[16]

The psalms included in *Psalmes, songs, and sonnets* form an intriguing group. The three-part *Sing ye to our Lord* and *I have been young*, like the four-part *Come let us rejoice*, are songs imbued with the spirit of the madrigal. *Sing we merrily unto God*, *Make ye joy to God* and *Arise Lord into thy rest* set joyful texts, and are anthems in Byrd's five-voice 'motet' style, which is now employed in a new manner. The references to instruments in the text of *Sing we merrily* provide every opportunity for a succession of illustrative motives.[17] Passages which Byrd could not have written before his flirtation with the madrigal occur in the other two songs as well. *Arise Lord* is a piece in which his anticipation of the baroque style emerges strongly, and is particularly noticeable in the bass voice. (Ex. 30.)

13   Kerman (1962, p. 116) draws attention to an inferior but far more madrigalian setting of the same words in Francis Pilkington's *The second set of madrigals and pastorals* (1624).

14   In the preface to his 1964 revision of Fellowes' edition of *Psalmes, songs, and sonnets*, Dart suggested (p. ii) that 'will' and 'reason' might refer to Byrd and John Reason, though he was mistaken in saying that the printed text of the song capitalized 'will' and 'reason'. While the idea that the song was a domestic joke cannot be dismissed entirely, there are two factors that render it doubtful. (1) The song appears to have been written about 1600, when − unknown to Dart − Reason was suffering severely for his Catholic beliefs. (2) The personification of wit, will and reason was sufficiently common to make the assumption of personal references unnecessary. An example occurs in Byrd's own *Where fancy fond* from *Psalmes, sonets, & songs of sadnes and pietie* (1588).

15   Morley, 1597, p. 167 (1952 ed., p. 276).

16   See note 5 above. Morehen (1987, p. 187) cites evidence that *How vain the toils* may have been adapted from a five-part work in order to make up a sufficient number of pieces for the six-part section of the collection.

17   Byrd substituted 'shawm' for the Prayer Book's 'psalm'.

Ex. 30

Arise Lord into thy rest, bars 43-52

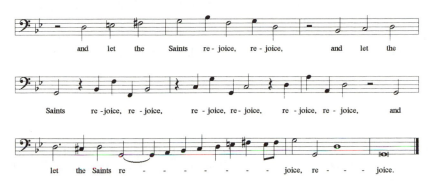

The three six-part psalms could hardly differ more from one another. The character of *Turn our captivity* (especially at 'they shall come with jollity') suggests composition after 1590. *Praise our Lord* is more even in style, but its climax is a succession of radiant repetitions of the word 'Amen', which seem to spring from the same inspirational source as the cries of 'Alleluia' in the *Gradualia*.[18] The penitential psalm *Have mercy upon me O God* is set as a verse anthem for a solo voice and five viols, with intermediate choruses for five voices and a final chorus for six voices.[19]

Most, if not all, of these psalms must belong to the last twenty or so years of Byrd's career as a composer, and it is puzzling to know why he should have written psalms with English texts at a time when his energies were concentrated on the setting of Latin texts for Catholic liturgical use. Were some made for recreational singing in Catholic households? Half a dozen of the translations set by Byrd have parallels in the Douai Bible.[20] Could some have been intended for the Chapel Royal? Three psalms have texts that seem to be related to those of the Prayer Book or other Anglican psalters.[21] Even though Byrd was living in semi-retirement he

18   Allowing for the variety of ways in which Byrd set the word 'Alleluia'.

19   Morehen (1987, p. 185) suggests that *Have mercy upon me O God* was adapted from a five-part work.

20   Kerman, 1962, p. 110. The translations which are close to the Douai Bible are *Sing ye to our Lord*, *Come let us rejoice*, *Arise Lord*, *Make ye joy*, *Praise our Lord*, and *Turn our captivity*. Kerman notes that Byrd could easily have known the Douai text many years before its publication.

21   Translations close to Anglican versions are *I have been young*, *Sing we merrily* and *Have mercy upon me*.

was still in touch with the court, and the emphasis on the God of Jacob in *Sing we merrily* suggests that it was intended for some occasion in the reign of King James.[22] The two carols *O God that guides* and *This day Christ was born* both came to be sung as Anglican anthems, whatever their original purpose. *O God that guides* is a consort song for solo voice and five viols, ending in a six-part chorus and a modestly extended 'Amen'. *This day Christ was born* could perhaps have been written as a church anthem. It has six singing parts, is in Byrd's latest style, and ends with a long and joyful 'Alleluia'.

Unpublished songs

Byrd's unpublished songs of this period appear in manuscripts compiled for Edward Paston.[23] Six can be linked to events that occurred between 1592 and 1612.

(a) There is some reason to suppose that *Quis me statim* (BE 15/37) was composed for a presentation of *Hippolytus* at Christ Church, Oxford, in 1591/2, when additional scenes by William Gager were performed.[24]

(b) *My mistress had a little dog* (BE 15/36) was written after 1596, since it describes an incident at Appleton Hall, Norfolk, which was built by Edward Paston in that year.[25] A probable pun at the end of the third stanza implies that 'my mistress' was Penelope Rich. If this is so, the song must date from before her divorce and re-marriage in 1605.

(c) The allocation of *Wretched Albinus* (BE 15/41) to the year 1601 depends on an assumption that the words of the song refer obliquely to the rebellion and execution of the Earl of Essex.[26]

---

22   The words are taken from Psalm 81, also set by Byrd as the anthem *Sing joyfully*. See p. 300.

23   See Brett, 1964(a). Relevant information in this article is repeated in Brett, 1970.

24   The case is argued by Jean Jacquot in Centre National, 1954, pp. 283-284. It should be noted that Byrd is no longer reckoned to be the composer of *Come tread the path* from *Tancred and Gismunda*, attributed to him by Fellowes (1948, p. 165) and referred to by Jacquot. (Brett, 1974, p. 177.) *Hippolytus* was attributed to Seneca.

25   Brett, 1964(a), pp. 53, 62.

26   In A.D. 197 Albinus, Governor of Britain, rebelled against the Emperor Septimus Severus, who had created him Caesar. After his defeat at Lyons he was executed, and his head was sent to Rome.

(d) *Though I be Brown* (BE 15/38) seems likely to have been written in honour of Mary Browne, perhaps on (but not after) the occasion of her marriage to Edward Paston's son Thomas in 1608.[27]

(e) *With lilies white* (BE 15/40) seems to be an elegy for Mary Browne's grandmother, the dowager Lady Magdalen Montague, who died in 1608.[28] Christopher Byrd's brother-in-law was her chaplain.[29]

(f) *Fair Britain isle* (BE 15/34) is an elegy for James I's eldest son, Henry, Prince of Wales, who died on 6 November 1612 and was buried at Westminster Abbey two days later.

Three more unpublished songs appear to belong to the same late period of Byrd's work, although they cannot be dated so narrowly. They are *An aged dame* (BE 15/33), *Where the blind* (BE 15/39), and *He that all earthly pleasure scorns* (BE 15/35).[30] The first two occur in Harvard College Library manuscript Mus. 30, and if this is correctly dated c.1605 they were probably composed during the first years of the century.[31] The last is in British Library Additional manuscripts 29401-5, of c.1613.

All these unpublished songs are for a solo voice and four viols, and *Psalmes, songs, and sonnets* obviously might have included more in this medium had Byrd wished. With the exception of *An aged dame, Quis me statim, Where the blind* and *Wretched Albinus*, the settings are stanzaic. All combine conservatism with Byrd's most mature, resourceful and supple contrapuntal manner. The elegy *Fair Britain Isle* is a worthy counterpart to the memorial pavan for the Earl of Salisbury, expressing a dignified grief. The conservatism is however relative. *An aged dame* transfers from the madrigal to the consort song the word-painting invited by 'Upon an hill', 'she tumbled to the ground', 'down fell the skulls', 'here and there they ran about the hill', and 'so varied they in their opinions all'. The most remarkable of Byrd's late unpublished songs, in terms of the trouble Byrd took over a trivial poem, and his ability to simulate a sorrow he could not have felt, is *My mistress had a little dog*.

27 Brett, 1964(a), p. 63. The marriage settlement is dated 12 January 1607/8.

28 Brett, 1964(a), pp. 63-64; Southern, 1954.

29 See p. 101.

30 *Quis me statim* and *An aged dame* are the only songs in this group which are not anonymous in the sources, but strong reasons for attributing the others to Byrd are set out by Brett, 1970, pp. ix-x. He points (p. 176) to an elaborate cadential progression which *He that all earthly pleasure scorns* shares with *With liles white* and *Ah silly soul*, the penultimate song of Byrd's 1611 collection.

31 Brett (1970, p. 178) suggests on grounds of style that *Where the blind* belongs to about the same time as *Though I be Brown*, though a few years must separate them if the date of the Harvard manuscript is correct and the latter song was written in 1608.

It is interesting for its form as well. The bright first section is sung three times with different words, each time with a repeated concluding couplet. The rest of the song consists of a slower mournful central section and a lively final section with a repeated refrain.

Byrd's last two verse anthems can best be dealt with in the context of his unpublished songs. Although *Hear my prayer O Lord* (BE 11/14) and *O Lord rebuke me not* (BE 11/15) survive with organ accompaniments, they are related to *Have mercy upon me*, a consort anthem from the 1611 collection. All three are settings of penitential psalms in Byrd's late manner, and there are similar alternations of soloist and chorus.

Songs of 1614

In 1612 Sir William Leighton published a collection of his verses under the title *The teares or lamentacions of a sorrowfull soule*.[32] Musical settings of many of these poems were published with the same title in 1614. Nothing is known of Byrd's acquaintance with Leighton, but the intensely religious poems were of a type calculated to appeal to his tastes, and he was among the twenty-one composers who made settings. His four pieces form a larger contribution than that of any composer but Leighton himself, and appear in the sections of the book devoted to unaccompanied songs of four and five parts.

Be unto me O Lord (BE 11/17) and *Look down O Lord* (BE 11/20) are for four voices; *Come help O God* (BE 11/18) and *I laid me down* (BE 11/19) are for five. Like many of Byrd's later songs they require two sopranos, but if their origin were unknown it would not be easy to date them to the end of Byrd's career. All are restrained and contain much homophonic writing. Apart from an occasional expression of joy, none is overtly emotional.

Byrd contributed nothing to the part of the book devoted to songs accompanied by a broken consort, made up of instruments of different kinds. This was one of several categories of music in which he never showed any interest. Another was music for the lute, either as an accompanying or solo instrument.[33] The implication must be that Byrd

---

32   A concise biography of Leighton (c.1565-1622) is given in Grove, 1980.

33   There are nevertheless plenty of arrangements by other people. There is an incomplete contemporary arrangement for broken consort of the fifth pavan from *My Ladye Nevells Booke*. The cittern part is in the Parton Collection, Mills College, Oakland, Cal.; flute and bass viol parts are numbered DDHO/20/1-2 in the Brynmor Jones Library, University of Hull. See Turbet, 1993(c), for a reconstruction of the treble viol, lute and pandora parts. Immediately Byrd's printing patent expired in 1596, Francis Cutting's arrangement of his 'Bray' pavan was published by William Barley in *A new*

was not a lutenist and was unwilling to try his hand at composing for an instrument of which he had no direct experience.

Keyboard music

The surviving keyboard music in Byrd's latest style includes over a score of pieces. Since they do not appear in *My Ladye Nevells Booke*, it can be assumed that they were written after 1591. Approximate dates can be attached to many of them.

(a) The first bar of Byrd's *Quadran pavan* is recalled in the first bar of the *Passamezzo pavan* by Morley. It is clear that the latter borrowed from the former, and thus Byrd's piece must have been written before Morley's death in 1602.[34] It may indeed have been written some ten years earlier, since its style recalls the *Petre* pavan and galliard of 1591.

(b) The last variation of Byrd's set on *Go from my window* seems to have suggested the imitative figure that begins Morley's second variation on the tune, so Byrd's set was obviously in existence before 1602.

(c) Morley's *First book of consort lessons* (1599) contains an anonymous setting of the tune *Mistress myne* (*O Mistresse mine* in the index). If the tune was then popular, Byrd may have composed his variations at about the same time. The possibility is strengthened by Shakespeare's inclusion of a song beginning 'O Mistris mine' in *Twelfth Night*, first mentioned in John Manningham's diary entry for 2 February 1601/2.[35]

(d) The piece which Tregian calls *Pavana Bray* may be named after William Bray, a Catholic gentleman, or Henry Bray, a Jesuit. There are a references to them in the State papers and other

booke of tabliture. A galliard by Byrd (MB 27/29b) appeared in the next year in *The Cittharn School* of Anthony Holborne. See North, 1976, for other lute arrangements of pieces by Byrd.

34 The main source of Morley's inspiration was Byrd's *Passing measures pavan* of about 1580. Bar six of Byrd's *Passing measures pavan* supplied the parallel passage in Morley's *Passamezzo pavan*, and there are other resemblances between the two pieces. Byrd's *Passing measures pavan* is echoed in Morley's *Quadran pavan* as well.

35 J. L. Hotson (*The first night of Twelfth Night*, 1954) argued that the play was presented at Whitehall a year earlier. Tomkins' index to Bibliothèque Nationale MS Réserve 1122 refers to a piece by Byrd, which is not in the manuscript, as 'o mistris myne I must'. There may have been a popular song with words differing from those of Shakespeare's verses, which do not readily fit the tune used by Byrd and Morley.

documents of the 1580s and 1590s. William Bray was in gaol with John Reason.[36] The pavan was transcribed for orpharion by Francis Cutting and included in William Barley's *A new booke of tabliture* (1596). Byrd may have written it in the early 1590s.

(e) Barley's book also contains John Dowland's *Lachrymae*. Dowland himself included it in *The second booke of songes or ayres* (1600) and *Lachrimae, or seaven teares* (1604). Peter Philips' setting of Caccini's *Amarilli*, dated 1603 by Tregian, echoes Byrd's setting of *Lachrymae*. When Byrd made the latter, perhaps about 1600, he may also have set James Harding's galliard to form a pair with it.

(f) Robert Cecil, who was created Lord Salisbury in 1605, died in May 1612. The pavans and galliards by Byrd and Gibbons which bear his name in *Parthenia* (published in 1612 or 1613)[37] were probably composed as memorial tributes.[38] Byrd wrote a pavan with two galliards. There is evidence that the second galliard (which, plainly in error, bears Mary Brownlow's name) was written somewhat later than the first. Byrd's pavan and first galliard have a different form of the F clef from all the other pieces in *Parthenia*, including the second galliard. The engraver may initially have been given a copy of the pavan and first galliard without the second galliard, which he received later in a copy made by a different hand.

(g) Byrd's galliard in C, which correctly bears Mary Brownlow's name, must have been written when she was of an age to appreciate the dedication, and perhaps to be Byrd's pupil.[39] She was born between 1589 and 1594, and was married in November 1613.[40] Resemblances between the *Brownlow* galliard and the *Salisbury* pieces may mean that it too was composed in 1612.

(h) The prelude (MB 27/1) which opens *Parthenia* was apparently written to precede the 'Petre' pavan and galliard, and perhaps for their publication. This places it after 1591 and most likely in 1612.

---

36   See p. 72, note 57.

37   Dart (1962, p. 39) proposed a publication date between 27 December 1612 and 14 February 1612/13. These were the days on which the dedicatees, Princess Elizabeth and her husband Frederick V, Elector Palatine of the Rhine, were engaged and married. (See Rimbault, 1872, pp. 161-166.)

38   Gibbons' pieces, indeed, were a tribute not only to the Earl of Salisbury, but to Byrd's development of keyboard dances to the point where they could bear the weight Gibbons imposed upon them.

39   See p. 363.

40   Cust, 1909, pp. 35, 39.

(i) A pavan in C (MB 27/33) appears anonymously in Forster's manuscript (British Library R. M. 24.d.3).[41] Late pieces by Byrd are typically anonymous in Forster's copies, so this supports stylistic evidence that the pavan is a late work.[42]

(j) Other apparently late pieces entered anonymously by Forster are a revised version of *The woods so wild*,[43] the *Echo* pavan and galliard, the galliard to the 'Ph. Tr.' pavan, Harding's galliard, the almain MB 55/30, and the prelude MB 55/3.

Byrd's total output of keyboard music during the two decades after 1591 amounted to no more than half of what he wrote in the preceding twenty years. It may be right to put this down to Byrd's increasing age, but his work shows no diminution in his powers and it is more probable that with his partial retirement and the arrival on the scene first of John Bull and then of Orlando Gibbons there was less cause for him to write new keyboard music.

It is the figuration and flamboyant runs that identify as a late work a C major setting of *Monsieur's alman* (MB 27/44), which Byrd had twice set in G (MB 28/87-88). A much more interesting alman in C (MB 55/30) occurs anonymously in Forster's manuscript, but Byrd's authorship is proclaimed by its balance and inventiveness, and by the attention given to every detail.

Byrd's late keyboard works include four preludes. Up to this point he had composed only one, the prelude in A (MB 27/12) apparently written to go with the fantasia in that key and dating from Byrd's years at Lincoln. From the beginning Byrd seems to have designed his preludes for specific works, as a means of extending them. Like the first, each of the later preludes has a distinct character conferred by its figuration, motives and textures.

A prelude in C (MB 27/24) was published in *Parthenia*, along with the prelude in G minor (MB 27/1) which Byrd probably wrote as an adjunct to the 'Petre' pavan and galliard. The prelude in C precedes and is in the same key as the Brounlow galliard, but appears independently of it in manuscript sources. Neighbour suggests that its 'rich surface ornament and relaxed harmonic progress' may — at least, as far as date goes — connect it with the late pavan and galliard in C (MB 27/33).[44] Some of its figuration strongly resembles passages in Bull's pavan and galliard *St Thomas wake*, and is one of several indications that Byrd

41   It is attributed to Byrd in New York Public Library MS Drexel 5612.
42   Neighbour, 1978, p. 23.
43   The original version dated 1590 was included in *My Ladye Nevells Booke*.
44   1978, pp. 223-224.

remained ready to absorb new ideas.[45] The prelude in F (MB 55/3) is without doubt another late piece, since its harmonies resemble those of the first strain of the 'Ph. Tr.' pavan, the galliard to which it precedes in Forster's manuscript. A prelude in G major (MB 55/4) is a larger, toccata-like work in three distinct sections. In Forster's manuscript it occurs only a few pages from Byrd's *Echo* pavan and galliard, with which it has clear motivic connections. Its figuration, like that of the prelude in C, contains intimations that Byrd had been listening to Bull.[46]

This is the place to say something about Byrd's adaptations as keyboard pieces of music by younger composers. These include an arrangement (MB 27/5) of the pavan and galliard *Delight*, by Johnson,[47] and another (MB 28/54-55) which combines John Dowland's *Lachrymae* pavan with a galliard by James Harding.[48] Byrd's treatment of Johnson's pieces preserves the basic melody and harmony, although his obvious dissatisfaction with the pavan's second strain led him to rewrite nearly half of it. His reinterpretation of the pieces by Dowland and Harding is more exuberant, and is plainly the later work. Harding's galliard is subjected to treatment it might have received from younger men like Bull and Gibbons, and the normally lively beat of Byrd's galliards is retarded by the many passages in semiquavers.

Byrd's 'Ph. Tr.' pavan and galliard (MB 28/60) are based on Morley's pavan and galliard in F.[49] Morley's popular pavan begins well, but it soon runs out of steam.[50] The first strain derives interest from

45   More flexible writing for the left hand and repeated notes in florid passages are among the features that Byrd seems to have incorporated into his late keyboard music from the work of younger men, but the question of priority is not always easy to determine. There is little doubt that Bull's arrival in the Chapel Royal stimulated Byrd, but behind references to Bull here and below there lurks the question of the part played by Byrd in initiating the development of a style that is fully formed in the work of the younger composer.

46   Left hand, bars 5-6, for example.

47   Tregian names Edward Johnson as the composer of the original. Lute sources ascribe it variously to R[obert], Richard and John Johnson.

48   There is a keyboard arrangement (MB 55/26) of Dowland's *Piper's galliard* (stemming from the composer's lute version), which may perhaps be by Byrd. See Neighbour, 1978, p. 165.

49   'Ph. Tr.' is the heading given to the pavan by Tregian; it may refer to his sister Philippa. (Cole, 1952-53.) A detailed comparison of Morley's original and Byrd's reworking is made by Neighbour, 1978, pp. 206-209.

50   Morley's pavan survives as a consort piece in Murhardsche Bibliothek der Stadt Kassel und Landsbibliothek 4° Ms. mus. 125. This may have been its original form. It was arranged by Philip Rosseter (*Lessons for consort*, 1609, where it is called *Southernes*

imitation between the treble and bass, but after that Morley's inspiration fails. The third strain, with no varied repeat, has a semibreve 'cantus firmus' in the treble. Therefore, while Morley can model the first two strains of the galliard on those of the pavan, he has to construct the third from new material. In Byrd's hands Morley's rather awkward dances are transformed into a lightly imitative pavan, and a sparely-textured galliard that is no longer constructed directly from the material of the pavan. The metamorphosis wrought by Byrd is a lesson in composition. If anything remains of the spirit of Morley's pieces, it is a hint of his ballett style.

Byrd's first step was to curtail and regularize the length of Morley's wandering and irregular strains. Morley's pavan has strains of twenty, sixteen and twenty semibreves; his galliard has strains of fourteen, thirteen and eleven dotted semibreves. Byrd tightens everything up so that the strains of his pavan consist uniformly of sixteen semibreves, and those of his galliard of eight dotted semibreves. Much other clutter is cleared away with the excess bars. The first strain of Byrd's pavan, like Morley's, is divided by a central cadence, and each half contains a contrapuntal subject. Byrd's second subject vaguely resembles Morley's, but beyond that very little remains of the original. In place of Morley's confused second strain Byrd fashions another from contrapuntal material, which echoes but does not precisely follow the shapes and rhythms of the first strain. The third strain of Byrd's pavan provides the clearest evidence that it was he who was copying Morley, not vice versa. Having turned Morley's cantus firmus into a subject for imitation, he takes the second part of Morley's countersubject as his own countersubject. The first part of Morley's countersubject appears later in inverted form. The strains of Byrd's galliard are subtly linked to its pavan by analogous harmonic progressions. The two subjects of Byrd's first galliard strain are borrowed from the first strain of Morley's pavan.

The third strain of Byrd's pavan in C (MB 27/33) quotes the beginning of *Lord Lumley's pavan* by John Bull.[51] This does not seem to be a tribute to Lord Lumley (who died in 1609) so much as a nod in Bull's direction.[52] Byrd does not attempt to emulate Bull's virtuoso passages, and although Bull's pieces are harmonically more purposeful than most of his pavans and galliards, Byrd's harmonies are more varied

---

pavan) and for keyboard by Giles Farnaby.

51   Bull quotes his own composition in a pavan-galliard pair published in *Parthenia* (nos. 12 and 13). See Neighbour, 1978, pp. 210-215.

52   There is no firm evidence to show that Bull's pavan-galliard pair was written in 1609, as assumed by Dart (1967, p. 236), who presumably thought it was a memorial to Lord Lumley. Bull's stylistic progress nevertheless suggests that this date may not be far out, and Byrd's pavan and galliard were probably written shortly after Bull's.

and their progress is more secure. Byrd however acknowledges certain features of Bull's style, by repeating notes in the last nine bars of the pavan and introducing rhythmic figures that are commoner in Bull's music than his own.

In experimenting with Bull's style Byrd was following a procedure that is frequent in his later keyboard pavans and galliards, namely conferring individuality on a work by means of a particular technique or device.[53] This is plainest in the *Echo* pavan and galliard (MB 28/114). Echo technique had played some part in Byrd's six-part consort fantasias in G minor (BE 17/12 and 17/13), but the keyboard pavan and galliard are likely to belong to the same period as the consort pavan and galliard in C (BE 17/15). Comparison of the two pairs of dances shows how far Byrd had travelled since transcribing his first keyboard pavan from a consort piece. It is difficult to imagine either pair of 'echo' dances being adapted for a different medium. Unusually for Byrd the keyboard dances are linked by identical harmonies at the beginnings of corresponding strains, but in the pavan the echo is handled largely in a contrapuntal manner, while in the galliard the echoed phrases are repeated at the original pitch in a varied setting. In each dance the harmonic context of a phrase is often altered when it is repeated.

The *Bray* pavan and galliard (MB 28/59) are if anything still further removed from consort style. The progressive separation of Byrd's keyboard and consort styles had been taking place for some time. It was well-advanced when Byrd wrote the fourth of his *Nevell* pavans (MB 27/30), and more or less complete by the time of the pavan in G (MB 28/71), from which *the Bray* pavan incorporates a near quotation.[54] In the *Bray* pieces Byrd weaves threads of sound, sometimes contrapuntal, sometimes imitative or lightly harmonized, into a fabric of great translucency. There are passages in a late pavan in D (MB 28/52) which revert to the consort manner,[55] but its galliard is connected structurally with the *Bray* galliard. Each piece has a second and third strain formed from transformations of its first strain.[56]

The Earl of Salisbury pavan and its galliards (MB 27/15) provide proof, if any is needed, that towards the end of his composing career Byrd's creative spirit was unimpaired and he was as eager as ever to

53   See Neighbour, 1978, p. 220.

54   The beginning of MB 27/30 also quotes part of an earlier pavan: the second strain of MB 27/17. Bars 19-20 of pavan MB 28/71 are remembered in bars 41-43 of pavan MB 28/59.

55   Particularly in the repeat of the first strain, where motives are passed from part to part.

56   See Neighbour, 1978, p. 205.

explore new paths. The pavan is the single mature example by Byrd to have eight-bar strains. The pavan and first galliard have only two strains, instead of the usual three. Perhaps because the strains of all three dances are repeated without variation, the pavan (uniquely among Byrd's pavans) has two galliards. Variation would be out of keeping with the work's surface simplicity, although the simplicity is more apparent than real and conceals much motivic development and linkage within and between the dances.[57] The cadential A-G#-A which appears in bars 3 and 4 of the pavan is repeated in the last two bars. At the start of the first galliard it reappears in the treble (bars 1-2) and in the bass (bars 2-3), and again at the end. The imitative motive which begins the first galliard is an inversion of a figure from the second strain of the pavan, which recurs in its original form in the second strain of the galliard. Both forms of this figure provide material for the second galliard, so confirming that the engraver of *Parthenia* made an error in heading it 'M[ris]: Marye Brownlo'.

The galliard correctly dedicated to Mary Brownlow (MB 27/34) precedes the *Salisbury* pieces in *Parthenia* and shares various features with them: the dotted rhythms, the motive that occurs in bars 12-13 of the *Brownlow* galliard and opens the third strain of the second *Salisbury* galliard, and the figure which appears in bars 9-10 of the *Brownlow* galliard and bars 5-7 of the *Salisbury* pavan. The *Brownlow* galliard is nevertheless exceptional in having motives formed from broken chords, and in the streams of semiquavers which, combined with a rapid harmonic pulse, make for a slower tempo than is usual in Byrd's galliards.

The Quadran pavan and its galliard (MB 28/70) form Byrd's only large-scale ground not included in *Nevell*. Byrd freely adds to the basic harmonies of the *passamezzo moderno* and spreads them over thirty-two semibreves.[58] After a varied repeat he adds a sixteen-semibreve reprise derived from part of the original ground, and varies that. The whole process is then repeated, so that the harmonic plan of the pavan is analogous to those of *Qui passe* and *My Lady Nevell's ground*.[59] The galliard consists of three double harmonic units.

---

57   Souris, 1955.

58   'Quadran' pavans were based on the eight basic harmonies of the *passamezzo moderno*, i.e. *passamezzo per B quadro* (B natural). The *passamezzo per B molle* (B flat) was the basis of the English *passing measures*.

59   A similar plan is adopted in the *Quadran* variations by other British composers. Byrd may have been inspired to compose his pieces by the variations on the ground written by Bull, who appears in turn to have known Morley's mediocre set. (See Neighbour, 1978, pp. 141-143.) Bull's three sets of *Quadran* pavans and galliards are

The *Quadran* pavan begins quite unlike any of Byrd's other grounds, with close imitations that announce immediately how compact the writing is to be. It holds an extraordinary concentration of musical thought. There is an equally breathtaking variety of manner and mood, controlled by the harmonic pattern, but sometimes slightly out of phase with it, so that nothing seems mechanical. The galliard is related to the pavan both by the ground and by recurring scalar motives, but is more relaxed. It is without the pressure of ideas contained in the pavan, and is not very different from Byrd's customary galliard style.

The other ground of Byrd's late years is *The bells* (MB 27/38), an astonishing feat of composition built on an alternation of the tonic and supertonic, the second of which occasionally functions as a constituent of the dominant chord. The piece is therefore a distant descendant of Aston's hornpipe, which inspired Byrd's early hornpipe and is built on the alternation of G and F. Although Byrd is generally strict in observing the limitations imposed by the brevity of the bass, he works mostly in units of four bars, grouping them to form larger units comparable to variations on a longer ground.

In his later years Byrd composed only four sets of variations on popular tunes. *Callino casturame* (MB 27/35) demonstrates the virtues of deliberate restraint. Above the same elementary harmonies on a bass that is sustained throughout much of the piece, Byrd repeats the poignant eight-bar tune six times. The uncomplicated decoration is not developed from the melody, but woven around it. Had *Callino casturame* been included in *Nevell* it might be taken for an earlier piece than it apparently is. Perhaps it is among the earlier of Byrd's post-*Nevell* variations, or was composed in an undemanding style for a pupil.

Go from my window also possesses something of the simplicity of earlier variation sets, and recalls those on *The maiden's song*. It has few of the features that link Byrd's late style to Bull's, but a late date is indicated by its melodic ease and invention, and by the skill with which details are fashioned. Several of the variations find parallels in those of *O mistress mine* and *John come kiss me now*.

In *John come kiss me now* (MB 28/81), the *passamezzo moderno* harmonies reappear, reduced to eight semibreves, without additions, and without the partial reprise. Ideas are present in profusion, amply compensating for the simplicity of the eight-bar tune, which is varied sixteen times. Byrd's endless invention in creating a web of rhythmic and

printed by Dart, 1967. Morley's and some anonymous sets are printed by Brown, 1989. National Library of Scotland MS 9447 contains a *Quadran* pavan and galliard by Kinloch. (See Brown, p. 178.)

melodic counterpoint and imitation only slightly obscures the pairing of variations of similar character.

The fourteen-bar stanza of *O mistress mine* (MB 28/83) permits a comparable lavishness within the space of six slower variations. The repetitions inherent in the stanza form A A B C D C D cause new ideas to well up before each reiteration of the tune has been completed. Rapid florid passages are concentrated in the central variations, and gradually die away before the last variation returns to the calm of the first. There is much in the style of *O mistress mine* that suggests Bull, for example the dotted broken chords of the second variation, and the shakes and left-hand figures of the fourth.

Consort pavan and galliard

Byrd's six-part pavan and galliard (BE 17/15) form an isolated pair. They are unusual among Byrd's pavans and galliards in that the first strain of the galliard is based on the melodic material of the pavan's first strain.[60] (Both dances in fact begin with two simultaneous points of imitation.) This can hardly be accounted an acceptance of a common practice which Byrd had studiously avoided hitherto, for the two dances, individually and together, are unified melodically and motivically to an extent not found outside Byrd's work.

A clue to their date lies in an apparent quotation from the pavan at the beginning of a five-part pavan by Richard Dering. If Dering's birth is correctly set at about 1580, he is unlikely to have borrowed from Byrd before the turn of the century. This strengthens the reasons advanced by Neighbour[61] for believing the pavan and galliard to be Jacobean, and possibly among Byrd's latest pieces. The antiphonal writing is matched by that in the late *Echo* pavan and galliard for keyboard (MB 28/114), and the density of motives calls to mind the *Brownlow* galliard (MB 27/34) and the *Salisbury* pavan and galliards from *Parthenia*.

60   The late *Echo* pavan and galliard have similar correspondences. See p. 354.
61   Neighbour, 1978, pp. 86-87.

POSTSCRIPT

Byrd's resolute recusancy and his repeated engagement in litigation no doubt exhibit one side of his character. On the other hand, he clearly possessed qualities of mind and personality that made him respected, and enabled him to mix easily with people at the highest social level and to be welcome in their homes: 'he is my frend', the Earl of Northumberland wrote to Lord Burghley.[1] It cannot have been his exceptional musical ability alone that impressed his contemporaries.

Many things about Byrd's life are nevertheless likely to remain obscure. None of his social letters or personal belongings is known to have survived, and there is little indication of his pursuits outside music, religion and his property. For all we know he rarely travelled more than thirty or forty miles from London after he left Lincoln. In 1580 he was Lord Paget's guest at Burton in Staffordshire;[2] there is no other indication that he went further afield than Boxley, Harlington or Stondon Massey. Although his musical interests and contacts were wide, there is scant evidence of what books he read (to judge by the verses he set, his tastes in poetry tended to the old-fashioned and moralistic), and none that he ever went to the public theatres.[3] He must have shared most of the beliefs of his age,[4] but whether he was curious about the scientific and geographical discoveries of the time is quite unknown.[5]

Byrd kept closely in touch with his brother John, and with his brothers-in-law Robert Broughe and Philip Smyth. He was in touch, too, with at least some of his many younger relations, but it is impossible to say whether his ties with them were close. There is no sign at all of his having kept up contacts with his wife's family.

Nothing has emerged to suggest that any of Byrd's brothers and sisters or their children adhered to the old religion, and some members of the family are known to have been Protestants.[6] A picture of Byrd as the paterfamilias of a household isolating itself as far as possible from the

1   BL, Lansdowne MS 29, f. 92^r, dated February 1579.

2   See p. 59.

3   Byrd's friend Sir William Petre may well have had a nodding acquaintance with Ben Jonson, if not with Shakespeare and other writers. He occasionally dined at 'the Mermaide', the tavern in Bread Street where Jonson held sway in the early years of the seventeenth century. (ERO, T/A/174; Jonson, 1925, p. 49.)

4   See, for example, Tillyard, 1943, but note the comments of Williams, 1995, p. 445.

5   Did Byrd smoke? Sir William Petre was in the habit of buying tobacco. (ERO, T/A/174.)

6   Byrd's brother-in-law Robert Broughe, and his nephew Thomas Byrd.

non-Catholic world cannot therefore be wholly true. Indeed, he had friends as well as relations who were firmly Protestant, among whom was a branch of the Herbert family. Byrd dined at Magdalen Herbert's house three times in 1601. John Bull and William Heyther were among her guests in the same year.[7]

Despite this, Byrd's friends and patrons appear to have belonged principally to the Catholic community, and to have been closely knit. Just how close and convoluted their relationships were can be illustrated by one example. Byrd's will mentions his lodging at the Earl of Worcester's house in the Strand. The fourth Earl of Worcester was Edward Somerset, whose father William, the third Earl, heads a list of 'Catholick*es* in Inglonde', drawn up in 1574.[8] The fourth Earl was one of those at Ingatestone Hall during the Christmas season of 1589-1590, when Byrd was also there. His daughter Katherine married William Petre, the son of Byrd's friend and patron, the Catholic first Lord Petre,[9] in a double wedding at which her sister Elizabeth married Henry Gilford. Mary, the daughter of Katherine and William Petre, married John Roper, later Baron Teynham, who was descended from Christopher Roper, a younger brother of the William Roper who married Sir Thomas More's daughter Margaret. Since Byrd's daughter-in-law Katherine (née Moore) was descended from Sir Thomas More, he could claim not only the friendship of the fourth Earl of Worcester, but a distant relationship with him. Through this marriage Byrd could additionally claim a relationship of sorts with Lord Lumley, who was descended from the Scrope family with which Katherine Moore was also connected. He could claim one as well with Lord Vaux of Harrowden, since in 1590 Vaux's son George, the child of his second marriage, became the husband of John Roper's daughter Elizabeth.

There are other testimonies of the friendship, as well as the relationship, of the Petres and Worcesters. William Petre's account book

---

7   Charles, 1974, p. 170. Richard Herbert of Montgomery married Magdalen Newport. Their ten children included Lord Herbert of Cherbury and the poet George Herbert. Magdelen Herbert was widowed in 1596, and married Sir John Danvers in 1608. Walton's biographies of John Donne and George Herbert give some account of her. (Walton, 1675.) On her death in 1627 Donne preached *A sermon of commemoration of the Lady Danvers*. If Byrd knew Donne, he would have been aware of his Catholic connections. Donne's maternal grandmother was a niece of Sir Thomas More; his parents remained Catholics, and his brother was imprisoned for harbouring a priest. For Byrd's possible connection with Heyther, see p. 27.

8   PRO, SP12/99/55.

9   Worcester was an overseer of Petre's will, and his wife received a legacy. (Probate copy: PRO, Prob. 11/122.

includes the entries 'To mie Lo: Worcesters Coche mañ for goinge wth mie wife & mee to ye Court twice 5[s]', and 'Lost at Gleeke y[t] day at Worcester house 20[s]'.[10] An inventory of the pictures hanging in the gallery at Thorndon Hall in 1613 shows that they included one of the fourth Earl of Worcester and 'a Catalogue of the Earles of Worcester in a Frame'.[11]

The relationship between the Petre and More families can probably be extended further, because the second wife of John Petre of West Hanningfield was Dorothy, a widow whose maiden name had been More or Moore. This John Petre was born at Ingatestone, and Robert Petre of Westminster was one of his godfathers.[12]

The Petres and Worcesters were friendly with the Talbot family. A portrait of Gilbert Talbot, the seventh Earl of Shrewsbury, was another that hung in the gallery at Thorndon Hall; and it was to him that Worcester wrote on 19 September 1602, to say: 'Wee are frolyke heare in Cowrt; mutche dawncing in the privi chamber of contrey dawnces before the Q. M. whoe is exceedingly pleased therw[th]: Irishe tunes are at this tyme most pleasing, but in wynter, Lullaby, an owld song of M[r] Bird's, wylbee more in request, as I think'.[13]

Byrd's friendships and relationships, however tenuous the latter, must have added to the social status he earned through his musical abilities, and facilitated his use of the Elizabethan system of patronage. The upper and middle classes in Elizabethan and Jacobean England were composed of a very small number of people. When Byrd joined the Chapel Royal in 1572 there cannot have been more than 25-30,000 families at all levels in London and Westminster, and the number of those who were prominent in political, commercial, religious and cultural life was far smaller. Many of them must have been on familiar terms. It would be intriguing to know more about their relationships, and a valuable study could be made of their family and social connections. Turbet hit the nail on the head when he wrote: 'A family tree for Byrd from the beginning of the Tudor dynasty to the Commonwealth noting every possible link would no doubt reveal much of interest'.[14]

10   ERO, T/A/174, ff. 50[r] and 124[r], November 1601 and June 1610.

11   ERO, D/DP F219.

12   Howard and Burke, 1887.

13   Lodge, 1791, iii, p. 148, quoting College of Arms, Talbot papers, vol. M, f. 18; Batho, 1971, p. 256. Worcester and Francis Talbot were among Thomas Paget's musical correspondents: see pp. 49-50. Among others well known to Byrd, whose portraits were at Thorndon Hall, were 'S[r] Thomas Hennage ... [and] Robert Earle of Salisbury'. (ERO, D/DP F219.)

14   Turbet, 1987, pp. 298-299.

Byrd's connections could be pursued almost indefinitely. The third name on the list of 'Catholick*es* in Inglonde' is that of the seventeenth Earl of Oxford, Edward de Vere, from whom Byrd proposed to buy the lease of Battyshall manor about the time the list was compiled. A slender link between William Byrd and the Vere family is suggested by the possible attendance of Byrd's brothers (and perhaps, briefly, Byrd himself) at St Paul's School, where Edward de Vere's cousin Francis was a pupil.[15]

The fifth person on the list of Catholics is Lord Paget, to whom Worcester, while still Edward Herbert, wrote about Byrd.[16] Another name on the list is that of Anthony Roper, who was associated with Byrd both as the owner of the property Byrd bought at Harlington, and as a friend of Tallis.

William and Clement Paston of Norfolk are also on the list, though Byrd's association with their family seems to have been through their nephew Edward Paston. Notwithstanding his Catholicism, Edward Paston apparently escaped the penalties for recusancy, and quietly pursued his interest in literature and music.[17] He was undoubtedly encouraged in the last by his father, Thomas, who may have taught Princess (later Queen) Mary to play the virginals.[18] Quite what his connection with Byrd amounted to is not known, but his large library of music is the sole source for many of Byrd's compositions. These include some which seem to refer to events in the life of Paston's family, celebrated in Paston's own verse.[19] A further link with Byrd is found in a music manuscript which is in the hand of one of Paston's copyists, but has John Petre's name on the cover.[20] In 1608 Edward Paston's eldest son, Thomas, married Mary, the daughter of Sir George Browne.

---

15   See p. 18.

16   See p. 50.

17   Brett, 1964(a) and 1993. Paston (1550?-1630) maintained a Mass-centre at a house close to Appleton Hall, near Sandringham. His home at Thorpe Hall can be assumed to have witnessed frequent musical gatherings, which Thomas Morley, among others, is likely to have attended when master of the choristers at Norwich Cathedral (1583-87). Morley may indeed have been the 'Norw[ch] Organest' whom Paston recommended as a suitable teacher for the Earl of Rutland's daughters. (Historical Manuscripts Commission, 1888 (Rutland), p. 223.) On Morley's Catholic sympathies, see Brown, 1959, and Dart, 1959.

18   Madden, 1831, pp. 5, 22, 26.

19   Brett, 1964(a), p. 64.

20   ERO, D/DP Z6/1, a single bassus-book of English and Continental motets. The supposition is that it is the survivor of a set presented to Petre by Paston. (Brett, 1964(a), p. 58.)

Mary's grandmother was the formidably pious Catholic, Lady Magdalen Montague, whose chaplain was Christopher Byrd's brother-in-law.[21] Byrd's songs *Though I be Brown* and *With lilies white* are thought to be connected with these two women.[22]

A connection with another Catholic family is revealed in a letter dated 28 May 1594, written by the informer Benjamin Beard to Morgan Jones at Gray's Inn. Beard's principal purpose was to convey information about Hill, a seaman who carried seminaries to England, but he added: 'meeting wth one Bird Brother to Bird of the Chappell I understand that M[rs] Tregion, M[rs] Charnock and M[rs] Sibill Tregion will be heere att the Court at this day. By whose comeing peradventure some good may be done'.[23] The 'good' he had in mind is obscure, but the letter establishes a link between William Byrd and the collector and copyist Francis Tregian, the compiler of the *Fitzwilliam Virginal Book* and other music manuscripts.[24] The association between Byrd and Tregian embraces Edward Paston, since a poem possibly written by the latter and set by Byrd concerns Penelope Rich, a relative of the Tregians.[25] The network can be extended still further, for another relative of the Tregians was Edward Parker, Lord Morley.[26] It was probably his wife Elizabeth, Lady Mounteagle, whose name is attached to a keyboard pavan ascribed to Byrd in the *Fitzwilliam Virginal Book*. It was she or Morley's second wife whose name is given to one of Byrd's settings of *La Volta* in the same source.[27]

Two more of Byrd's keyboard pieces carry the names of Kinborough Good and Mary Brownlow. It is possible that these young women were his pupils. Kinborough Good was the daughter of James Good of Malden

21   See p. 101.

22   See pp. 347.

23   PRO, SP12/248/118. The reference is to John Byrd, since Symond Byrd had died in 1579/80. Mention of the Byrd brothers is omitted by State papers, 1867, p. 511.

24   Thompson, 1992, casts doubt on the accepted beliefs (mostly based on Cole, 1952) concerning Tregian's imprisonment in the Fleet, whether he copied the manuscripts there or at all, and whether he died in 1619. Cuneo, 1995, in turn casts doubt on some of Thompson's conclusions. One of Byrd's keyboard pieces is called 'Pavana Ph. Tr.' in the *Fitzwilliam Virginal Book*; it may refer to Francis Tregian's sister Philippa.

25   The poem is *My mistress had a little dog*. See Brett, 1964(a), p. 62.

26   Lord Morley (c.1550-1618) married (1) Elizabeth (d. 1585), daughter of William Stanley, Lord Mounteagle, (2) Gertrude, widow of John Arundel of Trerice, Cornwall. Although Parker was apparently a Protestant, the Mounteagle family had Catholic sympathies.

27   The ascription is actually 'L. Morley', so there is a chance that it refers to Morley himself.

in Surrey. Her Catholic and musical connections with Byrd are suggested by Sebastian Westcote's will, which mentions 'M^res Good wydowe, latelye the wief of doctour Good Physicion ... and ... her dawghter Kynborowghe'.[28] The pavan was presumably written prior to Kinborough's marriage to Robert Barnewell, which must have been before 1589.[29] Mary Brownlow was born about the time her father, Richard, became chief prothonotary of the Court of Common Pleas in 1591. Their house was in Holborn. In November 1613 she married William Sanders of Northamptonshire.[30]

There are only two direct references to Byrd as a teacher of amateurs. One is in his petition of 1577 to the Queen, which claims that his income from teaching was reduced by his entering her service.[31] The other is in the letter already quoted, to Lord Burghley from the Earl of Northumberland, in which the latter refers to Byrd as 'scollemaster to my daughter in his artte'.[32]

As far as professional musicians are concerned, statements made by, or about, three men may imply that they were Byrd's pupils. In dedicating *A plaine and easie introduction to practicall musicke* (1597) to 'the most excellent Musician Maister William Birde', Thomas Morley invited him to 'defend what is in it truely spoken, as that which somtime proceeded from your selfe'. This could mean that Byrd gave his younger colleague lessons in composition, or it could mean no more than that Morley learned from the work of an admired older musician. Morley was deeply influenced by Byrd,[33] and called him 'my loving Maister (never without reverence to be named of the musicians)',[34] though when formal instruction could have taken place is unclear. There is doubt as to whether Morley lived in London much before 1588/9, when his son was buried at St Giles Cripplegate.[35] He was then about thirty years old, had

28   PRO, Prob. 10 box 105; probate copy, Prob. 11/64, ff. 99^r-100^v, confirmed at ff. 235^v-236^r; Honigmann and Brock, 1993, pp. 48-53.

29   PRO, Prob. 11/73, the will of Joan Good, dated 14 March 1588/9, proved 8 May 1589. This gives Good's Christian name and place of residence.

30   Cust, 1909, pp. 35, 39.

31   See p. 65.

32   BL, MS Lansdowne 29, f. 92^r.

33   See, for example, le Huray, 1978, p. 249; Brown, 1960; Beechey, 1981; Harley, 1992-94, ii, p. 46.

34   Morley, 1597, p. 115 (1952 ed., p. 202).

35   'Thomas, the sonne of Thomas Morley organist'. (GL, MS 64129/1.) Morley was described as 'Organist of Paules Church' in the anonymous printed account of *The honorable entertainment gieven to the Queenes Majestie in progresse, at Elvetham* (1591).

behind him several years of experience as Organist and Master of the Choristers at Norwich, and held an Oxford BMus.

Thomas Tomkins called Byrd his 'ancient, & much reverenced master'.[36] Again there is no doubt of Byrd's influence on Tomkins' music.[37] But although Tomkins had connections in London by about 1600 it is hard to see when he could have been Byrd's pupil.[38]

The third of the trio is Peter Philips, who grew up as a chorister of St Paul's.[39] A letter written in Spanish by Louis de Groote on 25 February 1609/10 refers to 'un musica famoso Uamado Burd, mro que fue de P°. flippi'.[40] Byrd and Philips are likely to have been brought into contact by their Catholicism as well as music; but any instruction Philips received from Byrd must have taken place before 1582, when as a young man he left England permanently. Henry Peacham was moved to say of Philips' vocal music, 'he affecteth altogether the *Italian* veine'.[41] It is in his keyboard music that Byrd's influence remained most clearly perceptible, and it seems in fact that Philips had access to some of Byrd's more recent keyboard compositions while he was living on the Continent.[42] Philips may also have been in touch with Francis Tregian, since the addition of dates to his pieces in the *Fitzwilliam Virginal Book* suggests that Tregian worked from copies closely associated with the composer.

Although it cannot be established that Byrd ever gave formal instruction to professional musicians, the likelihood that a number of others were his pupils has prompted suggestions as to who they might have been. Thomas Weelkes has been proposed as one on the strength of the possibility that he was the scribe of British Library Additional manuscript 30485, which contains good texts of Byrd's keyboard compositions.[43]

36   Dedication of *Too much I once lamented* in Tomkins' *Songs of 3. 4. 5. and 6. parts* (1622).

37   See, for example, Irving, 1992. Tomkins was the last composer to write directly under Byrd's influence.

38   The known facts of his life (1572-1656) are summarized in Grove, 1981, s.v. 'Tomkins'. Stevens, 1967, p. 27, suggests that Tomkins could have studied with Byrd only from 1594 to 1596.

39   Calendar of Philips' life (1560 or 1561-1628) in Steele, 1970, pp. xvi-xxi; modified by Smith, 1993, i, pp. 1-38.

40   'A famous musician William Byrd, who was the master of Peter Philips'. (Österreichisches Staatsarchiv, Vienna, Belgien PC 46.)

41   Peacham, 1622, p. 102.

42   Harley, 1992-94, ii, pp. 58-63; Smith, 1995.

43   Brown, 1969, i, pp. 43-44.

It is generally supposed that one of John Bull's teachers was John Blitheman, who in his will left forty shillings 'unto my felow John Bule'.[44] Blitheman's epitaph was once in St. Nicholas Olave, where he was buried, and stated that he

> A scholar left behind;
> John Bull, by name, his master's veyne
> Expressing in eche kynde.[45]

Bull's keyboard music makes this seem highly probable. Much of it is more strongly rooted in the organ style of the earlier sixteenth century than in developments pioneered by Byrd, and suggests a training on traditional lines such as could well have been given by Blitheman.[46] In a lecture delivered at Gresham College in 1597, however, Bull expressed not only his admiration for Byrd (who was evidently present) but sentiments which can be interpreted as acknowledging either the force of his example or instruction received from him.

> It is written, Right worshipful, that the Eagle onely soaring aloft unto the clouds, looketh with open eye upon the Sun: Such a quick sighted bird should now bee in this place who flying thro' heaven might fetch Apollo's harp and sound unto you the prayse of heavenlie Musick. My Master liueth and long [may he] lyve, and I his scholar not worthy in yours & his present to speak of this Art and Science.[47]

The pun on 'bird' is too obvious to be accidental, and Byrd made it himself in dedicating the first book of *Gradualia* to Henry Howard, the Earl of Northampton.

> *CYGNUM, aiunt, imminente iam morte, suaviùs canere. Huius ego* AVIS *suavitatem, in hac extrema aetate mea, Cantionibus istis, quas tibi dedicandus censui; ut ut assequi non potuerim, Illustrissime* Henrice: *ut ali quo saltem modo imitari conarer; duo habui non mediocria sive praesidia, sive incitamenta.*[48]

44   GL, MS 9171/1, f. 342ᵛ.

45   BL, Harleian MS 538. See also Stow, 1908 (ii, pp. 4, 357), where − apparently in error − Blitheman's Christian name is given as William.

46   Harley 1992-94, ii, pp. 47-48.

47   Bull, 1597. The transcription in King, 1959, of the faint off-print in mirror image, is a truly remarkable feat. The version above includes only two tiny amendments.

48   'They say the swan sings more sweetly when death is near. If, in my old age, that BIRD's sweetness has eluded me in these songs which I have decided ought to be

The author of a poem prefacing the second book of *Gradualia* made a similar pun:

> Those which of olde were skil'd in *Augurie*,
> By Flight, by Song, by Colour did devine...
> Loe heer's a *BYRDE* explaines the difference
> Twixt what hee shewes, and what they did inferre,
> And proves perspicuously that those did erre.

So did Worcester when, as Lord Herbert, he wrote to Lord Paget,[49] and so did Peacham in *The compleat gentleman*, where he called Byrd 'our Phoenix'.[50]

> For Motets, and Musicke of pietie and devotion, as well for the honour of our Nation, as the merit of the man, I preferre above all other our *Phoenix*, M. *William Byrd*, whom in that kind, I know not whether any man may equall. I am sure none excell, even by the judgement of *France* and *Italy*, who are very sparing in the commendation of strangers, in regard of that conceipt they hold of themselves. His *Cantiones Sacrae*, as also his *Gradualia*, are meere Angelicall and Divine; and being of himselfe naturally disposed to Gravitie and Pietie, his veine is not so much for light Madrigals or Canzonets, yet his *Virginalla*, and some others in his first set, cannot be mended by the best *Italian* of them all.

John Baldwin, the copyist of *My Ladye Nevells Booke*, devoted more than half his poem on famous musicians to praise of Byrd.[51] After

---

dedicated to you, most illustrious Henry, I have had two powerful defences or incentives in trying in some way to imitate it'.

49   See p. 50.

50   Peacham, 1622, p. 100. Another, briefer and more curious, list of England's 'excellent Musitians', including Byrd, is given by Francis Meres (1598, p. 288b). It has been suggested (Mateer, 1979, p. 287) that a version of the Byrd/bird pun may occur in John Sadler's music manuscripts, where a drawing of an owl appears with the legend 'I wyll not sing shut in a cage'. But there is no obvious connection with Byrd's music in the manuscripts, and it is difficult to explain why, in another instance, the owl should be accompanied by the words 'I am sycke for a mowse'. (Bodleian Library MSS Mus.e.1, f. 24ʳ, and Mus.e.3 f. 31ʳ.)

51   BL, MS R.M. 24.d.2, ff. iiᵛ-iiiʳ. The complete poem is printed in Andrews, 1926, pp. xx-xxiii; Hawkins, 1963, i, pp. 469-470; Boyd, 1962, pp. 310-312; and more accurately with regard to spelling in Brennecke, 1952. See also Bray, 1974.

including several foreigners in his list of the fifteen best composers, he went on:

> yet let not straingers bragg: nor they these soe commende:[52]
> for they maye now geve place: and sett them selves be hynd:
> an Englishe man, by name: willm̄ birde for his skill:
> w^c I should have set first: for soe it was my will:
> whose greate skill and knowledge: dothe excelle all at this tyme:
> and farre to strange countries: abroade his skill dothe shyne:
> famus men be abroade: and skilful in the arte:
> I do confesse the same: and will not from it starte:
> but in ewropp is none: like to our englishe man:
> w^c doth so farre exceede: as trulie I it scan:
> as ye cannot finde out: his equale in all thinges:
> throwghe out the worlde so wide: and so his fame now ringes:
> With fingers and with penne: hee hathe not now his peere:
> for in this world so wide: is none can him come neere:
> the rarest man hee is: in musicks worthy arte:
> that now on earthe doth live: I speake it from my harte:
> or heere to fore hathe bene: or after him shall come:
> none such I feare shall rise: that may be calde his sonne:
> O famus man of skill: and judgemente greate profounde:
> lett heaven and earth ringe out: thy worthye praise to sownde:
> ney lett thy skill it selfe: thy worthie fame recorde:
> to all posteritie: thy due deserte afforde:
> and lett them all which heere: of thy greate skill then saie:
> fare well fare well thou prince: of musicke now and aye:
> fare well I saie fare well: fare well and heere I end:
> fare well melodious birde: fare well sweete musicks frende:
> all these thinges doe I speake: not for rewarde or bribe:
> nor yet to flatter him: or sett him upp in pride:
> nor for affeccion: or owght might move there towe:
> but even the truth reporte: and that make knowne to yowe:
> Loe heere I end fare well: committinge all to god:
> who kepe us in his grace: and shilde us from his rodd:

There are other poetic tributes to Byrd. Robert Dow entered several in the manuscripts he copied in the 1580s.[53] Another was paid in the

---

52 Baldwin adds a decorative dash and dot after the colon at the end of each line.

53 Christ Church, Oxford, Mus. MSS 984-988; verses printed in Boyd, 1962, pp. 313-317.

eighteenth century. 'A Pindarick ODE, On Dr. Blow's *Excellency in the ART of* MUSIC. By *Mr.* HERBERT' says:

> Two great Improvers, Industry, and Time,
> To that Perfection rais'd, more than a Cent'ry since,
>   They yielded suich Fair, Golden, lasting Fruit,
>   As gain'd in *Rome* It Self, the best Repute ...

> Thus *Bird*, a *British Worthy*, spread his Name,
>   *And for his Country gain'd this early Fame.*[54]

The ode has a marginal reference to 'Bird's *Anthem in Golden Notes*'. This is the canon *Non nobis Domine*, to which Byrd's name somehow became attached, and which was believed to have been preserved in the Vatican Library.[55] If nothing else, the legend demonstrates the power of Byrd's name, but with the passage of time and changing tastes, his music fell into disuse. Manuscript copies indicate an interest in a few pieces of vocal music,[56] and John Barnard's *The first book of selected church musick* (1641) and William Boyce's *Cathedral music* (1760-73) in particular helped to ensure that a small number of works were widely available for the use of church choirs. For a time after Byrd's death, some of his keyboard pieces continued to circulate in manuscript. *Parthenia*, which was valued as a relatively accessible source of teaching material – though few pupils can have mastered all its contents – was reprinted in the 1640s and 1650s, but a change of taste had already been signalled by *Parthenia inviolata* (c.1625), which included none of Byrd's music. By the time Charles Burney wrote his *General history of music* (1776-89), Byrd's keyboard works appeared almost barbaric. Burney held the opinion that 'the loss, to refined ears, would not be very great, if [these old pieces] should for ever remain unplayed and undeciphered'.[57]

The story of the sad neglect of Byrd's music in the eighteenth century, and its rediscovery – falteringly at first – in the nineteenth, has been outlined by Turbet.[58] A prime event in the process of rehabilitation was the foundation in 1840 of the Musical Antiquarian Society, which published William Horsley's edition of the 1589

---

54   Blow, 1700, pp. vii-viii.

55   Hawkins, 1963, i, p. 468. The history of the piece is detailed by Brett, 1976, pp. viii-ix.

56   See Turbet, 1993(b), pp. 32-34; Thompson, 1996.

57   Burney, 1776-89, iii, p. 110 (1935 ed., ii, p. 96).

58   Turbet, 1993 (a).

Cantiones sacrae (1841) and Edward Rimbault's editions of the Mass for five voices (1841) and *Parthenia* (1847). In 1841 William Dyce founded the Motett Society, which set about issuing Rimbault's editions and adaptations of several of Byrd's motets and anthems. But it was the 'transmutation of antiquarianism into practicality that provides the genesis of the Byrd revival'.[59] The list of editors, publishers and performers who accomplished this is a long one, and the contribution they made has still to be recounted in the detail it deserves. Something of the excitement resulting from their efforts is conveyed by a notice in the *Musical Times* of 1891, from which it is clear that a performance of Byrd's four-part Mass at the Brompton Oratory struck the reviewer as a revelation.[60] The greatest achievement was Edmund H. Fellowes' edition in twenty volumes of *The collected works of William Byrd* (1937-50), and his book *William Byrd* (1936, second edition 1948). Though they can be seen to be flawed in the light of later scholarship, they are monuments to Fellowes' industry and his devotion to the composer.[61] The efforts of scholars of the nineteenth and early twentieth centuries created a foundation for the work of their successors in the second half of the century, notably Alan Brown's *Musica Britannica* edition of Byrd's keyboard works, and *The Byrd Edition*, which happily looks like being completed under its General Editor, Philip Brett.[62]

For most of this century Byrd has had a standing in English music equalled only by that of Purcell and Handel. What is it that gives Byrd this pre-eminence? Undoubtedly it is owing in part to the sheer quantity of his music, and the care he took to see that most of it was preserved in printed or manuscript copies for which he was responsible. A concern for what he wrote is an aspect of the self-criticism which led him perpetually to seek satisfaction in new and better solutions to problems of construction and technique. His attitude is never rigid. He tests the ideas of others in his own music, and usually manages to improve upon them. His attention to detail is matched by his large-scale planning. His longer works have an architectural distinction that results from an ability to visualize complete structures, and a technical assurance which enables him to work out details without jeopardizing the overall plan. If the qualities of Byrd's music had to be summed up in few words, they would include competence, invention, originality and unexpectedness. To these

---

59   Ibid., p. 125.

60   *Musical Times*, xxxii, 1891, p. 26.

61   An attempt to revise Fellowes' editions of Byrd's vocal music was begun in 1962 under the direction of Thurston Dart.

62   The preparation of this edition is the subject of Brett, 1980.

would be added sincerity, depth, and a controlled but profoundly experienced emotional content.

Byrd was well aware of the labour expended upon his works. His address, in *Psalmes, songs, and sonnets*, to 'all true lovers of *Musicke*' conveys his anxiety that they should be performed with care and that their merits should be appreciated.

> *Onely this I desire; that you will be but as carefull to heare them well expressed, as I have beene both in the Composing and correcting of them. Otherwise the best Song that ever was made will seeme harsh and unpleasant, for that the well expressing of them, either by Voyces, or Instruments, is the life of our labours, which is seldome or never well performed at the first singing or playing. Besides a song that is well and artificially made cannot be well perceived nor understood at the first hearing, but the oftner you shall heare it, the better cause of liking you will discover: and commonly that Song is best esteemed with which our eares are most acquainted. As I have done my best endeavour to give you content, so I beseech you satisfie my desire in hearing them well expressed: and then I doubt not, for* Art *and* Ayre *both of skilfull and ignorant they will deserve liking.* Vale.

Thine W. Byrd.

APPENDICES · BIBLIOGRAPHY · INDEXES

APPENDIX A

THE BYRD FAMILY

Pedigree of 1571

The Byrd family's genealogy was recorded by the Clarenceux King of Arms on 22 April 1571, and entered in 'The booke of the visitacion of the Citie and Suburbs of London taken by me Robert Cooke alias Clarencieulx kinge of armes of the Southe Easte and west partes of this Realme of England In anno doī. 1568 and In the tenthe yere of the reigne of owre sovereigne Ladie Quene Elizabethe'.[1] The discrepancy between the dates is easily explained. Mr P. Ll. Gwynn-Jones, Lancaster Herald, who has examined the 1568 Visitation of London at the College of Arms, says that 'The Byrd pedigree does not appear therein ... There is considerable evidence to suggest that Robert Cooke was preparing a later Visitation of London and was collating material which never reached full Visitation status thus entering the official records of the College of Arms. It would seem that the pedigree prepared by Cooke in 1571 of the Byrd family formed part of this material'.[2]

The record compiled by Cooke is as follows:

[*Arms: Sable, three stag's heads erased or, a canton ermine.*]

22 of April Aº 1571.

Richarde Birde of yenge at stone[3] in the cowntie of essex gentleman had issue
William Byrde of yenge at stonne sonne of Rychard had issue Thomas
Thomas Birde of London gent sonne of Wᵐ had issue John

---

1 The genealogy is on f. 72ᵛ of Queen's College, Oxford, MS 72, and was printed in London and Rawlins, 1963, pp. 73-74. See pl. 1.

2 Letter to the author. Mr Gwynn-Jones notes that 'Robert Cooke was a highly industrious Officer of Arms, but not always as painstaking as he might have been. His pedigrees are frequently found to be in error; and it seems that he accepted the word of the informer without checking the same or seeking corroborative evidence'.

3 Now Ingatestone. Some members of the the Byrd family who continued to live there in the sixteenth century left wills, though there is no indication that they retained any memory of their connection with the composer's branch of the family. The wills are at ERO, in the series D/ABW: nos. 3/219 (John Byrd, 1553), 4/345 (John, 1575), 6/82 (John, 1600), 7/93 (William 7/93).

John Birde of London gent sonne of Thomas maryd to his firste Wife Margery doughter of —[4] and by her had yssue Willm his sonne and heire and to his seconde Wife he maryd katheryn doughter of — by her hathe yssue John his seconde sonne Abbott of Boxeley[5] Thomas third sonne Robert forthe sonne & Rychard fifte sonne

Willm Birde of London gent[6] sonne and heire of John maryd — doughter of hunte and by her hathe issue Thomas his eldiste sonne John Bird of boxeley second Sonne[7]

Thomas Birde of London gent sonne and heire of W^m maryd Margery doughter of — and by her hathe issue Symon Birde of London sonne and heire John seconde Sonne, Willm third sonne maryd Julian doughter of Burley and hathe issue christopher the sayd thomas had issue Alis mar^d to W^m duffing Barbara mar^d to Robert broughe Mary mar^d first to Wm Ireland and after to Edward pryce martha maryd to philip Smythe.

Symond Birde of London gent Sonne and heire of Thomas maried Anne doughter of Brigges of London and by her hathe issue Mary his eldiste doughter is 2 yeres 9 moneths Martha second doughter is vi wekes old.

The parentage of Philip Smyth, William Byrd's brother-in-law, was also recorded in the course of the visitation:

Robert Smith of cossam[8] in the cowntie of wiltshire gent maried Agnes

---

4   Blank in the manuscript.

5   The younger John was the head of a Cistercian abbey. He is known to have flourished as the abbot of Boxley in Kent during the years after 1513 (Page, 1926, p. 155), and is therefore likely to have been born not later than about 1480. There is a difficulty in knowing exactly when John Byrd was abbot, since he was succeeded by a man with the same Christian name, John Dobbes, the last abbot of Boxley. It may be John Byrd to whom William Warham, Archbishop of Canterbury, referred in writing to Thomas Cromwell on 3 May 1524 that the abbot of Boxley was inclined to live precisely and bring the abbey out of debt. (Letters and papers, 1870, p. 127.) He may very well have been involved in the deception of the miraculous Rood of Grace, with the figure of Christ moved by a secret mechanism. (Lambarde, 1576, pp. 181-189; Letters and papers, 1892, p. 79. See also Cave-Browne, 1892, pp. 47-52, and Bridgett, 1888.) John Byrd apparently became vicar of Boxley in 1524. (Cave-Browne, p. 79-80.)

6   William was probably born no later than 1475. He must have retired to Boxley, where he died and was buried in 1540; see his will on p. 382. The extant Boxley parish register (at the Centre for Kentish Studies) starts at 1558.

7   An entry in the parish register shows that Alice, the wife of John Byrd, was buried at Boxley on 1 February 1560/1.

8   Corsham. The Smyth pedigrees are given in London and Rawlins, 1963, p. 80, and Squibb, 1954, pp. 180-182.

doughter of — and had yssue John Smyth first Sonne Phillip Smyth
seconde Sonne Maulde first maried to collymor after to Fowler

The 12 of February in A° 1571 Phillip Smyth of London gent second Sonne
to Robert maried Martha doughter of Thomas Byrde and by her had yssue
Thomas his sonne and here is i yere and vj moneths olde Elizabeth is ij
yers and vj moneths old

Pedigree of 1634

A further pedigree was drawn up during the visitation of Essex in 1634
by George Owen, York Herald, and Henry Lilly, Rouge Rose. The
original record is manuscript C 21 at the College of Arms. The version
printed in Metcalfe (1878-89, i, p. 366) was taken from copies.[9] One of
these, British Library Harleian manuscript 1542, carries the inscription
(f. 1*r): 'this was coppyed be ye original', and gives the pedigree set out
overleaf.

The Byrd arms

Mr Gwynn-Jones says: 'no reason is given for the grant nor for the
choice of charges. Nonetheless, the use of a canton in the 16th century
was found to be a convenient way of differencing Arms to which the
grantee was not properly entitled. If this is what was happening in this
instance, it infers that Symond Byrd may have made previous use of
three gold stags' heads on a black field. As I find no immediate trace of
any such Arms being used by a Mediaeval family, it may simply have
been a question of erroneous self-assumption by Symond Byrd or his
immediate forebears. Such erroneous usage was then brought to the
attention of Robert Cooke during his preparation of a London Visitation
and the matter was then rectified by a grant with an ermine canton'.

Mr Gwynn-Jones adds: 'I am conscious that many of Cooke's grants
have never found their way into the official records of the College of
Arms. He may have made something in the region of 100 new grants a
year, but his record keeping was not reliable.

'The above Arms are typical of a Cooke design. Some years ago, I
became conscious of four manuscripts which were prepared in Cooke's
office and which seemed to relate to grants or confirmations of Arms
made by him and his immediate predecessors. Many of these are not
listed in the official records of the College of Arms. I have therefore

9   ERO MS D/DQs 42 is a copy not listed by Metcalfe.

[Arms: Three stags' heads cabossed, a canton ermine] ex sigillo.[10]

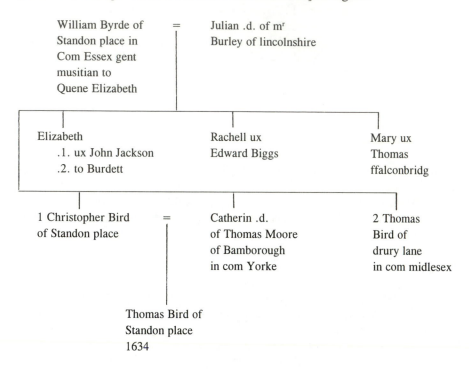

The Byrd pedigree of 1634 (Harleian MS 1542)

worked through these manuscripts and find an entry for Symond Byrd of London (College of Arms Ms Vincent 184 folio 309). The Arms in question may be blazoned as:-

Sable three stags' heads erased gold a canton ermine.

No crest was allowed.

'The inference is that a grant of Armorial Bearings was made by Robert Cooke to Symond Byrd in or about 1571. Unfortunately, there is

10   Cabossed' is the description used by Metcalfe, 1878; it means much the same as 'erased', used by London and Rawlins, 1963, i.e. separated from the body. The words 'ex sigillo' imply that for the record of the 1634 visitation the arms were taken from a seal. Could there be somewhere an unrecognized seal ring that belonged to the Byrd family? See the reference to a seal ring in John Byrd's will, p. 387.

no indication as to whether or not there was an extension of limitation to cover the brothers of Symond Byrd ... However, it is known that many Cooke grants had such an extension; and it is therefore likely that William Byrde being a person of substance would have been so comprehended.'

The earliest printed reference to the arms in question appears to be the one in Thomas Robson's *British Herald* (1830), where they are described as having a 'vert' field. Robson's source, in which the black field had apparently faded to green, presumably dated from before 1571 since there is no mention of a canton ermine. If the source was a monument that still exists, it will no doubt be recognized in due course. It may, on the other hand, have been in a London church which has been destroyed. Robson's description found its way into later volumes, e.g. Sir Bernard Burke's *General Armory* (1884). Fellowes must have consulted one of these, because he refers to a 'vert' field although the source he mentions (Metcalfe, 1878) does not give colours.

APPENDIX B

BYRD'S CHILDREN

It is not the purpose of this book to trace the history of the Byrd family beyond the composer's death, and the following notes are not the result of systematic research. Should anybody wish to investigate further there is undoubtedly more material, though no one descended directly from the composer is likely to bear the name Byrd.

Christopher Byrd's wife Katherine never remarried after his death. She continued to appear in assessment rolls for Stondon Massey,[1] and also in a list compiled about 1637 naming those taxed for ship money. This shows her to have been assessed at a level considerably above all but one of the other contributors in Stondon Massey. Mr Lathbury was assessed at £2. 0s. 0d, and Katherine Byrd at £1.10s. 0d. The next highest assessment was 15s., and others were 7s. 6d. or less.[2]

Katherine and her son Thomas continued to be fined for recusancy. In 1625 each suffered a fine of one hundred pounds, but such fines were often for offences committed over long periods and were cumulative, and may never have been collected.[3] She was listed as a recusant as late as 11 May 1638.[4]

Not long after William Byrd's death Stondon Place became the subject of a dispute in Chancery, in which Katherine and her son Thomas were opposed by her brother-in-law Thomas and her sister- and brother-in-law Rachel and Edward Biggs. This dragged on for more than ten years. Katherine argued that, as part of the arrangements surrounding the sale of Harlington manor and William Byrd's acquisition of Stondon Place, it was stated in writing that the latter should remain hers during her lifetime, and should then pass to her son Thomas and his heirs.[5] She claimed that the document prohibited John and Thomas Petre,[6] in whose

1   In a roll of 30 April 1629, unusually for a subsidy list, the word 'recusant' follows her name. (PRO, E179/112/617.)

2   PRO, SP16/358, p. 137; CSPD, 1868, pp. 177-178.

3   PRO, E377/57, mm. 18^r and 19^r.

4   Ibid., m. 26^v. Date read as 'Maij' by Campbell, 1959-65, though it is somewhat obscure. An assumption that Katherine was gaoled, repeated by J. G. O'Leary in *The Essex Recusant* (vii, 1965, p. 22), is due to a misinterpretation of the entry.

5   PRO, C3/334/3.

6   Thomas Petre of Cranham Hall (born at Ingatestone 1584, died 1625) was a son of Sir John Petre.

names Byrd bought Stondon Place, from disposing of it in any other manner. But, according to the account she placed before the court, after Christopher Byrd's death her father contrived a new arrangement in conjunction with the Petres, under which Stondon Place should be 'to the use' of her brother-in-law Thomas, and Rachel and Edward Biggs 'or of some other pson or psons to yor Orato^{res} unknown'.[7]

In Michaelmas term 1624 the elder Thomas, Rachel and Biggs struck back, and 'preferred their Bill of Complainte into this hon^{ble} Courte, against your Oratrix and Thomas Byrd her sonne to bee releaved against your Oratrix for two Annuityes or rentes [and charges of Twenty][8] pound*es* and Tenn pound*es* p ann and the arerages thereof'.[9] These were the sums Katherine was to pay under the terms of William Byrd's will.

In a submission dated 11 February 1627/8,[10] Katherine and her son reiterated their argument, asking that 'Thomas Petre the surviving ffeoffee[11] and the said Thomas Bird Edward Biggs and Rachell his wife and such other psons as did clayme anie interest in the said Stonden place and wood*es* and premisses ... be ordered to convey and assure the said Stonden place and premisses to yor Orato^{res} according to the true meaning of the said declara͡con of the said William Bird'.

The case continued at least until November 1635.[12]

Fellowes suggested that Elizabeth Byrd was the person described in Byrd's will as exhibiting 'undutifull obstinancie', because he thought she was unnamed in the will.[13] This was a slip of the pen. The daughter who did not receive a direct bequest was Rachel. Elizabeth is named, but in a way that indicates the unlikelihood of her ever having any children. She was fifty when the will was made.

Byrd's will anticipates that his son Thomas might attempt to contest it. It would not be in the least surprising if Thomas, as the younger son who was not scheduled to inherit the family estate, had reservations about Byrd's bequests. The will, probably made about 1619, when Thomas

---

7   This does not accord with Byrd's latest intention expressed in his will. See p. 394.

8   MS damaged.

9   PRO, C2/Charles I B105/16.

10   PRO, C2/Charles I B68/55.

11   But Thomas Petre had died in 1625.

12   PRO, C2/Charles I B105/16 is dated 1 June 1635. Entries in the court's books of orders and decrees arising from its consideration of the case in 1634 and 1635 are: C33/165, f. 747^v (25 June 1634); C33/167, ff. 481^r, 484^v, 527^r, 548^r, 663^v, 707^r, 727^r, 730^r, 751^{r-v}, 758^v, 776^v, 811^r; C33/169, f. 163^r (28 November 1635).

13   Fellowes, 1948, p. 31. Obstinacy seems to have been a trait of the Byrd family.

was forty-three, still allowed for the possibility that he might have heirs, but he was unmarried when the genealogy of 1634 was compiled.

In later life Thomas relied to a large extent on income from the farm at Stondon Massey. It was about this that Thomas submitted a petition in 1651 to the Committee on Compounding, claiming that he was seventy-five years old and had no other means.[14] The story is complicated, and really lies outside the scope of this book, but in brief it is this.

William Byrd's intention, expressed in his will, had been that the farm should pass to his daughter-in-law Katherine on certain conditions, one of which was that she should pay her brother-in-law Thomas an annual sum of twenty pounds. This was 'awarded unto him by the Arbitram[t] of one Samuell Symes'.[15] Thomas's complaint against Katherine for her failure to comply has been described above.

On 13 November 1634 the farm was let by the Byrd family to Thomas Warwick of Westminster 'for and in part security of a debt, owing by the said Thomas Bird the Elder'.[16] Warwick sublet the farm almost at once to Thomas Petre's son, Francis Petre of Cranham in Essex. Thomas Byrd's debt had been discharged by 12 April 1647, and he recovered his annuity. It was then paid until Francis Petre's property was sequestered on account of his recusancy. In 1651 the Committee for

14   Committee for Compounding, 1889-92, v, pp. 3284-3285 (giving references to the original documents); Howard and Burke, 1887, pp. 53-54. The Committee was also known as the Committee of Goldsmith's Hall, from the place where it frequently met.

15   Howard and Burke, 1887, p. 54.

16   Warwick may have been the keyboard player whom Robert Cecil employed around 1608-9. (Charteris, 1974, pp. 128, 130; Hulse, 1991, pp. 26, 31). Apart from Thomas Byrd's deputizing for Bull as Gresham lecturer, this is the only indication of his musical connections. Warwick married Elizabeth, a daughter of the Roman Catholic John Somerville of Edstone, Warwickshire, and a kinswoman of Sir Henry Goodyer. (Dictionary of National Biography, s.v. 'Somerville, John'; Historical Manuscripts Commission, 1976, p. 19, etc.) Goodyer was a friend of John Donne, who was in turn a friend of William Byrd's friends, the Herbert family. (See Donne's published letters to Goodyer.) Warwick succeeded Orlando Gibbons as organist of the Chapel Royal in 1625. (Rimbault, 1872, p. 11; Ashbee, 1986-96, iii, p. 7.) The Dean nevertheless forbade him to play verses because of his 'insufficiency' in 1629/30. (Rimbault, p. 78.) He was alive in 1650 but dead by 1660. (Ashbee, v, p. 25; i, p. 7.) He may at one time have held a post as Gentleman Usher to Queen Henrietta Maria. (Ashbee, v, p. xv.) The Thomas Warrock who became organist of Hereford Cathedral in succession to John Bull in 1586 (Shaw, 1991, pp. 133-134) seems to have been an older man, possibly the composer represented in the *Fitzwilliam Virginal Book*.

Compounding allowed Thomas's claim with arrears from 24 December 1649.[17] He was then described as living in Drury Lane, Westminster.

Mary Byrd's husband Henry Hawksworth appears to have been alive when Byrd's will was written. She was remarried, to Thomas Falconbridge, by the time the 1634 Visitation was made.

The younger Thomas Byrd, William Byrd's grandson, is shown in the 1634 genealogy as unmarried, like his uncle Thomas. He would have been in his forties when he (if it was he) supplied the information on which that genealogy was based. The last time Thomas was listed as a recusant in Stondon Massey appears to have been 11 May 1638.[18] It is to be assumed that the male line came to an end when Thomas died.

17   See Committee for Compounding, 1889-92, v, p. 3285, for the history of Stondon Place in the 1650s. The materials which Reeve gathered about Stondon Place after Byrd's death require fresh examination. (Reeve, 1902-11, and Reeve, 1906.) O'Leary (see note 4 above) attributed to 'PRO Recusant Rolls' the supposed statement of 1640 that 'Thomas Byrd late of Stondon, Gent, forfeits the Manor of Stondon Place', and said that the manor then reverted to the Crown. It has not proved possible to find any source for this, and doubt is cast on it by the inadequacy of the reference and the fact that Francis Petre's property was sequestered after 1640.

18   PRO, E377/57, m. 26^v.

APPENDIX C

WILLS

The will of William Byrd, the composer's grandfather[1]

In the name of god Amen / the xxvij daye of novemb̄ in the yere of o^r lorde god a m^{li} v^c xxxix / I willm̄ Byrde of the prish of boxlye in ye countye of Kent beinge of good Remēbrance & of hole mynde make cõstitute & ordeyne mye testament in man^r & fourme folowinge ffirst I cõmende & bequeth mye sowle to almightie god & mye bodye to be buryed in the churchard of boxlye aforesaid Also I bequeth at mye burieinge daye in funerall expens*es* vj^s viij^d Itm at mye trigintall[2] daye x^s to be bestowyd in massys dirig*es*[3] bredd & ale & other necessarye charg*es* The Resedewe of all mye moveable good*es* I bequeth to be devyded in thre pt*es* that is to saye one parte to mye wyffe And the ij other pt*es* to be equallye devydyd betwyne mye two Sonnys thom̄ byrd & John byrd mye[4] & legac*es* ffirst satisfied & payd / the which thom̄s byrd & John byrd I constitute & make myne executours. Witnesse Roger Johns vicar of boxlye John derbye & hugh holmys.

[Proved 4 October 1540 by Roger Johns, John Derbye, and John Byrd.]

The will of Thomas Tallis[5]

In the name of god amen. I Thomas Tallis of Est Greenwich in the County of Kente: one of the gentlemen of her Majesties Chappell beinge the xxth daye of August in the yeare of oure Lord 1583 whole in bodye of good and perfect memorye doe make and ordeine This my last will and Testament in mann*er* and fourme followinge. ffirst I bequeath my soule unto Allmightie god ou^r lorde and saviou^r Jesus Christ the only Redeemer of the worlde, and my bodye to be buried in the Churche of Saincte Alphe*ge* within the aforesaide Est Greenwich. and that there be given

---

1   Probate copy at the Centre for Kentish Studies: PRC 17/21, ff. 194^v-195^r.

2   Trental: a series of thirty masses.

3   The first antiphon in the first nocturn at Matins in the Roman Office for the Dead begins: 'Dirige, Domine Deus meus, in conspectu tuo viam meum'.

4   'dettes' omitted?

5   PRO, Prob. 10, box 115; probate copy: Prob. 11/68, from which the transcript in Buck, 1928, p. xxi, was made.

and distributed the day of my buriall to the poore people of the same pishe xl$^{s·}$ in mony or the value thereof in breade by the handes of those whome Joane my wieffe shall thinke good. Also I will that the said Joan mye wieffe doe give or cause to be given after my departure every ffrydaye duringe her Naturall lieffe sixe pen*ce* in mony or as much bread as it cometh to, to six poore people Besides that I give unto my Cosen John Sayer dwelling in the Ile of Thanett within the aforesaid County of Kent xl$^{s·}$ of good and lawfull mony of England. Lykewise I give unto Joane Pearc my wieffs sisters daughter xl$^{s·}$ Moreover I give & bequeathe to my company the gentlemen of her Ma$^{ties·}$ chappell towards their feast, iij$^{li·}$ vj$^{s·}$ viij$^{d·}$ ffurthermore I give and bequeath to Joane my wieffe my moyety for the printinge of musicall books, songs, and ruled paper duringe the Terme of the yeares to come, the which the Queenes Ma$^{tie·}$ gave joyntly betwene M$^{r·}$ Willm̄ Birde one of the gentlemen of her Ma$^{ties·}$ Chappell & mee. And if it soe happen the saide Joane my wieffe to depart this worlde before the expiraćon of the yeares I will that the saide moyetye duringe the yeares yett to come doe remayne to the use and proffitt of Thomas Bird my godson the sonne of the aforesaid Willm̄ Birde / Yf it please god to take to his mercy the saide Thomas Birde my godsonne before the yeares are fully ended I will that the saide moyety doe appertaigne wholye to the use and disposićon of the aforesaid Willm̄ Bird whilst the yeares doe laste. The Rest of all my good*es* my debt*es* being paid and funerall discharged I give fully and wholye moveables and removeables whatsoev*er* unto Joane my wieffe whom I ordeine and make my sole Executrix of this my laste will and Testament Also William Birde and Richard Cranwall[6] gentlemen of her Ma$^{ties·}$ chappel my overseers and for their paines taken herein, I give to eyther of them xx^{s} apeec*e* In wittnes whereof I have to this pnt*e* sett to my hand and seale the yeare and daye above written in the pnt*s* of theis parties whose names are heare subscribed

By me Thomas Tallis.

Also wheras I have given afore in my will to my Cozen John Sayer xl$^{s·}$ my will is the same be made iij$^{li·}$ vj$^{s·}$ viij$^{d·}$ And I will alsoe that Joane Pearc shall have the xl$^{s·}$ which I gave her in my will made also iij$^{li·}$ vj$^{s·}$ viij$^{d·}$ And also I will that my overseers shall have xx$^{s·}$ apeece more than is mentioned in my will / Sealed and deliv*er*ed as his last will in the

6 Also known as Granwall (apparently his own choice), Cranwell or Granwell. He was among the witnesses of Richard Farrant's will in 1580. (Copy in PRO, Prob. 11/63; printed by Honigmann and Brock, 1993, pp. 47-48.)

pr*esence* of us underwritten

By me Thomas ffryar
By me Willm̃ Birde.

[Proved 29 November 1585 by Joane Tallis.]

The will of Joane Tallis[7]

In the name of god amen the twelvethe of June in the nine and twentithe
yeare of the raigne of our soveraigne Ladye Elizabethe by the grace of
god of England ffraunce and Ireland queene defendor of the faiethe &c
And in the yeare of our Lorde god one thousand five hundred eightie
seaven I Joane Tallis of East Greenewiche in the Countie of Kent widowe
late wife to Thomas Tallis somtimes one of the gent of her majesties
chappell now deceased beinge at this present in good helthe and perfecte
memorie god be thanked for it and carryinge a mynde and purpose to
dispose of theis small thing*es* whiche god hathe lent me in this worlde so
that after my deathe no disquiet contention or dislyke may growe
amongest my kinsfolke and frendes in or aboute the same or any parte
therof and that every one maye accordinge to my intent and meaninge
quietly enjoye suche portion therof as I shall limitt and appoynte to him
or them doe make and ordeyne this my last will and testament in manner
and forme followinge ffirst in the dutie and profession of a christian I
humbly com̃end my sowle into the handes of almightie god creator
redeemer and comforter of the wholl worlde stedfastly hopinge throughe
the meritt*es* passian and pretius bludsheddinge of our Lord and saviour
Jhesus christ to be made partaker of eternall life and coheier withe him in
his fathers kingedome. Item I will that my bodye shall be buried in the
highe channcell of the churche of East Greenewiche aforesaide by the
bodye of my late husband Thomas Tallis deceased Item I give and
bequeathe to m͏ʳ Anthony Roper esquier one guilte bowle with the cover
therunto belonginge in respect of his good favors shewed to my late
husband and mee Item I give and bequeathe to William Bird one of the
gent of her majesties chappell one greate guilte cuppe withe the cover for
the same Item I give and bequeathe to Thomas Birde sonne to William
Birde aforesaide my husbandes godsonne thre silver spoones Item as well
for and in consideration of the great goodwill and frendshipp whiche

7   Probate copy: PRO, Prob. 11/74; previously transcribed by Buck, 1928, pp. xxii-
xxiv. There is a gap in the Prob. 10 series at this point, and the original will may no
longer exist.

was betwene my late husband deceased and Richard Granwall an other of the gentlemen of her majesties chappell as also for and in consideration of the continuall and tender care he hathe had of me ever synce my husbandes deathe I beinge then verye olde and unhable to take care for thing*es* my selfe whearin I have founde him to deale rather as a naturall childe towardes me then otherwise I give and bequeathe to him the saide Richard Granwall one cupp guilte withe the cover therunto belonginge and one guilte bowle ...[8]

Item I give and bequeathe fortie shilling*es* to be bestowed in bread and[9] to be distributed amongest the pore uppon the daye of my buriall by the discretion of my executors and overseers Item I give and bequeathe for dischardge of the churche duties twentie shilling*es* Item to be bestowed uppon a diñer for my neighbors and lovinge frendes uppon the daye of my buriall fortie shilling*es* Item I give to m^r William Birde m^r Richard Granwall and m^r Justice Greames my overseers xl^s a peece for their paines takeinge Item I give and bequeathe to the hospitall provided for the pore in Greenw^{ch} and the pore therin being x^s yearly for ever v^s therof to be paide out of the house I now dwell in and v^s out of the house whearin Thomas Palmer now dwellethe whiche Richard Granwall hathe of my gifte which house also I give and bequeathe to the saide Richarde his heiers and assignes for ever by this my Last will and testament[10] Item I give and bequeathe the rest of all my goodes moveables and immoveables herein before not bequeathed to my coozen[11] Joane Payre Item I give and bequeathe the house whiche I now dwell in wch I lately purchased of mr Lambert to the saide Joane Payer for and duringe her naturall life and after her decease to her son ffrannces and the heiers of his bodye lawfully begotten and for default of suche issue the remainder to Elizabethe daughter of the said Joane and the heiers of her bodye lawfully begotten and for default of such issue to the residue of the children of the saide Joane successively accordinge to their age and prioritie and to the heiers of their bodyes Lawfully begotten and for default of suche issue the remainder to the saide William Birde one of the gentlemen of her majesties chappell and his heiers and assignes for ever Item of this my Last will and testament I doe ordeyne constitute and appoynte my sayde cosen Joane Paire my sole executrix And overseers

8   The list of household goods which occurs at this point is printed on p. 53.

9   'to be bestowed in bread and' repeated.

10   When Granwall came to make his own will in February 1606/7 (copy in PRO, Prob. 11/109) he left all his houses and lands to his nephew 'Richarde Clarrke son of Willyam Clarrk late of London Taylor deceased'.

11   A term often applied to a niece.

therof they before named William Bird Richard Granwall and m^r Justice Greames Provided alwayes that if the saide Joane Payer my executrix of this my Last will and testament doe not within one monethe next after my deathe prove fulfill keepe and performe this my Last will[12] and testament in all poyntes accordinge to the tenor purport and trew meaninge hereof that then all the power libertie and authoritie unto her given as executrix by this my Last will and testament shall surcease and become utterly voyde and of none effect to all intent*es* and purposes and that then and from thenceforthe all and every Legacie and Legacies bequest and bequest*es* to her or her children or any of them by this my Last will and testament given or bequeathed shall remaine and be utterly frustrate thenceforthe the saide house wherein I now dwell shall remaine and be to the saide William Birde Richard Granwall and m^r Justice Greames their heiers and assignes to sell and dispose the same as they thinck good for the payment of my debts and Legacies accordinge to my appoyntment in this my Last will and testament whom also imediatly after suche defaulte made by my cosen Joane Paire as aforesaide I do appoynt make and ordeyne my executors of this my Last will and testament to see the same performed in all poynt*es* accordinge to the purporte trew meaninge and intent hereof In witnes whearof I the saide Joane Tallis to theis present*es* have sett to my hand and seale the daye and yeare first above written This is m̃ris Tallis marke Sealed and delivered as the last will and testament of the sayde m̃ris Tallis in presence of us Richard Granwall Thomas Palmer This is Richard Yeomans marke John Browne

[Proved 10 June 1589 by Joane Paier.]

The will of John Byrd, the composer's brother[13]

In the name of god amen: the Second daye of January in the yeare of our lord one Thousand six hundreth Twentye & one / I John Bird of London gent doe make this my last will & Testament in writing Revoking thereby both in deede & lawe, all former wills & Testam$^{ts.}$ ffirst I doe cõmend my soule into the hands of Almyghty god my maker hoping assuredly through the merytts of Jesus Christ my Saviour to be made p̱taker of life everlasting: And I doe cõmend my Body unto the earth whereof I was made: Itm̃ in what p̱ishe soever I dye: I give unto the p̱ish Church thereof xij^d Itm̃ I give unto the poore people of that p̱ishe six & Twenty Shillings & eight pence Itm̃ I give unto my Brother William Birdes

12   'will' repeated.
13   PRO, Prob. 10, box 389; probate copy: Prob. 11/139.

Children namely Thomas Elizabeth Mary & Rachell Birde Twenty pounds a peece: Itm̃ I doe give unto the five daughters of Martha Smith my sister deceased namely Elizabeth, Mary, Alice, Sara, & Judith, Twenty pounds apeece for ever: my Will is that my executor shall have the disposing of the said maryes porc̃on to her benifitt during her husbands life, and yf it happen that the said Mary doe dye before her husband, then my will is that her soñe & daughter shall have the said Twenty pounds betweene theym for ever: Itm̃ I give unto Mary ffarant my eldest Brothers daughter Twenty pounds Itm̃ I give unto William Cole Twenty pounds: Itm̃ I give unto Robt Chandler als Chantflower ffifteene pounds: Itm̃ I give unto Martha Camp my kinswoman tenn pounds: Itm̃ I give unto Thomas Campe my godsonne, tenn pounds Itm̃ I give unto John Bird my godson, soñe of Thomas Bird deceased tenn pounds And to my nephew John Bird upon condic̃on that he shall pay & make cleare with & to mine executor within six monethes nextafter my decease All such soñe or soñes of money as shall then happen to be Due by my said Nephew John Bird unto mine estate And likewise upon condic̃on that he do p̲cure his Brothers executor or executors to give a true account upon oath or oathes in the pᵣrogative court, for the true value that came to theyr hands in debts goods & money in the behalfe of his Brothers seaven Children being fatherless & motherless, And also to p̲cure sufficient security or mortgage of land to be taken for all such value, wᶜʰ by right & equity shalbe found due to them, or els to be removed into the hands of them that shall give the like security, And also to be p̲fected & done in my life time or within two yeares after my decease, Upon p̲formance of all which condic̃ons & not otherwise I give unto my said nephew John the soñe of one hundred pounds: Itm̃ I give unto Josiah Bird soñe of Symon Bird my nephew deceased fforty pounds and to Rebecca Bird his sister Twenty pounds to be paid her at the daye of her maryage or xxi yeares of age which first hapneth, And the foresaid soñe of fforty pounds to be paid to the said Josiah at his age of xxi yeares which said last recyted porc̃ons of Threescore pounds my will is that yf eyther the said Josiah or Rebecca doe dye beefore theyr Legacyes be paid then the survivor of them shall enjoye the said whole soñe of threescore pounds which said soñe of threescore pounds my will is to be disposed of to theyr best Com̃oditye & p̲fitt untill the time of the receipt thereof, at the discretion of my executor. Provided alwayes that yf the said Josiah Bird do recover (or any for him) his land in Lambeth or composition for it: then he shall give twenty of the said fforty pounds to his Sister Rebecca, which I give him. / Itm̃ I give unto William Ireland twentye pounds: Itm̃ I give unto Richard Bird sonne of John Bird my nephew my seall ring & unto his Sister Prudence my rubye ring: Itm̃ I give to Deborah Jones tenn pounds Itm̃ I give unto Robert

Blackwell towards the payment of his debts tenn pounds. Itm̃ I will that the tenn pounds which my nephew Phillip Smith hath in his hands & doth wrongfully detain from me, shall goe to the freeing of the estate of the children of the aforenamed Thomas Bird from the demand of one Rich /[14] Itm̃ I give unto Thomas Bird William Bird Symon Bird & Charles Bird tenn pounds a peece they being the sonnes of my nephew Thomas Bird Clerke deceased. / Itm̃ I give unyo my godsonne Roger Bridges being grandchild to Mr Willm̃ Rudstone deceased tenn pounds Itm̃ I give unto Mr Willm̃ Childe in Paules Churchyard tenn pounds All which Som̃es of money before named, my will is shalbe paid within six monethes after my decease (yf conveniently they may be.) Itm̃ I make & ordaine my loving Couzen Mr Willm̃ Campe my sole executor of this my last will & testam^t unto whom I give and bequeath all the rest of my goods & moneys whatsoever unbequeathed the Charges of my funerall & debts (yf any be) being first discharged: Also I intreat the said Willm̃ Child & Thomas Campe my godsonne to be overseers of this my last will & Testament: In witnes whereof I the said John Bird have hereuntoe set my hand & seall the daye & yeare first above written Last of all I doe give unto Hester the wife of my Couzen Sturges the som̃e of Twenty pounds to be disposed of by mine executor to her benifit during her husbands life Also I give unto her sister Mary the wife of my Cozen Spranger the som̃e of Twenty pounds. /

By me John Byrd

Signed sealed published &
declared in the psence of us
   Nicholas Wolleston
   William Ireland
   Willm̃ Tunnerdine

viij^vo die Januarii 1621

Memorand̃ that whereas I had given by my will within written unto Hester Sturges & Mary Spranger my kinswomen the som̃e of Twenty pounds a peece Now my will is that the said Hester & Marye shall have but tenn pounds apeece & that the said tenn pounds which the said Hester should have shalbe at the dispocõn of my said executor to her use as is

---

14   See p. 390, note 16. Sir Nathaniel Rich bought Stondon manor (distinct from Stondon Place) in 1610; the person named here may be one of his relations.

within mencõed.

By me John Byrd

Witnesses hereunto
    Thomas Purslowe
    Willm̃ Tunnerdine

xxiijth of January 1621

Md̃ that whereas I had given x^{li} to Roger Bridges by my Will, Now my Will is that the said Roger shall have but five pounds thereof, & thother v^{li} thereof I do give to m^{rs} Stannynought.

This is the marke of John Bird
Witnes Willm̃ Byrd

Wittnes
    Tho: Byrd
    Thomas Purslowe
    James Wynlow

[Proved 1 February 1621/2 by William Campe.]

Persons mentioned in the will of John Byrd

Witnesses are not legatees unless otherwise stated.

William Byrd, brother of the testator, witness to his will.
Thomas Byrd, son of the testator's brother William, witness to the will as well as legatee.
Elizabeth Byrd, daughter of the testator's brother William.
Mary Byrd, daughter of the testator's brother William.
Rachel Byrd, daughter of the testator's brother William.

Martha Smyth, née Byrd, the testator's dead sister.
Phillip Smyth, nephew of the testator, probably the son of Martha Smith.
Elizabeth Smyth, daughter of Martha Smyth.
Mary –, née Smyth, daughter of Martha Smyth.
Alice Smyth, daughter of Martha Smyth.
Sara Smyth, daughter of Martha Smyth.
Judith Smyth, daughter of Martha Smyth.

Unnamed son of Mary –, née Smyth.
Unnamed daughter of Mary –, née Smyth.

Mary Farrant, née Byrd, daughter of the testator's late brother Symond.
Roger Bridges, godson of the testator, perhaps a nephew of the testator's brother Symond, who married Anne Bridges.
William Rudstone, late grandfather of Roger Bridges.

William Ireland, the son of the testator's sister Mary by her first husband.

William Campe, the testator's cousin,[15] legatee and executor.
Martha Campe, the testator's kinswoman, probably the wife of his cousin William.
Thomas Campe, the testator's godson, probably the son of William and Martha.

Thomas Byrd, deceased clerk of Brightwell in Berkshire.
John Byrd, godson of the testator, son of Thomas Byrd of Brightwell.
Thomas Byrd, son of Thomas Byrd deceased.
William Byrd, son of Thomas Byrd deceased.
Symond Byrd, son of Thomas Byrd deceased.
Charles Byrd, son of Thomas Byrd deceased.
Seven children, possibly of Thomas Byrd and his wife, both deceased, if so including John, Thomas, William, Symond and Charles; their estate (in Lambeth?) not free, owing to the demand of 'one Rich'.[16]

William Cole, son of the late Hester Cole, née Byrd, the sister of the clerk Thomas Byrd.
Robert Chandler, *alias* Chantflower, the son of Hester, née Byrd, by her second marriage.

John Byrd, nephew of the testator, brother of Thomas Byrd deceased.
Richard Byrd, son of John Byrd the testator's nephew.
Prudence Byrd, daughter of John Byrd the testator's nephew.

Symond Byrd, late nephew of the testator, probably a brother of Thomas Byrd deceased.

15   'Cousin' and 'nephew' may denote kinship rather than a more precise relationship.
16   Court rolls in Lambeth Palace Library have not been examined for possible information about this.

Josiah Byrd, son of Symond Byrd the testator's nephew; apparently heir
    to the estate on which Rich made a demand.
Rebecca Byrd, daughter of Symond Byrd the testator's nephew; born
    after 1600.

– Sturges, the testator's cousin.
Hester Sturges, wife of the testator's cousin.
– Spranger, the testator's cousin.
Mary Spranger, sister of Hester Sturges and wife of – Spranger.

Deborah Jones.
Robert Blackwell.
William Child, dwelling in Paul's churchyard; probably not the future
    Gentleman of the Chapel, who was only about seventeen if the usually
    accepted date of his birth is correct.
Mistress Stanninate (Stannynought), in whose house the testator died.[17]
Nicholas Wolleston, witness to the will.
William Tunnerdine, witness to the will and first codicil.
Thomas Purslowe, witness to the codicils.
James Wynlow, witness to the second codicil.

The will of William Byrd[18]

In the name of the moste glorious and undevided Trinitye ffather sonne
holy Gost three distinct persons and one eternall God Amen / I William
Byrde of Stondon Place in the pish of Stondon in the Countye of Essex
gentleman doe nowe in the 80th yeare of myne age: but through y[e]
goodnes of God beeinge of good health and pfect memory make &
ordayne this for my last will & Testament: ffirst: I give & beequeth my
soule to God Almyghtye my Creattor & redemer and preserver: humblye
cravinge his grace and mercye for y[e] forgivenes of all my Synnes and
offences: past p[r]sent and to come. And y[t] I may live & dye: a true and
pfect member of his Holy Catholycke Church w[th]out w[ch] I beeleve theire
is noe Salvation for mee: my body to be honnestly buryed in that pish
and place: wheire it shall please God to take me oute of this lyve: w[ch] I
humbly desire: yf soe it shall please God maye bee in the pish of Stondon
wheire my dwellynge is: And then to be buried neare unto the place
where my wife lyest buryed: or eles where: as God and the tyme shall
pmytt & Suffer: And wheire I have beene longe desireous to setle my

17   GL, MS 590/1, f. 99[v]. The name is also found in the vicinity of Harlington.
18   PRO, Prob. 10, box 404; probate copy: Prob. 11/142.

poore estate in the ffearme of Stondon place accordinge to an awarde latlye made beetweene Catheren Byrde my daughter in law: & mee bee a verye good ffrend to hus bothe:[19] wch award wee bothe give our cristian pmisses to pforme: but havinge beene letted & hyndred theirein: by the undutifull obstinancie of one whome I am unwilling to name: do nowe ordayne & disposse of the same as followeth: ffirste the whole ffearme to remayne to my selfe & my assignes duringe my lyfe: and after my desscease: I give the same to my daughter in lawe m^ris. Catheren Byrd for hir life: uppon the condicõns folowinge vidz: to paye Twenty eight pounds fiftene shillinges & foure pence yearly to m^r Anthony Lutor or his assignes ffor the ffee fearme rent And to paye to m^ris Dawtrey of dedinghurst 15^s shillings yearly for the quitrent of Malepdus freehould: Allsoe to paye unto my sonne Thomas Byrde Twenty pounds yearly duringe his life: And to my doughter Rachell Ten pounds a yeare duringe her life And the same peaments to beegine at the next usiall ffeasts of peament after the day of my death: And after the disscease of my sayde daughter in law: m^ris Catheren Byrde & of the aforesayde lyffes: I give and beequeth the whole ffearme of stondon place to Thomas Byrde my granchild: sonne of Christofer Byrd my eldest sonne by the sayde Catheren: and to his heyres lawfully beegotten for ever: And for wante of suche heires: of the sayde Thomas Byrde sonne of ye sayde Christofer: I give the same ffearme of Stondon place to Thomas Byrde my sonne [and] to his heires lawfully beegotten: And for want of such heires: I give the Inheritance of the sayde ffearme to the foure sonnes of my daughter Mary Hawkesworth wiffe of Henrie Hawksworth gentleman as they are in age & Seniority vidz: ffirst to william Hawksworth & his heires lawfully beegotten and for want of such heires to Henrie Hawksworth his seconde brother & his heires lawfully beegotten & ffor want of such heires to George Hawksworth and his heires lawfully beegotten & for wante of such heires to John Hawksworth the fourth sonne of ye sayd marye hawksworth my daughter: And to his heires lawfullye begotten And for want of such heires of ye foure sonnes of Mary Hawksworth my daughter & her husband: To william hooke sonne unto Rachell Hooke my daughter and to his heires lawfully beegotten and for want of such heires: To the right heires of mee the said william Byrde for ever: It I give and bequeeth to my daughter in law m^ris Catheren Byrde & her sonne Thomas Byrde all my goods moveables and unmoveables at stondon place And alsoe all the woodes and Tymber trees wheiresoever they are groinge in & upon ye sayde ffearme: upon

19   The award probably arose from Katherine's misgivings about her entitlements under the arrangement which replaced the settlement of Harlington manor upon her at the time of her marriage. The good friend may have been Samuel Symes. See p. 380.

this condicõn only to see mee honestly buryed and my debts truly discharged to wch end & porposse: I doe make & ordayne Catheren Byrde my sayde daughter in law and Thomas Byrde her sonne whole executors of this my last will & Testament: It I give & bequeth unto my sonne Thomas Byrd all my goods in my lodginge²⁰ in the Earle of wosters howse in the straund:²¹ And wheire I purchassed a ppetuall anuytye or rent charge of 20^li a yeare of S^r ffrauncis ffortescue knight unto 200^li bee payde wch anuyty I have given to Elizabeth Burdet my eldest doughter for her lyfe: I doe now declare how it shall bee dispossed of after my sayde daughters desscease first yf my sayde sonne Thomas Byrde concurr wth this my last will & Testament & except of his Anuyty accordinge to ye same: Then I give the one halfe of y^t Anuyty beeinge Ten pounds a yeare ore one hundreth pound yf it bee payde in: to the sayde Thomas Byrd his heires executors and assignes And the other halfe of y^t anuyty I give & beequeth to Michaell walton wth marriage of his wiffe Catheren hooke my granchilde for her mariage portion Allwayes pvided y^t yf my sonne Thomas Bird do seeke by lawe or other wayes to disturb or troble my executors & not agree to ye same: Then I doe heireby declare That my will & intention is: That the sayde Thomas Byrde my sonne shall have noe parte of the sayde Annyty: but I doe heireby give y^t part of ye anuyty That I had given to my sonne Thomas Byrd: to Thomas Byrd my granchild to hym and his heires for ever And havinge now by the leave of god ffinished this my last will accordinge to the trew meaninge of the sayd awarde & our christian pmisses: I doe nowe by this my last will & Testament utterly revocke & annull all former grants writtings & wills as far as in mee lyeth whatsoever is contrary to this my last will & Testament: In wittnes wheirof I the sayd william Byrd have sett my hand & seale the ffifteenth day of November in the yeares of ye reigene of oure sov^ragne lord James by the grace of God Kinge of England ffraunce & Ireland the Twenteth and of Scotland ffiftie six defender of the fayth re: 1622:

By me Willym Byrde

Sealed & delivered in the psents of
 Han^y Hawksworth:

[Proved 30 October 1623 by Thomas and Katherine Byrd.]

20   End of leafe: signed 'By me Wyllm Byrd'.
21   If Thomas Byrd already had lodgings in Drury Lane (there is no sign in the parish books that he was a householder), he lived not far from the Earl of Worcester's house.

Provisions of Byrd's will

Byrd's intention was that his farm should pass first to his daughter-in-law Katherine, the widow of his eldest son, on the conditions that she should pay certain annual rents to Anthony Luther and Mrs Dawtrey, and should pay her brother-in-law Thomas and sister-in-law Rachel annual sums of twenty and ten pounds respectively. On her death it was to pass to her son Thomas and his heirs. If they died without heirs, the next in line were to be Byrd's second son, Thomas, and his heirs, followed by Byrd's younger daughter Mary and her heirs in order of seniority, and then Rachel's son and his heirs. The will was framed in the expectation that Byrd's eldest daughter Elizabeth would have no children.

The contents of Stondon Place, with the woods and timber trees growing on the farm (a valuable resource then as now), were left to Katherine and her son Thomas, provided they saw the testator honestly buried and his debts discharged. Byrd's belongings at the Earl of Worcester's house in the Strand went to his son Thomas.

Byrd had purchased an annuity from Sir Francis Fortescue. This was to go to Byrd's daughter Elizabeth. After her death half of it was to go to Byrd's son Thomas, and so to his heirs; but, if Thomas sought to upset the provisions of the will, his half would go to Byrd's grandson Thomas. The other half was to go to Michael Walton when he married Byrd's granddaughter Katherine Hooke, as her marriage portion.

The will of Thomas Byrd, Gentleman of the Chapel Royal[22]

In the Name of God Amen The xxi^{ti} daye of ffebruary in the yere of o^r Lord god 1560 I Thomas Byrd of Westm^r wthin the countie of Middelsex Jent beinge sick in bodye but thankes be unto almightie god of good and pfect remembrance doo make and ordeyne this my laste will and testament in manner and forme as followeth ffyrste I bequethe my sowle to almightie god my maker and redemer and my bodie to [be] buryed wthin the pishe churche of Ste Margarett in Westm^r aforsaid, Item I give & bequethe to the poore folkes cheste wthin the saide churche v^s· Item I give & bequethe to the poore people to be distributyd to them at the daie

22   Copy at Westminster Archives Centre, Accession 120, 188 Bracy, ff. 188^r-188^v, located by Dr Fiona Kisby. Another partial copy, ending with the words 'whatsoever they be' is at ff. 162^v-163^r of the same volume. Concerning the Commissary Court of Westminster, where the will was proved, see the introduction to Westminster Commissary Court, 1864.

of my buriall v^s· Item I give & bequethe to John Byrde my base sonne a table of Walnuttre wth a frame & fetherbed a boulster & pilloughe a pare of Blankett*es* and a coveringe of Irishe rugg*es* and my gowne of blacke wth a ffrynge faced wth taffata and lyned wth cottin a dublett of redd satten and fyve pounde in reddie monie, all the residue of my good*es* whatsoev^r they be after my dett*es* payd and my funeralle discharged I give and bequeth them to Johan Byrde my wief whome I make my sole executrix and I make myne overseers to see this my laste will and testame*nt* pformed fulfilled and kepte Richard Gibbes & Richard Garrett[23] and I give to every of them for theyre paynes x^s· a pece, In wytnes whereof I the said Thomas Byrde have caused this my Laste will & Testament to be wrytten & have sette my hand the daye and yere abovsaid in the presence of Christoffer Cosyn Henry Stilt and Nicholas Poole.[24]

By me Thomas Byrd.

[Will proved 18 March 1560.]

Thomas Byrd was buried at St Margaret's, Westminster, on 10 March 1560/1. (Westminster Abbey Muniment Room, registers of St Margaret's church; Burke, 1914.) Section 42 of the churchwardens' accounts for St Margaret's, 25 May 1560 to 9 May 1562, lists payments made for his grave, for the ringing of bells, and for 'herse clothes'.[25]

23   Payments by Gibbes and Garrett are listed in the parish Overseers' accounts. (Westminster Archives Centre).

24   Nicholas Poole was connected with the parish of St Margaret's; his name appears in the churchwarden's accounts (Westminster Archives Centre). Could Christopher Cosyn have been connected with the musicians John and Benjamin Cosyn?

25   Westminster Archives Centre, E4.

APPENDIX D

BYRD'S HANDWRITING

There are enough examples of Byrd's writing to enable some development to be discerned. His signature at Lincoln was upright and a little stiff, with flourishes added to the tops of *l*, *b*, and *d*. In a signature of 1567, written 'Wyllyam byrde' and too deliberately ornate, the flourishes added to *y, l, b* and *d* are carried to extremes.[1]

By 1580 Byrd had adopted a flowing, Italianate hand, better suited to writing at speed. This is the hand of the Battyshall and Tempest documents.[2] It is also the hand that enables a deposition made to the Court of Star Chamber in 1598 and a draft letter of 1603/4 to be identified as Byrd's.[3] His signatures of this period have similar characteristics. In addition to those of the deposition and the Tempest documents there is one added to Tallis's will, one in the books of decrees and orders of the Court of Exchequer,[4] and others added to a statement made in 1597/8 during Sir Edward Coke's enquiry into the running of the Fleet prison.[5]

The letter written to Lord Paget on 28 June 1573, and signed 'Willm̃ Byrde', must thus represent a transitional stage in the development of the composer's handwriting.[6] It has characteristics in common with later letters written by Byrd. The formation of the capitals 'A' and 'L', and the tail of 'y' are cases in point, though these features occur also in other hands of the period and cannot alone be accepted as conclusive of authorship.[7] The punctuation, which closely resembles that of Byrd's known letters, provides supporting evidence. Furthermore, the way in which the pen has been used and the ink applied betrays Byrd's hand.

The signature Byrd added to his brother John's will is essentially the same as that in the Tempest letters. It was only in signing his own will that his hand betrayed signs of age and weakness.[8]

1   LA, D&C Bi/2/1, in the 'liveries' section of the third part. See pl. 2a.

2   See pp. 54, 82, 90; pl. 4.

3   PRO, STAC5/B27/37 and SP15/36/5. See pp. 119, 140; pl. 6.

4   PRO, E126/1, f. 119^v (f. 128^v in modern numbering).

5   PRO, STAC5/A14/23.

6   See p. 47; pl. 3.

7   Similar characteristics can for example be found in a letter of 19 November 1581 from Herbert to Paget. (SRO, D603/K/1/7/41, photo-copied from the original at Keele University: see p. 46, note 26.)

8   Pl. 8a.

APPENDIX E

WILLIAM BYRD AND ST PAUL'S

Rimbault wrote that William Byrd was the senior chorister of St Paul's in 1554, 'when his name occurs at the head of the school in a petition for the resoration of certain obits and benefactions which had been seized under the Act for the Suppression of Colleges and Hospitals in the preceding reign. This petition, which is preserved among the records of the Exchequer (Michaelmas Term, 1 and 2 Philip and Mary), was granted and confirmed by letters patent, 14 Eliz. (see Dugdale's St. Paul's, edit. Ellis), and the payments are still received by the Almoner'.[1]

Some of Rimbault's biographical notes on William Byrd are clearly wrong. He thought, for example, that it was Byrd's son Thomas who married Katherine Moore, and he confused the composer with William Byrd of the the parish of St Helen's, Bishopsgate.

Rimbault's errors are due in part to his reliance on what others told him. 'For this and other valuable information', he wrote, 'I am indebted to the kindness of Miss Hackett, of Crosby Hall'.[2] Squire (1883) was quite scathing about this: 'On what was apparently merely a verbal statement by a certain Miss Hackett, of Crosby Hall, we are informed that Byrd lived in the parish of St. Helen's opposite Crosby Hall, and adjoining Sir Thomas Gresham's'. Maria Hackett seems to have known (or assumed) that one of Byrd's sons married a descendant of Sir Thomas More, and to have been led by Crosby Hall's connection with More to believe that the William Byrd who lived nearby was the composer.[3] He was in fact a different person, and is listed in the parish register as the father of Alice Byrd who was buried in 1587.[4]

It is quite possible that Rimbault never saw the document which he believed named William Byrd as head chorister. If, relying on second-hand oral information, he managed to confuse Christopher Byrd with Thomas Byrd it is likely that he also confused William Byrd with Symond or John Byrd.

1   Byrd, 1841, introduction; repeated in Rimbault, 1872, p. 189.

2   Byrd, 1841, introduction.

3   See Stowe, 1908, ii, pp. 299-300.

4   Bannerman, 1908, p. 255. It is probably this William Byrd who is listed as living in St Helen's parish in a list of citizens bound into Queen's College, Oxford, MS 72. A certificate of residence for 'Willm Burde of London esquyer' of St Helen's Bishopsgate is dated 2 December 1589. (PRO, E115/25/88.)

The account given by Hackett in *Correspondence and evidences respecting the ancient collegiate school attached to Saint Paul's Cathedral* (1832)[5] is as follows:

> (p. xlvii) When the revenues granted for the maintenance of Chantries and obits were seized by Henry VIII and Edward VI the Dean and Chapter were permitted to retain most of the Estates left to them for those purposes.

> (pp. l-li) Ten choristers appeared by Attorney to assert their claim to the obit money in the reign of Mary; and these payments were confirmed to ten choristers by the letters Patent of Elizabeth.

> (p. xlviii) When the Choir preferred their petition to the Throne for the restoration of these ancient benefactions, Sebastian Westcott, then Master of the Boys, appeared only in the character of Attorney for the Choristers, who are mentioned by name - see Records of the Exchequer, Mich. Term 1 & 2 Phil. and Mary.

Rimbault's words echo Hackett's very closely, though even she may not have seen the original documents, but relied on the work of Ralph Churton or John Pridden, both of whom had carried out research into the history of St Paul's.[6] The document Rimbault referred to, whether he and Hackett saw it or not, was probably among those in a set of memoranda of 1554-1555 (1 and 2 Philip and Mary), with the PRO number E159/334. These were known to Byrd's early biographers,[7] and the documents concerning St Paul's answer to the description given by Hackett. The memorandum that forms membrane 232 of the set explains the history of 'certeyn yerly rent[es] annuities and pencions' which the 'wardens and petycanons of the said churche tyme out [of] mynde have had and enjoed and of ryght ought to have and enjoye'. It says they 'have not ben paide the saide rent[es] annuities or pencions or any parte thereof for whych cause they have exhibited ther humble byll of

5   It should be noted that Maria Hackett's publications were often revised, in print and in manuscript, and bound together to form differing composite volumes in which one part of a work may be separated from another.

6   Churton wrote a life of Alexander Nowell, Dean of St Paul's (published 1809), to which Hackett refers on pp. 10 and 17. St Paul's Cathedral Library MS 51.D.6, 'Extracts from the statute-book belonging to the Dean & Chapter of St. Paul's Cathedral ... Collected by me John Pridden ... 1784', includes (ii, p. [157]ff) transcripts of letters written by Hackett in 1811-12 on the subject of cathedral choristers. Hackett sometimes drew on the same sources as Pridden, from whom she probably obtained transcripts.

7   Fuller Maitland (DNB) and Fellowes probably drew on Squire, 1883.

complaynt to the kyng[es] majesties moste hoñable counsell'. It was ordered that 'all tharrerage' should be paid from Easter in the second year of the reign, and that 'thys decre shalbe to the Treasourer of the said courte for the tyme beyng a sufficient Warrant and Discharge in that behalf'.

Membranes 238 and 262 deal (in Latin) with parallel problems experienced by the lay vicars and choristers, whose names are given. In conventionalized spelling they are:

vicars: Sebastian Westcote, Philip ap Rhys, Robert Saye, Thomas Martin, John More, Robert Bale

choristers: John Byrd, Symond Byrd, Richard Hughes, George More, John Alcock, Gilbert Moxsey, Roger Stackhouse, Richard Prince, John Farmer, Robert Chofe. Westcote is referred to as their attorney.[8]

These names appear subsequently in the rough books of payments formerly made by the Court of Augmentations.[9] It may be that John Byrd's position in the lists of choristers, which parallels Westcote's position in the lists of vicars choral, implies that he was the head chorister, but there is nothing else to suggest this.

How up to date the lists were is debateable, since it is clear that one list was copied from another. 'Chofe' was turned into 'Chosed' because the scribe confused 'f' and long 's', and assimilated part of the following word 'de' into the name. Philip ap Rhys became 'John', and Hughes was transformed from 'Hewse' into 'Howse'. Robert Saye became 'Roger'.

---

8   McDonnell, 1977, p. 35-36, includes the choristers among the pupils of St Paul's School, on the grounds of the close association between the choir and the school. He notes that John Farmer was probably the musician who later dedicated two books to Edward de Vere, the Earl of Oxford, whose cousin Francis was a pupil of St Paul's; that Roger Stackhouse may have matriculated as a sizar of Queens' College, Cambridge, in 1558; that George More may have been the son of John More, vicar choral; and that Richard Hughes may have become the father of a chorister of the same name who benefited under Westcote's will.

9   See p. 15. E405/508 (Easter, 3 & 4 Ph. and Mary) does not list the vicars and choristers, but the entry for St Paul's is signed 'Sebastyan Westcote' in acknowledgement of payment. A similar list of lay vicars is given by Pridden (St Paul's Cathedral Library MS 51.D.6, ii, p. [197]), whose notes record that 'A.D. 1554 3 & 4 Phil. & Mary. Nov: 18. John Fecknam Dean of Saint Pauls, with the Chapter let a Lease to Sebastian Westcote, Philip Apprice, Robert Say, Thomas Martin, Robert Ball, and John Moore, the 6 Lay Vicars of the Messuage by the name of Curlewes house adjoining to the Mansion house of the Penitentiarye for 99 years lying at the west end of Saint Pauls'.

These variations are of a different kind from the diverse spellings usual in Tudor documents. Examples of the latter can be found in the single membrane 238. Philip ap Rhys is 'P͠hus a pryce', 'P͠ho Apryce' and 'Philipps apryce', and Thomas Martin is 'Thomas mertyn' and 'Thome martyn'. John Farmer is both 'ffarmer' and 'ffarmar'. Numerous similar variations occur throughout the rough books.

The practice of copying from list to list is evident in the record of the visitation of St Paul's by Bishop Edmund Grindall in 1561. The scribe at first started the list of choristers (whose number had been reduced to nine) with John Alcock ('Halcocke') and Richard Prince, but crossed them out and wrote the names of John Reynolds, Anthony Pickering, William Fox, Richard Pridda[m?], Samuel Bush, Rufus Boker, Thomas Wilkinson, John Marshall and John Whalye. A revised list of vicars choral includes Sebstian Westcote, Philip ap Rhys, Robert Saye, Robert Grove, Thomas Wilder and William Mundy.[10]

---

10   GL, MS 9537/2, f. 17ᵛ. The lists are repeated on f. 19ᵛ without the names of Alcocke and Prince. The signatures of 'philip apryce' and 'willm̃ mundye' are among those of clergy and schoolmasters who (in 1559?) subscribed to the Act of Uniformity. (Lambeth Palace Library, Carte Antique et Miscellanee, XIII.57, f. 1ʳ.)

APPENDIX F

BYRD'S PORTRAIT

The only known representation of Byrd is an eighteenth-century engraving, in which he appears with Tallis. The plate is signed 'N. Haym delin. G. VanderGucht fecit'. Nicola Francesco Haym (1678-1729) included drawing among his many talents,[1] and in 1719-29 published a catalogue of Greek and Roman coins and medals in British collections, with his own illustrations. VanderGucht, an obscure figure about whom little has been written, presumably made his engraving from a drawing by Haym, reversing it in the process. Tallis is depicted as left-handed, and the music he is holding seems to have clef signs at the right-hand edge of the page.

No original has been found for either of the 'portraits'. They may have been purely fanciful, and engraved to meet a need that could not be filled by genuine portraits.[2] Some doubt lingers about this, because Haym was a collector of paintings and engravings, not only on his own account but on behalf of the second Duke of Bedford, and Sir Richard Walpole and others. It seems credible that he had access to pictures of Byrd and Tallis which have since been lost. A much less prominent musician, Thomas Whythorne, had his portrait painted four times,[3] and it might be expected that at least one portrait of Byrd would have been preserved by his descendants or in the collection of a noble friend. Nevertheless, until this is discovered, the authenticity of Haym's portrayal must be regarded with scepticism. The one thing that is certain about it is that it conveys no sense of the personality that emerges from either Byrd's music or the documents concerning his life.

1   Haym was born in Rome, but arrived in England in 1700 or 1701, where he was employed by the second Duke of Bedford. He was a cellist, literary editor, librettist, composer and antiquarian. See Grove, 1980, s.v. 'Haym, Nicola Francesco'.

2   There seems to be no solid evidence for the statement that they were engraved for a projected history of music by Haym. (Fellowes, 1948, p. 30.) It seems more likely that the engraving was made for the collectors supplied by Haym.

3   Whythorne, 1961, pp. 305-306. It would be no surprise to find that Byrd's portrait, like the picture of Whythorne painted in 1569 (ibid., frontispiece), bore his family's arms and his age.

APPENDIX G

MY LADYE NEVELLS BOOKE

My Ladye Nevells Booke is a manuscript devoted to keyboard music by William Byrd. It was compiled, probably under the composer's direction, by John Baldwin, who added a note to show that he completed the task in September 1591.[1]

The Lady Nevell for whom the book was intended has never been firmly identified. A glance at the genealogical tables printed by Rowland (1830) and Drummond (1846) is enough to show how wide the field is. Writing of Frances, the daughter of Thomas Manners, Earl of Rutland, who married into the Neville family, Drummond said: 'There is ... in the Earl of Abergavenny's possession a Book of Music which belonged to her'.[2] This is obviously impossible, since he adds: 'She died 1576'. Fellowes thought that Lady Nevell might have been Rachel, the wife of the younger Sir Edward Nevell, and that Byrd's daughter Rachel might have been named after her.[3] A later and more attractive theory favours Elizabeth, the wife of Sir Henry Nevell of Billinbear in Berkshire.[4] This, however, is inspired partly by the insertion in the book of a coat of arms once represented in a window at Billingbear House. As the arms were added at a late stage, they may be a red herring as far as the identity of the original owner is concerned. The Neville family had many branches, offering other candidates. One is Jane, the wife of Charles Neville, Earl of Westmorland (b. 1541 or 1543).[5] He was involved in plots on behalf of Mary, Queen of Scots, was attainted in 1571 and fled to Flanders, dying abroad in 1584. Jane was the daughter of Henry Howard, Earl of Surrey, who was attainted in 1546. Her mother was Frances, the daughter of John de Vere, fifteenth Earl of Oxford. Jane seems to have remained in England, where she died in 1593. She was buried in Kenninghall church, Norfolk.[6] Byrd was acquainted with members of both the Howard and Vere families, and while it cannot be asserted that it was Jane for whom *My Ladye Nevells Booke* was compiled, it would

1 Baldwin was at the time a lay clerk of St George's Chapel, Windsor. See p. 243, note 2.

2 Drummond, 1846, ii, 'Neville' section, p. 19.

3 Fellowes, 1948, pp. 14-16; Fellowes, 1949. See also Ford, 1979. The note transcribed on p. 403 suggests that the book was at one time in Sir Edward's possession.

4 Dart, 1964; Brown, 1968-69, pp. 29-30; Brown, 1969, i, pp. 33-40.

5 See p. 129, note 89, concerning a document among the Westmorland papers.

6 Rowland, 1830, pp. 48-49.

be risky to associate either Rachel or Elizabeth with it until more reliable information is forthcoming.

A clue to Lady Nevell's identity may be hidden in Byrd's original plan for the book, which apparently became distorted in the course of copying. If the structure of the *Cantiones sacrae* (1575) emphasized the number seventeen as a graceful compliment to Queen Elizabeth,[7] it may be that the originally intended division of *My Ladye Nevells Booke* into three sections containing nine pieces each also conveyed some meaning to those in the know.[8]

Part of the history of the book is recorded, anecdotally, in a manuscript note[9] glued to a blank leaf that follows the coat of arms:

This Book was presented to Queene Elizabeth by my Lord Edward Abergavennye Caled the Deafe, the queene ordered one s^r or m^r North one of her servants, to keepe it, who left it his son, who gave it m^r Haughton Atturny of Cliffords Inn, & .^{he} last somer 1668 gave it to me; this m^r North as I remember m^r haughton saide, was uncle to the last Ld North

N Bergevenny

The subsequent history of the book, including its ownership by Charles Burney and its reacquisition at some time between 1826 and 1833 by the Lord Abergavenny of the day, has been traced by Andrews and Fellowes.

As far as is known, *My Ladye Nevells Booke* has been exhibited publicly only once, at the Music Loan Exhibition in 1904.[10] It was loaned to Fellowes in 1947, to assist him in his work of preparing an edition of Byrd's keyboard music, but in order to avoid wear and tear permission to inspect it is nowadays given infrequently. The Marquess of Abergavenny has very kindly granted the author the rare privilege (rare in both senses) of examining the manuscript, enabling previous descriptions of it to be amplified.[11]

7   See p. 216.

8   See pp. 216, 243.

9   Reproduced by Fellowes (1949), who was unable to identify the writer and conjectured that his initial might have been an 'M', the last stroke of which became merged with the 'B' of 'Bergavenny'.

10   Reported in a cutting from the *Musical News*, 23 July 1904, enclosed loose in *My Ladye Nevells Booke*. See also Musicians' Company, 1909.

11   Fellowes, 1949; Andrews, 1926. There is a microfilm in the Pendlebury Library, Cambridge, which may be consulted with the permission of the Marquess of Abergavenny.

The book is an oblong volume bound in brown calf. The front and back boards are approximately 28 cm wide and 20.5 cm tall. The gold-tooling on both covers is typical of English bindings of the late sixteenth century. It consists of a ruled frame, with scroll-work inside each corner. In the centre is a strapwork design enclosing a blank oval. The words 'MY LADYE NEVELLS BOOKE' are enclosed by horizontal rules running between the designs in the top corners, the upper rule being about 1.5 cm below the inner edge of the frame. The remaining space is filled with rows of small ornaments made up of four dots.[12] The spine was replaced during repairs carried out in the nineteenth century.[13] The edges of the book were originally gilded, though they are now very much faded, and carry blind curlicued designs.

The leaves of the book measure approximately 27.5 cm by 19.5 cm. The music is written on ninety-six sheets of paper, foliated from 1 to 192, and apparently in gatherings of eight sheets (sixteen leaves).[14] Baldwin must have obtained the paper in these gatherings, or made them himself, since he writes continuously throughout each gathering and runs on from the end of one to the beginning of the next.

The music paper bears a watermark consisting of the letter B in outline, within a shield surmounted by a crown. It seems not to be precisely identifiable with any described by Briquet, but is related to a number of foreign marks which he illustrates.[15] Only the top half of the watermark appears, inverted at the top edge of leaves and at irregular intervals. Presumably the original sheets of paper were cut to provide leaves of the required size.

The music is followed by a table of contents. This forms part of the original volume but is written on a sheet of different paper, which has also been reduced in size and folded to give two leaves. It bears at the top edge part of a watermark that may be one of the many 'bunch of grapes' designs illustrated by Briquet, and again indicates a foreign origin.

At some, presumably later, stage a leaf of a paper not used elsewhere in the book was inserted at the beginning.[16] Glued to it is a piece of very

---

12   See plate between pp. x and xi of Andrews, 1926.

13   Fellowes, 1949.

14   This cannot be confirmed beyond doubt, as the binding is very tight, with head and tail bands. Folios 110 to 120 inclusive are numbered '1010' etc.

15   Briquet, 1968, iv, nos. 8067-8083. Dr David Mateer has noticed a similar watermark in Bodleian Library manuscript Mus. Sch. e.423 and elsewhere. See his forthcoming article *William Byrd, John Petre and Oxford, Bodleian MS Mus. Sch. E.423*.

16   The arms were present when Burney described the book. (Burney, 1776-89, iii,

thin paper on which the Nevell arms are painted, together with the initials HN and various devices.[17] Blank leaves at the ends of the volume, and the endpapers covered in pale blue-green silk, seem likely to have been added when repairs were effected.

The music pages carry four six-line staves drawn between two vertical lines about 22.5 cm apart and running from the top to the bottom of each page. Each staff is about 2 cm high. The spacing is variable, but the top of the first staff is generally a little more than 2 cm below the upper edge of the page, and the space between the staves is roughly 2.25 cm. The leaves containing the table of contents were ruled horizontally and headed before the number of titles to be entered was calculated, with the result that the last page was prepared but contains no entries.

Baldwin's literal and musical handwriting has been illustrated on a number of occasions.[18] When he noticed that he had made an error he corrected it. Having copied *all in a garden grine*, he noted on f. 145^v:

+ here is a falte, a=pointe left out, w^c ye shall finde prickte, after the end of the nexte songe, upon the .148. leafe:·

On f. 148^v he duly wrote in the missing music and observed:

this pointe bee longeth to the song before: $-\cdot$ .145. leafe: $-\cdot$.

The question of the hand or hands that made corrections and additions to what Baldwin wrote has also been widely discussed.[19] Fellowes thought that there was more than one corrector, and indeed a number of the alterations could have been made by anybody at any time. He rejected the idea that Byrd amended Baldwin's work, but others have concluded that some corrections are likely to have been made by the composer. To someone who has become familiar with Byrd's pen strokes in his letters and other documents, this seems altogether probable. Some amendments leap from the page and proclaim his authorship. It is hard to believe that so much personality can reside, for instance, in simple marks

p. 91; 1935 ed., ii, p. 79.)

17   Fellowes observed that the inserted leaf 'had been much torn and damaged before being placed in the book', and described the arms. The arms are pictured together with the cover and some music pages in the booklet accompanying Mr Christopher Hogwood's recording of the music from *My Ladye Nevells Booke* (L'Oiseau-Lyre D29D 4).

18   See, for example, Andrews, 1926; Brown, 1969; Gaskin, 1992. Colons, dashes and dots are frequent in Baldwin's work, here and in other manuscripts which he compiled.

19   In Fellowes, 1949; Brown, 1968-69; and other studies listed above.

like the added sharp signs on f. 179^r (*Munsers almaine*) and f. 181^r (the *Petre* pavan), but there can be little doubt who inserted them.

When Baldwin had completed 'The table: for this booke' he wrote:

ffinished & ended the leventh of september: in the yeare of our lorde God ·1591· & in the ·33· yeare of the raigne of our sofferaine ladie Elizabeth by the . $^{grace \ of}$ God queene of Englande: &^{c}

By me Jo: baldwine of windsore : — ·
· — : laudes:deo : — ·

The following table lists the contents of *My Ladye Nevells Booke*. It should be noted that pieces do not always begin at the top of a page. The spellings used here are those Baldwin employs in his index (but omitting his decorative dashes and single dots). They are not always the same as those he uses at the beginnings and ends of the pieces. Head and tail titles, together with Baldwin's various forms of ascription to Byrd, are given in the Textual Commentary of Brown's *Musica Britannica* edition of Byrd's keyboard music.

no.	fo.	
1	1^r	my ladye nevells grownde:
2	8^r	qui passe: for my ladye nevell:
3	13^v	the march before the battell:
4	18^r	the battell:
	18^r	— [*head title* the: souldiers: sommons:]
	19^r	the march of footemen:
	20^r	the march of horsemen:
	21^r	the trumpetts:
	22^v	the Irishe marche
	24^r	the bagpipe: & drone:
	25^r	the flute: & drome:
	28^r	the marche to fight:
	29^v	tantara:
	30^r	the battells be ioyned:
	31^r	the retreat:
5	32^r	the galliarde for the victorie:
6	34^r	the barlye breake:
7	43^r	the galliarde gygg:
8	46^r	the hunts upp:
9	52^v	ut. re. mi. fa. sol. la:
10	58^v	the first pavian:

11	61ʳ	the galiarde to the same:
12	63ʳ	the second pavian:
13	65ʳ	the galliarde to the same:
14	67ʳ	the third pavian:
15	69ᵛ	the galliard to the same:
16	71ᵛ	the fourth pavian
17	73ᵛ	the galliarde to the same
18	75ᵛ	the fifte pavian:
19	78ᵛ	the galliarde to the same
20	80ᵛ	− [*head title* pavana: the vi: Kinbrugh: goodd:
21	84ʳ	the galliarde to the same:
22	86ʳ	the seventh pavian:
23	89ʳ	the eighte pavian:
24	92ʳ	the passinge mesurs is: the nynthe pavian:
25	99ᵛ	Passa: measures gall: Bird
26	105ᵛ	the voluntarie lesson: [*head title* A voluntarie: for my ladye nevell:]
27	109ʳ	will you walk the woods soe wylde
28	103ʳ	the maydens songe:
29	109ᵛ	a lesson of voluntarie:[20]
30	126ʳ	the seconde grownde:
31	135ᵛ	have wᵗ you to walsingame:
32	142ᵛ	all in a garden greene:
33	146ᵛ	the: lo: willobies: welcome home
34	149ʳ	the carmans whistle
35	153ᵛ	hughe ashtons: grownde:
36	161ʳ	− [*head title* A fancie: for my ladye nevell:]
37	166ᵛ	sellingers rownde
38	173ᵛ	munsers almaine:
39	180ʳ	the tennth pavian: mr: w: peter:
40	184ᵛ	the galliarde: to the same:
41	186ᵛ	A fancie:
42	191ʳ	A voluntarie:

20   This looks like an error for 'A lesson *or* voluntary', but Baldwin gives the word 'of' both in the heading of the piece and in his index.

APPENDIX H

CATALOGUE OF BYRD'S WORKS

For other catalogues see Turbet, 1987 (arranged by genre), and Grove, 1980, s.v. 'Byrd, William' (compiled by Joseph Kerman).

A. MODERN EDITIONS

The following list sources and provide commentaries:

BE *The Byrd Edition*. General editor: Philip Brett. London, Stainer and Bell, 1970-. 17 volumes projected (some published as two or three); volumes 7a-b, 9, 12 and 13 not published at the time of writing.[1]

MB Alan Brown. *William Byrd. Keyboard music*. London, Stainer and Bell, 1976. *Musica Britannica*, 27-28. (Revised reprint of 28 issued in 1985.)

  Alan Brown. *Elizabethan keyboard music*. London, Stainer and Bell, 1989. *Musica Britannica*, 55.[2]

Byrd's works are identified below by reference to these editions, e.g. MB 27/5 means *Musica Britannica* edition, volume 27, piece number 5. For other editions see Turbet (1987) and Harley (1992-94).

B. PIECES COLLECTED DURING BYRD'S LIFETIME

Where collections contain music by several composers only Byrd's contributions are listed. Preliminary numbers show the positions of pieces in the original collections. Incipits of sections of multi-sectional works are separated by dashes. The number of voices is shown in parentheses, e.g. (*a* 5). Spellings are modernized. The identification of authors and sources of words of songs is based on Fellowes, 1967, and *The Byrd Edition*.

---

1 In the absence of BE 7a-b, the second book of *Gradualia* is available in an edition published by JOED Music (Carshalton Beeches), catalogue numbers B22, B28-32, B38, B43 and B63.

2 Brown and Turbet (1992) refer to *Elizabethan keyboard music* as 'EK', and follow Neighbour (1978) and Kerman (1981) in referring to the *Musica Britannica* edition of Byrd's keyboard works as 'BK'.

Cantiones, quae ab argumento sacrae vocantur, quinque et sex partium, autoribus Thoma Tallisio & Guilielmo Birdo ... Excudebat Thomas Vautrollerius typographus Londinensis ... 1575. Dedication: Queen Elizabeth. BE 1

4	Emendemus in melius quae ignoranter peccavimus − Adiuva nos Deus salutaris noster (*a* 5) BE 1/1	18	Memento homo quod cinis est (*a* 6) BE 1/8
5	Libera me Domine et pone me iuxta te − Dies mei transierunt (*a* 5) BE 1/2	19	Siderum rector (*a* 5) BE 1/9
6	Peccantem me quotidie (*a* 5) BE 1/3	23	Da mihi auxilium de tribulatione (*a* 6) BE 1/10
10	Aspice Domine quia facta est (*a* 6) E 1/4	24	Domine secundum actum meum − Ideo deprecor maiestatem tuam (*a* 6) BE 1/11
11	Attollite portas principes (*a* 6) BE 1/5	25	Diliges Dominum Deum tuum (*a* 8) BE 1/12
12	O lux beata Trinitas − Te mane laudem − Deo patri sit gloria (*a* 6) BE 1/6	29	Misere mihi Domine (*a* 6) BE 1/13
17	Laudate pueri Dominum (*a* 6) BE 1/7	30-32	Tribue Domine −Te deprecor − Gloria patri qui creavit (*a* 6) BE 1/14-16
		33	Libera me Domine de morte aeterna (*a* 5) BE 1/17

Psalmes, sonets, & songs of sadnes and pietie, made into musicke of five parts: whereof, some of them going abroade among divers, in untrue coppies, are heere truely corrected, and th'other being songs very rare and newly composed ... by William Byrd ... Printed by Thomas East, the assigne of W. Byrd ... Paules wharfe. 1588 ... Dedication: Sir Christopher Hatton. See Andrews, 1964, concerning later editions. BE 12 (for original versions of numbers 4, 6, 8, 10-16, 22-25, 27 and 29-35 see BE 16)

1	O God give ear *Psalm 55 John Hopkins*	5	O Lord how long wilt thou forget *Psalm 13*
2	Mine eyes with fervency of sprite *Psalm 123*	6	O Lord who in thy sacred tent *Psalm 15*
3	My soul oppressed with care *Psalm 119*	7	Help Lord for wasted are those men *Psalm 12*
4	How shall a young man prone to ill *Psalm 119*	8	Blessed is he that fears the Lord *Psalm 112*

9	Lord in thy wrath reprove me not *Psalm 6*		21	Although the heathen poets
			22	In fields abroad
10	E'en from the depth *Psalm 130 Thomas Sternhold*		23	Constant Penelope
			24	La verginella *Ludovico Ariosto*
11	I joy not in no earthly bliss			
12	Though Amaryllis dance in green		25	Farewell false Love *Sir Walter Raleigh*
13	Who likes to love		26	The match that's made for just and true respects
14	My mind to me a kingdom is *Sir Edward Dyer*		27	Prostrate O Lord I lie
15	Where Fancy fond		28	All as a sea
16	O you that hear this voice *Sir Philip Sidney*		29	Susanna fair
			30	If that a sinner's sighs
17	If women could be fair *Edward de Vere, Earl of Oxford*		31	Care for thy soul
			32	Lullaby my sweet little baby
18	Ambitious love hath forced me to aspire		33	Why do I use my paper ink and pen? *Henry Walpole?*
19	What pleasure have great princes For second version, perhaps a chorus, see BE 16/5		34	Come to me grief *Thomas Watson* or *Edward Dyer*
			35	O that most rare breast *Thomas Watson* or *Edward Dyer*
20	As I beheld I saw a herdsman wild			

Musica Transalpina. Madrigales translated of foure, five and six parts, chosen out of divers excellent authors, with the first and second part of La Verginella, made by Maister Byrd, upon two stanz's of Ariosto, and brought to speake English with the rest. Published by N. Yonge ... *Imprinted at London by Thomas East, the assigné of William Byrd. 1588.* Dedication: Gilbert, Lord Talbot.

44-45   The fair young virgin − But not so soon (*a* 5). *Adapted from* La verginella *in Psalmes, sonets, & songs.* BE 16/1

Liber primus sacrarum cantionum quinque vocum. Autore Guilielmo Byrd ... *Excudebat Thomas Est ex assignatione Guilielmi Byrd* ... *Londini. 25. Octob. 1589.* Dedication: Edward Somerset, Earl of Worcester. BE 2

1-2	Defecit in dolore − Sed tu Domine refugium BE 2/1	3-4	Domine praestolamur − Veni Domine BE 2/2

5	O Domine adjuva me BE 2/3	17	In resurrectione tua BE 2/10
6-7	Trisitia et anxietas – Sed tu Domine qui non derelinquis BE 2/4	18-19	Aspice Domine de sede – Respice Domine BE 2/11
8	Memento Domine BE 2/5	20-21	Ne irascaris – Civitas sancti tui BE 2/12
9-10	Vide Domine afflictionem – Sed veni Domine BE 2/6	22-23	O quam gloriosum – Benedictio et claritas BE 2/13
11-14	Deus venerunt gentes – Posuerunt morticinia – Effuderunt sanguinem – Facti sumus opprobrium BE 2/7	24-26	Tribulationes civitatum – Timor et hebetudo – Nos enim pro peccatis nostris BE 2/14
15	Domine tu jurasti BE 2/8	27	Domine secundum multitudinem BE 2/15
16	Vigilate BE 2/9	28-29	Laetentur coeli – Orietur in diebus tuis BE 2/16

Songs of sundrie natures, some of gravitie, and others of myrth, fit for all companies and voyces . Lately made and composed into musicke of 3. 4. 5. and 6. parts … Imprinted at London by Thomas East, the assigne of William Byrd, and are to be sold at the house of the sayd T. East, being in Aldersgate streete, at the signe of the blacke horse. 1589. Dedication: Sir Henry Carey. See Andrews, 1964, concerning later editions. BE 13 (for original versions of numbers 19, 31 and 32 see BE 16)

Second sections printed out of order with pieces for the same number of voices are repeated in square brackets in their correct places.

a 3

1	Lord in thy rage *Psalm 6*	7	Attend mine humble prayer *Psalm 143*
2	Right blest are they *Psalm 32*	8	Susanna fair
3	Lord in thy wrath correct me not *Psalm 38*	9	The nightingale so pleasant
4	O God which art most merciful *Psalm 51*	10-11	When younglings first – But when by proof
5	Lord hear my prayer *Psalm 102*	12-13	Upon a summer's day – Then for a boat
6	From depth of sin *Psalm 130*	14	The greedy hawk *Geoffrey Whitney*

a 4

15-16	Is Love a boy? − Boy pity me	22	O Lord my God
17-18	Wounded I am − Yet of us twain	23	While that the sun
19-21	From Cytheron − There careless thoughts are freed − If Love be just	24	Rejoice rejoice *Chorus of* 35
		25	Cast off all doubtful care *Chorus of* 40

a 5

26	Weeping full sore	33	O dear life *Sir Philip Sidney*
27	Penelope that longed		
28	Compel the hawk *Thomas Churchyard*	34	Love would discharge *Second section of* 29
29	See those sweet eyes − [34 Love would discharge the duty of his heart]	35	From virgin's womb (1 voice + 4 viols) − [24 Rejoice rejoice] *Francis Kindlemarsh*
30	When I was otherwise		
31	When first by force	36-37	Of gold all burnished − Her breath is more sweet
32	I thought that Love had been a boy		

a 6

38-39	Behold how good a thing- And as the pleasant morning dew *Psalm 133*	42-43	And think ye nymphs − Love is a fit of pleasure
		44	If in thine heart
40	An earthly tree (2 voices + 4 viols) − [25 Cast off all doubtful care (*or* Cease cares: *fragment* BE 16/36)]	45	Unto the hills *Psalm 121*
		46-47	Christ rising again − Christ is risen again (2 voices + 4 viols, 6 voices) *Romans 6.9, I Corinthians 15.20*
41	Who made thee Hob (2 voices + 4 viols)		

A gratification unto Master John Case, for his learned booke, lately made in the praise of musicke. Imprinted at London by Thomas East, the assigne of William Byrd ... 1589. Parts printed separately as broadsides, of which two survive: Cambridge University Library, Broadside A.1586 (cantus secundus, lacking

verse and colophon), and Bodleian Library MS Don. a.3.(3) (bassus). A copy of
the medius part is in Royal College of Music MS 2041. See Barnett, 1969.

> Let others praise — There may the solemn stoics (*a* 6) *Thomas Watson*
> BE 16/27

*The first sett, of Italian madrigalls Englished ... By Thomas Watson ... There
are also heere inserted two excellent madrigalls of Master William Byrds,
composed after the Italian vaine, at the request of the sayd Thomas Watson.
Imprinted at London by Thomas Este, the assigné of William Byrd, & are to be
sold at the house of the sayd T. Este, being in Aldersgate street, at the sign of
the black horse. 1590.* Dedication: Robert, Earl of Essex.

| 8 | This sweet and merry month of May (*a* 4) *Thomas Watson*? BE 14/9 Reprinted as no. 9 of *Psalmes, songs and sonnets,* 1611. | 28 | This sweet and merry month of May (*a* 6) *Thomas Watson*? BE 16/3 |

*Liber secundus sacrarum cantionum, quarum aliae ad quinque, aliae verò ad sex
voces aeditae sunt. Autore Guilielmo Byrd ... Excudebat Thomas Este ex
assignatione Guilielmi Byrd ... Londini, quarto Novemb. 1591.* Dedication:
Lord Lumley. BE 3

a 5

1-2	Laudibus in sanctis — Magnificum Domini — Hunc arguta BE 3/1	10-11	Domine exaudi — Et non intres in judicium BE 3/6
3-4	Quis est homo — Diverte a malo BE 3/2	12	Apparebit in finem BE 3/7
5	Fac cum servo tuo BE 33/3	13-14	Haec dicit Dominus — Haec dicit Dominus BE 3/8
6-7	Salve Regina — Et Iesum benedictum BE 3/4	15	Circumdederunt me BE 3/9
8-9	Tribulatio proxima est — Contumelias et terrores BE 3/5	16	Levemus corda BE 3/10
		17-18	Recordare Domine — Quiescat Domine BE 3/11
		19	Exsurge Domine BE 3/12
		20	Misere mei Deus BE 3/13

a 6

21-22	Descendit de coelis − Et exivit per auream portam BE 3/14	27-28	Afflicti pro peccatis − Ut eruas nos BE 3/17
23	Domine non sum dignus BE 3/15	29	Cantate Domino BE 3/18
		30	Cunctis diebus BE 3/19
24-26	Infelix ego − Quid igitur faciam? − Ad te igitur BE 3/16	31	Domine salva nos BE 3/20
		32	Haec dies BE 3/21

My Ladye Nevells Booke. Manuscript probably compiled under Byrd's direction, and inscribed: 'finished & ended the leventh of September in the yeare of our Lord God 1591 ... by me Jo. Baldwin of Windsore ... '. Title embossed on cover.

1	My Lady Nevell's ground MB 28/57	20-21	The sixth pavan (Kinborough Good) and galliard MB 27/32a-b
2	Qui passe MB 27/19	22	The seventh pavan MB 28/74
3	The march before the battle (*or* The Earl of Oxford's march) MB 28/93	23	The eighth pavan MB 27/17
4	The battle MB 28/94	24-25	Passing measures pavan and galliard MB 27/2
5	The galliard for the victory MB 28/95	26	A voluntary (for my Lady Nevell) MB 28/61
6	The barley break MB 28/92	27	Will you walk the woods so wild MB 28/85
7	The galliard jig MB 27/18	28	The maiden's song MB 28/82
8	The hunt's up MB 27/40	29	A lesson of voluntary MB 27/26
9	Ut re mi fa sol la MB 28/64	30	The second ground MB 27/42
10-11	The first pavan and galliard MB 27/29a-b	31	Have with you to Walsingham MB 27/8
12-13	The second pavan and galliard MB 28/71a-b	32	All in a garden green MB 28/56
14-15	The third pavan and galliard MB 27/14a-b		
16-17	The fourth pavan and galliard MB 27/30a-b		
18-19	The fifth pavan and galliard MB 27/31a-b		

33	Lord Willoughby's welcome home (*or* Rowland) MB 27/7	38	Mounsieur's alman MB 28/88
34	The carman's whistle MB 27/36	39	Pavan: William Petre MB 27/3a Printed as no. 2 in *Parthenia*, 1612-13
35	Hugh Aston's (*or* Tregian's) ground MB 27/20	40	Galliard [William Petre] MB 27/3b Printed as no. 3 in *Parthenia*, 1612-13
36	A fancy (for my Lady Nevell) MB 27/25	41	A fancy MB 28/46
37	Sellinger's round MB 28/84	42	A voluntary MB 27/27 Second part only

[*Mass for four voices*.] No title-page. 'W. Byrd' at top right-hand corner of each page. Printing ascribed to Thomas East, London, 1592-93.[3] Second edition 1598-1600. BE 4/1

Kyrie – Gloria – Credo – Sanctus – Agnus Dei

[*Mass for three voices*.] No title-page. 'W. Byrd' at top right-hand corner of each page. Printing ascribed to Thomas East, London, 1593-94.[3] Second edition 1598-1600. BE 4/2

Kyrie – Gloria – Credo – Sanctus – Agnus Dei

[*Mass for five voices*.] No title-page. 'W. Byrd' at top right-hand corner of each page. Printing ascribed to Thomas East, London, 1594-95.[3] BE 4/3

Kyrie – Gloria – Credo – Sanctus – Agnus Dei

A plaine and easie introduction to practicall musicke ... By Thomas Morley ... Imprinted at London by Peter Short dwelling on Breedstreet hill at the signe of the starre. 1597. Dedication: William Byrd.

On p. 103 Morley includes as an example a canon two in one by Byrd (1952 ed., p. 185). BE 16/32

3   Clulow, 1966.

Gradualia: ac cantiones sacrae, quinis, quaternis, trinisque vocibus concinnatae ... Authore Gulielmo Byrd ... 1605. Londini, Excudebat Thomas Este. Dedication: Henry Howard, Earl of Northampton. Reissued 1610. BE 5, 6a-b

a 5

Music for Marian Masses

1 Suscepimus Deus –
Magnus Dominus – Gloria Patri et Filio BE 5/1
2 Sicut audivimus BE 5/2
3 Senex puerum portabat BE 5/3
4 Nunc dimittis servum tuum – Quia viderunt – Lumen ad revelationem BE 5/4
5 Responsum accepit Simeon BE 5/5
6 Salve sancta parens – Eructavit cor meum BE 5/6
7 Benedicta et venerabilis BE 5/7
8 Virgo Dei genitrix BE 5/8
9 Felix es sacra Virgo Maria BE 5/9
10 Beata es Virgo Maria BE 5/10
11 Beata viscera BE 5/11
12 Rorate caeli – Bendixisti Domine – Gloria Patri et Filio BE 5/12
13 Tollite portas – Quis ascendet BE 5/13
14 Ave Maria BE 5/14
15 Ecce Virgo concipiet BE 5/15
16 Vultum tuum BE 5/16
17 Speciosus forma – Lingua mea BE 5/17
18 Post partum BE 5/18
19 Felix namque BE 5/19

20 Alleluia. Ave Maria – Alleluia. Virga Iesse floruit BE 5/20
21 Gaude Maria BE 5/21
22 Diffusa est gratia – Propter veritatem – Audi filia – Vultum tuum – Adducentur Regi – Adducentur in laetitia BE 5/22
23 Gaudeamus omnes – Assumpta est Maria BE 5/23
24 Assumpta est Maria BE 5/24

Non-liturgical

25 Optimam partem elegit BE 5/25
26 Adoramus te Christe (1 voice + 4 viols) BE 6a/1
27 Unam petii a Domino BE 6a/2
28 Plorans plorabit – Dic Regi BE 6a/3

All Saints

29 Gaudeamus omnes – Exultate iusti – Gloria Patri et Filio BE 6a/4
30 Timete Dominum – Inquirentes autem BE 6a/5
31 Iustorum animae BE 6a/6
32 Beati mundo corde BE 6a/7

a 4

Corpus Christi

1   Cibavit eos — Exultate
Deo/Gloria Patri et Filio
BE 6a/8

2   Oculi omnium — Aperis tu
manum — Caro mea
BE 6a/9

3   Sacerdotes Domini
BE 6a/10

4   Quotiescunque
manducabitis BE 6a/11

Antiphons and hymns for Corpus Christi and the Blessed Sacrament

5   Ave verum corpus
BE 6a/12

6   O salutaris hostia BE 6a/13

7   O sacrum convivium
BE 6a/14

8   [Chant Pange lingua] —
Nobis datus nobis natus —
Verbum caro — Tantum
ergo BE 6a/15

Antiphons and other settings of sacred texts

9   Ecce quam bonum — Quod
descendit BE 6b/1

10   Christus resurgens —
Dicant nunc Iudaei BE 6b/2

11   Visita quaesumus BE 6b/3

12   Salve Regina — Eia ergo
BE 6b/4

13   Alma redemptoris mater
BE 6b/5

14   Ave Regina caelorum
BE 6b/6

15   In manus tuas Domine
BE 6b/7

16   Laetinia BE 6b/8

17   Salve sola Dei genitrix
BE 6b/9

18   Senex puerum portabat
BE 6b/10

19   Hodie beata Virgo Maria
BE 6b/11

20   Deo gratias BE 6b/12

a 3

Marian hymns and antiphons

1   Quem terra pontus
aethera — Cui luna —
Beata Mater — Beata caeli
nuncio — Gloria tibi
Domine BE 6b/13

2   O gloriosa Domina —
Quod Eva tristis — Tu
regis alti — Gloria tibi
Domine BE 6b/14

3   Memento salutis auctor —
Maria mater gratia —

Gloria tibi Domine
BE 6b/15

4   Ave Maris stella — Sumens
illud Ave — Solve vincla
reis — Monstra te esse
matrem — Virgo singularis
— Vitam praesta puram —
Sit laus Deo Patri BE 6b/16

5   Regina caeli — Quia quem
meruisti — Resurrexit sicut
dixit — Ora pro nobis
BE 6b/17

Holy Week and the Easter season

6	Alleluia. Vespere autem sabbathi − Quae lucescit BE 6b/18
7	Haec dies BE 6b/19
8	Angelus Domini descendit BE 6b/20
9	Post dies octo − Mane nobiscum BE 6b/21
10	Iesum Nazarenum (Turbarum voces in Passione Domini secundum Ioannem) E 6b/22

Antiphon for the Candlemas procession

11	Adorna thalamum tuum Sion − Subsistit Virgo BE 6b/23

Gradualia: seu cantionum sacrarum quarum aliae ad quator, aliae verò ad quinque et sex voces editae sunt. Liber secundus. Authore Gulielmo Byrde … Excudebat Thomas Este Londini, ex assignatione Gulielmi Barley. 1607. Dedication: John, Lord Petre of Writtle. Reissued 1610. BE 7a-b

a 4

Mass of the Nativity

1	Puer natus est nobus − Cantate Domino − Gloria Patri et Filio
2	Viderunt omnes − Notum fecit Dominus
3	Dies sanctificatus
4	Tui sunt coeli
5	Viderunt omnes

Christmas Antiphons and responds

6	Hodie Christus natus est
7	O admirabile commercium
8	O magnum misterium
9	Beata virgo − Ave Maria

Mass of the Epiphany

10	Ecce advenit − Deus iudicium − Gloria Patri et Filio
11	Reges Tharsis
12	Vidimus stellam
15	Surge illuminare

Motets for the Mass of the Blessed Sacrament

13	Ab ortu solis
14	Venite comedite

Corpus Christi and the Votive Mass of the Blessed Sacrament

16	Alleluia. Cognoverunt discipuli
17	Ego sum panis vivus
18	O quam suavis *Hymn for the Ascension*
19	Iesu nostra redemptio − Quae te vicit − Inferni claustra − Ipsa te cogat − Tu esto nostrum gaudium

a 5

Mass on Easter Day

20	Resurrexi − Domine probasti me − Gloria Patri et Filio
21	Haec dies
22	Victimae paschali − Dic nobis Maria
23	Terra tremuit
24	Pascha nostrum

Mass of the Ascension and antiphon, second Vespers

25	Viri Galilei - Omnes gentes plaudite
26	Alleluia. Ascendit Deus
27	Dominus in Sina

28	Ascendit Deus
29	Psallite Domino
30	O rex gloriae

Mass of Pentecost and Magnificat antiphon, first Vespers

31	Spiritus Domini - Exsurgat Deus
32	Alleluia. Emitte spiritum
33	Veni sancte spiritus reple
34	Confirma hoc
35	Factus est repente
36	Veni sancte spiritus et emitte − O lux beatissima - Da tuis fidelibus
37	Non vos relinquam

a 6

Mass and antiphons, feasts of SS Peter and Paul and St Peter's Chains

38	Nunc scio vere - Domine probasti me − Gloria Patri et Filio
39	Constitues eos − Pro patribus tuis
40	Solve iubente Deo

41	Tu es Petrus
42	Hodie Simon Petrus
43	Tu es pastor
44	Quodcunque ligaveris

Miscellaneous motets

45	Laudate Dominum
46	Venite exultemus

Psalmes, songs, and sonnets ... Fit for voyces or viols of 3. 4. 5. and 6. parts. Composed by William Byrd ... 1611. London: printed by Thomas Snodham, the assigne of W. Barley. Dedication: Francis, Earl of Cumberland. BE 14

a 3

1	The eagle's force *Thomas Churchyard* BE 14/1

2	Of flatt'ring speech *Geoffrey Whitney* BE 14/2

3-4	In winter cold − Whereat an ant *Geoffrey Whitney* BE 14/3-4	6	Sing ye to our Lord *Psalm 149.1-2* BE 14/6
5	Who looks may leap *Geoffrey Whitney* BE 14/5	7	I have been young *Psalm 37.25* BE 14/7
		8	In crystal towers *Geoffrey Whitney* BE 14/8

a 4

9	This sweet and merry month *Thomas Watson*? Reprint of no. 8 in *The first sett, of Italian madrigalls Englished*, 1590 BE 14/9	12	Awake mine eyes BE 14/12
		13	Come jolly swains BE 14/13
10	Let not the sluggish sleep BE 14/10	14	What is life BE 14/14
		15	Fantasia in g (4 viols) BE 14/15, BE 17/4
11	A feigned friend BE 14/11	16	Come let us rejoice *Psalm 95.1-2* BE 14/16

a 5

17	Retire my soul BE 14/17	22	Crowned with flowers I saw fair Amarillis *Edward Paston*? BE 14/22
18	Arise Lord into thy rest *Psalm 132.8-9* BE 14/18		
19	Come woeful Orpheus BE 14/19	23	Wedded to will is witless BE 14/23
20-21	Sing we merrily − Blow up the trumpet *Psalm 81.1-4* BE 14/20-21	24	Make ye joy to God *Psalm 100.1-2* BE 14/24

a 6

25	Have mercy upon me (1 voice + 5 viols, 6 voices) *Psalm 51.1-2* BE 14/25	*day*: O God that guides the cheerful sun (1 voice + 5 viols) BE 14/28	
		29	Praise our Lord *Psalm 117* BE 14/29
26	Fantasia in g (6 viols) BE 14/26, BE 17/13	30	Turn our captivity *Psalm 126.5-7* BE 14/30
27	*A carol for Christmas day*: This day Christ was born *Translated from* Hodie Christus natus est BE 14/27	31	Ah silly soul (1 voice + 5 viols) BE 14/31
28	*A carol for New Year's*	32	How vain the toils (1 voice + 5 viols) BE 14/32

Parthenia or the maydenhead of the first musicke that ever was printed for the virginalls. Composed by three famous masters: William Byrd, D^r: John Bull, & Orlando Gibbons ... Ingraven by William Holt. Lond: print: for M^{ris}. Dor: Evans ... sould by G: Lowe print^r in Loathberry. [1612-13]. Dedication: Prince Frederick and Princess Elizabeth.

1	Prelude MB 27/1	5	Galliard: Mary Brownlow
2	Pavan: Sir William Petre		MB 27/34
	Revised from My Ladye	6	Pavan: the Earl of
	Nevells Booke *no. 39*		Salisbury MB 27/15a
	MB 27/2	7	Galliard [the Earl of
3	Galliard [Sir William Petre]		Salisbury] MB 27/15b
	No. 40 in My Ladye	8	Second galliard: Mary
	Nevells Booke MB 27/3		Brownlow [*recte* the Earl
4	Prelude MB 27/24		of Salisbury] MB 27/15

The teares or lamentacions of a sorrowfull soule: composed with musicall ayres and songs, both for voyces and divers instruments. Set foorth by Sir William Leighton ... London Printed by William Stansby. 1614. Dedication: Prince Charles.

a 4	*a* 5
Be unto me BE 11/17	Come help O God BE 11/22
Look down O Lord BE 11/20	I laid me down BE 11/19

C. PIECES NOT COLLECTED DURING BYRD'S LIFETIME

Arrangements by others of Byrd's music are not included.

Consort fantasias, grounds and dances	Fantasia in d (*a* 4) BE 17/7
	Authenticity uncertain
	Fantasia in F (*a* 6) BE 17/11
Fantasia in a (*a* 4) BE 17/5	Fantasia in G (*a* 4) BE 17/34
Fantasia in C (*a* 3) BE 17/1	Fantasia in g (*a* 6) BE 17/12
Fantasia in C (*a* 3) BE 17/2	Browning (*a* 5) BE 17/10
Fantasia in C (*a* 3) BE 17/3	Pavan in c (*a* 5) BE 17/14
Fantasia in C (*a* 5) BE 17/8	Pavan and galliard in C (*a* 6)
Fantasia in d (*a* 4) BE 17/6	BE 17/15
Authenticity uncertain	Prelude and ground (*a* 5) BE 17/9

Consort In Nomines

In Nomine (*a* 4) BE 17/16
In Nomine (*a* 4) BE 17/17
In Nomine (*a* 5) BE 17/18
In Nomine (*a* 5) BE 17/19
In Nomine (*a* 5) BE 17/20
In Nomine (*a* 5) BE 17/21
In Nomine (*a* 5) BE 17/22

Consort hymns and Misereres

Sermone blando (*a* 3) BE 17/23
   2 settings
Sermone blando (*a* 4) BE 17/30
   3 settings
Sermone blando (*a* 4) BE 17/31
   2 settings
Christe qui lux est (*a* 4) BE 17/24
   3 settings
Christe qui lux est (*a* 4) BE 17/25
   3 settings
Christe qui lux est (*a* 4) BE 17/26
   1 setting
Christe redemptor (*a* 4) BE 17/27
   2 settings
Miserere (*a* 4) BE 17/28 2 settings
Salvator mundi (*a* 4) BE 17/29
   2 settings
Te lucis ante terminum (*a* 4)
   BE 17/32 8 settings
Te lucis ante terminum (*a* 4)
   BE 17/33 4 settings

Consort songs

All for solo voice and four viols
except *Delight is dead*. BE 15 nos.
10, 17, 18, 26, 31, 34-36 and 38-41
are anonymous in the sources.

An aged dame BE 15/33
Ah golden hairs BE 15/13

As Caesar wept BE 15/14
Blame I confess BE 15/15
Come pretty babe BE 15/16
Content is rich BE 15/17
Crowned with flowers and lilies −
   O worthy queen BE 15/29
Delight is dead (2 voices + 3 viols)
   BE 15/30
E'en as in seas BE 15/18
Fair Britain isle BE 15/34
Have mercy on us Lord BE 15/3
He that all earthly pleasure scorns
   BE 15/35
In angel's weed BE 15/31
I will not say − Let fortune fail −
   My years do seek BE 15/19
The Lord is only my support
   BE 15/2
Lord to thee I make my moan
   BE 15/5
The man is blest BE 15/4
Mount Hope BE 15/20
My freedom BE 15/21
My mistress had a little dog − But
   out alas BE 15/36
O God but God BE 15/6
O Lord bow down BE 15/7
O Lord how vain BE 15/8
O Lord within thy tabernacle
   BE 15/1
O that we woeful wretches BE 15/9
Out of the orient crystal skies
   BE 15/10
Quis me statim BE 15/37
Rejoice unto the Lord BE 15/11
Sith Death at length BE 15/22
Sith that the tree BE 15/23
Though I be Brown BE 15/38
Thou poets' friend BE 15/24
Triumph with pleasant melody −
   What unacquainted cheerful
   voice − My faults O Christ
   BE 15/12

Truce for a time BE 15/25
Truth at the first BE 15/26
What steps of strife BE 15/27
Where the blind BE 15/39
While Phoebus used to dwell
     BE 15/28
With lilies white BE 15/40
Wretched Albinus BE 15/41
Ye sacred muses BE 15/32

Organ antiphons and hymns

Christe qui lux es MB 28/121 No.
     34 in Caldwell, 1965(b)
Clarifica me Pater MB 28/47
Clarifica me Pater MB 28/48
Clarifica me Pater MB 28/49
Gloria tibi Trinitas MB 28/50
Miserere MB 28/66
Miserere MB 28/67
Salvator mundi MB 28/68
Salvator mundi MB 28/69

Keyboard grounds

The bells MB 27/38
Ground in C MB 27/43
Ground in G MB 28/86
Ground in g MB 27/9
Hornpipe MB 27/39
Quadran pavan and galliard
     MB 28/70
Ut re mi fa sol la (MB 28/58)

Keyboard pavans and galliards

Galliard in d MB 28/53
Galliard in G MB 28/77
Piper's galliard MB 55/26
     Authenticity uncertain
Pavan in a MB 55/16 Authenticity
     uncertain

Pavan in d MB 55/15 Authenticity
     uncertain
Pavan in G MB 28/76
Pavan and galliard in a MB 27/16
Pavan and galliard in Bb MB 27/23
Pavan and galliard in C MB 27/33
Pavan and galliard in C MB 55/10
     Authenticity uncertain
Pavan and galliard in d MB 28/52
Pavan and galliard in G MB 28/72
Pavan and galliard in G MB 28/73
Pavan and galliard in g MB 27/4
Pavan: Bray and galliard MB 28/59
Pavan: Echo and galliard MB 28/114
Pavan: Lady Mounteagle MB 28/75
Pavan: Ph. Tr. and galliard
     MB 28/60
Johnson's *Delight* pavan and galliard
     MB 27/5 Arranged by Byrd
Dowland's *Lachrymae* pavan
     MB 28/54 Arranged by Byrd
Harding's galliard MB 28/55
     Arranged by Byrd

Other keyboard dances

Alman in C MB 55/30 *Listed*:
     MB 28/117
Alman in G MB 28/89
Alman in g MB 27/11
Coranto (*or* Jig) in C MB 28/45
The French coranto MB 27/21a
The second French coranto
     MB 27/21b
The third French coranto MB 27/21c
The ghost MB 28/78
Jig in a MB 27/22
La volta MB 28/91
La volta: L. Morley MB 28/90
Monsieur's alman MB 28/87
Monsieur's alman MB 27/44
The Queen's alman MB 27/10

Keyboard variations

Callino casturame MB 27/35
Fortune my foe MB 27/6
The gipsies' round MB 28/80
Go from my window MB 28/79
John come kiss me now MB 28/81
Malt's come down MB 28/107
  Authenticity uncertain
A medley (MB 28/112) Authenticity
  uncertain
O mistress mine MB 28/83
Wilson's wild (or Wolsey's wild)
  MB 27/37

Keyboard preludes

Prelude in a MB 27/12
Prelude in F MB 55/3 Listed:
  MB 28/115
Prelude in G MB 55/4 Listed:
  MB 28/116

Keyboard fantasias

Ut mi re MB 28/65
Fantasia in a MB 27/13
Verse (Fantasia) in C MB 27/28
Fantasia in G MB 28/62
Fantasia in G MB 28/63
Fantasia in a (and C) MB 27/27 The
  second part is no. 42 in *My Ladye
  Nevells Booke*

Keyboard arrangement

O quam gloriosum MB 55/48
Arrangement, perhaps by Byrd, of
Liber primus sacrarum cantionum
1589, nos. 22-23.

Latin motets and mass movement

Ad Dominum cum tribularer (*a* 8)
  BE 8/7
Ad punctum in modico (*fragmentary*)
  − In momento indignationis
  (*a* 5) BE 9
Alleluia. Confitemini Domino (*a* 4)
  BE 8/1
Audivi vocem (*a* 5) BE 9
Ave regina caelorum (*a* 5) BE 8/10
  Authenticity uncertain
Benigne fac (*a* 5) BE 9
[*Chant* Christe qui lux es] −
  Precamur sancte Domine (*a* 4)
  BE 8/3
[*Chant* Christe qui lux es] −
  Precamur sancte Domine (*a* 5)
  BE 8/4
Circumspice Ierusalem − Ecce enim
  veniunt (*a* 6) BE 9
Decantabat populus (*a* 5) BE 9
  Authenticity uncertain
De lamentatione Ieremiae
  prophetae − Heth. Cogitavit
  Dominus − Teth. Defixae
  sunt − Joth. Sederunt in terra −
  Ierusalem convertere (*a* 5)
  BE 8/5
Deus in adiutorium −Avertantur
  retrorsum − Exultent et
  laetentur − Et dicant semper −
  Ego vero egenus (*a* 6) BE 9
Domine ante te (*a* 6) BE 9
Domine Deus omnipotens − Ideo
  misericors (*a* 5) BE 9
Domine exaudi orationem meam et
  clamor (*a* 5) BE 9
Domine quis habitabit (*a* 9) BE 8/8
Ne perdas cum impiis − Eripe me (*a*
  5) BE 8/11
Omni tempore benedic Deum −
  Memor esto fili (*a* 5) BE 8/12

O salutaris hostia (*a* 6) BE 8/6

Peccavi super numerum (*a* 5) BE 9

Petrus beatus − Quodcunque vinclis
− Per immensa saecula −
Gloria Deo (*a* 5) BE 8/9

Quomodo cantabimus − Si non
proposuero (*a* 8) BE 9

Reges Tharsis (*a* 5) BE 9
Authenticity uncertain

[*Chant* Sacris solemnis] − Noctis
recolitur − Dedit fragilibus −
Panis angelicus (*a* 5) BE 9
Authenticity uncertain

Similes illis fiant (*a* 4) BE 8/2
Second section of *In exitu Israel*,
of which John Sheppard and
William Mundy wrote the first and
third sections

Vide Domine quoniam tribulor −
Quoniam amaritudine (*a* 5) BE 9
Authenticity uncertain

Sanctus (*a* 3) BE 9 Authenticity
uncertain

English services

Litany (*a* 5) BE 10a/4

Preces − Responses (*a* 5) BE 10a/1

First preces and psalms: Preces (*a* 5)
− O clap your hands (*a* 5) −
Save me O God (*a* 7) BE 10a/2

Second preces and psalms: Preces (*a*
5) − When Israel came out of
Egypt (*a* 5) − Hear my prayer O
God (*a* 5) − Teach me O Lord
(1, 5 voices + organ) BE 10a/3

Short service: Venite − Te Deum −
Benedictus − Kyrie − Creed −
Magnificat − Nunc dimittis (*a* 6)
BE 10a/5

Second service: Magnificat − Nunc
dimittis (1 and 5 voices + organ)
BE 10a/6

Third service: Magnificat − Nunc
dimittis (*a* 5) BE 10a/7

Great service: Venite − Te Deum −
Benedictus − Kyrie − Creed −
Magnificat − Nunc dimittis
(*a* 10) BE 10b

Full anthems

Arise O Lord − Help us O God
(*a* 6) BE 11/1

Exalt thyself O God (*a* 6) BE 11/2

How long shall mine enemies
triumph? (*a* 5) BE 11/3

O God the proud are risen (*a* 6)
BE 11/4

O God whom our offences have
displeased (*a* 5) BE 11/5

O Lord make thy servant Elizabeth
(*a* 6) BE 11/6

O praise our Lord − Extol the
greatness − Praise him on
tube − gladsome sound − all
the creatures (*a* 5) BE 11/21

Out of the deep (*a* 6) BE 11/7

Prevent us O Lord (*a* 5) BE 11/8

Save me O God (*a* 5) BE 11/9
Authenticity uncertain

Sing joyfully (*a* 6) BE 11/10

Verse anthems

Alack when I look back (*a* 1, *a* 5)
William Hunnis BE 11/11

Behold O God the sad and heavy
case (*a* 2, *a* 5) BE 11/12

Christ rising again/Christ is risen
(*a* 6) BE 11/13

Hear my prayer O Lord (*a* 1, *a* 5)
BE 11/14

O Lord rebuke me not (*a* 1, *a* 5)
BE 11/15

Thou God that guid'st (*a* 2, *a* 5)
  William Hunnis BE 11/16

Part-songs

O sweet deceit (*a* 5) BE 16/4
What pleasure have great princes
  (*a* 4) BE 16/5 Possibly a chorus to

no. 19 of *Psalmes, sonets, &
  songs*, 1588
What vaileth it to rule? (*a* 5)
  BE 16/6

Canon

Canon six in one and two in four
  BE 16/33

D. LOST WORKS AND FRAGMENTARY WORKS WHICH CANNOT BE RECONSTRUCTED

Ah youthful years BE 16/34
Behold how good BE 16/35
Behold O God, with thy all
  prosp'ring eye BE 11/22 Possibly
  a contrafactum of *Behold O God
  the sad and heavy case* BE 11/12
Calui curis (See p. ...)
Cease cares BE 16/36
Depart ye furies BE 16/37
I will give laud BE 16/38
If trickling tears BE 16/39
In tower most high BE 16/40

Let us be glad BE 11/23
Look and bow down BE 16/41
Medulla musicke (See p. ...)
O happy thrice BE 16/42
O trifling toys BE 16/43
Preces Deo fundamus BE 16/44
Psalm 100 (BE 10a/10)
Sing ye to our God BE 11/24
Sponsus amat sponsum BE 9
What wights are these? BE 16/45
While that a cruel fire BE 16/46
With sighs and tears BE 16/47

E. SPURIOUS WORKS

For a discussion of pieces attributed to Byrd inaccurately or on inadequate grounds, either in sources or editions, see *The Byrd Edition*; Brown, 1976; Neighbour, 1978; Kerman, 1981; and Turbet, 1987. The authenticity of some pieces printed in MB 55 is discussed by Neighbour, 1992. Contrafacta of Byrd's works and Byrd apocrypha are listed by Turbet, 1987, pp. 87-100.

A piece not mentioned in these works, and which is probably to be classified as spurious, is the four-voice motet *Haec est dies*, published as a supplement to *Annual Byrd Newsletter*, no. 2, 1996. On f. 116ᵛ of Bodleian Library manuscript Eng. th. b. 2 it is attributed to 'Mʳ. Byrd'. The manuscript, which is mentioned by Brett (1991, p. ix) as a source of information about Father Garnet, is the second volume of two (b. 1 and b. 2) completed early in the seventeenth century by someone calling himself 'Thomas Jollet', who says that Fathers Barkworth and Filcock sang *Haec est dies Domini: gaudeamus* on their way to execution in 1601.[4] On ff. 136v-137r is a four-voice setting of *Adoramus te Christe*, apparently signed by Jollet as composer. See Mary Clapinson and T. D. Rogers, *Summary catalogue of post-medieval western manuscripts in the Bodleian Library... Acquisitions 1916-1975... Vol. II ...* (Oxford, 1991), pp. 721-722, nos. 46532 and 46533. See also the note in *Early Music Review*, no. 21, 1996, p. 16.

4 It is possible that Jollet knew Byrd had composed settings of *Haec dies*, and assumed an anonymous *Haec est dies* to be by him. The music offers no obvious reason for its ascription to Byrd. See 'Is 'Byrd's' *Haec* a faec?' by John Morehen, in *Early Music Review*, no. 24, 1996, pp. 8-9.

ABBREVIATIONS AND PUBLIC RECORD OFFICE CLASSES

Abbreviations

BE	The Byrd Edition
BL	British Library
ERO	Essex Record Office
GL	Guildhall Library
GLRO	Greater London Record Office
LA	Lincolnshire Archives
MB	Musica Britannica edition
PRO	Public Record Office
SRO	Staffordshire Record Office

Public Record Office classes

ASSI 35	Assizes. Indictment files
C2	Chancery proceedings, series I indexes
C3	Chancery proceedings, series II
C33	Chancery entry books of orders and decrees
C66	Chancery patent rolls
C142	Chancery inquisitions post mortem, series II
CP25(2)	Court of Common Pleas feet of fines
E115	Certificates of residence
E117	Church goods
E123	King's Remembrancer entry books of decrees and orders, series I
E124	King's Remembrancer entry books of decrees and orders, series II
E126	King's Remembrancer entry books of decrees and orders, series IV (decrees)
E128	King's Remembrancer entry books of decrees and orders [no series number]
E134	Depositions by commission
E159	King's Remembrancer memoranda rolls
E179	Subsidy rolls
E310	Augmentation Office particulars for leases
E315	Augmentation Office miscellaneous books
E372	Exchequer. Pipe Office. Pipe rolls
E377	Exchequer. Pipe Office. Recusant rolls (Pipe Office series)
E401	Enrolments and registers of receipts

E405	Rolls and books of receipts and issues
E407	Exchequer of Receipt miscellanea
KB9	Ancient indictments
KB27	Court of King's Bench. Plea and Crown sides. *Coram rege* rolls
KB29	Court of King's Bench. Crown side. Controlment rolls
KB37	*Brevia regis* rolls.
LC2	Lord Chamberlain's Department. Records of special events
PRO 30/38	Registers of writs issuing from the Court of Star Chamber
Prob. 10	Original wills
Prob. 11	Probate copies of wills
PSO 5	Privy Seal Office. Docquet books
REQ1	Court of Requests. Books of orders and decrees
REQ2	Court of Requests. Proceedings
SP12	State papers domestic, Elizabeth I
SP14	State papers domestic, James I
STAC5	Star Chamber proceedings, Elizabeth I

BIBLIOGRAPHY

The following list is confined to books and articles mentioned in footnotes. Only the principal place of publication is given. For a full record of literature relating to Byrd see Turbet, 1987, and Turbet, 1994(a), extended by Turbet, 1994(b) and the *Annual Byrd Newsletter*.

Andrews, Hilda, ed. 1926. *My Ladye Nevells booke of virginal music by William Byrd* ... London. (With a new introduction by Blanche Winogron, New York, 1969.)

Andrews, H. K. 1962. 'Transposition of Byrd's vocal polyphony', *Music and Letters*, xliii, pp. 25-37.

– – – 1964. 'The printed part-books of Byrd's vocal music', *The Library*, 5th series, xix, pp. 2-10.

– – – 1966. *The technique of Byrd's vocal polyphony*. London.

Anglés, Higinio. 1944. *La música en la corte de Carlos V*. Barcelona. *Monumentos de la música española*, 2.

Anglin, Jay Pascal. 1965. The court of the Archdeacon of Essex, 1571-1609: an institutional and social study. Dissertation, University of California, L. A. (Typescript at Essex Record Office.)

Annual Byrd newsletter. 1995- . (No. 1 issued with *Early Music Review*, no. 11, June 1995.)

Anstruther, Godfrey. 1953. *Vaux of Harrowden*. Newport, Mon.

– – – 1969. *The seminary priests ... Elizabethan 1558-1603*. Ware, Durham.

Apel, Willi. 1972. *The history of keyboard music to 1700, translated and revised by Hans Tischler*. Bloomington, Ind.

Arber, Edward. 1875-94. *A transcript of the registers of the Company of Stationers of London; 1554-1640 A.D.* London. 5 vols.

Ashbee, Andrew. 1986-96. *Records of English court music*. Snodland (later Aldershot). 9 vols.

Baillie, Hugh. 1962. 'Some biographical notes on English church musicians, chiefly working in London (1485-1569)', *Royal Musical Association Research Chronicle*, 2, pp. 18-57.

Baker, J. H. 1990. *An introduction to English legal history. Third edition*. London.

Baker, T. F. T. 1976. *A history of Middlesex ... Volume V*. London. *Victoria county histories*.

Baldwin, David. 1990. *The Chapel Royal ancient & modern*. London.

Banks, Chris, ed. 1993. *Sundry sorts of music books. Essays on the British Library collections presented to O. W. Neighbour on his 70th birthday*. London. Co-editors: Arthur Searle, Malcolm Turner.

Bannerman, W. Bruce, ed. 1908. *The registers of St, Helen's, Bishopsgate, London*. London. *Harleain Society, Registers*, 31.

− − − 1913. *The registers of All Hallows, Bread Street, and of St John the Evangelist, Friday Street*. London. *Harleian Society, Registers*, 43.

Barker, G. F. Russell and Stenning, Alan H. 1928. *The record of old Westminsters. A biographical list*. London. 2 vols.

Barnard, John. 1641. *The first book of selected church musick, consisting of services and anthems, such as are now used in the cathedrall, and collegiat churches of this kingdome*. London.

Barnett, Howard B. 1969. 'John Case − an Elizabethan musical scholar', *Music and Letters*, l, pp. 252-266.

Batho, G. R., ed. 1971. *A calendar of the Shrewsbury and Talbot papers in Lambeth Palace Library and the College of Arms. Volume II: Talbot papers in the College of Arms*. London.

Beechey, Gwilym. 1981. 'Morley's church music', *Musical Times*, cxxii, pp. 625-629.

Bennett, John. 1988. 'A Tallis patron?', *Royal Musical Association Research Chronicle*, 21, pp. 41-44.

− − − 1992. 'Byrd and Jacobean consort music: a look at Richard Mico'. In Brown and Turbet, 1992, pp. 129-140.

− − − and Willetts, P. 1977. 'Richard Mico', *Chelys*, vii, pp. 24-46.

Bergsagel, John D. 1963. 'The date and provenance of the Forrest-Heyther collection of Tudor Masses', *Music and Letters*, xliv, pp. 240-248.

Blewett, P. R. W., ed. 1984. All Hallows by the Tower ... baptisms 1558-1575. (Computer script. Copy in Guildhall Library.)

− − − 1986. All Hallows by the Tower ... burials. (Computer script. Copy in Guildhall Library.)

Blow, John. 1700. *Amphion Anglicanus*. London.

Bossy, John. 1962. 'The character of Elizabethan Catholicism', *Past and Present*, no. 21, pp. 39-59.

− − − 1975. *The English Catholic community 1570-1850*. London.

Bowers, Roger. 1987. 'The vocal scoring, choral balance and performing pitch of Latin church polypony in England, c.1500-58', *Journal of the Royal Musical Association*, cxii, pp. 38-76.

− − − 1994. 'Music and worship to 1640'. In Owen, 1994, pp. 47-76.

− − − 1995. 'To chorus from quartet: the performing resource for English church polyphony, c.1390-1559'. In Morehen, 1995, pp. 1-47.

Boyce, William, ed. 1760-73. *Cathedral music: being a collection in score of the most valuable and useful compositions for that service, by the several English masters of the last two hundred years*. London. 3 vols.

Boyd, Morrison Comegys. 1962. *Elizabethan music and musical criticism ... Second edition*. Philadelphia.

Bradshaw, Henry, ed. 1892-97. *Statutes of Lincoln Cathedral, arranged by ...*

Henry Bradshaw ... edited ... by Chr. Wordsworth. Cambridge. 2 vols. in 3.

Bray, Roger W. 1969. 'British Museum Add. Mss. 17802-5 (the Gyffard part-books): an index and commentary', *Royal Musical Association Research Chronicle*, 7, pp. 31-50.

— — — 1971. 'The part-books, Oxford, Christ Church, MSS 979-983: an index and commentary', *Musica Disciplina*, xxv, pp. 179-197.

— — — 1974. 'British Library, R. M. 24 d 2 (John Baldwin's commonplace book): an index and commentary', *Royal Musical Association Research Chronicle*, 12, pp. 137-151.

Brennan, Michael G. 1993. 'Sir Charles Somerset's music books', *Music and Letters*, lxxiv, pp. 501-518.

Brennecke, E. 1952. 'A singing man of Windsor', *Music and Letters*, xxxiii, pp. 33-40.

Brett, Philip. 1961-62. 'The English consort song, 1570-1625', *Proceedings of the Royal Musical Association*, lxxxviii, pp. 73-88.

— — — 1964(a). 'Edward Paston (1550-1630): a Norfolk gentleman and his musical collection', *Transactions of the Cambridge Bibliographical Society*, iv, pp. 51-69.

— — — 1964(b). The songs of William Byrd. Dissertation, University of Cambridge. 2 vols.

— — — ed. 1970. *Consort songs for voice and viols.* London. *The Byrd Edition*, 15.

— — — 1971-72. 'Word-setting in the songs of Byrd', *Proceedings of the Royal Musical Association*, xcviii, pp. 47-64.

— — — ed. 1974. *Consort songs ... Second, revised edition.* London. *Musica Britannica*, 22.

— — — ed. 1976. *Madrigals, songs and canons.* London. *The Byrd Edition*, 16.

— — — 1980. 'Editing Byrd', *Musical Times*, cxxi, pp. 492-495, 557-559.

— — — 1981(a). 'Homage to Taverner in Byrd's masses', *Early Music*, ix, pp. 169-176.

— — — ed. 1981(b). *The Masses (1592-1595).* London. *The Byrd Edition*, 4.

— — — ed. 1989. *Gradualia I (1605) The Marian masses.* London. *The Byrd Edition*, 5.

— — — ed. 1991. *Gradualia I (1605) All Saints and Corpus Christi.* London. *The Byrd Edition*, 6a.

— — — ed. 1993(a). *Gradualia I (1605) Other feasts and devotions.* London. *The Byrd Edition*, 6b.

— — — 1993(b). 'Pitch and transposition in the Paston manuscripts'. In Banks, 1993, pp. 89-118.

Bridgett, T. E. 1888. 'The rood of Boxley; or, how a lie grows', *Dublin Review*, Third series, xix, no. 1, pp. 1-33.

Brigg, W., ed. 1890. *The register book of the parish of St. Nicholas Acons, London, 1529-1812.* Leeds.

Briggs, Nancy. 1968. 'William, 2nd Lord Petre (1575-1637)', *The Essex Recusant*, x, pp. 51-64.

Briquet, C. M. 1968. *Les filigranes ... ed. Allan Stevenson*. Amsterdam. 4 vols.

Brown, A. 1968-69. ''My Lady Nevell's Book' as a source of Byrd's keyboard music', *Proceedings of the Royal Musical Association*, xcv, pp. 29-39.

— — — 1969. A critical edition of the keyboard music of William Byrd. Dissertation, University of Cambridge. 3 vols.

— — — 1974. 'Keyboard music by Byrd 'Upon a plainsong'', *Organ Yearbook*, v, pp. 30-39.

— — — ed. 1976. *William Byrd. Keyboard music*. London. *Musica Britannica*, 27-28. 2 vols. Revised reprint of 28 issued in 1985.

— — — ed. 1981. *Cantiones sacrae II (1591)*. London. *The Byrd Edition*, 3.

— — — ed. 1989. *Elizabethan keyboard music*. London. *Musica Britannica*, 55.

— — — and Turbet, Richard, eds. 1992. *Byrd studies*. Cambridge.

Brown, David. 1957. 'William Byrd's 1588 volume', *Music and Letters*, xxxviii, pp. 371-377.

— — — 1959. 'Thomas Morley and the Catholics: some speculations', *Monthly Musical Record*, lxxxix, pp. 53-61.

— — — 1960. 'The styles and chronology of Thomas Morley's motets', *Music and Letters*, xli, pp. 216-222.

Buck, P., ed. 1928. *Thomas Tallis c.1505-1585*. London. *Tudor Church Music*, 6.

Bull, John. 1597. *The oration of Maister John Bull, Doctor of Musicke, and one of the Gentlemen of hir Majesties Royall Chappell. As hee pronounced the same, beefore divers worshipfull persons ... the 6. day of October. 1597*. London. (The title-page, with an off-print of the first page on the verso, is Harleian 5936, f. 118ᵛ, in the British Library's printed books department.)

Burke, Arthur Meredith. 1913. *Indexes to the ancient testamentary records of Westminster*. London.

— — — ed. 1914. *Memorials of St Margaret's church, Westminster. The parish registers, 1539-1661*. London.

Burke, Sir Bernard. 1884. *The general armory of England, Scotland, Ireland and Wales*. London.

Burney, Charles. 1776-89. *A general history of music from the earliest ages to the present period*. London. 4 vols. (With critical and historical notes by Frank Mercer, London, 1935.)

Butler, G. G. 1980. 'Music and rhetoric in early seventeenth-century English sources', *Music and Letters*, xix, pp. 280-294.

Caldwell, John. 1965(a). British Museum Additional manuscript 29996. Dissertation, University of Oxford.

— — — 1965(b). *Early Tudor organ music: I. Music for the Office*. London. *Early English church music*, 6.

— — — 1965(c). 'Keyboard plainsong settings in England, 1500-1600', *Musica*

Disciplina, xix, pp. 129-153. ('Addenda et corrigenda', *Musica Disciplina*, xxxiv, 1980, pp. 215-219.)

— — — 1991. *The Oxford history of English music. Volume I: from the beginnings to c.1715*. Oxford.

— — — ed. 1995. *Tudor keyboard music c.1520-1580*. London. *Musica Britannica*, 66.

— — — ed. 1990. *The well enchanting skill: music, poetry, and drama in the culture of the Renaissance. Essays in honour of F. W. Sternfeld*. Oxford. Co-editors: Edward Olleson, Susan Wollenberg.

Camden miscellany. 1853. *The Camden miscellany, volume the second: containing ... household account of the Princess Elizabeth, 1551-2*. London. *Camden Society, 1st series*, 55.

Campbell, Mother Joseph Mary. 1959-65. 'P.R.O. E.377/57: Essex recusants in an Exchequer document 1582-1642', *The Essex Recusant*, i, 1959, pp. 51-61, 104-109; iii, 1961, pp. 24-30, 124-128; iv, 1962, pp. 15-24, 71-76, 111-115; v, 1963, pp. 27-29; vi, 1964, pp. 90-95; vii, 1965, pp. 36-39. (The first article is signed 'Mother Joseph Mary Campbell'. Subsequent articles are signed 'Mother Joseph Mary' and 'Mother Nicholas'.)

Caraman, Philip. 1964. *Henry Garnet 1555-1606 and the Gunpowder Plot*. London.

Catholic Record Society. 1905. *Miscellanea · I*. London.

— — — 1906. *Miscellanea · II*. London.

— — — 1907. *Miscellanea · IV*. London, *Catholic Record Society, Publications*, 4.

— — — 1921. *Miscellanea XII*. London. *Catholic Record Society, Publications*, 22.

Cave-Browne, John. 1892. *The history of Boxley parish*. Maidstone.

Centre National de la Recherche Scientifique. 1954. *Musique et poésie au XVIᵉ siècle*. Paris. *Colloques Internationaux du Centre National de la Recherche Scientifique. Sciences humaines*, 5.

Chappell, William. 1893. *Old English popular music ... A new edition ... entirely revised by H. Ellis Wooldridge*. London. 2 vols. (In one volume, with a supplement by Frank Kidson, New York, 1961.)

Charles, Amy M. 1974. 'Mrs. Herbert's kitchin booke', *English Literary Renaissance*, iv, pp. 164-173.

Charteris, Richard. 1974. 'Jacobean musicians at Hatfield House', *Royal Musical Association Research Chronicle*, 12, pp. 115-136.

— — — 1981. 'New information about the life of Alfonso Ferrabosco the elder (1543-1588)', *Royal Musical Association Research Chronicle*, 17, pp. 97-114.

Chester, Joseph Lemuel, ed. 1876. *The marriage, baptismal, and burial registers of the collegiate church or abbey of St. Peter, Westminster*. London. *Harleian Society, Publications*, 10.

− − −   1880. *The parish registers of St. Mary Aldermary*. London. *Harleian Society, Registers*, 5.

− − −   and Armytage, George J., eds. 1886. *Allegations for marriage licenses issued by the Dean and Chapter of Westminster, 1558 to 1699*. London. *Harleian Society, Publications*, 23.

Clarke, A. W. Hughes, ed. 1939. *The register of St. Dunstan in the East London 1558-1654 ... Part I*. London. *Harleian Society, Publications*, 69.

Clulow, Peter. 1966. 'Publication dates for Byrd's Latin masses', *Music and Letters*, xlvii, 1966, pp. 1-9.

Cockburn, J. S., ed. 1978. *Calendar of assize records. Essex indictments Elizabeth I*. London.

− − −   1982. *Calendar of assize records. Essex indictments James I*. London.

Cole, Elizabeth. 1952. 'In search of Francis Tregian', *Music and Letters*, xxxiii, pp. 28-32.

− − −   1952-53. 'Seven problems of the Fitzwilliam virginal book', *Proceedings of the Royal Musical Association*, lxxix, pp. 51-66.

Cole, R. E. G., ed. 1917. *Chapter Acts of the Cathedral Church of St. Mary of Lincoln A.D. 1536-1547*. Horncastle. *Lincoln Record Society, Publications*, 13.

− − −   ed. 1920. *Chapter Acts of the Cathedral Church of St. Mary of Lincoln A.D. 1547-1559*. Horncastle. *Lincoln Record Society, Publications*, 15.

Collins, H. B. 1923. 'Byrd's Latin church music', *Music and Letters*, iv, pp. 254-260.

Colvin, H. M., ed. 1963-73. *The history of the king's works*. London. 6 vols.

Committee for Compounding. 1889-92. *Calendar of the proceedings of the Committee for Compounding, &c., 1643-1660 ... General proceedings. Edited by Mary Anne Everett Greene*. London. 5 vols.

Cuneo, Anne. 1995. 'Francis Tregian the younger: musician, collector and humanist?', *Music and Letters*, lxxvi, pp. 398-404.

Cunningham, Peter, ed. 1842. *Extracts from the accounts of the revels at court, in the reigns of Queen Elizabeth and King James I., from the original office books of the masters and yeomen*. London. *Shakespeare Society*.

Cunningham, Walker. 1984. *The keyboard music of John Bull*. Ann Arbor, Mich. *Studies in musicology*, 71.

Cust, Lady Elizabeth Caroline. 1909. *Records of the Cust family ... Series II. The Brownlows of Belton. 1550-1779*. London.

Daniel, Ralph T. and le Huray, Peter. 1972. *The sources of English church music 1549-1660*. London. *Early English Church Music*, Supplementary volume 1.

Dart, Thurston. 1959(a). 'Search for the real John Bull', *New York Times*, 1 November 1959, section 2, p. 1.

− − −   1959(b). 'Morley and the Catholics: some further speculations', *Monthly Musical Record*, lxxxix, pp. 89-92.

– – – 1960. 'An unknown letter from Dr. John Bull', *Acta Musicologica*, xxxii, pp. 175-177.

– – – ed. 1962. *Parthenia ... Second, revised edition*. London. *Early keyboard music*, 19.

– – – 1964. 'Two new documents relating to the royal music, 1584-1605', *Music and Letters*, lvi, pp. 16-21.

– – – ed. 1967. *John Bull. Keyboard music: II. Second revised edition*. London. *Musica Britannica*, 19.

– – – and Donington, Robert. 1949. 'The origin of the In Nomine', *Music and Letters*, xxx, pp. 101-106.

Daubney, Brian Blyth. 1992. *Aspects of British song*. Upminster, 1992.

Davison, Nigel. 1973. 'Structure and unity in four free-composed Tudor masses', *Music Review*, xxxiv, pp. 328-338.

Dawson, Giles. 1949-50. 'A gentleman's purse', *Yale Review*, xxxix, pp. 631-646.

Dent, Edward J. 1929. 'William Byrd and the madrigal'. In Lott, 1929, pp. 24-30.

Dictionary of national biography edited by Leslie Stephen [and Sidney Lee]. London, 1885-1900. 63 vols. with supplements.

Doe, P. 1976. *Thomas Tallis*. London. *Oxford studies of composers*, 4.

– – – ed. 1979-88. *Elizabethan consort music*. London. *Musica Britannica*, 44-45. 2 vols.

Doorslaer, G. van. 1921. *La vie et les oeuvres de Philippe de Monte*. Brussels. *Académie Royale de Belgique. Classe des Beaux-Arts. Mémoires*, i/1.

'Dotted Crotchet'. 1905. 'St Andrew's church, Holborn', *Musical Times*, xlvi, pp. 153-165.

Drake, Henry H., ed. 1886. *Hasted's history of Kent, corrected, enlarged and continued to the present time ... The hundred of Blackheath*. London.

Drake, Warren, ed. 1996. *Liber amicorum John Steele*. Stuyvesant, N. Y.

Drummond, Henry. 1846. *Histories of noble British families*. London. 2 vols.

Dugdale, Sir William. 1817-30. *Monasticon anglicanum ... A new edition ... by John Caley [et al.]*. London. 6 vols.

– – – 1818. *The history of St. Paul's cathedral ... with a continuation and additions ... by Henry Ellis*. London.

Duncan-Jones, Katherine. 1990. ''Melancholic times': musical recollections of Sidney, William Byrd and Thomas Watson'. In Caldwell, 1990, pp. 171-180.

Edwards, A. C. 1975. *John Petre. Essays on the life and background of John 1st Lord Petre, 1549-1613*. London.

Edwards, Warwick, ed. 1984. *Latin motets (from manuscript sources)*. London. *The Byrd Edition*, 8.

Eggar, Katharine E. 1934-35. 'The seventeenth Earl of Oxford as musician, poet and controller of the Queen's revels', *Proceedings of the Musical Association*, lxi, pp. 39-59.

Elder, John. 1555. *The copie of a letter sent in to Scotlande, of the arivall and landynge, and moste noble marryage of the most illustre Prynce Philippe, Prynce of Spaine, to the most excellente Princes Marye Quene of England.* London.

Elders, Willem. 1994. *Symbolic scores: studies in the music of the Renaissance.* Leiden.

Elliott, Kenneth, ed. 1964. *Music of Scotland 1500-1700 ... Second, revised edition.* London. *Musica Britannica*, 15.

— — — ed. 1971. *Consort music.* London. *The collected works of William Byrd*, 17. (Incorporated in *The Byrd Edition*.)

Elrington, C. R. and Herbert, N. M. 1972. *A history of the county of Gloucester ... Volume X.* London. *Victoria county histories.*

Emmison, F. G. 1961. *Tudor secretary: Sir William Petre at court and home.* London.

— — — 1978. *Elizabethan life: wills of Essex gentry and merchants.* Chelmsford.

— — — 1980. *Elizabethan life: wills of Essex gentry & yeomen.* Chelmsford.

Essex Record Office. Calendar of Queen's Bench Indictments Ancient relating to Essex in the Public Record Office. (Typescript at Essex Record Office.)

Fellowes, Edmund H. 1948. *William Byrd. Second edition.* London.

— — — 1949. 'My Ladye Nevells Booke', *Music and Letters*, xxx, 1949, pp. 1-7.

— — — 1967. *English madrigal verse 1588-1632. Revised and enlarged by Frederick W. Sternfeld and David Greer. Third edition.* Oxford.

Fenlon, Iain and Milsom, John. 1984. '"Ruled paper imprinted": music paper and patents in sixteenth-century England', *Journal of the American Musicological Society*, xxxvii, pp. 139-163.

Feuillerat, A. 1908. *Documents relating to the Office of Revels in the time of Queen Elizabeth.* Louvain.

Fitch, Marc, ed. 1974. *Index to testamentary records in the Commissary Court of London (London Division) ... Volume II 1489-1570.* London. *Historical Manuscripts Commission*, JP 13.

— — — ed. 1979. *Index to the testamentary records in the Archdeaconry Court of London now preserved in the Guildhall Library London. Volume I (1363)-1649.* London. *The Index Library.*

Flynn, Jane. 1995. 'The education of choristers in England during the sixteenth century'. In Morehen, 1995, pp. 180-199.

Foley, Henry. 1877-84. *Records of the English province of the Society of Jesus.* London. 8 vols.

Ford, Wyn K. 1979. 'Music at Knole', *National Trust studies*, 1, pp. 161-179.

Foster, C. W., ed. 1911. *Lincoln episcopal records in the time of Thomas Cooper, S. T. P., Bishop of Lincoln, A. D. 1571 to A. D. 1584.* London. *Lincoln Record Society, Publications.*

– – –   ed. 1915. *The parish registers of St Margaret in the Close of Lincoln 1538-1837.* Horncastle. *Lincoln Record Society, Publications.*

Foster, Joseph. 1887-88. *Alumni Oxonienses ... 1715-1886.* London. 4 vols.

– – –   1891-92. *Alumni Oxonienses: the members of the University of Oxford, 1500-1714.* Oxford. 4 vols.

Frere, Walter Howard, ed. 1910. *Visitation articles and injunctions of the period of the Reformation. Volume III 1559-1575.* London. *Alcuin Club, Collections,* 16.

Frost, Maurice. 1953. *English & Scottish psalm & hymn tunes c.1543-1677.* London.

Garton, Charles. 1983. Lincoln School 1500-1585: a draft history. (Typescript. Copies in Lincoln Cathedral Library and Lincoln Archives.)

Gaskin, Hilary. 'Baldwin and the Nevell hand'. In Brown and Turbet, 1992, pp. 159-173

Green, Vivian. 1977. *The commonwealth of Lincoln College 1427-1977.* Oxford.

Grove. 1980. *The new Grove dictionary of music and musicians, edited by Stanley Sadie.* London. 20 vols.

Guildhall Library. 1990. *A handlist of parish registers, register transcripts and related records at Guildhall Library. Part one: City of London ... Sixth (revised) edition.* London.

Gurr, Andrew. 1987. *Playgoing in Shakespeare's London.* Cambridge.

Hackett, Maria. 1832. *Correspondence and evidences respecting the ancient collegiate school attached to Saint Paul's Cathedral.* London.

Haines, Charles Reginald. 1930. *Dover Priory. A history.* Cambridge.

Hallen, A. W. Cornelius, ed. 1885-94. *Transcript of the registers of St. Botolph Bishopsgate.* London. 3 vols. *Hallen's London City church registers,* 2.

Harington, Sir John. 1769. *Nugae antiquae: being a miscellaneous collection of original papers in prose and verse.* London.

Harley, John. 1992-94. *British harpsichord music.* Aldershot. 2 vols.

Harper, John. 1991. *The forms and orders of western liturgy from the tenth to the eighteenth century.* Oxford.

Harrison, Christopher. 1990-91. 'William Byrd and the Pagets of Beaudesert: a musical connection', *Staffordshire Studies,* iii, pp. 51-63.

Harrison, Frank Ll. 1980. *Music in medieval Britain. Fourth edition.* Buren.

Hawkins, Sir John. 1963. *A general history of the science and practice of music ... With a new introduction by Charles Cudworth.* New York. 2 vols.

Henry, Leigh. 1937. *Dr. John Bull 1562-1628.* London.

Henson, T, ed. 1930. *Registers of the English College at Valladolid, 1589-1862.* Leeds. *Catholic Record Society, Publications,* 30.

Hill, Sir Francis. 1956. *Tudor and Stuart Lincoln.* Cambridge.

– – –   1965. *Medieval Lincoln.* Cambridge.

Hillebrand, Harold Newcomb. 1926. *The child actors: a chapter in Elizabethan stage history.* Urbana, Ill. *University of Illinois studies in language and literature,* 11.

Historical Manuscripts Commission. *Calendar of the manuscripts of ... the Marquis of Salisbury ... at Hatfield House, Hertfordshire.* London.
    1888. *Part II.*
    1899. *Part VIII.*
    1938. *Part XVII,* ed. M. S. Giuseppi.
    1968. *Part XX (A.D.1608),* ed. M. S. Giuseppi and G. Dyfnallt Owen.
    1976. *Part XXIV Addenda 1605-1668,* ed. G. Dyfnallt Owen.

— — — 1885. *The manuscripts of the Earl of Westmorland.* London. *10th report, Appendix, Part IV.*

— — — 1888. *The manuscripts of His Grace the Duke of Rutland ... Vol. I.* London. *12th report, appendix, part IV.*

— — — 1940. *Report on the manuscripts of the Marquess of Downshire ... Volume four Papers of William Trumbull the elder January 1613 - August 1614 Edited by A. B. Hinds.* London.

Hofman, May and Morehen, John. 1987. *Latin music in British sources c.1485-c1610.* London. *Early English Church Music,* Supplementary volume 2.

Holinshed, Raphael. 1807-8. *Holinshed's chronicles of England, Scotland and Ireland.* London. 6 vols.

Hollybande, Claude [i.e. Claude de Sainliens]. 1573. *The French schoolemaster.* London.

Holman, Peter. 1993. *Four and twenty fiddlers: the violin at the English court 1540-1690.* Oxford. *Oxford monographs on music.*

Honigmann, E. A. J. and Brock, Susan. 1993. *Playhouse wills 1558-1642. An edition of wills by Shakespeare and his contemporaries.* Manchester.

Hovenden, Robert, ed. 1884-91. *A true register of all the christeninges, mariages, and burialles in the parish of St James Clerkenwell, from the yeare of our Lorde God 1551.* London. 3 vols. *Harleian Society, Publications. Registers,* 9, 13, 17.

Howard, J. Jackson and Burke, H. Farnham, eds. 1887. *Genealogical collections illustrating the history of Roman Catholic families of England. Based on the Lawson manuscript ... Part I ... II. - Petre ...* Printed for private circulation.

Hudson, Frederick. 1970. 'The performance of William Byrd's church music. I. Music acceptable in the Anglican church', *American Choral Review,* xii, pp. 147-159.

— — — 1972. 'The performance of William Byrd's church music. II. Music for the Catholic rites', *American Choral Review,* xiv, pp. 3-13.

Hulse, Lynn. 1991. 'The musical patronage of Robert Cecil, first Earl of Salisbury (1563-1612)', *Journal of the Royal Musical Association,* cxvi, pp. 24-40.

Hume, Martin A. S. and Tyler, Royall, eds. 1912. *Calendar of letters, despatches, and state papers, relating to the negotiations between England and Spain … Vol. IX. 1547-1549.* London.

Humphreys, David. 1979-80. 'Philip van Wilder: a study of his work and its sources', *Soundings*, ix [*recte* viii], pp. 13-36.

Humphries, C. and Smith, W. C. 1954. *Music publishing in the British Isles.* London.

Hunter, George, ed. 1994. *Five-part consort music.* Urbana, Ill.

Irving, John. 1990. 'Penetrating the preface to *Gradualia*', *Music Review*, li, pp. 157-166.

− − − 1992. 'Byrd and Tomkins: the instrumental music'. In Brown and Turbet, 1992, pp. 141-158.

Jackman, James L. 1963. 'Liturgical aspects of Byrd's Gradualia', *Musical Quartley*, xlix, pp. 17-37.

Jacquot, Jean, ed. 1955. *La musique instrumentale de la renaissance.* Paris. *Journées internationales d'études sur la musique instrumentale de la Renaissance [1954].*

Jeaffreson, John Cordy, ed. 1886. *Middlesex county records volume I. Indictments, coroners' inquests-post-mortem and recognizances from 3 Edward VI. to the end of the reign of Queen Elizabeth.* London.

Jones, Stanley. 1984. *The survey of ancient houses in Lincoln. I: Priorgate to Pottersgate.* Lincoln. Co-authors: Kathleen Major, Joan Varley.

Jonson, Ben. 1925. *Ben Jonson edited by C. H. Herford and Percy Simpson … The first volume.* Oxford.

Josephson, David. 1976. [Letter], *Musical Times*, cxvii, p. 739.

Kerman, Joseph. 1950. 'Edmund H. Fellowes, ed. The collected works of Byrd, vols. X-XII, London, Stainer & Bell, 1948', *Journal of the American Musicological Society*, iii, pp. 273-277. (Review.)

− − − 1955. 'An Elizabethan edition of Lassus', *Acta Musicologica*, xxvii, pp. 71-76.

− − − 1961. 'Byrd's motets: chronology and dating', *Journal of the American Musicological Society*, xiv, pp. 359-382.

− − − 1962(a). *The Elizabethan madrigal: a comparative study.* New York. *American Musicological Society, Studies and documents*, 4.

− − − 1962(b). 'The Elizabethan motet: a study of texts for music', *Studies in the Renaissance*, ix, pp. 273-308.

− − − 1966. 'Byrd, Tallis, and the art of imitation'. In LaRue, 1966, pp. 519-37; also in Kerman, 1994, pp. 90-105.

− − − 1975. 'Old and new in Byrd's Cantiones Sacrae'. In Sternfeld, 1975, pp. 25-43.

− − − 1979. 'Byrd's settings of the Ordinary of the Mass', *Journal of the American Musicological Society*, xxxii, pp. 408-439.

− − − 1981. *The masses and motets of William Byrd.* London.

− − − 1992. '"Write all these down": notes on a song by Byrd'. In Brown and

Turbet, 1992, pp. 112-128; also, with minor amendments, in Kerman, 1994, pp. 106-124.

− − − 1993. 'The missa 'Puer natus est' by Thomas Tallis'. In Banks, 1993, pp. 40-53; also in Kerman, 1994.

− − − 1994. *Write all these down. Essays on music.* Berkeley, Cal.

Kimbell, John. 1816. *An account of the legacies, gifts, rents, fees &c. ... of the parish of St. Alphege Greenwich.* [Greenwich.]

King, A. Hyatt. 1959. 'Fragments of early printed music in the Bagford collection', *Music and Letters*, xl, pp. 269-273.

Kirk, R. E. G. and Kirk, Ernest F., eds. 1900-08. *Returns of aliens dwelling in the city and suburbs of London.* Aberdeen. *Huguenot Society, Publications*, 10.

Kirwan, A. Lindsey. 1973. *The music of Lincoln Cathedral.* London.

Knight, Ellen E. 1980. 'The praise of musicke: John Case, Thomas Watson, and William Byrd', *Current Musicology*, xxx, pp. 37-51.

Krummel, Donald W. 1975. *English music printing 1553-1700.* London.

Lambarde, William. 1576. *A perambulation of Kent ... Collected and written (for the most part) in the yeere. 1570.* London.

Land, J. P. N. 1882-91. 'Het Luitboek van Thysius beschreven en toegelicht', *Tijdschrift der Vereeniging voor noord-nederlands musikgeschiedenis*, i (1882-85), pp. 129-195, 205-264; ii (1887), pp. 1-56, 109-174, 177-194, 278-350; iii (1888-91), pp. 1-57.

Lang, R. G., ed. 1993. *Two Tudor assessment rolls for the City of London: 1541 and 1582.* London. *London Record Society, Publications*, 29.

LaRue, Jan, ed. 1966. *Aspects of medieval and Renaissance music: a birthday offering to Gustave Reese.* New York.

le Huray, Peter. 1978. *Music and the Reformation in England 1549-1660.* Cambridge. *Cambridge studies in music.*

− − − 1982(a). 'The Chirk Castle partbooks', *Early music history*, 2, pp. 17-42.

− − − 1982(b). 'Some thoughts about cantus firmus composition; and a plea for Byrd's *Christus resurgens*'. In Brown and Turbet, 1992, pp. 1-23.

Leland, John. 1964. *The itinerary of John Leland in or about the years 1535-1543 ... Edited by Lucy Toulmin Smith.* London. 5 vols.

Letters and papers. *Letters and papers, foreign and domestic, of the reign of Henry VIII.* London.

1870. *Vol. IV. − Part I*, ed. J. S. Brewer.

1892. *Vol. XIII. − Part I*, ed. James Gairdner.

1910. *Vol. XXI. − Part 2.* ed. James Gairdner and R. H. Brodie.

1929. *Addenda. Vol. I. Part I.*

Littlehales, Henry, ed. 1905. *The medieval records of a London city church (St. Mary at Hill) A.D. 1420-1559.* London. *Early English Text Society, original series*, 125, 128.

Littledale, Willoughby A., ed. 1895. *The registers of Christ Church, Newgate, 1538 to 1754*. London. *Harleian Society, Registers*, 21.

Lloyd, David. 1766. *State-worthies: or, the statesmen and favourites of England from the Reformation to the Revolution*. London. 2 vols.

Lodge, Edmund. 1791. *llustrations of British history, biography and manners ... selected from the manuscripts of the noble families of Howard, Talbot and Cecil*. London. 3 vols.

London, H. Stanford and Rawlins, Sophia W., eds. 1963. *Visitation of London 1568*. London. *Harleian Society, Publications*, 109-110.

London County Council and London Survey Committee. 1930. *Survey of London ... Volume XIII The parish of St Margaret, Westminster*. London.

Lott, Walter, ed. 1929. *Festschrift für Johannes Wolf*. Berlin. Co-editors: Helmuth Osthoff, Werner Wolffheim.

Lowinsky Edward E. 1946. *Secret chromatic art in the Netherlands motet ... translated from the German by Carl Buchman*. New York.

Machyn, Henry. 1848. *The diary of Henry Machyn, citizen and Merchant-Taylor of London, from A.D.1550 to A.D.1563. Edited by John Gough Nichols*. London.

McCann, Timothy J., ed. 1986. *Recusants in the Exchequer pipe rolls 1581-1592, extracted by Dom Hugh Bowler*. [No place of publication.] *Catholic Record Society, Publications (Records series)*, 71.

McClatchey, D. and O'Farrell, N. McNeil. Calendar of Essex Assize files in the Public Record Office. (Typescript in Essex Record Office. Despite a note on the title-page, it is not wholly superseded by Cockburn, 1978 and 1982.)

McDonnell, Sir Michael. 1977. *The registers of St Paul's school 1509-1748*. London.

McMurray, William. 1925. *The records of two city parishes*. London.

Madden, Frederick, ed. 1831. *Privy purse expenses of the Princess Mary, daughter of King Henry the Eighth, afterwards Queen Mary*. London.

Maddison, A. R. 1885. 'Lincoln Cathedral choir A. D. 1558 to 1640', *Reports and papers read at the meetings of the Architectural Societies of the Diocese of Lincoln, County of York [etc] ... during the year MDCCCLXXXV* [i.e. *Associated Architectural Societies reports and papers*, xviii, part I], pp. 110-122.

Manning, Roger B. 1969. *Religion and society in Elizabethan Sussex*. Leicester.

Marlow, Richard. 1974. 'Sir Ferdinando Heyborne alias Richardson', *Musical Times*, cxv, pp. 736-739.

Martin, Adam. 1819. *Index to various repertories, books of orders, and decrees, and other records, preserved in the Court of the Exchequer*. London.

Martin, Charles Trice, ed. 1870. 'Journal of Sir Francis Walsingham, from Dec. 1570 to April 1583'. In *The Camden miscellany, volume the sixth*, London, 1871.

Mateer, David. 1974. 'Further light on Preston and White', *Musical Times*, cxv, pp. 1074-1077.

− − − 1979. 'John Sadler and Oxford, Bodleian MSS Mus.e.1-5', *Music and Letters*, xl, pp. 281-295.

− − − 1986-87. 'Oxford, Christ Church Music MSS 984-8: an index and commentary', *Royal Musical Association Research Chronicle*, 20, pp. 1-18.

− − − 1993. 'The compilation of the Gyffard partbooks', *Royal Musical Association Research Chronicle*, 26, pp. 19-43.

− − − 1995. 'The 'Gyffard' partbooks: composers, owners, date and provenance', *Royal Musical Association Research Chronicle*, 28, pp. 21-50.

− − − 1996. 'William Byrd's Middlesex recusancy', *Music and Letters*. (Publication expected in 1996.)

− − − [Forthcoming]. 'William Byrd, John Petre and Oxford, Bodleian MS Mus. Sch. E.423'. (Publication expected in *Royal Musical Association Research Chronicle*.)

Meres, Francis. 1598. *Palladis Tamia. Wits treasury being the second part of Wits commonwealth*. London.

Metcalfe, Walter C., ed. 1878-89. *The visitations of Essex by Hawley, 1552; Hervey, 1558; Cooke, 1570; Raven, 1612; and Owen and Lilly, 1634. To which are added, miscellaneous Essex pedigrees from various Harleian manuscripts: and an appendix containing Berry's Essex pedigrees*. London. *Harleian Society, Publications*, 13-14. 2 vols.

Milsom, John. 1993. 'The Nonsuch music library'. In Banks, 1993, pp. 146-182.

− − − 1995. 'Sacred songs in the chamber'. In Morehen, 1995, pp. 161-179.

Monson, Craig. 1975-76. 'Byrd and the 1575 Cantiones Sacrae', *Musical Times*, cxvi, pp. 1089-1091; cxvii, pp. 65-67.

− − − ed. 1977. *Cantiones sacrae (1575)*. London. *The Byrd Edition*, 1.

− − − 1979. 'The preces, psalms and litanies of Byrd and Tallis: another "virtuous contention in love"', *Music Review*, xl, pp. 257-271.

− − − ed. 1980. *The English services*. London. *The Byrd Edition*, 10a.

− − − 1981. 'Through a glass darkly: Byrd's verse service as reflected in manuscript sources', *Musical Quarterly*, lxvii, pp. 64-81.

− − − 1982. 'Authenticity and chronology in Byrd's church anthems', *Journal of the American Musicological Society*, xxxv, pp. 280-305.

− − − ed. 1983. *The English anthems*. London. *The Byrd Edition*, 11.

Morant, Philip. 1768. *The history and antiquities of the county of Essex*. London. 2 vols.

Morehen, John, ed. 1987. *Psalmes, songs, and sonnets (1611)*. London. *The Byrd Edition*, 14.

− − − 1992. 'Byrd's manuscript motets: a new perspective'. In Brown and Turbet, 1992, pp. 51-62.

− − − ed. 1995. *English choral practice 1400-1650*. Cambridge.

Morley, Thomas. 1597. *A plaine and easie introduction to practicall musicke*.

London. (Edited by R. Alec Harman, London, 1952.)

Moroney, Davitt. 1993. "Bounds and compasses': the range of Byrd's keyboards'. In Banks, 1993, pp. 67-88.

Morris, John. 1872. *The troubles of our Catholic forefathers related by themselves. First series*. London.

––– 1875. *The troubles of our Catholic forefathers related by themselves. Second series*. London.

––– 1891. *Two missionaries under Elizabeth*. London.

Morris, R. O. 1922. *Contrapuntal technique in the sixteenth century*. Oxford.

Musicians' Company. 1909. *An illustrated catalogue of the music loan exhibition held ... by the Worshipful Company of Musicians at Fishmongers' Hall June and July 1904*. London.

Die Musik in Geschichte und Gegenwart. Kassel, 1949-68. 14 vols.

Nasu, Teruhiko. 1995. 'The publication of Byrd's *Gradualia* reconsidered', *Brio*, xxxii, pp. 109-120.

Navy Records Society. 1952. *The naval miscellany. Volume IV, edited by Christopher Lloyd*. [London.]

Neighbour, Oliver. 1971. 'New keyboard music by Byrd', *Musical Times*, cxii, pp. 657-659.

––– 1978. *The consort and keyboard music of William Byrd*. London.

––– 1992. 'Some anonymous keyboard pieces considered in relation to Byrd'. In Brown and Turbet, 1992, pp. 193-201.

Newcourt, Richard. 1710. *Repertorium ecclesiasticum parochiale Londinense: an ecclesiastical parochial history of the Diocese of London ... The second volume, comprising all the county of Essex*. London.

Nicholl, Charles. 1992. *The reckoning: the murder of Christopher Marlowe*. London.

Nichols, John. 1828. *The progresses, processions, and magnificent festivities of King James I*. London. 3 vols. in 4.

Nichols, John Gough. 1850. *The chronicle of Queen Jane, and two years of Queen Mary ... with illustrative documents and notes*. London. *Camden Society, first series*, 48.

Nixon, H. M. 1951-52. 'The book of XX songs', *British Museum Quarterly*, xvi, p. 335 and pl. XVI.

North, Nigel, ed. 1976. *William Byrd*. London. *Music for the lute*, 6.

O'Dwyer, Fr Michael. 1960. Catholic recusants in Essex c.1580 to c.1600. Dissertation, University of London.

Owen, Dorothy, ed. 1994. *A history of Lincoln Minster*. Cambridge.

Oxley, James E. 1968. *The Fletchers and Longbowstringmakers of London*. London.

Pacey, Robert. 1985. 'Byrd's keyboard music: a Lincolnshire source', *Music and Letters*, lxvi, 1985, pp. 123-126.

Page, William. 1926. *The Victoria history of the county of Kent ... Volume two*. London, 1926. *Victoria county histories*.

− − − and Ditchfield, P. H., eds. 1972. *The Victoria history of the county of Berkshire ... Volume four*. Folkestone. *Victoria county histories*.

Patent rolls. *Calendar of the patent rolls*. London.
  1916. *Henry VII. Vol. II. A.D. 1494-1509*.
  1964. *Elizabeth I Volume IV 1566-1569*.
  1966. *Elizabeth I Volume V 1569-1572*.
  1973. *Elizabeth I Volume VI 1572-1575*.
  1986. *Elizabeth I Volume IX 1580-1582*.

Payne, Ian. 1993. *The provision and practice of sacred music at Cambridge colleges and selected cathedrals c.1547 - c.1646. A comparative study of the archival evidence*. New York. *Outstanding dissertations in music from British universities*.

Peacham, Henry. 1622. *The compleat gentleman*. London.

Pevsner, Nikolaus. 1964. *The Englishness of English art*. Harmondsworth.

Phillimore, W. P. W. and Gurney, Thomas, eds. 1910. *Middlesex parish registers. Marriages ... Vol. II*. London.

Phillips, Peter. 1991. *English sacred music 1549-1649*. Oxford.

Pike, Lionel. 1992. 'The Great Service', *Musical Times*, cxxxiii, pp. 421-422.

Pine, Edward. 1953. *The Westminster Abbey singers*. London.

Pinks, William J. 1881. *The history of Clerkenwell ... with additions by the editor, Edward J. Wood. Second edition*. London.

Pollen, John Hungerford and MacMahon, William, eds. 1919. *The Venerable Philip Howard Earl of Arundel 1557-1595 ... English martyrs vol. II*. London. *Catholic Record Society, Publications*, 21.

Powell, W. R., ed. 1956. *A history of the County of Essex ... Volume IV*. London. *Victoria county histories*.

− − − ed. 1973. *A history of the county of Essex ... Volume VI*. London.

Price, David C. 1981. *Patrons and musicians of the English Renaissance*. Cambridge.

Privy Council. *Acts of the Privy Council of England*. London.
  1894. *New series. Vol. IX. A.D. 1575-1577*, ed. John Roche Dasent.
  1896. *New series. Vol. XIII. A.D. 1581-1582*, ed. John Roche Dasent.
  1897. *New series. Vol. XIV. A.D. 1586-1587*, ed. John Roche Dasent.
  1901. *New series. Vol. XXV. A.D. 1595-6*, ed. John Roche Dasent.
  1902. *New series. Vol. XXVII. A.D. 1596-7*, ed. John Roche Dasent.
  1903. *New series. Vol. XXVII. A.D. 1597*, ed. John Roche Dasent.
  1904. *New series. Vol. XXVIII. A.D. 1597-8*, ed. John Roche Dasent.
  1907. *New series. Vol. XXXII. A.D. 1601-1604*, ed. John Roche Dasent.
  1921. *1613-1614*.

Pulman, Michael Barraclough. 1971. *The Elizabethan Privy Council in the fifteen-seventies*. Berkeley, Cal.

Purser, John. 1992. *Scotland's music: a history of the traditional and classical music of Scotland*. Edinburgh.

Puttenham, George. 1936. *The arte of English poesie ... Edited by Gladys Doidge Willcock and Alice Walker*. Cambridge.

Rastall, Richard. 1996. 'William Byrd's string fantasia 6/g1'. In Drake, 1996.

– – – and Rayner, Julie. [Forthcoming.] *William Byrd's six-part fantasias in G minor*. Aldershot. (Publication scheduled for 1998.)

Reaney, P. H. 1935. *The place-names of Essex*. Cambridge. *Place-name Society*, 12.

Rees, Owen. 1992. 'The English background to Byrd's motets: textual and stylistic models for Infelix ego'. In Brown and Turbet, 1992.

Reese, Gustave. 1949. 'The origins of the English In Nomine', *Journal of the American Musicological Society*, ii, pp. 7-22.

Reeve, E. H. L. 1906. *Stondon Massey, Essex*. Colchester. ('Supplementary notes' form pp. 173-208 of 1914 ed., which contains an additional index.)

– – – 1902-11. A supplementary burial register for the parish of Stondon Massey, Essex with materials for a parish history gathered from divers sources. Essex Record Office, MS T/P 188/1-3. (Identifies sources of information not identified in Reeve, 1906.)

Reynolds, Susan, ed. 1962. *A history of the County of Middlesex ... Volume III*. London. *Victoria county histories*.

Rimbault, Edward F., ed. 1841. *A mass for five voices, composed between the years 1553 & 1558, for the old cathedral church of Saint Paul, by William Byrd; now first printed in score, and preceded by a life of the composer, by Edward F. Rimbault*. London. *Musical Antiquarian Society*, 1.

– – – 1847. *Bibliotheca madrigaliana*. London.

– – – ed. 1872. *The old cheque-book or book of remembrance of the chapel royal from 1561 to 1744*. London. (Reprinted, with an introduction by Elwyn A. Wienandt, New York, 1966.)

Robson, Thomas. 1830. *The British herald, or cabinet of armorial bearings of the nobility & gentry of Great Britain & Ireland*. Sunderland. 3 vols.

Rowland, Daniel. 1830. *An historical and genealogical account of the noble family of Nevill, particularly the house of Abergavenny*. London.

Sanders, Nicholas. 1571. *De visibili monarchia ecclesiae, libri octo*. Louvain.

Schofield, John. 1994. *Medieval London houses*. New Haven, Conn.

Shanahan, D. 1965. 'Thomas More IV, secular priest, 1565-1625', *Essex Recusant*, vii, pp. 88-91, 105-114.

Shaw, Watkins. 1967. 'William Byrd of Lincoln', *Music and Letters*, xlviii, p. 52-59.

– – – 1991. *The succession of organists of the Chapel Royal and the cathedrals of England and Wales from c.1538*. Oxford.

Sidney, Sir Philip. 1962. *The poems of Sir Philip Sidney, edited by William A. Ringler*. Oxford.

Simpson, W. Sparrow, ed. 1873. *Registrum statutorum et consuetudinum ecclesiae cathedralis Sancti Pauli Londinensis*. London.

Smith, Alan. 1965. 'The gentlemen and children of the Chapel Royal of Elizabeth I: an annotated register', *Royal Musical Association Research Chronicle*, 5, pp. 13-46.

— — — 1968. 'Elizabethan church music at Ludlow', *Music and Letters*, xlix, pp. 108-121.

Smith, David John. 1993. The instrumental music of Peter Philips: its sources, dissemination and style. Dissertation, Oxford University. 3 vols.

— — — 1995. 'Some stylistic correspondences between the keyboard music of Byrd and Philips: an introductory note', *Annual Byrd Newsletter*, no. 1.

Souris, A. 1955. 'Problèmes d'analyse'. In Jacquot, 1955, pp. 347-357.

Southern, A. C. 1954. *An Elizabethan recusant house comprising the life of the Lady Magdalen Viscountess Montague (1538-1608)*. London.

Spink, Ian. 1974. *English song, Dowland to Purcell*. London.

Squibb, G. D., ed. 1954. *Wiltshire visitation pedigrees 1623*. London. *Harleian Society, Publications*, 105-106. 2 vols.

Squire, William Barclay. 1883. 'A Father of Musick', *Musical Review*, i, pp. 299-300, 317-318, 331-332.

State papers. *Calendars of state papers, domestic series*. London.

    1856. *Edward VI., Mary, Elizabeth 1547-1580*, ed. Robert Lemon.

    1857. *James I. 1603-1610*, ed. Mary Anne Everett Green.

    1858. *James I. 1611-1618*, ed. Mary Anne Everett Green.

    1859. *James I. 1623-1625*, ed. Mary Anne Everett Green.

    1865. *Elizabeth, 1581-1590*, ed. Robert Lemon.

    1867. *Elizabeth, 1591-1594*, ed. Mary Anne Everett Green.

    1868. *Charles I. 1637*, ed. John Bruce.

    1870. *Elizabeth, 1601-1603; with addenda, 1547-1565*, ed. Mary Anne Everett Green.

    1871. *Elizabeth, addenda, 1566-1579*, ed. Mary Anne Everett Green.

    1872. *Elizabeth and James I., addenda 1580-1625*, ed. Mary Anne Everett Green.

State papers, Scotland. *Calendar of the state papers relating to Scotland and Mary, Queen of Scots, 1547-1603*.

    1910. *Vol. VI. A.D. 1581-1583*, ed. William K. Boyd. Edinburgh.

    1915. *Vol. IX. A.D. 1586-1588*, ed. William K. Boyd. Glasgow.

Steele, John, ed. 1970. *Peter Philips: select Italian madrigals*. London. *Musica Britannica*, 29.

Steele, Robert. 1903. *The earliest English music printing*. London. *Bibliographical Society, Illustrated monographs*, 11.

Sternfeld, F. W., et al, eds. 1975. *Essays on opera and English music in honour of Sir Jack Westrup*. Oxford. Co-editors: Nigel Fortune, Edward Olleson.

Stevens, Denis, ed. 1954. *The Mulliner Book. Second, revised edition*. London. *Musica Britannica*, 1.

— — — 1967. *Thomas Tomkins*. New York.

— — — ed. 1969 *Early Tudor organ music: II. Music for the Mass*. London. *Early English church music*, 10.

Stevens, John. 1961. *Music & poetry in the early Tudor court*. London.

— — — ed. 1969. *Music at the court of Henry VIII ... Second, revised edition*. London. *Musica Britannica*, 18.

— — — 1990. 'Sir Philip Sidney and 'versified music': melodies for courtly songs'. In Caldwell, 1990, pp. 153-169.

Stow, John. 1605. *The annales of England*. London.

— — — 1908. *A survey of London, reprinted from the text of 1603, with introduction and notes by Charles Lethbridge Kingsford*. Oxford. 2 vols.

Strunk, Oliver. 1952. *Source readings in music history from classical antiquity to the Romantic era*. London.

Strype, John. 1701. *Historical collections of the life and acts of the Right Reverend Father in God, John Aylmer*. London.

Thompson, Ruby Reid. 1992. 'The 'Tregian' manuscripts: a study of their compilation', *British Library Journal*, xviii, pp. 202-204.

Thompson, Robert. 1995. *The glory of the temple and the stage: Henry Purcell 1659-1695*. London.

— — — 1996. 'William Byrd and the late 17th century', *Annual Byrd Newsletter*, no. 2.

Tillyard, E. M. W. 1943. *The Elizabethan world picture*. London.

Turbet, Richard. 1985. 'Byrd's recusancy reconsidered', *Music and Letters*, lxvi, pp. 51-52.

— — — 1987. *William Byrd: a guide to research*. New York. *Garland composer resource manuals*, 7.

— — — 1988. 'Homage to Byrd in Tudor verse services', *Musical Times*, cxxix, pp. 485-489. (See also Turbet's letter, *Musical Times*, cxxx, 1989, p. 129.)

— — — 1990(a). 'A Byrd miscellany', *Fontes Artis Musicae*, xxxvii, pp. 299-302.

— — — 1990(b). 'The Great Service: Byrd, Tomkins and their contemporaries, and the meaning of 'Great'', *Musical Times*, cxxxi, pp. 275-277.

— — — 1992(a). 'Byrd throughout all generations', *Cathedral Music*, xxxv, pp. 19-24.

— — — 1992(b). 'The Great Service: a postscript', *Musical Times*, cxxxiii, p. 206.

— — — 1992(c). '"Melodious Birde": the solo songs of William Byrd'. In Daubney, 1992, pp. 10-14.

— — — 1993(a). 'The fall and rise of William Byrd, 1623-1901'. In Banks, 1993, pp. 119-128.

— — — 1993(b). *William Byrd 1543-1623: Lincoln's greatest musician*. Lincoln.

– – – ed. 1993(c). *The fifth pavan by William Byrd for broken consort.* Lincoln.

– – – 1994(a). *Tudor music: a research and information guide.* New York. *Music research and information guides.*

– – – 1994(b). 'Byrd at 450', *Brio*, xxxi, pp. 96-102.

– – – 1995. 'Byrd and Tomkins: the Great Service revisited', *Leading Notes*, no. 9.

Walton, Izaak. 1675. *The lives of D^r. John Donne, Sir Henry Wotton, M^r. Richard Hooker, M^r. George Herbert ... The fourth edition.* London. (With an introduction by George Saintsbury, Oxford, 1927.)

Ward, A. W. and Waller, A. R., eds. 1910. *The Cambridge history of English literature. Volume V.* Cambridge, 1910.

Ward, Jennifer C. and Marshall, Kenneth. 1972. *Old Thorndon Hall.* Chelmsford. *Essex Record Office publications*, 61.

Ward, John. 1740. *The lives of the professors of Gresham College.* London.

Ward, John M. 1969. 'Spanish musicians in sixteenth-century England'. In Reese and Snow, 1969, pp. 353-364.

– – – ed. 1983. *The Dublin virginal manuscript. New edition.* London.

Warren, C. W. 1968. 'Music at Nonesuch', *Musical Quarterly*, liv, pp. 47-57.

Welch, Charles. 1908. *Register of freemen of the City of London in the reigns of Henry VIII and Edward VI.* London.

Wells, Robin Headlam. 1994. *Renaissance mythologies. Studies in poetry, drama and music.* Cambridge.

Westminster Commissary Court. 1864. *A calendar of grants of probate and administration and of other testamentary records of the Commissary Court of the Venerable Dean and Chapter of Westminster, from the year 1504.* London.

Weston, William. 1955. *The autobiography of an Elizabethan. Translated from the Latin by Philip Caraman.* London.

Whythorne, Thomas. 1961. *The autobiography of Thomas Whythorne edited by James M. Osborn.* Oxford.

Williams, Penry. 1995. *The later Tudors.* Oxford. *The new Oxford history of England.*

Withycombe, E. G. 1977. *The Oxford dictionary of Christian names ... Third edition.* Oxford.

Wood, Anthony à. 1813-1820. *Athenae Oxoniensis ... to which are added the Fasti, or annals of the said university ... A new edition, with additions ... by Philip Bliss.* London. 4 vols.

Woodfield, Ian. 1984. *The early history of the viol.* Cambridge.

Woodfill, Walter L. 1953. *Musicians in English society from Elizabeth to Charles I.* Princeton.

Wrigley, E. A. and Schofield, R. S. 1981. *The population history of England, 1541-1871: a reconstruction.* London.

Wriothesley, Charles. 1875-77. *A chronicle of England during the reigns of the Tudors ... edited ... by William Douglas Hamilton*. London. *Camden Society, series II,* 20. 2 vols.

Wulstan, David. 1985. *Tudor music*. London.

− − − 1992. 'Birdus tantum natus decorare magistrum'. In Brown and Turbet, 1992, pp. 63-82.

− − − 1994. 'Where there's a will', *Musical Times*, cxxxv, pp. 25-27.

− − − 1995. 'Byrd, Tallis and Ferrabosco'. In Morehen, 1995, pp. 109-142.

Youings, Joyce. 1984. *Sixteenth-century England*. Harmondsworth. *The Pelican social history of Britain*.

Zouch, C. and Sherwood, P. T., eds. 1986. The parish registers of the church of St. Peter and St. Paul Harlington Middlesex. Transcription 1540-1850. (Typescript at the Greater London Record Office.)

INDEX OF BYRD'S WORKS

The articles 'A', 'An', 'La' and 'The' at the beginnings of titles are ignored in alphabetization. Sections of multi-sectional works are separated by dashes. References to so far unpublished volumes of *The Byrd Edition* (7a-b, 9, 12 and 13) are necessarily incomplete.

NAME AND SUBJECT INDEX